The Sculpture of the Hellenistic Age

The SCULPTURE of the HELLENISTIC AGE

by MARGARETE BIEBER

Columbia University Press: New York 1955

The Bollingen Foundation AND THE *Stanwood Cockey Lodge Foundation*
HAVE GENEROUSLY PROVIDED FUNDS TO ASSIST IN THE PUBLICATION OF THIS VOLUME

Columbia Bicentennial Editions and Studies

THE ENERGETICS OF DEVELOPMENT
By Lester G. Barth *and* Lucena J. Barth

NEW LETTERS OF BERLIOZ, 1830–1868
Text with translation, edited by Jacques Barzun

ON THE DETERMINATION OF MOLECULAR WEIGHTS
BY SEDIMENTATION AND DIFFUSION
By Charles O. Beckmann *and others*

Luigi Pirandello
RIGHT YOU ARE
Translated and edited by Eric Bentley

THE SCULPTURE OF THE HELLENISTIC AGE
By Margarete Bieber

THE ALGEBRAIC THEORY OF SPINORS
By Claude C. Chevalley

Henry Carter Adams
RELATION OF THE STATE TO INDUSTRIAL ACTION
and ECONOMICS AND JURISPRUDENCE
Edited by Joseph Dorfman

Ernst Cassirer
THE QUESTION OF JEAN-JACQUES ROUSSEAU
Translated and edited by Peter Gay

THE LANGUAGE OF TAXONOMY
By John R. Gregg

ANCILLA TO CLASSICAL READING
By Moses Hadas

James Joyce
CHAMBER MUSIC
Edited by William Y. Tindall

APOKRIMATA: DECISIONS OF SEPTIMIUS SEVERUS ON LEGAL MATTERS
Edited by William L. Westermann *and* A. Arthur Schiller

LIBRARY OF CONGRESS CATALOG NUMBER: 54-5783

COPYRIGHT 1955 COLUMBIA UNIVERSITY PRESS, NEW YORK
PUBLISHED IN GREAT BRITAIN, CANADA, INDIA, AND PAKISTAN BY GEOFFREY CUMBERLEGE
OXFORD UNIVERSITY PRESS: LONDON, TORONTO, BOMBAY, AND KARACHI
MANUFACTURED IN THE UNITED STATES OF AMERICA

GENERAL EDITOR'S PREFACE

THE MODERN university has become a great engine of public service. Its faculty of Science is expected to work for our health, comfort, and defense. Its faculty of Arts is supposed to delight us with plays and exhibits and to provide us with critical opinions, if not to lead in community singing. And its faculty of Political Science is called on to advise government and laity on the pressing problems of the hour. It is unquestionably right that the twentieth-century university should play this practical role.

But this conspicuous discharge of social duties has the effect of obscuring from the public—and sometimes from itself—the university's primary task, the fundamental work upon which all the other services depend. That primary task, that fundamental work, is Scholarship. In the laboratory this is called pure science; in the study and the classroom, it is research and teaching. For teaching no less than research demands original thought, and addressing students is equally a form of publication. Whatever the form or the medium, the university's power to serve the public presupposes the continuity of scholarship; and this in turn implies its encouragement. By its policy, a university may favor or hinder the birth of new truth. This is the whole meaning of the age-old struggle for academic freedom, not to mention the age-old myth of academic retreat from the noisy world.

Since these conditions of freedom constitute the main theme of Columbia University's Bicentennial celebration, and since the university has long been engaged in enterprises of public moment, it was doubly fitting that recognition be given to the activity that enlarges the world's "access to knowledge." Accordingly, the Trustees of the University and the Directors of its Press decided to signalize the 200th year of Columbia's existence by publishing some samples of current scholarship. A full representation was impossible: limitations of time and space exercised an arbitrary choice. Yet the Bicentennial Editions and Studies, the titles of which are listed on a neighboring page, disclose the variety of products that come into being on the campus of a large university within a chosen year. From papyrology to the determination of molecular weights, and from the state's industrial relations to the study of an artist's or poet's work in its progress toward perfection, scholarship exemplifies the meaning of free activity, and seeks no other justification than the value of its fruits.

JACQUES BARZUN

PREFACE

THIS BOOK could not have been written without the help of the Bollingen Foundation. At a time when the rules of Columbia University enforced my retirement while I felt that I might do better work than ever before, Bollingen gave me a new lease on life by a grant which enabled me to write this book and to have it adequately illustrated. My thanks are due particularly to Mr. John D. Barrett, as well as to Miss Vaun Gillmore, for advice and help.

Dr. Gisela Richter of the Metropolitan Museum of Art has read part of my manuscript and made some valuable corrections. Mrs. Agnes Brett of the Numismatic Society has provided me with information on many coins which form the basis of identification of the ruler portraits. Miss Mary Chamberlain of the Fine Arts Library at Columbia University has helped me greatly in the library work and by the encouragement and advice in difficult situations which only a true friend can give. Dr. Alice Muehsam has faithfully helped in trying to make the text clear and consistent. Miss Helen Stroop has worked tirelessly at the task of editing text and footnotes according to forms used by Columbia University Press, and Mr. Irwin Scollar has helped to put footnotes and bibliography in practical shape.

The forms for Greek proper names may appear to be inconsistent. At the insistence of Columbia University Press I have adopted familiar English forms, when such forms exist, for all names except the artists'. I regret the consequent appearance of inconsistent usage, but have been unable to avoid it.

The publication of this book, with its extensive text and numerous illustrations, has been made possible by the generous contributions of the Bollingen Foundation, the Stanwood Cockey Lodge Foundation of Columbia University, and Columbia University Press. I wish to express my warm gratitude to the members of these organizations.

I am happy that it has been possible to have this work included in the Columbia Bicentennial Editions and Studies, a series made possible by the generosity of the following: the Trustees of Columbia University, the Trustees of Columbia University Press, Mrs. W. Murray Crane, Mr. Herman Wouk, Mr. James Grossman, and friends of the late Robert Pitney, who wish to remain anonymous.

I owe the permission to publish many photographs to the courtesy of the directors of the Metropolitan Museum of Art in New York, to the directors of the Walters Art Gallery in Baltimore, to the Boston Museum of Fine Arts, the Fogg Art Museum, and to the Cleveland Museum. The photographs from museums in Athens, Istanbul, Rome, Naples, Florence, Paris, London, Dresden, and Berlin, and the Alinari, Anderson, and Brogi photographs, were acquired in Europe, mostly before 1933, when I planned to write a similar book in German.

On this occasion, I wish to extend my deeply felt gratitude to all the American institutions, colleagues, and friends who have helped me after my transplantation to grow new roots and branches in a new country. I hope that I have been able to write a better book here than would have been possible in Europe.

MARGARETE BIEBER
Columbia University in the City of New York
August 15, 1954

CONTENTS

Contents

The Sculpture of the Hellenistic Age

I

INTRODUCTION: CHARACTERISTICS OF HELLENISTIC ART

HELLENISTIC means late Greek. This word was first used by Johann Gustav Droysen in his history of the Hellenistic age, which appeared in 1833 (*Geschichte des Hellenismus,* 5th ed., 1917), and which for the first time treated the last centuries of Greek civilization as an important part of its history. Before Droysen's time everybody had regarded this period as the decline of Greek art, and it was neglected by historians as well as philologists and archaeologists. Most of the handbooks of ancient art devoted little or no space to this last period. The history of Greece seemed to end with or before Alexander the Great; for example, even in 1933 I found that in Oxford the requirements for the examination in Greek sculpture stopped around 330 B.C.

Droysen separated the history of Alexander the Great and of his first successors from the Hellenistic period and began his history of Hellenism proper with the date *c.*280 B.C., i.e., the period when the new states, founded by the successors of Alexander, were consolidated. In 1925 Richard Laqueur in his paper "Hellenismus" was, on the other hand, of the opinion that the Hellenistic period ought to be counted from *c.*400 B.C., because the new ideas which had shaped the new Hellenistic world in contrast to the classical Greek world really began with the sophistic movement at the end of the fifth century. He thus includes the whole fourth century in the Hellenistic period. His reason is that,

from 400 B.C. onwards, the Greeks had not confined themselves to their city-states as they had done in the fifth century, but had mingled with foreign states. By the middle of the fourth century, Isocrates had suggested to Philip of Macedon the idea of a great empire, an idea achieved later by Alexander. It is indeed true that the fourth century shaped the ideas which were realized in the following centuries. Thus we find a transitional period between the purely classical fifth century and the purely Hellenistic third, second, and first centuries B.C. We must therefore consider the fourth century first before contemplating the purely Hellenistic period. But on the other hand, the fourth century, principally its first half, is rightly considered to belong to the classical period, for in this century Plato, the greatest writer of the classical era, shaped classical ideas into their most perfect form. Plato's pupil Aristotle was the teacher of Alexander the Great and helped to shape the new age by influencing his pupil. With Alexander in history, and with his court sculptor Lysippos in art, the truly and purely Hellenistic period begins. I, therefore, consider the beginning of the reign of Alexander the Great as the true beginning of the Hellenistic period, and the earlier part of the fourth century as a transition from the classical to the Hellenistic age.

The end of the Hellenistic period has been put by Droysen in the beginning of the Augustan age, rightly as I believe. Some scholars, however—foremost historians of art such as Joseph Strzygowski and Charles Rufus Morey—refuse to see here the end of the Hellenistic age, believing rather that Hellenism is the most important part of the time of the Roman Empire. Indeed, the influence of Hellenistic art on Roman art has been considerable. But on the other hand, the new ideas which formed Roman art are purely Roman. It is very interesting to see how Hellenistic art took possession of Campania and later of Rome, and how in Rome it became the art of the Empire and later of the early Christian Church; how it wandered into the provinces with the Roman civilization, and how it lived through the Byzantine Empire in the East and through the Middle Ages in the West, and was then revived in the Renaissance period. But this was a continuation of Hellenistic influences into new periods, similar to the survival of classical forms in the Hellenistic period and of archaic forms in the classical, Hellenistic, and Roman periods. The new ideas, rather than those carried over from earlier times, are those which count in a period. I, therefore, think that with Augustus a definitely new epoch began, and that indeed we have to place the end of the purely Hellenistic period with the beginning of the reign of Augustus, while we have to put the beginning of the Hellenistic period with the beginning of the reign of Alexander. Thus 330—30 B.C. are the natural boundaries of this period, with transitional periods before the beginning and after the end.

This period between 330 and 30 B.C. is called Hellenistic to distinguish it from the preceding classical and the following Roman periods. The age of Alexander the Great (336—323 B.C.) was that of transition from the classical to the Hellenistic period, while the age of the Emperor Augustus (31 B.C.—A.D. 14) was the transition from the Hellenistic to the Roman imperial period.

The name Hellenistic owes its derivation to the fact that in the last centuries before Christ Greek art was no longer confined to originally purely Greek lands, but extended to many regions which up to then had had their own art and civilization, sometimes very little of both. This fact changed the character of Greek art, because art is influenced by new surroundings, by new knowledge of foreign countries and peoples, and by new patrons.

What are the distinctive characteristics of Hellenistic art in comparison with classical art? Droysen saw them in the mixture of Greek with foreign elements, particularly Oriental elements. This is too narrow a definition, for Egyptian and Italian elements were also largely absorbed into Hellenistic art. It is true that in contrast to classical art Hellenistic art is not purely Greek but, because it spread over large countries with individual and sometimes ancient civilizations, it took on new forms. These were better adapted to the different countries which had been conquered by Alexander and made by him and his successors provinces of Greek civilization. We might compare the situation to that of America today. The origin of American civilization is English. Today everyone in the United States speaks English, but only about half of the population is of English extraction. The minority of greatest size is of German extraction, the rest are of a variety of national and racial origins. Yet all are Americans or try to become Americans as soon as possible—influenced, of course, by the American language and the American civilization. It was the same with the Asiatic peoples—Persians, Syrians, Indians, Egyptians, and Hebrews; and from the second century B.C., cultivated Romans spoke Greek besides their native language. The Macedonians were not considered Greeks before the fourth century, but Philip, the father of Alexander, had already largely Hellenized them, and thus Alexander could become the leader of the Greek army. The word *Hellenistes* (ἑλληνιστής) instead of *Hellen* (ἕλλην) is first used in the Bible (Acts 14:1) for Jews using the Greek language and adopting Greek civilization in contrast to their own Hebrew language and civilization. But the cultivated Jew of the first century B.C. spoke Greek, as did the cultivated Syrian, Egyptian, and Roman. The admixture of foreign elements was of course of different strength in the different parts of the Greek world. A civilization which had lived on for several thousand years, such as that of Mesopotamia or Egypt, could not be abandoned easily for a new one. In other regions, such as the northern portion of the Balkan peninsula, people were too crude to absorb the Greek language and civilization.

Despite these facts, it is astonishing how homogeneous Hellenistic art is in comparison to classical art. In the classical period Athens was the leader of Greek culture, yet the Dorian art of the Peloponnese and the Ionic art of the coast of Asia Minor formed distinct schools. On the other hand, it has till now not been possible to attribute definite styles to the different schools of artists working in Pergamon, Antioch, Alexandria, the island of Rhodes, and other important centers of Hellenistic art. There have been, however, some attempts to find a solution, and we will make others.

One may define the difference between the classical and Hellenistic periods as follows: on the one hand the limited polis, the city-state with its particular moderation and all ideas confined to its own little community; on the other hand the empire, the general Greek civilization common to everyone living inside the large Hellenistic kingdoms. The individual citizen now takes no part in the life of the community, though he used to do so in the classical period. He is now a citizen of the whole world, a *cosmopolitan*. The difference between the citizens of city-state and empire is like that between a politician in America who is only interested in his native city or his state or the institution which has given him some position, and one who feels that he must be interested in the whole country. The artist in the classical period worked for a small democratic community. He built temples for the gods who protected his town, and he built public buildings for the people and adorned them with sculpture and painting. In the Hellenistic period he worked not only for the rulers, the princes of the different monarchies who needed palaces for themselves and brilliant buildings to commemorate their governments and to adorn their cities, but also for individual citizens who lived much more their own lives than did their earlier counterparts. There had been no domestic architecture or domestic sculpture of artistic merit before the Hellenistic period; then the Hellenistic private house also became an object for the arts and was adorned more and more with sculpture and painting. The luxury of public and private monuments increased and their dimensions grew with the growth of the cities and the states.

The Hellenistic horizon was extended greatly beyond the one of the classical period by the knowledge of foreign countries and people and by the development of science and philosophy. A deeper feeling for life invaded large circles. Passion and movement became distinctive characteristics of Hellenistic art. The study of foreign people led to the rendering of their distinctive personalities. The classical Greeks were not interested in barbarians, as all non-Greeks were called. Hellenistic art rendered the Gauls, the Italians, and the Negroes with deep understanding. Classical art, with few exceptions, knew only the Greek, and only the beautiful and young Greek. It is well known that even old women, with a few exceptions, were rendered as eternally young and beautiful. But the Hellenistic artists studied all ages—the wrinkled forms of old age as well as the delicate features of the children, whom classical art had rendered mostly as miniature grownups. Classical art knew only the well-educated citizen. Hellenistic art was interested in the lower classes also; for the first time herdsmen, fishermen, slaves, peasant women, and farmers were rendered with surprising naturalism.

This naturalism is another distinctive feature of the Hellenistic period compared to the idealism of the classical period. The feeling for life is much more intense in Hellenistic art than it is in classical art; all forms of nature—animals and plants, draperies and inanimate objects—are rendered with extreme fidelity.

This deep study of nature was one of the main reasons for the development of portraiture. Another reason was the age's greater interest in the individual character and in the peculiarities of the individual personality, as compared with the emphasis laid upon the type in the classical period. The New Comedy, the most important form of literature in the early Hellenistic period, beginning with Menander in the late fourth century, is the best example of this growing interest in the fate of the individual citizen.

Another characteristic of Hellenistic art is the contrast which we also find in the New Comedy —that of old age and youth, of man and woman, of strong and weak, of the beautiful and the ugly —often found in groups which only in this period were developed into real groups. Besides the beauty which was the only aim of classical art, the expressions in ugly, old, distorted forms grew in interest. Life had become richer and fuller of meaning, though less harmonious and less beautiful than the classical life; yet it did not lack beauty, for it remained Greek to the end.

Following the conquest of new countries by Alexander and his successors, new realms were also conquered for art. Many new fields came for the first time into the focus of the artist's eye: not only foreign peoples and lower classes, but also architectural and landscape backgrounds found their artistic form in the later part of this period.

As a consequence, the greatest peculiarity of this period is the great variety of styles which evolved in response to these many new tasks. The Hellenistic artists replaced the ideals of the classical period—serenity, harmony, and balance—with stormy passion, sincere realism, contrast of softest sweetness and distorted ugliness, violence of movement, figures crowded together in space or relieved against a rich background. To all of these, peculiar to Hellenistic art, was added an occasional return to earlier styles.

Thus when the Romans took over Greek art, they found a truly rich and manifold art which could be adapted to their taste and needs. Roman art is really built on Greek Hellenistic art, despite occasional returns to that of earlier periods. The importance of Hellenistic art to the world's history of art is indeed this fact: that as it had explored and sometimes exhausted all possibilities for artistic representation it was of a universal character and could form the base not only for Roman but for all European and, therefore, finally for American art.

The material for the study of Hellenistic sculpture is so rich and manifold that it is confusing. Up to now no clear and exhaustive representation has been published. Relatively few monuments are dated by external evidence. Gerhard Krahmer and Ernst Pfuhl, who have made the best investigations up to date, have grouped their limited material according to styles. Guy Dickins and A. W. Lawrence have grouped the material in their handbooks for the most part according to schools. Great scholars like Joseph Strzygowski and Charles Rufus Morey have added to the confusion by extending the name Hellenistic to the art in the eastern part of the Roman Empire in the early centuries after Christ. All these scholars have of course made use of dated monuments, but sometimes their dates are, in my opinion, incorrect.

In order to present a clear picture, I shall try to combine the three methods used up to now for arranging the material. I shall lay the stress on the monuments dated by external evidence, but I shall group them with related monuments in periods and in schools. It has become more and more evident to me that though definite schools did work exclusively in definite styles through definite periods, no one school maintained a monopoly over any specific style.

Thus the schools of Lysippos and Praxiteles dominated during the early Hellenistic age (c.330—250 B.C.), Athens led in portraiture, and Alexandria in that soft style which is often called Alexandrian, though it is also found in other parts of the Hellenistic world. In the middle Hellenistic period (c.250—160 B.C.) the school of Pergamon was foremost, due to the great building activity of the Attalids, the energetic rulers of this small kingdom. The same "baroque" style, however, was current also in other parts of the eastern Greek world, particularly Rhodes. Portraiture continued to flourish in Athens. A "rococo" trend was evident everywhere, with Alexandria as the leading center and with other centers in Asia Minor.

In the late Hellenistic period (c.160—c.30 B.C.) the earlier trends continued: the baroque tendency particularly in Rhodes, the rococo particularly in Alexandria, where it led to decadence. On the mainland classical forms were again taken up and mingled with baroque elements. When Rome became politically dominant, she attracted many artists who mingled Hellenistic art with classicized and archaistic motifs. Their eclecticism brought forth the creation of Roman art and marked the end of Greek art. Thus, during the Hellenistic period the leading schools of sculpture shifted from the Greek mainland first to the East, and finally to the West—to Rome.

II

GREEK SCULPTURE OF THE FOURTH CENTURY B.C.

GREEK SCULPTURE of the fourth century is generally neglected in handbooks on art. The chief reason for this is that this century was a period of transition between classical and Hellenistic art. Most scholars take it to be the second and less perfect period of classical art; others take it to be the as yet imperfect beginning of the Hellenistic period. The interest of most students of ancient art centers in the archaic period of the sixth century, when, with as yet insufficient training of hand and eye, the first heroic struggles were being made to reproduce in clear form the complicated tangible and visible forms of the world around. The interest of others centers in the classical period of the fifth century with its majestic, harmonious, and serious rendering of gods and men, its unity of body and soul. Others, again, find their main interest in the Hellenistic period of the third to first centuries B.C., with its heroic pathos, its mastery of the most complicated forms—whether of man or beast, objects or plants or furniture—and its rendering with equal skill of flesh, hair, and the material of dresses. The fourth century intervening between these clearly marked periods seems to many tame and dull.

Nevertheless, it is one of the most interesting and important periods of the history of art. The study of it is the best introduction to the study of Greek sculpture in general, and to Hellenistic sculpture especially.

The fact that the fourth century was one of transition allows the student to look from it both to the earlier and to the later periods, and so gives him a better impression of the whole field of Greek art than does any other century. At the beginning of the fourth century the schools of Polykleitos and Phidias, the two great masters of the fifth century, were still in full activity. The style of Polykleitos is found in many statues of athletes. It continued to be copied until first Skopas, then Lysippos, remodeled it. The style of Phidias is found in many grave reliefs, votive reliefs, and female statues, for instance the Eirene of Kephisodotos. Kephisodotos handed on this style to his great son, Praxiteles, who remodeled it with grace and softness. The peculiar style of the end of the fifth century, as found in the Nike Temple parapet (of c.410 B.C.), persisted in Epidaurus, where Timotheos worked; he, in old age, was a collaborator on the Mausoleum of Halicarnassus, which was built in the middle of the fourth century. Then Lysippos discovered and conquered a new province of art: the third dimension of depth, in addition to the two of height and breadth, to which plastic art had hitherto been confined. His time of activity was the second half of the fourth century, and so falls partly into the Hellenistic period, if we reckon that this began at around 330 B.C. or at the death of Alexander the Great in 323 B.C. We find Lysippos's pupils working for the successors of Alexander, the Diadochi, as did Bryaxis, another artist who in his youth worked together with Skopas and Timotheos on the Mausoleum. So we get a review of the whole development of Greek sculpture. Even the archaic period is not excluded, for in the fourth century began that imitation of archaic forms for religious and decorative purposes which we call archaistic and which persisted through classical and Hellenistic times to the Roman period, when it found much favor.

But the sculpture of the fourth century is distinguished by more than transition and tradition. It has very special characteristics of its own, which it owes to its three great artists, Praxiteles, Skopas, and Lysippos, just as the character of the fifth century is due to Myron, Polykleitos, and Phidias. The characteristics of the fourth century are often spoken of as softness and grace—characteristics of Praxiteles—and passion (pathos, πάθος), which characterizes Skopas; but the most important characteristic of fourth-century sculpture was contributed by Lysippos in the beginning of the Hellenistic period. Of his portraits of Alexander it is said that he alone expressed in bronze not only Alexander's external appearance, but also the vigor of his mind. That is to say, his work expressed not only beauty, but truth to nature. The new quality of faithfulness to nature was shown not only in exterior forms; he expressed the spirit and the soul of his subjects. The same is true of Praxiteles and Skopas in different ways. So the general characteristic of the fourth century is *faithfulness to nature.* The fifth century was not unfaithful to it, but subordinated truth to an ideal beauty. The face was beautiful, but was not a mirror of the soul. The artists of the Hellenistic period are literally more true to nature than those of the fourth century, but they often forget the subtleties of human nature in their joy in rendering external form. The fourth century maintained the balance between beauty of form and expression of soul, neglecting neither, and hence attained a charm in Praxiteles, passion in Skopas, and fire of life in Lysippos that we find in no preceding period.

The historical background for the culture of the fourth century is very interesting and accounts for the development of its art. The beginning of the fourth century found Athens, the leading city-state of the fifth century, weak and bleeding from the wounds inflicted by the long-drawn-out Peloponnesian War (431—404 B.C.), in which she finally suffered defeat. Sparta, the victor, had long since given up the arts of peace and concentrated on military virtues. Thus no state of the mainland was in a position to suggest great tasks for the artists, or to supply stimulus for their work. They continued to work on the lines taught them by the great masters of the fifth century. The Persians, defeated and repelled in the first half of the fifth century, profited by the weakness of the Greek states after the Peloponnesian War and extended their influence in the East. Their satraps, the masters of the provinces, grew rich. They summoned Greek artists to their capitals, commissioned them to design their coins and to build and to adorn their monuments, as did Mausolus in Halicarnassus, and as the rulers of Sidon and Lycia had done before him. But then a new great power arose in the north of the Greek mainland: Macedonia. Philip and Alexander conquered the quarreling city-states and put an end to their petty governments and wars. Alexander led his united army to Asia Minor, Egypt, and Persia, and gave new ideals and impulses to life and art. His court sculptor was Lysippos, and he, together with others and with his pupils, worked also for the friends and successors of Alexander. After the death of the great king, the generals began to quarrel among themselves, after the custom of the Greeks, but before the end of the fourth century the greatest of them founded new states in Macedonia, Syria, and Egypt. These became seats of art and science. The old cultures which the Greeks found in the East provided them with new subjects and new forms for life and art. New tasks were again set to the Greek artists and they fulfilled them, thanks to the good schooling they had had from the great masters of the fourth century.

It is evident, from this historical outline, that the fourth century does not allow such clear subdivisions as the fifth century, which can be sharply marked out into the late archaic, 500—480 B.C.; the early classic, 480–450; the Periclean age, 450–430; and the age of the school of Phidias, 430–400. We might indeed say of the fourth century that in the first quarter, 400–375, we have the tradition of the fifth century; in the second quarter, 375–350, the new styles of Skopas and Praxiteles; from 350–325, Lysippos; and from 325–300, early Hellenistic art.

But we should be making divisions where there are none, for these four periods overlap. The influence of the schools of Phidias and Polykleitos continued until the early years of Lysippos. Skopas and Praxiteles began to work about 370 at the latest, and continued until perhaps 340–330. Lysippos worked until the end of the fourth century. He may be regarded as the last classical, as well as the first great Hellenistic, master. His pupils were still at work in the third century.

We, therefore, had better say that the century was dominated from 400–360 by the tradition of the fifth century, from 370–330 by Praxiteles and Skopas, and from 350 to 300 by Lysippos and his school.

I. THE TRADITION OF THE FIFTH CENTURY (*c.*400—*c.*360 B.C.)

Of great help in dating Greek sculptures are reliefs found in connection with dated inscriptions. Thus, a relief above the inventory made by the treasurers of the Parthenon, dated 398/7 by the names of the archons at the head of the inscription, shows an Athena in the style of the Athena Parthenos of Phidias, and a representative of the demos in the style of the Parthenon frieze.[1]

Also helpful in dating the sculpture of the fourth century are the reliefs which we find on tombstones in the *Kerameikos,* the cemetery, where from the geometrical period of the eighth century down to Roman times the Athenians buried their dead. It is situated outside the Dipylon, the double gateway that led from the inner *Kerameikos,* the potters' district, to the outer portion, used as a burial place. This burial ground was reorganized at the beginning of the fourth century. Definite plots were given to the rich families, who made high terraces (Fig. 1). They placed high steles, crowned with *akroteria,* in the center; on these were inscribed the names of the buried members of the family. The members of the family were often shown on marble vases, mostly in the shape of oil flasks (*lekythoi*) (Fig. 2), which were set up at the corners of the terraces. Broad individual steles were set up, often with life-size figures, whenever members of the family, particularly young men or women, were buried [2] (Figs. 3–6).

The celebrated tombstone of Hegeso (Fig. 3) is still standing on one of these terraces, where the family had it erected at the beginning of the fourth century.[3] It is one of the tombstones which show the dead pursuing the daily occupations of their lifetimes. The deceased was, according to the inscription, Hegeso, the daughter of the Athenian Proxenos. The father certainly wanted the artist to make of his daughter, who had died in early youth, an image which portrayed her beauty, dignity, and grace. Inside a small shrine Hegeso is seated on a graceful chair, her feet resting on an artistic footstool. Her waiting maid stands before her and hands her a casket with jewelry. Hegeso's head is bent, and she looks with a gentle dreamy expression at the jewel in her hand, with which her fingers play gracefully. She is richly clad in a chiton buttoned over the shoulder, a mantle around her legs, and a veil falling over her head. Her elegant dress is emphasized by the coarser material of the chiton of the maid, which has tightly fitting sleeves, no belt, and no folds. The figure is reminiscent of the seated goddesses on the Parthenon east frieze, except that the dress, particularly the veil, is more delicate and transparent, and the spirit and mood softer than in the fifth century.

The tombstone of Dexileos stands in the middle of a corner terrace next to the city wall and near the Dipylon gate.[4] The inscription records that he fell in 394 B.C. in the Corinthian War. The terrace, as

---

[1] R. Binnebössel, *Studien zu den attischen Urkundenreliefs* (1932), p. 8, No. 24, and also pp. 47 f. P. Arndt and W. Amelung, *Photographische Einzelaufnahmen antiker Skulpturen* (1893—), No. 1212. See also H. K. Süsserott, *Griechische Plastik des 4. Jahrhunderts vor Christus. Untersuchungen zur Zeitbestimmung* (1938), pp. 27 ff., Pls. 1–5.

[2] A. Brückner, *Der Friedhof am Eridanos* (1909), pp. 13 ff., 35 ff., 70 f., Fig. 43. A good example of a normal family, consisting of father, mother, daughter, and little sister, is in the Metropolitan Museum of Art in New York; see G. Richter, *The Sculpture and Sculptors of the Greeks* (rev. ed., New Haven, Yale University Press, 1950), Fig. 495. Our Fig. 2 is a *lekythos* in Cleveland showing father, mother, little girl, and baby on the arm of her nurse (see M. Bieber in *Art in America,* Vol. XXXI [1943], p. 123, Fig. 9).

[3] H. Brunn and F. Bruckmann, *Denkmäler griechischer und römischer Skulptur* (1888—), Pl. 436. A. Conze, *Die attischen Grabreliefs* (Berlin, 1893–1922), Vol. I, pp. 21 f., No. 68, Pl. XXX. Brückner, *Friedhof,* pp. 104 ff., Fig. 66. H. Diepolder, *Die attischen Grabreliefs des 5. und 4. Jahrhunderts v. Chr.* (Berlin, 1931), p. 27, Pl. 20.

[4] Brunn-Bruckmann, *Denkmäler,* Pl. 438. Conze, *Grabreliefs,* Vol. II, pp. 254 f., No. 1158, Pl. CCXLVIII. Brückner, *Friedhof,* pp. 57 ff., Figs. 29, 34.

well as the relief, has the form of a shallow curve. Dexileos is shown in the bloom of youth, in vigorous combat with an enemy who has fallen to the ground and is looking up helplessly at his conqueror. The right arm of Dexileos is lifted, ready to strike the vanquished foe, and his cloak, the chlamys, flows in the wind. The horse is animated and full of life. The fragment of a similar tombstone belongs to the Berlin Museum [5] (Fig. 4).

Dexileos was one of many who fell for their country in 394 B.C. The grateful demos gave them a public memorial, part of which, with the inscription mentioning the Corinthian War, has been found.[6] The horseman and his horse, to the right, are even more animated than Dexileos. The bounding horse and the young knight are seen from the side in a momentary movement. A warrior on foot is seen in the front. He wears a short exomis, that is, a tunic leaving the right shoulder bare. He kills a naked adversary who has fallen to the ground. The drawing of this relief is splendid, the execution is delicate. The best artists available at this time must have been entrusted with the task of celebrating the deeds of the young warriors who gave their lives for their country.

Related to these war memorials of 394 is a big grave relief, now in the Villa Albani in Rome.[7] Here the warrior has sprung down from his fiery horse, which is seen in a most lively movement in the background. The knight, while still holding the bridle in his left hand, lifts the right with the weapon high over his head. His chiton and chlamys are flowing in the rush of the movement. The fallen enemy lifts himself feebly from the ground and tries to protect himself with the chlamys. The three figures fill the space in a beautiful diagonal composition, beginning from the lower left corner and ending at the upper right one.

Many scholars have believed the Villa Albani relief to be of the fifth century, disregarding its relationship to the dated war memorial of 394 B.C. It is

true that all three reliefs have many points in common with the horsemen and horses of the celebrated cavalcade of the north frieze and the knights of the west frieze of the Parthenon. The movements of the horses, their animated heads, and the movements of the knights are closely related. The artists trained by Phidias around 440 B.C. handed down their knowledge to their sons and pupils. These, however, adapted themselves to new tasks, and also to the softer mood of the fourth century.

Many other tomb reliefs belong to this group of the early fourth century, although they are not dated by external evidence. Related to the Hegeso relief is a fragmentary tombstone, now in Cleveland [8] (Fig. 6). The tombstone of Mynno, in Berlin, is less noble, but is very natural and simple.[9] Mynno is an alien, a *metoikos,* not an Athenian, since the tombstone does not name her father. She has short curly hair and her character as a good housewife is shown by representing her spinning, with the wool basket under her seat. Related in feeling to her monument is that of Tynnias, a dignified Athenian, seated on a chair with curved legs and back, as elegant as the one on which Hegeso is seated [10] (Fig. 5). He holds with loose fingers the long staff that the older citizens carried with them to the market place and on which they leaned when making conversation. These seated figures have their parallels in the seated gods of the Parthenon east frieze. They have the same easy elegance, although they lack the majesty and severity of the Olympian gods.

The school of Polykleitos, like the school of Phidias, lived on for a considerable part of the fourth century. The Doryphoros, Polykleitos's first masterpiece, became and remained for a long time the prototype for male statues. The statue was called the canon, because Polykleitos had used it to illustrate a book with this title, from which "the artists drew the rudiments of art as from a code" (Pliny *Nat. hist.* XXXIV. 55). The relative dimensions of the parts of the human body and the correct balance of the figure, achieved by the chiastic

[5] Conze, *Grabreliefs,* Vol. II, p. 256, No. 1160, Pl. CCXLIX. G. Blümel, *Staatliche Museen zu Berlin, Katalog der Sammlung antiker Skulpturen,* Vol. III (1939), p. 31, No. K30, Pl. 39.
[6] Conze, *Grabreliefs,* Vol. II, p. 253, No. 1157. A. Brückner in *Athen. Mitt.,* XIV (1889), 407, and in *Athen. Mitt.,* XXXV (1910), 183 ff., Pl. XI–XII.
[7] Brunn-Bruckmann, *Denkmäler,* Pl. 437. Conze, *Grabreliefs,* Vol. II, p. 252, No. 1153, Pl. CCXLVII. Diepolder, *Grabreliefs,* pp. 16 f., Pl. 9.

[8] M. Bieber in *Art in America,* Vol. XXXI (1943), p. 123, Fig. 8. Diepolder, *Grabreliefs,* pp. 32 f., Fig. 7.
[9] Conze, *Grabreliefs,* Vol. I, p. 15, No. 38, Pl. XVII. Blümel, *Berlin Katalog,* Vol. III, p. 26, No. K23, Pl. 33.
[10] Athens, National Museum, No. 902. See V. Staïs, *Marbres et bronzes du Musée nationale* (1910), p. 165. Conze, *Grabreliefs,* Vol. II, p. 131, No. 617, Pl. CXVIII.

arrangement of the arms and legs—the arm above the supporting leg hung down, while the arm above the relaxed leg was lifted—resulted in perfect formal beauty. A grave relief of a young knight of the early fourth century shows him beside his horse exactly in the position of the Doryphoros.[11]

The second masterpiece of Polykleitos, the Diadumenos, a youth who binds his hair with the fillet of victory, belongs to a later period, when the sculptor had come under the spell of the art of Phidias. The canon is adhered to, but the features are much smoother. Statuettes in the Cabinet des Médailles de la Bibliothèque nationale at Paris (Fig. 7) and in the Metropolitan Museum of Art in New York (Figs. 8–10) transpose the motif into the style of the fourth century.[12] The same is true of Polykleitos's youthful victors, like the so-called Westmacott athlete in the British Museum, who, in a graceful pose, places the wreath of victory on his head with his right hand.[13] An adaptation of this figure, with slimmer and softer forms belonging to the fourth century, has been found in Eleusis.[14]

Two pupils of Polykleitos—Naukydes and Daidalos—are known to us. Naukydes collaborated with Polykleitos in Argos, where he set up a statue of Hebe next to the Hera of the master. He may also have been responsible for the decorative sculptures of the Argive Heraion, as they show a mixture of Attic and Polycleitan style.[15] Naukydes's

fame, however, is based on single statues, among them the discus thrower. We have several copies of a discobolos belonging to the early fourth century which seem to be based on this work of Naukydes. The best preserved statue, which, however, is without its head, is in the Vatican Museum; the best in style is a torso with head in the Palazzo Caffarelli in Rome; another replica is in the Louvre.[16] All three replicas have the discus loosely held in the left hand. It is the moment before the action. The feet are wide apart, the head is bent towards the ground, as if seeking to find the best spot for placing the feet before throwing the discus. The forms of the body, with their strongly marked lines between the muscles, are clearly Polycleitan, as is also the head, with its clear-cut features and outlines of eyes and mouth. The hair, however, is rougher in texture and is arranged in a more lively manner than are the flat locks of the heads of Polycleitan athletes.

Daidalos of Sicyon, like Polykleitos, specialized in depicting athletes. About 370 B.C., working with other artists, he produced a group of nine figures dedicated at Delphi by the Arcadians in memory of their victory over the Spartans. Daidalos made two *apoxyomenoi*, boys scraping themselves with the strigil. One of them is probably reproduced in a bronze statue from Ephesus, now in Vienna.[17] A youth of heavy build stands firmly on his right leg; the left leg, with slightly bent knee, is put a little to the side. He scrapes the grease from his left hand with the strigil in his right hand, bending his head down to follow the action of the hands with his eyes. The head resembles somewhat the head of the discobolos of Naukydes, but it is in a younger style belonging probably to the period around 370 B.C. The eyes are narrow, the mouth has broad lips, the hair rises in rough and irregular tufts from the high forehead.

The other apoxyomenos of Daidalos is probably reproduced in numerous marble copies of a similar figure. The best is in the Uffizi Gallery in Florence. The hands, which are restored, probably held the strigil, and the thumb of one hand was being

---

[11] A. Furtwängler, *Masterpieces of Greek Sculpture* (1895), pp. 226 ff. For the grave relief from Argos (Athens, National Museum, No. 3153), see *ibid.*, p. 230, A. Furtwängler in *Athen. Mitt.*, Vol. III (1878), pp. 287 ff., Pl. XIII, and Brunn-Bruckmann, *Denkmäler*, Pl. 279a.

[12] Furtwängler, *Masterpieces*, pp. 238 ff. G. Richter in *A.J.A.*, XXXIX (1935), 46 ff. (for the statuettes see *ibid.*, Notes 10 and 11 and Fig. 4). Our Fig. 7, formerly in the Janzé collection, is now in the Cabinet des Médailles of the Bibliothèque nationale (E. Babelon and J.-A. Blanchet, *Catalogue des bronzes antiques de la Bibliothèque nationale* [Paris, 1895], p. 408, No. 927). G. M. A. Richter, *Handbook of the Greek Collection* (New York, the Metropolitan Museum of Art, 1953), p. 98, Pl. 79a and p. 110, Pl. 88d.

[13] Brunn-Bruckmann, *Denkmäler*, Pl. 46. Furtwängler, *Masterpieces*, pp. 249 ff., Figs. 102–5. A. H. Smith, *A Catalogue of Sculpture in the Department of Greek and Roman Antiquities of the British Museum* (3 vols., 1892–1904), Vol. III, pp. 106 ff., No. 1754.

[14] Furtwängler, *Masterpieces*, p. 255. Philips, in *Ephemeris Arch.* (1890), pp. 207 ff., Pl. 10–11.

[15] C. Waldstein (Sir Charles Walston), *The Argive Heraeum* (2 vols., 1902–5), Vol. I, pp. 146 ff., Plates XXX–XLI. F. Eichler, in *Oest. Jahreshefte* (1919), pp. 15 ff.

[16] L. Mariani in *Bollettino Comunale*, Vol. XXXIX (1911), pp. 97 ff., Pls. VI–VIII. Brunn-Bruckmann, *Denkmäler*, Pls. 131 and 682–85 (left-hand figures).

[17] Brunn-Bruckmann, *Denkmäler*, Pls. 682–85 (right-hand figures).

run along the hollow side of the instrument in order to clean it.[18]

Many gravestones of the fourth century found in Athens show *apoxyomenoi;* examples are those now in the Museum of the Piraeus and in the Metropolitan Museum of Art in New York.[19] Their motifs may have been taken from one of the athletes of Daidalos, or they may have been taken from life. The cleaning process they portray was necessary after athletic exercises. The body was anointed with oil, and the dust of the palaestra attached itself to the moist skin and made a layer of solid dirt. Thus the theme of scraping oneself became a favorite one long before Lysippos created his celebrated statue (Figs. 74–75).

The action of pouring oil was also a favorite subject in the school of Polykleitos. Again we have two types related to each other. The better one, in Munich, stands with legs wide apart in an attitude similar to that of the discobolos of Naukydes.[20] He lifts his right hand high over his shoulder and, bending his body backwards, lets the oil flow over it before he rubs it in with his left hand. The other type, exemplified by oil-pouring athletes in Dresden, Petworth, and in the Palazzo Pitti in Florence, has a similar but quieter pose.[21] The heads are of the same type—with elongated faces, high round skulls, rough bristling hair, high foreheads, clear-cut eyes, and strong mouths—as the other athletes of the Polycleitan school.

The school of Polykleitos continued to dominate until the middle of the fourth century. A bronze statue found in a ship sunken off Antikythera and now in Athens [22] has a body as heavy as the Ephe-

sus bronze and a head related to the heads of athletes of the Polycleitan school; the short curly hair rising from the forehead is arranged with the strands pushed to one side, as on the heads of the athletes of Naukydes and Daidalos. The features, however, are softer and the movement is more pronounced. The right arm is lifted; the hand was holding out an object of small size and light weight, which must have had some significance. It seems to have been round, and it may have been an apple. In the hanging left hand a bent object, perhaps a bow, was inserted. The suggestion of the Greek scholar J. N. Svoronos is that a weapon, the *harpe,* was in the left hand and the head of Medusa in the right hand, and that the figure represented Perseus after the killing of Medusa. My suggestion is that it might be the celebrated Paris (Alexandros) of Euphranor, in which the whole character of the Trojan prince was revealed: "the judge of the goddesses [shown by the apple], the lover of Helen [shown by his noble appearance], and the destroyer of Achilles [shown by the bow] could be detected at once" (Pliny *Nat. hist.* xxxiv. 77). Euphranor was considered to have been the first to represent heroes in their full majesty, and the first to have mastered the science of proportion. He was a painter as well as a sculptor, and he wrote on coloring and on proportions. His new proportions consisted of slenderer bodies, but his heads and limbs were considered too large in relation to these slender bodies. It seems to me that indeed the limbs of the Antikythera bronze are rather long in proportion to the body. In any case Euphranor could not substitute his new canon of proportions for the one of Polykleitos. It was not until Lysippos made a new canon that the one of Polykleitos was superseded.

A third trend, which beside the majestic art of Phidias and the academic perfection of the school of Polykleitos continued from the fifth into the early fourth century, is one which we might call manneristic. It developed during the Peloponnesian War, and found its full and finest realization in the parapet built *c.*410 b.c. around the little temple of Athena Nike on the bastion of the Acropolis of Athens.[23] The celebrated Nike loosening her sandal and the Nikes erecting trophies or lead-

[18] Furtwängler, *Masterpieces,* pp. 261 f. W. Amelung, *Führer durch die Antiken in Florenz* (Munich, 1897), pp. 21 ff., No. 25. Brunn-Bruckmann, *Denkmäler,* Pls. 523–24.

[19] Diepolder, *Grabreliefs,* p. 40, Pl. 40, No. 2, for the tombstone in the Piraeus; G. A. Richter, *Handbook of the Classical Collection* (New York, Metropolitan Museum of Art, 1930), pp. 258 ff., Fig. 181, and Richter, *Handbook* (1953), p. 108, Pl. 87b, for the tombstone of Sostratos. See also Conze, *Grabreliefs,* Vol. II, pp. 199 ff., Nos. 929–32, 954a, and 955, and Pls. CLXXX and CLXXXV.

[20] A. Furtwängler and P. Wolters, *Beschreibung der Glyptothek zu München* (2d ed., 1910), pp. 331 ff., No. 302. Brunn-Bruckmann, *Denkmäler,* Pls. 132–35, 557.

[21] Furtwängler, *Masterpieces,* pp. 259 ff., Fig. 107. Amelung, *Antiken in Florenz,* pp. 136 f., No. 190, Fig. 36. Arndt-Amelung, *Einzelaufnahmen,* Nos. 222–23.

[22] J. N. Svoronos, *Das Athener Nationalmuseum,* Vol. I (1908), pp. 18 ff., Figs. 2–14, Pls. I–II. M. Bieber in *Jahrbuch d. Inst.,* XXV (1910), 159 ff.

[23] R. Carpenter, *The Sculpture of the Nike Temple Parapet* (1929).

ing bulls are dressed in transparent Ionic chitons that allow the body to show through. Even where a mantle, the himation, is put over the chiton, the legs show clearly through the double clothing. The contrast between the veiled but practically nude body and the deep shadows of the surrounding drapery is striking.

This highly decorative effect was continued in the early fourth century in the sculptures of the sanctuary of Asclepius at Epidaurus, built about 395—375 B.C.[24] Building inscriptions recording contracts with several sculptors indicate Timotheos as the leading master sculptor. He carved the *akroteria* of one of the pediments of the temple of Asclepius, and *typoi*—that is, models—probably in the form of reliefs, for the pediment sculptures which were executed by other artists. The *akroteria* on the other pediment were made by an artist whose name begins with "Theo," and was perhaps Theon or Theotimos. The many fragments of the decorative sculptures are markedly similar in style. The *akroteria* show a Nike holding a bird and a Nike with particularly big wings as central figures, and so-called Nereids which are probably rather *Aurai* (Breezes), personifications of salutary winds, on horseback. Their transparent, delicate dresses are finely worked in a virtuoso manner, with sharply cut folds and big masses of material on the borders outside the body. The only head of a so-called "Nereid" found has youthful and clear-cut features. The fragments which come from the pediments, such as a well-preserved Amazon, are rather coarser, but the composition is similar to that of the "Nereids," and the lively movement is akin to the Dexileos relief.

In Copenhagen there is an original torso of a woman running, which shows a similar contrast between the transparency of the parts clinging to the body and the massed folds between the legs and on the borders.[25] It is beautifully and delicately carved. Also similar is a torso from the Agora in Athens[26] of a strong woman in a thin, transparent dress. The drapery is blown against the body, to which it clings so closely that the contours of the graceful figure are revealed. The folds of the garment are arranged in a beautiful but rather manneristic and unnatural way. As the back was left rough, this figure may have stood in the pediment of a fourth-century temple. The same contrast between the transparency of the parts clinging to the body and the massed folds between the legs and on the borders is found in a more clumsy and exaggerated manner in the statue of Leda, of which the best copies are in the Museo Capitolino and the Villa Albani in Rome and the Ashmolean Museum of Oxford.[27] The left breast covered by the chiton seems quite as nude as the right one that is really uncovered. The mantle, very heavy at the sides, is very thin where it is lifted to protect the swan in whose form Zeus, seemingly pursued by his eagle, has flown into her lap. This manneristic style could not be developed further, for it had reached its highest virtuosity. Timotheos's style was probably already out of date when he was called to help with the decoration of the Mausoleum of Halicarnassus.

The contrasting style, which we may ascribe to Agorakritos and Alkamenes, the great pupils of Phidias, and which is best represented by the caryatids (or *korai*) of the Erechtheum (*c.*421—415 B.C.), lived on, together with the Parthenon style, at least until the middle of the fourth century. We can see this in the relief above a treaty made at the instigation of the general Timotheos between Athens and Corcyra (Corfu), dated by the archontate of Hippodamas in the year 375/4 B.C.[28] The standing personification of the island of Corcyra reminds one of the goddesses of the fifth century and of the caryatids, while the seated figure representing the Demos of Corcyra recalls the seated gods of the Parthenon frieze. The style is almost the same in a relief above a treaty of Athens with

---

[24] P. Cavvadias, *Fouilles d'Épidaure* (Athens, 1891). A. Defrasse and H. Léchat, *Épidaure* (Paris, 1895). G. Lippold, in *Handbuch der Archaeologie*, Vol. III: *Die griechische Plastik* (1950), pp. 219 ff.

[25] G. Lippold, *Antike Skulpturen der Glyptothek Ny Carlsberg* (1924), pp. 13 f., Fig. 9. Brunn-Bruckmann, *Denkmäler*, Pl. 663. F. Poulsen, *Catalogue of Ancient Sculpture in the Ny Carlsberg Glyptotek* (Copenhagen, 1951), No. 397a; *Tillaeg til Billedtavler til Kataloget over Antike Kunstvaerker* (Copenhagen, Ny Carlsberg Glyptotek, 1915), Pl. VI.

[26] T. L. Shear in *Hesperia* (1935), pp. 374 ff., Figs. 4–7, Pl. IV.
[27] Jones, *Sculpt. Museo Capitolino*, Gabinetto della Venere No. 2, pp. 184 f., Pl. 45, No. 1. Brunn-Bruckmann, *Denkmäler*, Pl. 648.
[28] Athens, National Museum, No. 1467. Svoronos, *Athener Nationalmuseum*, Vol. II, Pl. CIII, Vol. III, pp. 588 ff., No. 240. Brunn-Bruckmann, *Denkmäler*, Pl. 533, No. 2. Binnebössel, *Urkundenreliefs*, p. 9, No. 34 (cf. pp. 53 f.). Diepolder, *Grabreliefs*, p. 36, Fig. 9.

the Arcadians, placed by the archontate of Molon in 362/1, and one above a treaty of Athens with Neapolis in Thrace, dated by the archontate of Elpinos in 356/5.[29]

The fact that this style lived on into the first quarter, and even the second quarter, of the fourth century allows us to date a tombstone found in Rhodes (which is, however, in Attic style) as a work of the early fourth century. The figure of the mother recalls statues of the school of Phidias, but the soft feeling in the rendering of the daughter, who embraces her mother, is of the fourth century.[30] To the same period belongs the tombstone of Sostrate[31] in the Metropolitan Museum: the father and mother are in the Parthenon style; the little girl is a miniature of a grownup, like the child in the following group.

The most important statue of a goddess in the early part of the fourth century is the Eirene with Plutus (Peace with Wealth) of Kephisodotos. The original of this cult statue stood on the slope of the Areopagus near the market place (Pausanias 1. 8. 2). In front of it stood an altar on which offerings to the goddess were laid every year after 375, the date of Timotheos's victory over the Spartans. The statue itself was probably erected in 372–368 (the Olympiad CII), in which Pliny dates Kephisodotos (*Nat. hist.* xxxiv. 50). However, the commission probably had already been given in 375, when the cult of Eirene was introduced at Athens. Her statue showed the goddess of Peace bearing the child Plutus (Wealth) in her arms (Pausanias IX. 16. 2). The Athenians at that time hoped that through peace prosperity would return to their impoverished city.

Coins of Athens show the goddess in a heavy peplos, with a scepter in her right hand and the child on her left arm.[32] She turns her face to the boy, who holds a big cornucopia in his left arm. The original parts of a statue in Munich have the same composition.[33] The right hand of Eirene, the arms and the head of the child, and the little pot held by both their left hands are modern restorations. In a replica of the child found in the harbor town of Piraeus,[34] the lower part of the horn of plenty is preserved. It was used by the museums of casts in Dresden and Rome in making excellent reconstructions.[35] The only mistake in the reconstructions is that the base is too short and, therefore, the scepter is not held up vertically as it appears on the coins. The best replica of the torso only is in the Metropolitan Museum of Art in New York.[36] The edge of the overfold and the pouch, which is drawn out of the belt, form long curved lines, and the folds over the breast and the heavy folds of the pouch also show manifold curves. This is in contrast to the straightness of the lower part, where the folds fall down in straight lines over the legs, with the exception of the part clinging to the relaxed upper right leg; the motif of the severe vertical folds is taken up again from the right knee down. This arrangement of drapery is also seen in the *korai* from the Erechtheum. Their severe outline and solid stance are emphasized by this arrangement, because they take the place of pillars in the portico over the tomb of the Attic hero Cecrops. Eirene is of severe appearance because she is a cult statue. She is broader and more matronly than the *korai*. Her head, on the other hand, shows a softer spirit, which is principally evident in the bending down to the child. The fall of the abundant hair and a certain softness in the features is in the spirit of the fourth century and in contrast to the severe rendering of the fifth century. Apart from this, however, the head does not show any sign of sentiment or tenderness. Portrayal of expression in the face was not to begin before the next generation.

The little boy on the arm of Eirene has a light linen shawl wrapped around his legs, which forms a marked contrast to the heavy peplos of the goddess. He puts out his arm in a babylike caress to

[29] Athens, National Museum, Nos. 480–81. Svoronos, *Athener Nationalmuseum,* Vol. II, Pls. CVI–CVII, Vol. III, pp. 298 f., 605 ff., Nos. 245, 248. Brunn-Bruckmann, *Denkmäler,* Pl. 533, No. 3. Binnebössel, *Urkundenreliefs,* p. 10, Nos. 37, 40 (cf. pp. 54 ff.). Arndt-Amelung, *Einzelaufnahmen,* No. 1213.

[30] G. Jacopi in *Clara Rhodos,* Vol. IV (1931), pp. 37 ff., Figs. 10–11, Pl. I, and Vol. V, Part 2 (1932), pp. 31 ff., Fig. 17, Pls. IV–VII. Jacopi dates this tomb relief much too early—in 460 B.C.

[31] Richter, *Handbook* (1930), pp. 256 ff., Fig. 180, and *Handbook* (1953), pp. 140 f., Pl. 121c; Richter, *Sculpture and Sculptors,* p. 133, Fig. 428. The inscribed pediment does not belong to this relief, but to a similar one.

[32] G. E. Rizzo, *Prassitele* (Milan and Rome, 1932), Pl. IV.

[33] *Ibid.,* pp. 4 ff., Pls. I–III. Furtwängler and Wolters, *Glyptothek,* pp. 216 ff., No. 219. Brunn-Bruckmann, *Denkmäler,* Pl. 43.

[34] Rizzo, *Prassitele,* Pl. V, No. 1.

[35] *Ibid.,* Pl. V, No. 2 and Pls. VI–VIII.

[36] *Ibid.,* Pl. IX. Richter, *Handbook* (1953), p. 140, Pl. 120c.

the face which is bent down in an attitude of motherly tenderness and care. But this is the only connection between the two, except that both together are holding the horn of plenty. The child is held to the side, and the right arm of the goddess holds her scepter without any relation to the child. Any other object on her left arm would produce the same outline of composition. That is to say, this grouping of a grown-up person and a small child is far from being perfect. Kephisodotos made perhaps the first attempt at such grouping, and, therefore, it is no wonder that the result is not yet satisfactory. The rendering of the child, as we know it also from the replicas in Athens, from the Piraeus, and in Dresden,[37] is in no way satisfactory. When we compare his size with that of Eirene, he ought to be about two years of age. But his proportions are those of a grown-up person in miniature, the head, in particular, being much too small in relation to the body.

Kephisodotos was interested in the representation of a child grouped with an adult, for we know that he also made a Hermes nursing the infant Dionysos (Pliny Nat. hist. xxxiv. 87). The composition is shown in an old drawing by J. B. de Cavalleriis and on coins of Athens.[38] The connection between the two persons is even looser than in the Eirene group, and, therefore, this may be an earlier work. The statue of Hermes in Madrid leaning his arm on a herm over which he has thrown his mantle is probably a copy of the Hermes of the group.[39] The forms of this statue in Madrid remind one of statues of the fifth century, just as does the statue of Eirene. The head of the herm, however, shows features in the style of the fifth century combined with a treatment of the hair in late-archaic manner. The same is true of a herm from the market place in Athens.[40] Over it a heavy cloak is hanging and on it a hand supports a child wrapped in a little thin mantle. The head of the herm has the same archaistic treatment of the hair and the beard as the herm in Madrid. Such a combination of contemporary features with stiffly curled archaic hair is first found in the Hermes Propylaios of Alkamenes. It was set up outside the

entrance of the Propylaia and it is preserved in many copies.[41] It is very likely that Alkamenes was the teacher of Kephisodotos, for we are told that Praxiteles, the son of Kephisodotos, was the third generation after Alkamenes (Pausanias viii. 9. 1). Kephisodotos thus may have used the Hermes Propylaios in making a kind of reverent quotation of the work of his teacher.

We thus can see how Kephisodotos handed down to his greater son, Praxiteles, the tradition of the fifth century.

2. PRAXITELES (c.370—c.330 B.C.)

Praxiteles was probably the son and pupil of Kephisodotos. He must have been born about 395 B.C. and have died about 330 B.C. Pliny (Nat. hist. xxxiv. 50) gives his date as Olympiad CIV, that is, 364 B.C. This is probably the date of his most celebrated statue, the Cnidian Aphrodite, the first that made him famous and thus a rather early one. He may have begun to work around 375–370. The painter Nikias, who lived until the second half of the fourth century, colored the marble statues of Praxiteles in his youth. Praxiteles used for his model Phryne, who was his friend and paramour; later Apelles, the court painter of Alexander the Great, also used Phryne as a model. Praxiteles's statue of Artemis Brauronia was dedicated in 346/5. An altar for the sanctuary of Artemis at Ephesus was probably finished around 330, as the sanctuary was not yet finished in 334, the date of the visit of Alexander the Great to Ephesus. Thus the years 370–330 are the possible limits of Praxiteles's activity.[42]

Praxiteles, as did his father before him, worked

---

[37] W. Klein, *Praxiteles* (Leipzig, 1898), p. 85, Fig. 8. Richter, *Sculpture and Sculptors,* pp. 256, 565, Figs. 662–63.
[38] Rizzo, *Prassitele,* Pl. IV, Nos. 3–4, and Pl. XII, No. 1.
[39] *Ibid.,* Pl. XII, No. 2.   [40] *Ibid.,* Pl. XIV.
[41] F. Winter in *Altertümer von Pergamon,* Vol. VII, Part 1, pp. 48 f., No. 27, Beiblatt 5, and Pl. IX. G. Mendel, *Catalogue des sculptures grecques, romaines et byzantines, Musées Ottomanes* (3 vols.; Constantinople [Istanbul], 1912–14), Vol. II, p. 234, No. 527. Richter, *Sculpture and Sculptors,* pp. 236 and 553, Fig. 628; B. Schröder, *Alkamenes-Studien (Winck.-Prog. Berlin,* No. 79 [1921]), p. 1, Fig. 1 and p. 10, Figs. 7–8. Blümel, *Berlin Katalog,* Vol. IV, pp. 8 ff., No. K133, Pl. 16. H. Schrader, *Phidias* (1924), pp. 195 ff., Figs. 175, 177–79. Eduard Schmidt, *Archaistische Kunst* (1922), p. 43, Pl. XXI.
[42] General works: W. Klein, *Praxiteles* (Leipzig, 1898); M. Collignon, *Scopas et Praxitèle* (1907); E. A. Gardner, *Six Greek Sculptors* (London, 1910), pp. 140 ff.; Ch. Picard, *Manuel d'archéologie grecque: La Sculpture antique,* Vol. III, Part 2 (1948), pp. 406 ff.; G. Lippold, *Die griechische Plastik* (Vol. III of *Handbuch der Archaeologie,* ed. W. Otto and R. Herbig; Munich, 1950), pp. 234 ff.

on the problems of the representation of a leaning figure and of the grouping of a grown-up person with a child. He even took over the archaistic herm as a support. We find it, for example, in the copies of his leaning Dionysos in Madrid and Varese,[43] and in one of his Eros figures reproduced on a coin, with the bust of Commodus on the other side.[44] Praxiteles, in turn, had the greatest influence on early Hellenistic art. His softness, his rejuvenating of gods, and his languid attitudes were accepted. Even such details as the figure leaning on an ancient image of herself was continued. In the statuette of Artemis from Larnaca of Cyprus, now in Vienna, a work ascribed to the sons of Praxiteles, and in any case belonging to the early Hellenistic period, the goddess stands in the graceful inclined pose familiar in the male figures of Praxiteles, and is supported by a stiff archaistic image[45] (Fig. 41). In another early Hellenistic statuette of Aphrodite, found in Pompeii and now in Naples, with painting well preserved, the youthful figure leans heavily on the archaistic image of herself.[46]

These statuettes have kept the easy and graceful beauty of form which is generally associated with the adjective "Praxitelean." The ancient writers praise Praxiteles for the consummate art with which he infused into his marble figures the emotions of the soul. The Hellenistic and Roman artists prized and imitated the sensuous beauty of his forms and the sweeping lines of his compositions.

The exquisite modeling of the surface of his marble statues can only be appreciated in an original. Fortunately the Hermes in Olympia, despite recent doubts, is such an original, for it was found during the German excavations in the Heraion on the same spot where Pausanias (v. 17. 3) had seen it seventeen centuries before[47] (Figs. 11–12). The statue, including the nose, is so well preserved because it had fallen face downward into the dissolved clay of walls and roofs composed of sunburnt bricks. Only some of the projecting parts of the body are lost: the right arm of Hermes, both his legs except the right foot (Fig. 13), and the left arm of the child.

It is not a solemn personification such as the Peace with Wealth of Kephisodotos. It shows how Hermes, the messenger of the gods who has been charged by Zeus to take his little brother Dionysos to the nymphs who are to nurse and raise him, rests on the way and plays with the child. He has, therefore, thrown his cloak, a chlamys with heavy folds, over a tree trunk, and he rests his left arm on it, supporting the child. His right arm was lifted, holding some toy or a bunch of grapes appropriate to the future god of wine. The child was looking at it and probably reaching out for it with his left arm. His right hand clasps the shoulder of his protector. Because the child reaches out with his left hand, the one more distant from Hermes, the connection between the two is closer than in the group of Kephisodotos. Both hands of Hermes are occupied with the child, while Eirene had a scepter in her right hand. Thus the son has learned from the father, but has improved the grouping.

The supporting tree trunk, together with the right leg, carries the weight of the body and produces the graceful and easy curve characteristic of Praxiteles. The light plays on the highly polished surface of the strong body. The nude parts are treated with wonderful subtlety and delicacy in the transitions. Technical skill and mastery of execution are combined with an inspired spiritual expression to fill the face with life (Fig. 12). The refinement of the features is in contrast to the hair, which is only roughly blocked out in irregular tufts of considerable depth which create shadows. When the hair was painted and seen from a distance it must have given the impression of reality. Even in the foot (Fig. 13), with its subtle swelling, there is a feeling for organic form, which is contrasted to the elegant but sober forms of the leather sandal. One can feel that this foot is a strong and able carrier.

The texture of the chlamys is also marvelously

---

[43] Rizzo, *Prassitele,* pp. 76 ff., 117, Pl. CXV.

[44] *Ibid.,* pp. 42 and 121, Pl. LXII, No. 8. Minted in Prusa ad Olympum.

[45] R. von Schneider, *Album auserlesener Gegenstände der Antikensammlung des Kaiserhauses zu Wien* (1895), Pl. IV. Rizzo, *Prassitele,* pp. 12 f., 113, Pl. XV.

[46] *Arch. Zeitung,* Vol. XXXIX (1881), Pl. 7. H. Bulle, "Archaisierende griechische Rundplastik," in *Abh. Bayr. Akad.,* XXX, Abh. 2 (1918), p. 13, No. 22, Pl. 3.

[47] G. Treu in *Olympia, Ergebnisse der Ausgrabungen,* Vol. III (1897), pp. 194 ff., Pls. 49–53. Brunn-Bruckmann, *Denkmäler,* Pls. 466–67. G. Rodenwaldt and W. Hege, *Olympia* (1937), pp. 50 ff., Pls. 85–91. Rizzo, *Prassitele,* pp. 66 ff., 116, Pls. XCIX–CIV. The Hermes has again been considered a copy by Rhys Carpenter in *A.J.A.,* Vol. LVIII (1954), pp. 155 ff., Pl. 3 (sketch of the supposed bronze original).

rendered and contrasted with the thin little mantle of the child as well as with the smoothness of the skin. When the first photos of the Hermes reached Germany, the eyes of the well-known scholar, Alexander Conze, were deceived so that he asked: "Why did they not remove the cloth before taking the photograph?" In this garment the naturalistic treatment has won over the former decorative one; but only at first sight does the arrangement of the folds look spontaneous and accidental. The rich folds are cleverly arranged with beautiful curves and resting points for the eye.

The motif of Hermes showing grapes to the child Dionysos on his left arm was used on Hellenistic silver vases. Hermes was changed to old Papposilenos (Father Silenus) in Hellenistic terra cottas and to a young satyr in Pompeian wall paintings.[48] Otherwise we have no variations or copies of this Olympian statue. But we have some of a closely related type of Hermes, called Hermes of Andros after the replica, which was found on the tomb of a young man on the island of Andros and is now in Athens[49] (Fig. 14), or Hermes Farnese, from another copy formerly in the Farnese collection and now in the British Museum,[50] or Antinous of Belvedere, from a misnamed copy in the Vatican.[51] This Hermes has a head of the same shape as the one in Olympia (the shape which is also found in the school of Polykleitos in the early fourth century), but the features are softer. The outlines of the cheeks are more elongated; the forehead projects more in its lower part, while the chin is more rounded. The expression is more serious than that of the Olympian Hermes, who looks dreamily into the distance. This expression and the fact that the type was used as a tomb statue make it likely that this statue represented Hermes Psychopompos, the guide of souls to the underworld. As we possess only copies, the exquisite finish and appearance of life and warmth which we admire in the Olympian Hermes is lacking. The expression was certainly more alert and the forms showed

more physical strength than the Olympian Hermes. We may imagine that these points were similar to an original head formerly in the Aberdeen collection and now in the British Museum.[52] Holes in the hair indicate that there was a bronze wreath. This may be the head of a young Heracles.

The comparison between the two Hermes of Praxiteles shows us how much we miss when we have only copies. Unfortunately this is the case with most celebrated masterpieces of Praxiteles—for example, his two satyrs. The satyr pouring wine[53] (Fig. 15), who raises his right hand with a jug above his head and pours into a cup once held in his left hand, is known in about twenty copies. It belongs among the early works of the master, for its style is simpler and more severe than that of the Hermes, and the composition is close to that of the athlete anointing himself from the school of Polykleitos (see above, p. 12). The satyr was perhaps grouped with Dionysos, for whom he poured wine. This was presumably not the celebrated satyr which was called "the world-famed" (Pliny Nat. hist. xxxiv. 69), for another Praxitelean satyr was copied even more frequently. The most familiar copy is in the Museo Capitolino.[54] Other good replicas are in the Glyptothek in Munich, in Berlin, and in the Museo Torlonia in Rome.[55] Like the Hermes in Olympia, the satyr supports himself with one elbow on a tree trunk. The inclination of the body is more emphasized. The right leg is bent at the knee and the right foot is placed just behind the left, so that the pose is more languid. The right hand holds a flute, with which the satyr has been amusing himself in the woods indicated by the tree. Now he is at rest, his left hand resting on his hip, and shifting to the side a skin which is draped elegantly around his

[48] Rizzo, Prassitele, p. 73, Pls. CVI–CVII.
[49] Brunn-Bruckmann, Denkmäler, Pl. 18. Rizzo, Prassitele, pp. 75 f., 117, Pls. CXIII and CXIV, No. 2.
[50] A. H. Smith, Brit. Mus. Cat., Vol. III, No. 1599, Pl. IV. Rizzo, Prassitele, Pl. CXII.
[51] W. Amelung, Die Sculpturen des Vaticanischen Museums (2 vols., Berlin, 1903–6), Vol. II, pp. 132 ff., Cortile del Belvedere 53, Pl. 12.

[52] A. H. Smith, Brit. Mus. Cat., Vol. III, No. 1600. Furtwängler, Masterpieces, pp. 346 f., Pl. XVIII. Rizzo, Prassitele, pp. 74 ff., 116, Pl. CXI.
[53] F. Weege, Der einschenkende Satyr aus Sammlung Mengarini (Winck.-Prog. Berlin, No. 89 [1929]). Klein, Praxiteles, pp. 190 ff. Rizzo, Prassitele, pp. 17 ff., Pls. XIX–XXVI. Blümel, Berlin Katalog, Vol. V, p. 18, No. K225, Pl. 37. Fragment in Metropolitan Museum: Richter, Handbook (1953), p. 107, Pl. 85 g.
[54] Brunn-Bruckmann, Denkmäler, Pl. 377. Jones, Sculpt. Museo Capitolino, I, 350 ff. Rizzo, Prassitele, pp. 34 ff., Pls. LII–LV.
[55] Furtwängler and Wolters, Glyptothek, pp. 233 ff., Nos. 228–29. Blümel, Berlin Katalog, Vol. V, pp. 16 f., Nos. K220–24, Pls. 34–36. C. L. Visconti, Catalogo del Museo Torlonia (1884), No. 113. Rizzo, Prassitele, Pls. XLVIII–LI.

body. The rough texture of the fur forms a marked contrast to the smooth skin of the body. There is a similar contrast between the abundant hair rising from the forehead and the round and smiling face. The wild creature of the woods has now become a handsome and delicate youth, loving music and dreamily enjoying his rest. The best torso, found on the Palatine in Rome, and now in the Louvre, may indicate the subtle execution of the original (Fig. 16).[56] Another headless replica, in Rome, gives him more slender forms and lets him lean more heavily.[57] It thus resembles the Apollo Sauroctonus, the young Apollo trying to transfix a lizard running up a tree, known in three replicas—in the Vatican (Fig. 18), the Louvre, and Villa Albani.[58] Here, as in other replicas of masterpieces, we cannot fully appreciate the execution of the original.

What we can see, however, in the existing copies is the perfect balance of form and content which must have been one of the main achievements of Praxiteles. This balance, as well as the subtleties of the execution, must have been very difficult to imitate. We can see this when we study the Apollo Lykeios of Praxiteles and its imitations in the Hellenistic period. The name of this statue is taken from a gymnasium in Athens in which there stood a statue of Apollo leaning on a column, one hand holding a bow and the other resting on the crown of the head (Lucian *Anacharsis* 7). Attic coins show a statue which agrees with this description,[59] as do Roman copies in the Louvre (Fig. 17) and in the museums of Dresden, Berlin, and other places. Most of these have wrong and fanciful supports added by the copyists or the modern restorers.[60] In an ivory statuette found in the market place of Athens by Professor Leslie Shear and restored by Mrs. Josephine Shear, the support is missing[61] (Figs. 20–21). The most beautiful part of the statue is the head, of which there are excellent copies in the Museo Barracco at Rome (Fig. 22) and in the British Museum.[62] The rich hair built up in a braid over the forehead frames the noble face, with its inspired expression.

The celebrated Apollino in the Tribuna of the Uffizi Gallery in Florence[63] is an early Hellenistic adaptation of this Apollo. Here he has become very young and soft, and the inspired expression is gone. In contrast, a Roman bronze head, formerly in the Museo Kircheriano in Rome and now in the Museo Nazionale Romano[64] (Fig. 23), although an exact and clear copy of the hair, has too-harsh features. The Youth of Sutri in the Museo Nazionale Romano in Rome, another bronze of the type of the Apollo Lykeios, goes still farther in the harsh forms of body and head[65] (Fig. 19). The sculptor of the Apollo from Cyrene in the British Museum has changed the leaning Apollo to a musician with the kithara in his arm and a cloak draped in effective lines around the legs[66] (Fig. 679). It is an elegant creation of the middle Hellenistic period, lacking the balance of form and content of Praxiteles's works.

The same changes in copying happened to the most famous among the female statues of Praxiteles, the Aphrodite of Cnidus. It was considered not only the finest statue by Praxiteles, but the finest in the whole world (Pliny *Nat. hist.* XXXVI. 20–22). Praxiteles had made and offered for sale two figures of Aphrodite, one nude and one whose form was draped. The people of Kos, to whom the choice of either figure was offered at the same

[56] Brunn-Bruckmann, *Denkmäler*, Pl. 126. Rizzo, *Prassitele*, Pl. LII.

[57] Formerly in the Museo Comunale, now probably in the Museo Nuovo.

[58] Rizzo, *Prassitele*, pp. 39 ff., Pls. LIX–LXIV.

[59] See F. Imhoof-Blumer and P. Gardner, *Numismatic Commentary on Pausanias* (repr. from *J.H.S.*, Vol VI–VIII [1885–87]), p. 145, Pl. CC, Figs. XVIII–XIX. Rizzo, *Prassitele*, Pl. CXIX, 1. O. Deubner, *Hellenistische Apollogestalten* (Athens, 1934), pp. 26 ff.

[60] Klein, *Praxiteles*, pp. 162 ff. Rizzo, *Prassitele*, pp. 79 ff., 117, Pls. CXIX–CXXI, CXXVI, CXXVIII–CXXIX. Blümel, *Berlin Katalog*, Vol. V, pp. 19 f., No. K227–29, Pls. 38–41. Deubner, *Apollogestalten*, pp. 62 f., No. 29.

[61] T. L. Shear in *Hesperia*, Vol. VI (1937), pp. 348 ff., Figs. 13–14.

[62] W. Helbig and G. Barracco, *La Collection Barracco* (Munich, 1893), pp. 45 f., Pl. 59. Rizzo, *Prassitele*, Pls. CXXII–CXXIII and CXXVII.

[63] Amelung, *Antiken in Florenz*, No. 69. Klein, *Praxiteles*, pp. 158 ff., Fig. 24. Rizzo, *Prassitele*, Pls. CXXIV–CXXV. Deubner, *Apollogestalten*, pp. 40 ff., 75, No. 30.

[64] The collection of the Museo Kircheriano has been transferred to the Museo Nazionale Romano and to the Museo di Villa Papa Giulio.

[65] R. Paribeni, *Le Terme di Diocleziano e il Museo Nazionale Romano* (Rome, 4th ed., 1922), p. 204, No. 546. Deubner, *Apollogestalten*, pp. 43 f., 75 f., No. 31.

[66] A. H. Smith, *Brit. Mus. Cat.*, Vol. II, No. 1380. W. Amelung in text to Brunn-Bruckmann, *Denkmäler*, Pl. 593. Rizzo, *Prassitele*, Pl. CXXVIII. Deubner, *Apollogestalten*, pp. 30 ff., 63 f., No. 30. See our Chap. XI, pp. 130 and 160.

price, preferred the one which was draped, as all figures of Aphrodite had been in the classical period, because they considered it more chaste and severe. The one which they rejected was bought by the Cnidians and became immeasurably more celebrated. Many sailed to Cnidus to see it. King Nikomedes of Bithynia wished to buy it from the Cnidians and offered to discharge the whole enormous debt of the city. But the Cnidians preferred to undergo the worst, and justly so, for by that statue Praxiteles had made the island of Cnidus famous.

The statue of the Cnidian Aphrodite is reproduced on Roman coins of Cnidus.[67] From these it has been possible to identify a number of Roman copies. The best known is in the Vatican [68] (Figs. 24–25). It is almost complete, but is of poor workmanship and was for a long time disfigured by a whitewashed lead cloak, wrapped stiffly around the legs; this has now been removed. A better copy has been found by Walter Amelung in the old dungeons, now storerooms, of the Vatican, where nobody had seen it for a hundred years.[69] But the body of this copy is also rather clumsy, and the head is dull compared to originals such as the Hermes. Yet the statue must have had a seductive beauty, as may be gathered from literary evidence. Phryne, the mistress of Praxiteles, is said to have been the model. Her beauty is brought home to us and emphasized by the story of how she took off all her clothes and bathed before the whole assembly at a festival at Eleusis. A young man is said to have become mad with passion for the marble statue in Cnidus. Although a mortal is said to have been the model, the image was believed to have been executed under the direct inspiration of the goddess. The head (Fig. 24) is particularly praised by the fine art critic Lucian (*Eikones* [*Imagines*] 6 and *Erotes* [*Amores*] 13). When he constructed an imaginary masterpiece of nature, taking it piece by piece from celebrated statues, he took the head from the goddess of Cnidus. "The hair and forehead and finely penciled eyebrows as Praxiteles made them, and in the melting gaze of the eyes with their bright and joyous expression he seeks also to preserve the spirit of Praxiteles. A haughty smile played gently over her parted lips." The head is best copied in a replica found in Tralles, formerly in the Kaufmann collection and in the Berlin Museum as a loan, and now in the Louvre.[70] Although it has simple and dignified features, which are gracious and strong at the same time, the melting gaze of the eyes can only be guessed at, particularly because the original colors are lacking. Praxiteles is said to have liked best those of his statues which the celebrated painter Nikias had colored. The hair of this replica is combed in soft waves to the side, twice surrounded by a fillet, formerly colored, and caught up in a graceful knot at the back. A fragment of another reproduction, found in Cnidus and now in the British Museum, must have been very near to the original.[71]

A head of another Aphrodite of Praxiteles, in the possession of Lord Leconfield at Petworth [72] and considered an original, allows us better to realize how Praxiteles could make his figures seem to live and breathe. The eyes are long. The lower lid is toned down almost to invisibility and contributes much to the soft and dreamy expression of the eye. The half-open lips give the impression of a sensitive nature. The forehead is high and triangular in shape. The hair is arranged in soft waves, with much display of light and shadow. The neck has the rounded folds called the collar of Venus. This head may be a later original by the hand of Praxiteles.

One of the followers of Praxiteles may have made the original head of a girl found in Chios, now in Boston.[73] Here the delicate forms are

---

[67] Coins of the time of Caracalla. Rizzo, *Prassitele*, Pl. LXX, Nos. 2–5.

[68] Brunn-Bruckmann, *Denkmäler*, Pl. 371. Klein, *Praxiteles*, pp. 248 ff., 115, Fig. 40. Rizzo, *Prassitele*, pp. 45 ff., Pls. LXXXII–LXXXIV. C. Blinkenberg, *Knidia* (1933), pp. 10 ff., Fig. 2, pp. 121 ff., No. I, 1, Pls. I, II.

[69] Rizzo, *Prassitele*, pp. 53 ff., Pl. LXXXI G. von Kaschnitz-Weinberg, *Sculture del Magazzino del Museo Vaticano* (1936–37), pp. 119 ff., No. 257, Pls. LI–LIII. Blinkenberg, *Knidia*, pp. 125 ff., No. I, 2, Pl. 3. Richter, *Sculpture and Sculptors*, p. 261, Fig. 670.

[70] Rizzo, *Prassitele*, Pls. LXXV–LXXXVI, pp. 54 ff. *Antike Denkmäler* (4 vols., Berlin, Kaiserlich Deutsches Archaeologisches Institut, 1891–1931), Vol. I, Pl. 40. Brunn-Bruckmann, *Denkmäler*, Pl. 161. Louvre, museum number 3518.

[71] A. H. Smith, *Brit. Mus. Cat.*, Vol. II, p. 208, No. 1314. Blinkenberg, *Knidia*, pp. 182 ff., No. V2, Figs. 67–69, Pl. 15.

[72] Rizzo, *Prassitele*, pp. 62, 73 f., 116, Pls. CVIII–CX. Furtwängler, *Masterpieces*, pp. 640 ff., Pl. XXXI. M. Wyndham, *Catalogue of the Collection Leconfield* (London, 1915), No. 73.

[73] L. D. Caskey, *Catalogue of Greek and Roman Sculpture* (Boston, Museum of Fine Arts, 1925), pp. 71 ff., No. 29. Richter, *Sculpture and Sculptors*, pp. 76, 267, Fig. 174.

treated in a rather impressionistic manner, with soft, flowing modeling impossible before Praxiteles set the example. Each part passes softly and imperceptibly into the adjoining one. A late Hellenistic adaptation of the Cnidian Aphrodite in the Metropolitan Museum of Art, New York,[74] (Figs. 26–27) shows her bending forward more than sideward; the changed style of her hairdress makes her seem more mortal and natural.

Another lesser follower of Praxiteles must have made an Aphrodite that is known to us from copies in Munich (Fig. 29), in the Museo Torlonia, and in the storerooms of the Vatican.[75] He has taken over the general outline of the composition of the Cnidian Aphrodite, which is as skillful and refined as in the Hermes. The nudity of the goddess in the original statue is explained by the bath, which in antiquity was taken by kneeling in the water and having water poured over the body from a jug. This vase is of beautiful shape, probably made of gilded bronze and richly ornamented with scrolls. From the hand of the goddess, her drapery falls over the vase in graceful folds. The garment was certainly originally painted, perhaps red or purple; just as the trunk and cloak of the Olympian Hermes contrasted with the flesh, the colored and rough material served to set off the soft skin of the nude body. The gesture of the right hand is taken from an old oriental representation of the goddess of love, but was remodeled to make it a gesture of unconscious protection against mortal observers. In the statue of Praxiteles's follower the serenity and divinity of the Cnidian Aphrodite are gone. Instead of allowing the drapery to fall onto the vase, the goddess lifts it with a gesture expressing fear of exposing her body to human eyes. The head is smaller and has rather insignificant features. Once begun by Praxiteles, the tendency to give to the gods human qualities instead of heavenly majesty made itself more and more felt.

A step further in this direction is made by the famous Medici Aphrodite (Venus de Medici) in the Tribuna of the Uffizi Gallery in Florence [76] (Figs. 30–31). Here the vase is replaced by two Erotes riding a dolphin. Thus both hands are free and shield the body—the right the breasts and the left the lower body—in a very conscious gesture of modesty. The beautiful head (Fig. 28) looks almost coquettishly to the side. It is unbroken in the New York replica. The features are sweet and soft. The hair is full and wavy, held by a ribbon, and bound into a small bow in front and a small knot at the back. The statue has occasionally been attributed to the sons of Praxiteles, and although this is not likely, it must belong to the early part of the third century, the same period during which Kephisodotos and Timarchos worked the statues for the altar in Kos.[77] The fragment of the body of a woman found in Kos near this altar, perhaps Aphrodite (Fig. 32), goes still further in the strong leaning and the sensuous rendering of the body, while the head from the same place (Fig. 33) is still softer and sweeter than the head of the Medici Aphrodite.

The Aphrodite in the Museo Capitolino (Figs. 34–35) and her replicas,[78] on the other hand, are much harsher in the forms of body and head than the Medici Aphrodite. The forms are mature and almost plump and the features are severe in comparison to the Medici Aphrodite. The bow on the crown of the head is large and luxurious, and long hair falls on the nape of the neck. It is probably a creation of the second century B.C.

Another nude figure by Praxiteles was called Pseliumene, the woman who puts on her necklace

---

[74] Metropolitan Museum of Art, No. 12173; perhaps from Asia Minor. See G. A. Richter, *Greek, Etruscan, and Roman Bronzes* (New York, Metropolitan Museum of Art, 1915), pp. 74 ff., No. 121, and *Handbook* (1953), p. 110, Pl. 88b.

[75] Furtwängler and Wolters, *Glyptothek*, pp. 266 ff., No. 258. Rizzo, *Prassitele*, pp. 131 ff., Pls. LXXI–LXXIII. Blinkenberg, *Knidia*, pp. 131 ff., No. I, 3, Figs. 52–55, Pl. 4, see pp. 1 ff., Fig. 1, and p. 148, No. I, 12, Pl. 8. Kaschnitz-Weinberg, *Magazzino del Vaticano*, pp. 116 ff., No. 256, Pls. XLVI–L.

[76] Amelung, *Antiken in Florenz*, pp. 46 f., No. 67. Klein, *Praxiteles*, pp. 276 ff., Fig. 41. Brunn-Bruckmann, *Denkmäler*, Pl. 374. The excellent replica acquired from a private collection in Silesia by the Metropolitan Museum of Art in New York has a different and more vigorous sidewards movement of the unbroken head than the Medici Aphrodite, and the facial and bodily forms are more rounded. The dolphin is at a different angle toward the goddess, and there is no riding Eros. The dolphin and the tree trunk play a smaller part in the composition, which was invented for a bronze original. The new statue has been published by Christine Alexander in the *Bulletin of the Metropolitan Museum of Art* (1953), pp. 241 ff., with 11 figures.

[77] M. Bieber in *Jahrbuch d. Inst.*, Vol. XXXVIII–IX (1923–24), pp. 242 ff., Pls. VI–VII.

[78] Jones, *Sculpt. Museo Capitolino*, pp. 182 ff., Gabinetto della Venere 1, Pl. 45. Brunn-Bruckmann, *Denkmäler*, Pl. 373. There is a list of replicas by B. Felletti-Maj in *Archeologia Classica*, III, No. 1 (1951), pp. 33 ff., 61 ff.

or bracelets (Pliny *Nat. hist.* xxxiv. 69). It has been recognized in bronze statuettes, the best one being in the British Museum[79] (Fig. 36). A beautiful woman, perhaps Aphrodite but more likely Phryne or another mortal woman, lifts both hands with a graceful movement to put the jewel around her neck. A similar movement is used for a series of Hellenistic statues and statuettes, most of which were called Anadyomene ("emerging from the sea") because Apelles painted an Aphrodite rising from the sea while removing the sea foam from her hair. But the statues and statuettes, like the one in Fig. 37, are actually engaged in lifting two side strands of the hair to finish the hairdress. As some of these already have a stephane in the hair, this might be the type of the Stephanusa, also established as a work of Praxiteles (Pliny *Nat. hist.* xxxiv. 69). A small bronze in the Metropolitan Museum of Art in New York may illustrate the gesture[80] (Fig. 38). Another adaptation of a similar type is the slender Hellenistic statuette in Dresden[81] (Fig. 39), who rests her left elbow on a pillar and holds an apple in her hand, while lifting a long strand of hair above the shoulder with the right hand.

A statue from Gabii, now in the Louvre,[82] has a graceful movement similar to that of the Pseliumene. With both hands she lifts a cloak to her right shoulder to fasten it there. Her chiton is girt and drawn through a second belt to form a pouch, thus shortening it. This statue is generally recognized as a copy of the image made by Praxiteles for the temple of Artemis Brauronia on the Acropolis of Athens (Pausanias I. 23. 7). Actual dresses were dedicated to this Artemis, who was a special protectress of women, particularly of mothers. The temporary arrangement of both dresses is meant to show how the goddess accepts and uses the garments offered by her votaries. The statue is first mentioned in 346/5, the probable date of erection;

it thus belongs to the middle period of Praxiteles.

Artemis was a favorite subject among the draped figures of Praxiteles. In Megara she stood beside her brother Apollo and her mother Leto (Pausanias I. 40. 3), a group repeated on coins.[83] This type is reproduced in sculpture in the round, the best copy being a statue in Dresden[84] (Fig. 40), wherefore it is known as the Dresden Artemis. There are many copies without the head: three are in Kassel, only one being good[85] (Fig. 42); others, with heads and arms which do not belong, are in the British Museum and in the Louvre.[86] The Dresden Artemis is a very young girl, clad in the ungirded peplos worn by young maidens. Her left hand hangs down and holds the bow, the right is lifted to take an arrow out of the quiver on her back. The head has very young and fresh features. The hair is combed back in simple waves and bound up in a thick bunch at the back. The composition is on very quiet lines. It must be an early work of Praxiteles, when he was still under the influence of Kephisodotos.

The torso of a peplos statue from the school of Praxiteles by his sons, the younger Kephisodotos and Timarchos, has been found in Kos. Probably it represents Hygieia[87] (Fig. 43). The peplos has a short overfold, with the pouch drawn out of an evident belt. The figure is broader and more matronly than the Artemis, but the treatment of the lower part of the dress, with the heavy vertical folds before the carrying leg and the one fold falling from the knee of the relaxed leg, is in the traditional manner of the fifth century, transmitted by the elder Kephisodotos to his son and through him to his grandsons.

The Artemis from Larnaca in Cyprus is also ascribed to the sons of Praxiteles (see Fig. 41, and p. 16, above).

Another group of Artemis with Apollo and Leto stood in the sanctuary of Mantinea. Pausanias (VIII.

---

[79] Klein, *Praxiteles*, pp. 282 ff., Figs. 45–50. H. B. Walters, *Catalogue of the Bronzes, Greek, Roman, and Etruscan, in the Department of Greek and Roman Antiquities* (London, British Museum, 1899), No 1084, Pl. V. Rizzo, *Prassitele*, pp. 60 f., Pl. LXXXIX.

[80] The Metropolitan Museum of Art number is 35. 122. Richter, *Handbook* (1953), p. 110, Pl. 88a.

[81] Furtwängler, *Masterpieces*, pp. 621 f., Fig. 122.

[82] Brunn-Bruckmann, *Denkmäler*, Pl. 59. Klein, *Praxiteles*, pp. 300 ff., Fig. 54. Rizzo, *Prassitele*, pp. 63 ff., 116, Pls. XCIV–XCVIII.

[83] Imhoof-Blumer and Gardner, *Numismatic Commentary*, p. 7, Pl. A, Fig. X (cf. p. 154, Pl. FF, Fig. II).

[84] Dresden Museum, No. 279. Klein, *Praxiteles*, pp. 308 f. Rizzo, *Prassitele*, p. 13 f., Pls. XVI–XVIII.

[85] M. Bieber, *Antike Skulpturen und Bronzen in Kassel* (1915), pp. 18 f., Nos. 17–19, Pl. XXI.

[86] A. H. Smith, *Brit. Mus. Cat.*, Vol. III, No. 1638c Ariadne (?), W. Fröhner, *Notice de la sculpture antique du Louvre* (4th ed., 1878), No. 390.

[87] See above, note 77.

9. 1) tells us that on the base were represented the Muses and Marsyas, who was playing the flutes. Pausanias names only one Muse, but that must be an error, for six Muses are preserved.[88] They are present at the musical contest between Apollo and Marsyas, who plays the flutes forbidden by the inventor Athena; he of course loses and is severely punished. The victorious Apollo is seated in a dignified pose on a rock, with his kithara. A Scythian slave holding the knife that is to flay Marsyas stands between them. The conception of the draped Muses is rich and beautiful. There is a balance between drapery and body which marks the culmination of classical harmony. The dress reflects and underlines the forms and the movements of the wearers. Some scholars assign the base to the younger Praxiteles, but as Pausanias, in speaking of the gods made by Praxiteles in Mantinea, mentions that he made the statues in the third generation after Alkamenes, with Kephisodotos being the second generation, there can be no doubt that this is a work of the most mature period of the great Praxiteles.

Several draped statues of females are related to these figures of the Muses. An Athena in bronze found in Arezzo, now in the Museo Archeologico of Florence [89] (Fig. 47), was often copied also in marble. Athena has the cloak slung around the body in varied folds following the attitude and the forms of the youthful and vigorous figure, similar to the Muses. The motif of the folds radiating over the whole left arm is also similar in both. The majesty of the Athena Parthenos of Phidias and other statues of Athena made in the fifth century is gone in this creation of a third generation, but the purity and restraint of this new creation is not without greatness of conception.

A very slender and graceful figure in Vienna, rightly called Kore or Persephone,[90] is very similar to the Muse with flutes on the base of Mantinea. It appears, together with a matronly Demeter wearing the peplos, on reliefs dedicated to the Eleusinian goddesses at Eleusis (in Eleusis, in Athens, and in the Louvre); one found in Mondragone is in Naples.[91] Praxiteles made statues of the Eleusinian goddesses for Athens, and it is very likely that these types are reminiscent of his work.

We find the same principles of draping, but with more complicated motifs and much differentiation, in the mourning women, perhaps the members of the harem of the deceased, on the sarcophagus from Sidon in Constantinople.[92] This work belongs probably to the school of Praxiteles. The same is true of the two celebrated "tall and small women" found in Herculaneum, now in Dresden.[93] The best copy of the small woman has been found in Delos and is now in Athens.[94] She has wrapped her mantle around her body and tightly around her left arm, while her right hand lifts the upper edge in a momentary movement up to her left shoulder. The statue of the tall woman, of which a good replica without a head has been found on the island of Andros and is now in Athens, has wrapped her mantle around her head also. She holds the upper edge in her right hand and draws it to the right side. These motifs result in a complicated crossing of folds and edges, which are beyond everything that we find in works attributed with certainty to Praxiteles himself.[95] The variously disposed folds circle the figures, however, still quite in the manner of Praxiteles. They are arranged so as to show the grace of the strong body of the tall woman as well as of the slim body of the small one. Originally the taller woman was probably meant to represent Demeter, the mother, and the smaller one Kore (Persephone), the daughter. Both figures were often copied in the Hellenistic and Roman periods; they were used for

[88] G. Fougères in *B.C.H.*, Vol. XII (1888), pp. 104 ff., Pls. I–III. W. Amelung, *Die Basis des Praxiteles aus Mantinea* (Munich, 1895). Rizzo, *Prassitele*, pp. 86 ff., 117, Pls. CXXX–CXXXII. Perhaps there were never more than six and the contest was in the center, with the seated Muse turned toward Apollo, the standing one turned away from Marsyas.
[89] Amelung, *Antiken in Florenz*, p. 256, No. 248, Figs. 45–46. Amelung, *Basis des Praxiteles*, pp. 16 ff. Rizzo, *Prassitele*, pp. 93 f., 118, Pls. CXXXIX–CXLII.
[90] R. von Schneider, *Jahrbuch der Kunstsammlungen des Kaiserhauses* (1894), p. 139, Pl. X–XI. R. von Schneider, *Album der Antikensammlung des Kaiserhauses zu Wien* (1895), pp. 2 f., Pl. 5. Klein, *Praxiteles*, pp. 362 ff., Fig. 73.

[91] Rizzo, *Prassitele*, pp. 100 ff., 118 f., Pls. CLI–CLIV.
[92] O. Hamdy-bey and T. Reinach, *Une Nécropole royale à Sidon* (Paris, 1892), pp. 238 ff., Pls. IV–XI. Details of the funeral procession (Pl. X) and of the hunting frieze (Pls. IX and XI) on the base confirm a date later than that of Praxiteles.
[93] Dresden Museum, Nos. 140–42. Brunn-Bruckmann, *Denkmäler*, Pls. 310 and 558. M. Collignon, *Les Statues funéraires dans l'art grecque* (1911), pp. 168 ff. Rizzo, *Prassitele*, pp. 91 f., 117 f., Pls. CXXXV–CXXXVI.
[94] Rizzo, *Prassitele*, Pl. CXXXVII.
[95] See M. Bieber, *Griechische Kleidung* (1928), pp. 63 ff., 81 f., Pls. XXIX–XXX, and LII, Nos. 3–4.

portrait statues and for gravestones, the older probably for married women, the younger for unmarried ones. Examples of their use on gravestones are the relief in the north wall of the Church of the Panagia Gorgoepikoos (the Little Metropolitan Cathedral) in Athens, and a late Hellenistic one, now in Munich.[96] The head of the best replica of the small woman, with its complicated melon coiffure, shows also that this type was created under Praxitelean influence in the early Hellenistic period.

The same is true of a group of Muses, the best replicas of which are in the Vatican Museum, and which has been attributed wrongly to Kephisodotos or to Praxiteles.[97] The figure of the so-called Polyhymnia, for example (Figs. 45–46) repeats the motif of the drapery of the small Herculaneum woman, but has still more refined motifs, like the hand shining through the veil-like mantle. The head crowned with roses (Fig. 46) also has Praxitelean features. The figure of Thalia with the comic mask beside her (Fig. 44) wears, however, the Hellenistic dress called *peronatris,* and has a Hellenistic mode of wearing the belt.

The influence of the tender and charming art of Praxiteles was very strongly felt in the minor arts. Tombstones, like the girl with a water jug,[98] and the mother and daughter exchanging caresses,[99] reflect his spirit. A head from a tombstone in Berlin [100] is similar to the heads of the Muses (Fig. 46), but it has still more strength and clearness in the features. Innumerable statuettes in terra cotta, the best of them found in Tanagra in Boeotia, for example some in the Louvre [101] (Figs. 49, 51, and 52), show girls in chiton and mantle, in

graceful poses and with endless variety of motifs in the drapery. Some recall the Muses on the base of Mantinea. Others, in the Metropolitan Museum of Art in New York (Figs. 48, 50, and 53), are colorful statuettes of seated boys and a kneeling girl, probably playing knucklebones.[102]

The exquisite art of Praxiteles lived on in his sons, the younger Kephisodotos and Timarchos (see pp. 20 f. and Figs. 32, 33, 43), who, however, were also influenced by Lysippos. The delicacy of rhythm in the work of Praxiteles had never been surpassed. The radiance and loveliness of his art appealed to the sculptors and artisans of the Hellenistic period, who, however, often missed the strength always present in his work, and thus sometimes produced effeminate creations, particularly in the school of Alexandria.

It was easier to imitate his great contemporary Skopas.

3. SKOPAS (c.370—c.330 B.C.)

The art of Skopas, contemporary of Praxiteles, is a supplement and at the same time a striking contrast to Praxiteles's art. While Praxiteles and his father Kephisodotos were Athenians, Aristandros, the father of Skopas, lived on the island of Paros, and in 405 B.C. was employed, together with the pupils of Polykleitos, on the memorial of Aegospotamos, the battle which destroyed the Athenian power and led to the surrender of Athens to Sparta at the end of the Peloponnesian War. Skopas's art, therefore, combines the traditions of Ionic and Peloponnesian art.[103]

Skopas's most important group of sculptures was made in the Peloponnese. He was employed in the rebuilding of the temple of Athena Alea at Tegea in Arcadia, which had been destroyed by fire in 394 B.C. Skopas, therefore, was an architect as well

[96] K. Michel and A. Struck in *Athen. Mitt.,* Vol. XXXI (1906), p. 305, Fig. 24. Furtwängler and Wolters, *Glyptothek,* p. 258, No. 249.

[97] G. Lippold, *Die Sculpturen des Vaticanischen Museums,* Vol. III, Part I (Berlin, 1936), pp. 21 ff., Pls. 4–9, Sala delle Muse 499, 503, 505, 508, 511, 515, 517. The correct date, a generation after Praxiteles, is given by Amelung and Lippold.

[98] Conze, *Grabreliefs,* Vol. II, p. 172, No. 805, Pl. 152.

[99] Conze, *Grabreliefs,* Vol. I, p. 73, No. 320, Pl. 78. Diepolder, *Grabreliefs,* p. 50, Pl. 47.

[100] Blümel, *Berlin Katalog,* Vol. III, pp. 39 f., No. K43, Pl. 51.

[101] Many examples are in E. Pottier, *Les Statuettes de terre cuite dans l'antiquité* (Paris, 1890). H. B. Walters, *Catalogue of the Terracottas in the Department of Greek and Roman Antiquities* (London, the British Museum, 1899). A. Köster, *Die griechischen Terrakotten* (Berlin, 1926). G. Kleiner, *Tanagrafiguren* (Berlin, 1942; Fifteenth Supplement [Ergänzungsheft] to *Jahrbuch d. Inst.*).

[102] Metropolitan Museum of Art, Nos. 07.286.26 and 14.146.4 (seated boys), Nos. 13.225.15 and 18.145.52 (kneeling or crouching girls). Richter, *Handbook* (1953), p. 112, Pl. 92 d-e. Anita Klein, *Child Life in Greek Art* (1932), pp. 17 ff., Pls. XVIII–XIX.

[103] General works: M. Collignon, *Scopas et Praxitèle* (1907), pp. 161 ff. E. A. Gardner, *Six Greek Sculptors* (London, 1910), pp. 177 ff. K. A. Neugebauer, *Studien über Skopas* (Leipzig, 1913). Ch. Picard, *Manuel d'archéologie grecque: La Sculpture antique,* Vol. III, Part 2 (1948), pp. 633 ff. G. Lippold, *Die griechische Plastik* (Vol. III of *Handbuch der Archäologie,* ed. W. Otto and R. Herbig, Munich, 1950), pp. 249 ff. P. E. Arias, *Skopas* (Rome, 1952).

as a sculptor. Pausanias (VIII. 45. 4–7) tells us that the large and remarkable temple erected after the fire was far superior to the other temples in the Peloponnese in size and magnificence. The first columns were of the Doric order, the next Corinthian, and inside the temple stood columns of the Ionic order. Pausanias says "The architect was Skopas of Paros, who was the sculptor of many statues in different parts of Greece." From this it seems clear that Skopas's most important work on the temple of Tegea were the decorative sculptures, just as the metopes, frieze, and pediment figures of the Parthenon were the most important part of the work of Phidias, who also had the supervision of the whole building and who influenced the architectural form in favor of the temple statue and the temple decorations. Skopas did not make the image of Athena Alea, for the temple statue was an ivory work by Endoios that had been rescued from the fire that destroyed the old temple. But Skopas supplied the marble statues of Asclepius and Hygieia that stood in the interior on either side of Athena.

The excavations of French scholars in Tegea have substantiated most of the description of Pausanias.[104] A beautiful original head in Parian marble, which might be a fragment of the Hygieia, has been found.[105] The face is serene but full of life, and the flesh is softly rendered. It was first fitted to a torso of a female figure, also carved in Parian marble, supposed to be Atalanta, the heroine of Arcadia, who was the first to wound the Calydonian boar in the chase represented in the front pediment[106] (Fig. 58). The torso wears a short hunter's dress which leaves the right breast and the right leg bare, because it opens in keeping with her active movement. She is just striking the wild boar. The head, however, does not fit the torso, and it is too calm for her lively action. Atalanta was the only female figure in the front pediment and, therefore, is of different marble from the rest of the sculptures, which are carved in a local stone from Dolianà near Tegea. Atalanta stood next to

the boar in the center, together with Meleager, who helped in killing the boar, but who gave the skin to Atalanta. This led to his premature death, as he quarreled with the brothers of his mother, who also took part in the hunt and objected to the honor given to a female. He killed them, and his mother in anger killed him. Theseus, Peirithoos, Heracles, Iolaos, Ankaios, who was wounded, and many others were also present. In the rear pediment the battle of Telephos against Achilles on the plain of the Caicus in Asia Minor was represented. Telephos was the local Arcadian hero, the son of Auge and Heracles, and the founder of Pergamon (see below, Chapter VIII, pp. 120 f., and Figs. 477–78).

No complete figure survives, but many fragments of these pediments have been found. The most important ones are some battered male heads, the best one with a helmet[107] (Fig. 55). Another, representing perhaps Telephos, the son of Heracles, has a lion's skin, and several heads are bare. The style of the heads is peculiar. They are massive and square, not oval as are those of Praxiteles. The forehead is low, instead of being high as in the works of Praxiteles, and has a marked projection of the lower part which is suggestive of force. The eyes, which in the Praxitelean heads are elongated and have soft eyelids, are short and wide open. They are overshadowed in the outer corner by a heavy roll of flesh curving out beneath the brow, so that the upper eyelid is actually embedded in it. The gaze is fixed upwards, while the gaze of Praxitelean heads is generally directed downwards. The nostrils are dilated. The mouth is half open, panting, while the mouths of the figures of Praxiteles are generally smiling. The expression is excited, pathetic, and intense, instead of being soft, calm, and dreamy as in Praxiteles. The emotional gaze is even found in the eye of the boar.[108]

The style of these sculptures is so peculiar that they have suggested the attribution of various other works to Skopas. A statue of Meleager is also connected in subject with Tegea. The best-preserved copies, each with a chlamys added by the copyist, are in Berlin and in the Vatican.[109] The head of

[104] C. Dugas, J. Berchmans, and M. Clemmensen, *Le Sanctuaire d'Aléa Athéna à Tégée* (Paris, 1924). Neugebauer, *Skopas*, pp. 1 ff., Pls. I–II.

[105] Dugas, *et al.*, *Tégée*, pp. 117 ff., No. 97, Pls. CXIII, CXIV a, CXV a.

[106] *Ibid.*, pp. 80 ff., No. 1, Pls. XCVI–XCVIII a. Richter, *Sculpture and Sculptors*, p. 270, Fig. 696.

[107] Dugas, *et al.*, *Tégée*, pp. 87 ff., Nos. 7–9, Pls. XCIX–CII. Richter, *Sculpture and Sculptors*, p. 270, Figs. 690–93. Arias, *Skopas*, pp. 120 ff., Fig. 27–31.

[108] Dugas, *et al.*, *Tégée*, pp. 84 f., No. 3, Pl. XCVII a.

[109] Blümel, *Berlin Katalog*, Vol. V, pp. 22 f., No. K235, Pl. 48. Amelung, *Vatican Kat.*, Vol. II, pp. 33 ff., Belvedere, Sala del

the boar and the hunting dog at Meleager's feet make the identification certain. Better worked copies are the torso in the Fogg Museum of Art of Harvard University [110] (Figs. 54, 56, 57), and a head in the Villa Medici in Rome.[111] The head in the Leonteion of Calydon is a coarse provincial adaptation.[112] In the torso at Harvard, the build of the body is powerful. The muscles are much more clearly marked than in the soft, youthful bodies of Praxiteles. The left hand held the spear of the hunter, the right hand rested behind the hip. The erect stance expresses vigor instead of languor. The wide-open eyes are deeply sunk under the brows and they have narrow lids like the heads of Tegea. The mouth is slightly open, and gives to the face a yearning expression. The emotion agrees with the sadness of the fate of the youth who had to die for his generosity. A head in the British Museum, found in the vicinity of Genzano, near Rome, gives similar emotional features to Heracles.[113]

A Bacchante of Skopas is described at length in a poem by Callistratus (*Descriptions of Statues II*). She was said to be depicted dancing in ecstasy, her head thrown back, her hair disheveled, and carrying a victim, the kid she has killed. This description applies to a small statuette in Dresden, which may therefore be identified as the Maenad by Skopas[114] (Figs. 59–60). Her dress, like that of Atalanta (Fig. 58), is fastened only on one shoulder and held together by a belt. It floats open, so that it leaves the left side of her body and the left leg bare. The edges frame the vigorous forms. On her left shoulder are traces of the body of the slain animal. Her right hand doubtless held the knife

with which she had killed it. It is a marvelous interpretation of orgiastic enthusiasm. The head is thrown back almost horizontally, so that the hair falls deep onto the back. Despite its being much damaged, it has the same squareness of shape and intensity of expression that we see in the Tegea heads (Fig. 55). Skopas certainly put passionate expression into a woman's glance when the subject was suitable.

We can be sure that he used the expression of passion and emotion to a large extent in the group of sea-gods and sea-creatures that had the highest reputation of all his works in antiquity (Pliny *Nat. hist.* XXXVI. 25–26). It represented Poseidon with Thetis and her son Achilles; Nereids riding on dolphins, huge fishes, or sea horses; Tritons, sea-monsters, and many other marine creatures. Pliny adds to the description that the group would have been remarkable even if it had been the work of a lifetime. It enjoyed the highest reputation in Rome, where it was set up in later times in a sanctuary near the Circus Flaminius by Cn. Domitius Ahenobarbus, who is supposed to have brought the group from Bithynia to Rome. The subject seems to have been the progress of Achilles to the Isles of the Blessed, accompanied by his mother Thetis, who was a Nereid, and all her relatives from the sea. The base, made in the first century B.C. for the group's re-erection in Rome, is thought to be preserved in the reliefs in Munich, showing the wedding procession of Poseidon and Amphitrite.[115] A single figure of the group is thought to have been copied in a beautiful Tritoness from Ostia,[116] whose features and disheveled hair remind us closely of the Maenad in Dresden (Figs. 59–60) and of the Tegea heads. The pathos, emotion, and yearning of sea creatures are very much emphasized; this emphasis must have been still stronger later in Hellenistic sculpture, under the inspiration of Skopas. Thus a Triton in the Vatican Museum[117] (Fig. 63) shows how the powerful creations of Skopas opened the way for the emotional sculptures of the Hellenistic period. Com-

Meleagro 10, Pls. 3 and 12. Brunn-Bruckmann, *Denkmäler*, Pl. 386.
[110] G. H. Chase, *Greek and Roman Sculpture in American Collections* (Cambridge, Harvard University Press, 1924), pp. 87 f., Fig. 97; cf. Figs. 98–101.
[111] *Ant. Denk.*, Vol. I, Pl. 40. Chase, *Greek and Roman Sculpture*, Figs. 100, 101, a; Richter, *Sculpture and Sculptors*, p. 274, Fig. 708.
[112] E. Dyggve, F. Poulsen, K. Rhomaios, *Das Heroon von Kalydon* (Copenhagen, 1948), p. 369, Figs. 91–93. G. Becatti in *Riv. del Ist. Arch.*, Vol. VII (1940), pp. 55 ff., Figs. 44–48.
[113] A. H. Smith, *Brit. Mus. Cat.*, Vol. III, p. 93, No. 1731, Pl. V, 2.
[114] P. Herrmann, *Verzeichnis der antiken Original-Bildwerke* (Dresden, Skulpturen-Sammlung, 1915), p. 35, No. 133. Neugebauer, *Skopas*, pp. 51 ff., Pls. III–IV. Arias, *Skopas*, pp. 126 f., Figs. 36–37.

[115] Furtwängler and Wolters, *Glyptothek*, No. 239, Brunn-Bruckmann, *Denkmäler*, Pl. 124.
[116] J. D. Beazley and B. Ashmole, *Greek Sculpture and Painting to the End of the Hellenistic Period* (Cambridge University Press, 1932), p. 56, Fig. 117.
[117] Amelung, *Vatican Kat.*, Vol. II, pp. 418 ff., Galeria delle Statue No. 253, Pl. 46. Brunn-Bruckmann, *Denkmäler*, Pl. 137.

pared with them, the Tritons and Nereids on the Munich base look rather tame.

The yearning expressed in the sea creatures was certainly intensified in the personifications of Himeros (Yearning) and Pothos (Desire) which stood next to an Eros in Megara (Pausanias I. 43. 6). Another figure of Pothos by Skopas stood next to Aphrodite at Samothrace (Pliny *Nat. hist.* XXXVI. 25). The statue of an Apollo-like youth in Florence, looking upward with a yearning expression (Fig. 62), of which several copies are known,[118] has rightly been recognized as the personification of Pothos. It is an unusual representation of a boy standing with crossed legs, a goose at his feet; over the back of the goose the boy's garment hangs down in long folds coming from the lifted left arm. For the same temple in Megara, Praxiteles worked the personifications of Paregoros (Consolation) and Peitho (Persuasion). The master of emotion very suitably chose the more violent, the master of grace the softer qualities connected with love—that is, with Aphrodite and Eros.

Skopas was a rival of Praxiteles in the representation of Aphrodite. A nude Aphrodite of Skopas, later in Rome, in the opinion of Pliny (*Nat. hist.* XXXVI. 26) surpassed even the famous Aphrodite of Praxiteles and would have been the fame of any place less full of works of art than Rome. Different types of Aphrodite have been attributed to Skopas, among others the Medici Aphrodite (Figs. 28, 30, and 31) and the Capitoline Aphrodite (Figs. 34–35), but both are Hellenistic adaptations of the Cnidian Aphrodite. To me, the best guess seems to be that the Aphrodite found in Capua and now in Naples, of which we have more than a dozen copies and adaptations,[119] is the Aphrodite which Skopas created, together with the figure of Pothos, for Samothrace. She crosses her body with her right

arm, as does Pothos (Fig. 62). A shield was probably held in both hands. Coins from Corinth give the outlines of the composition, which was often adapted later, as in the Hellenistic Aphrodite from Melos (Venus de Milo) (see Chap. XI, pp. 159 f., Figs. 673–75), in several representations of Nike, and in the Roman Victory.

An idea of the head of Aphrodite by Skopas might be gathered from the original head found on the southern slope of the Acropolis of Athens.[120] It probably represents, however, Ariadne or a reposing Maenad, for the remains of a hand are found on the crown of the head. The beautiful waves of the hair are encircled by a broad fillet arranged in such a way that it goes over the hairline and over the forehead. This is a fashion seen in representations of Dionysos and his followers. The eyes are wide open and look up, the mouth is slightly opened, as in breathing. It is interesting to compare this precious original head with a Roman copy in Berlin.[121] All the subtlety of modeling is gone from the hair and the intensity of expression is gone from the face.

A famous statue by Skopas was the Apollo that stood in Rhamnus in Attica until Augustus took it to Rome. There he put it into the temple of Apollo on the Palatine, built to commemorate the victory of Actium in 31 B.C. Propertius (II. 31. 5–8 and 15–16) tells us that Apollo was represented in a long garment playing the kithara, standing between his sister Artemis and his mother Leto. The Artemis was by Timotheos and the Leto by the younger Kephisodotos, the son of Praxiteles. All three statues are illustrated on a base from Sorrento. With the aid of this base, copies of the Apollo by Skopas have been traced.[122] There are, however, several types that are similar to the relief, without being identical with it or with each other. Most closely akin to the statue shown on the base are a statue in the Gallery of the Villa Borghese in Rome, a statue with the head preserved

[118] Amelung, *Antiken in Florenz*, pp. 2 ff., No. 4; p. 34, No. 46; p. 71, No. 96. H. Bulle in *Jahrbuch d. Inst.*, Vol. LVI (1941), pp. 121 ff. Brunn-Bruckmann, *Denkmäler*, Pls. 616–17. G. Becatti, "Il Pothos di Scopa," in *Arti*, Vol. III (1941), pp. 401–12, Pls. CXLII–CXLVI. P. Mingazzini in *Arti Figurative*, Vol. II (1946), pp. 137 ff., Pls. XLV–XLVI. Arias, *Skopas*, pp. 131 ff., Figs. 44–48. A replica in the Museo Archeologico at Florence, found at Ferento, has wings. L. A. Milani, *Il Museo Archeologico di Firenze* (2 vols., 1912), p. 306, Pl. 147.

[119] A. Ruesch, *Guida del Museo Nazionale di Napoli* (n.d.), pp. 76 ff., No. 251, Fig. 27 (cf. Fig. 28). Brunn-Bruckmann, *Denkmäler*, Pl. 297 (cf. W. Amelung in text to Pl. 593). Furtwängler, *Masterpieces*, pp. 628 ff., Fig. 127.

[120] No. 182 in the National Museum, Athens. Brunn-Bruckmann, *Denkmäler*, Pl. 174a. Arias, *Skopas*, p. 139, Fig. 49.

[121] Berlin Museum, No. 610. Blümel, *Berlin Katalog*, pp. 32 f., No. K251, Pls. 71–72. Richter, *Sculpture and Sculptors*, p. 180, Figs. 508–9. Brunn-Bruckmann, *Denkmäler*, Pl. 174b.

[122] W. Amelung in *Ausonia*, Vol. II (1907), pp. 16 ff., Figs. 1–7, Pls. IV–VIII, and Vol. III (1908), pp. 91 ff., Fig. 1. Deubner, *Apollogestalten*, pp. 5 ff., 21 f., 71, No. 22, and p. 73, Nos. 26–29.

which is in Candia in Crete, and the so-called Barberini Muse in Munich.[123] All these represent the god in a simple woolen garment with straight-flowing folds, carrying a kithara on his left arm. The *plektron,* the instrument with which one plays on the strings, is supposed to have been in the right hand. The heads of all the copies have lost the inspired expression which we must suppose Skopas had given to the god of music.

In contrast, we find such an expression in a noble head of Apollo found on the site of the Mausoleum of Halicarnassus.[124] His eyes are upraised as if to seek inspiration. The massive build of the head, the heavy overshadowing of the eyes at the side, and their intense expression remind us of the heads from Tegea (Fig. 55). This work, however, is of a much higher standard than the works of Tegea. It shows us Skopas at his best. This type of Apollo as an impassionate musician lived on in a head of Hellenistic times in the British Museum (Fig. 72), and was used also for Dionysos in ecstasy, for example in a head in Leyden.[125]

The smallest of the three friezes which decorated the Mausoleum of Halicarnassus, representing a chariot race, is also in the style of Skopas. The charioteers [126] (Fig. 64), bending forward in a lively movement with an eager gaze in their eyes, wear long dresses flowing in curved but otherwise similar folds as those of the Palatine Apollo.

The largest and best-preserved frieze, representing the battle of the Greeks and Amazons, also has many Scopadic elements [127] (Figs. 61 and 65). The heads have deep-set eyes, short mouths, and square faces. The slabs found on the east side where, as Pliny (*Nat. hist.* xxxvi. 30–31) tells us, Skopas worked, show motifs of the dress related to those of Atalanta of Tegea (Fig. 58) and the Dresden Maenad (Figs. 59–60). Thus in several

figures the vertical edges of the dress, held together only by a belt, open wide as a consequence of the lively movement and reveal the forms of the strong bodies [128] (Fig. 61). As Pliny tells us that the sculptures of the north side were by Bryaxis, those of the south by Timotheos, and those of the west by Leochares, scholars have tried to assign definite slabs to the different artists. Unfortunately each scholar prefers a different division.[129] I believe that all these attempts are futile. When we look closely, the differences are in the execution, and not in the composition, which is a unity. The figures are widely spaced, with flowing drapery more or less filling the gaps. The heads are often carelessly worked. Differences in their types or in the types of the horses are hardly as great as in the Parthenon frieze, whose composition is as a whole due to Phidias. If any artist was entrusted with the task of designing the friezes of the Mausoleum, it must have been Skopas. At that time he was at the height of his fame, while Timotheos was old and never very progressive (see p. 13), and Leochares and Bryaxis were gifted and young, but little known. Thus these three may have helped in the execution of Skopas's design.

I believe, moreover, that this frieze, which in contrast to the other two is so remarkably well preserved, was a decoration of the inside rather than the outside. An old report of the Rhodian knights, who took possession of and demolished the Mausoleum to build up their castle in Rhodes, tells of colored figures on the inside wall of the tomb chamber. As all Greek marble sculpture was painted, it is very likely that these were the reliefs with the original colors still preserved because they had been protected from the elements. It is more probable that the four great artists worked statues in the round which stood between the columns of the outer colonnade. A fine idealized, clear-cut, bearded head [130] (Fig. 73) is a masterpiece worthy

[123] Furtwängler and Wolters, *Glyptothek,* pp. 194 ff., No. 211.
[124] A. H. Smith, *Brit. Mus. Cat.,* Vol. II, pp. 127 f., No. 1058, Pl. XX, Fig. 2. W. Amelung in *Ausonia,* Vol. II (1907), p. 64, Fig. 32.
[125] A. H. Smith, *Brit. Mus. Cat.,* Vol. III, pp. 143 f., Pl. XII, No. 1858. Brunn-Bruckmann, *Denkmäler,* Pl. 155 (head in Leyden).
[126] A. H. Smith, *Brit. Mus. Cat.,* Vol. II, p. 119 f., Nos. 1036–37, Pl. XVIII.
[127] W. Amelung in *Ausonia,* Vol. III (1908), p. 107, Fig. 12. A. H. Smith, *Brit. Mus. Cat.,* Vol. II, p. 117, No. 1031, Fragment 4. *Ant. Denk.,* Vol. II, Pl. 18, No. 92. Arias, *Skopas,* pp. 108 ff., Figs. 8–15, 41.

[128] A. H. Smith, *Brit. Mus. Cat.,* Vol. II, p. 106, No. 1014, Pl. XVII. *Ant. Denk.,* Vol. II, Pl. 16. Brunn-Bruckmann, *Denkmäler,* Pl. 96.
[129] A. H. Smith, *Brit. Mus. Cat.,* Vol. II, pp. 98 ff. W. Amelung in *Ausonia,* Vol. III (1908), pp. 102 ff. P. Wolters and J. Sieveking in *Jahrbuch d. Inst.,* Vol. XXIV (1909), pp. 171 ff., Supplementary Pls. I–II. Neugebauer, *Skopas,* pp. 76 ff., Pls. VI–VIII.
[130] A. H. Smith, *Brit. Mus. Cat.,* Vol. II, p. 126, No. 1054, Pl. XX, Fig. 1.

of a great sculptor. It is perhaps the portrait of an ancestor of Mausolus.

The approximate period of Skopas's activity at the Mausoleum is determined by the death dates of Mausolus and his wife Artemisia. This dynast under Persian protection, satrap of Caria in Persian territory in Asia Minor, built his tomb-monument in his capital Halicarnassus, following the Oriental custom of beginning his tomb during his life. After his death in 353 B.C. and after the death of his widow Artemisia in 351, the artists completed the building on their own account, considering that it would redound to their own glory and be a standing proof of their genius. The leading artist of the Mausoleum was not Skopas but Pytheos, who was the architect and also worked on the monument as a sculptor. He erected the building in the form of a temple on a high base, surrounded by a colonnade of Ionic columns and crowned by a pyramid equal in height to the lower structure. On the apex stood a four-horse chariot in marble, the work of Pytheos. The statues and friezes carved by the four artists summoned by Mausolus must belong to the latest additions of the building. The decade 360–350, therefore, is the most likely period of their stay at Halicarnassus. It was due not only to the architecture but to the sculptures that the Mausoleum was counted among the Seven Wonders of the World; its name has become generic for tomb monuments in the form of great buildings.[131]

The activity of Skopas for the temple of Artemis at Ephesus can be dated at around 340 B.C. The great archaic temple was wantonly destroyed by Herostratos in 356, in the same night that Alexander the Great was born. The rebuilding was probably soon begun, but was not quite completed in 334, when Alexander visited Ephesus. He offered in vain to pay the expenses of the completion if allowed to dedicate it in his name to the goddess. At that time the columns, or at least their bases and

the lowest drums, must have been erected and finished. These parts were decorated with reliefs in imitation of the lower drums of the destroyed archaic temple. Pliny (*Nat. hist.* XXXVI. 95) tells that there were 36 such carved columns, and that one of them was made by Skopas. It so happens that the best preserved drum and base, both now in the British Museum, show an expression of pathos which is decidedly Scopadic[132] (Figs. 66–68). Thanatos, the god of death, with big wings and youthful but powerful form, with a sword in a long sheath hanging at his side, has brought to the underworld Alcestis, who has died to spare the life of her husband Admetus. She is fastening her mantle on her shoulder as if to part again. Indeed, Heracles has defeated the god of death, and on Alcestis's other side stands Hermes, the messenger of the gods, ready to take her back to life, to her husband and her young sons. He has a small cloak wrapped round his left arm, holds the herald's staff, and lifts his head to the light of the earth, while Thanatos is looking down. The features of both male heads are clearly Scopadic. Behind Hermes is the god of the underworld, Hades, seated, and his wife, Persephone, standing (Fig. 67). The drapery of all the figures is heavy, and is reminiscent of the Apollo of Skopas. It has, however, many details not found before; for instance, the small folds made not by the natural fall but by the folding of the garments when put away in a chest.[133] We find the same realism in the female figure on a base from one of the columns from Ephesus[134] (Fig. 68). It has the same style, and a movement full of life. We can hardly believe that this drum and base are actually from the one column carved by Skopas, but his spirit is certainly in these reliefs. Perhaps not just one, but several of the columns, were decorated by Skopas.

The influence of Skopas makes itself clearly felt in grave reliefs, where his kind of pathos is particularly effective and appropriate. This applies notably

[131] For the history, architecture, and restorations of the Mausoleum see A. H. Smith, *Brit. Mus. Cat.*, Vol. II, pp. 65 ff., Figs. 2–3; eight restorations made before 1899. More recent ones are by Krischen and Dinsmoor, and differ only in details: see F. Krischen, in *Jahrbuch d. Inst.*, Vol. XL (1925), pp. 22 ff., and in *Arch. Anz.* (1927), pp. 162 ff., Pl. 37, and *Die griechische Stadt* (1938), pp. 20 f., Pl. 37. W. B. Dinsmoor, *The Architecture of Ancient Greece* (3d ed., 1950), pp. 257 ff., Pl. LXIII, Figs. a-b. See also our Chap. V, pp. 71 f., note 4.

[132] A. H. Smith, *Brit. Mus. Cat.*, Vol. II, pp. 174 ff., No. 1206, Pl. XXIII. Brunn-Bruckmann, *Denkmäler*, Pl. 52. Richter, *Sculpture and Sculptors*, pp. 58, 105 f., 269, 273, Figs. 328 and 705. Bieber, *Griechische Kleidung*, p. 58, Pl. XXV, Fig. 2.
[133] Cf. M. Bieber, *Entwicklungsgeschichte der griechischen Tracht* (Berlin, 1934), p. 51, Pl. 31, Fig. 3.
[134] A. H. Smith, *Brit. Mus. Cat.*, Vol. II, pp. 171 f., No. 1200. Brunn-Bruckmann, *Denkmäler*, Pl. 173. Bieber, *Griechische Tracht*, Pl. 31, 4. Arias, *Skopas*, pp. 111 f., Figs. 16–18.

to the tombstone of a young man found near the river Ilissos [135] (Fig. 69). His old father expresses his grief in the memorial; he looks with deep-set eyes at the beautiful figure of the son, whose vigorous form reminds us of the Meleager of Skopas. Even the dog expresses sadness, as the boar's eye in Tegea expresses excitement. The little slave has wept himself to sleep. The difference in expression between the serene dead and the mourning father is very striking. A similar theme was treated on a fragmentary tombstone in Athens showing an old man with deeply furrowed face and sad expression and a warrior in full armor.[136] We also find Scopadic emotion in the tomb relief of the warrior Aristonautes.[137] He is running as if charging an enemy. He is fully clad, and wears a peculiar helmet which came to Greece from Thrace. His head, with deep-set eyes and a passionate expression, resembles the Meleager of Skopas. This tombstone has also been ascribed to both Timotheos and Leochares.[138]

It is not likely that any of the great artists carved these steles themselves. Their influence, however, made itself felt and affected the minor arts. The influence of Skopas was best adapted to the art of the cemetery. I believe that we can see it grow in the representations of Sirens, the birds with human upper bodies and heads. As embodiments of deceased souls they appeared as finials on many Attic gravestones.[139] The Sirens, in the first half of the

fourth century, play lyres and have serene expressions; in about the middle of the century they begin to express mourning, and in the second half they have abandoned the music and tear their long hair in passionate distress. The disordered hair strengthens the impression of emotion, as it does in the Dresden Maenad (Figs. 59–60) and in the Tritoness from Ostia.

The heads of these later Sirens reminds us of that of a seated Demeter discovered in the island of Cnidus and now in the British Museum [140] (Figs. 70–71). Her body is broad and matronly, and the heavy himation that surrounds it in inharmonious and restless folds shows nothing of her figure. The workmanship of the draperies is rather summary. The head and neck, in contrast, are carved out of a block of beautiful Parian marble and are of excellent workmanship. The face has not only external beauty, but a depth of expression that reminds one of later representations of the mourning Virgin Mary. Demeter mourns for her daughter Persephone, who has been carried away by the god of the underworld. The sorrow is expressed with restraint, but nevertheless the expression is intent—the eyes are deeply sunk into the sockets; the gaze is fixed in the distance, as if she hopes to see her child return; the mouth is shaped in beautiful curves with the corners drawn in as if by a sigh; the forehead and the rather hollow cheeks are smooth. The head is an original of the first rank. I would like to believe that it is one of the last works carved by Skopas himself. If not, it must be the work of an early Hellenistic artist who was imbued with the very spirit of the art of Skopas.

---

[135] Conze, *Grabreliefs*, Vol. II, p. 226, No. 1055, Pl. 211. Diepolder, *Grabreliefs*, pp. 51 f., Pl. 48. Staïs, *Marbres et bronzes*, pp. 167 ff., No. 869. Brunn-Bruckmann, *Denkmäler*, Pl. 469.
[136] Conze, *Grabreliefs*, Vol. II, p. 227, No. 1058, Pl. 212. Diepolder, *Grabreliefs*, p. 52, Pl. 49, Fig. 1.
[137] Conze, *Grabreliefs*, Vol. II, p. 251, No. 1151, Pl. 245. Diepolder, *Grabreliefs*, pp. 52 f., Pl. 50. A. von Salis, *Das Grabmal des Aristonautes* (Winck.-Prog. Berlin, No. 84 [1926]), Pls. I–III. Brunn-Bruckmann, *Denkmäler*, Pl. 470.
[138] F. Winter, in *Jahrbuch d. Inst.*, XXXVIII–XXXIX (1923–24), p. 54, ascribed the tombstone of Aristonautes to Timotheos, while von Salis assigned it to Leochares (see preceding note).
[139] Staïs, *Marbres et bronzes*, pp. 134 f., Nos. 774–75 and 2583. For Sirens as finials in relief: Conze, *Grabreliefs*, Vol. III, pp. 297 and 353 ff., Nos. 1369–71, 1663–79, 1733a, Pls. 288, 353,

355–56, 375; cf. also the painted Siren, No. 1124a, Pl. 311. Diepolder, *Grabreliefs*, p. 42, Pl. 37. Collignon, *Statues funéraires*, pp. 76 ff., 216 ff., Fig. 144. Blümel, *Berlin Katalog*, Vol. III, pp. 44 f., No. K55, Pl. 58. Caskey, *Catalogue*, pp. 97 f., No. 44.
[140] A. H. Smith, *Brit. Mus. Cat.*, Vol. II, pp. 203 f., No. 1300, Pl. XXIV. Brunn-Bruckmann, *Denkmäler*, Pl. 65. Richter, *Sculpture and Sculptors*, pp. 104, 147, Fig. 315. Arias, *Skopas*, p. 140, Fig. 57. B. Ashmole in *J.H.S.*, LXXI (1951), pp. 13 ff., Pls. I–VII.

III

LYSIPPOS AND THE EARLY HELLENISTIC AGE

THE GREATEST ACTIVITY of Lysippos of Sicyon was put by Pliny (*Nat. hist.* XXXIV. 51) in the Olympiad CXIII, that is, in 328—325 B.C. This was the time of his highest fame as court sculptor of Alexander the Great (336—323 B.C.). He was fittingly associated with Alexander, for as the conqueror initiated a new age in history, so Lysippos initiated a new age in art. He must have been a well-known sculptor when Philip of Macedon, the father of Alexander, commissioned portraits of Alexander as a boy. Before this he was a humble artisan, working for a coppersmith (Pliny *Nat. hist.* XXXIV. 61); this experience probably helped him acquire an excellent technique in bronze work. Most of his statues were in bronze, and he may have cast bronze for a living until his reputation as sculptor was made. He was not the pupil of any great artist. He is said to have declared himself the pupil of the Doryphoros of Polykleitos (Cicero *Brutus* LXXXVI. 296). This is understandable, because the school of Polykleitos continued at Sicyon during the early years of Lysippos. Lysippos was, however, a master pupil, one who learns all that can be learned from his master and then departs to build up new usages. Lysippos created a new canon of proportions that superseded the canon of Polykleitos. Lysippos's younger contemporary, Douris of Samos, tells a story, quoted by Pliny, and certainly well invented, if not true: Lysippos was inspired to attempt higher things by an answer of Eupompos, a celebrated painter of the Sicyonian school. Eupompos, when asked which of his predecessors he followed, pointed to a crowd of men and replied that Nature herself should be imitated, and not any artist. Such a tendency to naturalism is indeed characteristic of Lysippos, as it is throughout the second half of the fourth century.[1]

The earliest work by Lysippos known to us from literary evidence is the statue of the athlete Troilos who won two victories in the horse races at Olympia in 372 B.C. This is a *terminus post quem,* for the statue may have been erected later. The dedicatory inscription, which alone is preserved, has been dated at about 360—350.[2] The dates of all other works of Lysippos fall within the second half of the fourth century. A statue of Koreidas, who won the *pankration* for boys in the Pythian games at Delphi, is dated 342 or soon after.[3] This is in the period when Lysippos began to make portraits of Alexander as a boy.

When Alexander ascended the throne, Lysippos

---

[1] For Lysippos, see E. A. Gardner, *Six Greek Sculptors* (London, 1910), pp. 210 ff.; E. Loewy, *Lysipp und seine Stellung in der griechischen Plastik* (1891); F. P. Johnson, *Lysippos* (Durham, N.C., 1927); G. Richter, *The Sculpture and Sculptors of the Greeks* (rev. ed., New Haven, Yale University Press, 1950), pp. 287 ff.; G. Lippold, in Pauly-Wissowa *Real-Enc.,* Vol. XIV, pp. 48 ff., No. 6; G. Lippold, *Die griechische Plastik* (Vol. III of *Handbuch der Archaeologie*), pp. 276 ff. M. Bieber, "Lysippos," in Thieme-Becker, *Künstlerlexikon,* XXIII (1929), 496 ff.
[2] Johnson, *Lysippos,* pp. 59 ff. and 314 f., No. 82. The second reference is to the valuable Appendix (pp. 266 ff., Nos. 1–96), where the literary sources are given in the original language and in English translation. J. Overbeck, *Die antiken Schriftquellen zur Geschichte der bildenden Künste bei den Griechen* (Leipzig, 1868), is more complete but gives only the Greek and Latin texts without translations.
[3] Johnson, *Lysippos,* pp. 62 ff., 92 ff.

assumed the position of court sculptor (336–323). During this period he made his most renowned statues, in Tarentum, Sicyon, Corinth, Olympia, Delphi, Thespiae, Alyzia in Acarnania, and Dium in Macedon. He seems not to have followed Alexander to Asia, for no work of his is recorded to have been set up in the East. After the death of Alexander, Lysippos worked for Craterus and Cassander, the generals of Alexander. Craterus gave him and Leochares a commission to create a memorial of a lion hunt in which Craterus had come to the rescue of Alexander engaged in combat with a lion (Plutarch *Alexander* 40. 4). For Cassander Lysippos designed a special kind of jar as a container for wine. Wine was the chief export of Cassandreia, in Macedon, founded by Cassander. The artistic form of the jar was intended to attract the attention of customers. Cassandreia, a rebuilt city on the site of Potidaea, was established in 316. The latest work recorded for Lysippos is the portrait of Seleucus, the ruler of Syria, after this prince had taken the title of king in 306; the portrait was probably made soon after this date, about the end of the fourth century B.C.

We may assume from this evidence that the activity of Lysippos covered roughly the second half of the fourth century, beginning perhaps somewhat before the middle of the century and lasting until shortly before its end. Lysippos, therefore, must have been born about 375 B.C. and must have died about 300 B.C. A long life is indicated by the tradition recorded by Pliny (*Nat. hist.* XXXIV. 37) that Lysippos made 1,500 statues. It is said to have been the sculptor's custom to put into a money box a piece of gold out of the price he received for each statue, and that after his death his heir discovered 1,500 pieces. That he lived to be an old man is also attested by the fact that he is called *geron* (γέρων), old man, in an epigram about his statue of Aesopus (*Anthologia Palatina* XVI, *Appendix Planudea* 332).

I. LYSIPPOS AND EARLY HELLENISTIC SCULPTURE

Unfortunately, we possess no original work of Lysippos upon which we could base a judgment of his style and which we could use for stylistic comparison in order to attribute other works to him. But we have a number of good copies of his most celebrated works. Outstanding among these is the

Apoxyomenos, the athlete scraping himself with the strigil, which Pliny (*Nat. hist.* XXXIV. 61 *et seq.*) puts at the head of the list of Lysippos's works. Pliny tells us that Marcus Agrippa set it up in front of his baths in Rome. The emperor Tiberius, taking a great delight in the Apoxyomenos, could not refrain from having it removed into his private bedchamber. Although he put another statue in its place, the populace of Rome resented this deeply. They raised an outcry in the theater demanding restitution of the Apoxyomenos. The emperor had to yield, in spite of the passion he had conceived for the statue.

There is only this one mention of the Apoxyomenos in ancient literature, and there is only one copy known, now in the Vatican[4] (Figs. 74–75). The copy is well preserved. The only faulty restoration is that of the fingers of the right hand, which have been made to hold a die. The fingers were originally stretched out, continuing the movement of the arm, which is stretched forward almost straight from the shoulder. The left arm is bent almost at a right angle, and the left hand holds the strigil, with which the young man is scraping himself on the underside of the right arm just above the elbow. The feet stand rather wide apart, but they carry the body jointly. There is no distinction between the carrying and the relaxed leg such as is evident in the Doryphoros and many other works of Polykleitos and his school. One has the impression that the weight of the body at this moment is on the left leg, but in the next moment it will be shifted to the right leg. The whole figure seems to swing from one hip to the other. There is movement in every part. The left hand seems to glide along the right arm and the left arm will be stretched out toward the spectator in the next moment, as the right arm is now. When we compare the Apoxyomenos to the Doryphoros, we see the content of the new canon of proportions introduced by Lysippos. His figures had more slender bodies, and thus appeared to be of greater height. Pliny (*Nat. hist.* XXXIV. 65) says Lysippos made

[4] W. Amelung, *Die Sculpturen des Vaticanischen Museums* (2 vols., Berlin, 1903–6), Vol. I, pp. 86 ff., Braccio Nuovo, No. 67, Pl. XI. H. Brunn and F. Bruckmann, *Denkmäler griechischer und römischer Skulptur* (Munich, 1888—), Pls. 281, 487. H. Bulle, *Der schöne Mensch im Altertum* (Munich and Leipzig, 1912), pp. 117 ff., Fig. 22, Pls. 62, 106, 110 f., 196, 281. Johnson, *Lysippos,* pp. 81 ff., Pls. 12–13.

the heads smaller than older artists had done, and the bodies slimmer and with less flesh, thus increasing the apparent height of his figures. There is no Latin word for the canon of συμμετρία (symmetry) which he was so careful to preserve, bringing innovations which had never been thought of before into the square canon of the older artists. He often said that the difference between himself and them was that they represented men as they were, and he as they appeared to be.

This optical impression is due to the movement which pervades the whole figure. The body is firmly knit and free from superfluous fat. The play of the muscles, therefore, can be clearly seen. The back of the statue (Fig. 74) is also richly modeled, as are the sides, so that the figure is satisfying to look at from all angles. This also is quite new. Even Praxitcles, with his broad compositions, never tried to give more than one plane, putting the arms and their attributes to the side. Lysippos discovered the use of the third dimension, that of depth, for sculpture. Any view of the Apoxyomenos is pleasant and interesting, and presents beauty of line and of mass. While the right arm extends in front straight toward the spectator, the left arm crosses the body and gives the feeling for the differences in plane between the parts of the figure. By this means the spectator is directly invited to note the dimension of depth.

The importance of this new composition in the round cannot be overrated. Hellenistic sculpture, and all later sculpture, is based on the possibility of rendering every object in such a manner that the figure can be placed anywhere in space. No longer was a background, essential to all older sculpture, needed. Innumerable possibilities were opened for Hellenistic plastic art. The aesthetic value of the new discovery has been disputed by some writers,[5] but for the artists of all the world it has opened up vast horizons, just as Alexander's expedition did for politics, geography, science, and economics.

The Apoxyomenos illustrates in a striking manner the characteristics summed up by Pliny. The head is only one ninth of the length of the body, while the head of the Doryphoros is one eighth. The Apoxyomenos's head is dolichocephalic, that is, long, the breadth of the skull being less than four fifths of the length. The crown of the head is set low at the back. The hair is disordered and restless, as if in movement. (Pliny speaks of the vivid rendering of the hair by Lysippos.) The ears are remarkably well formed. The face is rather broad, almost round. The forehead has a horizontal groove, giving the impression of nervousness. The eyes are small and set deep under the brow, and are shaded by the upper lid. They are set close to each other, as the bridge of the nose is narrow. The mouth is finely shaped with lips slightly parted. The upper lip is well curved, the lower is thick, and a deep hollow divides it from the broad and solid chin. The expression of the face is pensive, rather restless and nervous. The muscles of the face also seem to be in movement.

The figure of the Apoxyomenos thus suggests the lifelike quality that all statues of Lysippos must have had. "The extreme delicacy of execution even in the smallest details" mentioned by Pliny is, however, lost in the obviously inferior copy.

The motif of the Apoxyomenos is one of many which occur while the athletes, after exercise in the palaestra, clean their bodies by scraping them with the strigil. Six different motifs are shown on a base in the small museum on the Acropolis of Athens[6] (Fig. 77). The first and fifth athletes hold their strigils in the hand, hanging down. The second scrapes his knee, the third the inside of his left arm below the elbow, the fourth his left side, and the sixth (on another fragment) his chest. The figures have Lysippean proportions, the movements are related to the Apoxyomenos, particularly in the third and fourth figures, and the inscriptions giving the names of the athletes are dated around 300 B.C. According to Pliny, Daippos, a son of Lysippos, made a *perixyomenos,* a youth scraping himself all around his body (*Nat. hist.* xxxiv. 87). The base may illustrate this process, which it would be impossible to render in a single statue. The base certainly belongs to the school immediately following Lysippos, and may well be by Daippos.

Another figure closely resembling the Apoxyomenos is the statue of a slender athlete in Berlin.[7]

---

[5] See A. Hildebrand, *Das Problem der Form in der bildenden Kunst* (5th ed., 1905), particularly pp. 107 ff.

[6] O. Walter, *Beschreibung der Reliefs im kleinen Akropolismuseum in Athen* (Vienna, 1923), pp. 195 ff., Figs. A-C. H. K. Süsserott, *Griechische Plastik des vierten Jahrhunderts vor Christus: Untersuchungen zur Zeitbestimmung* (Frankfurt, 1938), p. 121, Pl. 23, 1.

[7] Johnson, *Lysippos,* pp. 238 f., Pls. 53C and 54C. G. Blümel, *Staatliche Museen zu Berlin, Katalog der Sammlung antiker Sculpturen* (1938), Vol. V, p. 21, No. K233, Pls. 45-46.

The disordered hair, the mobile features, the stance of the feet, and the proportions—the figure has long legs and small head—are similar. Both arms are moved to the sides, however, and the feet are closer together than those of the Apoxyomenos. It may be an earlier work of Lysippos, while the Apoxyomenos is a mature work, belonging to the sculptor's best period, probably to the time during which he worked for Alexander the Great.

Certainly an earlier work is the Agias, found in Delphi with a series of statues dedicated by Daochos, tetrarch of Thessaly, residing in Pharsalus [8] (Fig. 76). The group represented Daochos himself, his son, his father, and five ancestors. The epigrams on the face of the base tell us that three of the group were statesmen, three were athletes, one was a warrior, one—the son—was a mere youth, and one statue had no inscription. Under the third statue was the epigram:

Coming from the land of Thessaly, Pharsalian Agias, son of Aknonios, you first conquered in the Olympic Pankration; five times at Nemea, thrice at Pytho [Delphi], five times at the Isthmus; and no one ever set up trophies by your hand.

No artist is named in the Delphi inscription, but a very similar inscription, with the signature of Lysippos, was copied by Baron Otto Magnus von Stackelberg in 1811 in Pharsalus, the native place of Agias and Daochos. It differs from the Delphic one only in crediting Agias with five Pythic victories instead of three. This smaller number is probably correct, as the official records in Delphi did not allow an exaggeration in favor of the ancestor.

The group in Delphi is placed by the official titles of Daochos between 344 and 334 B.C. The style of the Agias, however, appears older. It recalls the Meleager of Skopas (Fig. 56). Thus it is likely that the statue in Pharsalus was made first, and that the Agias in Delphi was copied or rather adapted from

it, for an exact copy was impossible at this time. The fine quality of the execution seems to point to the possibility that Lysippos himself worked the adaptation. The square build of the figure is evidence that the statue was worked in a period when Lysippos regarded the Doryphoros as his master. The stance, however, is much like that of the Apoxyomenos. The weight of the body seems about to swing from one leg to the other. The proportions are also approximately the same as those of the Apoxyomenos, but the body shows less anatomical knowledge and the shape of the head is different; the face is longer and narrower, the brow is serene, without grooves, the nose is broader, the chin is narrower. The thick lower lid, the shadow over the inner corner of the eyes, and the upward look remind us of the Tegea sculptures, as does the rather sketchy treatment of the hair. The Agias, therefore, is the adaptation, probably by the master himself, of a bronze made by Lysippos for Pharsalus in the early period of his activity.

Of the Delphi group, only the Agias can be connected with Lysippos. The other statues show different styles and certainly different hands at work. The figure of Agelaos, the younger brother of Agias, who won the stadium race for boys at Delphi, according to the epigram, is decidedly Praxitelean in conception. He leans with a graceful bend of his slender body on an archaistic herm, on which he rests his left arm, covered with his chlamys. Sisiphus I, on the other hand, the father of Daochos, who is praised in the epigram as a warrior ("never did you flee from foes nor receive any wound"), and represented wearing military chiton, chlamys, baldric, and high boots, is an insignificant work with no distinct style, apparently made by an inferior artist of the time.[9]

Probably at about the same time, Lysippos made the statue of another Thessalian hero, Polydamas, famous for his exploits at the court of the Persian king, Darius II (424–404), in Susa. Polydamas won a victory in Olympia about 408; thus his statue is a posthumous one, as is that of Agias. Only the pedestal, with some badly damaged reliefs, has survived.[10] The remarkable feats of Polydamas re-

[8] T. Homolle in *B.C.H.*, XXIII (1899), pp. 421 ff., Pls. IX–XII. École Française d'Athènes, *Fouilles de Delphes*, Vol. IV (1926), Pls. LXIII–LXVIII. C. Picard and P. de la Coste-Messelière, *Sculptures grecques de Delphes* (1927), pp. 35 ff. F. Poulsen, *Delphi* (1920), pp. 266 ff. W. Dinsmoor in *A.J.A.*, XIII (1909), pp. 473 ff. Johnson, *Lysippos*, pp. 117 ff., Pl. 20. P. de la Coste-Messelière, *Delphes* (1943), Pl. 187. C. Seltman, *Approach to Greek Art* (London, 1948), pp. 88 f., Pl. 80. E. Preuner, *Ein delphisches Weihgeschenk* (1899). *Insc. Graec.*, IX 2, No. 249.

[9] École Française d'Athènes, *Fouilles de Delphes*, IV (1926), Pls. LXV and LXVII. Poulsen, *Delphi*, Figs. 132, 138.
[10] *Olympia, Ergebnisse der Ausgrabungen*, Vol. III (1897), pp. 209 ff., Pl. LV, Figs. 1–3. Johnson, *Lysippos*, pp. 97 f., 312 ff., No. 81.

lated by Pausanias (VI. 5. 1–7) are represented. His struggle with the lion is shown in two episodes: in one he is wrestling with the beast, and in the other the struggle is finished. The heroic athlete is sitting on the dead animal. The idea is similar to the one in the early classical metope from the temple of Zeus in Olympia, where the youthful Heracles is standing wearily over the lion, resting his head on his hand.[11] The experiments of the early Hellenistic period often hark back to the experiments of the transitory period between the archaic and classical ages in sculpture, because Hellenistic art was undergoing a similar transition from the classical influence of the fourth century to the later baroque tendencies. The best-preserved scene shows Polydamas before Darius, who is seated on his throne, while the ladies of his harem are looking on. The Greek athlete has lifted one of Darius's strongest men in the air and is carrying him away. The reliefs are sketchy, but they must have been made after the design of Lysippos, either by himself or at least by his pupils under his supervision. They confirm the evidence of the Apoxyomenos regarding the slim proportions and lively movements of the works of Lysippos.

The statue of a young man with his foot raised on a rocky elevation busying himself with his sandal has been called an athlete preparing for the contest, or Jason who came to claim his kingdom from Pelias with only one shoe on, as the oracle had warned the king.[12] But the young man is fastening his sandal, not removing it, and the second sandal stands on the ground, preserved in a copy in Munich.[13] The right hand is occupied with the laces of the sandal he has just put on his right foot. The statue thus represents Hermes preparing for an errand from Zeus or some other god. The left arm and the chlamys of the Munich statue are reconstructed according to a replica in the Louvre,[14] in which these parts are wrong and bad restorations.

In both replicas, the heads are ancient but do not belong to this type. The head is preserved with the statue in an unfinished copy at Athens[15] and in a replica formerly in the Lansdowne collection in England, now in Copenhagen.[16] Here, as in the Louvre and Munich replicas, the thick tree trunk must be removed in order to perceive the almost nervous and nimble movement and the slimness which gives the figure its Lysippean character. The proportions are those of the Apoxyomenos. The best replica of the head is the Fagan head, found by Robert Fagan in Ostia and now in the British Museum.[17] It has nervous and eager features and an irregular arrangement of the hair like the Apoxyomenos, although each individual feature of the face is different. The forehead has no furrow, the eyes are large, and the lips are richly modeled. They are slightly parted and the head is turned and raised as if in anticipation of an urgent message to be received and delivered. The face expresses passionate desire to serve the higher gods.

The position of Hermes (the so-called Jason), with one foot raised, appears also in the Alexander Rondanini (p. 62, n. 22), probably made by Leochares for Philip when Alexander was crown prince and about eighteen years old; thus it can be dated at about 338 B.C. Later Leochares was the collaborator of Lysippos in the memorial of the lion hunt described by Plutarch (*Alexander* 40. 4). Lysippos himself used the motif in a statue of Poseidon made for Corinth, and reproduced on coins of that city. The same statue of Poseidon is also reproduced on a coin of Demetrius Poliorcetes[18] (Fig. 148). The best copy in colossal size is in the Lateran Museum.[19] The ship's prow and the dolphin are modern restorations. The raised leg rested on a rock, as the coins prove, in a position similar to that of the Hermes. The original was a bronze statue. Lucian (*Zeus tragoedus* 9) makes

[11] *Olympia, Ergebnisse der Ausgrabungen*, Vol. III (1897), pp. 153 ff., Figs. 175–78, Pl. XXXV, Fig. 1. R. Hamann and E. Buschor, *Olympia* (1924), Pls. XCIX–C.

[12] Johnson, *Lysippos*, pp. 170 ff.

[13] A. Furtwängler and P. Wolters, *Beschreibung der Glyptothek zu München* (2d ed., 1910), pp. 309 ff., No. 287.

[14] W. Fröhner, *Notice de la sculpture antique du Louvre* (4th ed., Paris 1878), pp. 210 ff., No. 183. Brunn-Bruckmann, *Denkmäler*, Pl. 67. Dickins, *Hellenistic Sculpture* (Oxford, The Clarendon Press, 1920), Fig. 30. *Encycl. Phot.*, Vol. III, Pl. 196.

[15] F. Studniczka, in *Athen. Mitt.*, Vol. XI (1886), pp. 362 ff., Pl. IX, Fig. 1. P. Arndt and W. Amelung, *Photographische Einzelaufnahmen antiker Skulpturen* (1893—), Nos. 733–34.

[16] Johnson, *Lysippos*, Pls. 30–31.

[17] A. H. Smith, *Brit. Mus. Cat.*, Vol. III, p. 119, No. 1785.

[18] F. Imhoof-Blumer and P. Gardner, *A Numismatic Commentary on Pausanias* (repr. from *J.H.S.*, Vol. VI–VIII [1885–87]), p. 16, Pl. D, Fig. LIII. For the type on coins of Demetrius Poliorcetes, see P. Gardner, *Types of Greek Coins* (1883), Pl. XII, Fig. 2, and our Fig. 148.

[19] Johnson, *Lysippos*, pp. 143 ff., Pl. 24. Brunn-Bruckmann, *Denkmäler*, Pl. 243.

Hermes say to the statue: "Lysippos made you a bronze and a pauper, because the Corinthians had no gold at that time." The Lysippean style of the head has been lost in the mediocre copy. Much nearer to the Apoxyomenos is a head in the Vatican of an old man, probably meant to be Poseidon.[20] The hair is rendered as if wet with sea water and disordered by storm. The face shows Lysippean character in the mobile rendering of the muscles. No sculptor before Lysippos achieved such naturalistic rendering of hair and skin.

A bearded head in the Taranto Museum[21] (Fig. 83) is similar in style to the Poseidon head in the Vatican, but it is more developed and, being an original, it is of a much higher quality than the Roman copy. It is an older man looking upward. The traces of the fingers of a hand are visible at the front of the beard. It seems that this hand had pushed up the chin, which explains the rather forced attitude of the head. Beard and hair are full and curly, with small locks lying close to each other. The mustache is slightly turned, with long thin ends which lose themselves between the strands of the beard. The forehead is full of deep furrows, with quite irregular design, giving the impression that part of these are not permanent wrinkles but momentary displacements of the skin. One almost sees the muscles move in nervous excitement. The eyebrows are drawn together over the bridge of the nose. The brows are strongly projecting. Thick muscular pads hang above the inner corner of the eyes, which are deeply sunk into their orbits. Outside the eyes are marked crows' feet, indicating either advanced age or early aging through excessive hardships. The eyes are turned toward heaven with a complaining, almost accusatory, expression. The full lips are loose, as if a low sigh had just escaped them. The cheeks are thin and hollow. The neck is stretched so that it has no folds. The ears are remarkably elegant, with elongated fine curves and distinctly marked edges. They resemble the ears of the Apoxyomenos.

The head must have some connection with the Heracles which Lysippos created for Tarentum, probably between 332 and 326. When Fabius Maximus conquered Tarentum in 209 B.C. he took the statue to Rome. From there it was taken to Constantinople in A.D. 325, where it was destroyed in 1204 when the Crusaders captured the city.

Before then, however, the statue had been fully described by Niketas Choniates (*De signis Constantinopolitanis* 5) and Constantine Manasses (*Ecphrasis* I. 21–32).[22] Heracles was seated on a woven basket, whereon was spread the lion's skin. "His left arm was supported at the elbow and the forearm raised, and on the palm of the left hand he was resting his head gently, full of despondency." The basket is the one in which he had removed the manure from the stables of Augeas—his most shameful, although not his most difficult, task. Thus are explained the despondency and the bitter complaint in the expression of the head (Fig. 83), if we assume that it is related in subject to the lost seated Heracles. It cannot be regarded as an exact copy, for it is only life size, while the original seated Heracles was "of such colossal bulk that the string which enclosed its thumb might serve as a man's belt and the shin of its leg was tall as a man." Thus, the head can only be either a smaller copy or an imitation of another original by Lysippos. Except for the play of the muscles and the form of the ear, reminiscent of the Apoxyomenos, it seems to be of a slightly later date. The passionate lifting of the head is more emotional than any other work of Lysippos. I believe, therefore, that some artist in Tarentum worked this copy of the colossus before it was taken to Rome. Thus, the head must be dated in the third century. It is a good example of early Hellenistic sculpture under the influence of Lysippos. Exact copying was unknown at this period.

A terra-cotta head in the M. H. de Young Memorial Museum in San Francisco seems to be a copy of the original. It has the same movement, a similar complaining expression, and hollow cheeks[23] (Fig. 82).

It has been supposed that the whole figure is reproduced on an ivory casket, dated in the tenth

[20] Amelung, *Vatican Kat.*, Vol. I, pp. 719 f., Museo Chiaramonti, No. 607, Pl. 77. Brunn-Bruckmann, *Denkmäler*, Pl. 140. Johnson, *Lysippos*, p. 150.

[21] Museo Nazionale di Taranto, Museum Number 3895. P. Wuilleumier, *Tarente* (1939; No. 148 in *Bibliothèque des Écoles Françaises d'Athènes et de Rome*), p. 283, Pl. VI, Fig. I. Johnson, *Lysippos*, pp. 194 f. Height 0.31 m.

[22] Overbeck, *Schriftquellen*, No. 1471 f. Johnson, *Lysippos*, pp. 193 ff., 287 ff., Nos. 40, 41, 43a.

[23] M. H. de Young Memorial Museum, San Francisco, Museum Number 55104. I owe the photograph to Penelope Dimitriou.

century A.D., now in Xanten.[24] Although Heracles is seated here on a basket, supporting his head with his hand, the head does not agree with the head in Taranto; it is beardless and rests sideways on the hand instead of being raised upward by it. The Byzantine master of the tenth century may not have studied the statue in Constantinople very closely. His immediate model was probably a miniature. The right arm in the ivory relief is bent, while according to the description of the original statue Heracles was "extending his right leg and right arm as far as he could."

The head of the statue, as well as the head in Taranto, is supported by the hand and expresses distress, but is, despite bitterness, not bent in humiliation. That Lysippos could use similar motifs in a quite different mood is shown in his two other celebrated statues of Heracles, one seated and one standing. The Heracles Epitrapezios, the Heracles on the table, was, in contrast to the bronze colossus made for Tarentum, a small silver table ornament. It is described and praised by Martial (*Epigrammata* IX. 43–44) and by Statius (*Silvae* IV. 6). Martial saw it in the house of Novius Vindex in Rome. He thought it was the work of Phidias, but then read the signature of Lysippos. Statius tells us that it was made for Alexander the Great and then passed to several celebrated men, such as Hannibal and Sulla. This fantastic story was told to enhance the value of the treasure. The description, however, seems to be exact. The hero was seated on a rock over which the lion's skin was placed. In his right hand he held a cup, in his left the club. His gaze was directed upward. About a dozen copies show this position, with various differences. Two of the best are in the British Museum[25] (Fig. 80). These still possess their heads, missing in most copies. The head as well as the right arm with the hand holding the cup are preserved in an enlarged

Hellenistic adaptation from Pompeii at Naples (Fig. 81). The body is well worked. The musculature is rich and treated with considerable detail. An early Hellenistic variation of the seated Heracles in New York shows similar powerful modeling, but is transposed into life size.[26] The hero is leaning on the club which he has put under the right armpit. The idea is that Heracles is feasting in Olympus, reposing and gaily lifting his drinking cup after his labors, while in the colossus in Tarentum he was shown overtired by the same labors.

Lysippos also carved these labors of Heracles in a series of statues for Alyzia in Acarnania. An epigram (*Anthologia Palatina* XVI, *Appendix Planudea* 96) describes the capture of the hind, saying that Heracles "rests all the weight of his knee on her, grasping her beautifully branched antlers with his hands, while she, panting hard with open jaws and forced breath, shows her heart's anguish by her tongue." This description fits a beautiful bronze group in Palermo[27] (Fig. 78). Heracles is in vigorous movement, apparently trying to break off the golden antlers which he has been ordered to take to Eurystheus. He turns his body to the side to give more strength to his arms. The sculptor thus has made use of the third dimension, depth, in a group, as Lysippos did in the single figure of the Apoxyomenos. The excellent rendering of the hind, full of life, confirms the literary sources which tell us of the excellent lions, horses, and dogs of Lysippos.[28] The struggle with the lion and the other labors of Heracles sculptured by Lysippos are perhaps imitated in some surviving Hellenistic groups and on Roman sarcophagi.[29]

The colossal seated statue in Tarentum showed Heracles tired by his labors, and lamenting the misfortune that made him a slave to the unworthy

[24] A. Furtwängler in *Sitzungsber. Bayr. Akad.* (1902), pp. 435 ff., fig. on p. 439. O. M. Dalton, *Byzantine Art and Archaeology* (1911), pp. 122, 181, 216. G. Schlumberger, *L'Épopée byzantine* (3 vols., 1896–1905), II, 271; frontispiece to Chap. V. K. Weitzmann, *Greek Mythology in Byzantine Art* (1951), p. 161, Pl. XLIX, Fig. 189.

[25] P. Weizsäcker in *Jahrbuch d. Inst.*, Vol. IV (1889), pp. 105 ff., Pl. 3. C. Picard in *Rev. Arch.*, XVII (1911), 257 ff. Johnson, *Lysippos*, pp. 98 ff., 288 ff., Nos. 45–57, Pls. 15–16. A. H. Smith, *Brit. Mus. Cat.*, Vol. III, p. 90, Nos. 1725 and 1726 (our Fig. 80). This is a late copy in limestone made by the artist Diogenes; it was found in Nineveh (Kuyunjik).

[26] Metropolitan Museum of Art, No. 11.55. A. W. Lawrence, *Later Greek Sculpture and Its Influence on East and West* (London, 1927), pp. 18 and 109, Pls. 25b and 26. G. A. Richter, *Handbook of the Classical Collection* (New York, Metropolitan Museum of Art, 1930), pp. 279 f., Fig. 198, and *Handbook of the Greek Collection* (1953), p. 142, Pl. 122b. For the well-preserved copy from Pompeii in the Museo Nazionale in Naples (Fig. 81), see R. Paribeni in *Notizie degli Scavi* (1902), p. 572. Cf. our Fig. 69a.

[27] M. Collignon, *Lysippe* (1904), Fig. 17. Johnson, *Lysippos*, pp. 190 ff., 297, Nos. 48–49.

[28] Johnson, *Lysippos*, pp. 316 ff., Nos. 88–95.

[29] *Ibid.*, pp. 190, 192 f.

Eurystheus. A similar motif—the contrast between the powerful and noble figure of the hero and his weariness—is used in the so-called Heracles Farnese [30] (Fig. 84). It takes its name from the family of the Farnese, into whose possession it came before it was transferred to Naples. It originally stood in the baths of Caracalla; its colossal size and exaggerated musculature are in keeping with the huge dimensions of the room in which it was found. It bears the signature, not of Lysippos, but of Glykon of Athens, who was probably commissioned at around A.D. 211—217 to make this copy for the new luxury establishment. Another copy, in the Palazzo Pitti in Florence, however, has the inscription "work of Lysippos." [31] Beside about two dozen more marble replicas of this figure there are more than a dozen in bronze, the original material; the largest of these, in the Villa Albani, has wrongly restored lower arms [32] (Fig. 79). The description of Libanius (*Ecphrasis* xv) matches the Farnese Heracles. The right arm is bent behind his back, the left is relaxed and hangs down toward the ground. His head is also bent toward the ground. The club, with the lion skin spread over it, supports him under the armpit. Heracles was thus represented after toil, bearing the tokens of his feats. The spectator could realize what sort of a man Heracles was even when the hero was shown resting from his labors.

The object of the composition is to make the spectator feel how enormous the work must have been that tired even this strong body. The particular task he has just fulfilled is indicated by the apples of life which he holds in his right hand behind his back, thus forcing the spectator to go around the statue in order to understand it. These are the apples he obtained from the Garden of the Hesperides, either fetching them himself or sending Atlas to get them, in the meantime supporting the sky in Atlas's absence. The achievement of this superhuman task explains why Heracles leans so heavily, and why he has one leg completely re-

laxed, putting it so far forward that the weight of the body cannot be carried by it. It is interesting to compare this Heracles to the leaning figures of Praxiteles. The Apollo Sauroctonus and the reposing satyr (Figs. 16, 18) of Praxiteles also have one foot behind the other, but the supporting leg is in front, the relaxed one helping to hold the balance. In Lysippos's Heracles the weight of the enormous body rests on one foot and the club; if the club were taken away the figure would collapse. Lysippos took the leaning posture much more seriously and used it more logically than Praxiteles, who used it to show the graceful lines of young and beautiful bodies.

It is possible that the original of the Farnese type of Heracles stood in Athens, for a similar figure appears on Athenian coins [33] and the copyist Glykon signed the statue made for the baths of Caracalla in Rome as an Athenian.

The singular position of the legs of the Farnese Heracles, with the relaxed leg in front resting on the outer side of the foot and the body leaning heavily to the side, is seen again in the figure of old Silenus carrying the infant Dionysos. The best copies are in the Vatican (Fig. 85), in the Louvre, and in Munich.[34] The theme reminds one of the Hermes of Praxiteles (Fig. 11), but the kinship in subject serves chiefly to emphasize the complete difference in style. Hermes is a handsome young man, who holds the child to the side, not allowing it to obscure the graceful forms of his own body. The Silenus is a kind old grandfather, holding the child in both his big hands before his chest, thus making a transverse line across his body. He bends his head to the child, the infant laughs and stretches both hands up to his protector. The grown person and the child form a unit; a real group composed of two persons is at last created. Only with the help of the third dimension was this perfection possible. The child's behavior is much more characteristic of his years than is that of Praxiteles's little Dionysos. The group is not mentioned in literature, but on stylistic grounds we must ascribe it to Lysippos.

[30] A. Ruesch, *Guida del Museo Nazionale di Napoli* (n.d.), p. 90, No. 280. Brunn-Bruckmann, *Denkmäler*, Pl. 285. Johnson, *Lysippos*, pp. 196 ff., 298, No. 51a.

[31] W. Amelung, *Führer durch die Antiken in Florenz* (Munich, 1897), pp. 31 f., No. 40 and p. 134, No. 186. Brunn-Bruckmann, *Denkmäler*, Pl. 284.

[32] S. Morcelli, C. Fea, and E. Q. Visconti, *La Villa Albani descritta* (1869), No. 933.

[33] Imhoof-Blumer and Gardner, *Numismatic Commentary*, pp. 147 f., Pl. DD, Fig. XI.

[34] Amelung, *Vatican Kat.*, Vol. I, pp. 16 f., Braccio Nuovo, II, Pl. II. Fröhner, *Notice sculpture Louvre*, pp. 265 ff., No. 250. Brunn-Bruckmann, *Denkmäler*, Pl. 64. Furtwängler and Wolters, *Glyptothek*, pp. 244 ff., No. 238. Johnson, *Lysippos*, pp. 184 ff., Pls. 33-34. *Encycl. phot.*, Vol. III, Pls. 232-33.

Another subject on which we are fortunately able to compare Lysippos and Praxiteles is the young satyr. Like Praxiteles, Lysippos made a satyr for Athens, mentioned by Pliny (*Nat. hist.* xxxiv. 64). It is generally agreed that the boyish satyr playing the flute, of which many copies exist, must be his. Among the best copies are those in the Louvre (Fig. 86) and in the Vatican, while another good one and one without a head are in the Museo Nazionale Romano in Rome.[35] Both arms cross the chest in raising the instrument to the mouth. Praxiteles had represented his satyr dreaming after having finished playing; Lysippos could show his satyr actually playing the flute, because he conceived his figures in the round. The rough animal's skin attached to the right shoulder and hanging down from the left arm is used by Lysippos as Praxiteles used it—to contrast with the smooth youthful human skin. It is, however, less artificially draped, and leaves the right shoulder bare. The head is not that of a dreaming musician, but of a happy, healthy, serious, and charming boy.

The image of Eros is the third subject treated by both artists. In Thespiae in Boeotia an Eros by Lysippos stood beside the celebrated one by Praxiteles. We know Lysippos's Eros better than the one of Praxiteles, for it has been generally recognized that the style of Lysippos shows in the Eros unstringing the bow, of which about forty replicas exist. Among the best are those in Benghazi, in the British Museum (Fig. 87), in the Louvre (found on the Palatine), in the Palazzo Ducale at Venice, and in the Museo Capitolino and the Vatican Museum in Rome.[36] The right foot is set to the side,

the knee slightly bent and the heel raised from the ground. The weight of the body rests in this moment on the left foot, but one has the feeling that it will be thrown on the right foot in the next moment. It is a movement similar to that of the Apoxyomenos. The left arm crosses the chest, as in the Apoxyomenos, and passes downward; the hand holds the middle of the bow. The right arm is stretched out almost horizontally and the hand holds the upper end of the bow. The lower end of the bow is pressed against the right leg. Some of the replicas press the end against the left thigh and represent Eros in the act of stringing the bow. The best replicas, however, show him unstringing it. It is evident that the bow is not bent sufficiently to allow the attachment of the string to the end of the bow. The shot must have been made, and Eros is looking at the object at which he has shot, while the fingers of his right hand loosen the string.

The body of Eros is like that of the Apoxyomenos, only more youthful. In its general outlines the face (Figs. 88–89) is like the face of the athlete, particularly in the narrowness of the nose and the form of the mouth. The eyes and the hair are, however, different. The eyes are larger and farther apart. The hair is long, falling in lovely locks; it is parted twice, and the hair between the partings is plaited along the middle line. The Eros of Lysippos is younger in years than Praxiteles's representations of the love god. Body and head have round and tender forms. Eros is here a charming boy, a forerunner of the still younger and sometimes babylike cupids of Hellenistic and Roman times, later imitated by Raphael and Venetian artists.

Active movement, instead of the dreamy repose of Praxitelean figures, pervaded the figures of Lysippos. Characteristic is his Kairos, the personification of the favorable moment or the brief period of opportunity in affairs. We have lengthy descriptions, according to which Kairos was standing on tiptoe, and "though standing still it showed that it had the possibility of starting off, and deceived one's eye, conveying the impression that it possessed the power of motion forward . . . leaving the hair for the breeze to wave wherever it wished" (Callistratus *Descriptions of Statues* vi. 1–3). The movement must thus have been mostly forward, with the hair also flying mostly in the same direction, for he had "long hair from the temples to the

---

[35] Fröhner, *Notice sculpture Louvre*, pp. 273 f., Nos. 262–63. *Encycl. phot.*, Vol. III, Pl. 205. Amelung, *Vatican Kat.*, Vol. I, pp. 55 f., Braccio Nuovo, No. 38A, Pl. V. Helbig, *Führer durch die öffentlichen Sammlungen klassischer Altertümer in Rom* (3d ed.; 2 vols., Leipzig, 1912–13), Vol. I, pp. 11 f., No. 12, and Vol. II, p. 167, Nos. 1389–90. Jones, *Sculpt. Museo Capitolino*, pp. 133 f., Galleria 60, Pl. 22 (cf. p. 93, Galleria 12, Pl. 18, with modern head).

[36] A. H. Smith, *Brit. Mus. Cat.*, Vol. III, pp. 64 ff., Nos. 1673–75. *Encycl. phot.*, Vol. III, Pl. 197. Jones, *Sculpt. Museo Capitolino*, pp. 87 f., Galleria, 5, Pl. 18. Amelung, *Vatican Kat.*, Vol. I, pp. 633 f., Museo Chiaramonti, No. 495, Pl. 67. Johnson, *Lysippos*, pp. 104 ff., Pls. 17–19. See also Blümel, *Berlin Katalog*, Vol. V, pp. 20 f., Nos. 230–32, Pls. 42–44. The best head (Fig. 89) is in the British Museum (No. 1680, A. H. Smith, *Brit. Mus. Cat.*, Vol. III, pp. 68 f., No. 1680, Pl. VI); another good one is in the Walters Art Gallery in Baltimore (Fig. 88).

forehead, but bare from the forehead back" (Himerius *Eclogae* XIV. 1), and is described "with the back part of the head bare" (Phaedrus *Fabulae* v. 8; Poseidippus, in *Anthologia Palatina* XVI. 275).[37]

While the Kairos had a forward movement, Lysippos's drunken flute player had a movement in the round. Copies of this figure have been recognized in a dancing woman in Berlin, in the Museo Nazionale Romano in Rome (Figs. 90–91), and in Frankfurt, and in a statuette in the Bibliothèque nationale in Paris [38] (Fig. 92). It is not a maenad in frenzy as has been assumed, for there is no animal's skin or other sign to support such an identification. There are traces of flutes on her left shoulder, and the lifted arms also show that she was playing the flutes, a musical instrument used by satyrs but not by maenads. Thus the statue represents a flute girl, hired for a festival. She is expected to play for the dancing and pleasure of others, not to dance herself. She, however, being drunk, begins to dance, twisting her charming body. Her rather voluptuous form is framed by the long curves of her half-open dress, fastened on one shoulder and held loosely by a belt. While the maenad of Skopas rushes along in one direction (Figs. 59–60), Lysippos's dancer moves her limbs in different directions—the arms to the left, the legs to the right—making full use of the third dimension.

A still stronger active twist of the body appears in a dancing satyr in the Gallery of the Villa Borghese in Rome [39] (Fig. 94). He also is playing the flutes as he dances. His arms are restored. The hands held the two flutes, not the cymbals as the restorer of the modern arms assumed. The head with the long beard and wavy untidy hair has Lysippean features. It reminds one of Socrates, whose portrait Lysippos made (see Figs. 128–30). The

two figures are so similar in their movement in the round that both are probably copied from statues of Lysippos, although the satyr, with his stronger twist, may be by one of Lysippos's pupils.

These dancing figures have many successors in the Hellenistic period. The twist of the body is brought to its utmost in a young satyr examining his tail and trying to catch it.[40] Such figures were not possible before Lysippos conquered the third dimension. One of the most charming Hellenistic creations is the dancing satyr from which the Casa del Fauno in Pompeii got its name [41] (Figs. 95–96). Here both arms and both legs go in different directions from the body and from each other. It is the fullest use which can be made of the third dimension conquered for sculpture by Lysippos.

Thus Lysippos's work marked the highest achievement in lifelike naturalism in the fourth century. It was carried on and developed further by his school during the early Hellenistic age.

Among the pupils of Lysippos were his three sons Daippos, Boidas, and Euthykrates; other celebrated pupils were Phanis, Eutychides, and Chares of Lindos. Definite works are known only of Boidas, Phanis, and Eutychides.

The only work of Boidas mentioned by Pliny (*Nat. hist.* XXXIV. 73) is the Adorer (*Adorans*). It has been recognized in the Praying Boy in Berlin [42]

---

[37] Johnson, *Lysippos,* pp. 163 ff., 281 ff., Nos. 33–39.

[38] Bulle, *Der schöne Mensch,* pp. 294 f., Pl. 138 (Berlin). S. Reinach, *Répertoire de la statuaire grecque et romain* (6 vols., 1906–30), Vol. II (1908), p. 809, Fig. 2 (Bibliothèque nationale). Johnson, *Lysippos,* pp. 249 f., Pl. 61 (Frankfurt). L. Murpurgo, in *Riv. del Ist. Arch.,* Vol. II (1930), pp. 178 ff., Pls. I–VII, Figs. 1–6 (Museo Nazionale Romano No. 108596, from Hadrian's Villa).

[39] Helbig, *Führer durch Rom,* Vol. II, p. 252, No. 1564. E. Von Mach, *University Prints,* No. 282. Brunn-Bruckmann, *Denkmäler,* Pl. 435. Bulle, *Der schöne Mensch,* pp. 148 f., Pl. 79, Fig. 30. A. Minto in *Bolletino d'Arte,* Vol. XIV (1920), p. 46, Figs. 6–7.

[40] A. Maviglia, *L'Attività artistica di Lisippo* (1914), pp. 104 ff. Bulle, *Der schöne Mensch,* p. 149, Fig. 31. W. Klein, *Praxiteles* (Leipzig, 1898), p. 217 f., Fig. 35 (sketch of a restoration). Helbig, *Führer durch Rom,* Vol. I, pp. 229 f., No. 357, and Vol. II, p. 117, No. 132b. Copies with heads are in the Museo Nazionale Romano (see G. Krahmer in *Ertesitö,* Vol. XLI [1927], p. 12, Fig. 9c) and in the Museo Archeologico of Florence (see A. Minto in *Bolletino d'Arte,* XIV [1920], pp. 47 f., Fig. 8). The black marble of the copy in Munich (Furtwängler and Wolters, *Glyptothek,* p. 404, No. 466) probably imitates bronze, the material of the original. The head is wrongly set on the body. See K. Riezler in text (pp. 4 f.) to Brunn-Bruckmann, *Denkmäler,* Pl. 578; L. Murpurgo, in *Riv. del. Ist. Arch.,* Vol. II (1930), pp. 190 ff., Figs. 8–9. See also the reliefs in the Metropolitan Museum of Art (Museum No. 19192.36): Arndt-Amelung, *Einzelaufnahmen,* No. 2032, and Amelung, *Vatican Kat.,* Vol. I, p. 797, Museo Chiaramonti, No. 708, Pl. 86.

[41] Dickins, *Hellenistic Sculpture,* p. 7, Fig. 3. A. Mau, *Pompeii in Life and Art* (1904), p. 442, Fig. 262. A. Ippel, *Pompeji* (1925), p. 170, Fig. 168. Bulle, *Der schöne Mensch,* p. 194, Pl. 102. E. Pernice, *Gefässe und Geräte aus Bronze* (1923; Vol. IV of F. Winter, *et al., Die Hellenistische Kunst in Pompeji*), pp. 2 f., Fig. 2.

[42] Brunn-Bruckmann, *Denkmäler,* Pl. 283. Bulle, *Der schöne Mensch,* p. 122, Pl. 64.

(Fig. 93). Although both arms are modern restorations, the upward glance and lifted shoulders do not leave any doubt that the arms were raised in worship. The arms and hands were certainly differentiated in their movements, as are the legs and feet. The long legs, slender body, and small head agree with the proportions laid down by Lysippos. The upward movement must have been emphasized by the arms.

The only work of Phanis mentioned by Pliny (*Nat. hist.* xxxiv. 80) is the Sacrificing Woman (*Epithyousa*). It has been recognized in the precious original statue found in an early imperial Roman villa at Anzio and now in the Museo Nazionale Romano in Rome [43] (Figs. 97–100). It is a girl deeply immersed in her sacred performance. She carries a sacrificial dish with incense stand, laurel, and fillet on her left arm, while the right hand, crossing the body, touched some object on the tray. In order to have her hands free, she has wrapped her mantle in a thick and ugly roll around her waist. In order to have her feet free, she has drawn her heavy crinkled chiton up under the belt, so that it falls in irregular and disordered folds. In order to have her eyes free, she has bound her hair in an untidy knot over her forehead. Her lovely face (Figs. 97–98) has a detached expression. She thinks only of her sacred task as the young priestess of a venerated godhead. The sweet young features resemble those of the flute-playing satyr of Lysippos (Fig. 86), and thus the identification with the work of one of his pupils is very likely. It shows progress in the realistic treatment of the dress—in the rendering of the material as well as in the natural and almost accidental arrangement—as compared to the formal and studied one found in Praxiteles's work. Beauty and realism are combined in this early Hellenistic masterpiece.

The third pupil of Lysippos, Eutychides of Sicyon, is well known through his Tyche (Fortune) of Antioch, the city founded on the river Orontes

in 300 B.C. by Seleucus of Syria as the capital of his Syrian empire (Pausanias VI. 2, 6). Coins issued by Tigranes, king of Armenia and Syria, dated 83—69 B.C., represent the Tyche seated with her foot resting on the shoulder of a youth representing the river god.[44] A marble statue in the Vatican (Fig. 102) agrees with the coin, and is supplemented by bronze statuettes in the Metropolitan Museum of Art in New York and in the De Clercq collection in Paris, and by a marble statuette in Budapest.[45] In these, Orontes is represented as if emerging from the water, and swimming. The city goddess sits on a rock representing the one on which the city was founded, her right foot on the shoulder of Orontes. Her legs are crossed, her left hand is laid at her side on the rock, while the right arm rests with the elbow on the right knee and the hand is lifted, holding a bunch of wheat or a palm branch. The head of the river god is turned to the left, that of Tyche to the right. Thus the movements of the parts of the group, as well as of the parts of the figures, are in different directions, making use of the third dimension of depth. The drapery of Tyche, also, is arranged so that the folds are much diversified. The main direction in the upper part follows the diagonal direction of the left arm from left to right, while in the lower part the folds are mostly vertical, but curving around the legs and meeting in zigzags above the head of Orontes. The complicated arrangement is used to clarify and emphasize the movement, which in the Tyche goes from her right to her left side, while the river god seems to swim in an opposite direction. Pliny (*Nat. hist.* xxxiv. 51) gives the *floruit* of Eutychides as the Olympiad CXXI, which is 296—93 B.C., the probable period of the creation of the Tyche.

Still more complicated is the movement of the

[43] Brunn-Bruckmann, *Denkmäler*, Pls. 583–84. Helbig, *Führer durch Rom*, Vol. II, No. 1352. Bulle, *Der schöne Mensch*, pp. 288 ff., Fig. 68, Pl. 136, pp. 544 f., Pl. 261. R. Paribeni, *The Roman National Museum in the Thermae of Diocletian*, trans. by Rose Binetti (Milan, Fratelli Treves, 1925), Pl. 20. S. Aurigemma, *Le Terme di Diocleziano e il Museo Nazionale Romano* (2d ed., Rome, 1950), pp. 75 f., No. 189, Pls. 32–33. A later date is suggested for the girl from Anzio by T. Horn in *Stehende weibliche Gewandstatuen in der hellenistischen Plastik* (1931), pp. 56 ff.

[44] W. Wroth, *Catalogue of the Greek Coins of Galatia, Cappadocia, and Syria* (1899), p. XIV, Pls. XX, XXIV–XXVII, Fig. 6. K. Regling, *Die antike Münze als Kunstwerk* (1924), p. 136, No. 857, Pl. XLII.

[45] Helbig, *Führer durch Rom*, Vol. I, pp. 232 f., No. 362. Brunn-Bruckmann, *Denkmäler*, Pls. 154, 610. G. A. Richter, *Greek, Etruscan, and Roman Bronzes* (New York, Metropolitan Museum of Art, 1915), pp. 130 f., No. 259, and *Handbook* (1953), p. 125, Pl. 104 i. A. Hekler, *Die Sammlung antiker Skulpturen* (*Die Budapester Sammlungen, die Antiken in Budapest*), 1. Abteilung: *Die Skulpturen* [1929]), pp. 63 ff., No. 52. J. Wollanka, *Katalogusa* (1912), pp. 12 f., No. 9 (Hungarian). Bulle, *Der schöne Mensch*, p. 378, Fig. 100. Lawrence, *Later Greek Sculpture*, pp. 102 f.

teen-age girl in the Palazzo dei Conservatori at Rome [46] (Fig. 101). The head shares the movement of the upper part in a direction opposite to that of the lower part of the body. All lines are in diverse diagonal directions.

A seated Ares from the Ludovisi collection, now in the Museo Nazionale Romano, is sometimes ascribed to Lysippos, and sometimes to Skopas [47] (Fig. 103). I believe, however, that it belongs to the Lysippean school. The contrast between the movement of the seated war god and that of the love god at his feet is similar to the one between Tyche and Orontes. It has, indeed, been assumed that Eros and a figure touching the left shoulder, probably Aphrodite, were later additions to a seated statue, copied from a colossal bronze Ares by Skopas that was set up in a temple of Ares near the Circus Flaminius about 130 B.C. (Pliny *Nat. hist.* xxxvi. 26). It has been said that the better replica of the torso from Puteoli, now in Naples (Fig. 105), and the other replicas, to which a torso in Pergamon must be added [48] (Fig. 104), do not show any of these additions. The torsos, however, all are broken through the left shoulder and the thighs, so that there is no possibility of ascertaining whether there were other figures. The strongly separated legs of all of them lead to the supposition that there was a figure behind the right and below the left leg, which is drawn up by the hands. A copy of the head from Albania has the left ear and the left side of the hair not fully worked out; this indicates that this part was certainly not visible because of the presence of another figure. [49] The

head is not in the style of Skopas. The hair is in confusion and expresses the restlessness of the mood of the god in the manner of Lysippos. The same restlessness is expressed through the motif of nursing the knees with both hands. The same motif had been used for Ares on the Parthenon east frieze, but this, of course, is a relief; it was much more difficult to execute it in the round. The use of depth by Lysippos made this possible. The presence of Eros serves not only to show the reason for Ares's restlessness, but like Orontes in the grouping with Tyche he moves differently from Ares, thus contributing to the crossing of lines. Eros and Aphrodite emphasize the idea that the god of love has conquered the god of war. A similar group by Lysippos, showing the mighty Heracles stripped of his arms by Eros, has been described: "Why did Lysippus mould thee thus with dejected visage and alloy the bronze with pain? Thou art in distress, stripped of thy arms" (Geminus in *Anthologia Palatina* xvi, *Appendix Planudea* 103; cf. Philip in *Appendix Planudea* 104). [50] Thus the idea as well as the form places the statue in the early Hellenistic period; it is a product of the school of Lysippos in the early third century B.C.

The impression of movement and activity in a seated figure, which Lysippos achieved in his colossal Heracles in Tarentum and his small Heracles Epitrapezios, is brought to a climax in the seated bronze Hermes from Herculaneum, now in Naples. [51] (Figs. 106–8). The marble rock is modern, but resembles the rock in the original as shown in small bronze adaptations, one of the best (found in Feurs, southern France) being in the Loeb collection [52] (Fig. 109), where, however, the posture of the figure is reversed. In all versions the body is inclined forward. One hand holds the messenger's staff, the caduceus; the other rests on the seat, to help Hermes get up quickly in case Zeus should

---

[46] Jones, *Sculpt. Palazzo Conservatori*, pp. 146 ff., Sala delle Orti Lamiani, No. 31, Pl. 53. Bulle, *Der schöne Mensch*, pp. 376 f., Pl. 171. Brunn-Bruckmann, *Denkmäler*, text to Pl. 610, Fig. 6 (cf. *ibid.*, Fig. 7, a bronze copy in the Louvre). Lawrence, *Later Greek Sculpture*, pp. 17 and 103, Pl. 23a. W. Klein, *Vom antiken Rokoko* (1921), Pl. I (frontispiece); cf. pp. 99 f.

[47] R. Paribeni, *Le Terme di Diocleziano e il Museo Nazionale Romano* (4th ed., 1922), p. 94, No. 72; *idem, Roman National Museum*, Pl. 22. Aurigemma, *Il Museo Nazionale Romano*, p. 107, No. 287, Pl. 71. Helbig, *Führer durch Rom*, Vol. II, pp. 91 ff., No. 1297. Brunn-Bruckmann, *Denkmäler*, Pl. 388. Bulle, *Der schöne Mensch*, pp. 359 ff., Pl. 165. E. A. Gardner, *Six Greek Sculptors*, p. 197, Pls. LIV–LV. Johnson, *Lysippos*, pp. 166 ff., Pl. 28 (the head). Arndt-Amelung, *Einzelaufnahmen*, Nos. 254–55 (the head). Ch. Picard, *Manuel d'archéologie grecque: La Sculpture antique*, Vol. III (Paris, 1948), pp. 720 ff.

[48] Ruesch, *Guida*, p. 95, No. 293. Arndt-Amelung, *Einzelaufnahmen*, Nos. 534–35. Johnson, *Lysippos*, Pl. 29.

[49] C. Praschniker in *Oest. Jahreshefte*, XXI–XXII (1924), 203 ff.

[50] Overbeck, *Schriftquellen*, p. 279, Nos. 1473–74. Johnson, *Lysippos*, pp. 296 f., Nos. 50–51.

[51] Ruesch, *Guida*, p. 208, No. 841. Brunn-Bruckmann, *Denkmäler*, Pl. 282. Bulle, *Der schöne Mensch*, p. 361, Pl. 166. Johnson, *Lysippos*, pp. 177 ff., Pl. 35.

[52] A list of replicas is in Johnson, *Lysippos*, p. 178; the statuette (our Fig. 109) is mentioned on p. 179. J. Sieveking, *Münchner Jahrbuch der bildenden Kunst*, Neue Folge 1 (1924), pp. 1 ff., Figs. 1–9. See also Sieveking, *Bronzen, Terrakotten und Vasen der Sammlung Loeb* (Munich, 1930), pp. 2 ff., Pls. 3–4. The modern rock is the work of the French sculptor Vallois.

require his services. When, however, Hermes gets up he will not run, but fly. His sandals have wings; one leg touches the ground only with the toes, the other, pushed far forward, only with the heel; the sandals have thick bronze knobs in the form of rosettes under the soles, to indicate that Hermes cannot walk on them—he must fly. The Hermes seated at the end of the assembly of the gods in the Parthenon east frieze is much like him, just as the Ludovisi Ares is like the Parthenon Ares. But on the Parthenon we have a relief, almost a drawing. Here we have a veritable figure in the round, of which the view is good from all sides. The god is all alertness and readiness. This is even expressed in the face, which is serious and tense. Otherwise the head is similar to those of the Apoxyomenos and the Eros. Thus again we have a creation which we can ascribe to the school of Lysippos at the beginning of the third century B.C. Small Hellenistic statuettes like one in the Metropolitan Museum of Art in New York [53] (Figs. 110–11) give variations of this interesting motif.

Besides the single figures, Lysippos made large dedicatory groups of figures in violent action, which we know only from descriptions; examples are the descriptions of Zeus and the Muses in Megara, in Pausanias I. 43. 6, and of Apollo and Hermes fighting over the lyre, in Pausanias IX. 30. 1; Alexander with his friends at the battle on the Granicus and Alexander with Craterus at a lion hunt, as well as many quadrigas, are mentioned in Pliny *Nat. hist.* XXXIV. 64. These accounts tell of his great power of composition. His realism, the grandiose scale of his compositions, and his new canon of proportions initiated a new age. In his work naturalism reached its high point of the fourth century; his school was to carry it to further heights in the Hellenistic age.

He also played a role in developing the art of portraiture.

2. LYSIPPOS AND EARLY HELLENISTIC PORTRAITURE

The activity of Lysippos was a turning point in the development of portraiture, as it was for sculpture in general. When Lysippos discovered the third dimension of depth—which made it possible to depict all the manifestations of the visible world —portraiture gained most by this new three-

[53] Metropolitan Museum of Art, No. 20.202.

dimensional quality. Not only could whole figures now move better in space, but also many more details of the features of the individual face could be rendered in a realistic manner.

There were real portraitists in Greece before Lysippos. Demetrios of Alopece was such a one, for he preferred truth and likeness to beauty; a maker "not of gods but of men" (Lucian *Philopseudes* [The Lover of Lies] 18, 20; Quintilian *Institutio oratoria* XII. 10. 9).[54] In the late fifth century Demetrios made a portrait of the Athenian cavalry officer Simon, the first to write a treatise on horsemanship (Pliny *Nat. hist.* XXXIV. 76). Simon is mentioned not only in Xenophon's *Peri hippike* ([On the Art of Horsemanship] 1. 1) but also as early as in Aristophanes's *Knights* (vs. 242), produced in 424 B.C. Thus this first realistic portraitist must have belonged to the late fifth and the early fourth centuries. The realism of Demetrios was particularly noticeable in the statue of old Lysimache, who had been priestess of Athena for 64 years; the base of this statue has been found on the Acropolis. A bronze statuette of an old woman, in Vienna, and the head of another, in the British Museum, have been tentatively assigned to Demetrios.[55] Another realistic portrait statue by the same master was that of the Corinthian general Pellichos, who was represented "as the image of the real man" (Lucian *Philopseudes* 18). He had a fat paunch, and was bald on the forehead, while the beard showed some of the hairs wind-blown.

A better known portraitist of the fourth century is Silanion,[56] who created a portrait of Plato about 360 B.C., and in his later period, when he was at his height in the Olympiad CXIII, that is, 328—325 B.C. (Pliny *Nat. hist.* XXXIV. 51), made an idealized statue of Corinna. He was a many-sided artist, as

[54] Overbeck, *Schriftquellen*, Nos. 897–903. H. Stuart Jones, *Select Passages from Ancient Writers Illustrative of the History of Greek Sculpture, with a Translation* (1895), pp. 188 ff., Nos. 234–35. W. Amelung in Thieme-Becker, *Künstlerlexikon*, IX, 52 f.; C. Robert in Pauly-Wissowa, *Real-Enc.*, IV, 2850 f.

[55] J. Banko and E. Reisch in *Oest. Jahreshefte*, Vols. XIX–XX (1919), pp. 296 ff., Figs. 191 and 195, Pl. VI. A. H. Smith, *Brit. Mus. Cat.*, Vol. III (1904), No. 2001, Pl. XIX. J. Six in *Röm. Mitt.*, Vol. XXVII (1912), pp. 83 ff., Pls. I–III. R. Delbrück, *Antike Porträts* (1912), p. XXXV, Pl. 21. L. Laurenzi, *Ritratti greci* (Florence, 1941), p. 89, No. 10, Pl. III.

[56] Overbeck, *Schriftquellen*, Nos. 1350–63. Jones, *Select Passages*, pp. 180 ff., Nos. 223 25. E. Schmidt in *Jahrbuch d. Inst.*, XLVII (1932), 238 ff., and XLIX (1934), 474 ff. G. Lippold in Pauly-Wissowa, *Real-Enc.*, Second Series, Vol. III, pp. 2 ff.

may be seen by comparing these two examples with each other and with the description of his bronze statue of the sculptor Apollodoros (Pliny *Nat. hist.* XXXIV. 81). It was said to look like "rage personified" because it expressed the madness of the sculptor in the insatiable longing for perfection that made him break into pieces his finished statues.

Plato (428–347),[57] a member of a distinguished aristocratic family in Athens and a pupil of Socrates, founded his school, the Academy, in 388/7 B.C. in the grove outside Athens that was named for the hero Academus. In dialogues and in his teaching he expounded belief in ideas as realities. But the members of his school were also taught arithmetic, geometry, astronomy, harmony, law, jurisprudence, and dialectics. They lived a community life, and in a kind of seminar the rational explanation of things was attempted by question and answer. Pupils came from all over the Greek world, the greatest being Aristotle, the future teacher of Alexander the Great. But non-Greeks were also among them, for example the Persian Mithridates. This foreigner set up in the Academy a portrait of Plato by Silanion, and dedicated it to the Muses (Diogenes Laertius *Lives of Eminent Philosophers* III. 25). Cicero later had a statue of Plato erected in a meadow at his villa in Tusculum (Cicero *Brutus* VI. 24). A bronze statue of him later stood in the Zeuxippos in Constantinople (Christodorus *Ecphrasis* [Description of Statues in the Zeuxippos], in *Anthologia Palatina* II. 97 *et seq.*). These may have been copies or adaptations of the portrait of Silanion.

Of the appearance of Plato we are told that he had a robust figure and a broad forehead (Diogenes Laertius *Lives of Eminent Philosophers* III. 4; Olympiodorus *Vita Platonis*). His back was bent, probably only in his later years, for he lived to the age of eighty (Plutarch *Quomodo adolescens poetas audire debeat* [How the Young Man Should Study Poetry] 8. 26b). He is said never to have laughed outright, to have looked gloomy,

frowning "with eyebrows lifted high like a snail" (Diogenes Laertius III. 26, 28). The members of his school were reported to have trimmed their hair and beards carefully (Ephippus, the comic poet, cited in Athenaeus *Deipnosophistae* X. 509 c), probably in imitation of the venerated teacher.

There can be no doubt that the portrait of Plato, of which we have 18 copies, may be traced back to the original portrait by Silanion in the Academy.[58] It is authenticated by a herm, now in Berlin but formerly in The Castellani collection, with the inscription ΠΛΑΤΩΝ on the uppermost part of the shaft[59] (Fig. 113). The best replica is in the Boehringer collection in Geneva[60] (Figs. 116–119). The very individual hooked nose is preserved in two copies in the Vatican, one in the Galleria Geografica and one in the entrance hall[61] (Fig. 112), as well as in a copy in the Fitzwilliam Museum in Cambridge, England.[62] A group of rather battered heads, one of which was used for the reconstruction in Figs. 114–15, represents late copies with an intensified, rather pathetic expression.[63] They may

---

[57] For Plato see Diogenes Laertius, *Lives of Eminent Philosophers;* B. Jowett, ed., *The Dialogues of Plato* (5 vols., 1937); U. von Wilamowitz, *Platon* (2d ed., 1920); A. E. Taylor, *Platonism and Its Influence* (1925), and *Plato, the Man and His Work* (1921); F. M. Cornford, in *C.A.H.,* VI, 310–32; E. Barker in *ibid.,* pp. 519–35; P. Shorey, *Platonism, Ancient and Modern* (1938; Sether Classical Lectures, No. 14); F. Solmsen, *Plato's Theology* (1942; Cornell Studies in Classical Philology, XXVII).

[58] J. J. Bernoulli, *Griechische Ikonographie* (2 vols., Munich, 1901), Vol. II, pp. 18 ff., Pls. IV–VI. E. Schmidt in *Jahrbuch d. Inst.,* XLVII (1932), 238 ff., and XLIX (1934), 181 ff. R. Boehringer, *Platon, Bildnisse und Nachweise* (Breslau, 1935); E. Pfuhl, *Die Anfänge der griechischen Bildniskunst* (Munich, 1927), pp. 28 ff., Pl. IV, 1–2.

[59] Bernoulli, *Ikonographie,* Vol. II, p. 27, No. 1, Pl. IV. P. Arndt, *Griechische und römische Porträts* (1891–1942), Pl. 5. Blümel, *Staatliche Museen zu Berlin, Katalog der Sammlung antiker Skulpturen,* Vol. V (1940), pp. 1 f., K192, Pl. IV. Boehringer, *Platon,* pp. 14 f., No. I, Pls. 1–5. It is damaged, but no restorations have been made.

[60] Boehringer, *Platon,* pp. 28 f., No. XVI, Pls. 78–92. K. Schefold, *Die Bildnisse der antiken Dichter, Redner, und Denker* (Basel, 1943), pp. 74 f., 205. H. Bloesch, *Antike Kunst in der Schweiz* (1943), pp. 80 ff., 179 f., No. 21, Pl. 45. No restorations.

[61] Galleria Geografica No. 63 and Galleria dei Arazzi No. 388, now in Ambulacro Superiore del Nuovo Ingresso. See Arndt, *Porträts,* Pl. 788; Boehringer, *Platon,* pp. 15 f., Nos. III and V, Pls. 11–14 and 18–22. In Fig. 112 the back part of the head, the lower part of the beard, and the neck are restored.

[62] Fitzwilliam Museum, No. 15. See Boehringer, *Platon,* pp. 20 f., No. IX, Pls. 40–48.

[63] Bernoulli, *Ikonographie,* Vol. II, p. 28, No. 8, Pl. VI, Fig. 2. Blümel, *Berlin Katalog,* Vol. V, pp. 2 f., K193, Pl. 5. Boehringer, *Platon,* pp. 19–21, 25–27, Nos. VII, X, XIII, Pls. 29–32, 49–54, 66–69, 70–72. A. Hekler, "Ein neues Platonbildnis in Athen," in *Praktika,* IX (1934), 80 ff.; *idem* in *Arch. Anz.* (1934), pp. 260 f., Figs. 7–8. E. Schmidt in *Jahrbuch d. Inst.,* Vol. XLIX (1934), pp. 181 f., Fig. 1. T. Dohrn, "Ein spätantikes Platonporträt," in *Athen. Mitt.,* LXIII–LXIV (1938–39), pp. 163 ff., Pl. 65.

belong to the period of the Neoplatonism of Plotinus, yet in details they agree with the other copies.

We, therefore, have a reliable likeness of Plato as he must have appeared to his pupils when he was between sixty and seventy years of age, or about 367—357 B.C. We see a personality of aristocratic distinction and of the highest dignity. The forehead is broad. The small eyes, shaded by drawn brows, have a deeply serious glance. The cheeks are thin, and the chin is rounded and protruding. The mouth is tightly shut as if in reticent silence. The hair is carefully arranged and the beard is laid in strands of equal shape and value. The significant head paints the ardent, but impractical and therefore disappointed, reformer and deep thinker. It was bent slightly forward and turned to his right in a statue with a bent back, of which only the casts of a small replica, now lost, are preserved [64] (Figs. 114–15). A heavy cloak is thrown over the left shoulder and arm, and laid around the lower body and legs. The right hand rests on the thigh, and the left hand holds a scroll that probably contains a lecture which the philosopher is reading to his students. The statue in the possession of Cicero may have been similar to this small replica.

While we may assume that this portrait of Plato is a contemporary one transmitted in reliable copies, the portrait of Corinna [65] by Silanion is an invented likeness, for this poetess was an older contemporary of her compatriot Pindar. In a painting on the wall of the gymnasium in her home town, Tanagra, she was represented winning a contest with the great poet; her picture there was said to show her as most beautiful, tying the fillet of victory around her head (Pausanias IX. 22. 3). The portrait by Silanion seems to be based on this tradition. A small copy in Compiègne is authenticated by the inscription KOPINNA on the base [66] (Figs.

120–22). Beside the tradition of the grace and beauty of the poetess, Silanion seems to have based his invented Corinna on the lovely Tanagra terracotta statuettes which were fabricated so plentifully in the fourth century (see Figs. 49, 51–53). The women of Silanion's own time may also have inspired him. The slender body and the high belt date the work in the later period of Silanion, about 330 B.C. For the head with the melon coiffure (Figs. 121–22) he could have used his contemporaries, or certain coins with idealized heads of young goddesses, such as one, representing Artemis, from Orthagoria in northern Greece [67] (Fig. 123), minted in about the middle of the fourth century. Silanion, in any case, created in this figure a lovable, idealized, and graceful image.

Lysippos, like Silanion, created contemporary as well as invented portraits. It is instructive to compare his Socrates with the older, probably contemporary portrait of the philosopher, and also with the portrait of Plato, the pupil of Socrates, by Silanion.

The subjects of these two portraits are very different. Socrates, the great educator and founder of Attic philosophy,[68] came from a lower-middle-class family. His father was a sculptor—that is, an artisan—and his mother was a midwife. Socrates said that he owed his method of teaching to her. He did not lecture, but brought the truth to life as children are brought to birth. From about 440 B.C. he taught in the gymnasia and in the market place, engaging people in conversation with the intention of discovering the truth and thus achieving moral and intellectual improvement. Philosophy for him was not only the love of wisdom, but also the right way of living. Through good education men would become good citizens. By 399 B.C., when he was seventy years old, he was accused of impiety on the ground that he had introduced new

[64] Casts are in German university museums, such as those of Leipzig, Bonn, and Kiel, and also in Karlsruhe and Strassburg. See G. Lippold, *Griechische Porträtstatuen* (Munich, 1912), p. 55, Fig. 7. F. Poulsen, *Iconographic Studies from the Ny Carlsberg Glyptothek*, I (1931), pp. 42 ff., Fig. 36. E. Schmidt in *Jahrbuch d. Inst.*, XLVII (1932), 255. A. Hekler in *Praktika*, Vol. IX (1934), pp. 190 ff., Pl. II; *idem, Bildnisse berühmter Griechen* (1940), pp. 21 ff., Fig. 6. Here the reconstruction is that shown in our Figs. 114–15. Schefold, *Bildnisse*, p. 210.
[65] For Corinna see P. Maass in Pauly-Wissowa, *Real-Enc.*, XI, 1393–97.
[66] Bernoulli, *Ikonographie*, Vol. I, pp. 88 ff., Fig. 14. S. Reinach in *Rev. Arch.*, XXXII (1898), pp. 164 ff., Pl. 5, and Vol.

XXXVI (1900), pp. 169 ff., Pls. II–III. E. Espérandieu, *Recueil générale des bas-reliefs, statues, et bustes de la Gaule romaine*, Vol. V. (1913), pp. 146 f., No. 3899. Arndt-Amelung, *Einzelaufnahmen*, Nos. 1188–89.
[67] H. Gaebler, *Die antiken Münzen Nord-Griechenlands*, Vol. III, Part 2: *Die antiken Münzen von Makedonia und Paionia* (1935), pp. 92 f., "Orthagoria" 1–3, Pl. XVIII, Nos. 21–23.
[68] For Socrates see Diogenes Laertius *Lives of Eminent Philosophers* II. 5. 18–47; W. E. Leonard, *Socrates, Master of Life* (1915); J. Burnet, *Greek Philosophy*, I (1914), 126 ff.; P. W. Stenzel in Pauly-Wissowa, *Real-Enc.*, Second Series, Vol. III, pp. 811–90; J. Bury in *C.A.H.*, V, 386–97.

gods and corrupted the young men of Athens. He refused to flee from the prison, and after some philosophical discussions with his pupils, he drank hemlock. Among his pupils were the celebrated statesman Alcibiades and the writers Plato and Xenophon.

We owe our knowledge of Socrates's life, appearance, and doctrine mainly to the works of Xenophon and Plato, for Socrates himself did not write anything. Both these writers agree in comparing him to the Silenus figures (Xenophon *Symposium* v. 5–7; Plato *Symposium* 215 A–B). His face is also compared to that of the torpedo (*narke*), a sea fish which has a broad flat body.[69] His eyes are said to have been small like those of a fish, to lie on the surface and wide apart, so that he can see more than other men. His snub nose is flat so that it does not obstruct his view, and his nostrils are wide open so that he can smell better. His mouth is big so that he can bite off larger pieces of food, and his lips are thick and soft, so that he can kiss better. He was fat and exercised to reduce his belly. He was content with frugal food and simple dress. He wore only one garment in winter and summer, and always went barefoot (Plato *Theaetetus*, p. 143 E; Xenophon *Symposium* v. 5–6).

These literary descriptions agree with the portraits of Socrates which have been preserved. Socrates must have made a strong impression on the artists with whom he associated. The personality of Socrates was, however, so rich that just as his followers founded various schools of different types, and just as the literary accounts of his personality and beliefs differ in the works of Xenophon, Plato, and the Cynics, so also the sculptured portraits are different in spirit, although the external features are the same.

We can divide the portraits of Socrates into three classes:[70]

A. Simple portraits which agree in details with the description of Socrates in Xenophon. The original was probably made during Socrates's lifetime.

B. Idealistic representations which agree with Plato's view of Socrates as an ideal teacher and ethical character. They are probably copied from an original by Lysippos.

C. Hellenistic portraits of Socrates which agree with the conception of Antisthenes and the later Cynics.

The simple type (A) of portrait head of Socrates is authenticated by a herm in the Sala delle Muse of the Vatican, which bears the inscription ΣΩΚΡΑΤΗΣ[71] (Fig. 125). Though the herm was taken from the Villa Negroni and the head was found in Roma Vecchia, they seem to fit together. The head agrees in its external features with Type B, which is well authenticated, and is also of the same kind as other replicas, except for the eyebrows. These are drawn in the way noticed by Aristotle. This is not the case in the best copy of Type A, in Naples,[72] and a bronze replica in Munich[73] (Figs. 126–27). Bronze was the material used in the original statue. All copies agree in having a high forehead indicating intelligence, small eyes lying on the surface and separated by the broad bridge of the snub nose, wide-open nostrils, and a big mouth; these features are just as they are described in the *Symposium* of Xenophon and the *Symposium* of Plato. The beard is broad and flat and helps to make the whole face suggestive of a torpedo fish. The hair recedes from the forehead, but there is one small tuft in the middle. Long strands fall on the nape of the neck and some are parted from the hair in the back above the ears. They form characteristic curved patterns above the temples.

This simple Type A head also appears on a figure in a relief in Naples[74] (Fig. 124). The figure

[69] See M. Bieber in *Athen. Mitt.* XXXII (1917), 118 ff.

[70] Bernoulli, *Ikonographie*, I, pp. 185 ff., Pls. XXI–XXIV. Bernoulli confuses the types; it was R. Kekule von Stradonitz ("Die Bildnisse des Sokrates" in *Abh. Preuss. Akad.* [1908]) who first divided the portraits into three types. Cf. G. Loeschcke in *Arch. Anz.*, XXIX (1914), 515 f., and Arndt, *Porträts*, Pls. 1031–50.

[71] Lippold, *Vatican Kat.*, III, pp. 55 f., Sala delle Muse, No. 514, Pl. 20. Bernoulli, *Ikonographie*, Pl. XXII, Fig. 2. Arndt, *Porträts*, Pl. 1037 and Fig. 1. The only parts of this head that have been restored are the tip of the nose and a small piece of the left side of the lower lip.

[72] Bernoulli, *Ikonographie*, Pl. XXII, Fig. 1. Arndt, *Porträts*, Pls. 1033–34. A. Hekler, Bildniskunst der Griechen und Römer (1912), Pl. 19. Schefold, *Bildnisse*, pp. 68 f., p. 204. The tip of the nose and part of the left ear are restored.

[73] Glyptothek, No. 448. See Arndt, *Porträts*, Pls. 1031–32. A few small repairs have been made.

[74] From a chest in Naples, found in Pompeii. R. Kekule von Stradonitz, "Die Bildnisse des Sokrates," in *Abh. Preuss. Akad.* (1908), pp. 43 f., Figs. 24 and 57 f. W. Amelung in *A.J.A.*, Vol. XXXI (1927), pp. 284 ff., Fig. 3. Poulsen, *Iconographic Studies*, Vol. I, p. 31, Fig. 24. E. Pernice, "Hellenistische Tische

is that of a short and sturdy man leaning on a staff placed under his right armpit, with his left hand behind his back. He talks to a seated woman and the figure of Eros stands between them, holding a writing tablet. There can be no doubt that the relief shows Socrates listening to Diotima, who is said to have instructed him in the power of the god of love (Plato *Symposium*, pp. 204–9). The fat belly of the philosopher is well indicated. He wears nothing but the one heavy garment which he used both in winter and summer, and he is barefoot. Here, then, Socrates is depicted as a man of the middle class who pretends to know nothing and therefore tries to learn by cross-examination of others. Thus he must have appeared as he stood in the market place and in the gymnasia, trying to teach his fellow citizens to think and act in accordance with right and justice. Even if the statue was made after his death, it must at least have been based on a clear recollection of the man himself, who was such a well-known personality as he walked in the streets of Athens. Thus Xenophon and others must have seen him, and contemporary artists must have represented him, in the clear and precise forms of the classical age.

Impressions of Socrates changed during the fourth century, as is shown by Type B. The simple search for truth which he had developed was taken over by Plato and used as the basis for his own doctrine, that of ideas as the only true reality. Plato enriched and broadened the teachings of Socrates by transferring his method of thought from the sphere of ethical and social problems to the whole field of knowledge. This wider application of the principles of philosophy prevailed when Lysippos was commissioned to make a bronze statue of Socrates (Diogenes Laertius *Lives of Eminent Philosophers* II. 43). It was erected about 340—330 B.C. in the Pompeion (Hall of Processions) near the Dipylon gate. This was certainly the model on which the Type B portraits of Socrates were based. There are many more copies of this posthumous portrait than there are of the contemporary one.[75]

The Lysippean head is authenticated by a herm in Naples which has inscribed on its shaft certain words attributed to Socrates by Plato (*Crito*, p. 46 B): "I am not the kind of man to obey anything else but the dictates of reason, and not only on this occasion but at all times I follow the one that seems to me best."[76] The best copies of this head are in the Museo Nazionale Romano in Rome[77] (Fig. 130) and in the Louvre[78] (Figs. 128–29). If we compare it to Type A we find that the artist has given spiritual life to the features and significant character to the ugly physical forms which as a whole he has retained. But the small eyes are deeper in their sockets than they were in the older portrait; the nose is not quite so broad; the upper lip is more concealed by the thick mustache, the beard is longer, and the hair, both of the beard and the head, is wavy and more plentiful, covering the upper part of the ears. That this type was accepted also by the Romans is shown by the facts that so many Roman copies existed and that it was used on the Roman mosaic of philosophers in Cologne, with the inscription ΣΩΚΡΑΤΗΣ[79] (Fig. 131).

The Type B head was part of a seated statue[80] (Figs. 132–35). It has been identified by means of an old drawing of the eighteenth century, in which the figure had a head of this type (Fig. 132). At the time that the statue came up for sale it had a head representing Trajan (Fig. 133). In this condition it was bought for the museum in Copenhagen, where the emperor's head was removed and a cast of the head of Socrates from the Museo Nazionale Romano (Fig. 130) was substituted (Figs. 134–35). The body, like the head, is in the

---

und Truhen," in F. Winter, *Die Hellenistische Kunst in Pompeji*, Vol. V (1932), pp. 79 ff., Fig. 34, Pls. 48, 2 and 49 (enlarged). H. Fuhrmann in *Röm. Mitt.*, LV (1940), 78 ff. Schefold, *Bildnisse*, p. 162 f., No. 2. Schefold believes that the woman is Aspasia, the friend of Pericles.
[75] R. Kekule von Stradonitz, "Die Bildnisse des Sokrates,"

in *Abh. Preuss. Akad.* (1908), pp. 46 ff., Nos. 1–16. F. Poulsen, *Iconographic Studies*, pp. 31 ff., Figs. 25–33.
[76] Bernoulli, *Ikonographie*, Pl. XXIV. R. Kekule von Stradonitz, "Die Bildnisse des Sokrates," in *Abh. Preuss. Akad.* (1908), pp. 18 ff., Fig. 13. R. Paribeni, *Il Ritratto nell' arte antica* (1934), Pl. XIX.
[77] R. Kekule von Stradonitz, "Die Bildnisse des Sokrates," in *Abh. Preuss. Akad.* (1908), pp. 23, 27 f., Figs. 26–27. Hekler, *Portraits*, Pl. 20. Schefold, *Bildnisse*, pp. 82 f. Both eyebrows, piece of forehead, tip of nose are restored.
[78] Bernoulli, *Ikonographie*, Pl. XXI. Arndt, *Porträts*, Pls. 1038–39. Restored are the front part of the nose and the herm.
[79] Bernoulli, *Ikonographie*, pp. 192 f., Fig. 36.
[80] G. Lippold in text to Arndt, *Porträts*, Pls. 1126–27, Figs. 9–12. Poulsen, *Iconographic Studies*, Vol. I, (1931), pp. 34 ff., Figs. 27–29, and Vol. II (1938), pp. 169 ff., Figs. 1–6. F. Poulsen, *Catalogue of Ancient Sculpture in the Ny Carlsberg Glyptotek* (1951), pp. 291 f., No. 415c.

characteristic style of Lysippos. There is the suggestion of motion in the feet, the right one being drawn back to the seat, while the left is stretched far forward. The heavy himation is draped in a grandiose manner. The old body is rendered realistically, though it does not have the exaggerated belly of Type A. Socrates has become a dignified professor seated in the gymnasium like Plato, instead of being the wandering philosopher of the streets and the teacher in the market place. If we compare the statue of Plato with this Lysippean Socrates, we find that Lysippos not only used deeper space, but had also deeper spiritual conceptions than Silanion. In revealing a beautiful soul in the ugly body, the freedom and reason in the character, Lysippos followed the advice of Socrates, who told artists that they must imitate not only a man's body but also his ethos and the feelings that affect the body and the activities of the soul (Xenophon *Memorabilia* III. 10. 6–8).

An eclectic Roman artist seems to have followed this Lysippean seated statue in making a side relief on a Roman sarcophagus in the Louvre.[81] Socrates, however, has here a head of the older type. His left hand is raised in lively gesticulation and his feet are crossed. He is speaking to Diotima, who is leaning on a pillar. Socrates is seated on a bench under an arch supported by two elegant pilasters, the dignified teacher in a gymnasium.

While in this sarcophagus Lysippean and older elements are combined, the artist of Type C in the Hellenistic period tried to represent the original Socrates once more. The sculptor of the head in the Villa Albani[82] (Figs. 136–37) exaggerated the eyebrows, drawn up as in Fig. 125, gave the nose the shape of a potato, made the lips and mustache thicker, and changed the expression to that of a martyr. This is the conception which the Cynic philosophers had of Socrates: he was the man who had suffered through the misunderstanding and nagging of his shrewish wife and through the ingratitude of his country. He had loved his country and tried to serve it, but for his devotion had been rewarded with a cup of hemlock. In the emotional Hellenistic age men felt the tragedy of the fate of Socrates much more deeply than they had in the classical period.

A small statuette from Alexandria in the British Museum is similar in character to the Villa Albani head[83] (Figs. 138–39). This statuette is also based on an older type, namely the Socrates represented on the relief (Fig. 124), but under the influence of Lysippos's conception much greater dignity has been added to his appearance. The folds of the himation are more carefully arranged. Both hands hold the edges of the drapery to indicate the concentration of thought. Socrates's head is turned to one side in a lively manner, as if he were deeply interested, but his expression is sad. If a relief in Naples is rightly interpreted as Socrates drinking poison, it would also give the Stoic conception.[84]

Thus it may be seen that just as Socrates's pupils changed his doctrines, so the artists of different periods altered the details of his appearance to suit their own ideas. The definitive conception, however, was that of Lysippos, which agrees with Platonic ideas.

The main task of Lysippos as the court sculptor of Alexander the Great was to make portraits of the great conqueror in all stages of his life. Plutarch tells us that

Alexander gave to Lysippos the sole patent for making all his statues; because he alone expressed in bronze the vigor of his mind, and in his lineaments represented the luster of his virtue; while others, who strove to imitate the turning of his neck and the softness and brightness of his eyes failed to observe the manliness and lion-like fierceness of his countenance. (*De Alexandri magni fortuna aut virtute* II. 2.)

The outward appearance of Alexander is best represented by the statues of him which Lysippos made, and it was by this artist alone that Alexander thought it fit that he should be modeled. For those peculiarities which many of his successors and friends afterwards tried to imitate, namely, the poise of the neck which was bent slightly to the left, and the melting glance of his eyes, this artist has accurately observed. (*Alexander* 4.1.)

---

[81] Lippold, *Porträtstatuen*, p. 54, Fig. 6.
[82] Bernoulli, *Ikonographie*, Pl. XXXIII. Arndt, *Porträts*, Pls. 1045–46. Hekler, *Bildniskunst*, Pl. 21. Paribeni, *Ritratto*, Pl. XIX, 2.
[83] H. B. Walters in *J.H.S.*, Vol. XLV (1925), pp. 255 ff., Pls. X–XIII. W. Amelung in *A.J.A.* (1927), pp. 281 ff., Fig. 1. Arndt, *Porträts*, Pls. 1049–50. Schefold, *Bildnisse*, pp. 84 f., p. 206. No restorations.
[84] Museo Nazionale, Naples, No. 6697. A. Ruesch, *Guida del Museo Nazionale di Napoli* (n.d.), p. 258, No. 1086.

When Lysippos had finished the first statue of Alexander, looking up with his face to the sky (as Alexander was wont to look with his neck slightly bent), he wrote on the pedestal, not inappropriately, the following epigram: "The bronze seems to look up to the god and say, I have set the earth under my sway; Zeus, you may keep Olympus." (*De Alexandri magni fortuna aut virtute* II. 2.)

Lysippos is also said to have quarrelled with the court painter Apelles because Apelles had painted Alexander's picture with a thunderbolt in his hand, thus likening him to Zeus, while Lysippos had given him a spear, which was natural and proper for him as the weapon which had given him the real glory of which time could not rob him (Plutarch *De Iside et Osiride* 24).

The copies of this celebrated Alexander with the lance—the Azara herm and a bronze statuette, both in the Louvre—are unfortunately rather poor, but they agree with the character of the Apoxyomenos in the shape of the face, the restlessness expressed by the treatment of the muscles and the hair, and in the mobile stance.[85] Still less can be learned of the style of the Alexander from the monument for the battle at the river Granicus (334 B.C.), represented in a bronze rider from Herculaneum in the Naples Museum.[86] This group of about twenty-five of the Companions of Alexander, killed at the first onset, was erected at Dium in Macedonia. The monument was executed at Alexander's order by Lysippos, who was chosen by him in preference to all other artists (Arrian *Anabasis* I. 16. 4). Metellus Macedonicus brought the group of equestrian statues to Rome and erected it before the temples in-

side the porticus of Octavia. Here the copy for the owner of the villa at Herculaneum may have been made. The features are handsome but do not express the importance with which Lysippos must have invested the portraits of the Macedonian king, who had conquered Greece and the then-known Eastern world. Lysippos certainly must have rendered the face of Alexander with many more details and in a realistic manner, judging from his Socrates (Figs. 128–30).

There is no doubt that Lysippos profited by the process of taking casts from the living face which was invented by his brother Lysistratos.[87] The trend toward realism, begun with Demetrios and continued by Silanion, led to the introduction of this new practice. Lysistratos took plaster casts of the faces for his portraits, then made wax models and worked them over. This led to the rendering of portraits with lifelike precision, "whereas previous artists had striven to make them as beautiful as possible" (Pliny, *Nat. hist.* XXXV. 153). The original bronze head in Olympia may give us an idea of Lysistratos's art [88] (Fig. 144). It shows exceedingly exact modeling of the features, sharp rendering of the thick locks of hair and beard, and many small detailed engravings which must have been added to the finished cast. The result is a sober and truthful portrait.

It is my belief that the purely human conception of Alexander by Lysippos was in the later period unfavorably received by the king, who in the meantime had become the great ruler of Persia and India. The other court artists, Apelles and the gem cutter Pyrgoteles, accepted the new conception of Alexander as the son of a god or as a god himself. Lysippos continued to work for Alexander's generals after the king's death. Thus Craterus erected a memorial of a lion hunt in which he came to the rescue of the king in combat with the lion (Plu-

[85] T. Schreiber, "Studien über das Bildnis Alexanders des Grossen," in *Abh. Sächs. Ges.,* XXI (1903), No. III, Pl. I. J. J. Bernoulli, *Die erhaltenen Darstellungen Alexanders des Grossen* (1905), pp. 21 ff., Pl. I and Fig. 1. Arndt, *Porträts,* Pls. 181–82. C. de Ujfalvy, *Le Type physique d'Alexandre le Grand* (1902), Pls. II, VIII, IX. F. Winter in *Arch. Anz.,* X (1895), 162. F. P. Johnson, *Lysippos* (1927), pp. 213 ff., Pls. 43–44, 47 (cf. pp. 298 ff., the references to Lysippos's statues of Alexander, in the original texts, with translations). M. Bieber, "The Portraits of Alexander the Great," in *Proceedings of the American Philosophical Society* (1949), pp. 382 ff., Figs. 13–18.

[86] Brunn-Bruckmann, *Denkmäler griechischer und römischer Skulptur* (1888–), Pl. 355b. Arndt, *Porträts,* Pls. 479–80. Bernoulli, *Darstellungen Alexanders,* Figs. 29–30. Ujfalvy, *Alexandre,* Pl. XVII. Johnson, *Lysippos,* pp. 225 f., Pl. 48. M. Bieber, "The Portraits of Alexander the Great," in *Proceedings of the American Philosophical Society* (1949), pp. 383, Figs. 22–24.

[87] For Lysistratos see Overbeck, *Schriftquellen,* Nos. 1513–15. Jones, *Select Passages,* pp. 206 f. M. Bieber in Thieme-Becker, *Künstlerlexikon,* XXIII, 500. G. Lippold in Pauly-Wissowa, *Real-Enc.,* Vol. XIV, pp. 66 f., No. 12. Johnson, *Lysippos,* p. 261.

[88] A. Furtwängler, *Die Bronzen,* in *Olympia, Ergebnisse der Ausgrabungen,* Vol. IV (1890), pp 10 f., Pl. II. Brunn-Bruckmann, *Denkmäler,* Pl. 247. Johnson, *Lysippos,* p. 236, Pl. 51. E. Schmidt (in *Jahrbuch d. Inst.,* XLIX [1934], pp. 193 ff., Fig. 48) believes the head to represent the athlete Satyros by Silanion. G. Rodenwaldt (*Olympia* [1937], pp. 53 f., Pls. 92–93) unfortunately has adopted this idea. The head shows a realism that is too advanced for Silanion.

tarch *Alexander* 40. 4). Some of the figures of the bronze group, which stood in Delphi, were made by Lysippos, the rest by Leochares. Leochares had already made statues of Alexander as crown prince. The Alexander Rondanini in Munich is rightly considered a copy of one of these early statues, showing Alexander as a young general, about eighteen years old, after he had won the battle of Chaeronea in 338 B.C.[89] The romantic conception, with the head surrounded by a mane of curled long hair, may have been similar to that of Apelles and Pyrgoteles. In any case, the successors of Alexander, when they minted coins with the portrait of Alexander, used a conception similar to that of the Alexander Rondanini. Thus the head of Alexander, on a coin minted by Lysimachus of Thrace and now in the Boston Museum of Fine Arts,[90] has the same big eye, elegant form of the nose, lively mouth, and luxuriant hair as the statue. Only more emotion, in the Hellenistic style, and the horns of Ammon have been added. Lysimachus was king from 306 to 281 B.C.; the coin was minted in the early third century. Whether the Alexander in the lion hunt was by Leochares, and if so, whether it was in the type of the Alexander Rondanini and the coin, we do not know. The only reflection of the group, on a relief from Messene, is too poor to be of any help.[91]

Lysippos certainly continued to work in his own style until the end of his life. We know this from the portrait of Seleucus, the general of Alexander who distinguished himself in the campaigns in Asia. He was only a few years younger than Alexander, but he survived him for about forty years. After the death of Alexander Seleucus became satrap of Babylonia and in 306/5 took the title of king of Syria. Lysippos, Bryaxis, and Aristodemos are said to have portrayed this mightiest and most noble among the successors of Alexander.[92] (Pliny *Nat. hist.* XXXIV. 73, 86). The Tyche by Eutychides, the son of Lysippos, decorated Seleucus's new capital, Antioch on the river Orontes (see p. 40 above and Fig. 102). The excellent bronze bust from Herculaneum, now in Naples[93] (Fig. 141–43), was early identified as a portrait of the founder of the dynasty of the Seleucids. The identification is based on coins minted between 281 and 263 B.C. by Philetairos of Pergamon, who had been under the protection of Seleucus (Fig. 140), and on those issued by his son Antiochus I as his coregent in 293–281 and as his successor in 281–261.[94] These last coins portray the deified king with the horn as the symbol of divinity. The features may have been taken from the portrait by Lysippos, for the coins as well as the bronze bust have decidedly Lysippean features. Both show Seleucus at about sixty to seventy years of age, with signs of old age in the face but with still abundant hair. The model, therefore, must be dated around 300 B.C. Statues of the king were erected in Antioch (Libanius *Oratio* XI, *Antiochus,* 92, p. R 301), and certainly in most of the many cities built by him in his large empire, which extended from the Aegean Sea to Bactria and India, including Asia Minor, Syria, Mesopotamia, and Persia. There is evidence that statues of Seleucus were erected in the Stoa Poikile (Painted Porch) in Athens (Pausanias I. 16. 1); in Olympia, where Seleucus appeared on horseback (Pausanias VI. 11. 1 and VI. 16. 2), and in the *Delphinion* of Miletus.[95]

[89] A. Furtwängler and P. Wolters, *Beschreibung der Glyptothek zu München* (2d ed., 1910), No. 298. Brunn-Bruckmann, *Denkmäler*, Pl. 105. Arndt, *Porträts*, Pls. 183–85. Bernoulli, *Darstellungen Alexanders*, pp. 44 ff., Fig. 10. Ujfalvy, *Alexandre*, pp. 84 ff., Pls. 10–11. Johnson, *Lysippos*, pp. 45 f., Pls. 6–7. M. Bieber, "The Portraits of Alexander the Great," in *Proceedings of the American Philosophical Society* (1949), p. 380, Figs. 9–11. Restored are a piece in the upper right part of the head, both arms, and the right leg. (See Chap. IV, p. 62, note 22).

[90] C. A. Robinson, *Alexander the Great* (1947), frontispiece. See our Fig. 415.

[91] G. Loeschcke in *Jahrbuch d. Inst.*, Vol. III (1888), p. 190, Pl. 7. Against the identification is J. J. Bernoulli in *Darstellungen Alexanders*, pp. 152 f. For the inscription and the room for the group in Delphi, see F. Courby in École Française d'Athènes, *Fouilles de Delphes*, Vol. II (1927), pp. 237 ff., and F. Poulsen, *Delphi* (1920), pp. 591 ff.

[92] E. Loewy, *Inschriften griechischer Bildhauer* (1885), No. 487. Overbeck, *Schriftquellen*, Nos. 1327, 1605.

[93] D. Comparetti and G. de Petra, *La Villa Ercolanese dei Pisoni* (1883), Pl. X, 1. Arndt, *Porträts*, Pls. 101–2. Johnson, *Lysippos*, pp. 67 f., 230 f., Pl. 49. Delbrück, *Porträts*, p. XXXV f., Fig. 11, Pl. 22.

[94] A good coin is in the Newell collection of the American Numismatic Society in New York. See E. T. Newell, *Royal Greek Portrait Coins* (1937), pp. 35, Pl. V, 1; F. Imhoof-Blumer, *Porträtköpfe auf antiken Münzen hellenischer und hellenisierter Völker* (1885), p. 28, Pl. I, 3–4. Our Fig. 140 is in the Bibliothèque nationale, Cabinet des Médailles. A similar one is in Brussels; it is dated between about 293–281 by Imhoof-Blumer, about 277—272 B.C. by Agnes Brett in a forthcoming book.

[95] G. Kawerau and A. Rehm, *Das Delphinion* (Vol. I, Part 3 of *Milet* [1914]), pp. 261 ff., 363 f., No. 158.

We do not know which statue was the model for the bronze bust. In any case it is one of the best existing portraits of a ruler. It depicts Seleucus as great, manly, and human. The forehead is protuberant, and the eyebrows are highly curved. The left eye still has the ancient filling of smalt, and the right eye has been restored accordingly. Thus we can divine the fire of the spirit from the eyes under their shadowing eyebrows. The nose is slightly curved. The upper lip is pouting. The chin is short and its underside is straight. Long folds, the sign of old age, furrow the cheeks. The bushy hair is arranged in irregular waves beginning at the vertex of the head. In front of the diadem, the royal band which Seleucus assumed in 306, heavy tufts of hair form an irregular and unsymmetrical crown. The execution of this copy is magnificent, and certainly close to that of the original. Even if Lysippos did not create the original, the copy shows that it is absolutely in his style. As in the Socrates, the features are realistic, but the nonessential has been subordinated to the significant.

Demetrius Poliorcetes, "the conqueror of cities," is another general and successor of Alexander who was portrayed in Lysippean style. He liberated Athens from Cassander, and in 306, together with his father Antigonos I (Antigonos Monophthalmos, "the one-eyed"), he took the royal title and diadem. When his father fell in the battle of Ipsus in 301, Demetrius fled and led an adventurous life until he was called back to Macedonia and made king. He ruled in Pella until his death in 283 B.C.

Demetrius Poliorcetes is said to have had features of rare and astonishing beauty. They had at once grace and strength, dignity and beauty. There was blended with their youthful eagerness a certain heroic look and a kingly majesty that were hard to imitate. He was regarded as a new Dionysos (Plutarch *Demetrius* 11). A statue was erected to him in Delphi (Pausanias x. 10. 2). Another was made by Teisikrates, a pupil of Euthykrates; his art, however, was nearer to that of the teacher of Euthykrates, Lysippos [96] (Pliny *Nat. hist.* xxxiv. 67). The art of Teisikrates was later appreciated

by the Romans, for a statue authenticated by an inscription stood in the porticus of Octavia in Rome.[97] It is quite possible, therefore, that the statue of Demetrius by Teisikrates was known in Italy.

Several scholars have recognized this portrait in a herm (Figs. 145–46) and in a bronze statuette (Fig. 149), both from Herculaneum, now in Naples.[98] In both the king has the same small horns of a bull as he has on his coins after 292 B.C.[99] (Fig. 147). Beside Demetrius, only Seleucus I was thus distinguished as a new Dionysos or Dionysos Tauros ("with the horns of a bull"). As we know the portrait of Seleucus, the identification of the herm and statuette as portraits of Demetrius is convincing. The herm (Figs. 145–46), with the chlamys of a general, is indeed very similar to the portrait on such coins as one minted in Amphipolis in 289/8. The upward gaze reminds one of idealized portraits of Alexander. The sober rendering of the

---

[96] See K. Jex Blake and E. Sellers, *The Elder Pliny's Chapters on Art* (1896), pp. 53 f.; G. Lippold in Pauly-Wissowa, *Real-Enc.*, Second Series, Vol. V, s.v. Teisikrates, pp. 149 f.; M. Bieber in Thieme-Becker, *Künstlerlexikon,* Vol. XXXIII (1939), s.v. Teisikrates, p. 217.

[97] *C.I.L.,* VI, No. 10043. Loewy, *Inschriften,* No. 493.

[98] For the herm (Museo Nazionale, Naples, No. 6149) see Ruesch, *Guida,* p. 273, No. 1146; Arndt, *Porträts,* Pls. 353–54; Comparetti and de Petra, *La Villa Ercolanese,* p. 275, No. 73, Pl. XX, No. 3; C. Picard in *Rev. Arch.,* Fourth Series, Vol. XXII (1944), pp. 5 ff., 22 ff., Figs. 5–6; C. Picard, in *Mon. Piot,* Vol. 41 (1946), pp. 79 ff., Figs. 3–6 and Pl. VIII; Laurenzi, *Ritratti greci,* p. 110, No. 50, Pl. XVIII; Hekler, *Portraits,* Pl. 72b; E. Pfuhl in *Jahrbuch d. Inst.,* XLV (1930), 10 f.; H. P. L'Orange, *Apotheosis in Ancient Portraiture* (1947), p. 42, Fig. 20. For the statuette (Naples, No. 5026) see Ruesch, *Guida,* p. 366, No. 1606; Arndt, *Porträts,* Pls. 355–56; T. Piroli, *Le antichità di Ercolano,* Vol. VI: *Bronzi di Ercolano, II* (1771), pp. 231 ff., Pl. LX, and Vol. V: *Bronzi, II* (1794), Pl. 31; C. Picard in *Rev. Arch.,* Fourth Series, Vol. XXII (1944), pp. 6 f., Figs. 1–2. While the Italian excavators of Herculaneum believed in 1771 that they recognized Seleucus, the right identification was made by E. Q. Visconti in his *Iconographie grecque,* Vol. II (1825), pp. 70 ff., Pl. III, and by P. Wolters in *Röm. Mitt.* (1889), p. 35. Mrs. Phyllis Williams Lehmann, *Statues on Coins of Southern Italy and Sicily* (1946), pp. 30 ff., Figs. 3 and 5, explains the statue as Demetrius in the guise of a young hunter or river god; she compares a tetradrachm of Segesta and a Campanian *lekythos* (Figs. 1–2).

[99] E. T. Newell, *The Coinages of Demetrius Poliorcetes* (1927), pp. 87 ff., Pls. VII–VIII. The coin in *ibid.,* Pl. XII, Fig. 3 belongs to the Newell collection in the American Numismatic Society, New York. I owe a photograph to the kindness of Agnes Brett. See also Newell, *Greek Portrait Coins,* pp. 27 ff., Figs. 2–3; Imhoof-Blumer, *Porträtköpfe,* Pl. I, Fig. 4 and Pl. II, Figs. 7 8; C. Picard, in *Rev. Arch.* (1944), pp. 17 ff., Figs. 3–4; K. Lange, *Herrscherköpfe des Altertums im Münzbild ihrer Zeit* (1938), pp. 50 f.; H. Gaebler, *Die antiken Münzen Nord-Griechenlands,* Vol. III, Part 2 (1935), pp. 181 f., Pl. XXXIII, 3–5, 7. The coin in our Figs. 147–48 belonged to the late George H. McFadden, to whom I owe the photographs.

features is near to Lysippos's conception of Alexander, which contrasted to that of other court artists. The features are handsome, although the mediocre copy does not show anything of the fiery character of the rather adventurous soldier. The movement of the neck seems to imitate that of Alexander. The Adam's apple shows in the portrait on the coin as well as in the bust.

Like the herm, the bronze statuette (Fig. 149) has the horns, the Macedonian chlamys, and the upward gaze of the eyes. The statuette has in addition the high *krepides,* the footwear of the soldier. It has the Lysippean stance, with one foot set up on an elevation, seen in the Alexander Rondanini as well as in the Poseidon in the Lateran, which is certainly a creation of Lysippos and which is also on the reverse of many coins of Demetrius Poliorcetes—for example, one in the collection of Mr. George H. McFadden (Figs. 147–48). Unfortunately, the execution of the small statuette is too coarse to permit comparison of its features with those of the herm. The former belongs to the first century B.C., the latter to the Augustan period.

The influence of Lysippos extended to artists outside his own school. The most interesting case is that of Kephisodotos and Timarchos, the sons of Praxiteles. As their father was not a portraitist, they were certainly influenced by Euthykrates, the son and pupil of Lysippos, with whom they made the statue of the poetess Anyte of Tegea.[100] This influence is seen in the statue of the poet Menander, the creator of the new Hellenistic comedy. His comedies are moral dramas, in which the destiny of man depends on his character as master of his fate. Menander presented for the first time in literature real individuals in ordinary situations taken from the contemporary life of the rich middle class of Athens. The plots are varied according to the qualities of the persons involved, and the characters are differentiated with vivid and subtle individual traits. Menander was influenced by his teacher Theophrastos, who in his book *Characters* had described individuals, such as the miser, the flatterer, and so on, for the first time. Theophrastos's teacher Aristotle, and before him Xenophon, had distinguished different people not as individuals, but according to the type of life they led, as military men,

active men, contemplative men, and so on. This development of biography was parallel to the development of portraiture: instead of types of the general, the politician, the philosopher, individual portraits were created in the school of Lysippos.

Menander is said to have been well dressed and handsome, but in delicate health (Phaedrus *Fabulae Aesopiae* v. 12). Statues were erected in his honor at Athens (Pausanias I. 21. 1) and a bronze statue later in Constantinople (Christodorus *Ecphrasis, Anthologia Palatina* II. 361 *et seq.*). Pausanias mentions the statue as being in the theater of Dionysos at Athens, where a base has been found, inscribed with the name of Menander and with the signatures of Kephisodotos and Timarchos.[101] This base was obviously designed for a seated bronze statue, approximately life size. It was probably set up in Menander's latter years, or shortly after his death in 291 B.C. It is to be assumed that most of the portraits of Menander which are preserved are based on this honorary statue.

Unfortunately, the busts of Menander authenticated by inscriptions are all late in date and poor in quality. The bust in a marble medallion in Marbury Hall, with a scroll in the background and the name on the lower part of the frame, shows Menander with a chiton and himation arranged on the left shoulder in the usual way[102] (Fig. 150). The technique for rendering the eyes is late Antonine. The bust agrees in general features with a now lost medallion of which drawings were made in 1578 by Theodorus Gallaeus, when it was in the possession of Fulvio Orsini (Fulvius Ursinus)[103] (Fig. 152). The profile is shown on theater tickets from Pergamon and Alexandria[104] (Fig. 153). These have the name ΜΕΝΑΝΔΡΟΣ and Roman

100 For the sons of Praxiteles see M. Bieber in *Jahrbuch d. Inst.,* XXXVII–IX (1923–24), 242 ff.

101 Loewy, *Inschriften,* No. 108. F. Studniczka, *Das Bildnis Menanders* (repr. from *Illberg's Neue Jahrbücher für das klassische Altertum,* Vol. XLI [1918]), pp. 3 f., Fig. 1.
102 Studniczka, *Das Bildnis Menanders,* p. 11, Pl. 4, Fig. 3; Pl. 6, Fig. 2; and Pl. 7, Fig. 2. Bernoulli, *Ikonographie,* Vol. II, pp. 105 f., Fig. 8. F. Poulsen in Arndt-Amelung, *Einzelaufnahmen,* Nos. 3113–14. J. F. Crome, *Das Bildnis Vergils (Reale Accademia Virgiliana di Mantova, Atti e Memorie,* Nuova Serie, Vol. XXIV [1935]), pp. 34 f., Pl. 20, Fig. 45. R. Herbig, "Zum Menander-Vergil-Problem," in *Röm. Mitt.,* Vol. LIX (1946), pp. 80 ff., Pl. 13.
103 Studniczka, *Das Bildnis Menanders,* pp. 6, 9, 12, 14, Pl. 4, Figs. 1–2 and Pl. 8, Fig. 2. Crome, *Das Bildnis Vergils,* pp. 29 ff., Figs. 46–47.
104 A. E. Kondoleon in *Athen. Mitt.,* XIV (1880), 130. E. Noir in *Bulletin de la Société royale d'Archéologie, Alexandrie,*

and Greek numerals on one side and the portrait of the poet holding a mask on the other side. The points in which all three sources agree are: the mantle on the left shoulder and the chiton covering both shoulders and the chest; the strongly protruding muscles and the Adam's apple in the hollow neck; the elongated form of the head; his short rounded chin sharply separated from the mouth; the short upper lip; the flat cheeks; his longish eyes with prominent lids only half open; the broad, high, and vaulted forehead; the hair only slightly wavy and brushed forward.

More than forty marble copies of a portrait head have been recognized as being copies of the portrait statue by the sons of Praxiteles because of their agreement with the medallions.[105] The most beautiful replica is in Boston[106] (Figs. 151, 154–55). Other excellent ones are in Venice[107] (Figs. 156–57), in Corfu (Corcyra),[108] and in Copenhagen, where a good reconstruction was made;[109] another, badly preserved, is in Ince Blundell Hall in

England.[110] To the features visible in the medallions these replicas add many subtleties and refinements of modeling in the style created by Lysippos.

The sculptured heads agree with the medallions in the division of the forehead into a high upper section and a lower one beneath it, and in the two horizontal furrows separating the two sides of the lower section and the eyebrows from each other. In the elegant and probably Augustan copy in Boston (Figs. 151, 154–55), however, the horizontal lines are much less emphasized and the two vertical creases, together with a slight horizontal furrow at the root of the nose, are used to give the expression of serious thought and of attentive observation. The eyebrows hang heavily over the almond-shaped eyes with their drooping eyelids. Together with the slightly open lips, they give an expression almost of sadness. The nose is bent slightly to its left, and as a result the heavy furrows running obliquely downward from the wings of the nose are differentiated. The flat hollow temples and cheeks contrast with the short and well-rounded chin. The features are in agreement with Menander's character as it may be inferred from his plays and as described in the literary sources. They show a handsome, physically frail, and sensitive person. The expression is that of an amiable and nervous personality.

The hair is laid in beautiful S-curves, with a general movement from the rear to the front, but bent backward again in beautiful bow lines at the sides. In front the strands are combed along the hairline from left to right, again in S-curves, with the points hanging over the right half of the forehead. The consequence is that on both sides of the face, above the left temple and above the middle of the right eye, more of the upper forehead is seen than in the center. This refined arrangement of the hair was ruined by some copyists, who, as in the Corfu head, inserted a few thin short strands in this space. This motif of inserted strands of hair was multiplied in the later medallion in Marbury Hall (Fig. 150), where, however, the original arrangement is still

Vols. XXXII–XXXIII (1938), N.S. 10, p. 157. R. Herbig, "Zum Menander-Vergil-Problem," in *Röm. Mitt.*, Vol. LIX (1946), p. 87, Fig. 4.

[105] Lists of replicas in Bernoulli, *Ikonographie*, pp. 103 ff.; Studniczka, *Das Bildnis Menanders*, pp. 1 ff.; Crome, *Das Bildnis Vergils*, pp. 1 ff., Pls. I–XXX, Figs. 1–62. Crome lists 38 replicas (pp. 67–71). To these must be added 3 more replicas: one is in Toronto (David M. Robinson in *The Royal Ontario Museum Bulletin of Archaeology* [1926], pp. 1 ff., S. Reinach in *Gazette des Beaux-Arts*, Vol. VI [1931], pp. 90 ff., Figs. 21–23, and David M. Robinson in *Proceedings of the American Philosophical Society*, Vol. LXXXIII, No. 3 [1940], pp. 470 f., Pl. III, Figs. 10–13); one is in the possession of David M. Robinson (*idem, Proceedings of the American Philosophical Society*, Vol. LXXXIII, No. 3 [1940], pp. 465 ff., Pl. I, Figs. 1–4); and one is in Rhodes (L. Laurenzi in *La Critica d'Arte*, Vols. XIX–XX [1939], pp. 28 ff., Pls. XVI–XIX, and *Ritratti greci* [1941], Pl. XLVII, Fig. 5).

[106] L. D. Caskey, Catalogue of Greek and Roman Sculpture (Boston, Museum of Fine Arts, 1925), pp. 168 f., No. 86. Bernoulli, *Ikonographie*, Pl. XIV. Crome, *Das Bildnis Vergils*, pp. 17 f., Figs. 19–21. M. Bieber, *Denkmäler zum Theaterwesen* (1920), Pl. 47. M. Bieber, *The History of the Greek and Roman Theater* (1939), pp. 164 f., Fig. 220.

[107] T. Campanile in *Bollettino Comunale*, Vol. LIV (1928), pp. 187 ff., Pls. I–II. Crome, *Das Bildnis Vergils*, pp. 15 f., Figs. 5–15. Schefold, *Bildnisse*, pp. 114, 116 f., Fig. 2. Laurenzi, *Ritratti greci*, pp. 139 f., Pl. XLVII, Fig. 1.

[108] Arndt-Amelung, *Einzelaufnahmen*, Nos. 610–11. Crome, *Das Bildnis Vergils*, p. 17, Figs. 16–18. Bieber, *Greek and Roman Theater*, Fig. 221. Laurenzi, *Ritratti greci*, Pl. XLVII, Fig. 2.

[109] Studniczka, *Das Bildnis Menanders*, pp. 17 f., Pl. 10, No. 3, and Frontispiece (reconstruction). *Billedtavler til Kataloget over Antike Kunstvaerker, Ny Carlsberg Glyptotek* (Copen-

hagen, 1907), No. 429, Pl. 31. F. Poulsen, "Ikonographische Miscellen," in *Vid. Sels. Skrift.*, Vol. IV, Part 1 (1921), p. 32, Fig. 10. Poulsen, *Catalogue Ny Carlsberg*, pp. 302 f., No. 429.

[110] B. Ashmole, *Catalogue of the Ancient Marbles at Ince Blundell Hall* (1929), p. 68, No. 176, Pl. 30, Nos. 1–5. The nose has been restored; the surface is corroded.

visible, though obscured by the set in filling. In the drawings by Gallaeus (Fig. 152) and perhaps in his model, the filled-in strands have overgrown the original central motif. In the original, as best represented by the Boston head, the treatment of the hair combines apparent casualness with artistic refinement in the same manner as that used in the Apoxyomenos by Lysippos.

Most scholars agree that these features are those of a Greek and thus of Menander,[111] but four scholars see in them a Roman, and believe the portrait to be that of Vergil.[112] But a relief in the Lateran, dated in the first century B.C., and a replica in the Art Museum of Princeton University show a poet studying the masks for a comedy;[113] that this seated poet of the New Comedy is Menander cannot be doubted, for the masks—one of which he holds in his hand, while two lie before him on the table—are masks of the three typical characters created by him: the elegant youth, the beloved woman, and the father. It seems even likely that these are the masks for Menander's comedy *Samia* or *The Girl from Samos*. The woman would be Chrysis, the girl from Samos, whom old Demeas has taken into his house as his common-law wife. When Moschion, the son, secretly engages himself to a poor girl and a baby is born, Chrysis pretends that it is her baby, in order to help the young lovers. The result is confusion ending happily with two marriages. The woman standing at the side in the relief must be Menander's beloved Glykera, described in his letters (Athenaeus *Deipnosophistae* XIII. 594). She was the model for Menander's delineation of decent and cultivated courtesans.[114] The head of the poet on the relief in the Lateran,

the unusual arrangement of the hair, the hollow temples and cheeks, the deep creases around the mouth and in the neck, the protruding Adam's apple, all agree with the sculptured heads. This head, therefore, must have been taken from some official portrait. The poet's attitude in this casual situation naturally would not be an exact copy of the attitude of an honorary statue, for in that he was undoubtedly represented in a more dignified and quiet position.

There may have been two portrait statues of Menander in Athens, one fully dressed and one with only a mantle around the lower part of the body, as in the relief; for the copies of the sculptured heads disagree in the treatment of the bust. Whereas the Boston bust has nude shoulders and chest, the bust in Venice (Figs. 156–57) has the same chiton and himation as occur in the medallions. Both garments are found also in a copy from the theater in Verona[115] and on a late Roman bust at Konya.[116] The Copenhagen bust has a mantle on the left shoulder. The honorary statue set up in the theater was probably of the second type. The draped statue may have been an earlier work of the sons of Praxiteles made in the lifetime of the poet (342–291). After the death of the poet, who drowned at about fifty years of age when he was swimming in the sea at Piraeus, Kephisodotos and Timarchos were commissioned by the city to erect a new statue in his honor in the theater. The dressed statue may have been distinguished by the wreath of the poet, as it appears on the Roman theater ticket (Fig. 153), on the mosaic made by Monnus in Trier,[117] and in a replica of the sculptured head in Oxford.[118] The wreath also reappears in two pictorial representations of Menander in full figure, the one from the Casa di Menandro in Pompeii[119] and the mosaic from Antioch on the

[111] Studniczka, Bernoulli, Poulsen, David M. Robinson, Hekler, Schefold, and Bieber, in works cited in notes 102, 105, and 109 above.

[112] Crome, *Das Bildnis Vergils*. Lippold, *Porträtstatuen*, pp. 89 ff. G. Lippold in *Röm. Mitt.* XXXIII (1918), 1 ff. Rhys Carpenter in *Mem. Amer. Acad. Rome*, XVIII (1941), pp. 96 ff., Pl. 30. R. Herbig, "Zum Menander-Vergil-Problem," in *Röm. Mitt.* LIX (1946). The explanation for this mistake of eminent scholars is the fact that some copies have features of Roman contemporary classicizing art.

[113] Studniczka, *Das Bildnis Menanders*, pp. 25 ff., Pl. 9, Figs. 1–2. J. Sieveking in text to Brunn-Bruckmann, *Denkmäler*, Pl. 625. Bieber, *Denkmäler zum Theaterwesen*, pp. 83 f., No. 30, Fig. 86, Pl. 47. Bieber, *Greek and Roman Theater*, pp. 165 f., Figs. 223–24. Schefold, *Bildnisse*, pp. 164 f., Fig. 3 (cf. p. 216).

[114] The replica of the Lateran relief, formerly in the Stroganoff collection and now in the Art Museum, Princeton University,

lacks the Glykera. See M. Bieber in *Festschrift Andreas Rumpf* (1952), pp. 14 ff., Pl. V.

[115] Crome, *Das Bildnis Vergils*, p. 18, Figs. 22–24.

[116] *Ibid.*, pp. 21, 35, Fig. 44. W. H. Buckler in *J.R.S.*, Vol. XIV (1924), p. 46, Pl. VII.

[117] *Ant. Denk.*, Vol. I, Pl. 48, No. 4. G. Lippold in *Röm. Mitt.*, XXXIII (1918), p. 12, Fig. 5.

[118] A. Michaelis, *Ancient Marbles in Great Britain* (1882), p. 557, No. 66. Crome, *Das Bildnis Vergils*, p. 19, Figs. 41–43. The eyebrows, the left part of the forehead, the nose, mouth, and bust have been restored.

[119] A. Maiuri, *Casa del Menandro* (1933), pp. 106 ff., Figs. 50, 52, 53, Pl. XII (in color). Schefold, *Bildnisse*, pp. 164 f., No. 1.

Orontes in the Art Museum of Princeton University.[120]

One reason why it has been assumed that the subject of the sculptured heads is not Menander, but Vergil, is that he also appears with an older bearded man, with a thick fillet in his hair, in two double herms, one in the Akademische Kunstmuseum in Bonn,[121] of which a replica is in Wilton House in England,[122] and one found on the Via Appia Nuova and now in the Museo Nazionale Romano in Rome.[123] This head of a bearded man has been identified with the so-called Apollonios, now definitely proved to be a portrait of Homer, created around 300 B.C., and thus contemporaneous with the portrait of Menander. On coins of Amastris it is inscribed ΟΜΗΡΟΣ. The combination of Menander with Homer in the double herm is a parallel to the epigram on a herm in Turin, which puts Menander second only to Homer:

Not without reason have I placed you, O dear Menander, alongside and opposite the gaze of the head of Homer, inasmuch as the wise grammarian Aristophanes, excellent judge of your writings, gave you second place immediately after the great genius.[124]

This high evaluation explains why so many copies of the portrait executed in Lysippean style by the sons of Praxiteles have been preserved.

Menander's philosophy was influenced by Epicurus, who was of the same age. The two had served together during their military training years, 323–321, and probably remained friends until the end of Menander's life. Epicurus founded his school first in 310 in Mytilene, later in Lampsacus, and in 306 in Athens in a garden outside the Dipylon gate. Here he taught and lived in close communication with his many friends and pupils, among whom were his lifelong friend Metrodorus and his successor Hermarchus. They revered him more as a religious than a scientific leader and as a savior and redeemer from evil. Epicurus's goal was not theoretical research, but the formulation of rules for right living. Just as Menander had replaced the religious content of Greek drama with moral content and dealt with subjects taken from actual life, so his contemporary Epicurus replaced the religious subjects of the earlier philosophical schools with secularism. He was in poor health, and perhaps partly because of his own sufferings he sought a theory of life which would free mankind from pain and anxiety. His motto was "live in retirement" (λάθε βιώσας), meaning to live— as he did—in philosophical serenity and cheerfulness. The sage must dedicate his life to pleasures, the spiritual pleasures to be preferred, for they are more lasting. He does not need laws, because he does the right thing for egoistic reasons: he is courageous, temperate, and just, because otherwise he could not secure tranquillity and happiness. The highest pleasure is reached when there is a complete absence of sensual pain and fear.[125]

The picture of the sage who has overcome his bodily sufferings which is transmitted by his writings and literary sources is borne out by the sculptured portrait of Epicurus. It is authenticated through a bronze bust, inscribed ΕΠΙΚΟΥΡΟΣ, found in the Epicurean library of a villa at Herculaneum, and now in Naples[126] (Fig. 159), and

[120] *Antioch-on-the-Orontes*, Vol. III: *The Excavations, 1937–1939*, ed. by R. Stillwell (1941), pp. 185 f., No. 131, Pl. 63. A. M. Friend, "Menander and Glykera in the Mosaics of Antioch," in *ibid.*, pp. 248 ff. The upper parts of the heads of Menander and Glykera, also with wreaths, are preserved in another mosaic (*ibid.*, p. 176, No. 110, Pl. 50).
[121] R. Kekule von Stradonitz, *Das Akademische Kunstmuseum, Bonn* (1872), p. 144, No. 688, Pl. 2. M. Bieber in *Röm. Mitt.*, Vol. XXXII (1917), p. 129, Pl. 7. Crome, *Das Bildnis Vergils*, pp. 14 and 24 ff. R. and E. Boehringer, *Homer, Bildnisse und Nachweise* (1939), pp. 69 ff., No. XV, Pl. 41.
[122] Michaelis, *Ancient Marbles*, p. 679, No. 35. Crome, *Das Bildnis Vergils*, p. 14. Boehringer, *Homer*, pp. 71 f., No. XVI, Pl. 42.
[123] R. Paribeni in *Notizie degli Scavi* (1929), pp. 351 ff., Pls. 16–17. Paribeni, *Ritratto*, Pl. LXIV. Poulsen, *Iconographic Studies*, Vol. I, pp. 26 ff., Fig. 21. Both Paribeni and Poulsen consider the head to be Aristophanes, while Crome, in *Das Bildnis Vergils* (pp. 14, 21 ff., Figs. 1–4), and the Boehringers, in *Homer* (pp. 68 f., No. XIII, Pls. 37–39), have identified the "Apollonios" as Homer. For a double herm of Menander and Aristophanes in the Villa Albani, see Chap. X, p. 143.
[124] Studniczka, *Das Bildnis Menanders*, p. 5, Fig. 3. G. Kaibel, *Epigrammata Graeca ex Lapidibus Conlecta* (1878), p. 490, No. 1085; cf. A. Körte, "Homer and Menander," in *Hermes*, LXXI (1936), 221 f. The translation of the epigram is by A. M. Friend, in *Antioch-on-the-Orontes*, III, 251.

[125] For Epicurus, see Diogenes Laertius *Lives of Eminent Philosophers* x; Cyril Bailey, *Epicurus, the Extant Remains* (with translation; 1926); E. Zeller, *The Stoics, Epicureans, and Sceptics*, tr. by W. Reichel (1892); H. von Arnim, in Pauly-Wissowa, *Real-Enc.*, Vol. VI, pp. 133–55, No. 4; R. D. Hicks, *Stoic and Epicurean* (1910), pp. 153–311; A. E. Taylor, *Epicurus* (1911).
[126] Museo Nazionale, Naples, No. 5465. Comparetti and de Petra, *La Villa Ercolanese*, Pl. XII, No. 7. Bernoulli, *Ikonographie*, Vol. II, p. 124, No. 6, Pl. XIX b. A. Hekler, *Bildniskunst*, p. XX, Fig. 11.

through the double bust of Epicurus and Metrodo- rus in the Museo Capitolino, with the same in- scription[127] (Fig. 160). The best copy of this head is in the Metropolitan Museum of Art in New York[128] (Figs. 161–62). About twenty-four rep- licas are preserved. The same portrait appears on a Roman gem[129] (Fig. 158), in agreement with the statement of Cicero (*De finibus* v. 3) that the portrait of Epicurus was even carved on cups and finger rings.

All replicas agree in representing a man of about fifty to sixty years of age—not much older than his friend and contemporary Menander, whom he out- lived by twenty years. The portrait, therefore, must have been made about 290—280 B.C. It is similar to the portrait of Menander, in a style still reminiscent of Lysippos. The head is elongated, with a well-rounded skull. The hair has the same free yet artistic arrangement seen in the Menander portrait. The thick hair in back is brought for- ward in horizontal strands; in front it hangs down with S-curves from the right to the left side, with three points hanging low over the high forehead above the left eye. On both sides short thick locks frame the face in front of the ears and approach the side strands of the long thick beard, which is di- vided in the center with the ends strongly curled. The mustache leaves a triangle of the deeply fur- rowed upper lip visible. The forehead has irregular wrinkles. The bushy eyebrows are broken in con- tour and hang heavily over the small deep-set eyes. The nose, preserved in the double herms in the Louvre and in the Museo Capitolino (Fig. 160), the bronze bust in Naples (Fig. 159), and the bust in the Museo Capitolino[130] (Fig. 171), has, like

the nose on the gem (Fig. 158), a great curve near the top, and the tip projects slightly downward. This, with the protruding forehead and the full wavy beard, gives to the head a clean-cut and re- fined profile. The cheeks are thin, narrow, and deeply furrowed with folds beginning at the inner corners of the eyes; on the temples are crow's-feet. The features betray rigorous intellectual labor and serious thinking. The distinguished character of the face would alone be sufficient to refute the ac- cusations made by enemies of Epicurus, and also the wrong interpretations given by later followers of his doctrine, that he was dedicated to the lower pleasures of the body.

The front of the neck in the best replica, that in the Metropolitan Museum (Figs. 161–62), has horizontal creases, showing that the head was bent forward. A thick mantle lies with broad folds over the left shoulder and high across the nape of the neck. The bronze bust in Naples (Fig. 159), and the bust in the Museo Capitolino (Fig. 171), as well as a bust in Ravenna,[131] add a continuation of these folds along and a little above the right shoul- der. This arrangement of the mantle led to the recognition of the statue to which this head be- longs. The best replica, originally inscribed EΠI- KOΥPOΣ, with a restored modern head, formerly in the Palazzo Margherita in Rome and now in Copenhagen[132] (Fig. 166), and other replicas of this statue in Ince Blundell Hall[133] (Figs. 163–64), in the Museo Archeologico in Florence (Fig. 165), and in the Magazzino Archaeologico in Rome,[134]

---

[127] Bernoulli, *Ikonographie*, Vol. II, pp. 122 ff., No. 1, Pls. XVI– XVII. Hekler, *Bildniskunst*, pp. XXI f., Pl. 100. Jones, *Sculpt. Museo Capitolino*, p. 244, Stanze dei Filosofi No. 63, Pl. 56. Arndt, *Porträts*, Pls. 1081–83. Found near Santa Maria Mag- giore. Only the patch over the left eye has been restored. Other double herms with Metrodoros are in the Louvre (Bernoulli, *Ikonographie*, No. 9; H. de Villefosse, *Catalogue sommaire des marbres antiques* [1896], No. 88), and in Copenhagen (Poulsen, *Catalogue Ny Carlsberg*, p. 301, No. 426, and Poulsen in Arndt-Amelung, *Einzelaufnahmen*, Nos. 4630–32).

[128] Delbrück, *Porträts*, p. XXXVIII, Pl. 25. G. Richter in Arndt, *Porträts*, Pls. 1124–25, and in *Handbook* (1953), p. 122, Pl. 100b. Schefold, *Bildnisse*, pp. 118 f., 210. No restorations.

[129] A. Furtwängler, *Antike Gemmen* (1900), Pl. XLIII, Fig. 5. G. Lippold, *Gemmen und Kameen* (1922), p. 178, Pl. LXVII, Fig. 6.

[130] Jones, *Sculpt. Museo Capitolino*, Stanza dei Filosofi, p. 244,

No. 64. Lippold, *Porträtstatuen*, p. 80, Fig. 18. Arndt, *Porträts*, Pl. 1084. Restored are the tip of the nose and the edge of the left ear.

[131] A. W. van Buren in *A.J.A.*, Vol. XLV (1941), pp. 465, 467, Fig. 15. Van Buren did not recognize Epicurus. Found in the Adriatic Sea near Porto Corsini.

[132] Arndt-Amelung, *Einzelaufnahmen*, Nos. 2092–93. Lippold, *Porträtstatuen*, pp. 77 ff., Fig. 17. F. Poulsen in *Gazette des Beaux-Arts*, XVII (1937), pp. 7 f., Fig. 7. Restored are the head, right arm, left hand, left shoulder, parts of folds of mantle, and parts of the seat. Cf. the reconstructed design in Poulsen, *op. cit.*, p. 2, Fig. 2. A sculptured reconstruction would be desirable.

[133] F. Poulsen, *Greek and Roman Portraits in English Coun- try Houses* (Oxford, The Clarendon Press, 1923), p. 43, No. 16. Ashmole, *Ince Blundell Hall*, p. 26, No. 4, Pl. 29. Restored are the head, which is a copy of the Albani Diogenes; neck, right arm from the middle of the upper arm, left hand with the scroll, plinth, both feet, and the end of the mantle in front.

[134] Hekler, *Bildnisse*, pp. 48, 57. L. A. Milani, *Museo Archeo-*

do not include the original heads, but the arrangement of the mantle is exactly the same as in the busts in Rome and Naples. In these statues the great teacher is seated on a throne, each end of which is shaped like the forepart of a griffin. His right leg is extended, with the foot probably protruding over the base; his left leg is drawn backwards, so that the feet in their elegant sandals are wide apart, in a natural and relaxed position. The left hand holds a scroll; the right arm is sharply bent and the now restored hand must originally have been lifted to the height of the shoulder or chin in a gesture of greeting or meditation. The left arm is wrapped in the mantle, which comes down from the shoulder and is laid in broad folds around the legs down to the ankles, with a broad overfold hanging from the lap and the left knee. The drapery, like the hair, is in a natural yet artistic arrangement. The main characteristic of this rich portrayal of the venerated teacher is the combination of movement with a form closed in quiet contours.

Portraits of Epicurus were frequent in antiquity. Bronze statues were erected in his honor at his birthplace, Samos. Many of the Romans who later followed the teachings of his school had his portrait in their private houses, and carried them with them from place to place (Pliny *Nat. hist.* xxxv. 5: "Epicuri voltus per cubicula gestant ac circumferunt secum"). Atticus (in Cicero *De finibus* v. 3) said it was impossible to forget Epicurus when one had once seen him. All these later portraits were certainly based on an official portrait, which must have been erected in his school. It may have been dedicated by his pupils, who adored Epicurus like a savior. It probably stood together with that of his faithful follower and friend Metrodorus, with whom he is connected in double herms [135] (Figs. 160 and 172). Metrodorus (330—277 B.C.) was only twelve years younger than his master, and died seven years before him. Epicurus instituted a me-

morial service for Metrodorus to be held in connection with his own birthday festival. It is possible that a portrait of Epicurus was erected for this occasion, in 277 B.C.

The features of Metrodorus in the double herm with the inscription ΜΗΤΡΟΔΩΡΟΣ (Fig. 172) are repeated in about a dozen replicas, the best ones being busts in the Museo Capitolino (Figs. 167–68) and in Athens [136] (Figs. 169–70). The head resembles that of Epicurus but is less distinguished, portraying a man not only younger but less worn by serious thinking. The strands of the hair are shorter and are brought forward more regularly. On the right side the strands are arranged in parallel curves, but above the inner corner of the left eye a lock is curved in the opposite direction to form a kind of calyx. A similar figure is repeated above the left temple. The full beard is also similar to that of Epicurus, but two large rolls of hair form a definite pattern below the chin. The lower part of the forehead protrudes and the eyebrows are straight. The nose, well preserved in the two busts (Figs. 167–70), has only a slight curve. The cheeks are more rounded than those of Epicurus. The portrait agrees with Cicero's saying that Metrodorus was almost another Epicurus. The portrait indicates, however, that he was a lesser man.

The statue of Metrodorus from which the head was copied is best preserved in the replica in Copenhagen, where it is restored with the cast of the head in Athens [137] (Figs. 173–74). The lower part, which is missing here, is preserved in a statuette in Newby Hall in England and there is another small replica in Naples.[138] The statue has been identified by the fact that the arrangement of the drapery on the left shoulder and behind the right shoulder agrees with that of the busts in the Museo Capitolino and in Athens (Figs. 167–70). The mantle lies

logico di Firenze, Vol. I (1912), p. 318, No. 89, and Vol. II (1912), Pl. CLVI, Fig. 2. G. Richter in text to Arndt, *Porträts,* Pls. 1124–25, Fig. 8. Schefold, *Bildnisse,* pp. 120 f., No. 1. The replica in the Magazzino Archaeologico in Rome was found on the Esquiline. The left hand holds the ancient scroll. Height 24 cm. A small replica is also in a storeroom at Ostia (Museum No. 1135).

[135] For Metrodoros see W. Kroll in Pauly-Wissowa, *Real-Enc.,* XV 1477–80. For the double herm see above, Note 127.

[136] Arndt, *Porträts,* Pls. 1085, 1089–90. Jones, *Sculpt. Museo Capitolino,* p. 244, Stanza dei Filosofi, No. 62, Pl. 56. The only part restored is the tip of the nose. Athens, National Museum, No. 368. The lower part of the bust is unfinished. No restorations.

[137] Lippold, *Porträtstatuen,* pp. 80 ff., Figs. 19–20. F. Poulsen, "Ikonographische Miscellen," pp. 73 ff., Pls. 31–35. Poulsen in *Gazette des Beaux-Arts,* Vol. XVII (1937), pp. 3 ff., Figs. 3–5. Poulsen, *Catalogue Ny Carlsberg,* p. 293, No. 416a. Schefold, *Bildnisse,* pp. 120 f., No. 4, p. 210.

[138] Michaelis, *Ancient Marbles,* p. 534, No. 35. F. Poulsen in *Gazette des Beaux-Arts,* Vol. XVII (1937), pp. 4 ff., Fig. 6. Ruesch, *Guida,* No. 1131. T. Birt, *Die Buchrolle in der Kunst* (1907), p. 87, Fig. 46.

in heavy masses on the lap and surrounds the back and the legs with elegant curves. A long end falls from the left shoulder to the cushion on the seat. The body is that of a man of about fifty, with flabby breasts and loose folds of skin. The statue therefore must have been done shortly before or at the time of the death of Metrodorus in 277 B.C. That it was based on the memorial statue ordered by Epicurus is probable. In any case it is a counterpart to the statue of Epicurus (Figs. 163–66). The right hand of Metrodorus, like the left of Epicurus, lies in the lap with a scroll; the left arm here, like the right of Epicurus, is bent with the hand before his shoulder, probably greeting the pupils. Thus the two stood together in the garden of Epicurus: the master represented at the end of a lecture, with a finished scroll in his left hand; the pupil and friend ready to start, with an unopened scroll in his right. Metrodorus followed the teachings of his master faithfully.

There probably stood in the garden also the statue of Hermarchus, the successor of Epicurus in the presidency at the Epicurean school. He became the head of the school after the death of the master in 270 B.C. at the age of about fifty-five.[139] His features are known through an inscribed bronze bust from the Epicurean library at Herculaneum in Naples [140] (Fig. 175). The head is preserved in about ten busts, the best being in Budapest (Figs. 177–78) and in the Sala delle Muse of the Vatican Museum; [141] the head in the Museo Capitolino, although not as good—it tends to flatness—is careful in details.[142] As in the other Epicurean heads and the head of Menander, the hair is swept over

the forehead to one side—here from the right to the left—leaving a free triangular space above the right eye. The beard is full like the others, but is not parted in the center. The strands in front of the chin have S-curves. The forehead of Hermarchus is less wrinkled than that of Epicurus. The nose, preserved in the bronze and in the bust of Budapest (Figs. 175, 177–78) is straight and long. Heavy furrows go from the nostrils to the outer corners of the mouth, which appears small under the hanging moustache. The expression is less thoughtful than the expressions of the other heads, rather defiant, and almost irritable. This agrees with the fact that Hermarchus was less docile than Metrodorus, who had to be guided, even dominated, by Epicurus (Seneca *Epistula* LII ["On Choosing Our Teachers"] 3).

The head, fortunately, is also found on a statue in Florence [143] (Fig. 176), and there is a replica from Ostia without the head in the Museo Nazionale Romano in Rome.[144] The drapery of the mantle agrees with that of the busts in Naples and Budapest. The arrangement of the drapery and the movement of the arms and feet are similar to those of Epicurus (Figs. 163–66). Hermarchus does not hold a scroll. His right elbow is sustained by the left hand, which is wrapped in the end of the himation.

The three portrait statues of the three Epicurean philosophers show not only a decline in the importance of the three personalities, but decidedly a decline of the Lysippean style. It becomes more commonplace with Hermarchus and returns to the forms which we find in Attic statues of around 340—330 B.C.: those of the three tragic poets set up in the theater of Athens by Lycurgus, and that of the orator Aeschines, the follower of Philip of Macedon, probably set up in the same period.[145] It thus seems that the school of Lysippos, like the school of Epicurus, underwent no further development during the middle and late parts of the Hellenistic period. The Lysippean school, which had been so influential, came to an end when Atticism became generally prevalent.

---

[139] For Hermarchos see Diogenes Laertius *Lives of Eminent Philosophers* x. 24 *et seq.*; H. von Arnim in Pauly-Wissowa, *Real-Enc.*, Vol. VIII, pp. 721 f., No. 1.

[140] Comparetti and de Petra, *La Villa Ercolanese*, p. 263, Pl. XII, Fig. 8. Hekler, *Bildniskunst*, Fig. 14 (p. XX, Fig. 13 is the same as in *La Villa Ercolanese*, Pl. XII, 2, which is also a portrait of Hermarchos; Pl. 102 is a portrait of Metrodorus. Hekler has confused the two types).

[141] From Asia Minor. No restorations. See A. Hekler, *Die Sammlung antiker Skulpturen. (Die Budapester Sammlungen. Die Antiken in Budapest.* I. *Abteilung: Die Skulpturen* [1929]), p. 54, No. 46; ill. on pp. 57 and 59. Lippold, *Vatican Kat.*, Vol. III, pp. 24 f., Sala delle Muse No. 509, Pl. 23. Hekler, *Bildniskunst*, Pl. 42 (labeled "unknown Greek"). Bernoulli, *Ikonographie*, Vol. II, pp. 139 f., Pl. XX (he questions the identification).

[142] Jones, *Sculpt. Museo Capitolino*, pp. 254 f., Stanza dei Filosofi No. 87, Pl. 60. Arndt, *Porträts*, Pls. 1091–92. Restored are the nose, ears, and bust.

[143] Milani, *Museo Archeologico di Firenze*, Vol. II, p. 318, No. 88, Pl. CLVI, Fig. 1. G. Richter in text to Arndt, *Porträts*, No. 1123, Fig. 7. Hekler, *Sammlung antiker Skulpturen*, fig. on p. 53. Schefold, *Bildnisse*, pp. 120 f., No. 2, p. 210.

[144] D. Vaglieri in *Notizie degli Scavi* (1913), p. 298, Fig. 4.

[145] See following chapter on Atticism.

IV

ATTICISM
IN THE LATE FOURTH AND
EARLY THIRD CENTURIES B.C.

ATHENS during the classical period was—besides the northern Peloponnese—the main seat of culture and art. In the Hellenistic period the city kept to the classical tradition more tenaciously than any other place. While the center of politics and luxury and a new kind of creative art shifted to the East, Athens remained a cultural center for philosophy. It became a kind of small university town, highly respected later even by the Roman victors. Main products of the fourth century and the early Hellenistic period were portraits of outstanding men. Leading were the sons of Praxiteles, Kephisodotos and Timarchos, who added the training in portraiture which they probably received in the school of Lysippos to the training in ideal sculpture which they had received from their father. They thus created the portrait of Menander (Figs. 150–57); the portraits of the philosopher Epicurus and his friends and successors were made in a similar style (Figs. 158–78).

During the period of Philip and Alexander of Macedon and the leadership of the statesman Lycurgus, other Attic artists must already have worked on portraits of celebrated personalities of the fifth century. The loss of political power led to a higher appreciation of the great past. Thus about 340—330 B.C. Lycurgus set up statues of the three great tragic poets in the theater (*Vitae decem oratorum* [Lives of the Ten Orators], included in Plutarch *Moralia* x, p. 841F), for their works at that time had become classics.

For Aeschylus there existed as a contemporary likeness probably only the portrait showing him as a valiant fighter in the battle of Marathon, painted in the Stoa Poikile by Mikon and Panainos during the leadership of Cimon (Pausanias 1. 15. 3 and 21. 2). An excellent literary portrait is given in Aristophanes's *Frogs,* produced in 405 B.C. The comic writer describes Aeschylus as solemn, simple, and heroic, with noble features and high forehead. This tradition, together with the grandiose character of Aeschylus's tragedies, and the fact that he is said to have "invented" the mask, was probably the basis for the Lycurgean statue, copied in the statue in the Vatican Museum.[1] The head is missing, as the one now on the statue represents Euripides. We must reconstruct the body with a head found in the sea near Livorno (Fig. 179), along with a head of Sophocles (Fig. 180), both now in the Museo Archeologico in Florence, and also together with a herm of Sophocles in the garden of the Villa Colonna at Rome.[2] The head in

[1] W. Amelung, *Die Skulpturen des Vaticanischen Museums* (2 vols., Berlin, 1903–6), I, 72. Braccio Nuovo No. 53, Pl. 9. M. Bieber, *The History of the Greek and Roman Theater* (Princeton University Press, 1939), pp. 32 f., Fig. 35.
[2] K. McDowell in *J.H.S.,* Vol. XXIV (1904), pp. 82 ff., Fig. 1 and Pl. II. W. Amelung in *Atti Pont. Accad. Rom.,* Series III, Memorie I, Part 2 (1924), p. 122, Fig. 6, Pl. XXXIV, Fig. 2.

Florence is made of bronze, the material of the original. It has a high forehead and solemn appearance, in agreement with the description of Aristophanes. The grandiose and simple arrangement of the mantle, the broad chest of the statue, and the rich hair and beard of the mask of Heracles render the later period's ideal conception of the perfecter of the tragedy, rather than his real appearance.

In contrast, there is a possibility of a genuine tradition for the Lycurgean Sophocles, best transmitted by the well-known statue in the Lateran.[3] It is authenticated by a bust in the Vatican, bearing the inscription [. . .]ΦΟΚΛΗΣ[4] (Fig. 181), which it once resembled even more than it does now. This is proved by the cast of the head taken before the statue was restored by Tenerani[5] (Fig. 183). It has serious features, a thick growth of hair combed over the forehead, and a carefully arranged beard. All this contributes to the distinguished appearance of Sophocles in this portrait, which was actually made about a hundred years after the point in his life at which he is represented. The beautiful drapery and the balanced pose depict the ideal poet of the Periclean age, the man equally well educated in body and in mind, handsome and good (καλὸς καὶ ἀγαθός), the favorite of his own time and of the following period. This conception of Sophocles

in the Lateran statue is repeated in a silver statuette in the museum at Ancona[6] and in many heads and herms.[7] The original material is used in the head in Florence (Fig. 180) found along with that of Aeschylus (Fig. 179).

While Sophocles in the Lateran type is represented as being in his best years, at perhaps fifty years of age, the author of the *Antigone,* a bronze head formerly in the Arundel collection and now in the British Museum depicts the old Sophocles, perhaps eighty years of age, the author of *Oedipus at Colonus*[8] (Fig. 182). Here the skin is dry and wrinkled and has shrunk around the deep-set eyes, which were originally inserted. The mouth seems toothless and is slightly opened. Hair and beard hang in long, thin strands, which have been carefully combed. This type was the model for a small statuette in the Bibliothèque nationale in Paris[9] (Fig. 184). Sophocles is reading from a scroll, with his back bent and his hair carefully arranged. This is how Sophocles must have looked when he appeared before the judges and refuted the accusation

---

Another replica is in Copenhagen: F. Poulsen, *Catalogue of Ancient Sculpture in the Ny Carlsberg Glyptotek* (Copenhagen, 1951), p. 297, No. 421, and F. Poulsen, *Iconographic Studies from the Ny Carlsberg Glyptotek,* Vol. I (1931), pp. 65 ff., Figs. 49–50. A. Hekler, *Bildnisse berühmter Griechen* (1940), pp. 26 f., Fig. 17.

[3] P. Arndt, *Griechische und römische Porträts* (Munich, Bruckmann, 1891–1942), Pls. 113–15. H. Brunn and F. Bruckmann, *Denkmäler griechischer und römischer Skulptur* (Munich, 1888—), Pl. 427. Bieber, *Greek and Roman Theater,* Figs. 55–56. Poulsen, *Iconographic Studies,* Vol. I, p. 67, Fig. 51. R. Delbrück, *Antike Porträts* (1912), Pl. 16b. A. Hekler, *Bildniskunst der Griechen und Römer* (1912), Pls. 52 and 54. Hekler, *Bildnisse,* Fig. 12. R. Paribeni, *Il ritratto nell' arte antica* (1934), Pl. XXVI. K. Schefold, *Die Bildnisse der antiken Dichter, Redner, und Denker* (1943), pp. 90–93, 207 f. Restored are the nose, parts of the eyebrows, part of the right cheek, right hand, both feet, the book box, and the base. The restorations were made by Tenerani.

[4] Lippold, *Vatican Kat.,* Vol. III, pp. 10 f., Sala delle Muse, No. 492, Pl. 19. Lower part of the nose has been restored. A drawing of the inscription is in W. Amelung, *Atti Pont. Accad. Rom.,* Series III, Memorie I, Part 2 (1924), p. 120, Fig. 3.

[5] Cast in the Villa Medici. See W. Amelung in *Atti Pont. Accad. Rom.,* Series III, Memorie I, Part 2 (1924), Pl. XXXV. Schefold, *Bildnisse,* pp. 90 f.

[6] G. Moretti, *Guida illustrato del Museo di Ancona* (1915), pp. 365, 387, Pl. 7. W. Amelung in *Atti Pont. Accad. Rom.,* Series III, Memorie I, Part 2 (1924), p. 122, Fig. 4. P. Marconi and L. Serra, *Il Museo Nazionale in Ancona* (1934), p. 39, Fig. 1.

[7] See J. J. Bernoulli, *Griechische Ikonographie* (1901), pp. 137 f. The list of replicas there, however, includes many copies of the so-called Farnese type. The most important replicas are the bronze head (Fig. 180) found in the sea near Livorno along with the head of Aeschylus (Fig. 179), both now in the Museo Archeologico at Florence (Katherine McDowell in *J.H.S.,* XXXIV [1904], pp. 81 f.; W. Amelung in *Atti Pont. Accad. Rom.,* Series III, Memorie I, Part 2 [1924], p. 123, Pl. XXXIV, Fig. 1; W. Amelung, *Führer durch die Antiken in Florenz* [Munich, 1897], p. 277, No. 274). For a marble head in Florence, Inscription Room, No. 287, see H. Dütschke, *Antike Bildwerke in Oberitalien,* III (1882), 363. F. Studniczka in *J.H.S.,* Vol. XLIII (1923), pp. 57 f., Fig. 2. Two herms in the Museo Capitolino: Jones, *Sculpt. Museo Capitolino,* pp. 232 f., Stanza dei Filosofi, Nos. 33–34, Pl. 58. F. Studniczka in *J.H.S.,* XLIII (1923), p. 61, Fig. 5. Herm in the garden of the Villa Colonna in Rome, originally in one piece with the herm of Aeschylus: W. Amelung in *Atti Pont. Accad. Rom.,* Series III, Memorie I, Part 2 (1924), p. 123, Figs. 5–6.

[8] H. B. Walters, *Catalogue of the Bronzes, Greek, Roman, and Etruscan, in the Department of Greek and Roman Antiquities* (London, the British Museum, 1899), p. 847; H. B. Walters, *Select Bronzes, Greek, Roman and Etruscan* (London, the British Museum, 1915), p. 64. Bernoulli, *Ikonographie,* p. 134, Pl. XV. Arndt, *Porträts,* Pls. 989–90. Poulsen, *Iconographic Studies,* Vol. I, p. 90, Fig. 70. F. Poulsen, "Collection Ustinow," in *Videnskaps Selskapets Skrifter,* Vol. II, Hist.-filos. Kl., No. 3, pp. 20 f., Fig. 22.

[9] Poulsen, *Iconographic Studies,* Vol. I, Fig. 71.

of incompetence raised by his family, by reading his last masterpiece, the *Oedipus at Colonus*. This is a Hellenistic conception, deepening the rather superficial conception of the Lycurgean statue with the advanced means of psychological analysis and emotional expression in the face and position.

The Lycurgean statue of Euripides, the third and last of the three great tragedians of Athens, is known only through the drawing of a figure without a head, which was formerly in the Orsini collection and is now lost [10] (Fig. 187). It was authenticated by the inscription ΕΤΡΕΙΠΙΔΗΣ. It seems to have been similar in style to the statue of Aeschylus. The mantle is draped in a similar grandiose manner. A head of Euripides, of the type associated with Lycurgus, on a herm found in Rieti (now in the Ny Carlsberg Glyptotek) is authenticated by lines from the *Alexandros* of Euripides [11] (Fig. 185). It is related in style to the heads of Aeschylus and Sophocles put up by Lycurgus (Figs. 179–80). The best among five replicas is a head found in Rome, now in the British Museum [12] (Fig. 186). It depicts the gloomy and embittered enemy of gaiety, who hated women and did not know how to smile—an impression due mostly to the writers of comedy. They considered Euripides, with his revolt against certain customs, with his discussion of educational, philosophical, social, and moral problems, his deep understanding of the good and the bad sides of women, and his ab-

horrence of the madness and horror of war, as a good target for their jokes. Aristophanes, in particular, attacked and ridiculed him as being too romantic, too realistic, too austere, and too immoral, as an unbeliever, and as an unintelligible author. Aristotle (*Poetics* p. 1453a) has called him the most tragic of poets and his plays the most tragic of all the tragedies. This is also the conception of the portrait. The influence and high estimate of Euripides were steadily growing after his death. His rationalistic attitude towards the gods, the human interpretation of the heroic characters, and his great creative power appealed to the fourth century. His high intelligence is shown in the high forehead with the finely modeled temples. His deeply shadowed eyes reflect his serious thinking. The thin lips seem to express the disgust for the lack of understanding displayed by his contemporaries which drove him to the court of King Archelaos of Macedon in 408, where he died in 406. He certainly hated to go into exile, for he loved his homeland, as is shown in the beautiful songs praising Athens, in the *Heracleidae* and in the *Phoenissae*. The full beard which broadens the lower part of the face is mentioned in the account of his life (Suidas *Vita Euripides*). Thus, of the three Lycurgean statues this is perhaps the most adequate likeness, because Euripides was nearer to the spirit of the late fourth century than were the two other tragic poets.

Similar in style to the portrait of Euripides is the one of Aristotle, the organizer of a great encyclopedic body of knowledge. He was a member of the Academy of Plato for twenty years. In 342, Philip of Macedon called him to Pella to educate the crown prince, Alexander. When Alexander became king in 336, Aristotle returned to Athens and founded his school in the Lyceum (*Lykeion*), near a grove dedicated to Apollo Lykeios; the covered walk (*peripatos*) of the garden has given the name Peripatetic to this school. Aristotle shifted the emphasis from the high philosophy, the doctrine of ideas, and the mathematics of Plato to the detailed facts of history and biology. Rhetoric, dialectics, ethics, poetics, literature, inscriptions, physics, metaphysics, psychology, logic, history, politics, animals, plants, and minerals were the fields in which teaching and research were undertaken. Aristotle thus tried to explore the whole universe.

[10] F. Ursinus, *Imagines* (1570), p. 27. F. Studniczka in *J.H.S.*, XLIII (1923), p. 64, Fig. 8.

[11] D. Comparetti in *Rendiconti dell'Accademia dei Lincei*, Fifth Series, Vol. VI (1897), pp. 205 ff. F. Poulsen, *Iconographic Studies*, Vol. I, Fig. 55; F. Poulsen, *Catalogue of Ancient Sculpture in the Ny Carlsberg Glyptotek* (Copenhagen, 1951), pp. 287 f., No. 414 b. Hekler, *Bildniskunst*, Pl. 89. Hekler, *Bildnisse*, Fig. 16. P. Arndt and W. Amelung, *Photographische Einzelaufnahmen antiker Skulpturen* (1893–), Nos. 1982–83.

[12] A. H. Smith, *A Catalogue of Sculpture in the Department of Greek and Roman Antiquities of the British Museum* (3 vols., 1892–1904), Vol. III, No. 1833. R. P. Hinks, *Greek and Roman Portrait Sculpture in the British Museum* (1935), p. 8, Pl. 4b, Mus. No. 1833. F. Studniczka in *J.H.S.*, XLIII (1923), p. 63, Fig. 7. Poulsen, *Iconographic Studies*, Vol. I, Fig. 56. E. Pfuhl, *Die Anfänge der griechischen Bildniskunst* (1927), Pl. III, Fig. 3. Schefold, *Bildnisse*, pp. 88 f., No. 3, and p. 207. Other good replicas: in Dresden, P. Herrmann, *Verzeichnis der antike Originalbildwerke* (1915), p. 54, No. 197, with plate. Poulsen, *Iconographic Studies*, Vol. I (1931), Fig. 57. Replicas in Rome: see V. Müller in *Arch. Anz.*, Vol. XXXVIII (1922), p. 131, Figs. 1–2. R. Paribeni, *Notizie degli Scavi*, (1921), pp. 56 f., Figs. 1–2.

His work laid the foundation for Hellenistic scholarship.

In appearance Aristotle is described as small, with thin legs and a large belly. He was well dressed and wore a short trimmed beard. His head was partly bald and his eyes were small. His mouth had an ironic expression, and he spoke with a lisp (Pseudo-Ammonius Alexandrinus *Aristoteles vita;* Diogenes Laertius *Lives of Eminent Philosophers* v. 1. 1 *et seq.;* Aelianus *Varia historia* III. 19). During his lifetime his pupil Alexander the Great set up a portrait of him in Athens, the inscription of which has been preserved on a herm.[13] It is dedicated to the divine Aristotle, possessor of all knowledge and all wisdom. Another portrait is said to have been put up by Alexander along with portraits of his own family at Delphi (Pseudo-Ammonius Alexandrinus *Aristoteles vita* 56; Aelianus *Varia historia* XIV. 1). A statue was also erected in Olympia, perhaps by Alexander or another pupil (Pausanias VI. 4. 8). In the testament of Aristotle (Diogenes Laertius *Lives of Eminent Philosophers* v. 1. 15) he ordered the finishing of some family portraits, among which may have been his own. The successor of Aristotle, Theophrastos, ordered portraits of his teacher and himself to be set up in the Lyceum (Diogenes Laertius *Lives of Eminent Philosophers* v. 2. 51). Cicero (*Ad Atticum* IV. 10) mentions a portrait of Aristotle standing in a niche of the house of Atticus at Rome. Under this portrait was a seat on which Cicero liked to sit. Juvenal (*Satire* II, line 6) testifies to the frequent purchase by the Romans of portraits of Aristotle, which certainly were not lacking in any of the larger libraries. A bronze statue in Constantinople is described in the attitude of Demosthenes with folded hands (Christodorus *Ecphrasis,* in *Anthologia Palatina* II. 16 *et seq.*).

Unfortunately we do not know the statue of Aristotle, except for the head, of which we have about fifteen replicas.[14] Franz Studniczka recognized that these were authenticated by drawings from a bust which was found in 1592 and which once belonged to Fulvio Orsini. One of the drawings is in the Codex Capponianus of the Vatican Library and the other is by Rubens [15] (Figs. 188–89). Both have at the base the inscription ΑΡΙΣΤΟΤΕΛΗΣ. They show a man of fifty to sixty years of age, with a short beard, a rounded skull, thin hair hanging over the forehead, a high brow, small eyes, a very individual, slightly aquiline long nose, and a broad mouth with thin and tightly closed lips.

All these features recur in the best sculptured head in Vienna [16] (Figs. 190–91), and in a bronze head from Herculaneum, in Naples [17] (Figs. 192–93). The rounded vault of the skull is impressive. The prominent forehead of the great thinker appears to arch forward under the thin strands of almost straight hair. The wrinkles and the hollow cheeks give testimony to hard spiritual work. The mouth seems to betray a mocking disposition, an ironical, ready wit, and some sensual inclination. The eyes have a critical look. Compared to the portrait of Euripides, the head shows an increase in the rational spirit. It is astonishing how much this universal Greek genius resembles the great German educator Melanchthon, as painted by Dürer.[18] Melanchthon had a nature sympathetic to Aristotle's ideals, and he defended Aristotle against the attacks of Luther. It is the spirit which shapes the form, and for Aristotle spirit was equal to soul: νοῦς καὶ Ἀριστοτέλους ψυχή (*Anthologia Palatina* 330).

[13] *Insc. Graec.,* 136. Bernoulli, *Griechische Ikonographie,* II, 85 f.

[14] F. Studniczka, *Das Bildnis des Aristoteles* (1908). Bernoulli, *Ikonographie,* II, 94 ff. Hekler, *Bildnisse,* pp. 27, 42. A reconstruction of the lost statue has been attempted with the help of the seated statue in the Palazzo Spada, which has an incomplete inscription; see G. Gullini, *Archeologia Classica, Rivista dell'Istituto d'Archeologia dell'Università di Roma,* Vol. I (1949), pp. 130 ff., Pls. XXXV–XXXVIII.

[15] Studniczka, *Bildnis des Aristoteles,* pp. 15 ff., Pl. II, Figs. 2 and 5. Delbrück, *Porträts,* p. XXXIV, No. 19, Fig. 9.

[16] R. von Schneider, *Album auserlesener Gegenstände der Antikensammlung des Kaiserhauses zu Wien* (1895), p. 6, Pl. 12. Studniczka, *Bildnis des Aristoteles,* p. 25, Pl. II, Fig. 3 and Pl. III, Fig. 1. Bernoulli, *Ikonographie,* Pl. XII. W. D. Ross, *Aristotle* (1923), frontispiece. Delbrück, *Porträts,* Pl. 19. Hekler, *Bildniskunst,* Pl. 87. Poulsen, *Ikonographic Studies,* Vol. I, p. 48, Fig. 39. E. Loewy in *Oest. Jahreshefte,* Vol. XXVI (1930), p. 131, Fig. 67. Schefold, *Bildnisse,* pp. 96 f., 98 f., No. 2. The back is cut away, indicating that this was probably originally a double herm. The nose, which must have been larger, judging from the other replicas, has been restored.

[17] D. Comparetti and G. de Petra, *La Villa Ercolanese dei Pisoni* (1883), p. 262, No. 10, Pl. IX, Fig. 1. Arndt, *Porträts,* Pls. 157–58. Hekler, *Bildniskunst,* Pl. 94. R. Paribeni, *Il ritratto nell'arte antica* (1934), Pl. LXVII, Fig. 2. Schefold, *Bildnisse,* pp. 104 f. Schefold labels the head "Solon (?)" and dates it about 300 B.C. The nose is ancient.

[18] V. Scherer, *Dürer,* in *Klassiker der Kunst,* Vol. IV (3d ed. translated as *The Work of Dürer,* 1907), Pl. 161.

As Aristotle is shown as a man between fifty and sixty years of age, the portrait must have been created about 335—325 B.C., and it may well be based on the portrait erected by Alexander the Great. We do not know the artist. It certainly was not Lysippos, whose sober manner of interpretation would not produce such a rational picture of such a rational spirit. It may be by the same artist who conceived the Lycurgean Euripides.

The statue of Aeschines, the champion of Macedon, in Naples [19] (Fig. 197), is related in style, though not in mood, to the statue of Sophocles, the tragic poet in whose *Antigone* Aeschines played the Creon, and in whose *Oinomaos* he fell in a ridiculous manner. This brought his theatrical career to an end, but his dramatic experience had provided him with good training for his magnificent voice and with expressive gesticulation for his later career as an orator. Two herms, one in the Vatican [20] (Figs. 194–95) and one in the British Museum [21] (Fig. 196), both inscribed ΑΙΣΧΙΝΗΣ, serve to identify the statue. The head is robust and handsome. The hair is laid carefully forward to cover the bald upper part of the high forehead. The beard is trimmed. The draping is similar in principle to that of the himation of Sophocles, but different in effect. The hand seems to be bandaged in the folds and unable to move, in keeping with the usage, praised by Aeschines, of the more dignified older orators, who held the hand inside the mantle instead of indulging in free gesticulation. (Aeschines *Against Timarchus* 25). The pose of Aeschines is theatrical. His right leg pulls the folds taut to the side, expressing tension. His features and his posture express the self-satisfaction of the successful partisan of Philip of Macedon. The figure had more movement but less harmony than the statue of Sophocles.

As the orator is portrayed at about fifty years of age, and as he lived from 390/89 to 314 B.C., the period of the statue seems to be that of his greatest influence and highest success, 340—330 B.C.; it is thus contemporaneous with the statues of the tragic poets. Another possible date would be 322–314, when he was about seventy years of age and had founded a school of oratory at Rhodes. But the head shows no sign of such old age.

The period 340–330 was a time of great activity in portraiture. Leochares, one of the collaborators of Skopas on the Mausoleum, made the bronze portrait of the orator Isocrates, who died in 338. After 338, the date of the battle of Chaeronea, which was won by Philip with the help of the young crown prince Alexander, Leochares was commissioned to set up the statues of Philip, his wife Olympias, his parents, and his son Alexander in gold and ivory for a round building, the Philippeion, in Olympia. At the same time he may have made the statue of the young general Alexander which is copied in the Alexander Rondanini in Munich.[22]

The most celebrated work of Leochares was the group of Ganymede with the eagle of Zeus. Zeus had sent the eagle to bring the beautiful Trojan boy to Olympus, to become his cup bearer. Pliny (*Nat. hist.* XXXIV. 79) tells us that the eagle seemed to feel what treasure he was stealing and to whom he was carrying it. He therefore used his talons gently, though the garment also protects the boy. A statuette in the Vatican answers to this description [23] (Fig. 198). The eagle, with widespread wings, lifts the boy by the shoulders, around which the cloak is wound, so that the claws do not touch the skin. The body of Ganymede is stretched and his head is lifted, as is that of the eagle. The dog sitting on the ground lifts his head also and watches

[19] Museo Nazionale, Naples, No. 6018. A. Ruesch, *Guida del Museo di Napoli* (n.d.), No. 1139. Comparetti and de Petra, *La Villa Ercolanese*, Pl. XVIII, No. 2. Brunn-Bruckmann, *Denkmäler*, Pl. 428. Arndt, *Porträts*, Pls. 116–18. G. Lippold, *Griechische Porträtstatuen* (1912), pp. 95 ff. Bernoulli, *Ikonographie*, pp. 62 ff., No. 4, Pl. X. Paribeni, *Ritratto*, Pl. XXIV. Hekler, *Bildniskunst*, Pl. 53. Hekler, *Bildnisse*, p. 47. Schefold, *Bildnisse*, pp. 102 f.

[20] In the Sala delle Muse, No. 502. Lippold, *Vatican Kat.*, Vol. III, pp. 26 f., Pl. 22. Bernoulli, *Ikonographie*, Vol. II, pp. 60 ff., Pl. 9. Arndt, *Porträts*, Pls. 641–42. Hekler, *Bildniskunst*, Pl. 55a. E. G. Suhr, *Sculptured Portraits of Greek Statesmen* (1931), p. 36. Restored are the left part of the forehead and the front of the nose.

[21] British Museum, No. 1839. A. Michaelis, *Ancient Marbles in Great Britain* (1882), Vol. XI, Pl. 18. Hinks, *Greek and Roman Portrait Sculpture*, p. 18, Pl. 5.

[22] A. Furtwängler and P. Wolters, *Beschreibung der Glyptothek zu München* (2d ed., 1910), pp. 323 ff., No. 298. Brunn-Bruckmann, *Denkmäler*, Pl. 105; Arndt, *Porträts*, Pls. 183–85. M. Bieber in *Proceedings of the American Philosophical Society*, Vol. XCIII, No. 5 (1949), p. 380, Figs. 9–11. See above, Chap. III, p. 49, note 89.

[23] Vatican, Galleria dei Candelabri, No. 118. Brunn-Bruckmann, *Denkmäler*, Pl. 158. F. Winter in *Jahrbuch d. Inst.*, Vol. XXXII (1917), pp. 226 ff., Figs. 1–2.

the ascent. Thus everything carries the eye upward, whither destiny is taking the astonished boy. The boy's feet are in the air; and this motif of hovering makes the group interesting, in spite of poor execution.

The outlines of the composition, particularly the movement of the legs of Ganymede, reappear in the Apollo Belvedere, and, therefore, this statue too has been associated with Leochares [24] (Figs. 199–200). This Apollo in the Belvedere of the Vatican has been praised in exaggerated terms by Winckelmann, and blamed with the same exaggeration in modern times. The execution by the Roman copyist, who has added the tree trunk, is inadequate. The composition, however, is beautiful, as Winckelmann and other writers of the eighteenth century have deeply felt. The god appears suddenly, walking before the spectator from right to left and extending the left arm, which probably held the bow, as can be concluded from the quiver on his back. In his right hand he held the laurel branch, fragments of which remain on the tree trunk of the copy. It represents the means of purification of repentant sinners, while the bow threatens to punish the evildoers. The head, despite the cheeks being too smooth and the hairbow being too luxurious in the copy, is beautiful, with its finely shaped large eyes, haughty mouth, and noble profile. Particularly when seen from the side to which it turns, the expression of proud aloofness, eternal purity, and disdain of all base and vile sinners is wonderfully rendered (Fig. 199). The movement suggests a sudden epiphany of the god. A head in Basel, Switzerland, is much damaged, but is a better replica than the Vatican one.[25]

The Artemis of Versailles, now in the Louvre, seems to have been conceived as a counterpart of the Apollo of Belvedere [26] (Fig. 201). She moves from left to right in the opposite direction from her brother—but the position of the limbs is the same. The youthful goddess is represented hunting, accompanied by her dog (the stag is a modern substitution). She has shortened her dress by means of two belts, pulling up the material in a long pouch. Her mantle is wound like a shawl around her waist. She moves quickly along, the fluttering dress emphasizing the movement, while she is taking an arrow out of the quiver on her shoulder. The bow was probably in her left hand. She turns her head back to the spectator as does Apollo, and, like the brother, she will be gone in the next moment.

Other works have been attributed to Leochares; an example is the stele of Aristonautes (see Chap. II, Note 138). But although the leading artists certainly influenced the artisans who carved these tomb monuments, it is not possible to assign them to definite masters. The general tendencies of the later fourth century, greater refinement and more intense expression of feeling, appear in many monuments which do not, however, show the definite style of a known artist.

The hound or lioness on a late fourth century tomb terrace in the cemetery outside the Dipylon gate in Athens [27] (Fig. 202), like the lion of Chaeronea erected after 338,[28] is a powerful beast with a passionate expression in his lifted face, which recalls the boar from Tegea. Some forms seem to be those of a lion, but the neck is stretched more like that of a dog, and most forms are more like a dog than a lion, which this artist surely had never seen. Dogs and lions were used not only for decoration but as symbols of protection of the tomb. This figure was probably set up at the corner of a terrace, with a companion piece at the other corner. Thus the mighty creature has taken the place of the *lekythoi* which were the usual ornaments at the ends of the family plots (see Figs. 1–2).

The loutrophoros, a vase used to carry water for

[24] Vatican, Cortile del Belvedere, No. 92. Amelung, *Vatican Kat.*, Vol. II, pp. 256 ff., Pl. 12. Brunn-Bruckmann, *Denkmäler*, Pl. 419. F. Winter in *Jahrbuch d. Inst.*, Vol. VII (1892), pp. 164 ff. K. A. Neugebauer, in *Arch. Anz.* (1946–47), pp. 1 ff., supports the attribution to Leochares by Winter.

[25] R. Kekule von Stradonitz in *Arch. Zeitung*, Vol. XXXVI (1878), pp. 8 f., Pl. II. W. Amelung in *Ausonia*, Vol. III (1908), pp. 128 f., Pl. IV, Fig. 2.

[26] W. Fröhner, *Notice de la sculpture antique du Louvre* (4th ed., Paris, 1878), pp. 122 ff., No. 98. Picard, *Manuel d'archéologie grecque. La Sculpture antique*, III (1948), 100. *Encycl. phot.*, Vol. III, Pls. 198–99. Brunn-Bruckmann, *Denkmäler*, Pl. 420. For detail of the fluttering dress, see J. Charbonneaux, *La Sculpture grecque au Musée du Louvre* (1936), Pl. XXXVII.

[27] A. Brückner, *Der Friedhof am Eridanos* (1909), pp. 74 ff., Fig. 45 (cf. Figs. 47–49). M. Collignon, *Histoire de la sculpture grecque* (2 vols., 1892, 1897), Vol. I, pp. 383 ff., Fig. 202; Collignon believed the animal to be a lion. Cf. A. Conze, *Die Attischen Grabreliefs* (4 vols., Berlin, 1893–1922), Vol. III, No. 1157, Pl. 258. B. Schröder's text to Brunn-Bruckmann, *Denkmäler*, Pls. 641–45, is an excellent discussion of the representations of lions in Greek art.

[28] B. Schröder in text to Brunn-Bruckmann, *Denkmäler*, Pls. 641–45, p. 15, Fig. 18.

the bridal bath, was an individual tomb monument used for women who died unmarried and thus had not had a bridal bath. It was usually richly decorated with fluting, plaited bands, scrolls, palmettes, and elaborate handles ending in spirals and sometimes enriched by acanthus leaves and fillets [29] (Fig. 203). The refinement of decoration is reminiscent of the subtleties introduced into sculpture by Praxiteles. The fact that these vases lack figurative representations seems to indicate that they may belong to the period after 317–307, when a law of Demetrius of Phalerum forbade the erection of luxurious sculptured tomb monuments, with their large family groups inside a deep shrine.

A good example of the last period before 317 is the stele of Demetria and Pamphile, two rich Athenian women.[30] It must be one of the last grave monuments erected before 317, because of its position in the cemetery. The figures do not face each other in the manner customary until the middle of the fourth century, but face the spectator. The height of the relief has increased so that parts of the figures are actually in the round, and strong shadows create a pictorial rather than a sculptural effect. The feeling for depth is like that of the compositions of Lysippos.

For the same reason I believe that the two tomb statues of slave women found in Menidi (Acharnai), belonging to the Museum in Berlin [31] (Figs. 204–5), were also created in the second half of the fourth century as corner decorations for a family plot. They make good use of the third dimension of depth by leaning forward and advancing the crossed feet toward the spectator. Their attitude expresses deep mourning and intense devotion to the deceased members of the family.

Such expression of mourning in the face is also not found in tombstones before the later period. A good example is a fragment in Athens [32] (Fig. 207), with a woman indicating mourning not only by the hair, which is cut short and lies in ringlets around her forehead, but in the expression of grief in eyes and mouth. She looks as if she is beginning to cry. The same is true in another fragment in the storerooms of the National Museum at Athens [33] (Fig. 206), where an older woman bends sorrowfully over the head of a little girl. With her left hand she lifts to her face her mantle, which covers her short curly hair, as if to stifle a cry or to dry her tears. The little girl, named Theophile ("the friend of gods"), is standing facing the front, holding the vertical edges of her mantle with both hands. She wears a peplos with long overfold, girt with a belt laid directly below her breasts, which are small but emphasized by crossing bands. The dress has many details and movements of the surface, which together with the frontal position date the relief in the period shortly before 317, when the decree of Demetrius killed a flourishing branch of art. We also see a similar frontal attitude and accidental creases and folds in the texture of the dresses in a tomb monument in the Metropolitan Museum [34] (Figs. 208–9).

This late date is confirmed by the close relationship between these reliefs and the figure of Athena Soteira which appears on a relief dated 323/2 and in a monumental statue. The relief is an honorary decree [35] dated by the archontate of Kephisodoros

---

[29] For *loutrophoroi*, see P. Wolters in *Athen. Mitt.*, XVI (1891), 371 ff. A loutrophoros similar to the one in Fig. 203 is shown in a relief in Conze, *Grabreliefs*, Vol. III, p. 293, No. 1350, Pl. 283; others are on pp. 363 ff. For the usage on tombs of those who died unwed, see Demosthenes's speech *Against Leochares* (No. 44). That this form persisted after the luxury decree of Demetrius is shown by the amphora in relief with ribbons and acanthus, similar to Fig. 203, dated after 317 (Conze, *Grabreliefs*, Vol. IV, p. 16, Pl. 379).

[30] Conze, *Grabreliefs*, Vol. I, No. 109, Pl. 40. H. Diepolder, *Die Attischen Grabreliefs* (1931), pp. 53 f., Pl. 51, Fig. 1. Brückner, *Der Friedhof am Eridanos*, pp. 95 ff., Fig. 62.

[31] G. Blümel, *Staatliche Museen zu Berlin, Katalog der Sammlung Antiker Skulpturen*, Vol. III (1929), pp. 13 f., No. K13, a–b, Pls. 18–21. Brunn-Bruckmann, *Denkmäler*, Pl. 534.

[32] For a similar emotional expression in a woman's face see the tomb relief from Rhamnus in Conze, *Grabreliefs*, Vol. III, p. 265, No. 1184, Pl. 261.

[33] Conze, *Grabreliefs*, Vol. II, No. 875, pp. 186 f., Pl. 169. Diepolder, *Grabreliefs*, p. 53, Pl. 52, Fig. 1. A girl seen in a similar front view and in a similar woolen dress appears on a tomb relief in Berlin: Blümel, *Berlin Katalog*, Vol. III, pp. 38 f., K40, Pl. 49.

[34] G. Richter in *M.M.A. Bulletin*, Vol. II, No. 8 (1944), pp. 48 ff. G. Richter in *A.J.A.*, XLVIII (1944), pp. 229 ff., Figs. 1–9. G. Richter in *Bulletin van de Vereniging tot bevordering der Kennis van de antieke Beschaving te 'S-Gravenhage*, Vol. XXVI (1951), pp. 42 ff., Figs. 2–4, and *Handbook* (1953), pp. 141 f., Pl. 120, a–b.

[35] Brunn-Bruckmann, *Denkmäler*, Pl. 533a. J. N. Svoronos, *Das Athener Nationalmuseum*, Vol. II (1911), Pl. 108, No. 1482. L. Curtius, *Die antike Kunst*, Vol. II (1938), pp. 339 f., 416, Fig. 494. F. Studniczka, "Artemis und Iphigenie," in *Abh. Sächs. Akad.*, Vol. XXXVIII, No. 5 (1926), p. 92, Fig. 74. L. Mariani in *Bollettino Comunale*, Vol. XXXV (1907), pp. 20 ff., Fig. 5. H. K. Süsserott, *Griechische Plastik des 4. Jahrhunderts vor Christus* (1938), pp. 67 f., Pl. 9, Fig. 4. He dates the relief 318/7 B.C.

in the year in which Alexander the Great died. It shows Athena in a quiet position, and a bearded man, perhaps Zeus Soter, who was worshipped together with Athena Soteira in the Piraeus. He may, however, be only a hero, as he is smaller than Athena. The worshipper is still smaller, and the slave, shown in an active movement trying to prevent the horse of the worshipper from intruding into the sacred scene, is quite small. The stable boy, like Athena, is seen from the front, the others from different points of view. Thus, even such a modest work of handicraft illustrates the mastery over space which was owed to Lysippos. The Athena is certainly a cult statue. Pliny (*Nat. hist.* xxxiv. 74) names the sculptor Kephisodoros as the maker of the Athena Soteira and an altar in the Piraeus; I would like to believe that this otherwise unknown Kephisodoros has been mistakenly called the sculptor rather than the archon, who may have dedicated the statue. It is certainly the same which we also possess in an excellent copy.

The copy [36] (Figs. 210–12) has been found in Rome near the site of the Castra Praetoria, the big military camp, and it is now in the Museo Nuovo (formerly Museo Mussolini) in Rome. The arms with the weapons—probably the lance in the right hand and the shield on the left arm—were worked separately and attached with dowels, for which the holes are preserved. She has the stance of the Athena Parthenos of Phidias, and her peplos is similarly arranged; but the style is fundamentally different. The heavy woolen cloth is rendered with many accidental details which characterize a rough surface, in a manner that did not appear until the third quarter of the fourth century in the Ephesus column drum (see Figs. 66–67). The aegis is a small collar laid double, originally decorated with bronze snakes at the edges. The Gorgon's head is small and tame in appearance. A thick, shawl-like mantle is laid in massed folds on Athena's left shoulder, and goes with deep folds down the back

to the right hip, from which it is lifted with a sharp turn to the right arm (Fig. 211). The head is slightly raised and Athena looks with an expression of interest into the distance (Fig. 212). The face is full and healthy. The hair falls in parallel waves in the back. The execution of the whole is effective but not refined.

The same may be said of the colossal statue of Themis, the goddess of Justice, found in Rhamnus and now in Athens [37] (Fig. 516). The interest of the artist here also was in the surface of the material of the dress, a crinkly crepelike thin wool with many narrow folds. The roll into which the upper part of the mantle is laid from her right hip to her left arm is similar to the shawl in the back of the Athena (Fig. 211). The sharp angle between the descending and ascending parts of this shawl is similar to the sharp angle with which part of the roll is drawn up to the armpit of Themis. This manneristic detail is matched by the puffed-up and rosette-shaped motif in the center of the roll. This shows that the Attic art forms of the fourth century had begun to be conventionalized, but were mixed with new elements to adapt them to more recent Hellenistic forms. The date of the Themis is given by the inscription, which names the dedicator as Megakles and the artist as Chairestratos, both otherwise unknown. The form of the letters, however, dates the statue at about 300 B.C. That Chairestratos followed models of the fourth century is also shown in the head, which has relation to such heads as those of the Attic sirens, to some Scopadic heads, and to the head of the woman in the tomb monument in the Metropolitan Museum [38] (Fig. 209).

Related to the Themis, and therefore also to be dated in the beginning of the third century, is the statue of a young man from Eleusis, now in Athens.[39] As he is wearing high boots of the Dio-

---

[36] L. Mariani in *Bollettino Comunale*, Vol. XXXV (1907), pp. 3 ff., Figs. 1–2, Pls. I–IV. L. Savignoni in *Ausonia*, Vol. II (1907), pp. 35 f., Fig. 14. W. Helbig, *Führer durch die offentlichen Sammlungen Klassischer Altertümer in Rom* (3d ed., 2 vols., Leipzig, 1912–13), p. 602, No. 1069. R. Horn, *Stehende weibliche Gewandstatuen in der hellenistischen Plastik* (1931; *Ergänzungsheft II to Röm. Mitt.*), pp. 8 ff., Pl. II, 2. D. Mustilli, *Il Museo Mussolini* (Rome, 1939), pp. 93 ff., Pls. LIV–LV, Figs. 218–21, No. 17.

[37] Athens, National Museum, No. 231. V. Staïs, *Marbres et bronzes du Musée nationale* (Athens, 1910), No. 231, pp. 63 f. Brunn-Bruckmann, *Denkmäler*, Pl. 476. R. Horn, *Gewandstatuen*, pp. 19 f., Pl. VI, Fig. 3, and Excurs 1, p. 95. V. Staïs in *Ephemeris Arch.*, Vol. III (1891), pp. 45 ff., Pl. 4. G. Dickins, *Hellenistic Sculpture* (Oxford, The Clarendon Press, 1920), p. 54, Fig. 40. G. Becatti in *Riv. del Ist. Arch.*, Vol. VII (1940), pp. 18 ff., Fig. 4.

[38] See Note 34 above.

[39] Athens, National Museum, No. 255. Staïs, *Marbres et bronzes*, p. 87. The head: Arndt-Amelung, *Einzelaufnahmen*, No. 637–38.

nysiac and Eleusinian cults, the statue probably represents either Iacchus or the torch-bearing boy serving in the Eleusinian cult. The statue, in the latter case, would have held torches in both hands.

How the tradition of the classical period lived on into the third century is well shown by the statue of a seated Dionysos in the British Museum [40] (Fig. 213). It stood originally as an addition to the monument of a victorious *choregos,* Thrasyllos, a wealthy citizen who had supplied the funds for a chorus at the feast of Dionysos, and with this chorus had won the victory in 319. The monument was erected on the south slope of the Acropolis inside the upper part of the sacred precinct of Dionysos Eleutherios. The statue was added to the top of the monument in 271 by Thrasykles. Dionysos is seated in a quiet pose. The drapery is arranged in grandiose and simple lines, and the skin of the sacred panther is tightly attached to the waist by a broad belt. If the inscription had not furnished the exact date, we would place the figure around the middle of the fourth century, near the date of the Mausoleum sculptures, at the latest. It even recalls some of the Parthenon pediment figures.

Attic art began to look backward to the great past. We can understand, therefore, why Pliny (*Nat. hist.* xxxiv. 52) reports that art ceased in Olympiad CXXI, that is, 296—293 B.C. There seemed to be no progress in ideal sculpture during that time in Athens, which was and which remained the venerated seat of all art. But this statement is neither true of other places nor true of Athens, when we consider the achievements of portraiture in Athens.

The portraits of Menander and Epicurus and his successors are excellent examples of seated statues treated in the first half of the third century (see above, pp. 51 ff. and 56 f., and Figs. 163–66, 173–74, 176). The best example of a standing portrait statue is the Demosthenes erected by Polyeuktos in 280—279 B.C., more than forty years after the death of the great orator and statesman in 322 B.C. While the portraits of the poet and the philosophers are contemporaneous with their subjects, we have in the Demosthenes portrait a posthumous pyschological interpretation of a man whose features were probably known, but whose physical appearance was interpreted with the new realistic means of expression developed in the third century B.C.

The features of Demosthenes, the ardent but unsuccessful champion of liberty in the struggle against Philip and Alexander of Macedon, are authenticated by a small bronze bust from Herculaneum with the inscription ΔΗΜΟΣΘΕΝΗΣ [41] (Fig. 214). The portrait shows an oval-shaped head with thick and lightly curled hair, growing thin at the temples, so that the forehead appears broad and high. Three horizontal wrinkles broaden the forehead still more. The thick eyebrows are drawn and shade the small eyes, giving them an ardent and bitter look. The cheekbones stand out sharply from the deeply furrowed face. The nose is long and straight, with a hanging tip and slanting nostrils. The thin, straight lips are shaded by the thick mustache. The beard is short and slightly wavy.

All these features, with the addition of a deep hollow at the root of the nose, reappear in better execution in a silver medallion from Miletopolis, near Pergamon, in the Berlin Museum [42] (Fig. 216). This relief was probably the center of a Hellenistic bowl of the second century B.C. A good Roman copy at Oxford also has the nose preserved, showing three prominent curved wrinkles at the root between the eyes [43] (Fig. 215). The same detail at the root of the nose, of which only the tip is restored, is also found in a replica in Copenhagen [44] (Fig. 217), and in a replica in Athens, where the nose is broken. [45] A gem by Dioskurides

---

[40] A. H. Smith, *Brit. Mus. Cat.,* Vol. I, pp. 257 ff., No. 432. Brunn-Bruckmann, *Denkmäler,* Pl. 119. V. Müller in *The Art Bulletin,* Vol. XX (1938), p. 385, p. 390, Fig. 31. G. Becatti, "Attika. Saggio sulla scultura attica del ellenismo," in *Riv. del Ist. Arch.,* Vol. VII (1940), pp. 20 f., Fig. 5.

[41] Comparetti and de Petra, *La Villa Ercolanese,* Pl. XII, No. 4 (cf. another replica, No. 1). Bernoulli, *Ikonographie,* Vol. II, p. 70, No. 7, Pl. XII a. Hekler, *Bildniskunst,* p. XVII, Fig. 3.

[42] H. Winnefeld, *Hellenistische Silberreliefs* (*Winck.-Prog. Berlin,* No. 68 [1908], pp. 13 ff., Pl. II).

[43] S. Casson in *J.H.S.,* Vol. XLVI (1926), pp. 72 ff., Figs. 1–5, Pl. V. Pfuhl, *Anfänge der Bildniskunst,* pp. 14 ff., Pl. IX, Figs. 1–2. E. Strong, *Catalogue of Antiques of Lord Melchior* (1928), p. 27, Fig. 14.

[44] Bernoulli, *Ikonographie,* pp. 72 f., No. 29, Pl. XII b. F. Poulsen in *Rev. Arch.* (1917), Part II, pp. 328 ff., Figs. 1–2. Arndt, *Porträts,* Pls. 1118–19.

[45] S. Casson in *J.H.S.,* Vol. XLVI (1926), p. 73, Fig. 2. Arndt, *Porträts,* Pl. 1117, text to Figs. 1–2. For other replicas see A. Michaelis in A. Schäfer, *Demosthenes und seine Zeit* (2d ed., 1885–87), pp. 401 ff.; Bernoulli, *Ikonographie,* pp. 66 ff.; Arndt, *Porträts,* text to Pls. 1111–20.

represents the portrait in three quarter view.[46]

All these replicas resemble one another, in spite of their different workmanship. There can be no doubt that we have here the real likeness of the unhappy champion of liberty, his face deeply lined by unselfish care for his beloved and ungrateful Athens. The expression agrees with the description in the comparison of Demosthenes with Cicero in *Vitae decem oratorum,* included in Plutarch's *Moralia:* "Gloomy seriousness was in his features. The expression of sorrow and meditation was seldom absent from his brow. His enemies, therefore, called him a sullen and stubborn person." This description is probably derived from the statue to which this head belongs. The same realistic and detailed rendering of the nervous countenance and the gloomy mood reappears in the heads of two statues, one in the Braccio Nuovo of the Vatican [47] (Figs. 218, 222–23) and the other in Copenhagen, formerly in Knole [48] (Figs. 219–21), as well as in a statuette now in private possession in New York [49] (Figs. 226–29). This statuette is not of good workmanship, but is in a perfect state of preservation. It is authenticated by the gesture of the hands clasped together. This agrees with the description of Polyeuktos's statue of Demosthenes "with his fingers twined together" (Plutarch *Demosthenes*

31), that is, with folded hands. The hollow thus made was said to have been used by a soldier to hide his purse. A marble replica of the hands was also found in Rome by Paul Hartwig.[50] As a consequence, the hands with a scroll, which were formerly considered genuine in the statue from Knole in Copenhagen, have been removed from this replica as well as from that in the Vatican Museum. Casts have been made with the hands restored in the correct attitude (Figs. 224–25).

Only now can the deep psychological value of the creation of Polyeuktos be appreciated. In contrast to the figure of Aeschines (Fig. 197), who has both hands inside his mantle, the hands of Demosthenes are twisted together as if in great distress, and the thin arms are completely bare. They form, with the shoulders, a kind of hexagonal pattern before the thin body. The mantle is bunched together on the left shoulder and hangs in front like a towel. Steep and ugly folds mount from the right to the left side. A thick roll under the hanging breast emphasizes the leanness of the frail body. The feet have an awkward stance. We can imagine how Demosthenes suffered when Meidias, in the theater before a large audience, attacked his weak and sickly body. The head is the crowning feature of this pathetic portrait of a noble and magnificent spirit, whose great passion and love for liberty were embodied in this frail frame. The fire of the spirit and of suffering which burns in the haggard face comes out in full power only when seen in connection with the body. It is a superb character portrait of the early Hellenistic period, based on a deep understanding of the tragic nature of Demosthenes's mission. He failed in Athens, but he gave the world the highest conception of the duties and tasks of a free democracy. Morally and spiritually, though not actually, Demosthenes achieved his goal. On the base of the statue was the epigram:

> If thou hadst had the same power as conviction
> The Macedonian Ares would never have reigned
>   over the Greeks.

The creative power of Athens in the third century was unimpaired in the field of portraiture, at

[46] Formerly in the collection of Sir Arthur Evans at Oxford. A Furtwängler, *Antike Gemmen* (1900), Vol. II, pp. 233 f., No. 7, and Vol. III, Pl. XLIX, Fig. 7.

[47] Amelung, *Vatican Kat.,* Vol. I, pp. 80 ff., Braccio Nuovo, No. 62, Pl. XI. Michaelis, *Ancient Marbles,* pp. 401 ff. Bernoulli, *Ikonographie,* p. 69, No. 2 and pp. 79 ff., Fig. 6, Pl. XI. Hekler, *Bildniskunst,* pp. 56 f. Brunn-Bruckmann, *Denkmäler,* Pl. 429. Arndt, *Porträts,* Pl. 574. Paribeni, *Ritratto,* Pl. XXIII. G. Krahmer, "Stilphasen der hellenistischen Plastik," in *Röm. Mitt.,* XXXVIII–XXXIX (1923–24), pp. 154 f. G. Fraser in *A.J.A.,* Vol. XLI (1937), p. 214, Fig. 2 (without the restored hands, from a photograph lent by M. Bieber). V. Müller in *The Art Bulletin,* Vol. XX (1938), pp. 385 ff., Fig. 24. M. I. Rostovtzeff, *The Social and Economic History of the Hellenistic World* (3 vols., Oxford University Press, 1941), Vol. II, p. 652, Pl. LXXI, Fig. 1. Restored are the front part of nose, right foot, most of the base.

[48] Michaelis, *Ancient Marbles,* p. 417, No. 1. Bernoulli, *Ikonographie,* Vol. II, pp. 71, 81, Fig. 1. Poulsen, *Catalogue Ny Carlsberg,* pp. 309 f., Nos. 436, 436a. Arndt, *Porträts,* Pls. 1111–14. Schefold, *Bildnisse,* pp. 106 f., 208. Restored are half of the nose, both hands and lower arms, toes of the left foot, two toes of the right foot. The scroll has now been removed.

[49] S. Reinach in *B.C.H.,* XLVIII (1924), pp. 504 f., Fig. 19. Arndt, *Porträts,* Pls. 1115–16. The statuette belongs to Mrs. Herbert Strauss.

[50] P. Hartwig in *Jahrbuch d. Inst.,* Vol. XVIII (1903), p. 26, Fig. 1. It is now in the Vatican Museum.

least. This is also shown by another portrait statue of a standing man, which cannot be much later in date than the Demosthenes. It is in the Metropolitan Museum of Art in New York, and has been tentatively identified as Hermarchus [51] (Figs. 230–31). If this is correct, it would establish the date as 270—260 B.C. The philosopher appears as a sturdy, thickset, and coarse man, standing in a clumsy position with thin legs set apart to the side. He has sloping shoulders, flabby breast, and fat belly. A heavy cloak, the *tribon* of the philosopher, is carelessly thrown around him in broad folds. The left hand clumsily gathers the hanging folds, while the right hand, with mobile fingers, hangs down. The face is furrowed and the nose is straight. The head, however, is less individual than the body. In any case we may recognize the character portrait of a man of humble origin and coarse manners, but with a face modeled by much serious thought.

Beside the seated statues of the Epicureans (Figs. 163–66, 173–74, 176) there is another seated philosopher represented in a bronze statuette found in Brindisi and now in the British Museum [52] (Fig. 233), of which four marble copies exist: one is in the Metropolitan Museum of Art in New York [53] (Fig. 232), restored with a cast from the head of the statuette in London, and others are in the Museo Barracco in Rome, the Galleria dei Candelabri of the Vatican, and the Skulpturen-Sammlung in Dresden.[54] The composition is less closed than in the statues of the Epicureans, while it is also related to, but less compact than, the composition of the statuette of Chrysippos discussed below. It therefore may be dated around the middle of the third century, and it could represent Cleanthes, the successor of Zenon, and the teacher and predecessor of Chrysippos. Cleanthes died in 233/2 B.C. The fact that a head of Chrysippos (Figs. 236–37) was found in the same place as the torso seems to confirm this interpretation as the portrait of some other Stoic. Both head and torso are in the Metropolitan Museum of Art in New York. The philosopher is seated with his feet crossed. The left arm and hand are wrapped in the mantle, while the bent right arm is free. The bronze and marble copies differ in the attitude of the hand. In the bronze the hand, with clenched fingers, is near the right cheek, while in the marble statuettes the hand seems to have rested on the edge of the mantle below the left shoulder. The looser composition of the bronze is probably the right one. The near relation to other Attic portraits of philosophers proves that it is also the work of an Attic artist.

The portrait of Chrysippos, who succeeded Cleanthes as head of the Stoic school in 233/2, is well known through coins of his birthplace Soli, from which he came to Athens about 260 and became an Attic citizen. The coins, minted in A.D. 163/4, but certainly based on an earlier portrait, show a bald-headed man about seventy years old, with high forehead, small eyes under protruding eyebrows, a thick nose, thin lips, deep wrinkles in his thin cheeks, and a short beard.[55] Chrysippos is looking upward. The shoulder is covered with a mantle. This portrait has been preserved in more than a dozen marble copies, the best of which are in the Galleria Geographica of the Vatican [56]

---

[51] G. Richter, *Greek, Etruscan, and Roman Bronzes* (New York, Metropolitan Museum of Art, 1915), pp. 70 f., No. 120. G. Richter in Arndt, *Porträts,* Pl. 1123 and Figs. 1–6, and *Handbook of the Greek Collection* (1953), pp. 124 f., Pl. 103a. Delbrück, *Porträts,* pp. XXXVIII f., Fig. 13, Pl. 26.

[52] British Museum, No. 848. Hinks, *Greek and Roman Portrait Sculpture,* p. 10, Pl. 11. K. A. Esdaile in *J.H.S.,* XXXIV (1914), pp. 47 ff., Pls. II–III. G. Lippold in *Röm. Mitt.,* Vol. XXXIII (1918), pp. 19 ff., Fig. 7. G. Lippold, *Griechische Porträtstatuen* (1912), p. 88, Fig. 24 (the head). G. Richter in *A.J.A.,* XXIX (1925), pp. 154 f., Fig. 5.

[53] G. Richter in *A.J.A.,* Vol. XXIX (1925), pp. 152 ff., Figs. 1–2. G. Richter, *Handbook of the Classical Collection* (New York, Metropolitan Museum of Art, 1930), p. 212, Fig. 147, and *Handbook* (1953), p. 123, Pl. 101d.

[54] W. Helbig and G. Barracco, *La Collection Barracco* (Munich, 1893), Pl. 64. K. A. Esdaile in *J.H.S.,* Vol. XXXIV (1914), pp. 48 f., Fig. 1, Pls. V–VI. G. Lippold, *Porträtstatuen,* pp. 86 f. Lippold in *Röm. Mitt.,* XXXIII (1918), 18 ff. Lippold will publish the replica in the Galleria dei Candelabri of the Vatican in the *Vatican Kat.,* Vol. III, Part 2 (in preparation). Replica in Dresden: Herrmann, *Original-Bildwerke,* p. 48, No. 194.

[55] Bernoulli, *Ikonographie,* Vol. I, Münztafel II, No. 11. F. Imhoof-Blumer, *Porträtköpfe auf antiken Münzen hellenischer und hellenisierter Völker* (1885), Pl. 8, No. 31. F. Imhoof-Blumer in *J.H.S.* (1898), p. 167, Pl. XII, 17. G. F. Hill, *Catalogue of the Greek Coins of Lycaonia, Isauria and Cilicia* (London, the British Museum, 1900), p. 154, No. 55, Pl. XXVII, 4. L. Bürchner in *Zeitschrift für Numismatik,* Vol. IX (1882), pp. 109 ff., Pl. IV, No. 13. Schefold, *Bildnisse,* p. 172 f., No. 27, p. 221. G. Becatti in *Riv. del Ist. Arch.,* VII (1940), 24 ff.

[56] Galleria Geographica, No. 13. Bernoulli, *Ikonographie,* Vol. I, pp. 166 f., Figs. 31–32; he wrongly called the type Hippocrates. Arndt, *Porträts,* Pls. 933–34. Restored: the nose, ears, the right part of the chin, and the bust.

(Figs. 234–35), in the British Museum,[57] and the Metropolitan Museum of Art in New York[58] (Figs. 236–37). This last-mentioned copy is a small one.

The portrait is striking, with its sharp, irregular lines on the forehead and the deep wrinkles between the eyebrows and around the eyes. It is an excellent likeness of the ingenious, highly intellectual, and acute scholar who had dedicated his life to the building up of an imposing system of logical knowledge. His books filled 705 scrolls. Although he neglected to perfect his style, he strengthened the Stoic dogmas with subtle and acute arguments so that they became the leading principles of life in Athens and later in Rome. He laid the main emphasis on ethics, and elaborated the ideal of the wise man who lives a purely rational life according to nature. Teaching and writing, he lived frugally, absorbed in his work and indifferent to his personal appearance.

The clever and subtle spirit of Chrysippos lived in an insignificant body (Diogenes Laertius *Lives of Eminent Philosophers* VII. 182). A statue in the *Kerameikos* at Athens was so small that it was almost hidden by an equestrian statue hard by. His adversary Carneades of the Academy mockingly called him Krypsippos ("hiding behind a horse") instead of Chrysippos ("golden horse"). Evidence of lively gesticulation in this statue, and probably in the original, is furnished by Cicero (*De finibus* I. 11. 39): "A seated statue of Chrysippos is in the *Kerameikos,* with his hand stretched out (*porrecta manu*)." The same gesture, or more probably another, similar one, is attested by Apollinaris Sidonius (*Epistulae* IX, Letter 9. 14); he says that the fingers were constricted to indicate numbers (*digiti propter numerorum indicia constricti*). The compressed or contracted fingers would seem rather to indicate bent fingers or a clenched fist, and one can imagine the little man alternately opening and bending his fingers in enumerating and emphasiz-

ing his arguments. "A man computing with his fingers (*digitis computans*)" by the artist Eubulides (Pliny *Nat. hist.* XXXIV. 88) has probably rightly been identified as a portrait of Chrysippos. In Rome and the provinces casts of his portrait were popular among his followers (*plena omnia gypso Chrysippi invenies* [Juvenal *Satires* II. 4]).

We can reconstruct this portrait statue with the help of a bust in Athens, inscribed ΧΡΥΣΙΠΠΟΣ, dedicated by one Akrisios to Mithras.[59] It has the same lean neck stretched forward and the same arrangement of the mantle on both shoulders as have the coin and the bust in the British Museum. The same treatment of the drapery is again found on a statuette, formerly with the modern addition of a head of Aristotle, but now with a cast of the head of Chrysippos, in the Louvre[60] (Figs. 238–39), and a replica of this statuette in Rome, in the Museo Nuovo[61] (Fig. 241). The drawings reconstructing this figure[62] (Figs. 240 and 242) show the eminent but insignificant-looking Stoic demonstrating with the fingers of his right hand, with his back bent and his head stretched forward and upward, a little toward his left. It is a lively picture of the eager and argumentative teacher who stresses his points vehemently with the gestures of the right hand. The heavy mantle is wrapped around his left arm and his right upper arm, leaving the chest free but deeply shadowed. Broad and deep folds with heavy shadows surround the back and the legs of the prolific, systematic, and dogmatic writer.

[57] A. H. Smith, *Brit. Mus. Cat.,* Vol. III, No. 1846, pp. 138 f., Pl. XII. Hinks, *Portrait Sculpture,* p. 10, Pl. 7b, No. 1846. Bernoulli, *Ikonographie,* Vol. II, p. 150, No. 3, Figs. 14–15; he wrongly called the head Aratus. Arndt, *Porträts,* Pls. 931–32; cf. Pls. 935–40. Schefold, *Bildnisse,* pp. 126 ff., No. 4, and p. 211. Restored: the nose, upper lip, and chin.

[58] G. Richter in *A.J.A.,* Vol. XXIX (1925), pp. 152 ff., Figs. 3–4, and *Handbook* (1953), p. 123, Fig. 101b. I owe to her kindness the photographs in Figs. 236–37, taken after the head was lifted to its right position.

[59] H. von Prott in *Athen. Mitt.,* XXVII (1902), 297 ff.

[60] Louvre, Museum No. 80. Bernoulli, *Ikonographie,* Vol. II, pp. 157 ff., Fig. 18. Lippold, *Porträtstatuen,* pp. 75 f., Fig. 16. F. Poulsen, *Ikonographische Miscellen* (Copenhagen, Host, 1921; K. Danske Videnskabernes Selskab, Copenhagen. Historisk-Filologiske Meddelelser, Vol. IV, 1, 1921) pp. 8 ff., Fig. 3. Schefold, *Bildnisse,* pp. 124 f., No. 3, p. 211. L. Laurenzi, *Ritratti greci* (1941), No. 76, Pl. XLVIII.

[61] Mustilli, *Museo Mussolini,* pp. 61 f., Pl. XLI, Figs. 166–67 (here is the list of 14 replicas of the head). G. Richter in *A.J.A.,* XXIX (1925), pp. 155 ff., Figs. 6–7.

[62] The first reconstructed drawing, by A. Milchhöfer (Fig. 242), in *Archaeologische Studien Heinrich Brunn dargebracht* (1893), pp. 37 ff., Fig. 1 on p. 2. The statue was first recognized as one of Chrysippos by A. Gercke in *Arch. Anz.,* V (1890), pp. 56 f. The new drawing (Fig. 240) is by Erika Schob in G. Kleiner, *Die Inspiration des Dichters* (1949), Pl. 11a. A sculptural reconstruction in a cast has been made in the Museo dei Gessi at Rome, and the statuette in the Louvre (our Figs. 238–39) has been given a cast of the head in the British Museum (G. Richter, *Three Critical Periods in Greek Sculpture* [Oxford, The Clarendon Press, 1951], Fig. 45).

The arrangement of the mantle and the movement of the body in the statuette of Chrysippos are more complicated and looser than in the statues of the Epicureans, with their closed composition. This indicates a more advanced and still developing style. It may well be the copy of the statue by Eubulides, who lived in the late third and early second centuries.[63] He thus may have known the venerable Chrysippos shortly before his death about 206 B.C. Chrysippos was born in about 280 B.C., and here appears as about seventy years of age, which would date the statue about 210 B.C.

Eubulides was probably the grandfather of the younger Eubulides who in about 130 B.C. worked in a classicized style. It appears, therefore, that pure Atticism, with still-creative powers, declined around 200 B.C. (see Chap. XI).

---

[63] W. Amelung in Thieme-Becker, *Künstlerlexikon*, XI, 69. C. Robert in Pauly-Wissowa, *Real-Enc.*, Vol. VI, Part 1, pp. 371 ff., Nos. 10–11. J. Overbeck, *Die antiken Schriftquellen zur Geschichte der bildenden Künste bei den Griechen* (1868), pp. 434 f., Nos. 2235–44. Eubulides appears on a list of *proxenoi* ol 191/90.

V

ASIANISM
IN THE
THIRD CENTURY B.C.

ASIATIC PEOPLE of native Carian stock living in Asia Minor, un-Hellenic by race and tradition, nevertheless had already fallen under the spell of Greek civilization in the archaic period.[1] This philhellenic tendency continued throughout the Hellenistic period.

I. GREEK ARTISTS IN THE SERVICE OF NON-GREEK ASIATICS

Persian kings and Persian satraps employed Greek artists as early as the late fifth century B.C. The Persian satraps Tissaphernes (in 411 B.C.) and Pharnabazus (in 410) struck silver tetradrachms which were certainly designed by Greek artists[2]

(Figs. 243–44). In about 360 B.C. the satrap Orontas, son-in-law of Artaxerxes II, struck both a silver tetradrachm at Colophon and a gold stater at Lampsacus, with his portrait in the Greek style of the fourth century[3] (Figs. 247–48).

At the same time Mausolus, the mighty dynast of Caria, erected his tomb monument, which has given its name—Mausoleum—to ostentatious tomb buildings ever since (see pp. 27 f.). The architects Satyros and Pytheos and the sculptors Skopas, Leochares, Timotheos, and Bryaxis voluntarily finished the monument after the death of the satrap and of his wife Artemisia, and it became one of the Seven Wonders of the World. In the tomb chapel, surrounded by an Ionic colonnade, stood the colossal figures of Mausolus and Artemisia, as cult statues. They were probably finished directly before or after the death of the satrap in 363 B.C. The stat-

---

[1] G. Karo, *Greek Personalities in Archaic Sculpture* (1948), pp. 212 ff. G. Richter, "Greeks in Persia," in *A.J.A.,* L (1946), 15 ff. G. Richter in *Archaeologia Orientalia: In Memoriam Ernst Herzfeld* (1952), pp. 189 ff.

[2] E. Babelon, *Traité des monnaies grecques et romains,* Part II, Vol. 2 (1910), p. 390, No. 583; Part III, Vol. 2 (plates), Pl. 108, Fig. 1; p. 1462, No. 2810 *bis;* Part III, Vol. 2, Pl. 178, Fig. 15 (Pharnabazus); Part II, Vol. 2, pp. 101 f., Nos. 51–54, Part III, Vol. 2, Pl. 188, Figs. 10–13 (Tissaphernes). F. Imhoof-Blumer, *Porträtköpfe auf antiken Münzen hellenischer und hellenisierter Völker* (1885), pp. 4, 23, 73, Pl. II, 1–2. B. V. Head, *Catalogue of the Greek Coins of Ionia,* ed. by R. S. Poole (London, the British Museum, 1892), p. 325, Pl. 31, Nos. 5–6. R. Delbrück, *Antike Porträts* (1912), p. LXIII, Pl. 61, Fig. 1. K. Regling, *Die antike Münze als Kunstwerk* (1924), p. 82, Pl. XIX, Nos. 424–25. K. Lange, *Herrscherköpfe des Altertums im Münzbild ihrer Zeit* (1938), pp. 32–35. M. Rostovtzeff, *Social and Economic History of the Hellenistic World* (1941), Vol. I, p. 76, Pl. XI, No. 2. G. F. Hill,

Historical Greek Coins (New York, 1906), pp. 57 ff., Pl. IV, No. 30. G. F. Hill, *L'Art dans les monnaies grecques* (Paris, 1927), p. 39, Pl. VII, No. 3. G. Richter in *Hesperia,* Supplement VIII: *Commemorative Studies in Honor of T. Leslie Shear* (1949), pp. 291 ff., Pl. 37, Fig. 1.

[3] Babelon, *Traité des monnaies,* Part II, Vol. 2, pp. 106 ff., No. 55, and pp. 111 f., No. 62; Part III, Vol. 2, Pl. 168, Fig. 25. Head, *Coins of Ionia,* Pl. IX, Fig. 14. Hill, *L'Art dans les monnaies,* p. 39, Pl. VII, Fig. 3. Delbrück, *Porträts,* p. LXIII, Pl. 61, Fig. 2. Imhoof-Blumer, *Porträtköpfe,* p. 73, Pl. III, Fig. 1. R. P. Hinks, *Greek and Roman Portrait Sculpture in the British Museum* (London, 1935), pp. 5 f., Pl. 2a. G. Richter in *Hesperia,* Supplement VIII: *Commemorative Studies in Honor of T. Leslie Shear* (1949), Pl. 37, Fig. 3.

ues [4] (Figs. 245–46, 249) would not have been so well preserved if they had fallen, as is generally assumed, from the quadriga on the high-stepped pyramidal roof. In style and size they do not agree with the fragments of the horses which belonged to the quadriga. The imposing over-life-size figure of Mausolus is clad in the Greek manner, in chiton and ample himation, draped in majestic folds around the vigorous body. Artemisia also wears the Greek chiton and the himation, drawn over the head. Her hair is wrapped in a cap and arranged over the forehead in small artificial curls. Her face has been destroyed, but that of Mausolus is decidedly Asiatic (Figs. 245–46). He has straight, long, sleek hair, combed back and streaming down the back. His beard is short and curly. The small eyes have a clever expression. The nose is flat, the mouth has sensual full lips. Both statues are important as draped figures dated exactly in the middle of the fourth century. They are dignified representations of leading personalities of Asia Minor. Asiatic features and Greek style are combined in a way which is a forerunner of Hellenism, that is, the spread of Greek civilization into new lands.

The conquest of the mighty Persian empire by Alexander brought more Greek artists into contact with Asiatic rulers. One of these was Abdalonymos, the last king of Sidon in Syria, appointed by Alexander in 332 B.C. In this town there was an old tradition of Greek sarcophagi; (see the discussion of the sarcophagus of mourning women, p. 22). The last of the group found in the royal necropolis of Sidon, now in the Museum of Istanbul, is, however, the most elaborate one.[5] It has the form

of a temple with a gable roof covered with tiles. The decoration is rich, almost luxurious. Along the top and edges of the roof are women's heads encircled by large leaves. Crouching lions are the *akroteria* at the four corners, while the central *akroteria* are palmettes flanked by griffins. Goats' heads serve as water spouts. In the frieze is a beautiful vine tendril surrounded by elaborate mouldings, which also are above and below the reliefs covering all four sides. Two more scenes are in the pediments. All parts are richly colored, the lively colors being very well preserved.

The subjects of the reliefs are four battle scenes and two scenes of hunting. The front depicts the same battle as does the celebrated mosaic showing Alexander winning the victory over Darius III in the battle of Issus in 333 B.C., copied from a painting by Philoxenos of Eretria.[6] In both representations Alexander is leaping forward on his celebrated horse Bucephalus, lifting his spear against a noble Persian who glides down from his wounded horse. (Fig. 251 is the Persian's head.) The sarcophagus has been named Sarcophagus of Alexander after this group. However, while Alexander is the only Greek hero on the mosaic, he shares the honors with two other Greek generals on the sarcophagus. At the right, as a companion piece to Alexander, we see an old man, perhaps Parmenion, Philip's general whom Alexander had retained. The center, however, is given to a young man, perhaps Hephaistion, the closest friend of Alexander, who died in 324, a year before Alexander's death, and who was honored like a hero with a magnificent funeral. This may be the reason for giving him the place of honor. The impression is that of a furious battle with wild scenes, yet there is a clear grouping underlying the seemingly accidental arrangement.

On the other long side is a lion hunt in which Persians are purposely combined with Greeks. Again the chief part is not played by Alexander, but in this case by a Persian. His horse is attacked

[4] A. H. Smith, *A Catalogue of Sculpture in the Department of Greek and Roman Antiquities of the British Museum* (3 vols., 1892–1904), Vol. II (1900), Nos. 1000–1001, Pl. XVI. H. Brunn and F. Bruckmann, *Denkmäler griechischer und römischer Skulptur* (Munich, 1888—), Pls. 241–42. A. Hekler, *Bildniskunst der Griechen und Römer* (1912), Pls. 37–38. R. Paribeni, *Il ritratto nell' arte antica* (1934), Pl. XXV. Hinks, *Portrait Sculpture*, pp. 6 f., Pl. 3. V. Müller in *The Art Bulletin*, Vol. XX (1938), pp. 369 f., Figs. 13, 15. G. F. Hill in *Anatolian Studies Presented to Sir William Ramsay* (Manchester University Press, 1923), p. 209, Pl. X. M. Bieber, in *Scritti archeologici e filologici in onore di Carlo Anti* (Padua, in the press). See also our Chap. II, p. 28, note 131.

[5] G. Mendel, *Catalogue des sculptures grecques, romaines et byzantines, Musées Ottomanes* (3 vols., Constantinople, 1912–14), Vol. I, pp. 171–200, No. 68. F. Winter, *Der Alexandersarkophag aus Sidon* (Strassburg, 1912). O. Hamdy-bey and T. Reinach, *Une Nécropole royale à Sidon* (Paris 1892), pp. 272 ff., Pls. XXV–XXX. M. Collignon, *Histoire de la sculpture*

grecque (2 vols., Paris, 1892, 1897), Vol. II, pp. 404 ff., Figs. 214–16, Pl. VIII. G. Richter, *Sculpture and Sculptors of the Greeks* (rev. ed., New Haven, Yale University Press, 1950), pp. 112, 152, 293, Figs. 399, 400, 748.

[6] F. Winter, *Das Alexandermosaik aus Pompeii* (1909). M. Bieber, "The Portraits of Alexander the Great," in *Proceedings of the American Philosophical Society*, Vol. XCIII, No. 5 (1949), p. 387, Fig. 27.

by a lion. Alexander and a young Greek, probably again Hephaistion, and a Persian, probably Abdalonymos, are coming to his aid. From the left another Persian and another Greek hurry to aid against the lion, while another Persian, together with another Greek, are killing the stag which has served to lure the lion.

In the other hunting scene, on one of the short sides of the sarcophagus, four Orientals (Fig. 250 is the head of one) surround a panther or leopard, while a fifth Persian throws himself against the rearing riderless horse, probably belonging to Abdalonymos, who must be the chief hunter, seen in full front. This shows clearly that the sarcophagus was made not for a Greek but for an Asiatic sovereign.

This becomes still more certain when one studies the three remaining battle scenes. In the gable above the hunting scene a Persian rider is in the center, while a Greek is in danger of being thrown down by the Persian's horse. At the right side a Persian defeats a Greek, while on the left a Greek has already been killed; his body fills the corner. On the other short side a Persian lifts his weapon against a Greek lying on the ground and protecting himself feebly with his shield, while as a compensation at both sides, Greek warriors are victorious against Persians. But in the gable above this battle scene we have an almost ignominious scene of Greeks fighting among themselves. Two fully armed Greek warriors murder a defenseless man, while another fight goes on at the right and a wounded man is supported by a servant in the left corner. This is probably an event from the wars of the Diadochi, the successors of Alexander. The fact, however, that in two scenes the Persians are victorious proves that the sarcophagus was made for a Persian, certainly Abdalonymos. The portraits of the Persians in their national dress, with the Persian tiaras surrounding their faces, and with very individual features—particularly the nobleman wounded by Alexander (Fig. 251) and the hunter next to Abdalonymos in the panther hunt (Fig. 250)—show that the artist must have known the Persians whom he represented.

The artist or artists of this sarcophagus must have come from the circle of sculptors working for Alexander and his successors. Lysippos himself, working in collaboration with Leochares, had made bronze figures of Alexander in combat with a lion, with Craterus coming to his aid (Plutarch *Alexander* 40. 4). Alexander galloping up to the aid of a hunting companion on the sarcophagus appears to be based on this celebrated group, which was set up after the death of Craterus in 321 by his son. But the sarcophagus is probably the work of a pupil of Lysippos working under his influence, such as Euthykrates, who enjoyed the greatest reputation among the sons of Lysippos.[7] Pliny (*Nat. hist.* xxxiv. 66) tells us that he imitated the strength rather than the grace of his father's work, trusting to an austere style, rather than a pleasant one. He was eminently successful in the following works: Alexander represented as a hunter in Thespiae, a cavalry battle, several four-horse chariots, and animals.

We may, therefore, get an idea of his style from the sarcophagus. The composition is crowded and the varied actions of the figures suggest a real battle, in marked contrast to the battle scenes on the Mausoleum (Figs. 61, 64–65), in which every figure stands out clearly against the background. Here there is the suggestion of depth. The figures sometimes seem to advance out of the background (see Fig. 251), or to recede into it. The figures in the round executed by the school of Lysippos were of course still more freely set into space.

2. THE DEVELOPMENT OF GROUPS

While the figures in the Mausoleum frieze are isolated from each other, those on the Alexander sarcophagus are arranged in groups which, particularly in the battle scenes, occasionally overlap. Somewhere between the two is the composition of the Amazon sarcophagus, now in Vienna (Fig. 252); it probably came originally from Cyprus.[8] The composition, like that of the Alexander sarcophagus, is divided into a center group and two side groups. The separation of the three is, however, much sharper on the Vienna sarcophagus, and the correspondence of the side groups is much stronger. On both long sides a Greek and an Amazon fight over a wounded Greek seated in the center between them. At each side a Greek,

[7] See J. Overbeck, *Die antiken Schriftquellen zur Geschichte der bildenden Künste bei den Griechen* (Leipzig, 1868), Nos. 1509, 1516, 1522–24.
[8] Brunn-Bruckmann, *Denkmäler,* Pl. 493. H. Schrader, *Phidias* (1924), pp. 98 ff., Figs. 80–83.

striding in the outward direction, turns back to fight an Amazon on horseback. The groups are clamped together by the two fallen Amazons between the center and side groups. Another striking feature of the sarcophagus in Vienna is the fact that all figures are frontal, at least in their upper bodies. One of the two fallen Amazons lies with her face to the spectator, the other with her back toward the spectator. There is much more variety in the Alexander sarcophagus. In both monuments, nevertheless, the composition of the single groups is similar. These groups are rather flat and loose. The Greeks who fight the Amazons are on the same plane with them, as are Alexander and his noble adversary on horseback, Hephaistion and the Persian kneeling near the hind legs of the Greek's horse, and the Persian falling from his horse before the onrushing Parmenion. Other groups form a flat segment of an ellipse or circle. Thus Abdalonymos, Hephaistion, and the Persian with the axe surround the lion in the center of the lion hunt, and the four Persians surround the panther in the other hunting scene. On the Vienna sarcophagus the Greek holding his wounded comrade by the arm and the Amazon lifting her weapon against him form such a flat rounded group. It is the same beginning of the use of the third dimension as we have in Lysippos's group of Heracles breaking the antler of the hind (Fig. 78). Both sarcophagi, therefore, may be attributed to the school of Lysippos.

The use of a motif for a group in the round, of course, differs from and presents many more difficulties than its use in a relief. In many cases a motif was first used in relief and only later transposed into a free group. The motif of one foot set on an elevation, already used in the Parthenon west frieze, becomes a motif for free statues in the Alexander Rondanini of Leochares (see pp. 49 and 62), in the Hermes binding his sandal (see p. 34), and in the Poseidon of Lysippos (Fig. 148). The restlessness of the seated Ares in the Parthenon east frieze is transferred to the round in the Ludovisi Ares (Fig. 103). These figures belong to the same period as the sarcophagi and the Heracles with the hind by Lysippos.

All these motifs—the one foot higher than the other, the restlessness expressed in the stance, and the groups which are only slightly rounded—are found in the much-discussed set of statues illustrating the story of Niobe and her children[9] (Figs. 253-64). The original must have been made in the last quarter of the fourth century, or in the first quarter of the third, somewhat later than the sarcophagi. It is identified with the group representing the death of Niobe's children which was brought from Asia Minor, perhaps Cilicia, to the temple of Apollo Sosianus in Rome. The copies, now mostly in Florence, preserve six sons and four daughters besides the mother and a pedagogue, so that certainly one son and three daughters, perhaps also the old nurse and the revenging gods, are missing. Niobe, the mother of fourteen children, had boasted that she deserved more veneration than Leto, the mother of only Apollo and Artemis, and therefore claimed that divine honors should be taken from Leto and given to herself. Apollo and Artemis thereupon cruelly punished Niobe by killing all fourteen of her children, shooting them down with arrows.

Pliny (*Nat. hist.* xxxvi. 28) tells us that it was doubtful whether Skopas or Praxiteles made the group. Some modern writers have assigned it to one or the other, but most have now agreed that the statement of Pliny carries little weight. There is hardly any Praxitelean element, and very little that is genuinely Scopadic in it, though some pathos in the style of the Tegean pediments may be found. But this was generally accepted after the middle of the fourth century. An attempt to identify the Niobid master with Timotheos[10] is impossible on account of chronological difficulties. Timotheos worked in the early fourth century and was certainly old when he worked on the Mausoleum. The composition of groups such as those of Niobe protecting her youngest daughter (Figs. 258 and 261), of the old pedagogue with the youngest boy, and the one of the eldest son with a younger sister (Figs. 253-57) were not possible before Lysippos's time, and are certainly a little later in date

[9] W. Amelung, *Führer durch die Antiken in Florenz* (Munich, 1897), pp. 115 ff., Figs. 32-35. J. Sieveking and E. Buschor in *Münchner Jahrbuch für bildende Kunst*, VII (1912), 114 ff. G. Lippold in *ibid.*, 136 ff. E. Buschor in *ibid.*, IX (1914-15), 191 ff. G. Rodenwaldt in *Röm. Mitt.*, XXXIV (1919), 53 ff. E. Loewy in *Jahrbuch d. Inst.*, XLII (1927), 80 ff., and XLVII (1932), 47 ff. F. Studniczka in *Abh. Sächs. Akad.*, XXXVII (1926), 60 f., 84 ff. K. Schefold in *Phoebus*, I (1946), 49 ff.

[10] F. Winter in *Jahrbuch d. Inst.*, XXXVIII-IX (1923-24), 49 ff.

than the use of the third dimension in the sarcophagi (Fig. 252).

The group of Niobe with the youngest daughter shows a particular advance in the grouping of a grown person and a child into a real unit. Niobe clasps the little girl close to her knees and holds a fold of her cloak over her head to shelter her from the destroying arrows of the gods (Figs. 258 and 261). With agonized expression she lifts her face to the sky. The group is a perfect one, the child being not an attribute but of equal value with the mother. The group of the eldest son with a younger sister must be reconstructed from the girl in Florence, with only the leg of the young man, and a better-preserved replica without the sister in the Vatican [11] (Figs. 253–55). The girl is wounded and sinks to the ground, fainting like a withered flower, supported by the brother. He strides forward, lifting his cloak over his head to protect her. He gazes anxiously into the distance from which the arrow has come. The chlamys, wrapped around the right arm, has slipped down with its big round pin from the shoulder to the thigh, where it is stopped by the advanced leg. The treatment of the drapery, with its rich heavy folds, reminds us of the Hermes of Praxiteles in Olympia (Fig. 11). The intensity of the expression, and the shadow thrown on the eye by the brow, resembles the heads of Skopas. Such figures as these explain the ancient dispute over the attribution of the work to Praxiteles or Skopas. But the movement and the grouping, both figures being of equal value, again are impossible before the time of activity of Lysippos. The group resembles most, however, the central group of a Greek supporting his wounded comrade on the Amazon sarcophagus in Vienna (Fig. 252), and because the group has been transferred into the round, must be later in date than the relief, and also later than any work of the two older masters. The third group, that of the youngest boy with the pedagogue (Figs. 254, 256–57), is more loosely constructed, and resembles such groups as those in the pediments of the Alexander sarcophagus.

The other sons and daughters are represented in various movements and postures—running, standing, crouching, kneeling, lying—all in poses that had been developed since the early fifth century, in order to fill the pediments of the temples with human figures of equal size that would fit into the space sloping down to the side corners. The boys are naked, or have small cloaks round their shoulders, or slipping down to their legs in their rapid flight. That is the case with the youngest boy, who is fleeing with the pedagogue (Figs. 254 and 256). He looks back and up, full of fear. Several of the sons are moving upward, one foot much higher than the other, anxiously looking backward (Fig. 259). One is kneeling with one leg on the ledge of a rock over which his mantle has fallen and over which he supports himself with his left hand. He, too, is looking back and upward. Of this figure we have three variations, two in the Uffizi Gallery in Florence and one in the Museo Capitolino in Rome.[12] One has already fallen on both knees, and his left arm reaches toward the wound in his back. Finally, one is dead, lying on rocky ground over which his mantle has fallen, with his feet crossed, his head falling backward, his left hand on his body, the right arm lifted over his head (Fig. 260). The pathetic figure has a replica, with slight variations, in Munich.[13] A third copy is in Dresden.

All these figures are conceived in such a way that the rocky ground is part of the composition. It is likely, therefore, that the figures were originally—or at least in their re-erection at Rome—arranged on rocky ground in the open air. Whether they stood in a row as assumed by many scholars [14] (Fig. 262), or in a more rounded arrangement, as in an old reconstruction by Arthur Milchhöfer (Fig. 263), is difficult to decide. A difference in height is certain from the many upward-turned heads and glances. Whether all these are directed toward the mother, or toward the gods—if these were part of the group—cannot be said. The fact that the statue of Artemis, on a slightly larger scale, has been found in Crete, together with Niobe protecting her youngest girl, speaks in favor of the

---

[11] The reconstructions (Fig. 254) are from J. Sieveking and E. Buschor in *Münchner Jahrbuch für bildende Kunst*, Vol. VII (1912), p. 114, Fig. 1. The group of the pedagogue and Niobid in Paris is illustrated in Amelung, *Antiken in Florenz*, Fig. 33.

[12] Jones, *Sculpt. Museo Capitolino*, pp. 121 f., Galleria 48, Pl. 21.

[13] A. Furtwängler and P. Wolters, *Beschreibung der Glyptothek zu München* (2d ed., 1910), pp. 280 ff., No. 269. Brunn-Bruckmann, *Denkmäler*, Pl. 43.

[14] J. Sieveking and E. Buschor in *Münchner Jahrbuch für bildende Kunst*, Vol. VII (1912), pp. 116 f., Figs. 2–4. Buschor in *ibid.*, Vol. IX (1914–15), figure on p. 200.

presence of the two revenging gods [15] (Fig. 261).

Among the daughters the most beautiful one is the running girl (Fig. 264). She advances rapidly, trying to reach her mother, her chiton flowing in long curved folds, her mantle flowing backward. She has long sleeves and ribbons around the shoulders. The closest counterpart, particularly in the treatment of the net of small folds over the breast, is the Themis of Rhamnus (Fig. 516). This gives the date—early third century—for the Niobid group. The frontal attitude of most of the figures is similar to those of the Vienna sarcophagus (Fig. 252). The date of the copies is probably the first century B.C., the earliest period of the art of exact copying.

Not a copy, but a Hellenistic variation, is the beautiful and vigorous statue of a running girl in the Vatican, called the Niobid Chiaramonti after the part of the Vatican in which she formerly stood [16] (Fig. 265). Her chiton has no small crinkled folds and long sleeves, but instead is of smooth material and has broad folds and short wide sleeves. Her cloak flows in rich and variegated folds. The whole figure is in a more impressive style and of a more tempestuous character than the copy in Florence. This spirited work has been regarded by some scholars as a figure from the original Niobid group, of which the dry and tame statues in Florence are faithful copies. I believe that it is an original which is somewhat later and does not necessarily belong to a Niobid group. There are many dangers from which a girl might run. The artistic merit of a type is not lessened if it is taken over, for it is the execution that counts, not the drawing of the outlines of the composition. The types of the single Niobids go back to the fifth century when Phidias adorned the throne of Zeus in Olympia with this story. They were copied in reliefs, and the decoration of a discus of Roman times mingles the figures of the Phidian re-

liefs with motifs from the group in Florence.[17]

Another figure which has been regarded as one of the Niobids is the so-called Ilioneus in Munich.[18] He is closely related in type to the kneeling Niobid, but he has no cloak and his flesh is more elastically modeled. The back is particularly rich and delicate, with many realistic details. He, therefore, is probably a somewhat later creation. His body bends forward, but the right arm and the head were directed upward. This shows that the figure was probably part of a group, but whether he is Ilioneus, the youngest son of Niobe, or Ganymede, or Troilus, it is impossible to say.

The youth from Subiaco in the Museo Nazionale Romano in Rome [19] (Fig. 266) is also sometimes associated with the Niobids. His closest parallel, to me, seems to be the Ilioneus in Munich. The Subiaco statue is probably a Hellenistic original which belonged to the Emperor Nero, in whose villa it was found. The boy's position has not yet been definitely determined. He is kneeling, or about to kneel, or rising from a kneeling position; the knee is a little above the ground. The ground has a wavy surface, probably indicating sand. The body is turned to the right, the right arm is stretched upward. Whatever the action may be, the artist has chosen it in order to display all the limbs in an active position. The third dimension of depth is abundantly used. Perhaps the figure was in a group with a second figure standing above him or even on horseback. It is completely thought out and executed in the round. The elasticity and warmth of the flesh, the sensitiveness and softness of the modeling, prove it to be an original masterpiece of the third century B.C.

The three figures last discussed are related in composition to the Niobid group. They are, however, more advanced in the treatment of the sur-

[15] E. Loewy in *Jahrbuch d. Inst.*, Vol. XLVII (1932), pp. 56 ff., Figs. 9–11. E. Kirsten in *Die Antike*, Vol. XIV (1938), p. 331, Fig. 14. Found in a Roman villa at Inatos on the island of Crete; dated about A.D. 200.

[16] W. Amelung, *Die Skulpturen des Vaticanischen Museums* (2 vols., Berlin, 1903–6), Vol. I, pp. 422 ff., Museo Chiaramonti, No. 176, Pl. 44. Brunn-Bruckmann, *Denkmäler*, Pl. 313. G. Lippold, *Kopien und Umbildungen* (1923), p. 165. E. Gabrici in *Mon. Accad. Lincei*, Vol. XLI (1951), pp. 680 ff., Figs. 2–5, Pls. I–II.

[17] E. Loewy in *Jahrbuch d. Inst.*, Vol. LXII (1947), pp. 93 ff., figure on Beilage 9. A. H. Smith, *Brit. Mus. Cat.*, Vol. III, pp. 260, No. 2200, Pl. XXVI. W. H. Schuchhardt in *Mitt. d. Inst.*, Vol. I (1948), pp. 95 ff., Pls. 41–44.

[18] Furtwängler and Wolters, *Glyptothek*, pp. 282 ff., No. 270. Brunn-Bruckmann, *Denkmäler*, Pl. 432.

[19] W. Helbig, *Führer durch die öffentlichen Sammlungen klassicher Altertümer in Rom* (3d ed., 1912–13), Vol. II, No. 1353. F. Studniczka, "Artemis und Iphigenie," in *Abh. Sächs. Akad.*, Vol. XXXVII, No. 5 (1926), pp. 74 f., Fig. 58. S. Aurigemma, *Le Terme di Diocleziano e il Museo Nazionale Romano* (Rome, 1950), p. 71, Pl. XXVII.

face and in the use of the dimension of depth. The groups to which they belonged had probably kept much less of the frontal arrangement than the Niobids. The third century was the great age for the creation of spatial groups.

The wrestlers in Florence are a closely knit group in a style similar to that of the Niobids; two heads of sons of Niobe have been used to replace the lost heads [20] (Fig. 267). The group has considerable depth and it is necessary to look at it not only from the front, but also from the back, in order to understand the action. The defeated young athlete kneels, with knees wide apart on the ground, which is characterized as sand as is the base of the youth from Subiaco (Fig. 266). His left hand supports his body, while his right arm is drawn back and upward by his adversary. The victor reaches out with his right hand for a decisive blow. He kneels over the defeated and with his left foot lifts the left leg of the other, so that he cannot raise himself from the ground. The group as a whole has a square form, inside of which is enclosed a complicated and lively movement. Seen from the back the form becomes more like a pyramid, the right shoulder and arm of the victor being the apex, his right leg one side, and the two heads the other side of the triangle.

The group of Artemis and Iphigenia in Copenhagen, reconstructed in a cast at Leipzig by Studniczka, belongs also to the early third century, judging from the style of the dresses [21] (Figs. 268–69). The small crinkled folds of the peplos of Artemis are reminiscent of those in the dress of the running Niobid (Fig. 264), while the treatment of the dress of Iphigenia, with its strongly emphasized groups of folds, has its closest parallel in the chlamys of the youngest son of Niobe (Fig. 256). The hair of Iphigenia is like the hair of the youngest daughter nestling against the knees of Niobe (Fig. 258); in both we see broad waves with strong curves and pointed ends.

The moment represented is the one when Iphi-

genia, destined to be sacrificed in expiation of the sin of her father Agamemnon, is rescued by Artemis, who brings a stag to the altar to be killed instead of the heroine. Iphigenia is torn away from the altar in such a manner that she hangs over the left thigh of Artemis. The goddess grasps Iphigenia's left arm with her left hand, and with her right hand she brings forward the stag. The stag stood outside her right thigh. Studniczka's reconstruction (Fig. 269) is unsatisfactory because he has put the altar on the wrong side. The nature of the action demands that the stag be forced to the altar while Iphigenia is torn away from it (see Fig. 271). The baroque form of the bow of Artemis, which was bound to the quiver on her back, has to be corrected. The struts should be eliminated, as they were probably made for the transportation of the group and through neglect were not removed after the work had been set up in a Hadrianic building.

When we place the altar on the right side of Artemis as in Fig. 271, it fills the gap below the rearing stag and before the right lower leg of Iphigenia. It is then in one plane with the left leg of the heroine and fits into the contour of this side, which goes from the antlers of the stag to the altar, while on the right side, in the reconstruction of Studniczka, it juts out and forward in an ugly way. When it is removed the two left arms of Artemis and Iphigenia form the other contour. Inside this rhomboid contour Artemis forms the central axis and the second layer, while the stag behind Artemis forms the third. We thus have a fine rhythmical balance between the stag and the heroine. The lines cross each other as in the Tyche of Antioch, but there are three figures involved instead of only two. The arrangement of the folds on the breast of Artemis, with the taut parts over the swelling forms, is more in the advanced style of the Niobid Chiaramonti than of the running Niobid in Florence. The motif, that of one helpless and one vigorous figure intertwined, is also stronger than in the Niobid and Wrestler groups.

This stag (Fig. 270) is related to the stag in the lion hunt on the Alexander sarcophagus, and to the hind in the Lysippean bronze group in Palermo (Fig. 78). Here again, however, there is a development toward a greater naturalism in the details

[20] Amelung, *Antiken in Florenz*, pp. 45 f., No. 66. Brunn-Bruckmann, *Denkmäler*, Pl. 431.

[21] F. Studniczka in "Artemis und Iphigenie," in *Abh. Sächs. Akad.*, Vol. XXXVII, No. 5 (1926). He dates the group too early in the fourth century. G. Rodenwaldt, in *Röm. Mitt.*, XXXIV (1919), 65, has given the right period—early Hellenistic.

of the antlers, the veins of the nervous head, and the finely penciled hair on the body.

The marble is said to be from Asia Minor. We can thus assume that the group was created in the East.

The arrangement of a figure supported by the arm of another who stands with wide stride is also found in small groups of two wrestlers, one from Antioch in Syria, and others from Egypt [22] (Fig. 643). The most grandiose creation of this type, however, is the group of Menelaos with the body of the dead Patroclus.

The group of a mighty hero carrying the body of a dead comrade has been excellently reconstructed by Bernhard Schweitzer from the remains of nine different replicas [23] (Figs. 272–77). It is sometimes called the Pasquino, from the mutilated group standing in the open air before the Palazzo Braschi in Rome (Fig. 273). (The name was derived from *pasquilli,* lampoons and other abusive documents attached to it during the sixteenth century.) Bernini considered it the most beautiful of ancient sculptures, despite its being already much defaced in his time. It is indeed not only of excellent workmanship, but the only copy that has the head of Menelaos preserved on the neck in the right position. The best-known replica, in the Loggia dei Lanzi (Fig. 272), has a modern restoration of Menelaos from the waist up. Better preserved is another replica, in the Palazzo Pitti, and of better workmanship are fragments of two copies, both of which stood in the Villa of Hadrian at Tivoli, and which are now in the Vatican Museum [24] (Fig.

277). Clear reflections of the group are on a bronze chariot in the Museo Capitolino, and on gems.[25]

The right interpretation of the group was found by Ennio Quirino Visconti. It is an illustration of Book XVII of the *Iliad.* Patroclus has gone forth, protected by the armor of Achilles, to help the Greeks against the Trojans, because Achilles, having been offended by Agamemnon, refuses to fight. Euphorbos and Hector have killed Patroclus and taken his armor and weapons. Around the naked body a violent fight has raged, with heavy losses on both sides. Menelaos, receiving strength from Athena, has taken the lead and killed Euphorbos, the friend of Hector. He has rescued the body of Patroclus, and thinking tenderly of the kindness of the dead, has lifted him from the midst of the Trojan enemies and carried him away. The group shows the moment when with a wide stride Menelaos bends forward, lifts the body so that it reposes for a moment on his left thigh, and rests the right arm of the dead against his shoulder. He looks back into the distance to make sure that the Trojans do not follow him. In the next moment he will lift the youth to his left shoulder and hurry on.

Thus the master of the group has caught the action in a fertile instant, full of movement and indications of earlier and following action. The contrast between the strong, muscular body of Menelaos, his raised head with tense features and sharply gazing eyes, and the soft delicate body of the youth whose lower legs and back of the left hand slide on the ground, while his head hangs helplessly backward and down on the other side, are indeed striking. While Menelaos wears his helmet, chiton with belt, and sword at the side, Patroclus is of course naked because his armor has been taken by the enemy. The two heads, that of Patroclus from the group in the Loggia dei Lanzi (Fig. 276), and that of Menelaos from the Villa of Hadrian (Fig. 277), are contrasts not alone in the one being bearded, with long fluttering hair and a richly decorated helmet, while the other has short curly hair. The expression of defiance in the living and the helplessness of the dead, with his

[22] F. Studniczka, "Artemis und Iphigenie," in *Abh. Sächs. Akad.,* Vol. XXXVII, No. 5 (1926), pp. 66 f., Fig. 50. R. Pagenstecher in E. Sieglin, *Expedition Ernst von Sieglin: Ausgrabungen in Alexandria* (1908–27), Vol. II: *Die griechisch-ägyptische Sammlung Ernst von Sieglin,* Part I A: *Malerei und Plastik* (1923), pp. 54 ff., Fig. 48, Pl. 23, 2. Group from lower Egypt, in the Louvre (Museum No. 365), Heracles subduing an adversary. The lower part of the defeated figure is broken. The excellent closed composition of this group is similar to that of the Pasquino. See Dorothy K. Hill, *Catalogue of Bronzes in the Walters Art Gallery* (Baltimore, 1949), pp. 66 f., No. 140, for the group from Egypt; *ibid.,* No. 141, for Heracles and Antaeus; our Figs. 643-644.

[23] B. Schweitzer in *Abh. Sächs. Akad.,* Vol. XLIII, Abhandlung 4 (1936), and in *Die Antike,* XIV (1938), 43 ff. Brunn-Bruckmann, *Denkmäler,* Pls. 346-47. G. Lugli in *Bolletino d'Arte,* Series II, Vol. IX (1929/30), pp. 207 ff., Fig. 1.

[24] Amelung, *Antiken in Florenz,* pp. 8 ff., No. 5. Amelung, *Vatican Kat.,* Vol. II, pp. 491, 506 ff., 563, 567 ff., Sala dei Busti, Nos. 293 J, 311, 377 F, 384 A, B, and D, Pls. 66, 68, and 73.

[25] Jones, *Sculpt. Palazzo Conservatori,* Sala dei Bronzi, pp. 179 ff., No. 13, Pl. 71, Group D, 12. A. Furtwängler, *Beschreibung der geschnittenen Steine* (1896), No. 2472, Pl. 22. B. Schweitzer in *Abh. Sächs Akad.,* Vol. XLIII, Abhandlung 4 (1936), pp. 74 f. and 125, Fig. 19, and *Die Antike,* Vol. XIV (1938), Pl. I and Fig. 6.

closed eyes and open mouth, are the work of a great master.

The many contrasts in the group do not, however, prevent its being one of the best and most closely built up groups of antiquity. It forms a pyramid, with the steeply lifted head of Menelaos as the apex. From here a line goes down the body of Menelaos to his right foot, and another from his shoulder to the shoulders and left arm of Patroclus. The left knee of Patroclus is the front point in the center between these two sides. The figures are held together by parallel lines. Thus the right leg of Menelaos parallels the right upper leg of Patroclus and his right arm, the hanging left arm of Patroclus. At the same time this parallelism brings out more emphatically the contrast of the tense, swelling muscles of the rescuer and the relaxation of the dead youth. The head of Patroclus is the only part which juts out of the closed contours of the group, thus emphasizing the helplessness of the dead. The shield of Menelaos forms the background from which the striding Menelaos, with the hanging body in his arms, is built forward in space. Although the main view is probably there, where both heads are in front view (Fig. 275), it is necessary to go around the figure to grasp all the rich details of the composition, and the pyramid form is visible all around. The problem of a three-dimensional group has found a perfect solution. The new artistic tasks of the world opened up by Alexander the Great and his successors have led to the development of a new plastic form.

The subject of a dead or wounded warrior supported by a comrade is of course much older. We find it in the friezes of Phigalia and of the Nike temple in the fifth century, and particularly in a bronze mirror of the fourth century, in the British Museum, the similarity is strong.[26] But these are reliefs, and several times we have found that it was not until the period of Lysippos and his successors that sculptors dared to transfer motifs from the ideal space of the relief into the real space of a free-standing group.

Bernhard Schweitzer has attempted to identify the artist of the group. The relief on the helmet (Fig. 277) shows a group of Heracles fighting the centaur, but also a leopard attacking a bird, and a miraculous bird similar to an eagle, but with snakes forming the tail. The leopard is characteristic of Libya; the miraculous bird, of Ethiopia. These are the utmost borders of the wanderings of Menelaos. Schweitzer concludes from this that the sculptor was also a scholar. He believes him to have been Antigonos of Carystus, on the island of Euboea, who later worked for Attalus I of Pergamon, and he sees Pergamene scholarship in the decoration of the helmet.[27] The theory is attractive but cannot be proved, particularly as we do not know whether the Antigonos named as one of the artists working for the Attalids (Pliny *Nat. hist.* xxxiv. 84) and who wrote books on art, is that Antigonos of Carystus who wrote biographies of philosophers and collected stories of rare events.

The group of Menelaos and Patroclus has a companion piece of the same size in the group of Achilles supporting Penthesilea, the queen of the Amazons, with whom he fell in love after having wounded her mortally. The work has been reconstructed by Giuseppe Lugli [28] (Figs. 278-80). The torso of a hero with a sword case hanging from a baldric (Fig. 280) and its replicas have been attributed to the Pergamene school and to the victory monument of Attalus.[29] It was then recognized as Achilles supporting the Amazon, whose torso has been preserved in the Museo Nazionale Romano at Rome and in a replica in the Palazzo Borghese which was found on Via Salaria near Sette Bagni (Fig. 278). The Amazon hangs from Achilles's left thigh and left arm in the same way as does Patroclus from the thigh and arms of Mene-

[26] B. Schweitzer in *Die Antike*, Vol. XIV (1938), pp. 69 ff., Figs. 17-18.

[27] B. Schweitzer in *Abh. Sächs. Akad.*, Vol. XLIII, Abhandlung 4 (1936), pp. 17 ff. and 104 ff.

[28] G. Lugli in *Bolletino d'Arte*, Series II, No. 6 (1925-27), pp. 193 ff., Figs. 1-12, and Series II, No. 9 (1929-30), pp. 207 ff., Figs. 1-17. See also E. Loewy in *Ausonia*, Vol. II (1907), pp. 77 ff., Figs. 2-5 (here is the first comparison with the Pasquino). G. Bendinelli in *Ausonia*, Vol. X (1921), pp. 53 ff., Pls. I-II, for the Amazon in the Museo Nazionale Romano; Brunn-Bruckmann, *Denkmäler*, Pl. 347 b, Amazon in Palazzo Borghese; and B. Schweitzer in *Abh. Sächs. Akad.*, Vol. XLIII, Abhandlung 4 (1936), pp. 82 ff., 147 f., Figs. 69-70, 72.

[29] P. R. von Biénkowski, *Die Darstellungen der Gallier in der hellenistischen Kunst* (Vienna, 1908), pp. 16 ff., Figs. 19-23, p. 28, Fig. 41a. The replica, formerly in the Museo Comunale, is now in the Museo Nuovo in Rome (Fig. 280); other replicas are in Geneva, Copenhagen, and Naples. P. Arndt and W. Amelung, *Photographische Einzelaufnahmen antiker Skulpturen* (Munich, Bruckmann, 1893—), Nos. 1884-85. P. Arndt, *La Glyptothèque Ny Carlsberg* (Munich, 1896-1912), Pl. 110.

laos. The powerful torso in the Museo Nuovo at Rome (Fig. 280) calls to mind, on the one hand, the body of Menelaos; on the other hand it is indeed related to the Attalid votive offerings, particularly to the most grandiose group, that of the Gaul who kills his wife and himself.

The wild hordes of the Gauls who had settled in 278 in Asia Minor were defeated in a decisive victory by Attalus I in 241, but the end of the war came only in 228. The wild chieftain represented in the group has probably fought on until the last moment. When he sees no hope and refuses to flee, he throws down his shield and scabbard, kills his wife, and is now killing himself.

This grandiose group in the Museo Nazionale Romano in Rome, formerly the Ludovisi collection [30] (Figs. 281–83), suffers from the wrong restoration of the right arm of the man and the left arm of the woman. The elbow of the lifted arm should be lower, so that the face is not covered in the main view, indicated by the center of the index tablet of the base.[31] The left arm of the woman should hang down much more vertically and limply, similarly to her right arm and her head, for the woman is already dead and could not stretch the arm to the side as in the restoration. The struts between the bodies of man and wife and the one from the man to his mantle would have to be removed in a reconstruction. This copy of a bronze original was made in marble from Asia Minor.

When the corrections are made, the group takes its well-deserved place beside the Pasquino as one of the most powerful creations of Greek art. With a wide stride the Gaulish chieftain puts his left foot on the edge of his shield and grasps his wife, who has followed him through all the dangers of his expeditions. He has killed her so that she cannot fall into the hands of the Greek enemy to suffer ignominy. Like a broken flower she sinks down

on the shield, sustained only by his left hand. Now he lifts his sword, and looking defiantly back at the pursuing enemy, he plunges the blade into his jugular vein. In the next moment he will sink down over the body of his dead wife.

Thus we have here, as in the Menelaos-Patroclus group, a fertile moment, indicating the preceding and following action. Here, just as there, we have a sharp contrast between the powerful nude body with its swelling muscles, the steeply erected head, with its defiant gaze, on one side, and the draped kneeling woman on the other side, her head and her arms hanging down, her lower legs on the ground and the tips of the fingers of her relaxed left hand just touching the ground beside the strong left foot of her husband. The energy and vigor of the man, the unconscious breaking down of the woman, are full of the highest pathos. The wild features of the chieftain with his moustache, thick eyebrows and thick, unruly, tossing strands of hair contrast sharply with the relaxed features of the wife, her hair hanging from the crown in long wavy strands in all directions. Defiance and resignation, strength and weakness, the pride of the defeated who prefers death to captivity, play on our emotions. It is the moment between life and death. These rich details and the transitory movement of both figures are again included in the sculptured form of a pyramid. In this case, however, the form is not quite so clear. The head is again the apex. One line leads down the body to the right foot, the other down the left arm and the body of the woman. The center is indicated by the right foot of the Gaul. The figures are more side by side and not as closely knitted together as are Menelaos and Patroclus, but we feel that they will cross each other in the next moment, when the Gaul will fall down like a felled tree. All axes of the bodies and the arms, the legs, and the heads go in different directions. The mantle flutters behind the back of the man. The drapery of the woman is laid in vertical, horizontal, and curved lines which cross each other at irregular angles. One has to go slowly around the group to grasp all motifs. The use of the third dimension here is perfect; the sides melt together to a round panorama in an ideal unity of space.

There can be no doubt that the three groups last discussed belong closely together. Schweitzer

[30] Biénkowski, *Gallier*, pp. 6 ff., Figs. 6–11, Pl. I. Helbig, *Führer durch Rom*, Vol. II, No. 1302. B. Schweitzer in *Abh. Sächs. Akad.*, XLIII, Abhandlung 4 (1936), pp. 85 ff., 114, 148, Fig. 72. F. Studniczka, "Artemis und Iphigenie," in *Abh. Sächs. Akad.*, Vol. XXXVII, Abhandlung 5 (1926), pp. 62 f., Figs. 46–47. G. Krahmer, "Stilphasen der hellenistischen Plastik," in *Röm. Mitt.*, XXXVIII–XXXIX (1923–24), pp. 160 f. Aurigemma, *Museo Nazionale Romano*, pp. 102 f., No. 273, Pls. LXII–LXIII.

[31] See A. D. Fraser in *A.J.A.*, XXXVI (1932), pp. 418 ff., on the correct position of the arm.

thinks that the Gaul and wife are by the same Antigonos of Carystus who made the Menelaos group. He dates the Menelaos group at about the middle of the third century, earlier than the Gaul group which belongs to the victory monument for the wars of 241—228 B.C. Others date the Menelaos group later, as late even as 200 B.C.[32] I believe that Schweitzer is right. The Gaul group is more advanced in its spatial form than the Menelaos group. It need not be by the same artist; the pyramidal form was a favorite of the Hellenistic period.

Three other artists of the Hellenistic period who are known to us used the pyramidal form. One of them comes from Thebes in Boeotia, but worked in Smyrna and in Pergamon. The other two are Asiatic Greeks.

The drunken old woman by Myron of Thebes is best preserved in the copy now in Munich (Fig. 284), while another replica, with restored head, is in the Museo Capitolino.[33] A very old woman with crumpled skin is seated on the ground, hugging her beloved bottle as if it were a child. She is dressed in the Hellenistic *peronatris,* a chiton held on the shoulders with a broad pin (*perone;* see Theocritus *Idylls* 15, *Adoniazusae* v. 21). The garment slips down from her right shoulder, and a heavy mantle is draped around her legs and slips down from her left shoulder. The lower part of her clothing forms cascades and waves on the ground, as if to represent the waves of intoxication on which she seems to be swimming. The head is thrown back in drunken ecstasy, showing the sinews of her lean neck. The almost toothless mouth is open. The cheeks are fallen in and the face and neck are covered with wrinkles. The rather elegant dress, the kerchief which covers the hair, the earrings and finger ring indicate that this woman has seen better days. Now her only consolation for the miseries of life, in her forsaken and lonesome old age, is the bottle, which she has decorated with ivy. The form of the flask is that of the *lagynos,* a festival wine jug used in the Hellenistic period. Five such

bottles have been given the shape of the creation of Myron.[34] They do not, however, keep the closed form of the original. While the terra-cotta imitations belong to the second century, the original creation, and with it Myron, may belong to the late third century. Myron worked in Pergamon at the time of the Attalids, as is testified by an inscription and a terra-cotta mould with the motif of the drunken woman found there. Although the other part is a jug rather than a human being, the drunken woman is actually a group, for the bottle takes the place of a child.

Another pyramidal group is by Boethos of Chalcedon, a city in Bithynia, to the south of the Bosporus. His work, called by Pliny (*Nat. hist.* XXXIV. 84) "an infant [meaning in antiquity a child about six years of age] who embraces and strangles a goose (*infans amplexando anseram strangulat*)"— has been preserved in several copies, the best ones being in the Museo Capitolino (Fig. 285) and in Munich; others are in the Louvre and in the Vatican.[35] The child stands with his round legs wide apart, like Menelaos and the Gallic chieftain. However, he bends his knees slightly, throws his fat body backward and embraces with all his might, and with both arms, the neck of a goose. The bird also stands with legs wide apart; the four feet form a trapezium on the base. The goose tries to draw away and forward, while the boy pulls backward. The transitory movements are caught in the form of a pyramid. The four corners of the base are indicated by the two feet of the boy and the left foot and the tail of the goose. The left foot of the child is in the center, like the left foot of the Gaul, and his head is the apex. The lovely head, with its smile of a healthy, playful, and contented child,

---

[32] G. Lippold, in *Die griechische Plastik* (Vol. III of *Handbuch der Archaeologie,* ed. W. Otto and R. Herbig [Munich, 1950]), pp. 362 f., dates *c.*200 B.C. F. Studniczka, in *Zeitschrift für bildende Kunst,* XIV (1903–4), pp. 178 ff., dates the Menelaos group later than that of the Gaul and his wife.

[33] Furtwängler and Wolters, *Glyptothek,* pp. 387 ff., No. 437. Brunn-Bruckmann, *Denkmäler,* Pl. 394. Jones, *Sculpt. Museo Capitolino,* pp. 89 f., Galleria, No. 8, Pl. 18.

[34] G. Leroux, *Lagynos* (1913), pp. 73 ff. R. Weisshäuptl in *Ephemeris Arch.* (1891), pp. 143 f., Pl. X. M. Fränkel, *Inschriften von Pergamon* (Vol. VIII of *Altertümer von Pergamon* [1890–95]), No. 136, "Myron Thebaios."
[35] W. Amelung in Thieme-Becker, *Künstlerlexikon,* IV, 208 f. Jones, *Sculpt. Museo Capitolino,* pp. 321 f., Stanza del Fauno, No. 16, Pl. 80. Brunn-Bruckmann, *Denkmäler,* Pl. 433. Furtwängler and Wolters, *Glyptothek,* pp. 278 ff., No. 268. H. Bulle, *Der schöne Mensch im Altertum* (1912), Pl. 190. R. Herzog in *Oest. Jahreshefte,* Vol. VI (1903), pp. 224 f., Figs. 119–20. W. Klein, *Vom antiken Rokoko* (1921), pp. 27 ff. and 178, Note 29. F. Studniczka in *Abh. Sächs. Akad.,* Vol. XXXVII (1926), pp. 68 ff., Figs. 53–54. On the date of Boethos see H. von Gaertringen in *Arch. Anz.* (1904), pp. 212 f., and A. Rumpf, "Boethoi," in *Oest. Jahreshefte,* XXXIX (1952), 86 ff.

and with the silky hair bound in a knot over the forehead, is in strong contrast to the worn features of the drunken old woman. The artists of this period were masters in the rendering of all ages, all social classes, and all moods, in all plastic forms.

Although there were several Boethoi, a second authenticated work by the same Boethos has been found in a ship sunk in the first century B.C. off the African coast near Mahdia in Tunisia; it is now in the Musée du Bardo in Tunis. An inscription naming Boethos of Chalcedon is on an archaistic herm, which, however, has turned out to be only part of a composition showing a winged boy leaning his right arm on the head of the herm [36] (Figs. 286-89). Both parts are in bronze and are an original work of the master of toreutics or *caelatura* (chasing or embossing metal), for which Pliny praises Boethos (*Nat. hist.* XXXIII. 155 and XXXIV. 84): *in admiratione . . . et Boethus quamquam argento melioris*. A nude gilded boy made by Boethos was dedicated in the temple of Hera at Olympia (Pausanias v. 17. 4), and a precious hydria, a water jar, of his making was stolen by Verres (Cicero *In Verrem* IV. 14. 32). When the connection between the figure and the herm in Tunis was not yet recognized, the winged figure was taken to be Eros and attributed to Praxiteles or Lysippos. The swinging movement, however, goes beyond both, and the face has neither the sweetness of Praxitelean features nor the nervousness of those typical of Lysippos. It is a serious and realistic face of an adolescent boy. The wreath which the boy puts on his head and the herm, which belongs in the palaestra, give the key to the right interpretation of the figure as Agon, the god of contests. He appears in a similar form on the throne of the priest of Dionysos in the Theater at Athens.[37] The strong stylization of beard and hair of the herm, particularly the stiff ringlets of the onkos, the artificial hair-do worn by tragic actors,[38] are in strong contrast to the realistic rendering of the cloth which lies above it and under the arm of Agon, supported by the herm.

This is not a real group, but the herm takes the place of a second figure at the side of the main figure. Groups which show the figures side by side had already been found next to groups in the round in the Niobid series, and we will find them all through the Hellenistic period.

The third master whose preserved work shows the pyramidal form is Doidalsas of Bithynia. His Bathing Aphrodite, however, is a single figure (see Figs. 290-93).

3. GREEK ARTISTS IN THE SERVICE OF HELLENISTIC RULERS

Boethos, whose figures of children and toreutic masterpieces were celebrated, also carved for Delos a portrait statue of Antiochus IV (Antiochus Epiphanes) of Syria, who reigned 175—164 B.C. This gives us a probable date for Boethos, who must have gotten this commission as an established artist. The portraits on the coins of Antiochus showing his own features, or those of his baby son, agree well with the style of the head of the Agon [39] (Figs. 286-87, 289). It is quite conceivable that the celator Boethos also cut some of the models for the coins of the king, or that his statue was used as a model for the coin cutter. In any case we see that the custom of working for the rulers, begun by Lysippos for Alexander the Great and carried on by his pupil, Eutychides, continued during the whole Hellenistic period. The statues represented on the reverse of the portrait coins of these rulers may be mostly such works commissioned by the kings. They still await a systematic investigation.

An example of a court sculptor in the third century is Doidalsas. King Nikomedes of Bithynia (c.278-250), who wished in vain to buy the Cnidian Aphrodite (Pliny *Nat. hist.* XXXVI. 21; see pp. 18-20, Figs. 24-25), commissioned Doidalsas, an artist of his own country, to create another Aphrodite for him. This bathing Aphrodite later stood in the porticus of Octavia in Rome (Pliny *Nat. hist.* XXXVI. 35) and has been copied, with many variations, in about fifteen marble statues, to which may

---

[36] A. Merlin and L. Poinsot in *Mon. Piot*, Vol. XVII (1910), pp. 31 ff., Pls. 2-4. A. Merlin, *Catalogue du Musée Aloui* (2d Suppl., 1921), p. 125, No. 106, Pl. 11. F. Studniczka in *Abh. Sächs. Akad.*, XXXVII (1926), pp. 69 f., Figs. 55 56. Klein, *Rokoko*, pp. 33 f., Fig. 9.

[37] M. Bieber, *The History of the Greek and Roman Theater* (Princeton University Press, 1939), p. 139, Note 54, pp. 240 f., Figs. 335-36.

[38] For the onkos see *ibid.*, p. 36, Fig. 41.

[39] E. T. Newell, *Royal Greek Portrait Coins* (New York, 1937), pp. 55 ff., Pl. V, Fig. 10, and Pl. VI, Fig. 12. Percy Gardner, *British Museum Catalogue of Coins, The Seleucid Kings of Syria*, Pls. XI–XIII.

be added some bronzes, terra cottas, and coins of the Roman period.[40] The best replica, unfortunately lacking the head, was found in Vienne, France, and is now in the Louvre (Figs. 290–91). Other good replicas are the one in the Louvre, from the Borghese Collection (Fig. 293), and those in the Museo Nazionale Romano and in the Vatican. An excellent bronze statuette from Beirut in Syria, now in a private collection (Fig. 292), reveals best the original composition without the addition of Eros (whose presence is indicated by his hand on the back of Figs. 290–91) or struts.[41] The best copies agree in that the composition is a closed pyramid, inside which the different movements of body, legs, and arms are arranged with much crossing of the lines. The left arm crosses the left thigh and the hand touches the right thigh. The right arm crosses the breast and the hand touches the upper left arm. The crouching body bends forward to receive a shower of water for her bath. It is supported only by the toes of the right foot and the sole of the left foot. The variations which show the right arm lifted destroy the closed form. This variation seems to be a combination with the characteristics of the so-called Anadyomene type, that of a woman or girl, sometimes probably Aphrodite, lifting both arms and holding a part of her long hair with each hand. The most lovely example of this type, in Rhodes,[42] (Figs. 294–95) and also many others, show Aphrodite

arranging her hair. She is about to lift the two strands to the crown of the head, and will bind the hair in a luxuriant bow such as is worn by some of the replicas of the bathing Aphrodite (Fig. 293).

The style of the Aphrodite from Vienne (Figs. 290–91) has been called baroque. It is indeed a type which might be compared to Rubens's nude women. The Bithynian artist undoubtedly agreed with the taste of his patron, who may have had some Oriental blood or inclination for sensuous and voluptuous forms in women. The coins of King Nikomedes "reveal to us the rugged features of a strong-willed, able and pertinacious man." [43] It is probably this same ruler who commissioned the Zeus Stratios for the temple of Zeus in his capital Nicomedia, founded in 264 B.C. This statue, a work of Daidalos of Bithynia, certainly the same as Doidalsas (Eustathius of Thessalonica *Commentary to Dionysius Periegetes,* p. 793) is represented on Bithynian coins of Prusias I (*c.*228—183 B.C.), and his successors.[44] This Zeus wears high boots and a large himation draped around the legs and with a great swing over his left shoulder. The god holds twigs in his outstretched right hand, and grasps a scepter in his lifted left hand.

Another court sculptor of the third century was Bryaxis, probably a grandson of the master who worked on the Mausoleum in the middle of the fourth century. The date of the younger Bryaxis is established by the fact that he created the statue of Serapis, a combination of the Greek Pluto and the Egyptian Osiris, for Ptolemy II (Ptolemy Philadelphus), who reigned from 285 to 247/6. We have many copies in marble, bronze, and dark stone of this statue, which was made of an alloy and was thus probably of dark color [45] (Figs. 296–97). Serapis sat like the classical Greek Pluto on a throne, richly and warmly clad in a chiton and himation, for the realm of the dead is cold. He had Cerberus, the dog of Hell, at his side. Serapis's fea-

[40] Lists of replicas are in J. J. Bernoulli, *Aphrodite* (1873), pp. 314 ff., and in W. Klein, *Praxiteles* (1898), pp. 270 ff. See also Klein, *Rokoko,* pp. 31 ff., Figs. 7–8; Amelung, *Vatican Kat.,* Vol. II, pp. 680 ff., Gabinetto delle Maschere No. 427, Pl. 16, and Amelung, *Antiken in Florenz,* p. 53, No. 76, Fig. 11. An over-life-size replica in the Museo Torlonia in Rome: C. L. Visconti, *I monumenti di sculture antichi, Museo Torlonia, reprodotti con la fototipia* (Rome, 1884), Pl. XLIII, No. 170.

[41] E. Michon, *Syria: Revue d'art oriental et d'archéologie,* Vol. VI (1925), pp. 312 f., Pls. XL–XLI. A. W. Lawrence, *Later Greek Sculpture and Its Influence on East and West* (London, 1927), p. 109, Pl. 25a. Another bronze statuette, in Copenhagen: F. Poulsen, *Catalogue of Ancient Sculpture in the Ny Carlsberg Glyptotek* (Copenhagen, 1951), No. 51; *Billedtavler til Kataloget over Antike Kunstvaerker. Ny Carlsberg Glyptotek* (1907), Pl. IV. See O. Brendel in text to Arndt-Amelung, *Einzelaufnahmen,* Nos. 3788–90, for earlier literature and discussion of the type of the bathing Aphrodite.

[42] A. Maiuri in *Bolletino d'Arte,* Series II, Vol. 3 (1923–24), pp. 385 ff., Figs. 1–3, and in *Clara Rhodos,* Vol. I (1928), pp. 22 ff., Figs. 5–6. G. Jacopi in *Clara Rhodos,* Vol. V, Part 1 (1931), pp. 16 ff., and in *Lo Spedale dei Cavalieri e il Museo Archeologico di Rhodi* (1932), p. 41, Pl. II.

[43] Newell, *Greek Portrait Coins,* pp. 37 f., Pl. III, Fig. 1.

[44] *Ibid.,* Pl. III, Figs. 2–5.

[45] See Clement of Alexandria, *Protrepticus* IV. 48; Overbeck, *Schriftquellen,* No. 1325. Clement clearly distinguishes the later Bryaxis from the older one, who came from Athens and worked on the Mausoleum. It is incorrect to assign the Alexandrian Serapis to the older Bryaxis, as has been done so often. See W. Amelung in *Ausonia,* Vol. III (1908), pp. 115 ff., Fig. 20; Lippold, *Vatican Kat.,* Vol. III, Part 1, pp. 135 ff., Sala Rotonda 549, Pl. 36; G. Lippold in *Festschrift für Paul Arndt* (1925), pp. 115 ff.; Brunn-Bruckmann, *Denkmäler,* Pl. 163.

tures are strong and serious. Long and thick curls fall over the brow, overshadowing the melancholy eyes and falling over the ears onto the shoulders, mingling at the sides with the luxurious beard. The head was crowned with the modius, the measure for grain and the symbol of the nether world.

Another work certainly by the younger Bryaxis was the statue of Apollo in Daphne, a suburb of Antioch on the Orontes, the capital of Syria, founded in 300 B.C., and the city for which Eutychides sculptured the city goddess, the Tyche (see Fig. 102). The statue of Apollo is represented on coins of Antiochus IV (Antiochus Epiphanes) of Syria (175—164 B.C.). Apollo is shown in a long chiton, with a bowl and a lyre in his hands.[46] This agrees with the description of the statue by Libanius (*Oratio* LX, *Monodia de temple Apollino Daphnaea,* 9-11, p. III, 334-35):

Imagination brings before my eyes that form, the bowl, the lyre, the tunic reaching to the feet, the delicacy of the neck in the marble, the belt about the chest which holds the golden tunic together, so that some parts fit closely and others hang loose. He seemed to be singing.

The portrait of Seleucus (Pliny *Nat. hist.* XXXIV. 73) was probably made by the older Bryaxis. But there can be no doubt that like Lysippos, Leochares, and Boethos many other artists created not only idealistic statues of gods, heroes, and men, but at the same time created portrait statues. The Hellenistic rulers gave a new kind of subject to the artists. The trend of the times required that they, like Alexander, had to be deified and lifted into a superhuman atmosphere. They often became gods even during their lifetimes, and were therefore represented as such in art. For example, a bronze statuette from Pompeii, now in Naples, is the portrait of a Hellenistic ruler with the diadem in his hair, but represented as Hermes, with wings attached to his sandals, the ribbon for the lost petasos preserved from his chin to the right ear, and a lost caduceus in his left hand [47] (Figs. 299-301). The ugly features—the bulging lower

part of the forehead, the small, deeply sunken eyes, the vulture-like nose with its subtle curve and slightly pendent tip, the short upper lip, and the flat chin—seem to agree with the portraits on the coins of Alexander Balas (152—144 B.C.) [48] Other scholars have identified the figure as Antiochus II (Antiochus Theos), who reigned from 261 to 246,[49] or Antiochus VIII (Antiochus Grypus, "with the hooked nose," 121-96).[50] These identifications, however, seem still less tenable. In any case the statuette must represent a ruler or a member of his family, for only a prince could be represented as Hermes. It is a good, and probably an early, example of statue types originally created for depicting the gods, but later used for portraits of mortal men. This usage began in the Hellenistic period and afterwards found much favor among the Romans. At the same time it is an example of the difficulties which we encounter when trying to identify sculptured portraits with the help of coins.

Another such example is the bronze statuette of a rider (the horse is lost), wearing an elephant skin like a chlamys, and with the scalp, including the trunk, lifted over his head.[51] (Fig. 298). It certainly represents a ruler imitating the elephant-skin helmet of Alexander. Such headgear was, for example, worn by Demetrios I of Bactria (*c.*200-190), who conquered parts of India;[52] but although the identification seems likely, it cannot be proved.

Many of the statues of rulers were worked in precious materials, like gold and ivory, silver, or at least bronze, and therefore they have not survived. Some contemporary copies may have been made

[46] Overbeck, *Schriftquellen,* Nos. 1321-24. Newell, *Greek Portrait Coins,* pp. 57 f., Pl. VI, 15.

[47] A. Ruesch, *Guida del Museo Nazionale di Napoli* (n.d.), No. 808. P. Arndt, *Griechische und römische Porträts* (Munich, 1891-1942), Pls. 929-30. E. Pernice, *Gefässe und Geräte aus Bronze* (Berlin, 1923; Vol. IV of F. Winter, *et al., Die hellenistische Kunst in Pompeji*), p. 2, Pl. I.

[48] F. Imhoof-Blumer, *Porträtköpfe auf antiken Münzen hellenischer und hellenisierter* Völker (1885), Pl. III, No. 24. E. Pfuhl in *Jahrbuch d. Inst.,* Vol. XLV (1930), p. 26, Pl. II, Figs. 1-3. Lange, *Herrscherköpfe,* pp. 58 f.

[49] Imhoof-Blumer, *Porträtköpfe,* Pl. III, No. 11. E. Pfuhl in *Jahrbuch d. Inst.,* Vol. XLV (1930), Pl. I, Figs. 8 and 12. The name Antiochus II Theos is given to the statue by Theodor Schreiber, "Studien über das Bildnis Alexanders des Grossen," in *Abh. Sächs. Akad.,* Vol. XXI (1903), pp. 272 ff., Figs. 30-31, and by G. Dickins in *J.H.S.,* XXXIV (1914), pp. 306 f., Fig. 10.

[50] Imhoof-Blumer, *Porträtköpfe,* Pl. IV, Nos. 4-5. The name Antiochus VIII Grypus is given to the statue by A. Ippel in *Arch. Anz.,* Vol. LIV (1939), pp. 355 ff., Figs. 7, 9-11. He quotes Hauser. For a prince represented as Hermes, see Horace (*Odes* I.2.41, *et seq.*). The young Caesar Octavianus, later Emperor Augustus, is meant.

[51] Arndt, *Porträts,* Pls. 1205-7.

[52] See Newell, *Greek Portrait Coins,* pp. 67 f., Pl. IX, No. 5.

for the different parts of their empires, but later copies in great numbers, such as we have for philosophers, orators, and poets, were rarely made. The founders of dynasties were the only ones to be continuously honored; examples are Ptolemy I of Egypt and Philetairos of Pergamon.

We do not have any inscribed busts to identify the rulers. We have, however, the coins of many of them. With the help of these we can get a good idea of their sculptured portraits, which were probably the models for the coin cutters. This trade reached its peak in the Hellenistic period, and it flourished particularly during the third century and the first half of the second.

Thus the portraits of Ptolemy I on his coins, which he began to issue in 305/4 after he had taken the official title of king, show the great and clever founder of the Greek dynasty of pharaohs, when he was over sixty years of age, as a robust and vigorous personality [53] (Figs. 304 and 306). The heavy hair strands are arranged around the vertex in a starlike, almost Polycleitan design, only much more lively. The curved ends of the strands lie in all directions and some slip over the borders of the diadem. The forehead curves strongly backward in its upper part and strongly forward in its lower part. The small eyes are deeply set under heavy brows. The nose curves like an eagle's beak. The mouth and the short, but round and protruding, chin betray energy. Ptolemy I, like Alexander, wears the aegis of Zeus.

A marble portrait found in Egypt, and now in Copenhagen [54] (Figs. 302-3), has similar grandiose forms in uniformly short and elastic curves and bulges for the forehead, eyelids, nose, and chin. The hair was originally added in stucco and gilded in imitation of the golden hair of a cult statue, which may have been the model for the head. Such a statue, carved in gold and ivory like the chryselephantine statues of various gods, stood in the temple of Ptolemy I (Ptolemy Soter) in Alexandria, built by his son and successor Ptolemy II (Ptolemy Philadelphus). It may be the same mentioned by Theocritus in *Idyll* XVII (vss. 123–25), which he wrote in praise of Ptolemy II. Though the head in Copenhagen is only a mask, it is a great work of art. It shows the great general and ruler as a stern-looking man, with large features and the expression of a fiery and powerful personality. If it really imitates the cult statue, it should be dated about 280 B.C., and therefore would be a posthumous portrait, but the agreement with the coins proves that here we have the features of the real man.

The same is true of the portraits on the coins struck by Ptolemy II (285–246) and Ptolemy III (246–222), with the portraits of Ptolemy I and his wife Berenice I as saviors, and that of Ptolemy II and his wife, Arsinoë II, with the inscription naming them brother and sister gods: ΘΕΩΝ ΑΔΕΛΦΩΝ [55] (Figs. 306 and 308). All these portrait coins of the first Ptolemy, like those of Seleucus I (see Fig. 140), show the Lysippean style, enriched with many individual traits and realistic details, at the same time with tense, curving forms which give to the grandiose heads an intense expression. On the brother-and-sister coins, minted by Ptolemy III to commemorate his grandparents and parents (Fig. 308), the heroic appearance is further enhanced, particularly by making the eyes large and wide open.

The portraits of the first Greek ruling couple in Egypt, Ptolemy I and Berenice I, appear also on a

---

[53] Our Fig. 304 is a silver coin and Fig. 306 a gold pentadrachm; both are in the Museum of Fine Arts in Boston. They were issued about 295 or 290–83, and thus are contemporaneous with Ptolemy I (died 283 B.C.). See Imhoof-Blumer, *Porträtköpfe*, p. 61, Pl. I, Fig. 2 and Pl. VIII, Fig. 2; R. S. Poole, *British Museum Catalogue of Coins, the Ptolemies* (London, 1883), pp. 9 ff., Pls. 2-3, and *passim*; J. N. Svoronos, *Die Münzen der Ptolemäer* (4 vols., 1904–8), Vol. III, Pls. 7–9, Vol. IV, pp. 53 ff.; E. Newell, *Greek Portrait Coins*, pp. 24 ff.; K. Lange, *Herrscherköpfe*, pp. 48 f.; E. Pfuhl in *Jahrbuch d. Inst.*, Vol. XLV (1930), p. 6, Pl. II, Figs. 9–13. W. Schubart, "Das Königsbild des Hellenismus," in *Die Antike*, Vol. XIII (1937), p. 276, Fig. 1.

[54] Arndt, *Porträts*, Pls. 853–54. E. Pfuhl in *Jahrbuch d. Inst.*, Vol. XLV (1930), pp. 6 ff., Figs. 2–3. E. Pfuhl, *Die Anfänge der griechischen Bildniskunst* (1927), p. 12, Pl. VIII, Figs. 1–2. Poulsen, *Catalogue Ny Carlsberg*, p. 322, No. 453a. Supplement (Tillaeg 1915) to *Billedtavler*, Pl. VIII. L. Laurenzi,

Ritratti greci (1941), p. 111, No. 52, Pl. XIX–XX. G. McFadden, in *Classical Studies Presented to David Robinson* (1951), pp. 713–19, Pls. 82–85, denies the identification as Ptolemy I.

[55] Our Figs. 306 and 308 represent a gold octadrachm struck under Ptolemy III; the coin is now in Boston. See Poole, *British Museum Catalogue of Coins, the Ptolemies*, pp. 40 f., Pl. 7. Svoronos, *Münzen der Ptolemäer*, Vol. III, Pl. XIV, Figs. 15–31, Pl. XXVIII, Figs. 1–2, Vol. IV, pp. 125 ff., 152 f. E. Pfuhl in *Jahrbuch d. Inst.*, Vol. XLV (1930), pp. 28 f., Pl. II, Figs. 14–16. Newell, *Greek Portrait Coins*, p. 86.

stucco relief in Alexandria [56] (Fig. 307). Front views of the head of Ptolemy I are on a plaster cast from a silver or bronze plaque in the Pelizaeus-museum in Hildesheim [57] (Fig. 305) and on a cameo in Vienna [58] (Fig. 309). The heavy and full hair in both agrees with that on the "savior" coins. All these monuments use similar forms for the eyes and mouth.

In the blending of realism and idealism on the early Hellenistic coins, realism predominates for the male rulers. In the female heads, in contrast, idealism prevails. In the beautiful heads of Berenice I on the "savior" coin and the stucco relief (Figs. 306–7), of Arsinoë II on the brother-and-sister coin (Fig. 308) and her own coin,[59] and on gems with these early Ptolemaic queens,[60] we have normal forms and the "Greek" profile, that is, the straight line of forehead and nose. The Ptolemaic princesses seem to have preferred a melon-like hairdress during the third century. It shows best in the gem which combines the melon arrangement with heavy braids made into a coil in the back. It probably represents Berenice I. A representation of Artemis on coins minted by Berenice's son-in-law Pyrrhos, who married Antigone, a daughter of Berenice by a former marriage, shows an identical hairdress [61] (see also Fig. 123). Perhaps Antigone lent her features to Artemis. It is, however, also possible that the type of Artemis of this period may have had an idealizing influence on the portraits of Berenice.

The grandiose forms of the early Hellenistic period were replaced in the middle Hellenistic era by a smaller form in which the often ugly and barbaric, but powerful, features are overgrown with many small details. Good examples are the coins of Mithridates III of Pontus (246–190) [62] (Fig. 314), struck about 230, which show many deep lines and furrows in the face, and of Ariarathes III, the first independent king of Cappadocia (230–220) [63] (Fig. 315), with deep wrinkles furrowing his strong and ugly features.

The most characteristic coins in this style are those of Euthydemos I of Bactria. Born in the Greek city of Magnesia, he overturned the Bactrian dynasty of Diodotos and made himself king; he reigned c.230—190 B.C. His portrait on tetradrachms struck in Bactria during his lifetime [64] (Fig. 310) shows him as an older man, at about fifty years of age. The short hair grows thin at the sides of the forehead, there are wrinkles outside the small eyes, and deep folds run downwards from his nose and mouth. The corners of the mouth are drooping, and there is fleshiness under the sagging chin. The nose is large, with a deep groove at the root and a strong curve at the bridge. The expression is that of a determined and strong character.

The main features of these coin portraits reappear in a marble head formerly in the Museo Torlonia, now in the Villa Albani, in Rome [65] (Figs. 311–13). The ugly face is here still more compressed and weather-worn. The eyebrows are irregular and surrounded by a network of little wrinkles. The cheeks are furrowed and the flesh of their lower part and the under part of the chin hangs limply. The age of Euthydemos appears to

[56] A. Adriani in *Bulletin de la Société royale d'Archéologie, Alexandrie*, N.S. X, Fascicules 32–33, 1938, pp. 77 ff., Pl. VI.
[57] O. Rubensohn, *Hellenistisches Silbergerät in antiken Gipsabgüssen* (Pelizaeusmuseum, Hildesheim, 1911), pp. 44 f., Pl. VI, No. 32 (cf. p. 24, Pl. X, No. 12). G. Roeder and A. Ippel, *Die Denkmäler des Pelizaeusmuseums zu Hildesheim* (1921), pp. 141 ff., No. 1120, Figs. 56–57. Delbrück, *Porträts*, p. LXII, Pl. 60, 5.
[58] A. Furtwängler, *Antike Gemmen* (1900), Vol. I, Pl. 59, Fig. 3, Vol. II, p. 266. Delbrück, *Porträts*, p. LX, Pl. 58, 14.
[59] Imhoof-Blumer, *Porträtköpfe*, Pl. 8, Fig. 3. Svoronos, *Münzen der Ptolemäer*, Vol. III, Pls. XV–XVI and IV, pp. 83 ff. Poole, *British Museum Catalogue of Coins: The Ptolemies*, pp. 42 ff., Pl. VIII. Newell, *Greek Portrait Coins*, p. 86, Pl. XV, Figs. 1–3. W. Schubart in *Die Antike*, Vol. XIII (1937), p. 276, Fig. 2.
[60] Furtwängler, *Antike Gemmen*, Vol. I, Pl. 32, No. 32, and Vol. II, p. 159. Delbrück, *Porträts*, p. LIX, No. 10, Pl. 58.
[61] B. V. Head, *British Museum, Coins of the Ancients* (2d ed., 1881), p. 84, No. 25, Pl. 46. B. V. Head, *A Guide to the Principal Coins of the Greeks in the British Museum* (1932), p. 66, Pl. 37, No. 16.

[62] Imhoof-Blumer, *Porträtköpfe*, Pl. IV, No. 23. E. Pfuhl in *Jahrbuch d. Inst.*, Vol. XLV (1930), p. 14, Pl. IV, Fig. 9. Lange, *Herrscherköpfe*, pp. 78 f.
[63] Imhoof-Blumer, *Porträtköpfe*, Pl. 5, No. 18. E. Pfuhl in *Jahrbuch d. Inst.*, Vol. XLV (1930), p. 18, Pl. IV, Fig. 8. Our Fig. 315 is a silver tetradrachm in Paris.
[64] Imhoof-Blumer, *Porträtköpfe*, p. 70, Pl. I, Fig. 6. P. Gardner, *The British Museum Catalogue of Indian Coins, Greek and Scythic Kings of Bactria and India*, ed. by R. S. Poole (1886), pp. 4 ff., Pl. II, Figs. 1–6. E. Pfuhl in *Jahrbuch d. Inst.*, Vol. XLV (1930), p. 18, Pl. IV, Fig. 13. Newell, *Greek Portrait Coins*, pp. 66 ff., Figs. 3–4. C. Seltman, *Greek Coins* (1933), p. 234, Pl. LV, Fig. 2. Our Fig. 310 is a coin in the Museum of Fine Arts, Boston. I owe the photograph to Agnes B. Brett.
[65] Museo Torlonia, No. 133. Delbrück, *Porträts*, pp. XLII f., Pl. 29. Paribeni, *Ritratto*, Pl. XLI. Laurenzi, *Ritratti greci*, pp. 120 f., No. 74, Pl. XXIX.

be more advanced than that shown in the coin portrait. The date may be around 200 B.C., when Euthydemos was fifty to sixty years of age. The modern retouching of the huge nose and of part of the skin simulates the impression of a Renaissance bust, but there is no reason to consider it a work of that period. The semibarbaric character of the face may indicate some Bactrian blood in Euthydemos which impelled him to conquer the kingdom for himself. The artist probably came from the king's home town, Magnesia, and the statue to which the head belonged may have been erected in his birthplace. From there the head came into the Giustiniani collection, which was made in Chios and Venice, and later was taken to Rome.

The diadem surrounds the straight hair below the wide-brimmed Macedonian helmet. Such a sun hat had already appeared on the Alexander sarcophagus, and later it is seen in the coin portraits of several Bactrian rulers of the second century, such as Eukratides and Antimachos [66] (Fig. 316). Antimachos, probably a son of Euthydemos I, is represented on his coins minted around 185 B.C. with very short, curly hair, encircled by a diadem over which he wears the flat, wide-brimmed sun helmet or *causia*. He has a high, sloping forehead. The eyebrows are drawn together and there are deep lines under the eyes. The corners of the lips are drawn up as if in a half-mocking smile. The portrait has been called by Newell "astonishingly modern," and Newell further says that it "suggests a person full of humor and bonhomie."

The same characteristics appear in a head in Copenhagen [67] (Figs. 317–18), carved of Asiatic marble. It has been identified as a likeness of Antimachos by my former student Janet Hawke. It has, indeed, the same forms of the projecting lower forehead, the heavy vaulted eyebrows, the thick lips, the nose at an angle to the forehead and with the tip slightly uptilted, the long overhanging upper lip, and the sharp incisions below the lower lip

and below the short chin. A wide-brimmed hat was attached by means of two holes on each side over the diadem, which encircles the short-cropped hair. This is certainly the same *causia* as on the coins of Antimachos and the head of Euthydemos.

Quite a different physiognomy, but a similar style, appears on the coins of Antiochus III of Syria, surnamed the Great, who ruled 223—187 B.C. and defeated Euthydemos in 208 B.C. The coins minted at Antioch between 208 and 200 [68] (Fig. 321) show Antiochus III with a high, sloping, and furrowed forehead, a receding hairline, heavy hanging eyebrows drawn together, a double-curved nose with a very long tip, high cheekbones, and a mouth with thin lips and puckered corners. The hair is becoming thin at the temples.

The same features appear in a head in the Louvre [69] (Figs. 319–20). It can be dated around 200 B.C. or a little later, for it shows the marks of age even more clearly than the coins. The thin strands of the front hair are combed onto the forehead. The cheeks are still more emaciated, so that the cheekbones are more prominent, and the forehead and brows are still more furrowed. Perhaps this excellent and realistic portrait was copied from the statue by the Athenian sculptor Meidias which was set up in Delphi, together with other statues of Seleucids, in 202 B.C. It showed Antiochus III on horseback, probably life size; a colossal bronze statue also stood in Delphi, on a round base.[70]

The portraits of the Bactrian kings have a passionate vigor which reminds one of the sculptures of Pergamon, but the rounding of forms is rather overdone, with the result that the underlying grandiose and powerful character is somewhat sup-

---

[66] For the coins of Eukratides and Antimachos I of Bactria with sun helmet, see Gardner, *Indian Coins*, Pl. V, Figs. 1–3 and 7–9, and Pl. VI, Figs. 1–11. C. Seltman, *Greek Coins*, p. 235, Pl. LV, Figs. 3 and 5. Hill, *L'Art dans les monnaies*, p. 41, Pl. XVI, Fig. 2. Newell, *Greek Portrait Coins*, pp. 67 f., Pl. IX, Fig. 8.

[67] Copenhagen, Ny Carlsberg Glyptotek, No. 455. Poulsen, *Catalogue Ny Carlsberg*, pp. 323 f., *Billedtavler*, Pl. XXXIV. Arndt, *Porträts*, Pls. 499–500. Hekler, *Bildniskunst*, Pl. 122. Laurenzi, *Ritratti greci*, pp. 129 f., No. 95, Pl. XXXVIII.

[68] Our Fig. 321 is from a coin in the Metropolitan Museum of Art, No. 26.59.14. I owe the photograph to the friendship of Gisela Richter. For coins of the young Antiochus see Laurenzi, *Ritratti greci*, p. 122, No. 77, Pl. XXVIII; Newell, *Greek Portrait Coins*, pp. 53 f., Pl. V, Fig. 8.

[69] Musée du Louvre, No. 1204. Arndt, *Porträts*, Pls. 103–4. Hekler, *Bildniskunst*, Pl. 123. E. Pfuhl in *Jahrbuch d. Inst.*, XLV (1930), 24. Paribeni, *Ritratto*, Pl. XL. *Encycl. phot.*, Vol. III, pp. 242 f., Figs. A-B. Laurenzi, *Ritratti greci*, p. 122, No. 77, Pl. XXVIII. The tip of the nose has been restored.

[70] *Insc. Graec.*, Vol. II, Part 3, p. 353, No. 1624b. H. Pomtow in Pauly-Wissowa, *Real-Enc.*, Suppl. IV, pp. 1353 ff., No. 87, and p. 1359, No. 87 E. F. Courby in École Française d'Athènes, *Fouilles de Delphes*, Vol. II (1927), "Terrasse du temple," p. 296. Laurenzi, *Ritratti greci*, p. 44, No. 160. For Meidias see M. Bieber in Thieme-Becker, *Künstlerlexikon*, XXIV (1930), 340.

pressed. The portrait of Antiochus the Great, on the other hand, is a masterpiece in which the baroque tendencies combine with a refined realism and strong modeling. The latter style easily tempted the artists to crowd too many details into the face. The coins of Nabis of Sparta, the tyrannical last king of Sparta, who reigned from 207 to 192 [71] (Fig. 322) and of his contemporary, the Roman general Titus Quinctius Flamininus [72] (Fig. 323), are in the same style. After Flamininus had set the Greeks free from Macedonian rule in 197/6 B.C., many statues of him were erected in Greek cities, and one by a Greek artist was erected in Rome. His portrait was put on his gold staters, struck in Macedonia about 197 to 195. This earliest contemporary portrait of a famous Roman renders his sober features, his long nose, half-open mouth, and fluttering thick strands of hair in an absolutely Greek, middle Hellenistic style, comparable to that of the coins of Nabis, against whom he fought in 195 B.C.

During the first half of the second century the style of the portraits on coins moved away from the baroque tendencies to a more refined style. Good examples are the coin portraits of Eumenes II of Pergamon (197–159), the builder of the great Altar of Zeus and of the library [73] (Fig. 417). The

high point of soft modeling is found in the handsome and delicate features of Orophernes of Cappadocia (158–7) [74] (Fig. 326). The heads of Agathokles of Bactria (170–159) [75] (Fig. 324) and of Mithridates IV (Mithridates Philopator) of Pontus (170–150).[76] (Fig. 325), on the other hand, with their un-Greek, coarse, and realistic forms, lead to such portraits as those of the young couple Alexander Balas and Cleopatra Thea (150–145) [77] (Fig. 327). These mark the end of the middle Hellenistic period and of a continuous development. From here on, blendings of different styles prevailed.

The portrait coins prove decisively that there was no decadence whatsoever in Greek art during the third century and the first half of the second century. On the contrary, there was even a new development which exhausted all the possibilities of sculptural presentation open to the Greek genius, and laid the foundations for all further progress. During this period a new grandeur blended with the continuation of the sober Lysippean style, and led to the "baroque" passionate art, which had its main center in Pergamon.

---

[71] Our Fig. 322 is a silver tetradrachm in London. For Nabis, see Holleaux in *C.A.H.*, Vol. VIII, pp. 146 f., 172, 188 ff., 203 ff., and C. T. Seltman in *C.A.H.*, Volume of Plates III, pp. 10 f., Fig. d.

[72] Hill, *Historical Greek Coins*, pp. 136 f., Pl. XI, No. 81. R. West, *Römische Porträtplastik* (1933), Vol. I, p. 35, Pl. LXVII, Fig. 6. P. Ducati, *L'Arte in Roma dalle origini al Sec. VIII* (1938), p. 59, Pl. XXV, Fig. 2 (our Fig. 323). O. Vessberg, *Studien zur Kunstgeschichte der römischen Republik* (1941), p. 124, Pl. III, Fig. 1. Lange, *Herrscherköpfe*, pp. 86 f. The statue of Flamininus on the Forum Romanum at Rome had a Greek inscription (Plutarch *Titus Quinctius Flamininus* I. 1), and therefore must have been made by a Greek artist.

[73] Imhoof-Blumer, *Porträtköpfe*, Pl. IV, Fig. 15. W. Wroth, *Catalogue of the Greek Coins of Mysia*, ed. by R. S. Poole (1892), p. 117, No. 47, Pl. XXIV, 5. H. von Fritze, "Die Mün-

zen von Pergamon," in *Abh. Preuss. Akad.* (Philol.-Hist. Klasse, Anhang 1910), p. 12, Pl. II, Fig. 14. Delbrück, *Porträts*, Pl. 61, No. 26. Polybius (XXXII. 23) describes Eumenes II as delicate and often ill, which agrees with the character of the portrait on his coins.

[74] Imhoof-Blumer, *Porträtköpfe*, Pl. 5, No. 21. W. Pfuhl in *Jahrbuch d. Inst.*, Vol. XLV (1930), p. 15, Pl. IV, Fig. 12. *C.A.H.*, Volume of Plates III, pp. 10 ff., Fig. e. Head, *Coins of the Greeks*, p. 72, Pl. 40, No. 19. Dated 158–157. Coins of Orophernes were found under the pedestal of the copy of the Athena Parthenos given by him to Priene. See E. L. Hicks, *The Collection of Ancient Greek Inscriptions in the British Museum*, III, 1 (1874), pp. 45, 424.

[75] Gardner, *Indian Coins*, pp. XXV f., 10 ff., Pl. IV.

[76] See Geyer in Pauly-Wissowa, *Real-Enc.*, Vol. XV, pp. 2161 f., No. 10; Newell, *Greek Portrait Coins*, p. 40.

[77] F. Imhoof-Blumer, *Monnaies grecques* (1883), pp. 433 f., No. 102, Pl. H 13. Delbrück, *Porträts*, p. LXV, Pl. 61, No. 23. E. Pfuhl in *Jahrbuch d. Inst.*, Vol. XLV (1930), pp. 26, 43, Pl. II, Fig. 5.

VI

THE ART OF ALEXANDRIA

ALEXANDRIA was built to the order of Alexander the Great in 331 by Deinokrates of Macedon, in the form of a Macedonian chlamys, that is, a square with rounded corners (for this form see Fig. 149). An excellent harbor was made by connecting the island of Pharos with the mainland by a jetty seven stadia long. On this island Sostratos of Cnidus erected the celebrated lighthouse of many floors and windows, a forerunner of the American skyscraper. The streets crossed each other regularly after the scheme of Hippodamus of Miletus. Central points were the Mausoleum of Alexander and the Museum, the prototype of our museums, with a large library. This was dedicated to the Muses and became the center of scholarship and literature, which nowhere flourished more than in Alexandria. Celebrated librarians were the poet Callimachus, the scholar Eratosthenes, and the grammarian Aristophanes. They made lists of the best epic, lyric, tragic, and comic poets, and also of the best historians and rhetors. These lists became canonical.

I. EARLY DEVELOPMENT

It is clear that the newly founded city, which became the residence of the Ptolemies, attracted not only poets like Apollonios of Rhodes, but also artists from all parts of the Greek world. Sculptors as well as architects went to Alexandria as they went to the royal residences in Asia Minor. We know that the sons of Praxiteles worked for the Ptolemies on the island of Kos (Figs. 32–33, 43), and it is very likely that they worked in Alexandria as well. In any case, the first distinct style which developed in Alexandria was one which may be called eclectic but which has, however, predominantly Attic features. A group of monumental

sculptures found in Alexandria itself decidedly has this character.[1] The torso of a seated man recalls the Dionysos from the Thrasyllos monument (see Fig. 213), while a female torso is a bad version of a figure in movement. The torso of a standing man [2] reminds one of the Hermes of Andros (Fig. 14), although it has a different arrangement of the chlamys and has the bent fingers of the right hand, not the left, touching the hip. In all these examples the nude parts are handled in the soft Praxitelean manner.

The softened Praxitelean style appears particularly well in heads. Walter Amelung was the first to assemble a group of female heads in an almost illusionistic style, which he characterized by the Italian words *sfumato* and *morbidezza*.[3] Heads of Muses like one in the Museo Nuovo in Rome (formerly in the Museo Comunale) and one in Dresden, both crowned with wreaths, and many others, like two heads from Alexandria now in Cleveland, show this softened Praxitelean style. Recently Adriani has added to this group some outstanding examples found in Alexandria itself, the most important of which is a head with artificially twisted locks, the so-called Isis headdress, and a fringed shawl covering the hair in a tight arrangement [4] (Figs. 328–29). Among the many examples of this

---

[1] A. Adriani, *Documenti e ricerche d'arte alessandrina,* Vol. I (1946), pp. 7 ff., Pls. I–VI.

[2] *Ibid.,* pp. 27 ff., Pl. VIII.

[3] W. Amelung in *Bollettino Comunale,* XXV (1897), 110 ff. The head of a Muse in Rome, *ibid.,* pp. 136 f., Pl. IX. See also A. W. Lawrence in the *Journal of Egyptian Archaeology,* Vol. XI (1925), pp. 181 ff., Pls. XVIII–XXI.

[4] Adriani, *Documenti,* Vol. II (1948), pp. 5 ff., Pls. I–II. For the heads in Cleveland see M. Bieber in *Art in America,* Vol. XXXI (1943), p. 125, Figs. 14–15. For other examples see *ibid.,* Pls. V–XI. See also Dorothy B. Thompson in *A.J.A.,* LIV (1950), 380 ff.

hairdress is a head in Paris which indeed wears the attributes of Isis—the uraeus and the half moon over the forehead [5] (Fig. 330). Another example is a head of which we know several copies, the best ones being in Florence and in the Metropolitan Museum of Art in New York, with a very sophisticated arrangement of hairband, twisted locks, and snaillike knot in the back [6] (Fig. 331). A similar coiffure is found on a head on a gem in Boston.[7] Statues with similar heads and a similar turbanlike arrangement of the shawl are in Ince Blundell Hall in England and in Florence [8] (Figs. 332–33). The interpretation of these figures is uncertain. The opinion that Hermaphroditos is represented cannot be proved.

2. PORTRAITS

To the *sfumato* of Alexandrian art was often added stucco for rendering the upper and rear part of the hair. Stucco lends itself to the soft modeling preferred by the Alexandrian artists. A good example is the head of Alexander the Great from Alexandria, now in Cleveland [9] (Figs. 334–35). As the hair was painted, the difference of material was not

striking in ancient times. There are many small heads of Alexander which were probably attached to statuettes of stucco, soft limestone, or wood. They may have been votive offerings at the tomb of Alexander, the apotheosized founder of Alexandria.[10] The Ptolemies also were represented in this guise, beginning with Ptolemy I (see Figs. 302–3). Good examples are the heads, now in Boston, of Ptolemy IV (Ptolemy Philopator), who ruled 222–205, and his wife-sister Arsinoë III [11] (Figs. 336–39). The couple was associated in the cult of their parents, grandparents, and Alexander as the "Father-loving Gods" and a temple was erected for them in Alexandria. The cult statues, probably executed in gold and ivory, seem to have been imitated in these heads. Ptolemy IV has disagreeable and heavy features, as he does on his coins (Fig. 403). He was the murderer of his mother and the first of the degenerate and less significant Ptolemies, although he had been educated under the guidance of Eratosthenes, the librarian of the Museum. This diverted his interest from problems of war and government to those of literature and the arts. He built a temple to Homer and patronized poets, grammarians, and philosophers. On the relief of Archelaos of Priene (Figs. 404 and 497) he is depicted as Chronos, the god of time. In the Boston head his sensual lips were originally hidden by a beard attached to the face through eight holes. The face of Arsinoë shows sadness. She must have led an unhappy life indeed at the side of her dissipated husband. While the decay of the male line of the Ptolemies began with her husband, she and all the succeeding women of the Ptolemy dynasty preserved the old

[5] Adriani, *Documenti,* Vol. II, p. 22, Pl. XVI. W. Fröhner, *Notice de la sculpture antique du Louvre* (4th ed., Paris, 1878), No. 559.

[6] P. Arndt, *Griechische und römische Porträts* (Munich, F. Bruckmann, 1891–1942), Pls. 219–20. A. Hekler, *Bildniskunst der Griechen und Römer* (1912), Pl. 65a. M. Bieber in P. Arndt and W. Amelung, *Photographische Einzelaufnahmen antiker Skulpturen* (Munich, F. Bruckmann, 1893—), Nos. 4727–29. Adriani, *Documenti,* Vol. II, p. 19, Pl. XIV, 1. G. M. A. Richter, *Handbook of the Greek Collection* (the Metropolitan Museum of Art, 1953), p. 122, Pl. 100 c.

[7] A. Furtwängler, *Antike Gemmen* (1900), Vol. I, Pl. XXXII, Vol. II, p. 159, No. 31. Adriani, *Documenti,* Vol. II, p. 18, Pl. XV, 4. The gem and the head of the princess probably belong to the second century B.C. G. Macurdy in *Hellenistic Queens* (Baltimore, the Johns Hopkins Press, 1932), pp. 104 f., Fig. 4c, expresses the belief that Berenice I is represented. She could, instead, be Cleopatra III, called New Isis, wife of Ptolemy VII (Ptolemy Euergetes II).

[8] Adriani, *Documenti,* Vol. II, pp. 5 ff., Pl. XIII. B. Ashmole, *Catalogue of the Ancient Marbles at Ince Blundell Hall* (1929), p. 13, No. 24. W. Amelung in *Bollettino Comunale,* Vol. XXV (1897), pp. 119 ff., Figs. 6–7.

[9] K. Gebauer in H. Brunn and F. Bruckmann, *Denkmäler griechischer und römischer Skulptur* (Munich, 1888—), Pls. 1201–2. K. Gebauer in *Athen. Mitt.,* LXIII–LXIV (1938–39), p. 44, No. K23. M. Bieber in *Art in America,* Vol. XXXI (1943), pp. 121, 124, Fig. 13, and in *Proceedings of the American Philosophical Society,* Vol. XCIII, No. 5 (1949), p. 391, Figs. 47–48.

[10] Examples are in T. Schreiber, "Studien über das Bildnis Alexanders des Grossen," in *Abh. Sächs. Ges.,* Vol. XXI, Philol.-Hist. Kl., No. 3 (1903), pp. 41 ff., Figs. 6–8, Pls. III–IV; J. J. Bernoulli, *Die erhaltenen Darstellungen Alexanders des Grossen* (1905), pp. 34 ff., Figs. 5–8; C. Watzinger in E. Sieglin, *Expedition Ernst von Sieglin, Ausgrabungen in Alexandria* (Leipzig, 1908–27), Vol. II: *Die griechisch-ägyptische Sammlung Ernst von Sieglin,* Part IB (1927), pp. 1 ff., Nos. 1–3, Pls. I–VI. K. Gebauer in *Athen. Mitt.,* 63–64 (1938–39), pp. 33 ff., Pls. 6–14.

[11] L. D. Caskey, *Catalogue of Greek and Roman Sculpture* (Boston, Museum of Fine Arts, 1925), pp. 120 ff., Nos. 57–58. A. W. Lawrence in *Journal of Egyptian Archaeology,* Vol. XI (1925), pp. 179 ff., 187, Pl. XXIV. E. R. Bevan, *A History of Egypt under the Ptolemaic Dynasty* (London, 1927), p. 219, Fig. 39, and p. 237, Fig. 41.

Macedonian nobility and spirit. On the relief of Archelaos she is portrayed as Oikoumene, the personification of the inhabited world.

Ptolemy III (Ptolemy Euergetes), who ruled 246—222 b.c., the father of Ptolemy IV and son of Ptolemy II, was the worthy and warlike successor of his grandfather Ptolemy I. By marrying Berenice, the daughter of Magas, he added Cyrene to his kingdom of Egypt. He invaded northern Syria, conquered all Asia Minor and the countries on the Euphrates, and achieved a great military triumph. When he returned in 243 he brought with him images of gods and sacred objects which Cambyses had taken from Egypt to Persia. He therefore received the surname Euergetes, "the benefactor." He tried to attach the Egyptian priesthood to the interests of the Ptolemaic rulers by favoring Egyptian religious ideas, by building a temple to Osiris in Canopus, completing the temple of Isis at Philae, and beginning the large temple for the god Horus at Edfu. He and his wife Berenice were represented on the pylon of the temple at Karnak in Egyptian style.[12] Thus, Egyptian forms began to mingle with Greek forms in Alexandria. The luxurious and soft living of Ptolemy III later brought him the nickname Tryphon (glutton), but he certainly was always a sober and vigorous ruler who also furthered art and science.

The coins minted in the lifetime of Ptolemy III[13] (Fig. 340) show strong and manly features. The forehead is high and divided by a horizontal wrinkle. The nose is slightly curved. The lips are full and the chin is strong and broad. The cheeks are rounded and the neck is rather fat. The aegis indicates that he was considered the benefactor God, likened to Zeus, and venerated as such in his lifetime.

The bronze cast from the model of a silver medallion from Galjub, near Cairo, now in Hildes-

heim[14] (Fig. 341), identifies Ptolemy III with Heracles, for he here wears a lion skin over his left shoulder and carries a club in his left arm. It shows a front view of him with the same features as the coins. Both views agree, again, with the bust from Herculaneum, now in Naples, wrongly labeled Ptolemy II[15] (Figs. 342–43). The arrangement of the hair and the sharply drawn eyelids are the same as on the coins.

The features of the face in the colossal head carved in black Egyptian granite, now in Copenhagen,[16] are also similar, but the hair is changed to resemble the *anastole* (that is, the hair rising over the forehead like a lion's mane) of Alexander the Great. The head in Alexandria and its replica in Cyrene[17] have been identified as Ptolemy III with less grounds for certainty, on account of their soft character. Many other small heads go, rightly or wrongly, under his name.[18]

To these examples of a flourishing portraiture in Alexandria can be added the portraits of the queens Berenice II and Arsinoë III. The coins of Berenice II are indeed masterpieces[19] (Fig. 344). She ruled

[12] Bevan, *History of Egypt*, p. 215, Fig. 35.

[13] R. S. Poole, *British Museum Catalogue of Coins: The Ptolemies* (London, 1883), pp. 56 ff., Pl. XII, Figs. 2–5. J. N. Svoronos, *Die Münzen der Ptolemäer* (4 vols., 1904–8), Vol. III, Pl. XXX, Figs. 1–8, Pls. XXXVI, Figs. 1–9, Vol. IV, pp. 477 ff. B. V. Head, *Guide to the Principal Coins of the Greeks in the British Museum* (London, 1932), p. 60, Pl. 34, No. 24. E. Pfuhl in *Jahrbuch d. Inst.,* Vol. XLV (1930), pp. 32 f., Pl. III, 9–13. E. T. Newell, *Royal Greek Portrait Coins* (1937), pp. 87 f., Pl. XV, Figs. 6–8. C. Seltman, *Greek Coins* (1933), pp. 242 f., Pl. LVIII, 10.

[14] A. Ippel, *Der Bronzefund von Galjub* (Berlin, 1922; Pelizaeusmuseum, Hildesheim, *Wissenschaftliche Veröffentlichung,* Vol. II), pp. 64 f., No. 73, Pl. VII; see also O. Rubensohn, *Hellenistisches Silbergerät in antiken Gipsabgüssen* (1911), pp. 24 f., Nos. 12 and 13, Pl. X; M. Rostovtzeff, *The Social and Economic History of the Hellenistic World* (Oxford, 1941), Vol. II, p. 730, Pl. LXXXI, Fig. 1.

[15] Arndt, *Porträts*, Pls. 97–98. Hekler, *Bildniskunst*, Pl. 72a. E. Pfuhl in *Jahrbuch d. Inst.,* Vol. XLV (1930), pp. 30 f., Figs. 14–15. L. Laurenzi, *Ritratti greci* (Florence, Sansoni, 1941), p. 112, No. 56, Pl. XXI.

[16] P. Arndt, *La Glyptothèque Ny Carlsberg* (Munich, 1896–1912), Pl. 208. G. Dickins in *J.H.S.,* Vol. XXXIV (1914), pp. 297 ff., Fig. 4. E. Breccia, *Alexandrea ad Aegyptum* (1922), p. 180, Figs. 85–86. F. Poulsen, "Gab es eine Alexandrinische Kunst?" in *From the Collections of the Ny Carlsberg Glyptothek*, Vol. II (1938), pp. 21 ff., Figs. 22–23.

[17] Breccia, *Alexandrea*, p. 180, Figs. 85–86. Poulsen, *From the Collections of the Ny Carlsberg Glyptothek,* Vol. II, pp. 18 ff., Figs. 16–19. G. Guidi in *Africa Italiana*, Vol. III (1930), pp. 95 ff., Figs. 1–8. Rostovtzeff, *History of the Hellenistic World*, Vol. I, p. 28, Pl. IV, Fig. 2.

[18] Bevan, *History of Egypt*, p. 189, Fig. 28. Breccia, *Alexandrea,* p. 181, Fig. 87. E. Pfuhl in *Jahrbuch d. Inst.,* Vol. XLV (1930), pp. 32 ff., Figs. 18–24. Poulsen, *From the Collections of the Ny Carlsberg Glyptothek,* Vol. II, p. 21 f., Fig. 21.

[19] Imhoof-Blumer, *Porträtköpfe auf antiken Münzen hellenischer und hellenisierter Völker* (1895), p. 87, Pl. VIII, 7. Poole, *British Museum Catalogue of Coins: The Ptolemies*, p. 59, Pl. XIII, 2–6. Svoronos, *Münzen der Ptolemäer*, Vol. III, Pl. XXVIII, Figs. 3–26, Pl. XXIX, Figs. 1–11, Pl. XXXI, Figs. 1–2,

as queen of Cyrene from 258 to 247 B.C., married Ptolemy III in 247, and for a short time after his death in 222 ruled together with her son Ptolemy IV until she was murdered at his instigation. The gold decadrachm struck in Alexandria between 235 and 220 shows her lovely profile with its high forehead, straight nose, and full and protruding chin. Her cheeks and neck are rather full, and heavy flesh hangs under the chin. She wears the melon coiffure, with small locks hanging over her forehead at the end of the furrows between the twisted rolls of hair. A head found in Cyrene, now in the museum of Benghazi, has the same features and the same hairdress [20] (Figs. 346–47). The hair was probably gilded, for the red sizing is preserved. This agrees with the description of her blonde hair in Catullus's translation of *The Lock of Berenice,* by the court poet Callimachus of Cyrene. (This poem tells of a lock of her beautiful hair that Berenice had dedicated in a temple at Alexandria when her husband went to Syria. When it disappeared, the astronomer Konon discovered it as a constellation, Coma Berenices, in the sky.) The eyes also still show traces of color. The expression is serious. The head gives a good picture of the energetic and brave woman.

Another portrait of Berenice II may possibly be preserved in a head in the Museo Nuovo in Rome [21] (Figs. 348–49). The stiff Egyptian peruke and the skin of a falcon as a headdress certainly indicate that it is the portrait of a Ptolemaic queen, possibly identified with Isis, or of a priestess of Isis. The protruding lips, the rounded cheeks, and the fleshy chin are of the same shape as those on the coins (Fig. 344). The soft treatment of the face agrees with the other heads in late Praxitelean tradition.

The stylization of the hair is a traditional one in Egypt, having already begun in the Old Kingdom. It is found, for example, in the head on the statue of black granite in Munich, dated in the Ptolemaic period, while the head has been dated in the preceding Saitic period; to me it seems to have been made separately, but to belong to the statue [22] (Fig. 350). This figure may be a priestess of Isis, or Isis herself. In her hands she bears a sistrum and the Egyptian hieroglyphic meaning "life." The mantle is bound together in a knot between the breasts. This is a dress of Egyptian women which the Greek artists transferred to Isis. Head and statue thus show the influence of the venerable Egyptian art on Ptolemaic art. Statuettes in the Metropolitan Museum of Art with the horn of plenty in their arms certainly represent princesses; one is without an inscription, while the other bears the name of a Cleopatra. It is uncertain which one of the seven queens of this name is meant [23] (Figs. 351–53).

The gold octadrachms of Arsinoë III show the fine and noble features of this queen in soft and delicate lineaments [24] (Fig. 356). The forehead is vaulted, the nose is almost straight with a clearly defined tip, the lips are compressed, and the chin is very small. The hair is parted and in the back lifted over the diadem to a finely curved roll.

An excellent bronze bust in Mantua agrees with this coin portrait in all essential points [25] (Figs.

11–26. E. Pfuhl in *Jahrbuch d. Inst.,* Vol. XLV (1930), pp. 41 f., Pl. III, 18. Newell, *Royal Greek Portrait Coins,* pp. 86 f., Pl. XV, 4–5. Seltman, *Greek Coins,* pp. 242 f., Pl. LVIII, 8–9. K. Lange, *Herrscherköpfe des Altertums im Münzbild ihrer Zeit* (1938), pp. 60 f.

[20] C. Anti in *Africa Italiana,* Vol. I (1927), pp. 164 ff., Vol. II (1928–29), p. 218, Fig. 2. C. Anti in *Die Antike,* Vol. V (1929), pp. 6 ff., Figs. 1–3, Pls. 2–5. W. Schubart in *Die Antike,* Vol. XIII (1937), pp. 277 f., Fig. 3. Laurenzi, *Ritratti greci,* p. 119, No. 71, Pls. XXV–XXVI. M. Rostovtzeff, *History of the Hellenistic World,* Vol. I, p. 40, Pl. VI, Fig. 2.

[21] W. Amelung in *Bollettino Comunale,* Vol. XXV (1897), pp. 118 ff., Pl. VIII. R. Delbrück, *Antike Porträts* (1912), pp. XLI f., Pl. 28. D. Mustilli, *Il Museo Mussolini* (1939), pp. 73 f., No. 16, Pl. XLVI, 184–85.

[22] A. Furtwängler and P. Wolters, *Beschreibung der Glyptothek zu München* (2d ed., 1910), pp. 32 f., No. 29. For the dress see Joseph Vogt in Sieglin, *Expedition Ernst von Sieglin,* Vol. II, Part 2: *Terrakotten* (1924), pp. 4 ff. W. Weber, *Mitteilungen aus der ägyptischen Sammlung der Museen Berlin,* Vol. II (1914): *Die ägyptisch-griechischen Terrakotten, pp.* 33 ff. These terra cottas prove that this Isis type was created in Alexandria.

[23] Metropolitan Museum of Art, No. 20.2.21. Nora F. Scott, *Egyptian Statuettes* (1946), p. 34, No. 36, tentatively identifies the other statuette as Arsinoë II.

[24] Imhoof-Blumer, *Porträtköpfe,* p. 87, Pl. VIII, Fig. 10. Poole, *British Museum Catalogue of Coins: The Ptolemies,* p. LIII, p. 67, Pl. 15, 6–7. Svoronos, *Münzen der Ptolemäer,* Vol. III, Pl. XXXIX, Figs. 1–15, Pl. XLII, Fig. 1, Vol. IV, pp. 216 ff. and 267; Delbrück, *Porträts,* p. LXIV, Pl. 61, No. 14. E. Pfuhl in *Jahrbuch d. Inst.,* Vol. XLV (1930), pp. 38 ff., Pl. III, 20. Seltman, *Greek Coins,* p. 243, Pl. LIX, Fig. 3.

[25] For the head of Arsinoë III and related Alexandrian heads, see Alda Levi in *Bolletino d'Arte,* Series II, No. 6, Vol. I (1926–27), pp. 548 ff., one plate, and Figs. 1–4. A. Levi, *Sculture nel Palazzo Ducale di Mantova* (Rome, 1931), p. 41, No. 64, Pls. XLIV–XLV. E. Pfuhl in *Jahrbuch d. Inst.,*

354–55). It adds to our knowledge of Arsinoë's appearance the broadness of the forehead and the serious expression. It is an excellent likeness of the noble and energetic woman who "endured insults and outrages inflicted on her during her whole life" (Polybius xv. 25). The superiority of her character over that of Ptolemy IV is quite marked in this portrait.

Statues of Berenice II as well as of Arsinoë III were set up in the temples of Alexandria and elsewhere. Thus Ptolemy V (Ptolemy Epiphanes) erected a temple in Alexandria in honor of his mother, Arsinoë III, which was cared for by a special priest. A statue of Berenice II was compared by Callimachus to one of the graces (*Anthologia Palatina* v. 146). We have only weak reflections of these statues on faience vases, which are identified by the names of the queens' husbands. Thus Berenice may be seen on a vase in the Bibliothèque nationale in Paris, inscribed "Ptolemy Euergetes"[26] (Fig. 345), and Arsinoë on a vase of greenish-blue faience from Alexandria, now in Stuttgart, inscribed "King Ptolemy Philopator"[27] (Figs. 357–59). Both queens carry cornucopias in their arms as benefactor gods and are pouring offerings from sacrificial bowls in their right hands. Berenice is very slender; Arsinoë is broader and shorter and her movement is stronger. Each is clad in a long chiton and a himation, which surround the figures with heavy and angular folds. The garment of Arsinoë spreads out at the bottom in a style which began in the middle Hellenistic period. Characteristic of this period is the arrangement of geometric figures, triangles, pentagons, and rhomboids as it appears in the drapery of the two queens.

Portraiture continued to flourish in Alexandria, as in other Hellenistic centers, until the middle of the second century B.C. The best example is a head in Alexandria of Ptolemy VI (Ptolemy Philometor), who ruled 181–145, carved in Pentelic mar-

ble[28] (Figs. 361–63). It has been identified by comparison with silver tetradrachms minted in about 148–146 at Ake (the Accho [Judges 1:31] or Ptolemais [Acts 21:7] of the Bible) in Coele-Syria, copies of which are in the Hague and in the Cabinet des Médailles of the Bibliothèque nationale in Paris[29] (Fig. 360). These were issued after Ptolemy VI had defeated Alexander Balas, had entered Antioch as victor, and was crowned with the diadem of Syria. The coins exhibit the remarkable features of the king, whom Polybius (xxxix. 7) describes as gentler and better than any previous king. His mind, however, in seasons of good fortune grew relaxed and weakened; and he suffered from a sort of Egyptian waste of energy and indolence. The portraits reflect this mixture of vigor, strength, benevolence, and moral weakness. The features express nervous energy through the strong lines at the corners of the mouth. The eyes look haughty and intense, but without firmness of purpose. The modeling of the flesh is fluent and soft. The head was probably broken from a statue marked by a strong movement in imitation of portraits of Alexander, for the neck is stretched to the right and the head is turned to the left side of the figure. The technique is the one so often used in Alexandria—that is, stucco was used to finish the hair at the upper and back part of the head. This portrait, on account of its exact date—around the middle of the second century—is an important cornerstone of the history of Hellenistic sculpture.

Two portraits on gems in the Louvre agree in their main features with the coins and the portrait head in Alexandria, and have therefore been identified as Ptolemy VI.[30] One represents Ptolemy VI as a Greek king with a diadem like the one he received at Antioch; he is wearing the Macedonian

Vol. XLV (1930), Fig. 25. A. Adriani in *Arti Figurative*, Vol. III (1947), pp. 51 ff., Pls. XXV–XXX.

[26] R. Horn, *Stehende weibliche Gewandstatuen in der hellenistischen Plastik* (1931; *Ergänzungsheft* II to *Röm Mitt.*), pp. 36 ff., Pl. 10, Fig. 1. Rostovtzeff, *History of the Hellenistic World*, Vol. I, p. 270, Pl. XXXVI, p. 368, Pl. XLI, Fig. 2.

[27] Horn, *Gewandstatuen*, Pl. 10, Fig. 2. R. Pagenstecher in Sieglin, *Expedition Ernst von Sieglin*, Vol. II, Part 3, pp. 207 f., Pls. XXXI–XXXII.

[28] A. Adriani in *Bulletin de la Société royale d'Archéologie, Alexandrie*, New Series, Vol. X, 1, No. 32 (1938), pp. 97 ff., Fig. 11, Pls. X–XII. Rostovtzeff, *History of the Hellenistic World*, Vol. I, p. 66, Pl. X, Fig. 2.

[29] Imhoof-Blumer, *Porträtköpfe*, p. 88, Pl. VIII, 13. Svoronos, *Münzen der Ptolemäer*, Vol. III, p. XLVIII, Figs. 19–20. Poole, *British Museum Catalogue of Coins: The Ptolemies*, p. LXV, Pl. XXXII, No. 8. B. V. Head, *Historia Numorum* (2d ed., Oxford, 1911), pp. 856 f. Adriani, in *Bulletin de la Société royale d'Archéologie, Alexandrie*, New Series, XI, No. 32 (1938), p. 97, Fig. 10.

[30] A. Furtwängler, *Antike Gemmen* (Leipzig, 1900), Vol. III, Pl. XXX, 35–36. G. Lippold, *Gemmen und Kameen* (Stuttgart, 1922), Pl. LXX, Figs. 2 and 5. G. Blum in *B.C.H.*, Vol. XXXIX (1915), pp. 23 ff., Pl. I, Figs. 4–5.

chlamys to indicate his ancestry. The other shows him as Pharaoh, crowned with the Egyptian double crown and two diadems for upper and lower Egypt. Here he wears an Egyptian decorated collar, and it is interesting to see that in this gem the chest appears in front view as in all Egyptian art since the Old Kingdom, while on the other it appears in perspective seen from the side, as in all Greek representations since the classical period.

A seal from a papyrus dated 181 B.C., the year in which Ptolemy VI began his reign, has a similar sensitive and intelligent face, big eyes, and a long nose.[31] It is supposed to represent Lysimachos, the writer of the letter.

Representations of Ptolemy VI with the accessories of a Pharaoh are attested in literature and also by a bust, now in Athens, inscribed with the name of Ptolemy VI in Egyptian hieroglyphics.[32] This portrait was found in the sea near Aegina and perhaps came from the temple of Isis at Methana in the Argolis, to the north of Troezen, opposite the island of Aegina. It has the Pharaonic headdress and crown. Although executed in severe Egyptian style, it has the same high and broad forehead, shape of eyebrows, heavy eyelids, powerful jaws, and energetic chin as the head in Alexandria. This makes it possible to identify another head as a portrait of Ptolemy VI carved in granite. It was found in Abukir and is now in Alexandria.[33] Though more conventionalized than the head in Athens, it is similar in the irregular arrangement of the hair, the elongated cheeks, and the puckered lips.

It is rare for portraits in the Egyptian style of this period to have so much individuality. A relief showing the figure of Ptolemy VI with his brother and sister, in the beautiful small temple at Der-el-Medineh on the Nile opposite Luxor, is fully stylized.[34] The portrait value of these conventionalized

Egyptian reliefs is slight. There is hardly any difference, for example, between the portrait of Ptolemy VI and that of his wicked brother Ptolemy VII (Ptolemy Euergetes II) on reliefs at Kom Ombo,[35] or between the portraits of these late Ptolemies and that of Ptolemy II on the relief in a temple of Isis built by him at Philae[36] (Fig. 370). The mixture of Greek and Egyptian elements did not produce satisfactory results.[37]

During the first century B.C., Greek art had degenerated in Alexandria. Even portraiture did not produce such excellent examples in this period as we have from other parts of the Greek world. The last ruler of Ptolemaic Egypt, the fascinating Cleopatra VII (51—30 B.C.), has not had an adequate representation. The best coins, a bronze in Alexandria (Fig. 364) and a silver coin of Ascalon dated 38/7 B.C.[38] (Fig. 365), show an interesting profile, with a high forehead and the long nose inherited from her father Ptolemy XI (Ptolemy Auletes) and other ancestors (see Fig. 360). She has large and deeply sunken eyes, a lively mouth, and a small but energetic chin. The melon-like arrangement of the hair is the same as that of early Ptolemaic queens (see Figs. 344, 346–47). The fine parallel curves of the hair are interrupted by the exceptionally broad diadem. The ends of the hair are bound in a rounded knob which hangs free from the nape of the neck. The fascination of Cleopatra must have lain particularly in her conversation, since the irresistible attractiveness that must have been hers when she enchanted Caesar and Marc Antony does not appear very clearly in her portraits. Unfortunately none of the statues set up

[31] W. L. Westermann, C. W. Keyes, and H. Liebesny, Zenon Papyri, Vol. II (New York, Columbia University Press, 1940), pp. 192 f., No. 122.
[32] J. Six in Athen. Mitt., Vol. XII (1887), pp. 212 ff., Pls. VII–VIII. A. Adriani in Bulletin de la Société royale D'Archéologie, Alexandrie, New Series, Vol. X, 1, No. 32 (1938), pp. 100 ff., Fig. 12. Bevan, History of Egypt, p. 303, Fig. 50.
[33] A. Adriani in Bulletin de la Société royale d'Archéologie, Alexandrie, New Series, Vol. X, 1, No. 32 (1938), pp. 101 ff., Figs. 13–14.
[34] Bevan, History of Egypt, p. 289, Fig. 49.

[35] Ibid., pp. 231 f., Figs. 53–54. G. R. Lepsius, Denkmäler aus Aegypten (1849–56), Vol. IV, pp. 101 ff. (text by E. Naville and K. Sethe).
[36] Bevan, History of Egypt, p. 186. Lepsius, Denkmäler, Vol. IV, p. 168.
[37] On this mixture see I. Noshy, The Arts in Ptolemaic Egypt: A Study of Greek and Egyptian Influences in Ptolemaic Architecture and Sculpture (1937).
[38] Imhoof-Blumer, Porträtköpfe, pp. 63 and 88, Pl. VIII, Figs. 14–15. Poole, British Museum Catalogue of Coins: The Ptolemies, pp. 122 f., Pl. XXX, Figs. 5–8, Pl. XXXI, Figs. 6–7. Svoronos, Münzen der Ptolemäer, Vol. III, Pl. LXIII, Vol. IV, pp. 371 ff., Pl. delta, 22 f. Head, Historia Numorum, p. 804a, Fig. 354, and p. 859. Head, Principal Coins of the Greeks, p. 81, Pl. 45, Fig. 20. Seltman, Greek Coins, pp. 244 f., Pl. LIX, Figs. 7–8. Our Fig. 364 is a bronze coin in the Museum of Fine Arts, Boston. Our Fig. 365, dated 38/7, is a silver tetradrachm in a private collection at Alexandria. I owe the photographs to Agnes B. Brett.

in her honor, not only in Egypt but elsewhere—for example the golden image which Caesar erected in the temple of Venus Genetrix in his new forum and the colossal statue erected along with one of Marc Antony on the Acropolis of Athens—are preserved.

Among the heads called portraits of Cleopatra the best is the one in the Vatican [39] (Figs. 366–67), with the same hair arrangement and unusually broad diadem as the coins. The nose has been restored, and the surface of the head is corroded. Thus little concrete evidence remains of the seductive beauty and grace with the queen must have possessed, judging from her successes and the evidence of literary sources. Something of her cleverness and energy, however, is discernible in the strong features.

The forms of the face and the melon coiffure seen on a head in the British Museum [40] (Figs. 368–69) agree with those on the coins and with those of the head in the Vatican. The nose also agrees with the coins. Unfortunately, however, the diadem is missing, and the arrangement of her hair in the back is different. Consequently the identification has been doubted. Otherwise we might have a more adequate picture of the great woman than we have in the authenticated heads.

A relief in the temple at Dendera depicts Cleopatra in Egyptianized style as the goddess Hathor. The relief retains the characteristic form of Cleopatra's nose, but otherwise it is without iconographic value [41] (Fig. 371).

Thus the Ptolemaic rulers adapted themselves much more to the ancient civilization which they found in their kingdom than did any other Hellenistic rulers. While the kings of Syria, Pergamon, and Bithynia tried to bring Hellenistic civilization to their subjects, the Ptolemies adopted the dress and crowns of the Pharaohs and allowed themselves to be represented as the earlier rulers of Egypt had been. When they restored or added to old temples, or built new ones, they used the forms and decorations that had been used in Egypt for several thousand years.

3. SUBJECTS OF DAILY LIFE

One has the impression that the Greek artists in Egypt were so awed by its monumental architecture and sculpture that they did not try to rival it. They rather turned to the daily life in the streets of cosmopolitan Alexandria. Sharp observation of the many races found in the streets of Alexandria resulted in many interesting works. Thus, because there were Gauls among the mercenaries of the Ptolemaic armies, we have a small head of a Gaul in Cleveland, and the celebrated head from Gizeh [42] (Figs. 372–73). These are quite different in character from the Pergamene Gauls.

A characteristic side of Alexandrian art is genre, which by its nature lends itself better to small than to monumental size. The grace of women and children attracted the artisans who worked small figures in bronze, marble, stucco, and, above all, in terra cotta. In the early Hellenistic period the young women wrapped in their mantles, with their hands lifting them slightly from the inside, portrayed in slow and elegant movements, look like imported Tanagra figurines [43] (Fig. 375). It is quite possible that not only molds, but also potters, were brought to Alexandria from Greece. The artisans liked to model in soft clay, or they chose the still softer stucco, materials very adequate to their style, for statues and heads of young girls, boys, and children. A little girl seated on the

[39] Lippold, *Vatican Kat.,* Vol. III, pp. 170 f., Sala a Croce Graeca No. 567, Pl. 62. The identification is due to Ludwig Curtius, in *Röm Mitt.,* Vol. XLVIII (1933), pp. 182 ff., Figs. 1–3, Pls. 25–27.

[40] A. H. Smith, *Brit. Mus. Cat.,* Vol. II, No. 1873, Pl. XXI. R. P. Hinks, *Greek and Roman Portrait Sculpture in the British Museum* (London, 1935), pp. 15 f., Pl. 18a. F. Poulsen, "Gab es eine Alexandrinische Kunst?" in *From the Collections of the Ny Carlsberg Glyptothek,* Vol. II (1938), pp. 28 f., Fig. 29. R. West, *Römische Porträtplastik,* Vol. I (Munich, 1933), p. 104, Pl. XXV, Fig. 102. P. Graindor, *Bustes et statues-portraits d'Égypte romain* (Cairo, 1939), pp. 39 f., Pl. 72, Figs. 2–3.

[41] Bevan, *History of Egypt under the Ptolemaic Dynasty,* p. 367, Fig. 62. Lepsius, *Denkmäler,* Vol. IV, Pls. 53 f.; text Vol. II, p. 185.

[42] T. Schreiber, *Der Gallierkopf des Museums in Gizeh bei Kairo* (1906); C. C. Edgar, *Greek Sculpture* (Cairo, 1903; Vol. IV of *Catalogue général des antiquités égyptiennes du Musée du Caire*), p. 20, No. 27475, Pl. X. Adriani, *Documenti,* Vol. II, pp. 31 ff., Pls. XVIII–XIX. For general discussions of Gauls in Alexandrian art, see A. J. Reinach, "Les Galates dans l'art alexandrine," in *Mon. Piot,* XVIII (1910), pp. 67 ff., Pls. VII–IX. P. Perdrizet, *Les terres cuites d'Égypte de la Collection Fouquet* (Paris, 1921), pp. 141 ff., Pls. XCII–XCIV. For our Fig. 437, in Cleveland, see M. Bieber in *Art in America,* Vol. XXXI (1943), p. 122, Fig. 17.

[43] J. Vogt in Sieglin, *Expedition Ernst von Sieglin,* Vol. II, Part 2: *Terrakotten,* pp. 63 f. and 129 f., Pls. XLV–XLVII. Our Fig. 375 is taken from his Pl. XLVI.

ground with a big garland in her hand is a good example [44] (Fig. 374).

In the third century an industry in small figures and reliefs of bronze, marble, terra cotta, and stucco had already developed. These works represented all kinds of street and low-class types. The most outstanding example is the bronze dancer in the Baker collection in New York; the figure probably represents a mime dancer of the third century B.C.[45] (Figs. 378-79). An actor of the popular New Comedy is the striking bronze figure in the Art Museum of Princeton University [46] (Figs. 382-83). Musicians, athletes (see Figs. 643-44), acrobats, and Negroes were portrayed in a great number of unambitious works of minor artists. Humor and mockery developed as a supplement to scholarship, and led to excellent representations of the lower-class characters observed in the streets. Among them were many Negroes and Ethiopians from the south of Egypt. One of the finest examples is the bronze statuette of a street boy in the Cabinet des Médailles in Paris [47] (Fig. 381). He was probably an Ethiopian, for Ptolemy II had again added Ethiopia on the upper Nile to Egypt. He stands in a lax position, his instrument (now lost), probably a *sambyke,* in his meager arms, his head bent backward and to his right, his face wearing a doleful expression. His meager body tells of a hard life of poverty. Other Negroes were represented running, like one in the Metropolitan Museum of Art in New York [48] (Fig. 380), or making love, or seated on the ground, lazy and sleepy.[49] Several times the upper part of a Negro slave was made into a bottle [50] (Fig. 384).

From central Africa came the pygmies. They had been known to the Greeks since the archaic period. Their battles with cranes were represented on the François vase and other black-figured vases of the sixth century B.C. They again came to the attention of the Hellenistic artists, who modeled the little men not only in their comic fight, but also in other situations.[51]

Grotesque individuals, particularly dwarfs, were used for public and private entertainment. Hunchbacks, even in the old Egyptian times, were considered to bring good luck. Dancing at religious festivals and at private banquets seems often to have been entrusted to such misshapen persons. A marble statuette of a hunchback from the Carnarvon collection, now in the Metropolitan Museum of Art in New York, seems to be dancing [52] (Fig. 376). A terra-cotta figurine in the same museum shows a dwarf with a heavy head, small pointed beard, bald pate, and mighty hunched

[44] For early Hellenistic heads of women see C. Watzinger in Sieglin, *Expedition Ernst von Sieglin*, Vol. II, Part 1 B, pp. 42 ff., Nos. 21-31, Pls. IV, XIX-XXV. M. Bieber in *Jahrbuch d. Inst.*, XXXVIII-XXXIX (1923-24), pp. 255 ff. For the heads of young men and women in stucco see R. Pagenstecher in *Expedition Sieglin*, Vol. II, Part 1 A, pp. 90 ff., Pls. XXXIX-XLIV. C. Watzinger in *Expedition Sieglin*, Vol. II, Part 1 B, p. 3, Fig. 1, and p. 31, Fig. 4. For the heads of children see Watzinger in *Expedition Sieglin*, Vol. II, Part I B, pp. 40 f., Nos. 18-19, and p. 129, No. 119, Pls. XVII-XVIII. For children in terra cotta see Weber, *Mitteilungen der Museen Berlin, Terrakotten*, pp. 224 ff., Nos. 392-99, Pl. 36. Our Fig. 374 is a statuette from Egypt, in the Louvre. J. Charbonneaux, *Les Terres cuites grecques* (1936), Pl. 65, Fig. 71.

[45] Dorothy B. Thompson in *A.J.A.*, Vol. LIV (1950), pp. 371 ff., Fig. 1-3, 11, 14.

[46] M. Bieber in *Record of the Art Museum, Princeton University*, Vol. IX, No. 2 (1950), pp. 5 ff., Figs. 1-2.

[47] E. Babelon and J.-A. Blanchet, *Catalogue des bronzes antiques de la Bibliothèque nationale* (Paris, 1895), No. 1009. G. Rodenwaldt, *Die Kunst der Antike* (Berlin, 1927; Propyläen-Kunstgeschichte III), p. 491. G. Richter, *The Sculpture and Sculptors of the Greeks* (rev. ed., New Haven, Yale University Press, 1950), p. 60, Figs. 58-60. J. Babelon, *Choix des bronzes de la Collection Caylus* (Paris and Brussels, 1928), pp. 55 f., No. 42, Pls. XXIII-XXIV.

[48] Metropolitan Museum of Art, New York, No. 18.145.10. G. A. Richter, *Handbook of the Classical Collection* (New York, Metropolitan Museum of Art, 1930), pp. 197 f., Fig. 136, and *Handbook* (1953), p. 125, Pl. 104 f.; *M.M.A. Bulletin*, Vol. XV (1920), p. 109, and Vol. XVI (1921), pp. 33 ff., Fig. 3. G. H. Beardsley, *The Negro in Greek and Roman Civilization* (1929), pp. 96 f., Fig. 19.

[49] C. C. Edgar, *Greek Moulds* (Cairo, 1903; Vol. VI of *Catalogue général des antiquités égyptiennes du Musée du Caire*), p. 24, No. 32085, Pl. VI; see Weber, *Mitteilungen der Museen Berlin, Terrakotten*, p. 229, Figs. 112-13, for Negroes—a man and a woman embracing on the relief of a drinking bottle. See also Perdrizet, *Terres cuites*, pp. 139 f., Pl. XCVII, for Negroes seated on the ground.

[50] M. Bieber in *Record of the Art Museum, Princeton University*, IX (1950), pp. 8 f., Fig. 3. Perdrizet, *Terres cuites*, p. 140, Pl. XCVI, No. 371. P. Goessler in *Antike Plastik, Amelung zum Geburtstag* (1928), pp. 80 f., Figs. 5-6.

[51] Edgar, *Greek Moulds*, p. 23, No. 32082, Pl. XXIV, and *Greek Bronzes* (Cairo, 1904; Vol. V of *Catalogue général des antiquités égyptiennes du Musée du Caire*), pp. 19 f., Nos. 27704-6, Pl. V. Weber, *Mitteilungen der Museen Berlin, Terrakotten*, p. 228, No. 402, Pl. 36 (lamp handle with pygmies fighting a crane). See also Perdrizet, *Terres cuites*, pp. 133 ff., Pls. XCVIII, CIV, CVIII.

[52] Metropolitan Museum of Art, No. 26.7.1403.

back, squatting on the ground.[53] (Fig. 377). The marble statuette of a *lantanarius,* a slave boy waiting with a lantern for his master, in the Egyptian department of the Metropolitan Museum of Art, may also represent a dwarf (Fig. 548).

Caricatures were popular in other parts of the Hellenistic world, but hardly anywhere were there executed such exaggerations, such figures with one-sided emphasis on abstruse and distorted forms, as in Alexandria[54] (Fig. 385). The idiot, with his backward-slanting forehead and his whistling mouth, and the dangerous-looking old woman with her thick lips, enormous nose, and severe glance of the eyes, in ridiculous contrast to her elegant hairdress, are little masterpieces of popular art. Such high hairdresses were frequently worn by lower-class women, often too fat or too lean, carrying thick wreaths, or baskets on their heads.[55] The so-called death brides, figures of concubines given as companions to dead men, have still more exaggeratedly high headdresses with wreaths and ornaments[56] (Fig. 386).

The coarse figures of women dancers with tambourines probably represent religious dancers, for in one case such a woman appears near an altar with the household god Bes dancing behind her.[57] I therefore believe that the female dwarfs found in the sunken ship near Mahdia, Tunisia, and now in the Musée du Bardo in Tunis, are such dancers used for banquets.[58] The big heads testify that they were dwarfs.

4. GODS

It is probable that his grotesque appearance made the Egyptian god Bes a favorite in Ptolemaic Egypt.[59] The gay humor of the Greeks gave him a wife, Besa or Beset[60] (Fig. 387). Her short squat body, puffy cheeks, staring eyes, protruding tongue, long hair, and feather crown above a thick wreath, which sometimes had been enriched with a shrine for the sacred bull Apis, matches not only her husband but also other grotesque figures of fat women, who seem to have been used as *apotropeia.*[61]

Of the other Egyptian gods, Isis (Figs. 330 and 350) and her little son Horus-Harpokrates (Fig. 392) became very popular.[62] Both Isis and Horus show Greek features combined with Egyptian dress and hairdress. Isis wears a tightly fitting dress with a knot between the breasts like that of Egyptian women, but the modeling of the body is in the Greek style. Harpokrates is a little Greek boy, usually shown seated on the ground with his finger in his mouth. Often he is nourished by his mother. Sometimes it is not possible to say whether Isis, a priestess, or some other mortal woman is represented, and whether the boy is Harpokrates or a mortal. The Ptolemaic princesses were venerated as Isis, and Cleopatra at her feasts with Marc Antony was dressed as Isis.

[53] Metropolitan Museum of Art, No. 17.230.50.

[54] Edgar, *Greek Bronzes,* Pl. V. Vogt, in Sieglin, *Expedition Ernst von Sieglin,* Vol. II, Part 2, pp. 55 and 138 ff., Pls. LIV–LX. Our Fig. 385 is his Pl. LIX; cf. his p. 146. See also A. Ippel, Bronzen von Galjub (Pelizaeusmuseum, Hildesheim, 1922), pp. 45 ff., Pl. IV, 30–35. For such grotesque types in general see R. Zahn in *Winck.-Prog. Berlin,* No. 81 (1923), pp. 9 f.

[55] Weber, *Mitteilungen der Museen Berlin, Terrakotten,* pp. 206 ff., Pls. 33–34. For high headdresses see *ibid.,* pp. 215 ff., Pls. 34–35, and Perdrizet, *Terres cuites,* Pls. VIII–IX.

[56] Vogt, in Sieglin, *Expedition Ernst von Sieglin,* Vol. II, Part 2, pp. 47 f. and 181 ff., Pls. XCI–XCVI (our Fig. 385 is equivalent to his Pl. XCV). Weber, *Mitteilungen der Museen Berlin, Terrakotten,* pp. 130 ff., Pls. 20–22. Perdrizet, *Terres cuites,* pp. 1 ff., Pls. II–V. Weber and Perdrizet believe these grotesque figures to be goddesses, not concubines.

[57] Weber, *Mitteilungen der Museen Berlin, Terrakotten,* pp. 153 ff., Pl. 24, Nos. 240–49. His Pl. 24, No. 249 is the relief with Bes and the dancer.

[58] A. Merlin in *Mon. Piot,* Vol XVIII (1910), pp. 5 ff., 9 ff., Pls. II–IV.

[59] Edgar, *Greek Moulds,* p. 21, Nos. 32074–76, Pls. IX, XXV. Weber, *Mitteilungen der Museen Berlin, Terrakotten,* pp. 158 ff., Nos. 250–64. Vogt, in Sieglin, *Expedition Ernst von Sieglin,* Vol. II, Part 2, *Terrakotten,* pp. 15 ff., 106 ff., Pls. XXI–XXIII. Perdrizet, *Terres cuites,* pp. 41 ff., Pls. XXXIX–XLII.

[60] Edgar, *Greek Moulds,* p. 22, No. 32077, Pl. XXV. Vogt, in *Expedition Ernst von Sieglin,* Vol. II, Part 2, *Terrakotten,* pp. 17 f., 109, Fig. 23, Pls. XXIV–XXV (our Fig. 387 corresponds to his Pl. XXIV). See also Perdrizet, *Terres cuites,* Pl. XLIII.

[61] For example, Edgar, *Greek Moulds,* p. 22, No. 32097, Pl. XXV. Weber, *Mitteilungen der Museen Berlin, Terrakotten,* pp. 165 ff., Nos. 271–79, Pl. 26.

[62] For Isis see C.C. Edgar, *Greek Sculpture* (Cairo, 1903; Vol. IV of *Catalogue général des antiquités égyptiennes du Musée du Caire*), pp. 18 f., Nos. 27470–73, Pl. IX, and *Greek Bronzes,* pp. 10 ff., Nos. 27669–79, Pl. IV, and *Greek Moulds,* pp. 14 ff., Nos. 32048–51, Pls. XXII and XXIV. Weber, *Mitteilungen der Museen Berlin, Terrakotten,* pp. 33 ff., Nos. 17–38, Pls. II–III. Vogt, in *Expedition Ernst von Sieglin,* Vol. II, Part 2, *Terrakotten,* pp. 4 ff., 89 ff., Pls. VII–VIII. For Harpokrates see Edgar, *Greek Bronzes,* pp. 13 f., Nos. 27680–88, Pl. III, and *Greek Moulds,* pp. 18 ff., Nos. 32061–70, Pls. XXIII–XXIV. Weber, *Mitteilungen der Museen Berlin, Terrakotten,* pp. 52 ff., Nos. 39–150, Pls. 4–14. Vogt, in Sieglin, *Expedition Ernst von Sieglin,* Vol. II, Part 2, pp. 8 ff., 95 ff., Pls. XI–XV. Perdrizet, *Terres cuites,* pp. 27 ff., Pls. XXI–XXXIV.

Osiris, the husband of Isis and father of the boy, disappeared from art during the Ptolemaic period. He was supplanted by Serapis (see Figs. 296–97). The many copies of the standing Serapis, as well as the seated figure, are the better and more Greek in character the earlier they are in date; the later copies of the statue, as well as of the head, are coarser and duller[63] (Fig. 388). As Osiris was merged with Pluto to become Serapis, Isis was gradually assimilated with Aphrodite, and Harpokrates with Eros, in cult worship and in figurines.[64]

There does not seem to have been any new monumental creation for a Greek god in Alexandria. The Greek gods were indeed treated with little respect. The best proof of the existence of this disdainful and skeptical attitude is the group of Ares and Aphrodite chained to their couch by Hephaistos, the outraged husband of Aphrodite[65] (Fig. 389). The story is very old and had already been represented in the sixth century B.C. Ares wanted Aphrodite, but Hephaistos got her. The adultery which followed the hated marriage is here represented for the first time and in a Hellenistic-Alexandrian spirit. With his right hand, Ares lifts his large sword, still in the scabbard, but is not able to draw it because his arm is fettered. Thus he is depicted in helpless rage, with his left arm around Aphrodite, who is clinging to him in fear and affection.

Aphrodite, then, is here a weak woman, needing the protection of the male, like a mortal woman. Next to those of Isis, her attributes were most frequently used in the representation of mortal women. For example, Arsinoë II was venerated as Aphrodite. The main cult statue seems to have been an Aphrodite binding up her hair. As such she appears in many marble statuettes, bronzes, and terra cottas, and in molds which were used for bronzes or terra cottas and thus testify to the local fabrication of these statuettes.[66] Some of these small figurines are still fine and delicate, like the Aphrodite with Triton in Dresden, found in Alexandria,[67] but others degenerated in the late Hellenistic period, like the statuette in the traditional Egyptian blue glazed faience in the Brooklyn Museum[68] (Fig. 390). In this, as in others, the preceding bath in the sea, rather than the rising from the sea, is indicated by a dolphin, as it is in the Medici Aphrodite (Fig. 30), or by a Triton, as in the Dresden statuette. Some earlier marble heads of Aphrodite have the *sfumato* of the better creations of Alexandrian art[69] (Fig. 393). I believe that this type of head belongs to the Aphrodite from Cyrene, which has the pictorial, sensual, and illusionistic quality of Alexandrian art[70] (Figs. 396–97). A similar cult statue may underlie the creations of the minor artisans.

There are many variations of the main type, in which both arms are lifted, the right arm higher than the left (Fig. 390 and Fig. 391, right). Sometimes the arms are lifted to fasten a *strophion*, the broad bandage used as a brassiere, over the

---

[63] Edgar, *Greek Sculpture*, pp. 4 f., Nos. 27432–37, Pl. II. Watzinger, in Sieglin, *Expedition Ernst von Sieglin*, Vol. II, Part 1 B, pp. 62 ff., Nos. 47–53, Pls. XXIX–XXXI. Vogt, in *Expedition Sieglin*, Vol. II, Part 2, pp. 3 f., 85 f., Pls. III–IV. For Serapis see also W. Amelung in *Rev. Arch.* (1903), Part II, pp. 177 ff.; G. Lippold in *Festschrift für Paul Arndt* (1925), pp. 115 ff. See our p. 83, note 45.

[64] For Aphrodite with the headdress of Isis see Edgar, *Greek Bronzes*, pp. 6 f., Nos. 27652–54, Pl. II. For Harpokrates with the wings of Eros see *ibid.*, pp. 15 f., Nos. 27689–91, Pl. III.

[65] Vogt, in Sieglin, *Expedition Ernst von Sieglin*, Vol. II, Part 2, pp. 22 and 122, Pl. XXVIII. Vogt doubts that the group is ancient, but neither Schreiber nor Pagenstecher had any doubt about it.

[66] Edgar, *Greek Sculpture*, pp. 11 f., Nos. 27454, Pl. VI, and *Greek Bronzes*, pp. 5 f., Nos. 27647–49, Pl. III, and *Greek Moulds*, pp. 2 f., Nos. 32004–9, Pls. I, XXIV. Weber, *Mitteilungen der Museen Berlin, Terrakotten*, pp. 122 ff., Nos. 179–80, Pl. 18. Pagenstecher, in Sieglin, *Expedition Ernst von Sieglin*, Vol. II, Part 1 A, pp. 63, 86. Watzinger in *Expedition Sieglin*, Vol. II, Part 1 B, pp. 87 ff., Nos. 71–77, Figs. 25–28, inserted plate no. 6. Vogt, in *Expedition Sieglin*, Vol. II, Part 2, pp. 22 and 125, Pl. XLII, Fig. 6. Ippel, *Der Bronzefund von Galjub*, pp. 28 f., Nos. 7–8, Pl. III. E. Michon, "Nouvelles statuettes provenant d'Égypte," in *Mon. Piot*, Vol. XXI (1913), pp. 163 ff., Pls. XVI–XVII. Jean de Mot, "Anadyomene," in *ibid.*, pp. 145–62, Figs. 1–2, Pls. XIV–XV.

[67] P. Herrmann, *Verzeichnis der antiken Original-Bildwerke* (Dresden, Skulpturen-Sammlung, 1915), pp. 48 f., No. 196. G. Dickins, *Hellenistic Sculpture* (Oxford, The Clarendon Press, 1920), p. 33, Fig. 25.

[68] From the Edwin Wilbour Memorial Collection, No. 44.7. Height 36 cm.

[69] Watzinger, in Sieglin, *Expedition Ernst von Sieglin*, Vol. II, Part 1 B, pp. 85 f., No. 68, Pl. XLI.

[70] E. Ghislanzoni in *Notiziario Archeologico*, Vol. II (1916), pp. 58 ff. L. Mariani in *Bolletino d'Arte*, Vol. VIII (1914), pp. 171 ff. G. Bagnani in *J.H.S.*, Vol. XLI (1921), pp. 232 ff. Dickins, *Hellenistic Sculpture*, p. 22, Fig. 11. L. Curtius in *Die Antike*, I (1925), 36 f. C. Anti in *Dedalo*, VI (1925–26), 683 ff.; G. Gullini in *Rivista d'Arte Antica e Moderna*, Vol. III (1947), pp. 67 ff. Gullini believes that the Aphrodite from Cyrene is a Rhodian work of c.100 B.C.; Cyrene was, however, part of Ptolemaic Egypt.

breasts[71] (Fig. 391, left). Sometimes a mantle is laid around the legs, seldom tightly knotted as in the Aphrodite Anadyomene of the Gabinetto delle Maschere in the Vatican,[72] mostly quite loose, but always arranged so that the ends of the mantle hang between the legs.[73] Thus one or both hands, instead of being raised to the coiffure, are busy with holding the mantle to prevent it from slipping. The type of Aphrodite lifting her left foot and stooping down to unfasten her sandal, so frequent in Asia Minor and in the islands, is also found in Alexandrian art; it is appropriate to this art circle.[74] A bronze statuette in the Louvre from Tell-Ramses, near Damanhur, a terra-cotta figurine (Fig. 395), and a small marble torso (Fig. 394), both in the Metropolitan Museum of Art in New York, well show the complicated and elegant movements.[75] (See our Figs. 606–7.)

Among the Greek heroes, Heracles was most frequently represented. The type preferred was the one created by Lysippos, the so-called Farnese type (see Fig. 398, from the Walters Art Gallery, and Fig. 84). There are remains of this type in marble and in terra cotta.[76] Characteristic is the addition of a big, overflowing wine jug in a statuette from Alexandria, now in Tübingen.[77] The weariness of the hero thus is not, as in the original creation, due to his superhuman deeds, but to excesses at banquets.

The deeds of Heracles are represented by the Alexandrians not in groups in the round, like those by Lysippos, but in medallions, of which the fights with the lion, bull, Stymphalic birds, and the Amazons are preserved.[78] Gypsum casts from wax models taken from the almost finished molds before the final cast was made seem to indicate that there was a complete series showing the hero's deeds. Some landscape elements, such as trees, were added in the way they are used in the Telephos frieze (see Fig. 477). These reliefs, therefore, do not belong to an earlier time than the second half of the second century.

The fight with the lion appears in a similar way in reliefs on a bowl as well as on a lamp found in Kom-esch-Schukáfa, in Alexandria (Fig. 399, bottom). Other lamps show Hellenistic groups, particularly from the story of Odysseus and Polyphemus[79] (Fig. 399, above, right). The one-eyed giant is seated holding one of the companions of Odysseus whom he has killed for his evening meal. He stretches out his hand to take the large wine cup which Odysseus hands him. Odysseus stands in an unstable pose, his right leg turned outward, while both arms are stretched to his left with the big cup, so that he can flee in the moment of danger. The same group is preserved in the Louvre in reliefs showing it below a tripod, and in fragments of the group in the round also: a bronze of Polyphemus in the Cabinet des Médailles and a marble Polyphemus in the Museo Capitolino (Fig. 400), and a marble statuette of Odysseus in the Museo Chiaramonti of the Vatican.[80] What is probably a

[71] J. Charbonneaux, *Les Terres cuites grecques* (Paris, Reynaud, 1936), Pls. 66–67, Nos. 73–74. They were found in Cyrene. See also the mould in Edgar, *Greek Moulds*, p. 3, No. 32007, Pl. XXIV, and Perdrizet, *Terres cuites*, Pl. X, Fig. 2. See our p. 139, note 26, and Fig. 558.

[72] Amelung, *Vatican Kat.*, Vol. II, pp. 696 ff., Gabinetto delle Maschere No. 433, Pl. 75.

[73] See Watzinger in Sieglin, *Expedition Ernst von Sieglin*, Vol. II, Part 1 B, pp. 87 f., No. 72, Fig. 26, and p. 92.

[74] Edgar, *Greek Sculpture*, p. 12, No. 27456, Pl. VI. See also W. Klein, *Vom antiken Rokoko* (Vienna, 1921), pp. 86 f. E. Pottier and S. Reinach, *La Nécropole de Myrina* (Paris, 1887), pp. 285 ff.

[75] *Encycl. Phot.*, Vol. III, pp. 90 f., Fig. D (bronze). Metropolitan Museum of Art, No. 23.160.20 (terra cotta), No. 20.49.1 (marble torso). Richter, *Handbook* (1953), p. 108, Figs. 86 e-f.

[76] Weber, *Mitteilungen der Museen Berlin, Terrakotten*, p. 181, No. 301, Pl. 29. Watzinger, in Sieglin, *Expedition Ernst von Sieglin*, Vol. II, Part 1 B, pp. 100 ff., Nos. 87–90, Fig. 37, inserted plate no. 7, Pl. XIII, 4. Vogt, in *Expedition Sieglin*, Vol. II, Part 2, pp. 25 f. and 118, Pls. XXXIV–XXXVI, 1. For our Fig. 398 see Dorothy K. Hill, *Catalogue of Bronzes of the Walters Art Gallery* (Baltimore, 1949), pp. 47 f., No. 97, Pl. 24; found in Alexandria.

[77] Vogt, in Sieglin, *Expedition Ernst von Sieglin*, Vol. II, Part 2, p. 118, Pl. XXXIV. For Heracles with a big drinking cup in his hand, see Pagenstecher in *Expedition Sieglin*, Vol. II, Part 1 A, *Malerei und Plastik*, pp. 67 f., Pl. XXVII, 2.

[78] A. Ippel, *Guss und Treibarbeit in Silber: Untersuchungen zu antiken Modell-Abgüssen im Pelizaeus Museum, Hildesheim* (*Winck.-Prog. Berlin*, No. 97 [1937]), pp. 29 ff., Pls. 2–3. For groups of Heracles with Antaios see Fig. 644 and R. S. Poole, *British Museum Catalogue of Coins: Alexandria and the Nomes* (London, 1892), Pl. VI, Nos. 1054 and 1479.

[79] Pagenstecher, in Sieglin, *Expedition Ernst von Sieglin*, Vol. I: *Die Nekropole von Kóm-Esch-Schukáfa* (1908), pp. 313 f., Figs. 231–32, Pl. LXX, Figs. 2 and 5, and in *ibid.*, Vol. II, Part 1 A, p. 57, Fig. 54. R. Zahn in T. Wiegand and H. Schrader, *Priene: Ergebnisse der Ausgrabungen und Untersuchungen in den Jahren 1895–1898* (Berlin, 1904), p. 453, No. 188, Fig. 561.

[80] Bronze statuette in Cabinet des Médailles, No. 812. Jones, *Sculpt. Museo Capitolino*, Atrio, No. 35, pp. 36 f., Pl. 5. Amelung, *Vatican Kat.*, Vol. II, pp. 790 ff., Museo Chiaramonti No. 704, Pl. 85. For the relief with the group below a tripod see E. Petersen in *Festschrift für O. Benndorf* (1898), p. 13.

figure of Odysseus from the same group has been found on the sunken ship off Antikythera.[81] From the same set of Homeric groups stems a ram in the Villa Albani and one in the Palazzo Doria, each with Odysseus, who hides in the thick wool, clinging to the animal's belly [82] (Figs. 401–2). A replica, in which Odysseus is lost, is in the Museum of Toledo. It is quite possible that this set of Homeric groups was created in Alexandria, although no other heroic groups have been found there.

5. SCHOLARSHIP

Homer was venerated like a god in his temple founded by Ptolemy IV (Ptolemy Philopator). The interior of this sanctuary is represented in the lower tier of the relief signed by Archelaos of Priene, now in the British Museum [83] (Figs. 404 and 497). The father of epic poetry had been deified, and therefore he is shown in his temple enthroned like Zeus. The founder of the temple, Ptolemy IV, stands behind Homer holding scrolls, probably the poems of Homer, whose manuscripts were kept in the library in the custody of Ptolemy's teacher Eratosthenes. The king is depicted with large wings and his figure is inscribed ΧΡΟΝΟΣ, the name of the god of time. He has been identified with the help of coins which show the same disagreeable and heavy features of this first degenerate and less significant Ptolemy [84] (Fig. 403). He

has short, flat curls, a vertical forehead, to which the inward curve of the nose is set at a sharp angle, and thick, sensual lips. The cheeks and neck are fat. In contrast, his wife, Arsinoë III, has fine and noble features as on her coins (Fig. 356). They are, however, coarser in execution on the relief. Her himation is drawn like a veil over her head. She is portrayed as Oikoumene, the personification of the inhabited world, and she crowns Homer. The central idea of the relief is that the fame of Homer is for all time and has pervaded all places. Another idea, that all literary arts are dependent on Homer, is expressed in the figures adoring and sacrificing to him: Myth, History, Lyric Poetry, Tragedy, Comedy, and Human Nature (Physis), the latter educated through Homer to all virtues. All of this smacks of Alexandrian scholarship. The relief may, indeed, refer to a contest in poetry won by the poet whose statue is shown near the tripod (the prize of victory), and whose poem may have been inscribed on a scroll which Klio, the Muse of History, hands to Apollo.

Yet this is not an Alexandrian work, but probably a Rhodian one. The Muses of the upper part are types found in Rhodes, Kos, Miletus, and other parts of southern Asia Minor and the neighboring islands (see Chap. IX). No such types, with perhaps one exception,[85] have been found in Alexandria. The Muse with kithara, Terpsichore, found there in a statuette (Fig. 406), is a typical Alexandrian work, lovely and delicate, perhaps modeled on an Apollo Citharoedus of the type used also on the relief of Archelaos [86] (Fig. 497). For Alexandrian heads of Muses see above, p. 89.

Scholarship is also reflected in the Alexandrian representations of the river Nile. The Egyptians represented him as a standing stout man with lotus or papyrus, the plants growing in the Nile valley. The Greeks chose their usual personification of river gods, a strong and bearded man, either seated or reclining. To distinguish the Egyptian river, the Nile was shown with the horn of plenty, so fre-

A colossal head of Polyphemus in marble, with a big eye at the root of the nose and the two closed eyes in their normal places, was on exhibition in the Walters Art Gallery in 1949–50, on loan from a private collection.

[81] J. Svoronos, *Das Athener Nationalmuseum* (3 vols., Athens, 1908–37), Vol. I, Pl. XIII, Figs. 1–4.

[82] Group in Galeria of Palazzo Doria: Arndt-Amelung, *Einzelaufnahmen* No. 2281; in Villa Albani (now in the possession of the Torlonia family): photo German Inst. Rome, 35.81. C. L. Visconti, *I monumenti di sculture antichi, Museo Torlonia, riprodotti con la fototipia* (Rome, 1884), Pl. CXII, No. 438. M. Bieber in *A.J.A.,* XLVII (1943), pp. 380 ff., Figs. 1–3.

[83] C. Watzinger, *Das Relief des Archelaos von Priene* (*Winck.-Prog. Berlin,* No. 63 [1903]), pp. 18 ff., Figs. 8–9. Watzinger, in Sieglin, *Expedition Ernst von Sieglin,* Vol. II, Part 1 B, pp. 12 f. M. Bieber, *The History of the Greek and Roman Theater* (Princeton University Press, 1939), pp. 1 and 3, Fig. 1. Alda Levi in *Bolletino d'Arte,* Series II, No. 6 (1926–27), p. 353, Fig. 3. For the whole relief, see our Chap. IX, p. 127 f., and Fig. 497.

[84] Our Fig. 403 is a silver tetradrachm, now in the possession of Mrs. E. T. Newell, who kindly allowed its publication. It was minted by the finance minister Sosibius at Sidon in Phoenicia. For other coins see Newell, *Royal Greek Portrait*

Coins, p. 88, Pl. XV, 9. Poole, *British Museum Catalogue of Coins: The Ptolemies,* pp. 63 f., Pl. XIV, 6–10, Pl. XV, 1–2. Svoronos, *Münzen der Ptolemäer,* Vol. III, Pl. XXXVI, Figs. 1–9, Pl. XXXVII, Fig. 1, Pl. XLIII, Figs. 1–3, 6–10 (cf. Vol. IV, pp. 201 ff.); Seltman, *Greek Coins,* p. 243, Pl. LIX, 2.

[85] Edgar, *Greek Sculpture,* p. 16, No. 27465, Pl. V.

[86] C. Watzinger in Sieglin, *Expedition Ernst von Sieglin,* Vol. II, Part 1 B, pp. 109 f., No. 97, Pl. XLII.

quent on Egyptian coins and in the arms of gods and royal persons. He leans on a hippopotamus, a crocodile, or a sphinx, the symbols of Egypt, and water flows from an urn [87] (Fig. 405) or from under his mantle—an allusion to the mysterious, then unknown sources of the Nile. On coins and in the well-known statue in the Vatican, which is a Roman adaptation of an Alexandrian creation [88] (Figs. 407–9), the right hand of the Nile holds a papyrus branch or sheaves of wheat as symbols of fertility. He is surrounded by 16 boys, each representing one of the 16 cubits which the Nile rises in flood, and through which he brings fertility and prosperity to the Nile valley (cf. Lucian *Rhetorum praecepta* 6, and Philostratus Lemnius *Imagines*, Loeb ed., pp. 17 f., with Fig. 1). The boy seated in the cornucopia indicates the highest level of the flood. Some of the boys play with a crocodile (Fig. 408) and an ichneumon, animals characteristic of the Nile. The front of the base is carved to represent streaming water in which reeds grow. At the side, cattle are feeding, an ichneumon and a crocodile are fighting, and a hippopotamus is attacking a boat with pygmies. Water birds, other crocodiles, boats, and hippopotami fill the other sides. Although the statue was made in the imperial period for the sanctuary of Isis and Serapis in Rome, the motifs, as well as the playing children, belong to Alexandrian art.

The best example of a seated personification of the Nile is on the celebrated Tazza Farnese, a large cameo in the form of a flat cup, in the Museo Nazionale in Naples [89] (Figs. 410–11). The figure representing the Nile is leaning against a tree at the left side, while in the center below him is a sphinx against which reclines Euthenia, the goddess of prosperity and wife of the Nile. She wears the dress of Isis and holds sheaves of wheat in her hand. Triptolemus, identified with the Egyptian

Horus, is characterized as bringer of agriculture, with the plow, knife, and seed bag. To the right side are two graceful seated women, probably the Horae, and above them two youthful wind gods, representing the winds which help to stem the waves of the Nile during the inundations. This entire symbolic representation of the fertility of Egypt is in the same spirit as Alexandrian learned poetry.

This beautiful large cameo, the outside of which is decorated with a very sophisticated aegis with a head of Medusa in the center (Fig. 411), is at the same time an example of the great luxury which existed in the courts of all the Hellenistic rulers, but probably nowhere more lavishly than in the residence of the Ptolemies. Cameos like the Tazza Farnese, gems, silverware, flowers, and paintings adorned their life and particularly their festivities. The famous tent of Ptolemy II and the boat of Ptolemy IV built for taking pleasure rides on the Nile are described as filled with all kinds of luxuries (See Athenaeus *Deipnosophistae* V pp. 196a–197c, 204d–206c).[90] Noble metalware and carefully wrought jewelry were specialties of the Alexandrian artisans.[91] Among the celebrated sets of silver tableware, the death-dance cups, showing the skeletons of poets and philosophers, and the bowl with the personification of Africa, or perhaps Alexandria, represented with an elephant skin over her head, a cornucopia on her arm, and surrounded by the attributes of many gods, found in Boscoreale and now in the Louvre, are indeed replete with the spirit of Alexandrian scholarship and love of luxury.[92]

In summation, it can be said that Alexandrian

---

[87] *Ibid.*, pp. 111 f., No. 98, Fig. 42, Pl. XLIII. See also Edgar, *Greek Moulds*, pp. 1 f., No. 32002, Pl. I, and Perdrizet, *Terres cuites*, pp. 61 ff., Pl. L. For Nilus on coins see Poole, *British Museum Catalogue of Coins: Alexandria and the Nomes*, Pls. XIX–XXI.

[88] Amelung, *Vatican Kat.*, Vol. I, pp. 124 ff., Braccio Nuovo No. 109, Pl. XVIII. W. Klein, *Geschichte der griechischen Kunst* (Leipzig, 1907), Vol. III, pp. 104 ff.; E. Schmidt in *Festschrift für Paul Arndt* (1907), p. 110.

[89] Furtwängler, *Antike Gemmen*, Vol. I, Pls. 54–55, Vol. II, pp. 235 ff. Noshy, *Arts in Ptolemaic Egypt*, p. 132, Pl. XIV, Fig. 3.

[90] J. Overbeck, *Die antiken Schriftquellen zur Geschichte der bildenden Künste bei den Griechen* (1868), Nos. 1985–90. F. Studniczka, "Das Symposion Ptolemaios II," in *Abh. Sächs. Akad.*, Phil.-hist. Klasse, Vol. XXX, Abhandlung 2 (1914).

[91] T. Schreiber, "Alexandrinische Toreutik: Untersuchungen über die griechische Goldschmiedekunst," in *Abh. Sächs. Akad.*, Vol. XXXIV, Abhandlung 1 (1894). O. Rubensohn, *Hellenistisches Silbergerät in antiken Gipsabgüssen* (Hildesheim, Pelizaeusmuseum, 1911; Wissenschaftliche Veröffentlichungen, Vol. I), and Ippel, *Bronzefund von Galjub* (ibid., Vol. II, 1922). Rostovtzeff, *History of the Hellenistic World*, Vol. I, p. 390, Pl. XLVII. B. Segall, *Museum Benaki: Katalog der Goldschmiede-Arbeiten* (1938), pp. 31 ff., 49 ff., Pls. 8 et seq.

[92] Héron de Villefosse in *Mon. Piot*, Vol. V (1899), pp. 64 ff., 224 ff., Pls. VII–VIII (death dance) and 39 ff., Pl. I (Alexandria).

art is distinguished from other branches of Hellenistic art by a continuation of Attic (particularly Praxitelean) style, preference for low-class street types and caricatures, an unhappy mixture of old Egyptian and Greek Hellenistic styles in architecture and figures of gods, and a taste for scholarly personifications and great luxury. It is not really great art. Callimachus advised the writers of Alexandria to avoid the highways of literature, where so many had traveled before them, and to find some little bypath where few had gone before. It seems that the artists of Alexandria followed similar advice. We must, therefore, abstain from calling all great art of the Hellenistic period Alexandrian.

VII

THE ART OF PRIENE

IT IS INTERESTING to compare Priene, a small but cultivated city built high above the Meander plain of Asia Minor, with the large capitals of the Attalids and Ptolemies. Priene is better known to us than any other ancient city except Pompeii, with which it has often been compared. It was, indeed, about the same size. It was similarly situated on irregular ground, making an irregular city wall necessary. Its streets, market place, sanctuaries, and civic buildings are equally well known to us. Like Pompeii, it had its best period during the third and second centuries B.C. Pompeii, however, was not only older, but it still flourished in the first centuries before and after Christ. It had a mixed civilization—Oscan and Roman, following each other, both strongly influenced by Greek civilization—while Priene was a Hellenistic town of a purely Greek culture. Like Alexandria, it was built in the time of Alexander the Great.

We know Priene so well because of the excavations conducted there in 1895–98 and followed by a model publication, with the best available specialists responsible for the detailed description of city planning, sanctuaries, public buildings, houses, sculpture, terra cottas, vases, and implements.[1]

Despite the difficult formation of the slope of Mount Mycale, where Priene is situated on several terraces, the old plan devised for flat ground by Hippodamus, from neighboring Miletus, was strictly adhered to. The streets running north to south had to be made very steep and were often merely staircases; the main streets running east to west were absolutely straight despite the fact that the market place, the exact center of the city, lay higher than the other parts of the street leading to it from the west and from it to the east gate of the city wall.

One temple, that of Asclepius, is connected with the market place. The main sanctuary of Athena is near it. A sanctuary of Demeter is higher up, one of the Egyptian gods farther to the east, and the sanctuary of Cybele, the Great Mother of the Gods, near the west gate. Near this gate is also the Sacred House, in which a statuette of Alexander has been found [2] (Figs. 412–14). Alexander had given the money to finish the temple of Athena; therefore he was venerated as a benefactor and his image was set up on a podium in a large banquet room. Only the upper part and the left hand, with part of a sword, have been preserved. The statue is a sketchy but able work of about 300 B.C. showing the high forehead, the wide-open eyes gazing with liveliness into the distance, the curved lips, and the turn of the neck and head as we know them from contemporary portraits of the great conqueror (see Chap. III, pp. 47 f.). The features also are related to the coins issued by Lysimachus in neighboring Magnesia on the Meander in the early third century, after 297 B.C.[3] (Fig. 415).

Before the temple of Athena an altar was erected where figures of women were set up between columns on a high balustrade. The arrangement thus

[1] T. Wiegand and H. Schrader, with contributions by G. Kummer, W. Wilberg, H. Winnefeld, and R. Zahn, *Priene: Ergebnisse der Ausgrabungen und Untersuchungen in den Jahren 1895–1898* (Berlin, 1904). Hereafter referred to as *Priene*.

[2] R. Kekule von Stradonitz, in *Sitzungsber. Preuss. Akad.* (1899), pp. 281 ff. C. de Ujfalvy, *Le Type physique d'Alexandre le Grand* (Paris, 1902), pp. 92 ff. H. Winnefeld in *Priene*, pp. 180 ff., Figs. 176–77. M. Bieber, "The Portraits of Alexander the Great," in *Proceedings of the American Philosophical Society*, Vol. XCIII, No. 5 (1949), pp. 390, 407, Figs. 38–40.

[3] M. Bieber, "The Portraits of Alexander the Great," in *Proceedings of the American Philosophical Society*, Vol. XCIII, No. 5 (1949), Fig. 41.

is similar to that on the sarcophagus of mourning women (see p. 22). Only one figure, headless, is preserved.[4] Its style is similar to that of the statuette of a priestess of Demeter which stood at the entrance to the sanctuary of Demeter and Kore on the uppermost boundary of the city[5] (Fig. 517). On both, the mantle is draped in such a way that diagonal folds cross over the breast and the body, while one horizontal fold, sharp but narrow, goes from one upper arm to the other. The folds of the chiton are clearly distinguished in their fall over the feet; those over the supporting left leg are almost vertical, while those over the relaxed right foot fall in rounded hooks. The mantle of the priestess of Demeter is of a crinkly material which was the fashion in the early Hellenistic period (cf. Figs. 99–100, 201, 516, 542). The hair falls in long locks over the shoulders and at the outer sides of the breasts. In the same sanctuary have been found two female heads with the archaistic hairdress of three rows of little curls over the forehead and broad fillets binding the hair.[6] The ears are pierced for metal earrings. All of these are careful early Hellenistic works.

The same is true of a group of small marble statuettes which were used in the houses.[7] These show a marked Praxitelean character, to be compared to the works of the sons of Praxiteles (see Figs. 32–33). A young man with a chlamys hanging from his forearm, leaning on a pillar,[8] recalls the Hermes of Praxiteles in Olympia (Fig. 11). A Dionysos with his right hand on his hip, leaning toward the right where a panther looks up to him,[9] reminds one of the Hermes of Andros (Fig. 14). An Aphrodite with a mantle around the lower part of her body[10] recalls Praxitelean Aphrodites. All of these, and particularly some very lively seated women with similar drapery,[11] are, however, more advanced in movement, and are not imitations or adaptations but original small creations of minor but gifted artists.

The same may be said of the many terra-cotta statuettes found in the houses.[12] They may have been made in Priene, for molds and inscriptions of artists not found elsewhere have been excavated.[13] There are few figures of gods—Cybele, Isis, Athena—reflecting the local cults.[14] Aphrodite is represented in a well-known and popular type, bending down and unfastening her sandal[15] (Figs. 394–95, 606–7). Eros was popular, too, as in all Hellenistic sites. Most interesting are the statuettes of flying *Erotes*, which were pressed out of molds as nudes and then differently dressed in small mantles and hats added freehand.[16] Very sweet is a little Eros seated on the ground with outstretched hand like the boy from Ephesus[17] (Fig. 534). The genre figures and caricatures are much more restrained than in Alexandria. Pan teaching a winged young man (Eros?), and a pedagogue, bent by age, teaching a young child,[18] are fine studies in the contrast of grotesque old age and blooming youth. The street boy pulling a thorn out of the sole of his foot[19] is a masterpiece: the whistling mouth, the blinking eyes, the stupid expression, the thick arms and legs all massed together, both hands and the wounded foot obscuring a great part of the body, show an advanced and mature art. The caricatures of slaves and Negroes, without the exaggerations which we find elsewhere, are fine studies.[20]

Among the female figures, two half-figures of beautiful women represent a rare and original type.[21] Two dancers (one is signed by Theodotos)[22] are particularly lovely. The draped standing girls and women show great variety;[23] some are similar to the types found in the neighboring My-

[4] *Priene*, pp. 120 ff., Figs. 91, 95, 96. R. Horn, *Stehende weibliche Gewandstatuen in der hellenistischen Plastik (Ergänzungsheft II to Röm. Mitt.*, 1931), pp. 62 f., Pl. 26, Fig. 1.
[5] *Priene*, pp. 147 ff., Figs. 118, 120, p. 200, Fig. 196. Horn, *Gewandstatuen*, p. 24, Pl. 8, Fig. 1.
[6] *Priene*, pp. 155 f., Figs. 124–27.
[7] H. Winnefeld in *Priene*, pp. 366 ff.
[8] *Priene*, pp. 367 f., Figs. 461–62.
[9] *Priene*, pp. 368 ff., Figs. 463–64.
[10] *Priene*, pp. 370 f., Fig. 465.
[11] *Priene*, pp. 372 f., Figs. 468–69.

[12] H. Winnefeld in *Priene*, pp. 329 ff.
[13] *Priene*, pp. 364 f., Figs. 454–60.
[14] *Priene*, pp. 330 ff., Figs. 366–75.
[15] *Priene*, pp. 336 ff., Figs. 377–81.
[16] *Priene*, pp. 336 ff., Figs. 382–90.
[17] *Priene*, pp. 339, 341, Fig. 391.
[18] *Priene*, p. 346, Figs. 407, p. 356, Fig. 433.
[19] *Priene*, p. 357, Figs. 434–35. G. Rodenwaldt, *Die Kunst der Antike* (Berlin, 1927; Propyläen-Kunstgeschichte III), p. 470. J. Charbonneaux, *Les Terres cuites grecques* (Paris, 1936), Pl. 90.
[20] *Priene*, pp. 358 f., Figs. 436–43.
[21] *Priene*, pp. 354–55, Figs. 428–30.
[22] *Priene*, p. 348, Figs. 410–11.
[23] H. Winnefeld in *Priene*, pp. 349 ff., Figs. 412–27.

tina, but many, particularly those made for the sanctuary of Demeter,[24] are distinguished by a marked inventiveness, especially in those carrying water and in the little dancing girls. The figures of Baubo, found in many examples in the same sanctuary,[25] may have been influenced by Alexandrian grotesques, but they also manifest great variety in the hairdress and the attributes—the lyre, the torches of Kore, and the little pig whose blood was used for purification of the initiates in the mysteries of Demeter.

House furnishings and implements found in Priene are distinguished by simplicity and pure form. Thus the bronze horse and bust of Artemis

[24] H. Winnefeld in *Priene*, pp. 157 ff., Figs. 128–47.
[25] *Priene*, p. 161, Figs. 149–56.

which decorated a couch,[26] the lamps,[27] and even the coal stands[28] have much more refined forms than similar objects found in Pompeii. Most of these objects belong to the third century.

In the second century a copy of the Athena Parthenos was set up in the temple of Athena here, as it was in the library of Pergamon. A frieze representing the battle of the gods and the giants and the fight of the Greeks with the Amazons was also carved in this period.[29] It was definitely influenced by the great altar of Pergamon.

[26] *Priene*, pp. 378 ff., Figs. 480–82.
[27] *Priene*, pp. 384 f., Figs. 485–89.
[28] R. Zahn in *Priene*, pp. 460 f., Figs. 565–69.
[29] *Priene*, pp. 111 ff., Figs. 81–89. A. H. Smith, *Catalogue of Sculptures in the Department of Greek and Roman Antiquities* (London, the British Museum), Vol. II (1900), Nos. 1165–76.

VIII

THE ART OF PERGAMON

THE STATE AND DYNASTY of Pergamon were founded by Philetairos. Born in Bithynia near the Pontos Euxeinos, the Black Sea, and made a eunuch by an accident in his childhood, he served nevertheless as an officer in the Macedonian army, after 302 under Lysimachus of Thrace. In 284 he was entrusted with guarding the fortress of Pergamon, where a treasure of 9,000 talents was deposited. Philetairos surrendered the city to Seleucus I of Syria in 282, but kept the money for himself. He counted his rule from this time on, although he recognized Seleucus I as his suzerain, surrounded as he was on all sides of his small state by Syrian territory. After Seleucus was killed in 280, Philetairos minted coins with the portrait of the deified Syrian king (see Fig. 140). In order to secure the sway of Pergamon for his house, he adopted his nephew Attalus and married him to a Seleucid princess. When Attalus died, Philetairos adopted his nephew Eumenes, the son of his other brother. In 277 he consolidated his rule still further by driving the invading Gauls from his territory. With sagacious political principles, he laid the foundation for expansion of the power of the Attalid dynasty. He also began the building activity at Pergamon by erecting a temple of Demeter.

After Philetairos died in 263 at the age of eighty, his adopted son and successor, Eumenes I (263–241) and all the other Attalids venerated him as the deified founder of the dynasty. They put his portrait on their silver tetradrachms.[1] On the coins

(see Fig. 416) a laurel wreath encircles the massive head. The hair strands are arranged around the vertex of the head in a way similar to those of Ptolemy I (see Fig. 304), but they are more differentiated in their movement over the forehead and on the nape of the neck.

The features of the coin portrait agree remarkably with those of the marble bust from the villa of the Pisones in Herculaneum, now in Naples[2] (Figs. 418–19). It has been identified with the help of the coins bearing the portrait of the founder of the dynasty which were minted by Philetairos's successors. The bust may have been copied from the same statue from which the coin portrait was drawn. Such statues must have been erected in his honor in Pergamon; we know of a statue erected in the theater of Delos by Eumenes I and of an equestrian bronze statue set up by the Athenians at Olympia.[3] The turning of the marble head toward the left shoulder certainly has been taken from a statue. The chlamys indicates the officer. Like the coin portraits, the statues were probably all posthumous and, in a certain sense, must have been idealized. But they are clearly based on the actual appearance of Philetairos, and they well express his strong, brutal, and ruthless personality.

---

[1] H. von Fritze, "Die Münzen von Pergamon" in *Abh. Preuss. Akad.* (1910), Abhandlung I, pp. 7 f., 24 ff., Pl. II, Figs. 3–13, 15, Pl. III, Figs. 1, 2, 4. G. F. Hill, *L'Art dans les monnaies grecques* (Paris, 1927), p. 40, Pl. XI, Fig. 2. K. Lange, *Herrscherköpfe des Altertums im Münzbild ihrer Zeit* (1938), pp. 62 f. M. Rostovtzeff, *Social and Economic History of the Hellenistic World* (Oxford, 1941), Vol. I, p. 46, Pl. VII, Fig. 4. W.

Schubart, "Das Königsbild des Hellenismus," in *Die Antike,* Vol. XIII (1937), p. 285, Fig. 6. Our Fig. 416 is a coin issued by Eumenes II, now in the Boston Museum of Fine Arts. I owe the photograph to the kindness of Agnes Brett.

[2] D. Comparetti and G. de Petra, *La Villa Ercolanese dei Pisoni* (Turin, 1883), p. 176, No. 78, Pl. XXI, Fig. 2. P. Arndt, *Griechische und römische Porträts* (Munich, Bruckmann, 1891–1942), Pls. 107–8. F. Winter, *Altertümer von Pergamon,* VII, 151. A. Hekler, *Bildniskunst der Griechen und Römer* (1912), Pl. 70. L. Laurenzi, *Ritratti greci* (Florence, 1941), p. 111, No. 54, Pl. XXI.

[3] *Insc. Graec.,* Vol. XI, Part 4, No. 1106. W. Dittenberger, *Sylloge Insc. Graec.* (3d ed., 1915–24), Nos. 628–30, 641.

The bloated face combines energy and guile. The exceptionally small and narrow eyes, buried in fat, regard the world with a mixture of slyness, shrewdness, and superiority. The powerful and heavy jaw and the broad projecting chin indicate great energy.[4]

The nephews and successors of Philetairos, Eumenes I and Attalus I (241–197), inherited a small territory, but a rich treasury. They used it to carry out a grandiose city plan which is better known to us than any other residence of a Hellenistic ruler, thanks to the systematic excavations and publications of such eminent scholars as Karl Humann, Alexander Conze, Wilhelm Dörpfeld, Theodor Wiegand, and others.[5] With the help of high substructures, the royal architects erected such buildings as sanctuaries, palaces, a library, a theater, a market place, and gymnasia on terraces of different heights. The library became the second seat of scholarship after Alexandria. It also contained a collection of older masterpieces. Attalus I defeated in 238 B.C. the Galatians, Gallic tribes who had settled in 278 in Asia Minor, and had repeatedly plundered it. Therefore Attalus earned for himself the title of king and the surname Soter (Savior). When Antiochus Hierax of Syria hired Galatians as mercenaries, and when family quarrels broke out in the house of the Seleucids, Attalus used these as excuses for attempting to make himself ruler of all Asia Minor as far as the Taurus Mountains. In 228/7 he won a decisive victory over Antiochus. In 222, however, Antiochus III threw Attalus back to his homeland. Attalus realized that he needed support for his plans of expansion, and in 211, therefore, he joined the Aetolian League and Rome against Philip V of Madedonia. With the help of Rome he actually attained rule over a large part of Asia Minor.

I. THE FIRST PERGAMENE SCHOOL (SECOND HALF OF THE THIRD CENTURY B.C.)

In contrast to the Ptolemies, the Attalids, unhampered by the traditions of an old civilization, used their power and treasury mainly for monumental buildings and sculpture. They summoned artists from all Greek lands, particularly Attica, which they emulated, considering themselves—much as did the Athenians in the classical period—the cultural leaders of the Greeks. From Athens itself came Phyromachos, who created the statue of Asclepius for the sanctuary of this god [6] (Polybius XXXII. 25; Diodorus Siculus *Bibliotheca historica,* Excerpta Book XXXI, Fr. 35). The statue, represented on coins of Pergamon,[7] resembled an older Attic cult statue. The head has been recognized in a copy now in the Museo Nazionale Romano in Rome (Fig. 423), while of the body there are only small replicas preserved in Pergamon, which may have served as votive offerings.[8] The head distinctly combines Attic tradition with the beginning of the "baroque" style which was to become characteristic of the Pergamene school.

Another Attic artist working for the Attalids was Nikeratos. An inscription with his signature has been found on the island of Delos near the statue of a fallen warrior, which, therefore, has been attributed to him [9] (Fig. 422). The warrior

---

[4] For Philetairos, see W. Hoffmann in Pauly-Wissowa, *Real-Enc.,* XIX, 2157–61; W. W. Tarn in *C.A.H.,* VII, 97 ff.

[5] *Altertümer von Pergamon,* Vols. I–IX (1885–1910). E. Pontremoli and M. Collignon, *Pergame: Restauration et description des monuments de l'Acropole* (Paris, 1900). E. Hansen, *The Attalids of Pergamon* (1947). A. Schober, *Die Kunst von Pergamon* (Vienna, 1951).

[6] J. Overbeck, *Die antiken Schriftquellen zur Geschichte der bildenden Künste bei den Griechen* (Leipzig, 1868), Nos. 1998–99.

[7] H. von Fritze, "Die Münzen von Pergamon," in *Abh. Preuss. Akad.* (1910), Abhandlung I, Pl. I, Fig. 17, Pl. IV, Figs. 10 and 20, Pl. V, Figs. 13–16, Pl. VIII, Figs. 1, 2, 4, Pl. IX, Figs. 13, 15, 16, 24.

[8] For the Attic prototype see K. A. Neugebauer, *Asklepios* (*Winck.-Prog. Berlin,* No. 78 [1921]); O. Deubner, *Das Asklepieion von Pergamon* (Berlin, 1938), pp. 7 ff., Fig. 1 (title picture) and Figs. 2–3 (coins). Deubner also assumes that the cult statue has been copied from the Athenian prototype, tentatively ascribed to Alkamenes, the pupil of Phidias. This seems to be confirmed by the small statuettes of the same type, which were probably votive offerings to the Asclepius of Pergamon (Winter, *Altertümer von Pergamon,* Vol. VII, pp. 190 f., Nos. 193–95). For the head in the Museo Nazionale Romano (Fig. 423) see L. Savignoni in *Notizie degli Scavi* (1901), pp. 372 ff., and Savignoni in *Röm. Mitt.,* Vol. XVI (1901), pp. 376 f., Fig. 2; Helbig, *Führer durch die öffentlichen Sammlungen klassischer Altertümer in Rom* (2 vols., Leipzig, 1912–13), Vol. II, No. 1340. For the statue see W. Amelung in *Röm. Mitt.,* XVI (1901), pp. 372 ff., and Vol. XVIII (1903), pp. 1 ff., Figs. 1–4. D. Mustilli, *Il Museo Mussolini* (Rome, 1939), pp. 146 f., Sala XI No. 11, Pl. LXXXVII, Fig. 326.

[9] P. R. von Biénkowski, *Die Darstellungen der Gallier in der hellenistischen Kunst* (Vienna, Hölder, 1908), pp. 21 ff., Figs. 42–43. H. Brunn and F. Bruckmann, *Denkmäler griechischer und römischer Skulptur* (Munich, 1888—), Pl. 9. G. Leroux in *B.C.H.,* XXXIV (1910), pp. 478 ff. A. J. Reinach in *Mélanges Holleaux* (1913), pp. 233 ff.

is supported by his right knee, while the left leg is stretched widely to the side and the body is bent to the right side. The upper part is lost, but the movement seems to indicate that he tried to protect himself with his shield against an attacker above him. His helmet is lying on the ground next to his left knee. It has been assumed that a head found in Delos, now in Mykonos, belongs to this warrior, or at least to a monument including both [10] (Figs. 420–21). The hair, standing up in stiff strands over the forehead, and the shrieking mouth seem to indicate a Gaul. The connection, however, cannot be proved.

Nikeratos was not among the artists who, according to Pliny (*Nat. hist.* xxxiv. 84) represented the fights of Attalus and Eumenes against the Gauls. These were Phyromachos, Stratonikos of Cyzicus, Isigonos, and Antigonos, who was a writer on art. As the Antigonos named is probably identical with Antigonos of Carystus on Euboea, the main group of the victory monument of Attalus I, the Gaul killing his wife and himself, has been attributed to him (Figs. 281–83, 424). It is assumed that this grandiose group stood in the center of a round base, surrounded by four dying Gauls. [11] The best preserved of these is the celebrated so-called Dying Gladiator in the Museo Capitolino [12] (Figs. 426–27). The ancient base is indeed rounded, and the composition invites one to walk around it, as can be done in the Sala del Gladiatore where this figure is the effective center. The "gladiator" is actually a trumpeter, who has blown retreat and now awaits death while lying on his shield, the broken trumpet before him. There seems to be no doubt that this is the trumpeter of Epigonos, of whom Pliny (*Nat. hist.* xxxiv. 88) says "Epigonos omnia fere praedicta imitatus praecessit in tubicine." Epigonos may be identical with the otherwise unknown Isigonos mentioned pre-

viously by Pliny. In any case, this work is a masterpiece of the new "baroque," the passionate art of Pergamon. The attempt to hold the body up while the blood streams from the wound under the right breast, the bitterness expressed in the head which sinks helplessly forward, the eyebrows drawn together in agony—all are deeply moving. The torques around the neck, the thick leatherlike skin, the short mustache, and the greased hair standing stiffly around forehead and cheeks characterize the Gaul. Compared to the head of the chieftain (Fig. 424), the expression is less defiant and less haughty. There probably were other variations in the heads of the three other Gauls who surrounded the leader. We would like to know the one belonging to the torso in Dresden, [13] and one would like to assign to the same monuments some other large heads of Gauls, like the bearded one in the Museo Chiaramonti in the Vatican, with its brutal realism. [14] In any case, we can imagine that the monument, standing in the center of the sanctuary of Athena, must have been very impressive. It was the oldest free-standing monument in a city square, to which so many others, down to our time, have succeeded. The date of its erection was probably after 228 b.c., when the war with the Gauls ended.

While the Athenians had celebrated their triumph over the Persians by representing the victorious battles of the gods against the giants, of the heroes of the past against the Trojans, and of Theseus against the centaurs and the Amazons, the Attalids commissioned monuments of their own victories in battle. It seems, however, that in the large victory monument of Attalus I there was represented the battle of the Greeks against the Persians as a parallel to the Attalids' own victories. The head of a dying Persian, wearing the tiara, is of the same size, style, and emotional appeal as that of the Gauls [15] (Fig. 425). The thick hair and

[10] Biénkowski, *Gallier*, pp. 32 ff., Figs. 46–47. C. Picard, *La Sculpture antique de Phidias à l'ère byzantine* (1926), p. 239, Fig. 93.

[11] A. Schober in *Röm. Mitt.*, Vol. LI (1936), pp. 104 ff., Figs. 4–5.

[12] Jones, *Sculpt. Museo Capitolino*, pp. 338 ff., Sala del Gladiatore, No. 1, Pl. 85. Biénkowski, *Gallier*, pp. 1 ff., Figs. 14 and 18. A. Schober in *Röm. Mitt.*, Vol. LI (1936), p. 115, Fig. 2. A. W. Lawrence, *Later Greek Sculpture and Its Influence on East and West* (London, Cape, 1927), p. 20, Pl. 32. Pontremoli and Collignon, *Pergame*, pp. 126 ff. Brunn-Bruckmann, *Denkmäler*, Pl. 421.

[13] Biénkowski, *Gallier*, p. 4, Fig. 5. A. Schober in *Röm. Mitt.*, Vol. LI (1936), p. 119, Fig. 3. Pontremoli and Collignon, *Pergame*, pp. 131 f.

[14] W. Amelung, *Die Skulpturen des Vaticanischen Museums* (2 vols., Berlin, 1903–6), Vol. I, pp. 663 f., Pl. 70, Museo Chiaramonti, No. 535. Brunn-Bruckmann, *Denkmäler*, Pl. 704. See also Biénkowski, *Gallier*, p. 13, Figs. 15–17, and Pontremoli and Collignon, *Pergame*, p. 132 (figure showing face and profile).

[15] R. Paribeni, *Le Terme di Diocleziano e Il Museo Nazionale Romano* (5th ed., Rome, 1932), Pl. 26. Lawrence, *Later Greek Sculpture*, p. 20, Pl. 33. Brunn-Bruckmann, *Denkmäler*, Pl.

small whiskers are similar. The eyes are beginning to close, and the mouth is opened for the last sigh; the right eyebrow is drawn up in a triangle. The passive dying of the Oriental is in contrast to the wild obstinacy of the dying Gauls.

It is a question whether the defeated Syrians and the victorious Pergamenes were also represented. A head in the Museo Comunale in Rome (Fig. 428) might give an idea of the style of the Syrians,[16] and a grandiose torso of a Hellenistic ruler from Pergamon in Berlin [17] (Fig. 429) might suggest the style of the Pergamenes. These heroic groups were probably set up not long after the decisive victory over the Gauls.

There are later, smaller groups which were dedicated on the Acropolis of Athens near the south wall (Pausanias I. 25. 2). These included fighting Gauls, all wounded but still bravely defending themselves. Copies are scattered in different museums. Thus, there is one in Venice of a Gaul with a garment thrown wide open, showing his broad and ugly form, and with wild hair and beard.[18] Another in the same museum is young and unclothed [19] (Fig. 430). He seems to have been run over by a horse and rider, is falling backward, and is supporting himself with the heel of his outstretched left foot, his right foot, and his right hand. One in the Louvre (Fig. 431) is wounded in the thigh, from which the plastically rendered blood spouts. He has thrown away his sword and his shield, on which his wounded leg is kneeling.[20] He looks defiantly up, frowning under his mop of wild, disheveled hair. In contrast, a statue in the Museo Nazionale in Naples [21] (Fig. 435) is that of a Gaul already dying from the wound in his left breast. He holds himself up with his left hand, but the head and the right arm hang helplessly for-

ward and the legs are spread apart, the knees cramped. The attitude resembles very much that of the dying trumpeter of Epigonos (Fig. 427). Different again is the dead young giant in Venice [22] (Fig. 436), marked as such by the twisted belt around his naked and vigorous body, whose musculature is exaggeratedly modeled. The left arm with the shield is stretched upward. The young face surrounded by curly hair is thrown back in the deep sleep of death.

This dedication enhanced the deeds of Attalus by adding to his own victories over the Gauls the defeat of the giants by the gods, and the defeat of the Amazons by the Greeks. Added, moreover, to these two subjects—with which the Athenians, on the Parthenon and elsewhere, had symbolically celebrated their victories over the Persians—was the battle of Greeks and Persians, now used as a parallel and symbol of the Attalids' own deeds. The statues of the Persians show attitudes of defense, pain, and terror that go still farther in realism and variety than those found among the other groups. A crouched Persian in full Oriental dress, in the Museum of Aix in the south of France [23] (Fig. 437), kneels and supports himself with his right hand, which is laid on the ground before his right knee. His distorted face, with thick eyebrows and open mouth, expresses unrestrained terror. Another Persian in the Vatican, with the Phrygian cap but otherwise nude, shows his sinewed and muscular body in a contorted position, lifting his right arm while supporting the body with the left.[24] His head (Fig. 433) expresses pain but not defiance, as do the heads of the Gauls. The hair is shorter and smoother. Pain only is expressed also in the head of the dead Persian from the figure in Naples [25] (Fig. 432 and Fig. 435, left front). He lies on his side; his eyes are almost closed and his thick lips are opened in a last sigh. The right hand

515. S. Aurigemma, Le Terme di Diocleziano e il Museo Nazionale Romano (2d ed., Rome, 1950), No. 199, Pl. XXXVII b.
[16] Rome, Antiquario Comunale. Biénkowski, Gallier, pp. 25 f., Figs. 37–38.
[17] Berlin Museum, No. 1486. See W. Reinecke, Einführung in die griechische Plastik an der Hand von Meisterwerken im Alten Museum (1931), p. 97 f., Fig. 73.
[18] Biénkowski, Gallier, pp. 40 f., Figs. 53–55. Lawrence, Later Greek Sculpture, p. 22, Pl. 37b.
[19] Biénkowski, Gallier, pp. 44 ff., Figs. 57–59.
[20] Ibid., pp. 51 f., Figs. 63–65. Encycl. phot., Vol. III, p. 248A. R. Horn in Röm Mitt., Vol. LII (1937), pp. 147 ff., Pl. 41, No. 1.
[21] Biénkowski, Gallier, pp. 47 f., Fig. 60. R. Horn in Röm. Mitt., Vol. LII (1937), p. 160, Pl. 33. A. Ruesch, Guida del Museo Nazionale di Napoli (n.d.), pp. 99 ff., No. 302.

[22] Biénkowski, Gallier, pp. 37 ff., Figs. 50–52. A. Ruesch, Guida, p. 100, Fig. 35.
[23] R. Horn in Röm Mitt., Vol. LII (1937), pp. 151 f., Pl. 35, No. 2. A. Schober in Röm. Mitt., Vol. LIV (1939), p. 92, Fig. 1. P. Arndt and W. Amelung, Photographische Einzelaufnahmen antiker Skulpturen (Munich, Bruckmann, 1893—), No. 1396.
[24] R. Horn in Röm. Mitt., Vol. LII (1937), pp. 156 f., Pl. 43, No. 2. Brunn-Bruckmann, Denkmäler, Pl. 481, No. 1. A. Schober in Röm. Mitt., Vol. LIV (1939), p. 93, Fig. 2.
[25] Ruesch, Guida, pp. 99 ff., No. 300, Fig. 37. R. Horn in Röm. Mitt., Vol. LII (1937), pp. 156 f., Pl. 43, No. 1.

loosely holds the curved sword of the Persians, of the kind still used as a sabre by the Turks.

In contrast to this quiet death, the giant in Naples [26] (Fig. 435, upper right), also lying flat and helpless on the ground, still seems to brandish his sword violently over his head. His broad chest is expanded. His hair flutters like flames above his forehead and behind his cheeks and on the back of his head (Fig. 434). He forms an effective contrast not only to the Persian, but still more so to the dying Amazon [27] (Fig. 435, lower right). Giant and Amazon are in similar positions, the right leg bent and the left leg extended; the right arm is lifted over the head. In both, the leg is bent in the agony of death, but in the Amazon it is soft and relaxed, as are her arms; the left arm is extended along her side, the right hand lies open and tired behind her head. It holds no weapon, for her spear is broken and she has fallen over it. Her garment is open on the right side, unveiling her womanly breast. An old drawing of 1540 showed a child next to her.[28] She thus may be a copy of a statue by Epigonos who, as Pliny (*Nat. hist.* xxxiv. 88) tells us, "surpassed his predecessors by his infant pitiably engaged in caressing its murdered mother." Pliny does not say whether this mother was an Amazon —she might have been a Gaul—but the motif is certainly related.

These four groups were probably dedicated by Attalus I around 201 B.C., when he visited Athens. There is a tendency among German scholars to assign the groups to Attalus II (159-138), thus to date them much later than the larger figures.[29] It

seems to me that the relation between the large and small figures is too close for such a long interval.

Again, by no means do we know all the figures of the group. It has been assumed that Amazons on horseback belong to the smaller group, but the style of the existing figures seems different to me.[30] There certainly were figures of the victorious gods, heroes, Athenians, and Pergamenes, for a Dionysos belonging to the gigantomachy was thrown by a storm wind from the Acropolis into the theater of Dionysos in 32/31 (Plutarch *Antonius* 60). There probably are not as many copies of them as of the defeated, who are not only in most interesting and diverse attitudes, but are always represented with dignity and deep feeling for their fate. They have been the models for many Roman monuments of victories over Gauls, like the celebrated sarcophagus in the Museo Capitolino;[31] the victors on these monuments, however, are always the Romans, and thus the sarcophagi are no help in identifying copies of the victorious Attalid fighters.

Another group rightly attributed to the first Pergamene school is the punishment of Marsyas, who is shown about to be skinned alive by a Scythian slave because he has dared to compete in music with Apollo and has been defeated.[32] It is characteristic that Myron in the fifth century represented the prelude to this event—the satyr appropriating the flutes, which Athena has thrown away and cursed; Praxiteles in the fourth century showed the unhappy contest itself and the preparation for the punishment, on the base of Mantinea (see above, pp. 21 f.); the Pergamene artist of the third century goes farther toward representing the severe punishment itself. He shows old Marsyas fastened to a tree and the Scythian sharpening his knife at his feet, in order to flay him, while Apollo placidly

---

[26] Ruesch, *Guida*, p. 102, No. 301, Fig. 38. R. Horn in *Röm. Mitt.*, Vol. LII (1937), pp. 158 f., Pl. 42, No. 1.
[27] Ruesch, *Guida*, pp. 102 f., No. 303, Fig. 40. M. Collignon, *Histoire de la sculpture grecque*, Vol. II (Paris, 1897), pp. 507 ff.
[28] A. Michaelis, "Der Schöpfer der attalischen Kampfgruppen," in *Jahrbuch d. Inst.*, Vol. VIII (1893), pp. 119 ff., Figs. 2–4. E. Petersen, "Amazzone Madre?" in *Röm. Mitt.*, Vol. VIII (1893), pp. 251 ff. S. Reinach, "L'exvoto d'Attale et le sculpteur Epigonos" in *Revue des Études Grecques*, Vol. VII (1894), pp. 37 ff.
[29] R. Horn, "Hellenistische Köpfe, I: Zur Datierung des 'kleinen attalischen Weihgeschenks,'" in *Röm. Mitt.*, LII (1937), 140 ff. A. Schober, "Zur Amazonengruppe des attalischen Weihgeschenks" in *Oest. Jahreshefte*, XXVIII (1933), pp. 107 ff.; *idem*, "Zu dem Weihgeschenk eines Attalos in Athen," in *Röm. Mitt.*, LIV (1939), 82 ff. and *idem, Die Kunst von Pergamon*, pp. 121 ff.; cf. M. Bieber, "Archaeological News," in *A.J.A.*, XXIV (1940), pp. 241 f. H. Kähler, *Pergamon: Bil-*

derhefte antiker Kunst (1949), pp. 146, 195 f., accepts the late date, because he sees in the heads of the small Gauls a "classicising numbness" (*klassizistische Erstarrung*) which escapes me.
[30] A. Schober, "Zur Amazonengruppe des attalischen Weihgeschenks," in *Oest. Jahreshefte*, Vol. XXVIII (1933), pp. 102 ff., Figs. 38–40.
[31] Jones, *Sculpt. Museo Capitolino*, pp. 74 f., Stanza Terrene a Dritta, II, No. 5, Pl. 14. Biénkowski, *Gallier*, pp. 105 ff., Ergänzungs-Tafel IV.
[32] W. Amelung, *Führer durch die Antiken in Florenz* (Munich, 1897), p. 48.

looks on. The group is reproduced on a disk in Dresden.[33] Only the Marsyas of the group was often copied; we have several variations of his figure, in statues in Constantinople (Fig. 438), the Louvre (Fig. 439), the Uffizi Gallery in Florence (Fig. 440), the Palazzo dei Conservatori in Rome, and in other museums.[34] The horror of the approaching torture is more or less emphasized in all of these, the worst being a torso in red marble in the Palazzo dei Conservatori; in this the veins of the body stand out as if they are going to burst and the muscles are stretched as if they will be torn. The head has thick hair, which seems to be drenched in sweat, and the mouth is drawn obliquely awry, as if reacting against the sharpening and grinding of the knife of the Scythian. Dumb despair has never been rendered more effectively in the features of a distorted face.

The Scythian is preserved in only one copy, in Florence. This might even be the original[35] (Figs. 441–42). It is, like the figures of the Gauls, a first-rate study of a foreign race. He is seated on the ground sharpening the knife on a stone, and is in an ugly position. This makes an excellent closed pyramidal composition. One has to go around the figure to grasp it in its entirety as it rises from the square base and forms a triangle which looks like a pyramid from all sides. Both knees are between the two lines formed by the two arms. The face (Figs. 443–44) is of the type still found among the South Russians or Cossacks. The skin is stretched over the protruding cheekbones. Little irregular tufts of hair are scratched below the lower lip, on the chin, and on the lower cheeks near the ears. The policeman (the Scythians were used as such in Athens also) looks up with callous wonder at Marsyas, his forehead furrowed, his eyebrows drawn together, his gaze dull and dumb, his lips half open. The forehead is receding, the hair grows on the back of the long skull only and is thrown

forward in long, thick strands. The execution is smooth and polished.

As to the third figure of the group, only the torso of Apollo has been found in Pergamon[36] (Fig. 445). In contrast to the two others he has a youthful, well-developed body with soft skin. He probably sat, fully relaxed, with the kithara in the (now lacking) left arm, while the right seems to have been lifted, with the hand reposing on the head. This group thus contained a rare richness of forms and motifs, with contrasting moods. The agony of Marsyas is contrasted to the indifference of the executioner and to the serenity of the soft and reclining Apollo.

The Marsyas of Myron seems to have been adapted to Pergamene taste in a bronze statuette in the British Museum[37] (Fig. 446). As in Myron's group, the moment portrayed is that when Marsyas spies the flutes, thrown away by Athena. He stretches out his left arm and grasps the shaggy hair of his head, bent down in wonder to the flutes.

The Hellenistic period shows several other examples of the use of motifs of the early classical period which the Periclean age had discarded because the sculptors of that era lacked interest in lively movement. The Pergamene artists, for example, used the satyr again as a vehicle of unbridled emotion. Thus a bronze statuette of a rather coarse but very gay young satyr has been found in Pergamon[38] (Fig. 449). The raised right arm probably held an object with which he teased a panther at his right side. He pulls back, standing only on the toes of both feet, the panther skin over his left arm swings, and the hand is holding the shepherd's pipe. This is a far departure from the elegant young satyrs of Praxiteles and Lysippos. A running satyr, found in the ship sunk near Mahdia and now in the Musée du Bardo in Tunis,[39] is so closely related to these two satyr statuettes that it certainly also

[33] Amelung, *Antiken in Florenz*, pp. 63 f., Fig. 16. *Jahrbuch d. Inst., Anzeiger* (1889), p. 99.

[34] Amelung, *Antiken in Florenz*, pp. 61 ff., Nos. 86–87, Figs. 14–15. *Encycl. phot.*, Vol. III, pp. 232 f. Brunn-Bruckmann, *Denkmäler*, Pls. 423–24. Jones, *Sculpt. Palazzo Conservatori*, pp. 165 ff., Sala degli Orti Lamiani No. 18, Pl. 59. Lawrence, *Later Greek Sculpture*, pp. 18, 22, Pls. 29 and 39.

[35] Amelung, *Antiken in Florenz*, pp. 47 ff., No. 68. Brunn-Bruckmann, *Denkmäler*, Pl. 425. Lawrence, *Later Greek Sculpture*, p. 18, Pl. 30a.

[36] F. Winter in *Altertümer von Pergamon*, Vol. VII, pp. 128 f., No. 111, Pl. XXVI. Amelung, *Antiken in Florenz*, p. 63, Fig. 17.

[37] H. B. Walters, *Catalogue of the Bronzes, Greek, Roman, and Etruscan, in the Department of Greek and Roman Antiquities* (London, the British Museum, 1899), p. 35, No. 269. O. Rayet, *Monuments de l'art antique* (Paris, 1884), Vol. I, Pl. 34.

[38] A. Furtwängler, *Der Satyr aus Pergamon* (*Winck.-Prog. Berlin*, No. 40 [1880]), Pl. I.

[39] A. Merlin in *Mon. Piot*, Vol. XVIII (1910), pp. 15 f., Pl. V.

belongs in this orbit of Pergamene satyr creations. He stretches out his arms, while at the same time he bends forward and looks upward. His face is full and round, his eyebrows are drawn, his hair is standing up in a manner similar to the giant's (Fig. 434). Two excellent bronze statuettes in the Metropolitan Museum, one a satyr with torches, the other dancing [40] (Figs. 447–48), are also related in style. All these satyrs are full of tension, expressed in the meager and slim bodies. The sinews stand out and the muscles are harsh under a thin upper layer of fat. The strong muscles of the legs show that these satyrs are gay dancers. They are boorish, but jolly and harmless. They are the best exponents of the sparkling lusty life of the best period of Hellenistic civilization. There are many Hellenistic and Roman variations of the satyr (see Chap. X, pp. 139 f.).

Probably also to the same period (about 200 B.C.) and to the Pergamene school belongs the celebrated sleeping Barberini satyr in Munich [41] (Figs. 450–51). It was found between 1624 and 1641 near the Castello Sant' Angelo, the mausoleum of the Emperor Hadrian, in Rome. The missing right leg, part of the left leg, the ugly left arm, and the rock with plants and a tree at the back were added by the great baroque sculptor Lorenzo Bernini (died 1680). The right leg is too strongly bent; the place for the heel can be seen below the toes of the modern foot. Otherwise this is a valuable Hellenistic original. The satyr is depicted as if tired after a gay banquet, intoxicated with wine, the gift of his god Dionysos. At the moment when he sinks back on the rock, his panther skin, which hangs from his left shoulder, spreads over the rustic seat. The seat originally must have been a little lower, so that the body, like the right leg, was stretched out more than now. The right arm is lifted and laid over the rear part of the head. The head reclines on the left shoulder. The left arm must have hung in a much more relaxed way, similarly to the arms of the dead Patroclus and the dying wife of the Gaul (Figs. 272, 274–75, and 281–83). Only the left side of the torso reclines firmly on the rock. Therefore his

back, with a short tail, is free; it is as excellently modeled as the front of the torso.

The head is crowned with a wreath of ivy leaves and berries that covers most of his shaggy hair, which grows upward over the forehead. Thus hair and ivy form an effective frame for the coarse and individual face. The forehead has swelling muscles. The eyebrows are grown together over the broad nose. The eyes are deeply sunk into their orbits. The cheeks are meager, with broad cheekbones; the chin is harsh. The mouth is broad and slightly open, so that the upper teeth are visible. One has the impression that he is snoring. It is the moment before the beginning of a deep sleep, when the tension of the preceding revel is not yet quite gone.

Several later versions of this motif of beginning sleep are known to us. The rendering of sleep in its different forms is indeed one of the great achievements of the Pergamene school. How different from the satyr's rest is the sleep of death of the Persian, the giant, the young Gaul, and the Amazon! (Figs. 432, 434–36.)

Closely related to the Barberini satyr is the head of a sleeping Erinyes, or more probably a Maenad, in the Museo Nazionale Romano in Rome [42] (Figs. 452–53). It is the same moment of beginning sleep. The preceding ecstatic reveling is suggested by the long disheveled hair, the sunken eyes, and the slightly open mouth. The head, with its long wavy hair strands, sinks forward, the eyes have just closed, and the eyebrows are relaxed. The hair seems to be wet with sweat. The features are reminiscent of the wife whom the Gaul has killed. The head, therefore, has also been identified as that of the dead mother whose child was trying to caress her, a statue by Epigonos (see above, p. 110). In any case, this work is closely related to the Gauls and consequently belongs to the Pergamene school.

Other examples of restless sleep are the Ariadne and the Hermaphrodite (Figs. 623–25). Examples of sweet and undisturbed sleep are Endymion

[40] Metropolitan Museum of Art, New York, Nos. 41.11.6 and 29.73. G. M. A. Richter, *Handbook of the Greek Collection* (1953), p. 125, Pl. 104b–c.

[41] Brunn-Bruckmann, *Denkmäler*, Pl. 4. A. Furtwängler and P. Wolters, *Beschreibung der Glyptothek zu München* (2d ed., 1910), pp. 209 ff., No. 218. E. Buschor, *Die Plastik der Griechen* (Berlin, Rembrandt-Verlag, 1936), p. 97.

[42] Helbig, *Führer durch die öffentlichen Sammlungen klassischer Altertümer in Rom*, 3d ed., Vol. II, No. 1301. Paribeni, *Le Terme di Diocleziano*, Pl. 28. C. Kleiner, *Das Nachleben des Pergamenischen Gigantenkampfes* (*Winck.-Prog. Berlin*, No. 105 [1949]), pp. 13 f., Fig. 8. R. Exner in *Museum Helveticum*, Vol. VIII (1951), pp. 185 ff., Fig. 2. She explains this head as that of a Hydra. S. Aurigemma, *Le Terme di Diocleziano e il Museo Nazionale Romano*, pp. 106 f., No. 283, Pl. LXX a.

(Figs. 621–22), the head of a girl in the Museo
Nazionale Romano, and Eros (Figs. 616–20). Thus
sleep was represented in all stages: the drunkenness of the satyr; the ecstasy of the Maenad; the
restless sleep of Ariadne forsaken by Theseus; of
Endymion, whom Selene will awaken; the sweet
sleep of innocent youth, and the sleep of Eros (see
Chap. X, pp. 145 f.).

2. THE SECOND PERGAMENE SCHOOL (FIRST HALF OF THE SECOND CENTURY B.C.)

The development of the Pergamene school from
realism to passion is shown by the differences in
the two great works: the representations of the
Gauls in the dedication of Attalus and the gods and
giants on the great altar, dedicated by Eumenes II
(197–159). It already is evident, however, in the
difference between the portraits of Philetairos on
coins and the portrait of the dedicator of the altar [43]
(Fig. 417). It was exceptional for a ruler of Pergamon to put his own portrait on the coins instead
of the portrait of Philetairos (Fig. 416). In place
of the brutal and powerful features of the unscru-
pulous military ancestor, on this coin there appear the refined features of Eumenes, with deeply
shaded eyes, slender hanging nose, expressive
mouth with thin lips, the folds under the eyes and
the meager cheeks expressing restlessness and emotion. The hair is thick and curly.

The same turn from realism to emotion can be
seen in a marble head which has been almost generally recognized as the portrait of Attalus I; however, because he did not put his likeness, but that
of Philetairos, on his coins, it cannot be verified by
a coin portrait. It is an original head of the highest
quality, found on the slope of the Acropolis of
Pergamon and last seen in the Pergamon Museum
in Berlin [44] (Figs. 454, 456–57). This head underwent a curious transformation in antiquity. At first
it had a simple arrangement of the straight hair,
with the strands placed in flat layers. A diadem was
knotted together in the back. Then the hair was
cut down in front and above the temples, and a
long-haired wig of thick, curled strands was added.
Such luxurious hair was favored in the second century at the time of Eumenes II. It may be seen on
his coins (Fig. 417) as well as on the great altar
(see Figs. 460, 462). The effect of the wig is to give
a heroic character to the features. The swelling
under the eyes gains significance. The mouth becomes more lively. The expression is more emotional; there is less evidence of burdening thought
and more of serious passion and concern. There is,
no doubt, a certain disunity introduced into the
composition by the wreath of locks.

The original head probably dates from about
200—197 B.C., the last years of Attalus I. Then his
son and successor, Eumenes II, in an attempt to
make his father look like a hero and to heighten
the expression according to the taste of his time,
had the wig added. The same means were used by
the Diadochi to idealize Alexander (see Fig. 455),
and later by Mithridates Eupator (see pp. 121 f.
and Figs. 480–81).

The same taste can be seen in the most grandiose
work of the Pergamene school, and perhaps of all
Hellenistic art, the great altar of Pergamon, built
by Eumenes around 180–160 B.C. The large frieze
may have been carved between 182 and 165. When
this monument was discovered by Karl Humann
in 1880, he sent a telegram to the Museum in Berlin, saying: "We have found a whole new epoch
of art; we have in our hands the greatest work remaining to us from antiquity." It was at once compared to works of the Italian baroque, particularly
those of Michelangelo; to Flemish baroque, particularly Rubens, and German baroque, particularly Schlüter. But, like the baroque, it also found
enemies among classicists who missed the "noble
simplicity and serene greatness" of Greek art.
Only later were scholars able to make the right
evaluation of this powerful Asiatic style, which
contrasted to, yet was based on, Attic style. The ex-

---

[43] F. Imhoof-Blumer, *Porträtköpfe auf antiken Münzen hellen-
ischer und hellenisierter Völker* (1885), p. 32, Pl. IV, No. 15.
H. von Fritze, "Die Münzen von Pergamon," in *Abh. Preuss.
Akad., Anhang* (1910), Abhandlung I, Pl. II, No. 14. *Alter-
tümer von Pergamon*, Vol. VII, p. 146, Fig. 130 c. See also
Chap. V, p. 88, note 73.
[44] F. Winter, *Die Skulpturen* (Vol. VII of *Altertümer von
Pergamon*), pp. 144 ff., No. 130, Figs. 130 a-c, Pls. XXXI-
XXXII. R. Delbrück, *Antike Porträts* (1912), pp. XXXVIII ff.,
Fig. 14, Pl. 27. Hekler, *Bildniskunst*, Pl. 75. E. Pfuhl in *Jahr-
buch d. Inst.*, XLV (1930), pp. 46 f., Fig. 28. V. Müller in *Art
Bulletin*, Vol. XX (1938), Fig. 28. Müller dates it in 195–185
B.C., without distinguishing the two different phases. See H.

P. L'Orange, *Apotheosis in Ancient Portraiture* (Harvard
University Press, 1947), p. 41, Fig. 19. Kähler, *Pergamon*
(pp. 9 f., 33, frontispiece), names the head Eumenes II. The
coins (Fig. 417) refute this identification.

cellent reconstruction in the Berlin architectural museum has been of great help [45] (Fig. 458).

The altar was the center of the great terrace dedicated to Zeus below the sanctuary to Athena, which was above the theater auditorium and the upper market place. It is described by Ampelius in his *Liber memorialis* (8. 14) as one of the wonders of the world: "At Pergamon is a great marble altar, forty feet in height, with colossal sculptures. It contains the battle of the giants." The Bible mentions the altar as the throne of Satan (*Revelation* 2. 12). The general shape is found on a coin of Septimius Severus.[46] It shows a broad staircase at the front, and over a high pedestal a colonnade with entablature and *akroteria*. The reliefs are not indicated. The coin may have been minted on the occasion of a renovation in the period of Septimius Severus, when a baldachin was erected over the altar proper, above the staircase inside the colonnades. The builder seems to have been Menekrates of Rhodes. He is mentioned as one of seven celebrated architects in the *Mosella* of Ausonius (vs. 307), a poem written in A.D. 371, based on Book x of Varro's *Imagines*. Ausonius classes Menekrates with Daidalos, the creator of the labyrinth, Iktinos, the builder of the Parthenon, and others. The name "Menekrates, the son of Menekrates of Rhodes" appears with other sculptors' names on the socle of the Pergamon altar. Menekrates thus was the architect and leading sculptor of the altar, just as Skopas had been in Tegea, and Pytheos had been for the Mausoleum of Halicarnassus. Under

Menekrates, or with him, worked other sculptors from Pergamon, Rhodes, Attica, and Ephesus.[47] Yet here, as in the votive offerings of Attalus, a unified, very advanced, especially characteristic "baroque" Pergamene style developed through the collaboration of many artists in a great task.

The design was not made by the artists alone. As Phidias, together with Pericles, worked out the democratic program of the sculpture of the Parthenon for a democratic state, so here probably the leading artist, together with a kind of a learned society which had gathered at the court of the Attalids, worked out the plan for the arrangement of the frieze, in which scholarship was combined with connoisseurship of older art. The battle of the gods and giants was to celebrate the victories of Eumenes, as on the east metopes of the Parthenon the same battle had been represented to celebrate the victory of the Greeks over the Persians. The Attalids considered themselves the true heirs to Attic leadership in the fields of politics, art, and science, only the Attalids did everything on a much larger scale than their predecessors. Thus, not only the twelve Olympic gods, but about seventy-five gods and their adversaries, were represented to celebrate the Attalid victory. To make up such a total, all available gods had to be pressed into service. The main source for the mythology seems to have been Hesiod's *Theogonia*, and for the representations of stars and constellations, the *Phaenomena* of Aratus, a description of the astronomical system. The arrangement was certainly prescribed by the scholars. On the east side, not in the center but more to the north, opposite the main entrance to the precinct, Zeus fights, standing between his children Athena and Heracles. As a parallel, near the south corner of the east side Leto is in battle between her children Apollo and Artemis. Between these two groups, each containing a parent with one son and one daughter, were Hera, Hebe, Hephaistos, and Demeter. At the north end was Ares, turning his horses inward; at the south end is Hecate, turned outward. She is represented in this position because she does not belong to the main group of Olympian gods to whom this side is dedicated. On the other side of the southeast corner fights Asteria with the other Titans and

[45] J. Schrammen, *Der Grosse Altar* (Vol. III, Part 1 of *Altertümer von Pergamon*), p. 4, pp. 24 f. (plan), Pls. XVIII–XIX (reconstruction). A. von Salis, *Der Altar von Pergamon* (Berlin, Reimer, 1912). W. H. Schuchhardt, *Die Meister des grossen Frieses von Pergamon* (Berlin, de Gruyter, 1925). H. Kähler, *Der grosse Fries von Pergamon: Untersuchungen zur Kunstgeschichte und Geschichte Pergamons* (Berlin, Gebrüder Mann, 1948), and Kähler, *Pergamon, in Bilderhefte antiker Kunst*, Vol. IX (Berlin, 1949), pp. 16 ff., Pls. 6–40. Pontremoli and Collignon, *Pergame*, pp. 59 ff. H. E. Stier, *Aus der Welt des Pergamonaltars* (Berlin, 1932). A. E. Napp. *Der Altar von Pergamon* (Munich, 1936). W. von Massow, *Führer durch das Pergamon-Museum* (2d ed., 1936). G. Bruns, *Der grosse Altar von Pergamon* (Berlin, 1949). A. Schober, *Die Kunst von Pergamon* (Vienna, 1951).
[46] H. von Fritze, "Die Münzen von Pergamon," in *Abh. Preuss. Akad.*, Anhang (1910), Abhandlung I, Pl. IX, No. 3. J. Schrammen in *Altertümer von Pergamon*, Vol. III, Part I, p. 5. W. Wroth, *Catalogue of the Greek Coins of Mysia*, ed. by R. S. Poole, (London, the British Museum, 1892), Pl. XXX, No. 7.

[47] M. Fränkel, *Die Inschriften von Pergamon* (Vol. VIII of *Altertümer von Pergamon*), Nos. 70–84, pp. 55 ff.

heavenly lights, to whom the south side is given—Phoebe, Themis, Uranus, Aither, Theia, Adrasteia, and Cybele; and before all is Helios, preceded by Eos and followed by Selene—Sun, Dawn, and Moon. On the north fights Nyx, the night, surrounded by stars and constellations. To them are added the Gorgons and the Erinyes. At the northeast corner Aphrodite fights next to her mother, the Titan Dione, and so makes the transition to the east side, where behind the corner Aphrodite's lover Ares is fighting from his chariot. The southwest corner is similarly decorated with two lions going in opposite directions, one carrying Cybele and the other preceding Rhea; like Ares and Aphrodite, the goddesses are turned away from each other. Rhea is placed as a counterpart to Dionysos, who, followed by his satyrs, fights at the short end of the podium near the staircase. The declining space at the side of the stairs is filled with figures of Hermes and of the nymphs. Thus the gods of the earth are the counterparts of the gods of the water on the other side of the staircase. Triton and Amphitrite have their adversaries between them, while Nereus, Doris, Oceanus, and Tethys fill the narrowing space near the steps.

It is clear that a grandiose and very learned plan underlies the arrangement, and though not all the identifications are certain, the chief idea was plainly to group the Olympians on the main side, the heavenly lights and venerable Titans in the south, the night and stars to the north, earth and water divinities in the west.

One might expect a frosty representation of this purely intellectual scheme, but the opposite is true. Hellenistic art here shows an inventiveness in original creation, a great variety of moods, interesting details, and full-blooded personalities, proving that the words "degeneration" and "decline" are not to be used in describing this art.

The greatest innovation lies in the diverse forms of the giants. In the archaic and classical periods they had human forms and weapons. On the shield of Athena Parthenos they fight with stones, facing upward toward the gods, who, as dwellers on Olympus, naturally fight from a higher level.[48] Then occasionally, beginning in the late fifth or early fourth century, the giants were represented with snake legs. This symbolizes the fact that the giants were the children of Ge, the earth goddess, and snakes are supposed to live in the earth. The Pergamene artists, however, varied in their depiction of the giants; some remained completely human, some were endowed with other animal attributes, such as claws, birds' wings, a lion's head, bull's horns, and napes of the neck like a bull's. The snake legs—where applied—are useful for making the giants appear lower than the gods, since the difference of level, as Phidias used it, was not possible in this long frieze where there is no space above the heads of the upright-standing figures. There also is no background of importance left. The fury of battle is reflected in the fact that nowhere is there a piece of neutral ground, as we still have it in the Mausoleum and the Alexander sarcophagus. The snake legs, the wings, and the fluttering hair and draperies fill every available spot.

If we look at the group of Zeus and his three adversaries[49] (Fig. 459) we at once get an idea of the richness of forms and the virtuosity of Menekrates and his collaborators. The outspread arms of the highest god fill three fourths of the available space. His powerful torso, surrounded by the veil-like arrangement of the upper part of his mantle, stands out as if in full roundness. The folds of the lower part of the himation underline the swing of the movement of the legs to his right, while his head is turned to the left to look at his most powerful adversary, Porphyrion, against whom he wields the thunderbolt in his right hand. His left arm, wrapped in the aegis, is stretched out toward the left arm of Porphyrion, which is wrapped in a lion's skin. Porphyrion, seen from the back, is lifting himself up on his snake legs. His eyes were inlaid with sparkling stones. He alone still defies the god. Between the two, a young giant, fully human, has fallen to his knees. With his right hand he nurses his shoulder, pierced by a thunderbolt of Zeus. On the other side of Zeus another youthful and fully human giant is falling backward under the impact of a still flaming thunderbolt which has pierced his left thigh. He still holds his shield on the left arm and his sword in the right hand, while

---

[48] A. von Salis in *Jahrbuch d. Inst.,* Vol. LV (1940), pp. 91 ff., Figs. 1–8, 17–25.

[49] H. Winnefeld, *Die Friese des grossen Altars* (Vol. III, Part 2 of *Altertümer von Pergamon*), pp. 50 ff., Pls. XI, XXIV, and XXIX, No. 4.

the scabbard hangs at his left side. Above him hangs the end of the lion skin of Heracles, filling the space, as the eagle of Zeus fills the space above Porphyrion. Of the four figures one appears full front, one full back, one in three quarter view, and one in profile. Despite the impression of wild unrest there is a clever and clear composition.

The same is true of the neighboring Athena group [50] (Fig. 460), and also for both groups taken together. Athena moves in the opposite direction from Zeus, just as she moves away from Poseidon in the west pediment of the Parthenon. She also recalls the Athena in the east pediment. It is quite possible that the Pergamene artists wanted their gods to resemble the Attic gods, which now were serving the Attalids as they had formerly served the Attic people. Athena, like Zeus, spreads out both arms, the left bearing her shield. The right hand grasps the luxuriant hair of her adversary Alcyoneus [51] (Figs. 460 and 462). He is perfectly human except for big wings. Snake legs would be out of place, for the sacred snake of Athena is attacking him. The reptile curls around his left upper arm and his right thigh, then lifts itself up to bite into his right breast. Alcyoneus stretches out his left arm in a gesture of supplication, while with his right hand he tries to tear the hand of the goddess away from his hair. The long winding strands surround his face like snakes. His features reflect deep anxiety. The mouth is open as if shouting for mercy, the nostrils are dilated, the eyes look up imploringly, full of deep anguish. The eyebrows are drawn, the forehead is wrinkled. His supplication is supported by his mother Ge, the earth, whose upper body appears; both hands are lifted to Athena. The richness and movement of Ge's hair even surpasses that of her son's. Her pleading is in vain. Nike has appeared to give Athena the crown of victory. Here again, the figure of Nike is similar to the Nike in the east pediment of the Parthenon, another proof that the Pergamene artists adopted the Attic forms of the gods.[52] Nike

counterbalances the movement of Athena, while her wings balance the big wings of Alcyoneus and fill, like these, the upper part of the relief to the right and to the left of the head of Athena.

Quite different is the grouping in the other family, where Leto fights standing between her son and daughter [53] (Fig. 461). With a wide stride she pushes a torch into the face of her adversary Tityus, so that he falls backward, holding himself up with the left claw, which has been given him instead of a hand. He is scratching Leto with the birds' talons which serve him as feet. He has curved wings which seem to be scorched. Leto has her hair bound up. Over the chiton she has a mantle with open seam and fringe. She has rolled this into a thick pad near the belt below her breast, while the end flutters behind her back. The inside seen here is crinkled, in contrast to the smooth outside. She wears sandals with many straps, held together by a leaf-shaped ornament on the instep of the foot.

To the right of Leto, Apollo—often compared to the Apollo of Belvedere (Figs. 199–200)—has hit Ephialtes in the eye with an arrow. This giant recalls the dying Gaul in Naples [54] (Fig. 435, upper left). To the left of Leto, Artemis and her adversary are represented in what amounts to a romantic love story [55] (Fig. 463). Artemis is a particularly beautiful girl. Her full hair is bound up nicely, her mantle is rolled around her waist in a thick pad, with the ends floating before and behind her; her shoes are a wonderwork of the shoemakers' craft: high boots with elegant fur cuffs and finely drawn scallops and scrolls. With these she strides over bodies lying on the ground between her and Otos, and aims at him a deadly arrow which she has taken from the quiver on her back and put into her bow. Otos stands rigid, as if fascinated. His right arm with the sword sinks to his side. He holds the shield on his left arm, but he does not protect himself. He is like the Greek hoplite as he appeared in archaic art, in a helmet decorated with a long horse's tail. In the next moment he will sink down

[50] *Altertümer von Pergamon*, Vol. III, Part 2, pp. 53 ff., Pls. XII, XXIV. A. von Salis, *Altar von Pergamon*, pp. 45 ff., Figs. 1–2.

[51] *Altertümer von Pergamon*, Vol. III, Part 2, Pl. XXVI, No. 4. For the head of Alcyoneus, see *Altertümer von Pergamon*, Vol. III, Part 2, Pl. XXVI, No. 4; for Ge, see *ibid.,* Pl. XXVIII, No. 2.

[52] Salis, *Altar von Pergamon*, pp. 53 f.

[53] *Altertümer von Pergamon*, Vol. III, Part 2, pp. 38 ff., Pl. IX. For the head of Tityus, see *ibid.,* Pl. XXVIII, No. 2.

[54] *Altertümer von Pergamon*, Vol. III, Part 2, pp. 46 f., Pl. IX. Salis, *Altar von Pergamon*, pp. 70 ff.

[55] *Altertümer von Pergamon*, Vol. III, Part 2, pp. 43 f., Pl. VIII. Salis, *Altar von Pergamon*, p. 72, Fig. 8. For the head of Artemis, see *Altertümer von Pergamon*, Vol. III, Part 2, Pl. XXXV, Fig. 2; for Otos see *ibid.,* Pl. XXVIII, Fig. 1; for Aphrodite, see *ibid.,* Pl. XIV.

on the heap of bodies between him and the cruel goddess. Between his legs are the snakes of the bearded giant Aigaion, who lies on his side, his wavy hair grasped by a big hunting dog, the companion of Artemis. The dog's bushy tail appears between her and Leto (Fig. 461). The giant lifts his arm and pushes his finger into the eye of the attacking dog (Fig. 464). His left hand lies weakly on the elegant boot of Artemis's right foot, which she has put on the chest of a dead young giant. Similarly, Aphrodite has put her foot into the face of a slain giant, over whom she bends, probably to extract a weapon from his chest. The contrast of beauty and brutal behavior in the same person is used for strong effect.

A very original creation is the Hecate from the south end of the east frieze [56] (Fig. 465). Alkamenes had represented this goddess as three equal figures, with their backs leaning against one another. The fourth century had many variations of this type. The Pergamene artists, however, wanted her to be in action and fighting. They thus represented only one figure in full, seen from the back. A broad belt holds her wide chiton and mantle, the end of which is drawn through the belt, and goes in a roll over the left shoulder. Her left arm holds a shield, her lifted right hand a torch. When we follow this torch, we see that a second face appears in front of the full head, and a second hair-knot behind the full hair. Below the lifted arm appear an arm with a sword and a hand with a spear. In front of the shield is a hand with a scabbard. We thus can piece together three bodies of Hecate, fighting against the giant Klytios. He has a dignified head with full hair and beard. With both hands he holds a rock over his head. His snake legs have particularly hideous dragons' heads, one of which ineffectively bites into the shield of Hecate, while her dog bites the left thigh of Klytios. The gap between Hecate and Otos is filled with a snake of the giant Aigaion, with the scabbard of Otos, the three arms of Hecate, and the helm bush of Otos. The snake of Aigaion is placed between the legs of Otos and bites into the folds of the dress of Hecate. Nowhere is there an empty space.

The center of the north side is given to one of the most beautiful figures of the frieze: Nyx, the personification of night [57] (Fig. 466). Her heavy dress and diagonally laid mantle surround her matronly form in large and diversified curves. A veil and the ends of a pearl fillet binding her hair-knot flutter around her head. In her right hand she lifts a vase around which a snake is coiling. It is the constellation Crater with the Hydra, the water snake. She wants to throw this missile, which she has torn from the starry sky, at a bearded giant who is falling to his left knee. She tries to tear away the shield with which he attempts to protect himself. A snake belonging to the next figure, which is missing, fills the space above the helmeted head of the attacked giant. Behind Nyx fights a giant in full armor, including a corselet; he is seen from the back. His shield has stars and thunderbolts as decoration on its rim. He thus may be Aster or Asterios, one of the personified stars who fight around their mother Nyx.

Of the two short sides on the west near the staircase, the one to the right, or to the south, has only one figure well preserved—that of Dionysos [58] (Fig. 468). He advances with both arms stretched out horizontally, probably wielding his thyrsus, the sacred wand, in the right hand, while with the left he probably grasped his adversary. He is crowned with ivy, has a chiton with two belts and a long pouch drawn out over the lower belt, a small mantle wrapped around the shoulders and fluttering behind him, a nebris (the skin of a fawn) over his breast, and high decorated cothurni. He is helped in the fight by his panther, which is between his legs, and two small satyrs behind him.

The left wing, to the north, is well preserved. On the short side an excellent and severe composition puts three giants between Triton and his mother Amphitrite [59] (Fig. 458). A standing giant in the center attacks Triton with his left arm, around which he has wrapped a lion's skin. Between him and the gods two young giants have fallen on their knees. The one below the lion's skin is completely human; the other has snake legs which wind high up behind him and behind Amphitrite. The goddess threatens him with a spear. Triton is the most

[56] *Altertümer von Pergamon,* Vol. III, Part 2, pp. 40 ff., Fig. 5, Pl. VIII. For the head of her adversary Klytios, see *ibid.,* Pl. XXIX, Fig. 1.

[57] *Altertümer von Pergamon,* Vol. III, Part 2, pp. 66 ff., Pl. XVII; for her head, see Pl. XXV, Fig. 1.
[58] *Altertümer von Pergamon,* Vol. III, Part 2, pp. 13 ff., Pl. I.
[59] *Altertümer von Pergamon,* Vol. III, Part 2, pp. 83 ff., Pl. XXI.

complicated figure on this side. He has a human body, wings made of fish fins, and the legs and breast of a horse, ending in a long eellike fish tail. He has a knife in his right hand, while his left hand tries to tear away the lion skin of the standing giant. The composition on the south end was probably similar—a symmetrical one, with many details.

The narrowing space near the steps is excellently filled, and again is better preserved on the north side than the south [60] (Figs. 467, 470). The movement becomes more and more lively. It begins with the dignified, quietly standing figure of Nereus, the Old Man of the Sea. His head is covered with a cap made out of fishskin. The same material is used for the boots of his wife, Doris. She is grasping the hair of a giant with particularly long snake legs, which are spread out to both sides (Fig. 467). She puts her foot on one snake leg, while the other lies on two steps of the stairs, as if helpless. Behind this coiled snake leg fights Oceanus, the god of the sea, as the last and one of the most magnificent figures. He probably lifted an oar with his right hand. His exomis opens in the violent movement. Behind him is his wife Tethys, who wielded a branch of a tree. Before them a pair of smaller giants flee up the stairs, one kneeling on one step and supporting himself with his hand on the next step. The other is seen from the back, seated on the next higher step, trying to protect himself with a shield. One of his snake legs is seen on the step above him and was probably struggling against the eagle which filled the narrow angle between the podium and the uppermost steps. This use of the stairs is a particularly "baroque" motif (Fig. 470).

On the roof above the colonnade were figures of Tritons as *akroteria* [61] (Fig. 469). The two best preserved have strong bodies with powerful muscles, recalling those of Zeus and Porphyrion (Fig. 459). Both are in strong movement. Of the heads only one, with thick hair, is partly preserved. The one without a head holds an elongated shell in his left arm. He probably lifted another such "Triton shell" to his mouth, using it as a trumpet. Both have cuffs of leaves below their hips to separate the hu-

man and animal parts of their bodies. Below the cuffs are large acanthus leaves with strong ribs and sharp fin-like edges; behind and under these begins the featherlike covering of the legs. Most characteristic of the period are the sharp and diverse points of the acanthus leaves.

All the sculptures decorating the outside of the altar have a luxurious and grandiose style. Light and shade play over the surfaces of the nude bodies as well as over the draperies, wings, shoes, and furs. The draperies underline in a dramatic fashion the grandiose movements of the bodies. They flow in a picturesque manner over the front and fall in big masses to the side and to the ground, surrounding breasts, heads, and arms in great curves and broken lines. They underline in a sophisticated and often refined manner the differences in movement of the two sides. There are fine differentiations of material: the textures of the inside and outside of wool and furs are indicated. Thin linen with a dull surface and silks of shining lustre are well distinguished. Perhaps the first pure silk ever to reach Greece was brought to Pergamon, as were elegant furs, precious woolens, and the thin linen of Egypt and the island of Cos. The boots show a preference for decoration with scrolls, pointed leaves, and irregular scallops. Everything is full and rich; a substantial body of material is used for the dresses. The direction of the folds, the feathers of the wings, and the points of the scallops are as diversified and divergent as possible. The ideals of the classical period—symmetry, balance, and harmony—are disregarded or, rather, are seen from an entirely new angle.

Several single statues found in Pergamon have the same sumptuous style, although the restless movements of the great battle scenes had of course to be toned down in the statues. But, for example, the statue of Zeus [62] (Figs. 471–72) found in the temple of Hera built under Attalus II (159–138) recalls the mighty torso of the Zeus of the frieze.

---

[60] *Altertümer von Pergamon*, Vol. III, Part 2, pp. 86 ff., Pl. XXII.

[61] J. Schrammen, *Altertümer von Pergamon*, Vol. III, Part 1, pp. 76 ff., illustration on p. 78. Winter, *ibid.*, Vol. VII, Part 2, pp. 173 f., Nos. 166–67, Beiblatt 24.

[62] A. Ippel in *Athen Mitt.*, Vol. XXXVII (1912), pp. 261, 316 ff., Figs. 11–15, Pls. 22a and 26. M. Schede, *Meisterwerke der türkischen Museen zu Konstantinopel*, Vol. I (1928): *Griechische und römische Skulpturen des Antikenmuseums*), p. 12, Pl. 20. *Ant. Denk.*, Vol. III, Pl. 19. R. Horn, *Stehende weibliche Gewandstatuen in der hellenistischen Plastik* (1931; *Ergänzungsheft II* to *Röm. Mitt.*), pp. 49 ff., Pl. 20, No. 2. Ippel and Horn see a relaxation of intensity and evidence of academic traits in this statue, a view which I cannot share.

However, the wide stride of the feet, clad in elegant sandals like those on the frieze, the raising of the right arm, and the hand holding the thick upper roll of the overfold of the himation express movement even in the quietly standing figure. The light plays on the surface of the full mantle, with its deep and variegated folds.

A seated statue of similar style is the Cybele [63] (Fig. 474). Here also we have the broad forms surrounded by substantial draperies with many deeply cut folds, which vary from finely drawn sharp ridges to deep unruly shaded grooves. Like the Athena and the Apollo of the frieze, this is an adaptation of an older Attic type created in the late fifth century by Agorakritos.[64]

The most "baroque" single statue is the one probably rightly interpreted as Tragoidia [65] (Fig. 473). A magnificent figure of a woman, unfortunately without head, hands, and left foot, with a broad belt directly below her breasts and a sword at the side, she is wrapped in ample garments which broaden out outside the legs and are broken into the most diverse patterns by deep shadow-filled pits. A large mantle thrown over the left shoulder and arm hangs down the back, while in front it is rolled up into a thick pad at its upper edge, and into a flat strip at the lower edge, running diagonally across the body from the right knee to the left hip. The triangle between the knee and the hip is filled in the upper part with bow-lines, which begin with delicate ridges and become more elevated until they meet thick horizontal folds over the thigh. Thus many small motifs divide the surface into contrasting planes and light areas.

The so-called Juno Cesi, a statue of a goddess in the Museo Capitolino, has often been compared to the Tragoidia.[66] She has, indeed, a similar voluminous chiton, a high belt, a mantle arranged over the left shoulder, with a thick roll at the upper edge and a triangular field below it. The mantle, however, has a triangular overfold, with the tip hanging over the left thigh, not the right one, and the main part is not lifted to the left hip but hangs quite flat. The hollow grooves are much flatter, the motifs of the mantle much more simplified. We have here the copy or adaptation of a Pergamene statue of the second century, not an original made in Pergamon. The head, however, may give some idea of the type of head which we might expect for the Tragoidia.

A similar original head, although much more expressive, is the so-called Beautiful Head of Pergamon, until 1945 in the Pergamon Museum in Berlin [67] (Fig. 475). The upper part of the hair, as well as the nose, lips, and chin, are rubbed off; at the left side a piece of the hair was worked separately and fastened with two dowels. Enough remains, however, to show the silken quality of the hair, which is parted and laid in soft strong strands. The eyes have a dreamy expression and the mouth is opened as if in longing. The mood is softer than that of any head remaining on the frieze, but the head of Nyx (Fig. 466) is of a similar type.

An over-life-size head of Heracles from Pergamon, in Berlin [68] (Fig. 476), is a kind of male and more masculine counterpart of the Beautiful Head. The hair is raised in soft short wisps around the hairline. The eyebrows, with irregular hair, throw a deep shadow on the small eyes, which look up as if in sorrow. The lips are slightly parted. The beard is well groomed and has thick curls, irregularly parted in the center. The head was slightly bent to the right. Heads like that of Klytios (Fig. 465) are its closest parallel.

The head of the so-called Dying Alexander has long since been recognized as that of a dying giant.[69] The head pathetically thrown back, sur-

---

[63] *Altertümer von Pergamon*, Vol. VII, pp. 69 f., No. 45, Pl. XII.

[64] A. von Salis in *Jahrbuch d. Inst.*, XXVIII (1913), pp. 1 ff., Figs. 1–2. The best fifth-century figure: M. Bieber in *Athen. Mitt.*, Vol. XXXVII (1912), pp. 159 ff., Fig. 3, Pls. XI–XII.

[65] *Altertümer von Pergamon*, Vol. VII, pp. 76 ff., No. 47, Pls. XIV–XV. Horn, *Gewandstatuen*, pp. 51 f., Pl. 18, No. 2. Horn wrongly assumes that the mantle is small; it is actually large, but rolled together. For other draped statues in the style of the altar, see *Altertümer von Pergamon*, Vol. VII, Part 2, pp. 80 ff., Nos. 49–89, Pls. XVI–XXIV.

[66] Brunn-Bruckmann, *Denkmäler*, Pl. 359. Jones, *Sculpt. Museo Capitolino*, Stanza del Gladiatore, No. 2, pp. 340 f., Pl. 85. F.

[——] Winter in *Altertümer von Pergamon*, Vol. VII (text), p. 80, Fig. 47d.

[67] *Altertümer von Pergamon*, Vol. VII, pp. 117 f., No. 90, Pl. XXV. Brunn-Bruckmann, *Denkmäler*, Pl. 159. Pontremoli and Collignon, *Pergame*, figure on p. 204. Lawrence, *Later Greek Sculpture*, p. 28, Pl. 44.

[68] Berlin Museum, No. 1675. W. Reinecke, *Meisterwerke im Alten Museum*, p. 98, Fig. 74.

[69] Amelung, *Antiken in Florenz*, pp. 95 f., No. 151. Brunn-Bruckmann, *Denkmäler*, Pl. 264.

rounded by thick, long locks like creeping snakes, the drawn eyebrows, the anxiously lifted eyes, and the sobbing mouth remind one of the Alcyoneus (Fig. 462) and other wounded young giants of the frieze. But here we have a copy, with forms and mood flattened when compared with the full passion of the frieze.

The Pergamene artists' conception of the real Alexander shows in a head found in Pergamon and now in Istanbul [70] (Fig. 455). It is Alexander portrayed in his later years as the romantic conqueror of India, too soon aged by inhuman tasks, loss of friends, and revolts of the army. His lion's mane is rendered with long heavy strands, characteristic of the Pergamene style. His eyes look up in sorrow and longing; his mouth is open in passion and emotion. The best parallel for the expression on the frieze is the face of Otos (Fig. 463).

Among reliefs closest in style to the large altar relief is the beautiful dancer found in Pergamon and now in Istanbul. With her left hand she is gracefully lifting her finely pleated dress, dancing on tiptoe, whirling her body so that the end of the shawl over her shoulders floats behind and beside her [71] (Fig. 479). The torsion is emphasized by the swing of the drapery, similar to that of the Helios on the frieze.

The small frieze inside the colonnade around the upper platform on which the sacrificial altar was erected was certainly carved last among the decorations of the great building, for it is partly unfinished. It may, therefore, even belong partly to the time of Attalus II (159–138), and can be dated about 164—158 B.C. It tells the story of Telephos, the founder of the dynasty of Pergamon, in a long sequence of scenes, where for the first time in art history a genuine narrative style is used.[72] The figures are smaller and more numerous than in the large frieze. About a hundred and twenty-five—less than half of them—are preserved. The arrangement and interpretation have been attempted by Carl Robert and Hans Schrader, without absolute certainty being achieved.[73] The general outline of the tale has, however, been established.

The story begins with the grandfather of Telephos, Aleos, who consults the oracle of Delphi and receives the prophecy that a child of his daughter will kill his sons [74] (Fig. 477, left). We see him standing before the statue and laurel tree of Apollo, receiving the oracle, with a servant who seems to write down the words. There follows the story of the parents of Telephos, Heracles and Auge, the daughter of Aleos. Heracles comes as a visitor to Tegea and is kindly received by the royal couple [75] (Fig. 477, center). Neaira, the queen, is seated on a high throne; next to her stands a young man, who may be one of the sons later killed by Telephos. The following scene shows Heracles behind an oak tree spying on Auge (Fig. 477, right). He falls in love with her and seduces her in the woods. Telephos is born, and when this is discovered he is exposed to die in the Parthenian mountains. Fortunately, he is suckled by a lioness and found by his father, who provides for his education. Auge is condemned to be tossed into the ocean inside a chest. The building of this box is represented in detail [76] (Fig. 478). Under the supervision of an overseer, perhaps Aleos himself, four laborers work on the oval chest and its cover. Auge, bowed down in grief, her head covered with her himation, is seated on rocks with two maids standing near her. It is not certain whether the fragment with a goddess seated high on a rock, and a girl lighting a fire under a kettle with the help of a torch, belong to this or to another, later scene.

Auge is rescued. The ark lands in Mysia in Asia Minor, where King Teuthras receives her kindly

[70] *Altertümer von Pergamon*, Vol. VII, pp. 147 ff., No. 131, Beiblatt 21, Pl. XXXIII. J. J. Bernoulli, *Die erhaltenen Darstellungen Alexanders des Grossen* (1905), pp. 80 ff., Figs. 23–24. M. Bieber in *Proceedings of the American Philosophical Society*, Vol. XCIII, No. 5 (1949), pp. 392 f., Figs. 57–58.
[71] *Altertümer von Pergamon*, Vol. VII, pp. 272 ff., No. 344, Pl. XXXVIII. Lawrence, *Later Greek Sculpture*, p. 28, Pl. 45. G. Mendel, *Catalogue des sculptures grecques, romaines et byzantines, Musées Ottomanes* (1912–14), Vol. II, pp. 298 ff., No. 575. For the Helios, see *Altertümer von Pergamon*, Vol. III, Part 2, Pl. IV.
[72] H. Winnefeld in *Altertümer von Pergamon*, Vol. III, Part 2, pp. 157 ff., Pls. XXXI–XXXVI. Pontremoli and Collignon, *Pergame*, pp. 90 ff.

[73] K. Robert in *Jahrbuch d. Inst.*, II (1887), 244 f., and III (1888), 45 ff., 87 ff. Schrader in *ibid.*, XV (1900), 97 ff.
[74] *Altertümer von Pergamon*, Vol. III, Part 2, pp. 157 ff., Pl. XXXI, No. 1. Pontremoli and Collignon, *Pergame*, figure on p. 91.
[75] *Altertümer von Pergamon*, Vol. III, Part 2, pp. 159 f., Pl. XXXI, No. 2.
[76] *Altertümer von Pergamon*, Vol. III, Part 2, pp. 162 ff., Pl. XXXI, No. 3, Pl. XXXII, No. 3, Pl. XXXVI, No. 11. For the goddess on the rock and the maid lighting the fire, compare the arrangement of Robert in *Altertümer von Pergamon*, Beilage 6, and of Schrader in *ibid.*, Beilage 7.

and adopts her as a daughter. When Telephos is grown he kills his uncles, as prophesied, and leaves Arcadia. He, too, comes to Teuthras, whom he helps in a dangerous war. For this he is to be rewarded with the hand of Auge. They recognize each other as mother and son. Telephos marries Hiera, and accompanied by this Amazon-like wife he fights against the Greeks under Agamemnon when they invade Asia Minor on their expedition against Troy. Hiera is killed and Telephos is wounded by Achilles. He travels to Mycenae to be healed, where, according to the oracle, only that spear which has wounded him can cure him. He forces the healing by threatening to kill little Orestes. Telephos then returns to Mysia, founds Pergamon, and establishes there the cults of Dionysos and Athena, and finally dies as a venerated hero.

All this is told in a series of scenes in which the main heroes appear again and again; the scenes are not isolated, but are separated from each other only by trees, pillars, or columns belonging to the story. The laurel tree of Apollo indicates his sanctuary; the curtain in the banquet scene indicates the interior of the palace; the oak tree indicates the woods in which Heracles finds and seduces Auge (Fig. 477, right). Another interesting feature is that the figures do not all reach from the bottom to the top of the relief as in the large frieze, but that either empty space is above them, or they are standing or are seated on higher ground, thus giving several levels to the scenes (Fig. 478). This pictorial style was to have a great future.

The mood of the story—quiet, idyllic, and in places cozy—is in contrast to the stormy passion of the large frieze. The small details—of objects, furs, dresses, weapons, the leaves of the trees—are carved with loving care. The women are in graceful attitudes. The men are not superhuman or heroic.

The style of the small frieze, as well as that of the large one, lived on not only outside Pergamon, but also in Pergamon itself. The last Greek ruler who resided in Pergamon was Mithridates VI (Mithridates Eupator) of Pontus. He lived from about 132 to about 63 B.C.; his mother was Laodike, the daughter of Antiochus IV of Syria. When Mithridates was about twelve, his father died, murdered, it was rumored, by Laodike and relatives who also wanted to kill the young prince. He

was rescued, however, and taken into the woods, where, although he developed great physical power and mental energy, he became a suspicious and friendless personality.

When about twenty years old, Mithridates returned to Pontus, punished his mother, relatives, and guardians, created an army and navy, and in 112 began to conquer all the lands around the Black Sea. In 100/99, he conquered Bithynia. The mighty Roman senate forced him to give it up, but he again conquered it in 95/4. This led to the Mithridatic Wars, during the first of which (88–84) he resided in Pergamon. He was regarded as a liberator by the Greeks of Asia Minor, who suffered under the harsh Roman rule. With the help of the Greek cities he conquered the whole of Roman Asia. He killed not only all Roman prisoners, but had 80,000 Roman citizens murdered in one day. Taking their property, he became immensely wealthy. The Greeks honored him with many statues, among them some of silver and gold which later, when Mithridates was defeated by Lucullus in 72 and by Pompey in 66 B.C., were carried in the triumphal processions of the Roman generals.

At about the period of his greatest fame he minted silver tetradrachms with Pegasus on the reverse side. One in the Royal Ontario Museum of Toronto bears the Pontic date 209, which is 89/8 B.C.[77] The hair is thick and falls in heavy strands; there are marked sideburns. The upper part of the forehead recedes sharply. The nose is straight. The full lips are slightly parted, the corners of the mouth strongly marked. The short rounded chin is separated from the lower lip by a deep groove. The head is held high on a strong neck. The character of the face is rather barbarian and reveals a mixture of energy and passion.

This character is intensified on two coins in the Museum of Fine Arts in Boston: the earlier (Fig. 480) is more realistic, the other (Fig. 481) more idealized.[78] In both, the hair is lifted over the fore-

[77] I owe a photograph to Professor Homer Thompson, then of the Royal Ontario Museum and Professor at the University of Toronto, now at the Institute for Advanced Study at Princeton. See similar coins in E. Babelon and T. Reinach, *Recueil général des monnaies grecques d'Asie Mineure* (1925), p. 16, Pl. II, Fig. 9 (also dated 89/8), and in C. Seltman, *Greek Coins* (1933), pp. 237 f., Pl. LVII, No. 3.
[78] I owe the photographs for Figs. 480–81 to Agnes B. Brett. For similar coins see Babelon and Reinach, *Monnaies grecques,* pp. 13 ff., Pls. II–III, No. 6, and Supplementary Plate B-C 6.

head and flutters wildly behind the head, in a manner similar to that used on contemporary coins of the Macedonian quaestor Aesillas, with the portrait of Alexander the Great.[79] There is no doubt that the ambitious Mithridates felt himself a genuine heir to Alexander, the world conqueror. Therefore on the coins minted in Odessus, which imitate the coins of Lysimachos showing the portrait of Alexander, the features of the Macedonian king are replaced by those of Mithridates [80] (Fig. 484). The lion skin, the *anastole,* and the exalted expression are imitations of portraits of Alexander the Great.

The lion skin was taken by Alexander as a symbol of his descent from Heracles. Mithridates considered himself, like Heracles, a benefactor of mankind, engaged in liberating it from the evils brought by the Romans. Certainly, then, he must also have been represented as such. A head in the Louvre has generally been accepted as having come from a portrait statue which must have represented Mithridates as Heracles [81] (Figs. 482–83). The lion skin hides the hair, but the long sideburns are visible and the features agree with those on the coins.

The marble head is turned to the left and must have been part of a statue exhibiting strong movement, in accordance with the high-spirited and violent character of the king. In the portrait Mithridates appears to be about forty years of age; hence the head can be dated around 92—90 B.C.

When Mithridates resided in Pergamon, 88—85 B.C., at the height of his power, he was celebrated there as the liberator of the Greeks; in a symbolic group he appeared in the guise of Heracles liberating Prometheus [82] (Figs. 485–87). Again he wears the lion skin, which covers the rear part of his head and his back. He is shooting an arrow vigorously at the eagle that is torturing Prometheus. The diadem appears between the head of the lion (broken away) and Mithridates's thick and curly front hair. The profile of the head is the same as that on the coins, but the deep wrinkle in the forehead indicates that he may have been five years older here than in the other portraits. The lips appear fuller and more widely opened. The passionate expression is heightened. We see here the conception of Mithridates as the savior and liberator of Asia. It is in the same baroque spirit which we know from the remodeled portrait of Attalus I (Figs. 456–57) and from the large frieze of the Pergamon altar. The arrangement on several levels, however, probably against a landscape background of rocks, is the same as on the small frieze.

The practice of combining a portrait head with an idealized statue was soon to be imitated by the Romans. The whole ancient world, and with it the style of its art, became Roman during the first century B.C.

Imhoof-Blumer, *Porträtköpfe,* p. 34, Pl. V, Nos. 3–4. Delbrück, *Porträts,* p. LXV, Pl. 61, Fig. 27. E. T. Newell, *Royal Greek Portrait Coins* (New York, 1937), pp. 40 ff., Fig. 3. Lange, *Herrscherköpfe,* pp. 82 f.

[79] M. Bieber, "The Portraits of Alexander the Great," in *Proceedings of the American Philosophical Society,* Vol. XCIII, No. 5 (1949), p. 394, note 56, and p. 415, Fig. 67.

[80] I owe the photograph of this coin in the Newell collection to Agnes B. Brett. On the change of the features of Alexander to those of Mithridates, see Seltman, *Greek Coins,* p. 238. Another coin from Odessus: G. F. Hill, *Historical Greek Coins* (New York, 1906), p. 106, Pl. VII, No. 60.

[81] F. Winter, "Mithridates VI Eupator," in *Jahrbuch d. Inst.,* Vol. IX (1894), pp. 245 ff., Pl. 8. E. Pfuhl in *Jahrbuch d. Inst.,* Vol. XLV (1930), pp. 15 f. Valentine Müller in *Art Bulletin,* Vol. XX (1938), pp. 408 f., Fig. 30. Müller dates the head 85–75, which is probably a little too late.

[82] F. Winter, *Die Skulpturen* (Vol. VII of *Altertümer von Pergamon*), pp. 175 ff., No. 168, Supplementary Plate 25, Pl. XXXVII. G. Krahmer, "Eine Ehrung für Mithridates VI Eupator in Pergamon," in *Jahrbuch d. Inst.,* Vol. XL (1925), pp. 183 ff., Figs. 1–2, 11–12.

IX

RHODES AND THE SOUTHWEST OF ASIA MINOR

THE ISLAND OF RHODES is situated near the southwest coast of Asia Minor, being the most easterly of the islands in the Aegean Sea, and the largest of the Sporades ("scattered islands"). The nearest land on the Asiatic continent is Caria. Rhodes was inhabited by Dorians; their main cities in the archaic period were Camirus, Lindos, and Ialysus. In the fifth century Rhodes was a member of the Delian League under the leadership of Athens. During the Peloponnesian War, however, Rhodes fell away from Athens. In 408 the city of Rhodes was founded with an excellent harbor in a place favorable for trade. But Rhodes remained part of Persia until the expeditions of Alexander again gave it autonomy. In 304 it defended itself successfully against an attempt by Demetrius Poliorcetes to conquer it. From 301 on it remained a free city, built up a small empire including Caria and Lycia on the mainland, and attained commercial leadership during the third and early second centuries. These possessions it lost to the Romans in 168 when it had antagonized them. It lost its trade in favor of the island of Delos, which established a free port in 166. Although Rhodes recovered during the later second century and the first half of the first century B.C., it was a dependent ally of the Romans. When it sided with Pompey against Caesar it lost all its political importance, and after the death of Caesar was plundered by Cassius (43/2) when he took over the province of Syria.[1]

Rhodes was the leader not only in politics, but also in science, rhetoric, and art in southwestern Asia Minor during the Hellenistic period. Aeschines, the rival of Demosthenes, had already founded a school of rhetoric in which, during the third century, Apollonius Rhodius, the author of the poem *Argonautica,* taught. Later Apollonius became librarian in Alexandria. His style, and probably the style of the school, is "Asiatic," that is, pompous and showy, much like some of the Rhodian sculpture. The literary schools of Rhodes continued to flourish under the Romans, just as the philosophical schools continued in Athens under the Macedonian sway.

I. EARLY DEVELOPMENT

From the beginning the tendency of the Rhodian art school seems to have been toward the colossal and showy, qualities corresponding to the rhetoric of its literature. A quadriga with four rearing horses is represented on amphora stamps found in Rhodes. This representation may be derived from the four-horse chariot and the figure of the Sun made for the Rhodians by Lysippos, for which, according to Pliny (*Nat. hist.* xxxiv. 63), the artist won fame above all others. It must have been a late work, probably commissioned after the successful defense against the siege of Demetrius Poliorcetes in 304, and thus one of the last works of the master.[2] Soon thereafter, probably upon the death of

[1] M. Rostovtzeff, "Rome and the Mediterranean, 218—133 B.C.," in *C.A.H.,* VIII (1930), 619–42. B. Ashmole in *ibid.,* pp. 672–79. H. von Gaertringen in Pauly-Wissowa, *Real-Enc.,* Supplement V (1931), pp. 731–840.

[2] A. Maiuri in *Atene e Roma,* Vol. I (1920), 133 ff. Franklin P. Johnson, *Lysippos* (1927), pp. 73, 152 f. Amphora stamps with Helios on his car: A. Maiuri and G. Jacopich in *Clara Rhodos,* Vol. I (1928), p. 36, Fig. 15 (cf. p. 34) and V. Grace in *Hesperia,* Vol. III (1934), pp. 197 ff. (esp. p. 240).

Lysippos, his Rhodian pupil, Chares, born in Lindos, was given the task of representing Helios standing near the harbor. The assertion that the colossus stood astride the harbor is wrong, for even if it was, with its height of 105 feet, the greatest in size of the statues of the Hellenistic period and therefore, like the altar of Pergamon, one of the Seven Wonders of the World, it would have hampered the lively commerce in the harbor. An earthquake destroyed this statue in 223/2 B.C., but the fragments remained undisturbed during both ancient and medieval times, until in 1360 a merchant bought the bronze for scrap and carried it away loaded on 980 camels. This bronze had originally been taken from the machines and tools left by Demetrius Poliorcetes after his unsuccessful siege of Rhodes.[3]

A metope from the temple of Athena in Troy, in the Prehistoric Museum (Museum für Vor- und Frühgeschichte) in Berlin, may give us an idea of the composition of the quadriga with Helios made by Lysippos [4] (Fig. 488). It also can teach us something of the style of his pupil Chares, who certainly, like other pupils of Lysippos, continued to work during the early third century in the style of his master (Chap. III, pp. 39, 50). The fiery horses, with their bulging muscles, and Helios, with the great swing of his body, his fluttering drapery, and passionate turn of his head, recall the horses of Ares and the Helios on the Pergamene frieze. A like observation can be made for another metope from Troy, showing Athena dealing the death blow to the fallen giant Enceladus.[5] The similarity to the same group on the frieze (see Fig. 460) is so strong that it has been assumed the temple in Troy was erected by one of the Attalids. The temple, however, seems definitely to be of the early third century.[6] We can, therefore, assert that the

style of the Pergamene altar had precursors in other Asiatic cities, and if the metopes reflect the Rhodian school, whose founder was Chares, we may assume that this baroque style was formed not first in Pergamon, but existed even earlier in Rhodes. This assumption tallies with the fact that the leading architect and sculptor of the great altar was Menekrates of Rhodes (see Chap. VIII, p. 114).

Of the conception of the head of Helios as formed by Lysippos and Chares we may get some inkling from the Trojan metope, as well as from the coins minted in Rhodes in the late fourth and in the third centuries,[7] and from a grandiose head found on the island of Rhodes, last seen in the possession of Freiherr Friedrich Hiller von Gärtringen in Berlin.[8] It stems from Scopadic heads, but has added movement and intensified expression.

A similar relation between a type created in Rhodes and one made in Pergamon seems to be attested by a hermaphrodite, one of which, a life-size example, has been found in Pergamon and one, in statuette form, on the island of Rhodes. The Pergamene statue, now in Istanbul, lacks only the right arm and left hand.[9] The left arm is lean-

---

[3] See J. Overbeck, *Die antiken Schriftquellen zur Geschichte der bildenden Künste bei den Griechen* (Leipzig, 1868), pp. 291 ff., Nos. 1539–54.

[4] W. Dörpfeld, *Troja und Ilion* (Athens, 1902), p. 429, Beilagen 49–51. C. Schuchhardt, *Schliemanns Ausgrabungen* (Leipzig, 1890), pp. 104 ff., Fig. 94 (trans: *Schliemann's Excavations*, pp. 80 ff., Fig. 90). H. Brunn and F. Bruckmann, *Denkmäler griechischer und römischer Skulptur* (Munich, 1888—), Pl. 162a.

[5] Schuchhardt, *Schliemanns Ausgrabungen*, Fig. 95; *Excavations*, Fig. 91.

[6] A. W. Lawrence, in *Later Greek Sculpture and Its Influence on East and West* (London, Cape, 1927), p. 166, dates the

temple and its metopes in the early second century. H. Schleif, in *Forschungen und Fortschritte* (1935), p. 534, and W. Zschietzschmann, *Die hellenistische und römische Kunst* (1939; Vol. II, Part 2 of *Handbuch der Kunstwissenschaft*), p. 59, both date it around 290 and consider that it was built by Lysimachos. A volume on this temple, planned by these two authors in *Denkmäler antiker Architektur*, has, as far as I know, not appeared.

[7] B. V. Head, *Catalogue of the Greek Coins of Caria, Cos, Rhodes* (London, the British Museum, 1900), pp. 240 ff., Pls. XXXVI–XXXVIII (cf. Introduction, pp. CIII and CVI); B. V. Head, *Historia Numorum* (2d ed., Oxford, 1911), p. 639. G. Jacopi, "Monumenti di Scultura II," in *Clara Rhodos*, Vol. V, Part 1 (1931), p. 46, Fig. 26. C. Seltman, *Greek Coins* (1933), Pl. XXX, Nos. 13–15.

[8] B. Gräf, "Helioskopf aus Rhodos," in *Strena Helbigiana* (1900), pp. 99 f. See also G. Jacopi in *Clara Rhodos*, Vol. V, Part 1 (1931), pp. 42 ff., No. 7, Figs. 23–25, for a similar head from Rhodes. The head from Rhodes which was published by T. L. Shear (in *A.J.A.*, Vol. XX [1916], pp. 283 ff., Pls. VII–VIII), on the other hand, seems to reflect the type of Helios before Lysippos and Chares created the more grandiose figures. A similar style is found in the head of an athlete (A. Maiuri, "Monumenti di Scultura I," in *Clara Rhodos*, Vol. II [1932], pp. 30 f., Figs. 14–15, Pl. I); this is certainly a fourth-century work.

[9] F. Winter, *Altertümer von Pergamon*, Vol. VII, p. 132, No. 115, Pl. X and Beiblatt 16. G. Mendel, *Catalogue des Sculptures grecques, romaines et byzantines, Musées Ottomanes* (3 vols., Constantinople [Istanbul], 1912–14), Vol. II (1914), pp. 368 ff., No. 624. E. Pontremoli and M. Collignon, *Pergame: Restaura-*

ing on a tree trunk. This motif and the soft rendering of the body, as well as the sweet features of the face, recall the works of Praxiteles, only with added sensuality. This points to a date early in the third century when the school of Praxiteles was active in Kos, the island nearest to Rhodes. Indeed there has been found in Rhodes an exact parallel to this figure, the only one known, in the private possession of Mr. Piero Tozzi of New York[10] (Fig. 492). This statuette is leaning on a pillar.

We cannot decide whether this Hermaphrodite is identical with the "noble Hermaphrodite" by Polykles, which Pliny (*Nat. hist.* xxxiv. 80) mentions, since we know neither the time nor the native place of this Polykles. A younger Polykles is mentioned as the artist of a work in the porticus of Octavia at Rome (Pliny *Nat. hist.* xxxvi. 35), while an older one, of Athens, who created a statue of Alcibiades, is mentioned under Olympiad CII, that is 372—368 B.C. (Pliny *Nat. hist.* xxxiv. 50).[11]

There is another connection between this figure and Rhodes. The closest stylistic parallel is the figure of Dionysos with Ariadne on a bronze in the British Museum which comes from the island of Chalke near Rhodes.[12] The group was probably attached to the handle of an amphora. It has the same leaning position and the same arrangement of the mantle, also a similar pillar on the left side. One might even consider whether the statuette in the collection of Mr. Tozzi originally likewise had Ariadne on the other side of the pillar. This would make it a Dionysos who then might have held a wine cup, the cantharus, in his right hand. The

Ariadne of the bronze relief indeed recalls the statue in Florence to which the name Ariadne has been given, and which appears as a goddess on a relief in Munich, attributed to the Rhodian school by Luciano Laurenzi (see Figs. 489 and 491).

2. EARLY BAROQUE ART (SECOND CENTURY B.C.)

The magnificent Nike which originally stood on a ship's prow in the sanctuary of the Cabiri on the island of Samothrace has now with certainty been ascribed to Pythokritos of Rhodes[13] (Figs. 493–96). This proves that Rhodian artists were called to work also at places outside the Rhodian empire. The statue, now in the Louvre, was originally identified with a Victory dedicated by Demetrius Poliorcetes, because it was believed to be the same as that represented on coins minted after Demetrius's victory near Salamis on the island of Cyprus in 306 B.C.[14] But the Nike on the coins not only lacks the mantle which plays such a prominent part in the Nike of Samothrace, she also lacks the swing of the drapery, the movement of the wings, and the twist of the body. Nike has just alighted from the air on the prow of the ship. Her wings are still open, at different heights. With a wide

---

tion et description des monuments de l'Acropole (Paris, 1900), figure on p. 205. G. Dickins, *Hellenistic Sculpture* (Oxford, The Clarendon Press, 1920), pp. 5, 65, and Fig. 1 on frontispiece. Dickins's chapter on the Rhodian school is a chaos of all kinds of sculptures from the most diverse places and by the most diverse artists, many of which are not at all connected with Rhodes. An exception is the Nike of Samothrace, which he rightly attributes to Rhodes, although with a wrong date.

[10] Mr. Piero Tozzi of New York, the owner of the statuette, which was found in Rhodes, kindly provided the photograph.

[11] Overbeck, *Schriftquellen*, Nos. 1138, 1145–46, 2206–12.

[12] H. B. Walters, *Catalogue of the Bronzes, Greek, Roman, and Etruscan, in the Department of Greek and Roman Antiquities* (London, the British Museum, 1899), No. 311, pp. 46 f., Pl. XI, No. 5. G. Richter in *A.J.A.*, Vol. L (1946), p. 364, No. 12, Pl. XXVI, Fig. 14. The Eros on the hydria in the Metropolitan Museum of Art (Richter, *op. cit.*, pp. 361 ff., Pls. XXII–XXIII) has a similar arrangement of the himation and leans similarly to his left. G. M. A. Richter, *Handbook of the Greek Collection* (1953), pp. 110 f., Pl. 90a and c.

[13] O. Benndorf, *Neue Untersuchungen auf Samothrake* (1880), Vol. II, pp. 52 ff., Figs. 25–42, Pl. LXIV. A. S. Murray, in *A History of Greek Sculpture* (London, 1890), II, 373 ff., first recognized the Nike as a Rhodian work. See Brunn-Bruckmann, *Denkmäler*, Pls. 85, 85a; G. A. Richter, *The Sculpture and Sculptors of the Greeks* (rev. ed., New Haven, Yale University Press, 1950), p. 64, note 80, Fig. 95. *Encycl. Phot.*, Vol. III, plates on pp. 219–22; A. W. Lawrence in *J.H.S.*, XLVI (1926), 213 ff.; Lawrence, *Later Greek Sculpture*, pp. 13, 97 (he dates it much too early—in the last quarter of the fourth century); Dickins, *Hellenistic Sculpture*, pp. 46 ff., Fig. 34 (he dates it after the battle of Cos in 258—about 250 B.C.); H. Thiersch, "Pro Samothrace," in *Sitzungsberichte der Akademie der Wissenschaften Wien*, No. 212, Abhandlung 1, pp. 21 ff., and "Die Nike von Samothrake, ein rhodisches Werk und Anathem," in *Nachrichten Gött. Ges.* (1931), pp. 338 ff.; C. Seltman, *Approach to Greek Art* (London and New York, 1948), Pl. 84 (both Thiersch and Seltman give the date as about 190 B.C., which is probably right); E. Pfuhl in *Jahrbuch d. Inst.*, XLVII (1932), 69 ff.; Chr. Blinkenberg and K. F. Kinch, *Lindos, Fouilles de l'Acropole, 1902–1904*, Vol. II: *Inscriptions* (1941), pp. 431 ff., No. 169, Figs. 1–6. For Pythokritos, see *ibid.*, pp. 53 f., 395 ff., Nos. 147–48, 150, 155, 159, 199, 203. K. F. Kinch, in *Second Report on Lindos* (1907), pp. 31 ff., dated about 180 B.C. L. Laurenzi, "Problemi della Scultura ellenistica—La scultura Rodia," in *Riv. del Ist Arch.*, VIII, Fasc. I (1940), p. 29, also dates rightly in 200—180 B.C.

[14] See this coin in *C.A.H.*, Volume of Plates II (1928), pp. 10 f., Fig. k; E. T. Newell, *Royal Greek Portrait Coins* (New York, 1937), p. 28, Fig. 1.

stride, and probably only with the forepart of her feet, she touches ground, while the lower ends of her long mantle already sweep the ground. The upper end flutters behind her. The chiton is thrown against her body by a strong wind and the violent movement. Some parts, therefore, like the left leg, the abdomen, and the breast, appear as if nude, while folds waving like foam, with unruly lights and shades, cover the other parts. Big streams of folds fall between the striding legs. The directions of all folds change in every part, much more so than in earlier works, such as the Tyche of Antioch (Fig. 102). Characteristic is the crossing of the upper edge of the mantle over the uppermost right thigh to the end of the mantle sweeping the ground. It separates the folds at the lower part of the overfold and those on the remaining part of the right thigh, which go in the opposite direction. The rhythm is rather choppy. Details emerge and disappear again. There is, indeed, continuous change of direction in all parts. The organic continuity is sometimes interrupted. For example, the beginning of the fluttering end of the mantle is not clear. The separation of chiton and mantle is not carried through, for example, over the right lower leg. But the effect of stormy movement and gale on the drapery has hardly ever been more gloriously handled. Pythokritos was a great master who saw nature with knowing eyes. Here we have, indeed, a parallel to the Asiatic baroque of Rhodian literature.

The connection of the Nike of Samothrace with Rhodes has been firmly established by Hermann Thiersch, who investigated its base, which is in the form of a prow, and the fragment of an inscription found with this base. The inscription on a relief representing a similar ship's prow in Lindos on the island of Rhodes and several inscriptions signed by Pythokritos of Rhodes have the same letters as the inscription in Samothrace. The form of the letters date Pythokritos in the early second century, thus probably shortly before the altar of Zeus at Pergamon, where indeed the closest parallels to the style of drapery of the Nike are found. The same date is indicated for Pythokritos by the date of his son Simias, who was active about 150 B.C.[15]

A parallel to the Nike of Samothrace in Rhodes itself is a mutilated statue of a Nike, with a similar swing in the movement of the body and in the folds of the drapery.[16] It is dated at about the end of the third, or the beginning of the second, century. This is the period when the navy of Rhodes fought successfully side by side with the Romans against the Macedonians and Syrians. This, therefore, is the best period for a splendid victory monument like the Nike of Samothrace.

A statue called Ariadne, but probably representing some goddess, of which we do not possess the original but only two copies—one in the Louvre and one in the Uffizi Gallery in Florence [17] (Fig. 491)—has some affinity to the Nike of Samothrace, despite the fact that it is a quietly standing figure in strong contrast to the violent movement of the Nike. The head does not belong, and the arms are restored. The goddess has put her left foot on a little elevation, so that the knee is slightly bent and a gathering of folds falls, radiating from the knee downward. Between the supporting right leg and the left leg there is a group of deep garland folds becoming broader in the lower part. The lower edge of the peplos drags on the ground outside the feet. The edge of the overfold seems to have been lifted by the lost right hand. A drawing by J. B. de Cavalleriis, made in 1585, indicates that the elbow reclined on a tree trunk. The thin and sharp folds which are modeled over the abdomen recall the same area in the Victory of Samothrace.

That this figure is connected with the Rhodian school appears from the use made of it on a relief in Munich, which Luciano Laurenzi, by comparing Rhodian altars and reliefs, has rightly proved to be a local product of Rhodes [18] (Fig. 489). The goddess here holds a long scepter in her right hand and is leaning on a pillar. She is standing next to

---

[15] G. Lippold in Pauly-Wissowa, *Real-Enc.*, Second Series, Vol. III A, p. 143, s.v. Simias, No. 3.

[16] A. Maiuri in *Clara Rhodos,* Vol. II (1932), pp. 9 ff., Fig. 1.
[17] W. Amelung, *Führer durch die Antiken in Florenz* (Munich, 1897), No. 33, p. 28 f., Fig. 6. L. Laurenzi in *Röm. Mitt.,* Vol. LIV (1939), pp. 42 ff., Fig. 2, and Pl. 12.
[18] A. Furtwängler and P. Wolters, *Beschreibung der Glyptothek zu München* (2d ed., 1910), No. 206, pp. 183 ff. H. Bulle, *Der schöne Mensch im Altertum* (Munich, 1912), Pl. 279. E. Buschor, *Die Plastik der Griechen* (Berlin, Rembrandt-Verlag, 1939), figure on p. 98. Lawrence, *Later Greek Sculpture*, p. 24, Pl. 41a. L. Laurenzi, in *Clara Rhodos*, Vol. V. Part 2 (1932), pp. 9 ff., Figs. 1–8, Pl. I, and in *Röm. Mitt.,* LIV (1939), Pl. 11 (for the Rhodian reliefs, see Figs. 3–4). A. Maiuri, in *Clara Rhodos*, Vol. II (1932), pp. 45 f., Fig. 22.

a dignified god who also holds a long scepter and is seated on an elaborate throne supported by griffins. Behind the two gods is a curtain attached to a big sycamore or plane tree, the trunk of which is decorated with a broad sacred fillet. Under it stands a pillar with archaistic statuettes of a male and a female god. Between the pillar and the goddess is an altar, behind and to the side of which a family of eight—father, mother, and six children —bring sacrifices. The oldest boy has set a basket, into which the father puts his right hand, on the altar. Behind him is his wife, wrapped in her mantle. Nearest to the left side of the altar, a small girl brings a large box, covered with a cloth, on her head. Behind her a little brother brings a bird, perhaps a chicken, and a pail. The youngest child, behind him, is fully wrapped in a mantle, as are also two daughters standing before the tree, both with their mantles over their heads; one wears in addition a round pointed hat.

This is perhaps the oldest framed relief with landscape elements which reach higher up than the figures, so that much space is left over their heads. The relation of the figures to the free space, the curtain, and the leaves of the plane tree, which are laid parallel to the ground, are similar to the Telephos frieze (Figs. 477–78). Thus this relief may be dated around 160 B.C., while the type of the Ariadne used on it may be a little older. We have here the beginning of the pictorial reliefs which were not developed to full landscapes before the Augustan period. (Chap. X, pp. 153–55.)

Another example of a Rhodian relief of about the same period—the second quarter of the second century—is the tomb relief of a Rhodian schoolmaster, perhaps a member of one of the celebrated schools for rhetors [19] (Fig. 490). It was last seen in the possession of the late Hiller von Gärtringen in Berlin. The name of the deceased Hieronymos, son of Simylinos, from Tlosos, is written above the frieze; the artist's name, Damatrios (a Doric form of Demetrios), without patronym, is written below. In the first of the four scenes (from left to right) are the teacher seated with four pupils, two of whom are seated and two standing, listening to the lecture. A pillar built of squares of stone separates this scene from the next: Hades is seated on a large throne, with Persephone holding a scepter standing before him and Hermes beside her, indicating the lower world. In the next scene a standing man, another young man, and a woman, the last two seated on rocks, probably represent the blessed; the field of the blessed is indicated by a tree behind them. The last scene may indicate two penitents, one seated wrapped in her mantle, the other coming up from or sinking down into the ground. A woman with butterfly wings and a rod in her hand seems to watch over them.

The seated penitent resembles Auge (Fig. 478) and the seated figure in three-quarter view resembles the queen, Neaira (Fig. 477). Pillar and tree are used here as indications of locality in the same manner as on the Telephos frieze. Thus again we see a relation between Rhodes and Pergamon during the first half of the second century.

Another relief, the Apotheosis of Homer, with rocks and curtain as background, seems related to Rhodes, although it was made by Archelaos, an artist of Priene. It has the portraits of Ptolemy IV and Arsinoë in the guise of Chronos and Oikoumene crowning Homer [20] (Fig. 497; see also Fig. 404). There was in Alexandria the most celebrated sanctuary of Homer, built by Ptolemy IV (Ptolemy Philopator), who reigned 222 to 205, and that is why he and his queen are represented here. This, however, is only a *terminus post quem,* and probably an indication that the unidentified poet, shown on a pedestal at the right edge, has won a victory in a literary contest in this celebrated center of scholarship. If he had been an Alexandrian, he would not have commissioned an artist from Asia Minor, but rather an Alexandrian artist, to carve this memorial of his victory. The lowest tier smacks, indeed, of Alexandrian scholarship. Homer is represented as a god, with scepter and scroll. Personifications of the Iliad (with sword) and the Odyssey, with aphlaston (the ornament of the stern of a ship), are kneeling at the feet of Homer. A frog and a mouse play around the footstool—an allusion to the *Batrachomyomachia (The Battle of Frogs and Mice)*, a poem credited to Homer.

[19] Brunn-Bruckmann, *Denkmäler,* Pl. 579. L. Curtius, in *Mitt. d. Inst.,* Vol. IV (1951), pp. 20 ff., Pl. 8.

[20] A. H. Smith, *Brit. Mus. Cat.,* III (1904), pp. 244 ff., No. 2191, Fig. 30. C. Watzinger, *Das Relief des Archelaos von Priene (Winck.-Prog. Berlin,* No. 63 [1903]), Pl. I. Brunn-Bruckmann, *Denkmäler,* Pl. 50. W. Amelung, *Die Basis des Praxiteles aus Mantinea* (Munich, 1895), pp. 43 ff., 79 ff. A. Levi in *Bolletino d'arte,* Series VI, No. 6 (1926–27), p. 353, Fig. 3.

Before Homer stands an altar on which Myth, depicted as a little boy, serves with sacrificial jug and bowl. History, the continuation of Myth, strews incense on the altar, behind which a humpbacked bull, found in this form in Caria, is standing as a sacrifice. There follow Poetry with two torches, and Tragedy and Comedy in stage costume. (The order in which lyric poetry, serious drama, and comedy are represented is the same in which these types of literature developed.) Finally a child, representing Human Nature, lifts hand and head to the Four Virtues, in which the study of Homer educates children: Courage, Good Memory, Trustworthiness, and Wisdom.

Not Homer alone, however, but all the Muses are supposed to have contributed to the success of the poet. Their father Zeus is seated at the peak of the mountain, which may represent Olympus, Helicon, or Parnassus. To Zeus's right is his eagle, to his left directly below him on a ledge is Mnemosyne (Memory), the mother of the Muses. Terpsichore, the Muse of the dance, is skipping down the slope which leads to the second tier. Here Euterpe, the Muse of song, is seated, pointing with her double flutes to the inscription of Archelaos below the seat of Zeus. Her neighbor, Erato, the Muse of lyric poetry, holding the small lyre, is also looking up in the same direction. The other seated Muse in this tier, reading from a diptych, must be Kalliope, the Muse of epic poetry, while the slender woman wrapped in her himation must be Thalia, the Muse of comedy.

In the third tier the seated woman with the large kithara is Polyhymnia, the Muse of hymns and other choral songs. Before her stands Urania, the Muse of Heaven, handling and looking at the globe lying before her on a pilaster. The remaining space of this tier is taken by Apollo between two Muses. The god, dressed in a long floating robe held together by a belt high on his chest, his large kithara held in the left arm and the *plektron* in his right hand, stands in front view inside a cave beside his omphalos. His head, now restored, probably also faced front. To his right is Melpomene, the Muse of tragedy, leaning on a rock pillar projecting from the entrance of the cave. On the other side, inside the cave, but resting her hand on another pillar at the opening of the cave, is Klio, the Muse of history, presenting a scroll to the god.

Such a scroll is also in the hand of the statue of a poet standing on the pedestal outside the cave, outlined against a tripod with covered kettle. One may assume that the scrolls contain the poem with which the victory in the literary contest has been won. The figure of Homer in the lowest tier leads us to think that this has been an epic victory, but the figure of Melpomene, and the fact that before Homer the personifications of the drama, with Tragoidia as the largest figure, are worshipping, might also lead us to think of a dramatic victory. It may be, too, that the presence of all the Muses indicates the victories of some many-sided writer who has won several contests.

The date of this relief, according to the inscription, is about 125 B.C.[21] The original types of the Muses, however, of which many replicas and variations are known in statues, must belong to a period shortly before they were used on the relief of Archelaos and before some of them appeared on a round base from Halicarnassus.[22] Replicas of the types were first collected by Walter Amelung, but many more copies have since been found. The most popular seems to have been the Muse of the dance, Terpsichore, who is uppermost on the relief. At least twenty replicas are known,[23] among them one from the Faustina baths in Miletus[24] (Fig. 498), and one in Dresden.[25] Klio comes next, with at least twelve replicas,[26] among them one from the baths in Miletus,[27] another in Istanbul[28] (Fig. 499), and one from Kos[29] (Fig. 500). A variation of this type has also been found in the

[21] M. Schede in *Röm. Mitt.,* XXXV (1920), 65 ff.
[22] C. Watzinger, *Relief des Archelaos,* Pl. II.
[23] M. Bieber in *Antike Plastik: Walter Amelung zum sechzigsten Geburtstag* (1928), pp. 18 f., footnote 3.
[24] Mendel, *Catalogue Musées Ottomanes,* Vol. I (1912), pp. 326 f., No. 119. K. A. Neugebauer in T. Wiegand, ed., *Milet: Ergebnisse der Ausgrabungen und Untersuchungen seit dem Jahre 1899* (Berlin, 1906–28), Vol. I, Part 9: Von Gerkan, Krischen, and Neugebauer, *Thermen und Palaestren,* pp. 107 f., Pl. XXX.
[25] P. Herrmann, *Verzeichnis der Originalbildwerke* (Skulpturen-Sammlung, Dresden, 1915), No. 319. K. B. Stark, *Niobe und die Niobiden* (1863), p. 285, Pl. 11.
[26] M. Bieber in *Antike Plastik,* pp. 19 f., footnote 2.
[27] Mendel, *Catalogue Musées Ottomanes,* Vol. I, pp. 321 f., No. 116. Neugebauer in Wiegand, *Milet,* Vol. I, Part 9, pp. 101 f., Pl. XXIX. This figure has been wrongly described as the Muse with lyre. The rock pillar at her side identifies her as Klio.
[28] Mendel, *Catalogue Musées Ottomanes,* Vol. III, pp. 11 ff., No. 809.
[29] M. Bieber in *Antike Plastik,* p. 19, Fig. 4.

baths at Miletus[30] (Fig. 501), with a replica in Munich.[31] The Muse on the other side of Apollo is best copied in a statue in Berlin, which, however, has a head, in a wrong frontal position, added by Christian Rauch[32] (Fig. 502). The right head, in profile as on the relief of Archelaos, is on a fragment formerly in the possession of Walter Amelung. The best-preserved head is in Dresden, with the characteristic bunch of long hair hanging free behind the back.[33]

A great number of these copies and variations have a peculiar treatment of the drapery which is characteristic of the late Hellenistic period but which began, according to new investigations by Dorothy Thompson,[34] in the late third century. Over the thick woolen dress, which is probably the *peronatris* described by Theocritus (*Idylls* 15, *Adoniazusae*, v. 21), a thin veillike mantle is laid, through which the folds of the heavier main dress are shown.[35] The result is a gay play of lines, the vertical lines interrupted by the thin backs of the curved or diagonal folds of the shawl. There can be no doubt that this is the diaphanous byssus or Coan *vestis* of the late Hellenistic and early Roman periods, made either of thin linen or fine silk spun on the island of Kos. The same dresses are rendered in the same style on many terra-cotta figurines; examples are two in the Metropolitan Museum of Art in New York. One leans on a pil-

lar (Fig. 503), and the other resembles the Pudicitia type (Fig. 513); others spread out their wide mantles with their left hands[36] (Fig. 601).

As many examples of this treatment have been found in Kos itself (Fig. 500) or in southwestern Asia Minor, it seems safe to assume that this style is characteristic of Rhodes and the neighboring islands and mainland. Not all copies, however, have this style, particularly not the Roman copies from Miletus, for example Figs. 498 and 501. We miss this style, above all, in the various seated Muses which have been connected with the group represented on the relief of Archelaos and the base of Halicarnassus.[37] There is also great uncertainty about which, if any, of these seated Muses were originally part of the same set. On each relief there are three seated Muses, but they do not agree with each other either in attitude or in style. The statuary replicas of these seated figures also do not agree exactly, either with the reliefs or with each other. The best candidate for placement in the original set seems to me to be the seated Muse in the Museo Nazionale Romano in Rome (Fig. 504), found on the Palatine, which has a certain similarity to the one from the baths of Faustina in Miletus, both being, of course, Roman copies.[38] The Roman Muse is related to a number of the seated Muses on both reliefs. She is seated on rocks. She turns strongly to her side, like Kalliope and two seated Muses on the relief of Halicarnassus. She puts her left hand on the rock, like Euterpe and Klio. Her right arm crosses her body, as do those of Polyhymnia and Erato. Thus she may give us an idea how the seated Muses of the original group may have looked, at least as to composition. It may, however, also be that the sculptor of the original

---

[30] Mendel, *Catalogue Musées Ottomanes*, Vol. I, pp. 323 f. Neugebauer in Wiegand, *Milet*, Vol. I, Part 9, pp. 111 f., Fig. 120, Pl. XXXIII. He identifies her tentatively as the comic Muse, Thalia. See also R. Horn, *Stehende weibliche Gewandstatuen in der hellenistischen Plastik* (1931; *Ergänzungsheft II to Röm. Mitt.*), p. 69, Pl. 21, No. 3.

[31] Furtwängler and Wolters, *Glyptothek*, pp. 276 f., No. 266.

[32] Berlin Museum, No. 221. See Watzinger, *Relief des Archelaos*, pp. 4 f., Fig. 1.

[33] For the fragment in the possession of Amelung, see Watzinger, *Relief des Archelaos*, p. 6, Fig. 2. For the head in the Skulpturen-Sammlung, Dresden (No. 173), see P. Herrmann, *Originalbildwerke*, p. 44, and W. Klein in *Oest. Jahreshefte*, XVI (1913), pp. 183 ff., Figs. 90–96. For a small replica at Pompeii, in the garden of the house of Laomedon, see *Dedalo*, IV (1923–24), p. 671, and A. Ippel, *Pompeji* (1925), p. 112, Fig. 105. See also D. Mustilli, *Il Museo Mussolini* (Rome, 1939), pp. 78 f., No. 24, Pl. XLVI, Fig. 187. Mustilli lists 14 replicas.

[34] D. Thompson's article on the bronze statuette in the Baker collection (our Figs. 378–79), in *A.J.A.*, LIV (1950), 371 ff. For the date of this kind of drapery see also G. Lippold in W. Otto and R. Herbig, *Handbuch der Archaeologie*, Vol. III: *Die Plastik* (Munich, 1950), pp. 333–35.

[35] M. Bieber, *Entwicklungsgeschichte der griechischen Tracht* (Berlin, 1934), p. 35, Pl. 34.

[36] G. M. A. Richter, *Handbook of the Greek Collection* (1953), p. 112, Pl. 92a (our Fig. 513; others p. 128, Pl. 108e–f, and our Fig. 601).

[37] See G. Lippold in *Röm. Mitt.*, XXXIII (1918), 64 ff.

[38] Neugebauer in Wiegand, *Milet*, Vol. I, Part 9, pp. 108 f., Pl. XXXI. Cf. the discussion of the whole group in *ibid.*, pp. 114 ff. The nine Muses and Apollo stood in niches in a room connected with the *apodyterion* of the baths. This room, therefore, has been called the Museion. See Krischen in Wiegand, *Milet*, Vol. I, Part 9, pp. 60 f., Pl. XXII. For the group of Muses and Apollo of the types of the Archelaos relief found in Delos, see Fayence and Leroux, in *B.C.H.*, Vol. XXXI (1904), pp. 389 ff., Figs. 1–5. For the Muse from the Palatine (Fig. 504) see S. Aurigemma, *Le Terme di Diocleziano e il Museo Nazionale Romano* (2d ed., 1950), pp. 74 f., No. 187, Pl. XXXI b.

group included only six Muses, the number we find on the base of Mantinea (see pp. 21 f.). Originally there were only three Muses in mythology; they were first doubled, and then tripled.

Unfortunately most of the heads of the Muses are missing, or are preserved in lifeless Roman copies only—such as those of the Polyhymnia in Dresden and three Muses found in the baths of Faustina in Miletus (see Fig. 501). Of these the best is the variation of Klio (Fig. 506). Her features appear to be similar to an original head from Kos, which has the same attitude—turned slightly to the right—and the same hairdress, with the parting of the soft waves which cover the upper part of the ears [39] (Fig. 505). This head, found by Rudolf Herzog, is twice life size. The hair is confined in a broad fillet and a metal ring, over which a shawl is wound, with holes for the attachment of rosettes or other ornaments. This rich headdress testifies that a goddess is represented. The high forehead, the form of the eyelids and of the lips, and the shape of the cheeks are the same as those of the Muse. But everything shows the hand of an original Greek artist. The hair is soft, like silk, the skin is that of a delicate female, the glance of the eyes and the slightly opened lips are much more expressive than in the Roman copies of the Muses. The realistic rendering of hair and skin agrees with the rendering of the texture of the original head from Kos (Fig. 33).

There is no doubt that the group of Muses, as it can be reconstructed (although not all parts can be restored with absolute certainty), must be the work of a great Hellenistic sculptor of the first half of the second century, in the region covered by most of the finds discussed in connection with the relief of Archelaos (Fig. 497). Who was this artist? Most scholars, beginning with Walter Amelung, have identified him with Philiskos of Rhodes, whose nine Muses, together with a draped Apollo, his mother Leto and his sister Artemis, and another nude Apollo, stood in the Porticus of Octavia in Rome [40] (Pliny *Nat. hist.* XXXVI. 34). This porticus was built by Q. Caecilius Metellus Macedonicus, so named after he won the fourth Macedonian War (148–146). Whether the works mentioned by Pliny were booty of the victorious general, or

whether the artists whose works stood in this porticus created new statues or made adaptations of celebrated masterpieces for him, is not yet decided (below, p. 160). As the Rhodians lost the favor of the Romans in consequence of this war, both are possible. Beside Philiskos's, there were works of Attic artists like Timarchides I, whose Apollo holding a kithara seems to have been copied in the Apollo with the Muses in the baths at Miletus [41] (see Figs. 678–81). The only known signature of Philiskos is written on a base found on the island of Thasos and now in Istanbul: "Philiskos, son of Polycharmos, a Rhodian, made it." The base supported a statue of Are, daughter of Neon, whose son Antiphon had dedicated her statue to Artemis [42] (Fig. 507). The letters of the inscription belong to about 100 B.C. The lower part of a female statue was found lying before this base, but the connection does not seem quite certain.[43] In any case this statue cannot be by the same master as the Muses, for the treatment of chiton and mantle are different. Whereas the mantles of the Muses have many small folds, crossing each other, dividing into smaller folds and losing themselves in a smooth surface in imitation of a delicate thin material, the Are has some very deep folds while others are flatter, lying mostly in parallel bowlines. Whereas the chitons of the Muses have deep grooves and baglike folds, between which the surface is covered with many engraved, thin, irregular lines, imitating a heavy woolen material, Are (if it is Are) has mostly vertical, alternatingly deep and flat, rather wearisome folds. If this is a work of Philiskos, his Muses must have been classicized statues like those of Timarchides and his sons, which also stood in the Porticus of Octavia (Pliny *Nat. hist.* XXXVI. 35). Philiskos, in this case, would be an adapter of the early first century B.C.

3. DEVELOPMENT OF DRAPERY

In any case, the Muses are creations of an artist from Rhodes or its neighborhood. The same style

---

[39] M. Bieber in *Antike Plastik*, pp. 16 ff., Fig. 1, Pl. 3.
[40] Overbeck, *Schriftquellen*, p. 429, No. 2207.

[41] Neugebauer in Wiegand, *Milet*, Vol. I, Part 9, pp. 104 ff., Pl. XXVIII. Mendel, *Catalogue Musées Ottomanes*, pp. 317 ff., No. 114. G. Becatti in *Riv. del Ist. Arch.*, Vol. VII (1940), p. 30, Fig. 9.
[42] Th. Macridy-Bey in *Jahrbuch d. Inst.*, Vol. XXVII (1912), pp. 17 f., No. 7, Pl. IV. Mendel, *Catalogue Musées Ottomanes*, pp. 345 f., No. 136. Bieber in *Antike Plastik*, pp. 21 ff., Fig. 10.
[43] M. Schede in *Röm. Mitt.*, XXXV (1920), pp. 65 ff.

appears in other works of the same region. Thus two fragments of the lower part of female statues from Kos, in the British Museum, have the same deep grooves and baglike folds spreading out on the ground around their walking legs as some of the Muses [44] (Figs. 508–9). The torso of a woman found in Kos in the wall of the castle has, besides these folds, the finely engraved surface lines imitating a heavy woolen material and over it the thin veillike mantle with delicate and variegated thin-backed folds [45] (Fig. 510). The closest parallel to this statue is the one found in the Heraion of Samos, leaning on an unidentified object at her left side and turning toward it [46] (Fig. 512). This support might be a pillar or a musical instrument, which would make her a Muse. In any case, the fine design of the thin folds of the veil, the interesting composition with the folds from all directions crossing near the right hand, and the animated movement make this an outstanding example of the group. The heavy vertical folds of the woolen underdress show very clearly, but not too sharply, through the clinging mantle.

Related, but probably a little later, is the well-known Cleopatra from Delos, the wife of an Athenian, Dioskurides, who had settled in Delos. By an inscription referring to Dioskurides, the statue of his wife can be fairly accurately dated by the name of the archon, Timarchos, in 138/7 B.C.[47] (Fig. 511). Here the veil has less refined and less numerous motifs, while the vertical folds of the woolen chiton, although variegated in the lower part, have become monotonous and parallel to each other where they shine through the veil. This may be the work of a Rhodian artist who followed the trend of commerce from Rhodes to Delos after 168. The attitude is that of the Pudicitia (see Figs.

522–25), which makes the upper part of the figure very narrow, while the hips are particularly broad. These proportions are similar in a terra-cotta statuette in the Metropolitan Museum of Art [48] (Fig. 513) and a statue from Pergamon, which, however, has much more swing in the attitude as well as in the design of the folds [49] (Fig. 514). The folds in the chiton of the Pergamene statue, as well as in her mantle, are much deeper and more variegated than in the Pudicitia, and sometimes massed in such a way that the continuity of the surface is interrupted by rolls and pads such as those below the breast and around the hips. This baroque motif is also found on another statue from Pergamon with somewhat broader proportions in the upper part [50] (Fig. 515). Here the vertical folds are quite schematic between the two curved rolls going from the right side to the left hip. A torso in the British Museum found in the Ionian city of Erythrae is very close in style to these baroque figures from Pergamon [51] (Fig. 521). The artist signs himself as Apollodoros, son of Zenon, from Phocaea. In this figure a triangular overfold of the mantle allows the rising folds of the lower part of the shawl to shine through the bowlines of the overfold, while some of the heavy folds of the woolen chiton between the legs are continued through the lowest part of the shawl, ending at the tip of the overfold. A statue in the Louvre (Fig. 519) is perhaps the richest development of the overrich Hellenistic drapery.[52]

A statue from Magnesia shows the high point and at the same time the manneristic achievement of this virtuoso's rendering of several layers of drapery [53] (Fig. 520). The richness of the lower

---

[44] Bieber in *Antike Plastik*, pp. 20 ff., Fig. 8. A. H. Smith, *Brit. Mus. Cat.*, Vol. III, pp. 205 f., No. 2075 and p. 211, No. 2097. Cf. also the fragment from Rhodes in the British Museum, in Horn, *Gewandstatuen*, Pl. 19, No. 2.

[45] Bieber in *Antike Plastik*, pp. 21 ff., Fig. 9.

[46] M. Schede in *Röm. Mitt.*, XXXV (1920), pp. 74 ff., Pl. I. G. Krahmer in *Röm. Mitt.*, XXXVIII–XXXIX (1923–24), pp. 142 ff., Fig. 1.

[47] J. Chamonard, *Exploration archéologique de Délos* (École française d'Athènes), Vol. VIII, Part 1 (1922), pp. 218 ff., Fig. 95. Fayence and Leroux in *B.C.H.*, Vol. XXXI (1907), pp. 415 ff., Fig. 9. E. Buschor, *Die Plastik der Griechen* (Berlin, Rembrandt-Verlag, 1939), figure on p. 103 (best illustration). M. Collignon, *Les Statues Junéraires dans l'art grecque* (1911), Fig. 188.

[48] Metropolitan Museum of Art, No. 30.117. Richter, *Handbook* (1953), p. 112, Pl. 92a.

[49] F. Winter in *Altertümer von Pergamon*, Vol. VII, pp. 88 f., No. 54, Pl. XXI. Horn, *Gewandstatuen*, p. 69, Pl. 21, No. 2.

[50] F. Winter in *Altertümer von Pergamon*, Vol. VII, pp. 100 f., No. 69, Pl. XXIII.

[51] A. H. Smith, *Brit. Mus. Cat.*, Vol. III, p. 70, No. 1684. G. Krahmer in *Röm. Mitt.*, XXXVIII–XXXIX (1923–24), pp. 175 f., Pl. VII. M. Bieber, *Entwicklungsgeschichte der griechischen Tracht*, p. 51, Pl. 35, No. 2.

[52] J. Charbonneaux, *La Sculpture grecque au Musée du Louvre* (Paris, 1936), Pl. 38. He illustrates the upper part only.

[53] K. Humann, J. Kohte, and K. Watzinger, *Magnesia am Maeander* (Berlin, Reimer, 1904), pp. 185 ff., Pl. 9. W. Klein, *Vom antiken Rokoko* (Vienna, Hölzel, 1921), pp. 118 f., Fig. 50. W. Klein in *Oest. Jahreshefte*, Vol. XVI (1913), pp. 204 f., Fig. 101. S. Besques-Mollard, in *Mon. Piot*, XLV (1951), p

part of the chiton, with its irregular masses of heavy, broad, and small broken folds, the clear continuation of the steep vertical folds under the tensely drawn, cobweb-thin shawl with its converging sharp-backed folds, the angular position of the right arm, the leaning to the left side, all give a kind of nervous energy to this figure. This probably belongs to a somewhat later date, and to a new conception, away from the heaviness of the Pergamene baroque as well as from the graceful poses of Rhodian art to a more restless and pictorial surface pattern, disregarding the body inside the dress. It is fascinating to follow the development of drapery during the Hellenistic period from the simple Themis of Rhamnus (Fig. 516) of the early third century, to the later third-century statue from Priene (Fig. 517), to the figures of the second century (Figs. 499–504, 508–15, 518–19, and 521), and finally, in the statue of Magnesia (Fig. 520), to the first century B.C.

The so-called Pudicitia type is a good example of this development. The veiling of the whole body, including both arms, and the consequential crossing of the folds of the dress before the body, begins with the types of the mother and daughter of Herculaneum (see Chap. II, pp. 22 f.). But in the Pudicitia the crossings are emphasized and multiplied by the fact that the arms also cross the body. A statue in the Ashmolean Museum at Oxford [54] (Fig. 522) has the left arm laid firmly and horizontally below the breast, crossing the body to the right hip. The right arm is sharply bent and the hand is wrapped in the upper part of the mantle, which she lifts from her right shoulder, while the fringed vertical edge of the mantle hangs from the left lower arm down to the left upper leg. The next development from this attitude is that the right arm is pressed more closely to the body, that the left arm goes diagonally over the body, sustaining the right elbow, and that the mantle is drawn over the head. In this form the Pudicitia type appears on many tombstones of Rhodes, Smyrna, and other places of Asia Minor, for example in the monument of Menephila, daughter of Artemidoros

from Ephesus, in the Louvre [55] (Fig. 523). She is standing between her two little servants. Many statues agree with this conception, for example one in the Vatican (Fig. 524), while others add more crossings by letting the right hand grasp the edge of the mantle on the left instead of the right side of the neck; an example is a statue in the Louvre [56] (Fig. 525). The result is that the upper part of the figures becomes very narrow in contrast to her broad matronly hips and the spreading out of the dress at the ground. Since this scheme is the same as in the Cleopatra, dated about 138/7 (Fig. 511), we may date the creation in the later part of the second century. It has, indeed, been credited to Athenodoros I, the father or grandfather of Agesandros and Athenodoros, masters of the Laocoon, who created the portraits of noblewomen (Pliny *Nat. hist.* xxxiv. 86).[57] There can be no doubt that most, if not all, of the figures represent such portraits, as proved by the tomb reliefs. The name Pudicitia, taken from a similar type on Roman coins, should be discarded. The Romans also used this type for tombstones and for honorary statues of noble ladies, with distinct portrait character, in the first century B.C.[58] Often the end of the mantle

[55] *Encycl. phot.*, III, 252. For other tombstones from Rhodes, see A. Maiuri in *Clara Rhodos*, Vol. II (1932), No. 32, Figs. 37–38; L. Laurenzi, "Monumenti di scultura del Museo archaeologico di Rhodi [Part IV] e dell' antiquario di Coo [Part II]," in *Clara Rhodos*, Vol. IX (1938), pp. 97 f., Fig. 63, are those from Kos. For one in Venice, see M. Guarducci in *Rivista d'Archeologia*, Vol. XX (1942), pp. 30 ff., No. V, Mus. No. 67. For tombstones from Smyrna, see O. Walter in *Oest. Jahreshefte*, Vol. XXI–XXII (1922–24), Beiblatt, pp. 242 ff., Figs. 136–38, and Horn, *Gewandstatuen*, Pl. 23, No. 2; for one in Oxford (the Ashmolean Museum), see Horn, *Gewandstatuen*, Pl. 25, Fig. 2. For others, see E. Pfuhl, "Beiwerk auf den ostgriechischen Grabreliefs" in *Jahrbuch d. Inst.*, Vol. XX (1905), pp. 52 ff., Figs. 5–8, 14, pp. 123 ff., Figs. 20, 23, 26, Pls. 4 and 6. For one of many Roman republican examples in the Museo Nuovo, see Horn, *Gewandstatuen*, Pl. 40, Fig. 1, and Mustilli, *Museo Mussolini*, p. 15, No. 36, Pl. VI, Fig. 22.
[56] *Encycl. phot.*, Vol. III, Pl. 249 c; here it is dated correctly into the first century B.C. Amelung, *Vatican Kat.*, Vol. I, Braccio Nuovo, No. 23, pp. 33 ff., Pl. 4. For other statues of the Pudicitia type, see R. Horn, *Gewandstatuen*, pp. 65 f., 78, Pls. 40–45; Humann, Kohte, and Watzinger, *Magnesia*, pp. 202 f., Fig. 204; L. Laurenzi, "Monumenti di scultura, I" in *Clara Rhodos*, Vol. V, Part 2 (1932), pp. 118 ff., Pls. XI and XIV.
[57] See L. Laurenzi in *Röm. Mitt.*, LIV (1939), pp. 42 ff. Laurenzi also wants (pp. 53 f.) to assign to Athanodoros I the Isis standing next to Zeus-Serapis in his Fig. 3 and repeated in the statuette in Vienna illustrated in his Figs. 5–6 and Pl. 13.
[58] See Horn, *Gewandstatuen*, Pl. 40, No. 2 and Pl. 41, Nos.

66, Pl. IX. He dates it 160–150. For Tanagra statuettes in a transparent mantle see *ibid.*, pp. 54 ff., Figs. 1–10, Pls. VII–VIII.
[54] P. Gardner in *J.H.S.*, XLIII (1923), pp. 53 f., Pl. II. Restored are the upper part of the head, nose, right hand, some ends of drapery, and the lower part of the body.

hangs down from the right hand in the middle of the body instead of from the left lower arm to the left leg.

Many of these "Pudicitia" figures and other draped female figures of the first century show the beginning of a certain stiffening of form, a return to a more linear conception, away from the almost confusing play of light and shade in the second century. It is instructive to compare the statue in the Louvre [59] (Fig. 519) with one of the statues from the island of Thasos [60] (Fig. 518), found together with the Are (Fig. 507). The pictorial variegated folds on breast and body, surrounded by the deep trenches of the mantle folds in the former, has made way for a more even and flatter arrangement of folds in the latter. The first classicizing tendency begins to show. Among the older figures (particularly Fig. 522, in Oxford), there is, on the other hand, a tendency which we may call "rococo" (see Chap. X).

This rococo tendency, which is entirely absent in Pergamene art although it was present in an earlier period in Alexandria, is shown in works from Rhodes and its vicinity. The tendency is also verified by the fact that a style similar to the one for draped women was also used for draped men, like the husband of Cleopatra, Dioskurides; [61] and several tombstones, Hellenistic as well as Roman republican, [62] depict such a male type as a parallel to the "Pudicitia."

The tendency toward the rococo shows best, however, in the fact that many nude and semi-draped figures, probably mostly of Aphrodite, have come to light in this region. [63] It certainly is significant that, with the exception of the Hermaphrodite, probably of Rhodian origin (Fig. 492), not one such figure has been found in Pergamon. The Attalids were too serious to care for such figures, and perhaps felt a certain prudery.

Most of the semidraped figures, like the Aphrodite found in the harbor of Rhodes [64] (Fig. 527) and a similar small marble torso in the Metropolitan Museum [65] (Fig. 526), are of a late date, with elongated proportions characteristic of the late Hellenistic period. The arrangement of the drapery sometimes recalls that of the Hermaphrodite (Fig. 492), as does a torso in the Fogg Art Museum of Harvard University. [66] The long massed folds at the upper edge, falling from the right hip over the advancing left leg and hanging down outside the left side, occur also in a female torso from Rhodes; this figure of a woman seated on rocks has been considered either Aphrodite or a nymph [67] (Fig. 528). It so happens that this torso agrees astonishingly with the Dirce from the celebrated Farnese Bull group (Fig. 529); this dates these types of semidraped figures at about 100 B.C.

4. LATER BAROQUE ART (FIRST CENTURY B.C.)

Apollonios and Tauriskos of Tralles, sons of Artemidoros, were adopted by the Rhodian Mene-

---

1-2. O. Vessberg, *Studien zur Kunstgeschichte der römischen Republik* (1941), Pl. XXVII. See also Mustilli, *Museo Mussolini*, p. 102, Sala VI, No. 9, Pls. LVI–LVII, Figs. 225, 227–30.

[59] Charbonneaux, *La Sculpture grecque au Musée du Louvre*, Pl. XXXVIII.

[60] Th. Macridy-Bey in *Jahrbuch d. Inst.*, Vol. XXVII (1912), pp. 12 f., Pl. IIA. M. Schede, *Meisterwerke der türkischen Museen zu Konstantinopel* (Berlin, 1928), Bd. I: *Griechische und römische Skulpturen des Antikenmuseums*, Pl. 30. Horn, *Gewandstatuen*, p. 60, Pl. 22, No. 2. Horn compares it to a Pergamene statue.

[61] J. Chamonard, *Exploration archéologique de Délos* (École française d'Athènes), Vol. VIII, Part 1 (1922), pp. 39 f., Fig. 14, pp. 218 ff., Fig. 95.

[62] See E. Pfuhl, "Beiwerk auf den ostgriechischen Grabreliefs," in *Jahrbuch d. Inst.*, Vol. XX (1905), pp. 128 ff., Figs. 22–26; Vessberg, *Kunstgeschichte der römischen Republik*, Pls. XXVII, XXIX, XXXII, Pl. XXIV, No. 3, Pl. XXXVI, No. 2, Pl. LVIII, No. 1, Pl. LXXXV.

[63] See *Clara Rhodos*, Vol. I (1927), pp. 24 f., Figs. 5–6; Vol. V, Part 1 (1932), pp. 5 ff., Figs. 1–8, Pl. I, Vol. V, Part 2 (1932), pp. 143 ff., Figs. 34–35, Pl. XV, Vol. IX (1938), pp. 50 f., Fig. 31. L. Laurenzi even assigns the celebrated Kallipygos or Callipygian Venus (Brunn-Bruckmann, *Denkmäler*, Pl. 578) to Rhodes because a relief from Kos shows the same motif (*Clara Rhodos*, Vol. IX [1938], p. 112 f., Fig. 77). The motif, however, is described in Athenaeus (XII. 80, 554) for a sanctuary of Aphrodite in Syracuse.

[64] G. Laurenzi in *Clara Rhodos*, Vol. V, Part 1 (1931), pp. 5 ff., Figs. 1–8, Pl. I. G. Jacopi, "L'Afrodite pudica del Museo archeologico di Rodi," in *Bolletino d'Arte*, Series II, No. 9 (1929–30), pp. 401 ff., Figs. 1–9. G. Jacopi, *Lo spedale dei Cavalieri e il museo archeologico di Rhodi* (1932), pp. 49 f., Pl. III.

[65] Metropolitan Museum of Art, No. 24.97.88. The head was removed in 1951.

[66] A similar torso in Madrid is shown in Klein, *Rokoko*, p. 99, Fig. 41, and P. Arndt and W. Amelung, *Photographische Einzelaufnahmen antiker Skulpturen* (Munich, Bruckmann, 1893—), No. 1542. The latter authors list 14 replicas.

[67] A. Maiuri in *Clara Rhodos*, Vol. V, Part 2 (1932), pp. 30 f., No. 38, Fig. 19–21, Pls. III–IV. Jacopi, *Lo Spedale dei Cavalieri*, p. 65, Fig. 35. B. Schweitzer, "Dirke," *Winckelmannsblatt Leipzig* (1940). G. Gullini, in *Arti Figurative*, Vol. III (1947), pp. 61 ff., Pl. XXXIII, shows similar Hellenistic works, for example the nude girl from Beroea on Pl. XXXII.

krates, perhaps the leading artist of the altar of Zeus at Pergamon. They created a group of "Zethus and Amphion, also Dirce and the bull, including the rope, all out of the same stone" (Pliny *Nat. hist.* XXXVI. 33-34). The original was certainly not so overloaded with accessories as the preserved group in Naples [68] (Fig. 529). This is a copy made in the early third century A.D. for the baths of Caracalla (211-217). The main additions are the figure of Antiope (who had been threatened with the punishment which her sons now mete out to the wicked queen Dirce), and the rear part of the base on which Antiope stands, which has changed the pyramidical composition to a square one, better adapted to the center of a large hall in the bath establishment. Probably the shepherd, or personification of the Cithaeron mountain, and all animals except the dog are also additions. The modern restoration—all the heads, the upper part of Dirce, and the right arm of Amphion, who originally grasped the hair of Dirce—also add to the disfigurement of the group. When we use the torso (Fig. 528), a coin from Thyatira, and a cameo in Naples for models in restoring the upper part of Dirce, we get a much more natural turn of the strong womanly body. The rich rocky landscape, used as support and for letting the drapery fall over it, shows a further step in the direction of the development of landscape, here used for a group in the round instead of in reliefs as on the Telephos frieze and Munich relief (Figs. 477-78 and 489). Perhaps the torso (Fig. 528) is an original work of Apollonios and Tauriskos and can help us to visualize their original group.

The Farnese Bull group testifies to a reawakening of the baroque spirit which began with the Nike of Samothrace in Rhodes (Figs. 493-96). The highest point and at the same time the end of this Hellenistic tendency is the Laocoon [69] (Figs. 530-

33). This is the joint work of Agesandros, Polydoros, and Athenodoros of Rhodes, and was later set up in the house of the emperor Titus (Pliny *Nat. hist.* XXXVI. 37), which is the Golden House built by the emperor Nero. Here it was found in 1506 and set up in the Belvedere of the Vatican. The sculptor Giovanni Angelo Montorsoli restored the missing right arms of the father and the younger son. A restoration in Dresden (Fig. 530) shows the right attitudes. [70]

The group depicts the punishment of Laocoon, a priest of Apollo, whose laurel is shown in the wreath, of which only a few leaves are preserved in the back of the head. Laocoon has violated the sanctity of the temple of the god; therefore, while he is sacrificing at an altar, assisted by his two sons, two snakes attack the three. One serpent comes from the right, winds around the legs of all three, binds together the legs of father and younger son, entwines the shoulders of the child, and bites into his breast. The second snake comes from the left, winds around the right arm of the father, his tail hanging on the back of Laocoon, continues behind his back to his left and encircles the older son's right arm; this snake returns to the father, who grasps its neck, but is nevertheless wounded in the hip. It is necessary to understand these movements of the two snakes in order to understand the group. One of the snakes attacks from the front, the other from the back, but their main movement is to the side of father and younger son, who will die, while the older son will escape. He is already pulling out his right arm and pushing the end coil of the snake from his left foot. His movement is to the right, toward liberty, while the two others are sinking backward and to the left, toward the altar of the god who has sent them death.

The difference in age is expressed in the bodies as well as in the heads. The strong swelling muscles of the father, the mature body of the older son, and the soft body of the younger boy are finely graded. Even in the feet there is the difference of age. In the heads, not only this difference, but the difference of mood, is expressed with virtuosity. The dis-

[68] A. Ruesch, *Guida del Museo Nazionale di Napoli* (n.d.), pp. 80 f., Fig. 29, No. 260. Brunn-Bruckmann, *Denkmäler*, Pl. 367. F. Studniczka in *Zeitschrift für bildende Kunst*, New Series, Vol. XIV (1903), pp. 171 ff., Figs. 1-13.

[69] Amelung, *Vatican Kat.*, Vol. II, pp. 181 ff., Pl. 20. Brunn-Bruckmann, *Denkmäler*, Pl. 236. Gotthold Ephraim Lessing, *Laokoon* (1766). Goethe, *Über Laokoon* (first published in 1798 in *Propylaeen*, a periodical art review published by Goethe). M. Pohlenz in *Die Antike*, IX (1933), 54 ff. M. Bieber, *Laocoon: The Influence of the Group since Its Rediscovery* (New York, Columbia University Press, 1942). G. Lippold in *Jahrbuch d. Inst.*, LXI-LXII (1946-47), pp. 93 f. G. Highet,

The Classical Tradition: Greek and Roman Influences on Western Literature (Oxford, 1949), pp. 16, 371-74, 665.

[70] A similar restoration has been made in the Cast Museum at Rome. See E. V. Caffarelli in *Archeologia Classica*, Vol. I (1949), pp. 75 f., Pl. XII.

torted features of the father (Fig. 531), repeated also in a replica in the Palazzo Spada in Rome, are modeled with the same arbitrary arrangement as we find in some heads of the Pergamon frieze. The rumpled hair and beard, with deep shadows between the thick strands, continue the style of Pergamon. The face of the father expresses unrestrained agony. The face of the older son, in contrast, expresses only deep concern, while the younger son, his round boyish face framed with short curls, is beginning to succumb to the bitterness of death. Marco Dente in his engraving (Fig. 532), and even the master of the baroque, Baccio Bandinelli, in his group (Fig. 533), have brought out and emphasized this distinction.

The Laocoon is an example of a late Hellenistic one-sided group, that is, one in which all important motifs can be seen from the front.[71] This is not a return to the flat arrangement of the classical period, for the group has considerable depth, and although a view from the side or the back adds nothing essential, yet many details are necessary for better understanding—for example, the tail of the snake in the back of Laocoon. The best view of the Laocoon is from a certain distance, where the multiplicity of the forms is less evident. There is, decidedly, a certain tension between the front and the deep space in which the figures are set, with dark parts in irregular contours (see p. 122).

This characteristic applies to a number of groups, most of which, particularly the group of Pan and Daphnis by Heliodoros of Rhodes (Fig. 628), show the rococo trend of the later Hellenism. The Laocoon certainly is one of the latest groups. Athenodoros carved a group of Philippos and Agauris in 42 B.C. He and Agesandros became priests of Athena Lindia in 22 and 21 B.C. respectively; this was an honor bestowed only on older people. The Laocoon, therefore, must have been created around 50 B.C., shortly before Rhodes was plundered by Cassius, in 42 B.C.[72]

[71] G. Krahmer, "Die einansichtige Gruppe und die späthellenistische Kunst," Nachrichten Gött. Ges. (1927), pp. 53 ff.

[72] For the date see C. Blinkenberg in Röm. Mitt., Vol. XLII (1927), pp. 178 ff., and Blinkenberg and Kinch, Lindos, Vol. II: Inscriptions I, pp. 29–32, No. 27. Good reasons for the late dating of the Laocoon are given by R. Horn in Röm. Mitt., LII (1937), p. 147. G. Richter, in her Sculpture and Sculptors, pp. 48, 300 f., dates c.150 B.C. See also "The Date of the Laocoon," in her Three Critical Periods in Greek Sculpture (1951), pp. 67–70. Her wish to date the Laocoon so early stems from her attempt to describe the first century as "a period of wholesale copying," which it by no means is. See pp. 150 ff. and my Chap. XI.

X

ROCOCO TRENDS
IN HELLENISTIC ART

THE TERM "ROCOCO" was first used in France in the reign of Louis XV (1715–74) for the decorative arts, chiefly those used in interiors. It is derived from *rocaille,* rock, and *coquille,* shell, motifs prominent in interior decoration in France, Germany, and Italy in the eighteenth century. It was an outgrowth of, but also a reaction against, the sobriety and heaviness of the preceding baroque style. Lightness and delicacy are its chief characteristics. This spirit is perhaps best expressed in porcelain, particularly in the eighteenth-century products of Dresden and Meissen in Germany and Sèvres in France.

The term was first transferred to a similar trend in Hellenistic art by the Austrian scholar Wilhelm Klein.[1] He is right in understanding the graceful, light, and playful side of Hellenistic art as a parallel to eighteenth-century art. He is wrong, however, when he transfers baroque-rococo in chronological sequence to the Hellenistic period. There is no doubt that in ancient art this rococo trend began in the early third century and lasted through all the following periods, including the Roman. Just as Dresden china is still popular today, so this lighter side of Hellenistic art won many more admirers than the voluminous and pretentious baroque art. Like porcelain in the eighteenth century, terra cotta, bronze, and ivory, in addition to marble, were favorite materials for rococo figures.

The main subjects of rococo art are children, male and female adolescents, and old men and women. All these ranged from the higher classes to the lower groups living on the sidewalks of the capitals or in rural districts—peasants, fishermen, and shepherds—down to caricatures. The lust for life is expressed in satyrs, maenads, and pans. Among the gods Dionysos, Aphrodite, and Eros became the favorites of an era which enjoyed song, dance, wine, and love.

I. SINGLE FIGURES

A center for this rococo trend in the third century was Alexandria (see Figs. 374–97), though at the same time it had already spread to Asia Minor, as testified by Herondas (*Mimiamb* IV. 30–34). He describes the figure of a boy seated on the ground, probably the votive offering of a fond mother, in the temple of Asclepius on the island of Kos. He smothers (πνίγει) his pet goose, looking as natural as if alive. The statue found in Ephesus, of an infant lifting his head and right arm as if wanting to speak or to be lifted up, agrees so well with this description that here we almost have an illustration of Herondas, certainly a contemporary work and thus one of the early third century[2] (Fig. 534). The boy presses down a fox goose, a kind of goose more like a duck. His heavy head has the right proportions for his chubby body. Both his knees are bent. His left leg is lying fully on the ground;

[1] W. Klein, "Studien zum antiken Rokoko," in *Oest. Jahreshefte,* XIX–XX (1919), pp. 252 ff. W. Klein, *Vom antiken Rokoko* (Vienna, Hölzel, 1921).

[2] R. Herzog in *Oest. Jahreshefte,* Vol. VI (1903), pp. 215 ff., Pl. VIII. Klein, *Rokoko,* p. 29, Fig. 6. Cf. G. von Kaschnitz-Weinberg, *Scultura del Maggazzino del Museo Vaticano* (1936–37), pp. 163 ff., No. 352, Pl. LXIX.

his right, with the foot turned out, touches the ground only with the heel. This movement shows that he is not yet able to get up and walk.

A variation of this motif is found in the infant Heracles strangling the two snakes sent by Hera to kill him in his crib [3] (Fig. 536). The statue in the Museo Capitolino is a Roman copy, therefore the execution is hard and lifeless. But the movement of the infant hero is full of life. His left hand chokes the neck of one snake by forcing it against the ground, while the lifted right hand squeezes the other snake. The head is turned toward the action of his right hand.

Children of all ages were favorite subjects in this period. Twins in their crib are shown in a terra cotta in Athens [4] (Fig. 535). A little boy holding grapes lies on his mattress playing with his dog, in Munich [5] (Fig. 537). From Smyrna, now in the Louvre [6] (Fig. 538), is the little boy reaching out for grapes on the tombstone of Metrodoros and Matreas, while another boy with crossed feet is looking on. On the tombstone of Amyntas, also from Smyrna and in the Louvre, we see a child seated on the ground holding fruits to the side, away from his favorite cock [7] (Fig. 539). Around him are his toys; among them, below the inscription, are three knucklebones, a ball, and a milk bottle. Behind and above him are a herm and a framed wreath.

A charming terra-cotta group in the Walters Art Gallery in Baltimore shows two little boys at a cockfight [8] (Fig. 540). The owner of the victorious bird claps his hands, his dimpled face all smiles. The other boy, whose cock has been defeated, despondently leans his head on his hand, his elbow on a chest. Between the two, a girl stands (her upper part is missing). Children with their pets are frequently represented; an example is Boethos's boy strangling a goose (Fig. 285). Terra cottas from Myrina, now in the Louvre, show a little boy with his young deer, and a little girl with a hare [9] (Fig. 543). Statuettes of little girls from the sanctuary of Eilithyia at Agrae which are now in Athens represent them seated on the ground, or holding their pets in their arms or in the folds of their mantles [10] (Fig. 542). A marble statue in the Metropolitan Museum depicts a little girl in two heavy dresses, which are wide and long, so that she may not outgrow them too quickly. She lifts her outer garment to hide her pet in a kind of pouch before her body [11] (Fig. 541). Young boys are shown in a multitude of terra cottas; they are seated, with or without hats, wrapped in mantles or dressed in chlamydes, holding a bag of knucklebones or masks, or supporting their heads with their hands; many other motifs were also used [12] (see Figs. 48 and 50). Girls from about ten to twelve years of age are seated on the ground playing knucklebones, in terra cottas [13] (Fig. 53) and marble statuettes. The best known of these is in Palazzo Colonna; [14] this statuette has

---

[3] H. Stuart Jones, *A Catalogue of the Ancient Sculptures Preserved in the Municipal Collections of Rome. The Sculptures of the Museo Capitolino* (Oxford, 1912), Galleria No. 54b, pp. 128 f., Pl. 25. For other statuettes of the infant Heracles strangling the serpents, see G. Cultrera, *Saggi sull' arte ellenistica e greca-romana*, I (1907), 77 f. The motif is found earliest in painting; see P. Herrmann and F. Bruckmann, *Denkmäler der Malerei des Altertums* (Munich, 1904–31), pp. 53, 111 ff., Pls. 41, 83. Cf. G. Lippold in *Jahrbuch d. Inst.*, LXI–LXII (1946–47), p. 90, and in *Röm. Mitt.*, LI (1936), 99 ff. Many children were represented as the young Heracles, little Hermes, or the child Dionysos. See Klein, *Rokoko*, pp. 133 ff.

[4] National Museum, Athens, No. 12649. Anita Klein, *Child Life in Greek Art* (Columbia University Press, 1932), pp. 1 ff., Pl. IA.

[5] Munich, Museum antiker Kleinkunst. Klein, *Child Life in Greek Art*, p. 3, Pl. IB.

[6] *Encycl. phot.*, Vol. III, p. 253D. E. Pfuhl, "Beiwerk auf ostgriechischen Grabreliefs," in *Jahrbuch d. Inst.*, Vol. XX (1905), pp. 78 f., No. 22, Fig. 15.

[7] E. Pfuhl, "Beiwerk auf ostgriechischen Grabreliefs," in *Jahrbuch d. Inst.*, Vol. XX (1905), p. 78, No. 17, Pl. 5.

[8] Walters Art Gallery, No. 48,1714. Found in Samsun on the Black Sea. Dated in the third century b.c.

[9] E. Pottier and S. Reinach, *La Nécropole de Myrina* (Paris, Thorin, 1887), pp. 335 f., Pl. XVII, No. 2 and pp. 457 f., Pl. XLIII, No. 5. Louvre Nos. 112 and 312. Compare the marble statue of a little girl protecting a dove, in the Museo Capitolino, Stanza del Gladiatore, No. 9 (Jones, *Sculpt. Museo Capitolino*, p. 349, Pl. 87). Other children with pets: Klein, *Child Life in Greek Art*, pp. 10 ff., Pls. X–XIV.

[10] J. N. Svoronos in *Ephemeris Arch.* (1917), p. 78, Pls. 1–2. Idem, *Athener Nationalmuseum*, (3 vols., Athens, 1908–37), Nos. 693–96. Cf. *Oest. Jahreshefte*, Vol. IV (1901), p. 211, Figs. 227–28.

[11] Metropolitan Museum of Art, No. 26.60.89. Christine Alexander in *M.M.A. Bulletin*, Vol. XXV (1930), pp. 168 f., Fig. 5.

[12] J. Charbonneaux, *Les Terres cuites grecques* (Paris, Reynaud, 1936), pp. 44 f., Figs. 47–48.

[13] L. Heuzey, *Les Figurines de terres cuites du Musée du Louvre* (Paris, 1883), Pl. 52, No. 2. E. Pottier, *Les Statuettes de terre cuite dans l'antiquité* (Paris, 1890), p. 89, Fig. 33. Other examples are in the Metropolitan Museum of Art.

[14] H. Heydemann, *Knöchelspielerin in Palazzo Colonna* (*Hallisches Winckelmanns-Programm* [1877]), Pl. I. Replicas of this statue are in the Berlin Museum (No. 494) and the Louvre (No. 1425). See also A. H. Smith, *A Catalogue of*

a badly restored right arm. This type was very popular among the Romans for portraits of little girls. A bronze statuette of a girl about four years of age, in the Palazzo Grazioli, is looking down at her hands, which evidently held some object. Her careful melon headdress and full peplos testify to her being a child of rich parents [15] (Fig. 544). Her eyes and the buckle of her belt were inlaid with silver. The bronze statue of a boy, in Madrid, running merrily and eagerly, with an elegant braid over the parting of the hair and small locks bound to a tuft on the crown of his head, also testifies to his parents' prosperity [16] (Fig. 545). All these happy children are smiling or looking pleased, and there are attractive heads of such smiling children, like the boy in the British Museum [17] (Fig. 546) and the healthy but sleepy child in Munich [18] (Fig. 547).

There are, however, less fortunate children. The street boy in Priene, pulling a thorn from his foot (see Chap. VII, p. 104) and the similar marble statue in the British Museum [19] (Fig. 550), has hurt his foot while running around barefoot. Boys playing in the streets get into quarrels; thus in the group in the British Museum the knucklebones testify to the reason why the one boy (who is well preserved) bites into the arm of his playmate, the other parts of whom have been lost.[20] The poor slave boy has to wait for his master who is enjoying a banquet, in order to light the master's way home with the lantern [21] (Figs. 548–49). He has

drawn his cape over his head to protect himself against the cool night and has fallen asleep.

Teen-age girls, with their restless and nervous moods, are excellently rendered from the early third century on. To this period certainly belongs the girl in the Museo Capitolino, who is so nearly related to the Tyche of Antioch by Eutychides, the pupil of Lysippos, that she has been attributed to the same artist [22] (see Fig. 101). Others of these young girls, holding each others' hands, play in a terra-cotta group in the Louvre [23] (Fig. 551), or carry each other on their backs in a game probably called *ostrakinda,* in groups of which several variations exist [24] (Fig. 552). Above all, they like to dance and to throw their heads back, lifting their arms or one foot and twisting their slender bodies in all directions [25] (Figs. 553–57). Bronze and terra cotta are the favorite materials for these dancers. The finest and one of the earliest is the bronze statuette from Alexandria, now in the Baker collection in New York (see Figs. 378–79). The sweeping movements are underlined by the movement of the garments. The breasts are lifted up by

Sculpture in the Department of Greek and Roman Antiquities of the British Museum (3 vols., London, 1892–1904), Vol. III, No. 1710. Replica in Dresden, Museum No. 726. Replica in Hanover, P. Arndt and W. Amelung, *Photographische Einzelaufnahmen antiker Skulpturen* (F. Bruckmann, Munich, 1893—), No. 1073. P. Arndt in text to H. Brunn and F. Bruckmann, *Denkmäler griechischer und römischer Skulptur* (Munich, 1888—), Pl. 520, lists seven replicas.
[15] Brunn-Bruckmann, *Denkmäler,* Pl. 540.
[16] Brunn-Bruckmann, *Denkmäler,* Pl. 514.
[17] A. H. Smith, *Brit. Mus. Cat.,* Vol. III, No. 1934, Pl. VI.
[18] A. Furtwängler and P. Wolters, *Beschreibung der Glyptothek zu München* (2d ed., 1910), No. 349.
[19] A. H. Smith, *Brit. Mus. Cat.,* Vol. III, No. 1755, Pl. VIII.
[20] *Ibid.,* pp. 110 f., No. 1756. Brunn-Bruckmann, *Denkmäler,* Pl. 54.
[21] Our Fig. 549 is in Rome, Museo Nazionale Romano No. 125587. Our Fig. 548 is in the Egyptian Department of the Metropolitan Museum of Art (No. 23.160.82). R. Zahn, in "Lanternarius," in *Jahrbuch der Preussischen Kunstsammlungen,* XXXVII (1916), 14 ff., discusses a bronze figurine in Berlin. Other examples are in P. Perdrizet, *Terres cuites grec-*

ques d'Égypte de la Collection Fouquet (Paris, 1921) p. 19, No. 74, Pl. LXXX. Silver figure of a lanternarius from France, in the British Museum: H. B. Walters, *Catalogue of the Silver Plate in the British Museum* (London, 1921), pp. 38 f., No. 145, Pl. XXIII; other examples are cited there.
[22] H. Stuart Jones, *A Catalogue of the Ancient Sculptures Preserved in the Municipal Collections of Rome. The Sculptures of the Palazzo dei Conservatori* (Oxford, 1926), pp. 146 f. Orti Lamiani, No. 31, Pl. 53. Brunn-Bruckmann, *Denkmäler,* text to Pl. 610, Figs. 6–7. Klein, *Rokoko,* Pl. I (frontispiece; cf. pp. 99 f.). See our Chap. III, p. 41, note 46.
[23] Louvre, Museum No. 246.
[24] Terra-cotta group, Metropolitan Museum of Art, No. 07.286.4. G. M. A. Richter, *Handbook of the Greek Collection* (1953), p. 112, Pl. 92i. For others see M. Bieber in *Classical Studies Presented to David Robinson,* I (1951), 556–58. There also is an explanation of the game *ostrakinda,* played by throwing a disk colored black on one side, white on the other. The members of the team whose color wins are carried on the backs of the losing players. See Charbonneaux, *Terres cuites,* Pl. 31, No. 33, for a group from Tegea, and P. Perdrizet, "Terres cuites de l'Asie Mineure," in *Mon. Piot,* Vol. IV (1897), pp. 209 ff., Pl. XVII, for a group from Myrina.
[25] Fig. 554 is in Baltimore; see D. K. Hill, *Catalogue of Bronzes in the Walters Art Gallery* (Baltimore, 1949), p. 104, No. 235, Pl. 44. The snail under her left foot contrasts her quick movement with the slow one of the animal. Fig. 552 is in the Bibliothèque nationale at Paris. Fig. 555, from Tarentum, and Fig. 557 are in the Metropolitan Museum of Art, Numbers 11.212.20 and 13.232.12. Richter, *Handbook* (1953), p. 128, Pl. 108g–i. Fig. 556, from Egnatia, is in the Louvre: Charbonneaux, *Terres cuites,* p. 86, Fig. 98.

the *strophion*, the soft broad ribbon serving as brassiere [26] (Fig. 558; see Fig. 391, left).

The dance is the favorite pastime, too, of the satyr who had already, in the works of the school of Lysippos, become the exponent of the lust for life of this period (see Fig. 94). The satyr in the house at Pompeii which is named from this figure "La Casa del Fauno" throws his head and both arms up in an exuberant expression of the joy of life (Figs. 95–96). The variation in Athens,[27] although under suspicion, seems to me a genuine work of this gay trend. The bearded dancing satyr, a bronze statuette in the Bibliothèque nationale in Paris (Fig. 561), is more restrained than the flute-playing Borghese satyr (Fig. 94), while the small bronze figure from Herculaneum gives a still more restrained variation [28] (Fig. 559). Much more frolicsome is the dance of the young satyr swinging a thyrsus, from Herculaneum [29] (Fig. 560). His left leg is swung backward into the air, both arms are stretched out, and his head is lifted and turned to the right in the direction of the movement. His face expresses gaiety and satisfaction. The playful character of the satyr is well expressed in the satyr looking for his tail, which he has discovered while dancing.[30]

As on vases of the fifth century B.C., the satyrs of this period not only dance, but also make dance music for their companions, nymphs and maenads. An excellent discovery of Wilhelm Klein is that the celebrated satyr in the Tribuna of the Uffizi Gallery in Florence is himself not dancing, but is inviting a seated nymph to dance for him [31] (Figs.

562–67). His right foot beats the rhythm on a clapper (*kroupezion*), while his arms wave in the air, fingers snapping, and his head is bent down to the nymph. The girl responds by looking up at him laughingly while she puts the sandal on her left foot, which she has lifted over her right knee. This grouping of the figures (Fig. 564) is verified by a coin from Cyzicus (Fig. 565). The figures are not closely combined into a group, but the connection is attained by the heads smiling at each other. The best copies of the nymph are in Florence (Fig. 563) and in Brussels (Fig. 566). Both have wrong heads. The right head is best copied in a large head in Venice (Fig. 567), together with a replica of the satyr's head. Both figures have considerable depth, though together they have only one main view. This is a so-called one-sided group, to be dated probably in the second half of the second century B.C.

Often the satyr plays with the panther, the sacred animal of Dionysos; examples are a statuette from Pergamon (Fig. 449) and a statue in the Villa Albani [32] (Fig. 568). The Albani satyr has collected fruits in the skin which he has hung around his neck and over his left arm, and he is showing grapes to the thirsty animal. Old Papposilenos (Father Silenus), in a statue in the Vatican, feeds the panther from a wine jug. In another statue carved in red stone, in the Vatican, with a replica in the Museo Capitolino, a satyr who has collected fruits in the skin looks laughingly up at a bunch of grapes in his right hand [33] (Fig. 573).

The good-natured satyr, however, is not only a joyful but a helpful fellow. He allows little Dionysos to ride on his shoulder, for example in the statue in Villa Albani [34] (Fig. 569), in a fragment

---

[26] Metropolitan Museum of Art, No. 13.232.13. On the *strophion* see M. Bieber in Pauly-Wissowa, *Real-Enc.,* Second Series, Vol. 4A, 2, pp. 378 ff., s.v. Strophium.

[27] Mylonas in *Ephemeris Arch.* (1885), pp. 227 ff., Pls. V–VI. H. Bulle, *Der schöne Mensch in Altertum* (Munich, 1912), Fig. 44 in text to Pl. 102. Klein, *Rokoko,* pp. 52 f. J. Sieveking in text to Brunn-Bruckmann, *Denkmäler,* Pl. 760, Fig. 1. For the satyr from the Casa del Fauno, see Chap. III, p. 39, note 41.

[28] From the villa of the Pisones, now in Naples. See D. Comparetti and G. de Petra, *La Villa Ercolanese dei Pisoni* (Turin, 1883), p. 268, Nos. 34–35, Pl. XIII, No. 1, Pl. XV, No. 1.

[29] *Ibid.,* Pl. XVI, No. 6. See also Klein, *Rokoko,* p. 50, and figure on p. 82.

[30] See Chap. III, p. 39, note 40.

[31] W. Klein in *Zeitschrift für bildende Kunst,* Vol. XX (1909), pp. 101 ff., Figs. 1–10. Klein, *Rokoko,* pp. 45 ff., Fig. 14. W. Amelung, *Führer durch die Antiken in Florenz* (Munich, 1897), Nos. 65, 84. A. W. Lawrence, *Later Greek Sculpture and Its Influence on East and West* (London, 1927), p. 19, Pl. 30b (reconstruction) and Pl. 31 (heads in Venice).

[32] Villa Albani, No. 124. See A. Furtwängler, *Der Satyr aus Pergamon* (*Winck.-Prog. Berlin,* No. 40 [1880]), pp. 4 ff., 20, Pl. I, Pl. III, No. 1.

[33] For Papposilenos, see Brunn-Bruckmann, *Denkmäler,* Pl. 198. Amelung, *Vatican Kat.,* Vol. I, pp. 671 f., Museo Chiaramonti, No. 544, Pl. 71. For the satyr in rosso antico, found in the Villa of Hadrian, see *Vatican Kat.,* Vol. II, pp. 694 ff., Gabinetto delle Maschere, No. 432, Pl. 76. For the replica in rosso antico in the Museo Capitolino, also found in the Villa of Hadrian, see M. Squarciapino, *La Scuola di Afrodisia* (1943), pp. 33 f., Pls. V and F, b; Jones, *Sculpt. Museo Capitolino,* pp. 309 f., Stanza del Fauno, No. 1, Pl. 77; cf. a replica in white marble in *ibid.,* p. 279, Salone No. 6, Pl. 67.

[34] Villa Albani, No. 148. Replicas in the Vatican: Amelung, *Vatican Kat.,* Vol. I, pp. 43 f., Braccio Nuovo, No. 29, Pl. V; W. Helbig, *Führer durch die öffentlichen Sammlungen klas-*

in the Walters Art Gallery [35] (Fig. 571), and in a terra-cotta statuette from Myrina in the Louvre [36] (Fig. 570). The grown Dionysos is also often sustained by a smaller satyr, as in a bronze group in the Walters Art Gallery [37] (Fig. 572). The features of these Hellenistic satyrs always mirror keen observation, good nature, and alertness, as in a head in the Louvre (Fig. 574).

The satyr, being a follower of the god Dionysos, naturally loves wine. He is rarely really drunk, but rather ecstatic, or sometimes tired by dancing and revel. He is shown in drunken sleep in the Barberini Satyr (above, Figs. 450-51), but is more frequently just at the moment of falling asleep. This instant is shown in a series of statues, the best being a bronze found in Herculaneum and now in Naples [38] (Fig. 576). Another good statue in marble is in the Vatican Museum [39] (Fig. 575). The bronze shows the beginning of relaxation in the hanging left arm, while the right seeks to hold up

the head, which is sinking backward. The torso is still upright, the feet seeking a hold on the rock which forms his seat. The marble satyr has spread a skin over his rock seat. His left hand holds a wineskin, which originally was used as a fountain spout. His body is stretched backward and the head with the sustaining hand will, in a moment, fall to the seat. Thus the transitory moment between waking and sleeping is rendered in a strong momentary movement.

Quite different is the drunkenness of Heracles in bronze statuettes, one in the Metropolitan Museum of Art in New York (Figs. 577-78, 580) and one in the Walters Art Gallery in Baltimore [40] (Fig. 579). Here the hero leans his rather dignified head, with full hair and beard, forward, while his unstable legs let the heavy body lean slightly backward, and the right arm tries to keep the balance.

The influence of wine on the wild centaurs had already been depicted in the classical period on the occasion of the wedding feast of Peirithoos. When they tried to carry away the bride and her friends, they were defeated by the Lapiths and Theseus. This fight became a symbol of the victory of civilization over brute force. The Hellenistic period had a different conception of the centaurs. Zeuxis, in the fourth century, had painted a family idyll, giving a wife of the same half-equine race to the centaur (Lucian *Zeuxis* 3-6). A Hellenistic artist, probably of the second century B.C., showed the influence of love on a young centaur and an old one, in a contrasting pair, recalling Hellenistic love epigrams. We know the group only through Roman copies, the best having been carved in dark grey stone by Aristeas and Papias of Aphrodisias in the second half of the second century A.D. for the Villa of Hadrian in Tivoli [41] (Fig. 584). They are now in the Museo Capitolino. Replicas of the young centaur, in red marble in the Palazzo Doria and in white marble in the Vatican,[42] as well as one

---

sischer Altertümer in Rom (3d ed., Leipzig, 1912-13), Vol. II, p. 247, No. 384, Galleria dei Candelabri, No. 148. Another replica, in Copenhagen, signed by Flavius Zenon of Aphrodisias: P. Arndt, *La Glyptothèque Ny-Carlsberg* (Munich, 1896-1912), pp. 222 ff.; Arndt-Amelung, *Einzelaufnahmen*, Nos. 166-70; G. Lippold, *Antike Skulpturen der Glyptothek Ny Carlsberg* (1924), p. 26, and Squarciapino, *Afrodisia*, pp. 41 f., Pl. XII a. For other figures of a satyr with the child Dionysos see Klein, *Rokoko*, p. 51, Fig. 17 and pp. 54 f.; A. Minto, "Satiro con Bacco fanciullo," in *Ausonia*, VIII (1913), 99 ff. Many examples are on Roman sarcophagi.

[35] Unpublished; Walters Art Gallery, No. 23.69. Acquired 1920.
[36] Pottier and Reinach, *Myrina*, pp. 372 ff., Pl. XXVI; Charbonneaux, *Terres cuites*, p. 62, No. 67.
[37] Walters Art Gallery, No. 54.1035. See Dorothy K. Hill, *Bronzes*, p. 26, No. 46, Pl. 14. For the best example in marble, in Florence, see Amelung, *Antiken in Florenz*, p. 90, No. 140; Klein, *Rokoko*, pp. 77 ff., Fig. 32; Arndt in Brunn-Bruckmann, *Denkmäler*, Pl. 620 (other replicas are Figs. 1-5 in the text). See also P. Ducati in *Oest. Jahreshefte*, XVI (1913), pp. 107 ff., Figs. 57-58; Amelung, *Vatican Kat.*, Vol. I, pp. 705 f., Museo Chiaramonti, No. 588, Pl. 75; A. Ippel, *Der Bronzefund von Galjub: Modelle eines hellenistischen Goldschmeids* (Berlin, 1922; Pelizaeusmuseum, Hildesheim, Wissenschaftliche Veröffentlichung, Vol. II), pp. 32 ff., No. 11, Pl. I (he lists 19 variations of the group). W. Technau, in *Die Antike*, Vol. XV (1939), pp. 293 ff., Figs. 294-95, dates the original in the early Hellenistic period. Roman versions build the group loosely from single figures.
[38] Comparetti and de Petra, *La Villa Ercolanese*, Pl. XIII, No. 1. A. Ruesch, *Guida del Museo Nazionale di Napoli* (n.d.), p. 209, No. 842. Brunn-Bruckmann, *Denkmäler*, Pl. 594 (replicas are listed in the text by Riezler). See also H. Bulle, in *Jahrbuch d. Inst.*, XVI (1901), pp. 14 ff.
[39] Amelung, *Vatican Kat.*, Vol. II, pp. 463 f., Galleria delle Statue No. 267, Pl. 50.

[40] See Dorothy K. Hill, *Bronzes*, p. 48, No. 98, Pl. 22, for example in the Walters Art Gallery (No. 54.732). The Metropolitan Museum of Art statuette is No. 15.57. Richter, *Handbook* (1953), p. 125, Pl. 104d.
[41] Jones, *Sculpt. Museo Capitolino*, pp. 274 ff., Pl. 64, Salone No. 2 and 4. Brunn-Bruckmann, *Denkmäler*, Pl. 392. Squarciapino, *Afrodisia*, pp. 32 f., Pls. VI-VII. A. della Seta, *Il nudo nell' arte* (1930), pp. 483 ff.
[42] Palazzo Doria: Arndt-Amelung, *Einzelaufnahmen*, Nos. 2271-72. Vatican: Amelung, *Vatican Kat.*, Vol. II, p. 346, Sala degli Animali, No. 138, Pl. 35.

of the old centaur in the Louvre [43] (Figs. 581 and 583), show a little Eros on the back of each centaur. The subject matter is the difference with which the youth and old age react to love. The young centaur gallops gaily along, snapping his fingers of the right hand, shouldering his pedum, lifting and waving his tail. The old centaur has his hands bound to his back by his torturer, who seems to try to pull the hair of the old man. He turns around to Eros and tries to lash him with his tail. The heads are an excellent study in contrast: the coarse but smiling face of the young centaur, closely related to the so-called Fauno colla Macchia in Munich [44] (Fig. 582), with short hair and wisps falling to the forehead, on the one hand; and on the other hand, the rather dignified head of the old centaur [45] (Fig. 581), with heavy masses of long hair which stand up over the forehead and frame the cheeks, their ends mingling with the broad and long beard. The features, particularly the eyebrows and forehead, are drawn out of form, as in some heads on the Pergamon altar as well as the Laocoon head. The bearded head makes an effective contrast not only to the young centaur, but also to the smooth and childish rounded face of the ivy-crowned Eros (see Fig. 581). A variation of the centaur's head, in Berlin,[46] emphasizes still more the tragedy of the love of an old man, which brings him only pain, sorrow, and ridicule.

Drunkenness in an old woman has been expressed by Myron in a pathetic figure, where the dress and adornment, and the elegant form of the bottle with a wreath around it, hint at better times in the past (Fig. 284). The motif is also used very adequately in a terra-cotta wine bottle and in the bronze bottle in shape of a woman in the Louvre [47] (Fig. 586). The repeated emptying of the cup in her right hand has apparently made her sick. She crouches on the ground, her heavy head hangs forward, and both wrists recline on her knees while the hands hang down slackly. The mouth is open and deep folds hang down from the cheeks to the chin, as if the old woman were nauseated. It is an excellent study of a debased female.

An old nurse in distress seems to be the motif of a head, related in style to the sick woman [48] (Fig. 585). It was bought in Rome and is in the possession of Dr. Hermann Vollmer in New York. The material, Pentelic marble, may indicate that it was carved in Athens. Head and neck are meager, covered with dried skin and hollowed by deep furrows. The mouth is open as if lamenting, showing a few irregular teeth. A cap covers the still rather full hair. A stocky old nurse with an apelike face, carrying a little girl, and an old pedagogue with too large a head, bald pate, potato nose, meager arms, and a fat belly, teaching a little boy to write on a *diptychon,* are represented in terra-cotta figurines in the Metropolitan Museum of Art in New York [49] (Figs. 587–88).

Pleasanter than these old derelicts are the figures of peasant women who carry their wares to market. An example, in the Metropolitan Museum of Art, is a woman, stooped with age, who takes her chickens and vegetables to market [50] (Fig. 590). One in the Palazzo dei Conservatori at Rome carries a lamb against her right side [51] (Fig. 591). These old women are lean, but still alert and not starved, unlike their male counterparts in the Palazzo dei

[43] W. Fröhner, *Notice de la sculpture antique du Louvre* (4th ed., Paris, 1878), pp. 293 ff., No. 299. M. Collignon, *Histoire de la sculpture grecque* (2 vols., Paris, 1892 and 1897), Vol. II, p. 678, Fig. 355. *Encycl. phot.,* Vol. III, p. 238. Squarciapino, *Afrodisia,* Pls. E and F, a.

[44] Furtwängler and Wolters, *Glyptothek,* pp. 223 ff., No. 222. Brunn-Bruckmann, *Denkmäler,* Pls. 5a and 740. A replica in Aix: Arndt-Amelung, *Einzelaufnahmen,* No. 1391.

[45] J. Charbonneaux, *La Sculpture grecque au Musée du Louvre* (Paris, 1936), Pl. 47. A good replica in the Barracco collection: W. Helbig and G. Barracco, *La Collection Barracco* (Munich, 1893), Pl. 66, No. 1. Helbig, *Führer durch Rom,* 3d ed., No. 1125. Another, in the Berlin Museum (No. 205): W. Reinecke, *Einführung in die griechische Plastik an der Hand von Meisterwerken im Alten Museum* (1931), p. 110, Fig. 84.

[46] Berlin, Altes Museum No. 206. Another, in the Vatican: Amelung, *Vatican Kat.,* Vol. I, p. 753, Museo Chiaramonti, No. 652, Pl. 81.

[47] Musée du Louvre, Room of Bronzes, No. 2936; Mus. No. A 784. Found in Vichy. A. de Ridder, *Les Bronzes antiques* (1913), Fig. 64. *Encycl. phot.,* Vol. III, p. 126 B.

[48] M. Bieber in Arndt-Amelung, *Einzelaufnahmen,* Nos. 4738–39.

[49] Richter, *Handbook* (1953), p. 112, Pl. 92h and pp. 128 f., Pl. 109c. Klein, *Child Life,* p. 29, No. 346, Pl. 28C.

[50] G. A. Richter, *Handbook of the Classical Collection* (New York, Metropolitan Museum of Art, 1930), pp. 276 ff., Fig. 196. G. A. Richter in Brunn-Bruckmann, *Denkmäler,* Pl. 730, and *Handbook* (1953), pp. 143 f., Pl. 124c–d. Lawrence, *Later Greek Sculpture,* p. 41, Pl. 68c.

[51] Jones, *Sculpt. Palazzo Conservatori,* p. 145, Sala degli Orti Lamiani, No. 28, Pl. 50. Brunn-Bruckmann, *Denkmäler,* Pl. 393a.

Conservatori and in the Metropolitan Museum of Art [52] (Fig. 593). All these have scanty dress, carelessly arranged. A fisherman in the British Museum wears an exomis, the dress of slaves and artisans, fastened on only one shoulder because it is too narrow to be fixed on both [53] (Fig. 592). It seems to consist of rough felt or of irregularly shorn fur. Fishermen sometimes were too poor even for such dress, and are shown wearing just a scanty loincloth. An example is the stooping old chap, the best copies of which are the one in black marble, with alabaster for his small mantle, in the Louvre [54] (Fig. 595) and two, both in white marble, in the Museo dei Conservatori and in the Vatican.[55] The knees are slightly bent as if trembling; the head has thin cheeks fallen in, small eyes, pathetically raised, a bald forehead, irregular beard, and thick lips. A good copy of this lined and weather-beaten head is in the Museo Capitolino.[56] The type has been misunderstood and used for the dying Seneca in the painting by Rubens in Munich. The fisherman should be reconstructed with a pail in the left hand for his catch, and the fishing rod in his right hand. Thus he stands on the beach, a picture of misery, bent with age and want. The head of such a fisherman, or perhaps a peasant, in Dresden, with small felt hat, has harsh and furrowed features.[57]

Old age and perhaps arthritis have bent the back and knees of an old shepherd, represented in a relief formerly in the possession of Dr. Ludwig Pol-

lak in Rome [58] (Fig. 594). He moves painfully forward, leaning heavily on his shepherd's staff, warmly dressed in fur trousers, short woolen chiton with sleeves, and small mantle, knotted in front. A second, smaller figure puts a hand under the old man's chin as if to hold him upright. A terra cotta in the Louvre represents an old stooping servant (Fig. 589, right).

The sordid side of life in the large cities is best represented in Alexandria (see Figs. 378–86), but is also found elsewhere. Thus two ithyphallic street venders from Pompeii [59] are hawking with wide-open mouths, holding one hand to their throats so that their vocal cords may not break, and with the other hand offering a tray with their wares. Their ugly, un-Greek features match their lean bodies, long meager arms, and the stretched sinews of their legs.

Figures of actors, particularly of New Comedy and farce, with padded bodies, grotesque masks, and enormous noses decorated with warts, are found in Alexandria, and also in Asia Minor; statuettes of actors from Myrina, near Smyrna, are in the Louvre.[60] (See Figs. 382–83.)

In Athens, the seat of philosophy, we find much more restrained representations of daily life. The old man in a terra cotta from Athens, with bent head and long, dignified beard, may be a pedagogue or teacher of philosophy [61] (Fig. 589, left). The head of an old man, found in the American excavations of the market place of Athens, seems to be that of a priest.[62] He wears a rolled fillet around his head; the hair was painted; the forehead has three sharp wrinkles; many lines surround the eyes, and sharp folds go from the nose to the corners of the mouth, where fleshy pockets are formed. The expression is serious, discontented, and rather disagreeable.

[52] Jones, *Sculpt. Palazzo Conservatori,* p. 144, No. 27. Richter, *Handbook* (1930), p. 276, Fig. 195, and *Handbook* (1953), p. 144, Pl. 124b.

[53] A. H. Smith, *Brit. Mus. Cat.,* Vol. III, p. 115, No. 1766. M. Bieber, *Entwicklungsgeschichte der griechischen Tracht* (Berlin, 1934), p. 60, Pl. 37, No. 2.

[54] Héron de Villefosse, *Catalogue sommaire des marbres antiques* (Paris, Louvre, 1896), No. 1354. *Encycl. phot.,* Vol. III, pp. 266 f.

[55] Jones, *Sculpt. Palazzo Conservatori,* Sala degli Orti Lamiani, No. 27, p. 144, Pl. 50. Vatican, *Galleria dei Candelabri,* No. 177. Helbig, *Führer durch Rom,* Nos. 385 and 934. Brunn-Bruckmann, *Denkmäler,* Pls. 164, 393b. An excellent torso from Aphrodisias, in Berlin: Reinecke, *Meisterwerke im Alten Museum,* pp. 90 f., Fig. 67; K. Wiegand, "Torso eines Fischers," in *Jahrbuch der preussischen Kunstsammlungen,* XXXVII (1916), 1 ff.

[56] Jones, *Sculpt. Museo Capitolino,* Stanza dei Filosofi, No. 39, p. 234, Pl. 59.

[57] P. Herrmann, *Verzeichnis der antiken Original-Bildwerke* (Dresden, Skulpturen-Sammlung, 1915); the head is in the Hellenistic Room, No. 178. It is related to the head in the same collection (No. 176), a replica of the peasant woman in New York (Fig. 590).

[58] It is of Pentelic marble, and there are traces of red color; it is 18.5 cm. high, 17 cm. long. Dr. Pollak believed the scene to be from a comedy and the old man to be Socrates. I do not know where the relief may now be.

[59] *Bolletino d'Arte* (1925), p. 270. *Arch. Anz.* (1927), p. 159. S. Reinach, *Répertoire de la statuaire grecque et romaine,* Vol. VI (1930), p. 92, Fig. 7 and p. 182, Fig. 1. I owe photographs to Professor Amadeo Maiuri.

[60] For grotesque figures and actors see Pottier and Reinach, *Myrina,* pp. 464 ff., Pls. XLV–XLVII.

[61] Charbonneaux, *Terres cuites,* p. 77, No. 85

[62] T. L. Shear in *Hesperia,* Vol. IV (1935), pp. 402 ff., Figs. 30–31. Evelyn Harrison, *The Athenian Agora,* Vol. I: *Portrait Sculpture* (1953), pp. 12 ff., No. 3, Pl. 3.

The head of a poet, probably an invented portrait of Aristophanes, was created in the second century B.C.[63] (Figs. 596–97). It is connected in double herms—one from Herculaneum in Naples and one in the Villa Albani—with the portrait of Menander (see Figs. 150–57). Therefore it can only be the naughty and often coarse poet of Old Comedy, set against the refined poet of the comedy of manners. The many replicas, particularly the bronze head in Naples (Figs. 596), the marble head in the Musée du Bardo in Tunis, the one with the ivy wreath in the Museo Nazionale Romano in Rome, and the one in Florence (Fig. 597), agree in all essential features with each other and with the many other replicas. The long, slick strands of hair are combed irregularly onto the high forehead; there are deep sacks below the eyes; the mouth is slightly opened; the tufts of the beard grow irregularly; the neck is crumpled with folds.

This portrait is probably contemporary with, or a little earlier than, the most celebrated of all invented portraits of antiquity, that of Homer[64] (Figs. 598–99). We again have a rich and very homogeneous tradition. The best head is in the Louvre (Fig. 599), but the bronze bust in the Museo Archeologico in Florence (Fig. 598) and the late copies in the Museo Capitolino in Rome and the Museo Nazionale in Naples agree in all essential features. The hair, thin over the high forehead, full at the sides, is confined by a narrow fillet; the eyes are deeply sunk into their orbits because all the flesh has been wasted away by blindness, the mouth is slightly open; the beard is full and well kept. The expression is that of a prophet who, despite blind eyes, can look by inspiration into the essentials of the world. The conception of this invented portrait is that of a blind seer and a great singer. The artist could use all the developed possibilities of realistic portraiture for these spiritualized heads. He was able to reflect deep thoughts and ideas through his mastery of the outer form.

The range of the rococo trend thus goes from the innocent baby in his crib to the old men and women in all walks of life, embracing all those between childhood and old age. Graceful women are favorites. They are much more numerous in terra-cotta statuettes than are athletic young men. In long sweeping dresses and mantles they stand, walk, or sit; sometimes the head and the arms, including the hands, are covered, but always so that the swelling forms of the body and the pleasant movements of the young ladies are not obscured[65] (Figs. 600–602). Sometimes it is difficult to say whether a mortal or a divine person is represented. The marble statuette of a woman with a lyre in her arms, from Alexandria and now in Tübingen, could represent a young musician as well as a Muse[66] (Fig. 406).

The same problem—whether the subject is a goddess or a mortal woman—is often raised by the representations of nude women, most of whom are occupied with their grooming, bathing, arrangement of hair, dressing, or undressing (cf. Figs. 390–91). Thus a kneeling woman of terra cotta in the Louvre, from Myrina[67] (Fig. 603), recalls the Aphrodite of Doidalsas and the Rhodian kneeling Aphrodite (Figs. 290–95). She is apparently taking a shower bath which she receives on her back, turning her head sidewise and her bent arms forward. Often these nude young women are hold-

[63] Comparetti and de Petra, *La Villa Ercolanese*, pp. 38 ff., Pl. III, Nos. 3 and 7, Pl. IV, Nos. 3–5, Pl. V. J. J. Bernoulli, *Griechische Ikonographie* (2 vols., Munich, 1901), Vol. II, pp. 160 ff., Pls. XXII–XXIII, Fig. 19. M. Bieber in *Röm. Mitt.*, Vol. XXXII (1917), pp. 122 ff., Figs. 3–7. J. F. Crome, "Das Bildnis Virgils," in *Reale Accademia Virgiliana di Mantova, Atti e Memorie*, Nuova Serie, Vol. XXIV, pp. 59 ff., Fig. 62. G. de la Valles in *Rendiconti dell' Accademia dei Lincei*, Series 12, Vol. VI (1936), pp. 571 ff. K. Schefold, *Die Bildnisse der antiken Dichter, Redner, und Denker* (Basel, Schwabe, 1943), pp. 134–38, p. 212 (40 replicas). L. Laurenzi, *Ritratti greci* (Florence, Sansoni, 1941), p. 138, Appendix A, Pl. XLVI. *Encycl. phot.*, Vol. III, p. 246.

[64] Bernoulli, *Ikonographie*, Vol. I, pp. 1 ff., Pls. I–II. Amelung, *Antiken in Florenz*, pp. 276 f., No. 272. P. Arndt, *Griechische und römische Porträts* (Munich, Bruckmann, 1891–1942), Pls. 1–2, 1011–20. Jones, *Sculpt. Museo Capitolino*, Stanza dei Filosofi, Nos. 44–46, pp. 235 f. *Encycl. phot.*, Vol. III, p. 247. R. Boehringer and E. Boehringer, *Homer, Bildnisse und Nachweise* (Breslau, 1939), Pls. 51–102, pp. 73 ff. Laurenzi, *Ritratti greci*, pp. 136 f., No. 113. Schefold, *Bildnisse*, pp. 142–43, 213. There are 24 replicas. The dates given to the original range between 200 and 25 B.C.

[65] Fig. 600 is in the Walters Art Gallery, Baltimore. Figs. 601–2 are in the Metropolitan Museum of Art; Richter, *Handbook* (1953), p. 128, Pl. 108 f. (our Fig. 601); see her Pl. 108 d and e. See dozens of examples in Pottier and Reinach, *Myrina*, pp. 421 ff., Pls. XXXV–XXXIX, and in all terra-cotta collections.

[66] Watzinger, in Sieglin, *Expedition Ernst von Sieglin: Ausgrabungen in Alexandria*, Vol. II: *Die griechisch-ägyptische Sammlung Ernst von Sieglin*, Part 1 B: *Malerei und Plastik* (1927), pp. 109 ff., No. 97, Pl. XLII.

[67] Pottier and Reinach, *Myrina*, pp. 269 ff., Pl. III, No. 1. Charbonneaux, *Terres cuites*, p. 68, No. 75.

ing long strands of their loose hair in one or both hands, probably to bind them together on the crowns or at the backs of their heads. Thus a marble statue in the Palazzo Colonna in Rome [68] (Fig. 604) has, beside the two thick strands in both hands, others hanging at the back. The ladies often look into a mirror held in one of their hands or by a second person. Others bind a fillet around their hair, as does the Stephanusa of Praxiteles (see Fig. 38). Thus a marble statuette in Baltimore has the motif of the Diadumenos of Polykleitos, transferred to a slender woman with a soft and delicate face [69] (Fig. 605).

Perhaps the most popular and most characteristic creation representing Aphrodite in connection with her bath is the one of which more than 70 representations are known: 39 in bronze (see Figs. 606–7), 17 in marble (see Fig. 394), 5 in terra cotta (see Fig. 395), and 10 on gems.[70] There are many variations in the hairdress and jewelry and in the accessories, which comprise rocks, a vase, and a dolphin (to indicate the bath in the sea). The goddess is, however, always represented as standing on her right leg, lifting the left and moving the hand down to the sole or sandal of the left foot. The upper part of the body is bent forward and the left arm is moved to the side in order to keep balance. Whether Aphrodite is taking off her sandal before her bath, or putting it on afterwards, is difficult to determine. I prefer the first alternative. It seems to me that this must have been a favorite

votive offering, perhaps by sailors, in sanctuaries of Aphrodite all over the Mediterranean area.

Beside the nude there are many denuded Aphrodites—that is, draped figures whose dress opens in such a way that all parts of the body are visible. Perhaps the most charming is in the Louvre [71] (Fig. 609). Here she has lifted her right hand to the back of her head, probably to her hair. This movement allows her mantle to glide down from her shoulders. She catches it with her left elbow and left hand, but it opens wide and sweeps the ground behind her uncovered legs. The swing of the movement of body and drapery provide an interesting arrangement of lines, forms, light and dark areas. A small statuette from Egypt in the Louvre [72] (Fig. 608) uses the opened mantle as a background for the whole body, from head to foot. The girl leans to her left; the mantle seems to slip from her head and she catches it with her left elbow and her right hand. Finally we have this motif: although the mantle laid around the hips has been knotted together, it slips from the hips and opens in front [73] (Fig. 610). The upper part of this figure, in the Gabinetto delle Maschere of the Vatican, including head and arms, is modern. She made the gesture of the Venus of Syracuse; the remains of the left hand are still visible above the bowknot in front. This is the most sensuous representation of Aphrodite. It belongs to the late Hellenistic period.

Eros, the son of Aphrodite, had already become a young boy in the hands of Praxiteles and Lysippos. But now he becomes a real child with childish manners [74] (Figs. 611–13). A new conception shows him hovering in the air. That had been done in many paintings of the fourth century, but in sculpture it is only now that he was shown really flying in space. The best terra cottas of this type come from Myrina in Asia Minor [75] (Figs. 614–15).

[68] Arndt-Amelung, *Einzelaufnahmen*, No. 1144. For the type see Amelung, *Vatican Kat.*, Vol. II, pp. 697 f., text to Gabinetto delle Maschere, No. 433; D. Mustilli, *Il Museo Mussolini* (Rome, 1939), p. 38, No. 8; H. Bloesch, *Antike Kunst in der Schweiz* (Zurich, 1943), pp. 112 f., Pl. 64.

[69] Walters Art Gallery, Baltimore, No. 23.83. Formerly in the Nelidow collection.

[70] Pottier and Reinach, *Myrina*, pp. 285 ff. A list of replicas is in *ibid.*, pp. 285–87, Note 1. See also J. J. Bernoulli, *Aphrodite* (1873), pp. 329 ff. Klein, *Rokoko*, pp. 86 f. Our Fig. 606 is in Naples. Our Fig. 607, from Paramythia, is in the British Museum: H. B. Walters, *Catalogue of the Bronzes, Greek, Roman, and Etruscan, in the Department of Greek and Roman Antiquities* (London, the British Museum, 1899), pp. 37 f., No. 280, Pl. VII; W. Klein, *Praxiteles* (Leipzig, 1898), p. 298, Fig. 53. Other good bronzes, one with golden earrings, another from Egypt, in the Louvre (Nos. 4244 and 389): *Encycl. phot.*, Vol. III, pp. 90 f., Figs. C and D. A terra-cotta figurine and a marble torso in the Metropolitan Museum of Art, our Figs. 394–95: Richter, *Handbook* (1953), p. 108, Pls. 86e and f.

[71] Klein, *Rokoko*, p. 88, Pl. III. Fröhner, *Notice sculpture Louvre*, pp. 185 f., No. 144.

[72] From Horbeit in Egypt, in the Louvre. E. Michon in *Mon. Piot*, Vol. XXI (1913), pp. 163 ff., Pl. XVI.

[73] Vatican, Gabinetto delle Maschere, No. 441. Amelung, *Vatican Kat.*, II, pp. 713 ff., Pl. 75; see also pp. 696 ff., No. 433, for the himation closed in front. Charbonneaux, *La Sculpture du Louvre*, Pl. VII. *Encycl. phot.*, III, 225.

[74] Metropolitan Museum of Art, Nos. 06.1130–31, 22.139.5. Richter, *Handbook* (1953), p. 128, Pl. 108b–c.

[75] Pottier and Reinach, *Myrina*, pp. 324 ff., Pls. XI–XVII. The terra cotta in our Fig. 614 is shown in *ibid.*, p. 324, Pl. XI,

the hermaphrodite very light. This seems to point to the possibility that in the group the satyr was of bronze or dark stone, the hermaphrodite of white marble, which would contribute to the grasping of the complicated crossings. Clearly the painting was adapted from a sculptured group, and was not, as has been wrongly assumed, the original for the sculpture.[87]

The group has been attributed to Kephisodotos, the son of Praxiteles,[88] because Pliny (*Nat. hist.* XXXVI. 24), calling Kephisodotos an heir to his father's art, describes "a noble *symplegma* at Pergamon, which was praised and in which the fingers seemed to be impressed in the body truer than it could be in marble." It seems unlikely to me that scholarly and sober Pergamon bought such a sensuous group as our satyr and hermaphrodite. There are also related groups for which the same claim might be made, particularly the young satyr who is seated on the ground and who has drawn a nymph between his knees[89] (Fig. 627). Of this creation there exist seven copies, the best being in the Museo Nuovo in Rome. The satyr has caught the nymph from behind and embraces her with both arms around the waist while she grasps his full hair on the left side and vigorously pushes his head back. The expression of his round and healthy face is half gay, half grievous, for she hurts him by pulling his hair. The lively torsions in both bodies are only possible in a group of considerable depth. Again the side views are unsatisfactory. All this makes these groups too late to be the *symplegma* of Kephisodotos.

There is, however, another *symplegma* called "noble" by Pliny (*Nat. hist.* XXXVI. 35). This was made by Heliodoros, an artist of about 100 B.C. Pliny describes it as a fight between Pan and Olympos, and gives as its place the Porticus of Octavia in Rome. Another group of Pan and Olympos is mentioned by Pliny (*Nat. hist.* XXXVI. 29); he says it was in the Saepta Julia, with a companion piece, Achilles and Chiron. Of this we have a painted copy from the so-called Basilica in Herculaneum, now in the Naples Museum.[90] We do not have a copy of Pan and Olympos, and probably there never was such a group. Olympos was a pupil of Marsyas, not of Pan. The counterpart to the painted Chiron and Achilles group in Herculaneum was a much-damaged group depicting Marsyas teaching the flute to Olympos. Pliny, therefore, must have misunderstood his source. Pan fights with Eros on wall paintings, and he teaches music to the shepherd Daphnis, just as Chiron teaches music to Achilles. Thus the noble *symplegma* of Heliodoros probably represented Pan teaching Daphnis to play the shepherd's pipe. Such a group is indeed preserved in about twenty replicas, the best of which is in the Museo Nazionale Romano[91] (Fig. 628). It is a *symplegma,* for Pan, seated on rocks next to his pupil, turns toward him and lays his left arm around Daphnis' shoulders, correcting with his right hand the left hand of his pupil. The delicate boy, represented in front view, holds the pipes in both hands and crosses his feet as if to move away from contact with the goat's leg of the boorish god of the woods. The two bodies, as well as the heads, form a striking contrast.

This contrast between the hairy Pan and a delicate human body is still further heightened in the "pantoufle" group of Pan and Aphrodite, so called from the sandal with which the goddess tries to ward off the attack of Pan[92] (Figs. 629–30). It was

---

[87] E. Schmidt in *Festschrift für Paul Arndt*, p. 101, Fig. 9. His deductions in this article are wrong. Painting and sculpture develop in a parallel way and both have the same trends and motifs. Occasionally one is influenced by the other, but in ancient art more often the sculptor inspired the painter.

[88] F. Hauser and G. Lippold in text to Brunn-Bruckmann, *Denkmäler,* Pl. 731.

[89] Brunn-Bruckmann, *Denkmäler,* Pl. 732 and Figs. 1–7 in text. G. Krahmer, "Die einansichtige Gruppe und die späthellenistische Kunst," in *Nachrichten Gött. Ges.* (1927), pp. 86 f., Pl. IV, Figs. 9–10. Mustilli, *Museo Mussolini,* pp. 77 f., Sala IV, Nos. 22–23, Pl. XLVIII, Figs. 195–96. Klein, *Rokoko,* pp. 58 f., Fig. 24. W. Zschietzschmann, *Die hellenistische und römische Kunst* (Vol. II, Part 2 of *Handbuch der Kunstwissenschaft*), p. 58, Fig. 58, dates both groups in the third century. His list of Hellenistic sculpture (pp. 58 ff.) is useful but full of wrong datings.

[90] P. Herrmann and F. Bruckmann, *Denkmäler der Malerei des Altertums* (Munich, 1904–31), pp. 109 ff., Pl. 82 (Chiron and Achilles), Pl. 87 and Fig. 29 (Marsyas and Olympos). M. Gabriel, *Masters of Campanian Painting* (1952), pp. 8, 31 f., Pls. 9–12.

[91] W. Klein in *Oest. Jahreshefte,* Vol. XIX–XX (1919), pp. 260 ff., Fig. 178. Text to Brunn-Bruckmann, *Denkmäler,* Pl. 731. K. Wernecke in Roscher, *Lexikon der Mythologie,* Vol. III (1901), s.v. Pan, pp. 1453 ff., Fig. 21. L. Laurenzi, in *Riv. del Ist. Arch.,* VIII, Fasc. I (1940), pp. 36 f., Fig. 9.

[92] M. Bulard in *B.C.H.,* Vol. XXX (1906), pp. 610 ff., Pls XIII–XV. G. Krahmer, "Die einansichtige Gruppe und die späthellenistische Kunst," in *Nachrichten Gött. Ges.* (1927), pp. 66, 89. Lawrence, *Later Greek Sculpture,* pp. 38 f., Pl. 63. The

created about 100 B.C. for a Syrian merchant in Delos. Pan has laid his right arm around Aphrodite's back and has placed his right leg behind her legs, while with his left hand he grasps her left wrist, turning sideways toward her. However, he is not only threatened by the shoe which she has taken from her left foot, but also hindered by little Eros, who helps his mother. Hovering over the left shoulder of Aphrodite, he has grasped the right horn of the goat-god and pushes the head away. The group needs to be studied from front and back; again the side views are of no importance. Pan in contrast to the fair goddess is also represented in an incised design on the cover of a mirror from Corinth, in the British Museum [93] (Fig. 632). Here he squats on the bench on which she is seated, and they are playing a game, with little Eros standing on the bench behind his mother as an interested spectator. Pan is not only made a lover, he also gets a wife in the Hellenistic period, just as the centaur got one in the painting of Zeuxis. The Panisca in the Villa Albani in Rome, playing the flute, her slender body decorated with a panther skin in coquettish arrangement, is a true rococo creation [94] (Fig. 631).

A much more congenial partner for Pan than Aphrodite is the satyr. Several small groups depict Pan as a good friend who operates on the foot of the satyr when he has hurt himself by stepping with his naked sole on some sharp object. A group in the Louvre shows the satyr seated on a rock, head thrown back, sustaining himself with his hands on the seat, while Pan, seated with crossed legs on the ground, carefully inspects the sole of the satyr's foot, laid horizontally over the rock and right knee [95] (Fig. 634). Here we have a very deep group, built up in three steps: from the little Pan to the shoulders, and then to the head of the satyr. The satyr's face, with drawn eyebrows and shouting mouth, recalls the Laocoon. It is likely that this group belongs to the same period as the Laocoon, about the middle of the first century B.C.

There are several variations of this humorous subject. In a group from Ostia [96] (Fig. 633), the satyr, with the help of his left hand, lifts his leg high up, and Pan bends backward instead of forward. He is seated between the two legs of the wounded friend. In a group in the Vatican, originally used as a fountain, both are of the same height [97] (Fig. 635). The contour is rectangular. The satyr leans back, pressing on a wine skin from which originally water flowed; he lifts his right leg horizontally with his outstretched right hand and Pan, holding the leg and foot with both hands, carefully inspects the sole. The upper frame is given by the two heads and by the right arm and leg of the satyr; the side frame is given by the skins bound around their necks and falling vertically behind their backs. The composition combines diagonal and parallel directions into a deep but frontal view.

Satyrs in distress are represented in two groups which look like a rococo edition of the Laocoon group. In a group now in the Palazzo dei Conservatori,[98] a young satyr and two companions, of whom only fragments remain, are attacked by a snake-legged giant. The satyr in the center sinks down, supporting himself on his right hand, in a position recalling the dying trumpeter of Epigonos (Fig. 427) and the dying Gaul of the small victory monument of Attalus (Fig. 435, upper left). Satyrs as companions of Dionysos also fight against the giants on the Pergamon altar (Fig. 468). The head of the young satyr shows unkempt and full hair; the eyebrows are contracted, the eyes are beginning to close in death, the mouth is open in agony. A similar group of three satyrs attacked by a gigantic snake which connects the three figures, just as the two snakes bind Laocoon and his sons together, has

name of the Syrian owner is Dionysios, son of Zenon. He came from Beirut, now the capital of Lebanon.

[93] Walters, *Catalogue of Bronzes*, pp. 41 f., No. 289.
[94] Brunn-Bruckmann, *Denkmäler*, Pl. 391. Helbig, *Führer durch Rom*, No. 1873. Bulle, *Der schöne Mensch*, Pl. 163.
[95] Klein, *Rokoko*, p. 65, Fig. 27. Another small replica: Kaschnitz-Weinberg, *Magazzino del Vaticano*, pp. 91 f., No. 183, Pl. LXVII.

[96] Raissa Calza, *Il Museo Ostiense* (1947), No. 35, figure on p. 39. Guido Calza, *La necropoli del Porto di Roma* (1940), p. 238, Fig. 137.
[97] G. Krahmer, "Die einansichtige Gruppe und die späthellenistische Kunst," in *Nachrichten Gött. Ges.* (1927), pp. 88 f., Pl. IV, Fig. 11. In a group in the Casa di Lucrezio in Pompeii the action is reversed: the satyr operates on the sole of the foot of Pan, regardless of the fact that the hoof of the goatman can hardly be wounded. This artist apparently had little knowledge of natural history.
[98] Jones, *Sculpt. Palazzo Conservatori*, pp. 81 f., Galleria, No. 88, Pl. 28. Beazley and Ashmole, *Greek Sculpture and Painting*, p. 83, Figs. 174, 178.

been found in Salona, near Split (or Spalato) in Dalmatia.[99]

The group of the three Graces is another good example of a late Hellenistic one-view group. The best-known copy is the one in the library of the cathedral of Siena; two others, one in relief, are in the Louvre; three have been found in Cyrene; one was rediscovered in the storerooms of the Vatican and is now in the Gabinetto delle Maschere, and one was in the Ferroni collection.[100] All three heads are preserved only in the larger group from Cyrene and in the Vatican copy. The group in Siena and a variation, from a sanctuary of Isis at Cyrene, have two heads each, and only one is preserved in the smaller Cyrene group. The heads in the Louvre are modern. The main line of the composition agrees in all these seven replicas. The central Grace is seen from the back, with her left hand on the left shoulder of the Grace standing to the left, while with her right arm she crosses the body of her companion on the right. Both of these side figures are in front view. Their heads are turned outward. Their arms cross behind the back of the central figure and are laid on her shoulders. In most replicas, slender vases, over which drapery is thrown, stand outside the side figures. Their outer hands hold fruits, ears of wheat, flowers, or twigs. The central Grace is nearer to the right than to the left. The bodies are slender and graceful. The group appears twice on Pompeian wall paintings.[101] Eduard Schmidt has again assumed, as in the case of the group of the satyr and hermaphrodite, that we have here a painting transferred to sculpture.[102] Again, the assumption seems impossible to me. In both paintings the figures are plastically conceived, sharply relieved against a background enlivened only in one of them by dim rocks and plants. The heads of the Graces vary greatly in features and hairdress. Some have ribbons, some are crowned with flowers. The motif also reappears on Roman reliefs. A fine silver bowl from Gaul in the British Museum shows twigs in the hand of the left Grace and one vase near the right figure.[103] A relief in the Vatican and two others in Sofia, from Thrace, dedicated to the nymphs, depicts them as healing goddesses of springs. The one in Rome in the Vatican shows them together with Asclepius, Hermes, and the kneeling donor.[104] Finally, many sarcophagi show them probably in the guise of healing goddesses. There is one in the Vatican, defaced by a modern loincloth,[105] another in the Musée du Bardo, in which the Graces are in the center between personifications of the four seasons,[106] and many others. They also appear on medallions of Faustina and Lucilla of the Antonine period. On

[99] A. Schober, "Eine neue Satyrgruppe," in *Röm. Mitt.*, Vol. LI (1936), pp. 83 ff., Pls. 23–26. He mentions the fact that a similar satyr group in Rome was thought by F. Weege (in *Jahrbuch d. Inst.*, XXVIII [1913], 232 ff.) to be a replica of the Laocoon group.

[100] Brunn-Bruckmann, *Denkmäler*, Pl. 259. Bulle, *Der schöne Mensch*, Pl. 161 (Siena). E. Ghislanzoni in *Notiziario Archeologico*, Vol. II (1916), pp. 51 ff., Figs. 29–30 (Cyrene). L. Curtius in *Die Antike*, Vol. I (1925), pp. 50 ff., Fig. 12. Arndt-Amelung, *Einzelaufnahmen*, Nos. 2975–78 (Schloss Tegel). R. Lullies, "Zur Drei Grazien-Gruppe" in *Mitt. d. Inst.*, Vol. I (1948), pp. 45 ff., Pl. 6 (Siena), Pl. 7 (Ferroni), Pl. 8 (Head). E. Schmidt in *Festschrift für Paul Arndt*, pp. 102 ff., Figs. 12–15. G. Becatti in *Bolletino Comunale*, Vol. LXV (1937), pp. 41 ff., Figs. 1–12, Pls. I–IV (here is a list of copies). Kaschnitz-Weinberg, *Magazzino del Vaticano*, pp. 136 f., N. 284, Pl. LIX (cf. p. 192, No. 426, Pl. LXXIX).

[101] Herrmann, *Denkmäler der Malerei*, pp. 61 ff., Pls. 49–50. Bulle, *Der schöne Mensch*, Pl. 318. G. E. Rizzo, *Pittura ellenistico-romana* (1936), Pl. 137.

[102] E. Schmidt in *Festschrift für Paul Arndt*, pp. 104 ff.

[103] Walters, *Silver Plate, British Museum*, pp. 33 f., No. 132, Pl. 18. The group is also used on the cult statue of Aphrodite of Aphrodisias (C. Fredrich in *Athen. Mitt.*, Vol. XXII [1897], pp. 361 ff., Pls. XI–XII).

[104] Lippold, *Vatican Kat.*, Vol. III, pp. 140 f., Sala Rotonda, No. 550a, Pl. 48. The relief from Thrace, in Sofia: B. D. Filow, *L'Art antique en Bulgarie* (Sofia, 1925), pp. 67 f., Fig. 56, and Filow, *Sofia, Führer durch das Nationalmuseum* (Sofia, 1923), p. 133. Similar reliefs, coming also from Thrace, in *B.C.H.*, XXI (1897), pp. 124, 126. The Villa Albani examples (in Canopus) have the museum numbers 708 and 709. (Phot. German Arch. Inst., Rome, No. 1931, 21.) Compare also the relief on the *pulpitum* of the theater at Sabratha in *Africa Italiana*, Vol. III (1930), pp. 26 ff. Fig. 26 (cf. p. 23, Fig. 19).

[105] Vatican, Galleria Lapidaria, No. 12. Amelung, *Vatican Kat.*, Vol. I, pp. 172 f., Pl. 24.

[106] From Sainte Marie du Zit, in Musée du Bardo, Tunis. See Robert, *Sarkophagreliefs*, Vol. II, Pl. 4, No. 10 and Pl. 5, No. 11. For others in Tunis, see E. Schmidt in *Festschrift für Paul Arndt*, p. 103, Fig. 11; for those in the Museum of Ostia and Withington Hall in Chelford, Cheshire, see G. Rodenwaldt in *J.R.S.*, Vol. XXVIII (1938), pp. 61 ff., Pls. VI–VII. W. Déonna, in "Le Groupe des trois Graces nues et sa descendance," in *Rev. Arch.*, Vol. XXXI (1930), I, pp. 274 ff., deals with the type of the three Graces from the Hellenistic period into modern times. The Graces on a sarcophagus from Aguzzano sulla Via Tiburtina, in the Museo Nazionale Romano (No. 113226; Aurigemma, *Museo Nazionale Romano*, p. 15, No. 3) stand on a column; this was perhaps the original erection of the group.

one dated A.D. 164—69, Lucilla hands a small replica of the group of the Graces to the seated Vesta.[107]

If the question arises whether sculpture or painting has the priority in the creation of a certain motif, it can be said that in most cases the sculpture was the model for the painting. This is even clearer than in the case of the three Graces in the example of the nymphs carrying fruit on a big tray or shell. In the newly excavated house of Romulus and Remus in Pompeii such nymphs are painted standing at the two sides of a fountain and are certainly conceived as statues (Fig. 636). Such a statue has indeed been found not far away and may have been the direct model for the painter [108] (Fig. 637).

A closely knit group of only two persons with considerable depth is that of Eros and Psyche in the Museo Capitolino [109] (Fig. 638). The two children have no wings, but replicas in terra cotta and bronze, with wings, warrant the interpretation. Boy and girl are turned toward each other, the boy advancing his left leg. He lays his left arm around the head of the girl and seems to open her mouth with the right hand. The girl leans toward him and places her arms around his waist. It has been assumed that he counts her teeth, and the group has also been called "the invention of the kiss." In any event, it is a rococo motif. The draping of the mantle of the girl is the unstable one which we find in

the Aphrodite of Melos and other late Hellenistic statues (see Figs. 674–75, 679–81, 709–11).

A one-sided deep group with a true rococo motif is the Triton carrying off a Nereid in the Vatican [110] (Fig. 640). It was used as a fountain figure and originally it probably stood in the center of a large water basin, now supplanted by the restorer's big artificial wave. Triton is carrying off the woman, holding her in his right arm, while his left is stretched forward (the triton-shell trumpet is modern). She throws both arms out widely, with the left hand pulling his hair. Two cupids are seated on the windings of the Triton's tail. The upper one puts his finger on his mouth in order to silence the girl; the other cups his ear as if, in the roar of the sea, he cannot understand what she is shouting. Her dress is slipping down from her right leg and makes fine garland folds over the fish body of Triton. Her left leg is caught between the legs of the sea-centaur. This group is in the same spirit which we find in the centaurs carrying cupids (Figs. 583–84). The group belongs to the first century B.C., the same in which Arkesilaos created centaurs who carried nymphs (*centauri nymphas gerentes*—Pliny *Nat. hist.* xxxvi. 33).

A group in the Louvre, in which a Triton carries old Papposilenos in the same way as he carries the graceful Nereid in the Vatican group, looks like a parody of this work (Fig. 641). Silenus holds on to the Triton, while he looks down into the water, which in this case is sculptured and in which a dolphin is swimming, indicating that the scene is not the crossing of a river but the ocean. The right arm of Silenus is modern and has been removed.

Late Hellenistic one-sided deep groups are also found in terra cotta. The best example is the young couple on their bridal couch, in the Louvre, from Myrina [111] (Fig. 642). The bride is seated in front view, wrapped in her mantle, which covers both arms. The left hand lying on the right knee sustains the elbow of the right arm. This and the advanced right foot are the front axis from which the two sides recede diagonally into the background.

---

[107] F. Gnecchi, *Medaglioni romani* (1912), No. 10, Pl. 76, Fig. 7. A. Grueber, *Roman Medallions* (London, the British Museum, 1874), Pl. XXIV, Fig. 3. Agnes Brett, "Six Roman Bronze Medallions," in *Numismatic Notes and Monographs*, Vol. VI (1923), pp. 23 ff., Pl. IV. For later adaptations of the group see E. Panofsky, *Studies in Iconology* (1939), pp. 168 f., Pl. LXVIII, Figs. 123–24. A. von Salis, *Antike und Renaissance* (1947), pp. 153 ff., Pls. 44a, 45–49.

[108] I owe the photograph for Fig. 637 to the kindness of Professor Amadeo Maiuri. See A. Maiuri in *Notizie degli Scavi* (1927), pp. 60, 70 f., Fig. 32. Height 33 cm.; with base, 38 cm. Found in the *aedicula* for a fountain in the back of the garden near the summer *triclinium* in the house of the Ephebus, Regio I, Insula VII, Casa No. 10–12.

[109] Brunn-Bruckmann, *Denkmäler*, Pl. 375. Jones, *Sculpt. Museo Capitolino*, pp. 185 f., Gabinetto della Venere, No. 3, Pl. 45. Terra-cotta group with wings from Alexandria: J. Vogt, in Sieglin, *Expedition Ernst von Sieglin*, Vol. II, Part 2: *Terrakotten*, p. 121, No. 1. The group is here used for a bottle. Another, dated in the second century B.C.: A. Furtwängler, *La Collection Sabouroff* (1883–87), Pl. CXXXV. The bronzes are reliefs under the vertical handles of Hellenistic bronze hydrias. See G. Richter in *A.J.A.*, Vol. L (1946), p. 364, Pls. XXIV–XXV, Figs. 5–9. Her date, in the late fourth century, seems too early to me. Cf. Klein, *Rokoko*, p. 155, Fig. 68.

[110] Amelung, *Vatican Kat.*, Vol. II, pp. 386 ff., Sala degli Animali, No. 228, Pl. 43. Brunn-Bruckmann, *Denkmäler*, Pl. 258. Klein, *Rokoko*. p. 109 f., Fig. 47. The group in Fig. 641 is now in the storerooms of the Louvre.

[111] Pottier and Reinach, *Myrina*, pp. 442 ff., Pl. XL, No. 4.

The bridegroom is turned toward her, his left foot on the footstool before the couch, his right dangling. He stretches both arms toward the woman, who shyly and slowly turns her head toward him. Her head is adorned with broad fillets, his with a thick wreath from which fillets hang down. The moment before the marital union is delicately rendered.

Another one-sided group in terra cotta is that of Dionysos and Ariadne from Myrina, in the Louvre.[112] Ariadne is seated high on rocks; Dionysos is seated on a lower level, and leans his head against her shoulder. Ariadne is shown in front, Dionysos in three-quarter view. The space between them is filled by the figure of a panther.

Finally, let us look back from the one-sided late Hellenistic groups to earlier forms of groupings during the Hellenistic period. A typical one-view group in bronze is now in Vienna[113] (Fig. 639). Heracles is fighting with a centaur. He swings his club, the centaur wields a branch. The centaur rears his horse part vertically upward and throws back his human upper part, while Heracles throws his whole body back. The hero seizes with his left hand the left foreleg of the centaur. He puts his foot on the left hind leg of the horse-man. In the background there is a tree, which contributes to the feeling of deep space which is characteristic of these groups, despite the fact that all their motifs are clear from a front view.

A bronze wrestling group in the Walters Art Gallery in Baltimore is a good example of the open or centrifugal form prevailing in the second half of the second century B.C.[114] (Fig. 644). One pancratiast has lifted his adversary from the ground. He holds his enemy before him and to the left side, both arms encircling his waist. The defeated tries in vain to pull away from the encircling arms.

There is neither a definite contour nor a definite frontal view.

Another bronze wrestling group from Alexandria in the same gallery shows the closed pyramidal form characteristic of the second half of the third century[115] (Fig. 643). The fallen athlete kneels between the legs of the victor, who pulls the athlete's right arm backward with his left hand and presses down the head of his helpless opponent with his right hand. The contour is closed, and the whole group has the pyramidal form which we found in the Menelaos group and in the group of the Gaul killing his wife from the Attalid victory monument (Figs. 272–75, 281–83; cf. also Fig. 279).

Finally, we come back to the early third century when, under the influence of Lysippos, groups were constructed in the form of a segment of a circle. Such a one is the terra-cotta group of three girls from Tanagra, now in the Louvre[116] (Fig. 645). All three kneel on the ground, the central figure in full front, the two others turned inward. They place their graceful heads, with melon coiffures and hair bunched on the crown, close to each other and seem to whisper about some important secret. The central figure lays her arms around the shoulders of the two others, the one to the right lays her right hand on the knee of the central figure, the one to the left places her left hand on her own knee, while both gesticulate in a restrained manner with their outer hands. There is still much of the balance, symmetry, and harmony of classical art in this early Hellenistic group.

Thus these Hellenistic groups reflect, perhaps more clearly than any other type of monument, the main phases of Hellenistic sculpture: the early period, shown in the gossiping girls (Fig. 645) and the Alexander sarcophagus (pp. 72–73); the high period, shown in the Pergamene groups and our wrestling group (Fig. 643); and the late Hellenistic, shown in the group of Heracles fighting a

---

[112] Ibid., pp. 366 ff., Pl. XXV. Charbonneaux, Terres cuites, Pl. 84.

[113] Vienna, Kunsthistorisches Museum, No. 3.

[114] Walters Art Gallery, No. 54.742. Dorothy K. Hill, Bronzes, p. 67, No. 141, Pl. 30. She mentions other replicas. See particularly Sieglin, Expedition Ernst von Sieglin, Vol. II, Part I A, Pl. XXIII, Figs. 2a, 2b. Another similar group is in the Louvre (No. 366), dated 150—100 B.C. See this group as Heracles and Antaeus on coins from Alexandria in R. S. Poole, British Museum Catalogue of Coins: Alexandria and the Nomes (London, 1892), pp. 123, 188, Pl. VI, Nos. 1054 and 1479.

[115] Walters Art Gallery, No. 54.1050. See Dorothy K. Hill, Bronzes, pp. 66 f., No. 140, Pl. 30. Replica in the British Museum: Walters, Catalogue of Bronzes, p. 154, No. 853, Pl. XXVII. See p. 78, note 22.

[116] For a similar group, see H. B. Walters, Catalogue of the Terracottas in the Department of Greek and Roman Antiquities (London, the British Museum, 1903), p. 244, No. C529, Pl. XXX; in this group, two girls are talking, seated on a couch.

centaur (Fig. 639) and in most examples given in this chapter, ending with the Laocoon [117] (Fig. 530).

3. HELLENISTIC RELIEFS

The term "Hellenistic reliefs" was introduced by Theodor Schreiber, who collected a group of reliefs, many with landscape elements and in a pictorial style, which he attributed mostly to Hellenistic Alexandria.[118] His thesis was opposed by Franz Wickhoff, who considered these reliefs Roman.[119] More recently some scholars, particularly Johannes Sieveking and Arnold Schober, have distinguished both Greek and Roman reliefs.[120] I believe that pictorial reliefs began in the Hellenistic period, but not before the first century B.C., with modest forerunners in the second century.

Slight indications of landscape are found on Rhodian votive reliefs of the second century B.C. (Figs. 489–90), on the Telephos frieze (Figs. 477–78), and on tombstones from Pergamon and Smyrna [121] (Figs. 646–47). Characteristic of these reliefs is one large tree growing at the side, with the foliage spread out flat against the background.[122] Sometimes a snake, the symbol of death, coils around the trunk or the branches. The deceased is often a young knight, represented riding on, or standing beside, his horse. In the Pergamene relief his wife stands under the tree. In the relief from Smyrna in Berlin (Fig. 647) a boy plays with two dogs at the foot of the tree, while a servant has put the large helmet of the heroized dead on his small head and holds the reins (originally in bronze) of the horse, which turns his head back toward the master. All figures are in front view, standing plastically against the smooth background. On the Pergamene relief only the woman in the attitude of the so-called Pudicitia (Fig. 524) stands in front view; the rider is in profile. On a relief in the Baker collection in New York the rider is in profile, as in the Pergamon relief. Behind the tree a boy is partly visible. As on the relief in Berlin, he wears the helmet of his master, and in addition carries his large lance and his shield, which reaches from the boy's feet to his neck. From the tree trunk behind which he stands, some foliage is spread out flatly on the background. The covering of the figure by the tree, and the type of horse with the bulging muscles of the head, date the relief in the Hellenistic period.[123] Hero reliefs in Pergamon, and the provincial "Thracian rider" reliefs, of which many hundreds are in the Museum of Sofia, often show this combination of rider and tree around which the snake coils.[124]

A more plastic rendering of the foliage of an oak tree is seen in the relief found on the island of Capri, now in Naples. This represents a youth and a girl riding together on one horse led by a servant [125] (Fig. 648). The torch in the hand of the girl shows that we deal here with an adventure at night. Behind the tree stands a statue on a high pillar decorated with a garland. Perhaps we have an elopement which ends in a sanctuary. The horse and three figures are in high relief set against a smooth background.

[117] For similar differentiation of the phases of Hellenistic sculpture see G. Krahmer, "Stilphasen der hellenistischen Plastik," in *Röm. Mitt.*, Vol. XXXVIII–XXXIX (1923–24), pp. 138 ff.; G. Krahmer, "Die einansichtige Gruppe und die späthellenistische Kunst," in *Nachrichten Gött. Ges.* (1927), pp. 62 ff.; G. Rodenwaldt, "Die klassische Periode der hellenistischen Kunst," in *Arch. Anz.*, XLVIII (1933), 748 ff.

[118] T. Schreiber, *Die hellenistischen Reliefbilder* (1894); *Die Wiener Brunnenreliefs aus Palazzo Grimani: Eine Studie über das hellenistische Reliefbild mit Untersuchungen über die bildende Kunst in Alexandrien* (1888); and "Die hellenistischen Reliefbilder und die augusteische Kunst," in *Jahrbuch d. Inst.*, XI (1896), 78 ff.

[119] F. Wickhoff, *Einleitung zur Wiener Genesis* (1895), pp. 17 ff. (trans. as *Roman Art* by Eugenie Strong-Sellers [London, 1900]; pp. 35 ff.).

[120] J. Sieveking in text to Brunn-Bruckmann, *Denkmäler*, Pls. 621–30. Sieveking in *Festschrift für Paul Arndt*, pp. 14 ff. A. Schober, "Vom griechischen zum römischen Relief," in *Oest. Jahreshefte*, XXVII (1932), 46 ff. Cf. also Cultrera, "La corrente Asiana," *Saggi sull'arte ellenistica e greca-romana*, I (1907), pp. 1 ff., 176 ff.

[121] Berlin Museum, No. 809. See Lawrence, *Later Greek Sculpture*, p. 34, Pl. 58b; Reinecke, *Meisterwerke im Alten Museum*, p. 101, Fig. 76.

[122] E. Pfuhl, "Beiwerk auf ostgriechischen Grabreliefs," in *Jahrbuch d. Inst.*, Vol. XX (1905), pp. 47 ff., 123 ff., Figs. 1–15, 20–28, Pls. 4–5. For trees on tomb reliefs, see *ibid.*, pp. 93 f.

[123] D. von Bothmer, *Antiquities from the Collection of W. C. Baker* (New York, 1950), p. 10, No. 55, dates late in the fifth century. Single trees appear, of course, in the fifth century, for example on the frieze from Phigalia, but not with figures directly in front or partly hidden behind them.

[124] F. Winter in *Altertümer von Pergamon*, Vol. VII, Part 2, pp. 248 ff., Nos. 302–16, 320–27, Beiblatt 33–34. Filow, *L'Art antique en Bulgarie*, pp. 34 f., Fig. 26, and 66 f., Fig. 54.

[125] Museo Nazionale, Naples, No. 6691. Picard, *La Sculpture antique de Phidias à l'ère byzantine* (1926), pp. 298 f., Fig. 115. On related reliefs from Sorrento see Alda Levi in *Mon. Linc.*, Vol. XXVI (1920), pp. 181 ff., Pls. I–V. Cf. also J. Sieveking in Brunn-Bruckmann, *Denkmäler*, Pl. 629a.

A similar style of relief is found in the relief of Dolon, on whom Odysseus and Diomedes are spying, in Vienna [126] (Fig. 650). Here the tree, with full foliage, is betweeen the Trojan on one side and the Greeks on the other, the latter being on a higher level. Odysseus is seated on rocks, against which Diomedes leans. An eagle is flying above Diomedes; otherwise the background is smooth.

Another relief, in the Villa Albani in Rome, representing Polyphemus seated under a large tree, has more landscape elements [127] (Fig. 649). The branches of the tree are spread out in different directions. A goat stands against the rock on which the Cyclops is seated with the lyre on his arm. Otherwise, again, only rocks and a tree are used.

Pillars are another frequent addition to the human figures on Hellenistic reliefs (see Figs. 489 and 648). A rare bronze relief offers a good example [128] (Fig. 650). It was found set into a stele at the entrance to the temple of Agathe Tyche (Good Fortune) on the island of Delos. The statuette of a goddess on a high pillar is probably Artemis, for she carries a torch, just as does the Artemis who stands in the center of the relief with two large torches before an altar on which a small satyr deposits a basket with offerings. Another brings an *oinochoe* and a patera with a long handle. Probably this relief represents a sacrifice made by Artemis to Dionysos, assisted by his followers, the satyrs.

A high pillar is used as the seat of Peitho, the goddess of persuasion, in the relief in Naples (Fig. 653). The celebrity of this work is attested to by several copies, one being a fragment with Peitho in the Metropolitan Museum of Art in New York [129] (Fig. 652). On a chair which partly crosses this pillar, Aphrodite is seated with Helen, around whose shoulders she lays her right arm, pointing with her left hand to Paris (Alexandros). Eros, Aphrodite's son, has laid his hand on the shoulder of the reluctant lover, looking up to him. Eros's large wings fill the otherwise empty center of the relief.

A relief in Naples, called Alcibiades among the Courtesans, is of much higher relief and gives almost the impression of a one-sided, deep group set before a smooth background [130] (Fig. 654). A young man, presented in front view with a kithara in his left arm and a *plektron* in his right hand, leans heavily on the shoulder of a girl represented in side view. She looks back and up to him adoringly. Two courtesans on a couch try to catch the attention of the youth. One, in front view, touches his kithara from below; the other, seen in three-quarter view, reaches out behind the back of the first and tries to draw his mantle to her. The draperies of all the figures are open, denuding their youthful and charming bodies. Horizontal lines (couch, outer arms of side figures), vertical and diagonal lines (of the bodies), and bow-lines (of inner arms and draperies) make a rich and variegated composition, as in free-standing one-sided groups.

It seems to me that a continuous pictorial background—that is, one filled with architecture or landscape which serves as background for the figures—does not occur before the first century B.C., and probably not before the second half of this century. This at least is what happened in the Roman and Pompeian wall paintings of this period. The older second style, as seen in the Villa of Mysteries in Pompeii and the Boscoreale frescoes in New York and Naples, sets the large figures against big slabs in one color, an element of the architectural style. In the second half, in the transition to the third style, for example, in the Odyssey landscapes in the Vatican and in the House of Livia on the Palatine in Rome, a continuous architectural or

[126] J. Sieveking in Brunn-Bruckmann, *Denkmäler*, Pl. 627b; Schreiber, *Hellenistische Reliefbilder*, Pl. XLV.

[127] J. Sieveking in Brunn-Bruckmann, *Denkmäler*, Pl. 627a. Schreiber, *Hellenistische Reliefbilder*, Pl. LXV.

[128] R. Vallois in *B.C.H.*, Vol. XLV (1921), pp. 242 ff., Fig. 2. Picard, *Phidias à l'ère* byzantine, pp. 249 f., Fig. 96. F. Studniczka, "Artemis und Iphigenie," in *Abh. Sächs. Akad.*, Vol. XXXVII, No. 5 (1926), p. 119, Fig. 89. J. Sieveking in text to Brunn-Bruckmann, *Denkmäler*, Pl. 621, Fig. 1.

[129] Ruesch, *Guida*, pp. 84 f., No. 268. Brunn-Bruckmann, *Denkmäler*, Pl. 439b. Cf. Arndt, *Glyptothèque Ny-Carlsberg*, Pl. 55; Klein, *Rokoko*, pp. 146 f., Fig. 63; Bulle, *Der schöne Mensch*, Pl. 284; Amelung, *Vatican Kat.*, Vol. II, pp. 150 ff., Cortile del Belvedere, No. 58d, Pl. 16. Our Fig. 651, fragment with Peitho, is in the Metropolitan Museum of Art (No. 10.210.27). Richter, *Handbook* (1953), p. 109, Pl. 87 f. The Paris-Helen relief is used for a neo-Attic crater: Jones, *Sculpt.*

Palazzo Conservatori, pp. 39 f., Salone No. 1, Pl. 15. See G. Lippold in *Abh. Bayr. Akad.*, Phil.-Hist Klasse, New Series, Vol. 33 (1951), pp. 21 ff., Fig. 13; he compares vases and Pompeian wall paintings. He assumes that the model for the reliefs was a classical painting. In any case the relief itself seems to me to belong to the Hellenistic period.

[130] Ruesch, *Guida*, pp. 168 f., No. 578; Klein, *Rokoko*, pp. 145 f., Pl. V.

landscape background with many different motifs detracts from the figures.[131]

Good examples of this process are the so-called "Icarius reliefs." One in the Louvre has an undecorated background [132] (Fig. 655). An older man in chiton and mantle lies on his couch, a table with fruit and cakes before him. He wears the ivy wreath of a poet and has an expressive head with deep-set eyes, sunken cheeks, and wrinkles in the neck. A little servant pours wine from an *oinochoe* (a wine jug) into the cup in his (lost) left hand. A woman is seated at the end of the couch. The man lifts his hand in greeting to the young Dionysos who, leaning on his big thyrsus and a small satyr, seems to be intoxicated. He wears a short chiton, small mantle, and high boots, his cothurni.

This subject has been enlarged on a relief of which copies in marble are preserved in the Louvre, in the British Museum, and in Naples (Fig. 656). A relief found in Kephisia copies only the left part of the composition [133] (Fig. 657). The man on the couch is young. He retains the same attitude of the arms, but his head and the head of the woman who is stretched out on the couch in the Naples and Kephisia reliefs are turned to the other side. The woman lies on the couch instead of being seated (her upper part is lost on the London relief, Fig. 656). Dionysos enters, held up by a small satyr, but he is the dignified bearded god, wrapped in a large mantle. A second small satyr removes his shoes so that he may lie down on the couch behind him. He is much taller than both the mortals and his followers, who enter with him. A satyr, dancing and looking backward, carries the long thyrsus of the god. Then follows old Silenus wearing a small mantle and cothurni, playing the double flutes.

Another satyr, carrying a wineskin on his left shoulder, dances behind him. The last group, partly restored, consists of a satyr supporting an intoxicated maenad, who carries the hind part of a kid. A curtain, attached to a pillar supporting a votive tablet, serves as immediate background for the couch. The thiasos is set against a low wall. Above curtain and wall appear a large building and a small one, both with gable roofs. The large building has double windows in front and at the side. In the right corner of the scene (missing in Naples) the replica in London (Fig. 656) has another satyr who fastens a garland to the large building and a palm tree. On the votive tablet on the pillar, a victor driving a chariot is sculptured in relief. The gable of the large building shows two Tritons supporting the head of Medusa. The British Museum, Louvre, and Kephisia replicas (Figs. 656–57) have four masks and scrolls on a small podium instead of the footstool of the Naples relief. Probably all these accessories were originally painted on the latter relief. The explanation of the relief as a visit of the god, patron of the theater, to Icarius, the founder of the Attic tragedy, is possible, but a visit of the god to his priest or to a victorious poet is more probable.

A similar relationship between the figures, which are all in the foreground, and the architecture behind them on a second plane, is found on the so-called Kitharoidos reliefs, the best of which are in the Villa Albani, in Berlin, and in the Louvre.[134] Behind a round altar, on which dancing women are sculptured in relief, Nike gracefully lifts her right hand in the action of pouring wine into a bowl, which she hands to Apollo. The god holds his large kithara in his left arm. He is followed by Artemis with the quiver on her back, carrying a torch in her left hand, while with the right hand she holds onto the mantle of her brother. Behind her Leto, the mother, holds a scepter in her left hand, while with the right hand she draws her mantle over her right shoulder. The figures are in the archaistic style of the first century B.C. They are set against a smooth wall, behind which, on a second plane, a large temple is represented. Corin-

[131] C. M. Dawson, *Romano-Campanian Mythological Landscape Painting* (New Haven, Yale University Press, 1944; Yale Classical Studies, No. IX), pp. 28 ff.

[132] Héron de Villefosse, *Marbres antiques* (1896), No. 741. *Archäologische Zeitung* (1881), Pl. 14. Found in the Piraeus harbor.

[133] Ruesch, *Guida*, pp. 87 f., No. 272. Schreiber, *Hellenistische Reliefbilder*, Pl. XXIX. Replica in the Louvre, from the Albani collection: Héron de Villefosse, *Marbres antiques*, No. 1606; Fröhner, *Notice Sculpture Louvre*, pp. 225 ff., No. 204; Schreiber, *Hellenistische Reliefbilder*, Pl. XXXVIII; *Encycl. phot.*, Vol. III, p. 257 A. For the British Museum relief, see A. H. Smith, *Brit. Mus. Cat.*, Vol. III, pp. 240 ff., No. 2190, and Schreiber, *op. cit.*, Pl. XXXVII. The relief (Fig. 657) in Kephisia is said to have been found in Patras. I owe the photograph to Professor Otto Walter.

[134] Brunn-Bruckmann, *Denkmäler*, Pl. 344a. Schreiber, *Hellenistische Reliefbilder*, Pl. XXXIV (Villa Albani), Pl. XXXV (Berlin), Pl. XXXVI (Louvre). E. D. van Buren, in *Mem. Amer. Acad. Rome*, III (1919), pp. 91 ff., Pl. 75 (Berlin). *Encycl. phot.*, Vol. III, p. 257 B.

thian columns carry the architrave, above which a frieze with a chariot race is sculptured in relief. The gable is decorated in the center by a shield with the head of Medusa, supported by two Tritons.

A similar rather loose relationship between the figures in the foreground and the objects in the background exists on the relief of a peasant watering his cow at a fountain, in the Vatican Museum [135] (Fig. 658). The cow, which takes two thirds of the foreground, and the calf which she is suckling, are outlined against a low wall behind which a temple appears. The temple has Ionic columns and a mask of Medusa in the gable. The peasant, carrying two ducks hung from his pedum over his left shoulder and a bunch of vegetables in his right hand, stands on the other side of the fountain. Behind the basin is the pillar from which, through a lion mask as water spout, the water flows into the basin. Between the peasant and the pillar a large and knotty plane tree grows; its plastically carved foliage spreads above the heads of man and animals. The relation of the figures to their surroundings in this part is similar to the one on the Polyphemus relief (Fig. 649), but the background is more variegated.

A still more variegated background is in the celebrated relief of the peasant driving his cow to market, in Munich [136] (Fig. 659). The figures are strongly rounded. The old man is stooping under the load of a hare which he carries on a bent pole over his shoulder and the basket with fruit in his right hand. The cow carries on her back two sheep bound together by their feet. They pass a rural sanctuary through the entrance porch of which a knotty old tree sends out a large branch. The upper part of the wall has partly fallen, so that the curved pillar in its center, upon which stands a basket full of fruit, becomes visible. A torch is leaning against it, while two tambourines are set up on top of the wall. In the left upper corner a small shrine with

a herm of Pan is set on a rock which protrudes from the left side. This relief has rightly been dated in the late first century B.C., that is, the Augustan period. Its closest parallels are the Grimani reliefs and the Ara Pacis of Augustus, the latter dated 13—9 B.C.

Most of the so-called Hellenistic reliefs are of an even later date. In the period of Trajan or Hadrian belong the large panels in the Palazzo Spada, of which the scene with Paris minding his herd, approached by Eros, is a good example.[137] The rock here fills two thirds of the background, and the cattle in the lower part are outlined against it. On the ledge which protrudes about half way up, Paris is seated in Phrygian dress, next to a small sacred enclosure around a large oak tree. His dog is at his feet. Eros lays his arms around Paris's shoulders and persuades him to give the apple to Aphrodite in exchange for the love of Helen.

Reliefs of all these types were used for the inner decoration of houses, palaces, bath establishments, and other public buildings. The older ones mostly have idyllic scenes of small size; the later ones, probably all made for rich Romans, are mythological scenes of large size. We see here the influence of the nature-loving and luxurious Romans on the Greek artists who worked for them.

4. ANIMALS

One outstanding feature of these reliefs is the excellent and almost psychological rendering of animals. There is a fine differentiation between the meager cow suckling her calf (Fig. 658), the heavily loaded cow driven to market (Fig. 659), and the well-fed, contented cows of the Trojan prince on the Spada relief.

The dog also was rendered with fine shades of character: the eager watchdog of Paris on the Spada relief, the two playful slim hounds in the Vatican [138] (Fig. 661), and the powerful bulldogs, of which about ten copies exist, the best ones being two in the Vatican [139] (Fig. 660). This dog lifts

[135] Schreiber, *Hellenistische Reliefbilder*, Pl. LXXIV, and Schreiber, *Brunnenreliefs*, p. 96, No. 69. Amelung, *Vatican Kat.*, Vol. II, pp. 358 f., Sala degli Animali, No. 157, Plates 35, 38. J. Sieveking, Fig. 3, in text to Brunn-Bruckmann, *Denkmäler*, Pl. 617.

[136] Furtwängler and Wolters, *Glyptothek*, p. 397, No. 455. Schreiber, *Brunnenreliefs*, pp. 6 ff., Fig. 2. Schreiber, *Hellenistische Reliefbilder*, Pl. LXXX. J. Sieveking, Fig. 2, in text to Brunn-Bruckmann, *Denkmäler*, Pl. 627.

[137] Schreiber, *Hellenistische Reliefbilder*, Pl. IX. Brunn-Bruckmann, *Denkmäler*, Pl. 625b. Wickhoff, *Wiener Genesis*, pp. 23 ff. (cf. the fragment in Berlin: Schreiber, *op. cit.*, Pl. XXVIII, No. 2).

[138] Amelung, *Vatican Kat.*, Vol. II, pp. 332 f., Sala degli Animali, No. 116, Pl. 31.

[139] *Ibid.*, pp. 162 ff., Cortile del Belvedere, Nos. 64–65, Pls. 17–18.

himself up on his widely stretched front legs, turns his head up and to the side, and with grim mouth, showing the teeth, is ready to bite any intruder. The little pet dog, in contrast, sleeps peacefully on a couch, in a terra cotta in the Berlin Museum [140] (Fig. 664). The bronze figurine of a lean and slender greyhound, formerly in the possession of Paul Jacobsthal, now in the Metropolitan Museum of Art in New York, represents him hungrily gnawing a bone [141] (Fig. 663). In the same museum is the fine head of a lively mule, in bronze with silver inlays, which once decorated, as one of a pair, the curved headrest of an elegant couch [142] (Fig. 662). The different characters of all these animals are well understood and strikingly rendered.

[140] C. R. Williams, *Couches and Beds: Studies in Ancient Furniture* (1905), p. 34, Pl. XXIX a. G. Richter, *Ancient Furniture, Greek, Etruscan, and Roman* (1926), pp. 133 f., Fig. 316. W. Weber, *Mitteilungen aus der ägyptischen Sammlung der Museen Berlin*, Vol. II: *Die ägyptisch-griechischen Terrakotten* (1914), No. 461, p. 41.

[141] Metropolitan Museum of Art, No. 36.11.12. Richter, *Handbook* (1953), p. 126, Pl. 105 f.

[142] Metropolitan Museum of Art, No. 18.145.133. G. Richter, *Bronzes*, pp. 91 f., No. 133.

XI

CLASSICISM IN THE SECOND AND FIRST CENTURIES B.C.

WHILE BAROQUE and rococo tendencies prevailed during the Hellenistic period in the Eastern countries, Attica, through all the centuries of ancient civilization, kept to the tradition of its great past, the classical period of the fifth and fourth centuries. The great masters of the past—Phidias, Polykleitos, and Praxiteles—became classics, that is, models who seemed so perfect that they could not be improved upon. Not only the Athenians, however, but the cities of the northern Peloponnese, where the school of Polykleitos continued to flourish, and also some of the Eastern rulers, held this opinion. The Ptolemies collected mostly the books of classical writers, such as the manuscripts of the great tragic poets of the fifth century. The Attalids, in contrast, collected classical works of art, or had copies made for their collections. An early classical Athena, a copy of the Athena Parthenos of Phidias, and a Demeter from his school were in the possession of the Attalids,[1] and the Hermes of Alkamenes, the greatest pupil of Phidias, also was known in Pergamon.[2] The large frieze of the altar of Eumenes had, beside its new baroque style, at least some quotations of older types. The same love for Athenian classical art induced Antiochus IV (Antiochus Epiphanes) of Syria (175–164 B.C.) to order a copy of the Zeus of Phidias in Olympia to be set up at Daphne near his capital, and a copy of the Athena Parthenos to be placed in Antioch itself. Soon afterwards the satrap Orophernes gave another copy of the Athena Parthenos to Priene (Pausanias VII. 5. 5); it is represented on the later Roman coins of this city.[3] These cities considered themselves the inheritors of the intellectual and artistic leadership of Athens. Thus during the Hellenistic period began the high esteem for classical forms and content, for harmony, beauty, grandeur, and balance, which the Romans

[1] See F. Winter in *Altertümer von Pergamon*, Vol. VII: *Die Skulpturen*, pp. 13 ff., No. 22, Pls. II–V (Athena), pp. 25 ff., No. 23, Pls. VI–VII (Demeter), pp. 33 ff., No. 24, Beiblatt 22–23, Pl. VIII (Athena Parthenos).

[2] *Altertümer von Pergamon*, Vol. VII, pp. 48 ff., No. 27, Beiblatt 5, Pl. IX.

[3] The Zeus on coins of Antiochus IV and later Seleucid kings: Percy Gardner, *British Museum Catalogue of Coins, The Seleucid Kings of Syria*, ed. by R. S. Poole (1878), p. 42, Pl. XIII, 7, 12, 14; pp. 51 f., Pl. XV, 6; p. 57, Pl. XVII, 5; p. 59, Pl. XVII, 9. The Athena, *ibid.*, p. 52, Pl. XV, 5; p. 56 f., Pl. XVI, 12; p. 59, Pl. XVII, 10; p. 89, Pl. XXIV, 2; p. 95, Pl. XXV, 7, 12. The Athena on coins of Priene: B. V. Head, *Catalogue of the Greek Coins of Ionia* (London, the British Museum, 1892), p. 239, Nos. 55–58. K. O. Regling, *Die Münzen von Priene* (Berlin, 1927), p. 10, No. 211, Pl. V. For the remains of the statue in London, see A. H. Smith, *A Catalogue of Sculpture in the Department of Greek and Roman Antiquities of the British Museum* (3 vols., 1892–1904), Vol. II, pp. 152 f., No. 1150, 1–4 (marble), and H. B. Walters, *Catalogue of the Bronzes, Greek, Roman, and Etruscan, in the Department of Greek and Roman Antiquities* (London, the British Museum, 1899), No. 1728 (wings of Nike). Cf. T. Wiegand and H. Schrader, *Priene: Ergebnisse der Ausgrabungen und Untersuchungen in den Jahren 1895–1898* (Berlin, 1904), pp. 110 f.

accepted as their standard ideal also, and which again came to the fore during the Renaissance and, particularly, during the second half of the eighteenth century, the best-known period marked by tendencies toward classicism.

Until about the end of the second century B.C. there were no real copies made of the older works. The Athena Parthenos in Pergamon is Pergamene in style, even though the composition was taken from Phidias. On the mainland also, in Attica and the Peloponnese, the new Hellenistic tendencies were not ignored but blended with the traditional forms so as to make genuine new creations. The best and earliest examples of this are the statues by Damophon of Messene.

The writer Pausanias (IV. 31. 6) tells us that Damophon was commissioned to repair the Zeus of Phidias, probably as a consequence of an earthquake in 183 B.C. which caused the seams of the ivory to open. He did this with the greatest possible precision. He thus learned the technique of fitting together a colossal statue from different pieces and was able to study a great classical work. Through this he became an admirer and imitator of the style of Phidias, and he applied it when he had to set up a number of cult statues in the Peloponnese: in Messene, Aigion, Megalopolis, and in the sanctuary of Demeter and Despoina (Persephone or Kore) near Lycosura in Arcadia. This temple and the statues are described by Pausanias (VIII. 37). Many fragments of the group have been found, and with their help the group has been reconstructed. A coin gives the outline of the four figures [4] (Fig.

668). Despoina and her mother Demeter were seated, while Artemis and the Titan Anytos were standing. Thus the composition is the old classical one with all figures in one row without any depth. Pausanias gives some details:

The images of the goddesses themselves, Despoina and Demeter, and the throne whereon they are seated and the footstool beneath their feet, all are of one block. Demeter bears a scepter and a cista, as it is called, in her lap. With one hand she holds the cista. On each side of the throne is a figure. Beside Demeter stands Artemis clad in a deer skin, with a quiver on her shoulder. In one hand she holds a torch, in the other two snakes. Beside Artemis lies a bitch, like those used in hunting. Close to the image of Despoina stands Anytos, attired as a warrior in full armor. The attendants of the temple say that Despoina was reared by Anytos and that he is of the number of Titans, as they are called.

The well-preserved heads of Anytos (Figs. 665–67) and Despoina (Fig. 670) show a mixture of the grandeur of Phidias and the refinement of Praxitelean style, with some of the excitement of the contemporary Asiatic style in the features, hair, and beard of Anytos. It is the beginning of an eclecticism which was to be an outstanding characteristic of the mainland school of sculpture. The back of the head of Anytos is hollowed out and prepared to receive separate pieces with the help of metal dowels (see Fig. 667). This is the technique used for gold and ivory, or marble and wood, but the statues were wholly of marble. Among the fragments is a piece of the hanging garment of the main goddess, Despoina, the mistress of the house; it is decorated in flat reliefs imitating a rich embroidery with figures of Nike, dancing daimons, laurel wreaths, and a wave pattern.

Damophon was not the only artist to work in this manner during the second century B.C. Eubulides worked in a similar style in Athens in the second half of the second century. A torso of a Nike and a head of Athena (Fig. 669) show a cold imitation of Phidian style.[5] Eukleides was the artist of a colossal statue of Zeus in Aegira, three times life size, in a similar classicized style and of Pentelic

[4] P. Cavvadias (Kabbadias), *Fouilles de Lycosura* (1894). G. Dickins in *Ann. Brit. Sch. at Athens*, XII (1905–6), 109 ff.; see pp. 132–35, Figs. 8–10 for the inscription and Fig. 11 for the votive offering dedicated by Damophon; Vol. XIII (1906–7), pp. 356 ff., Pls. XII–XIV and Figs. 1–25 for the restoration of the groups; also Vol. XVII (1910–11), pp. 80 ff., Fig. 1, for the coin and Fig. 2 for the restoration of the group. H. Brunn and F. Bruckmann, *Denkmäler griechischer und römischer Skulptur* (Munich, 1888—), Pls. 478–80. G. Becatti, "Attikà, saggio sulla scultura attica dell'ellenismo" in *Riv. del Ist. Arch.*, Vol. VII (1940), pp. 40 ff., Figs. 18–23. G. Dickins, *Hellenistic Sculpture* (Oxford, The Clarendon Press, 1920), pp. 60 ff., Figs. 45–48. A. W. Lawrence, *Later Greek Sculpture and Its Influence on East and West* (London, Cape, 1927), p. 30, Pls. 54–55. M. Bieber, "Pliny and Graeco-Roman Art," in *Hommages à Cumont, Collection Latimus,* Vol. II (1949; *Revue des Etudes Latines Brussels*, Vol. XXVII), pp. 39 ff., Pls. I–II. On the earthquake see W. B. Dinsmoor in *A.J.A.*, XLV (1941), pp. 399 ff., and M. Bieber in *ibid.*, pp. 94 f. On the mechanical reconstruction of the group see

K. Kourouniotes in *Ann. Brit. Sch. at Athens*, XIII (1906–7), pp. 384 ff., Figs. 24–25.

[5] L. Julius in *Athen. Mitt.*, VII (1882), 81 ff. Brunn-Bruckmann, *Denkmäler*, Pls. 48–49. Dickins, *Hellenistic Sculpture*, pp. 58 f., Figs. 43–44. G. Becatti in *Riv. del Ist. Arch.*, Vol. VII (1940), pp. 48 ff., Figs. 30–31.

marble, but made in imitation of the chryselephantine technique [6] (Figs. 671–72). According to Pausanius (VII. 26. 4) the statue of Zeus was seated. The head, which has survived, is of the type with oversized forehead with the hair standing up above it and the full beard which, in Rome, led to the type of the Jupiter Capitolinus by Apollonios.

This type of work, which combined classical and baroque grandeur in a new style which was neither as simple as that of earlier times nor so exaggerated as later sculpture, was considered a revival of art by Pliny (*Nat. hist.* XXXIV. 52), when he says that art died in Olympiad CXXI (296 B.C.)—that is, with the school of Lysippos—and was not revived before Olympiad CLVI (156 B.C.). The great Alexandrian and Pergamene periods were probably unknown to Pliny; and Athens, although it still led in portraiture and philosophy, had not recently given any great tasks to artists. The earthquakes in the Peloponnese during the second century necessitated new works, which were executed in a taste appealing to the Romans, an eclectic mixture of ancient and modern forms. Classical grandeur and Hellenistic vivacity, conservative and progressive trends, were combined into a late Hellenistic style.

This eclectic style certainly had its origins in Attica and the Peloponnese. It was, however, also accepted in the second half of the second century in Asia Minor. The best example is the much-discussed Aphrodite of Melos (Venus de Milo).

This Aphrodite, found on the island of Melos and now in the Louvre [7] (Figs. 673–75), has been dated by some scholars in the classical period, but by most, however—and rightly—in the later Hellenistic period. The latter date is documented by the inscription which was found with the statue and which gives the name of the artist: "[Agesor Alex-] andros, son of Henidos, from the city of

Antioch on the Meander." Unfortunately the part of the plinth with the inscription (Figs. 676–77) has been lost. It contained a square into which a pillar could be fitted; the goddess certainly rested her lost left arm on this pillar, for the left shoulder is raised. With the right hand she grasped the drapery which is slung loosely around her hips. The end hangs between the legs; the left leg is set forward with slightly bent knee. The drapery looks very unstable, and below the roll of the upper edge at the right side it looks as if it is fastened with a fibula to prevent it from slipping down. The upper torso and the head are turned slightly to the left; the left knee, however, turns to the right. This makes for a complicated and inharmonious double movement. Breast and hips are matronly, broad, and very realistically modeled. The head (Fig. 673), on the contrary, is in an idealistic style. The features of the face are serene and finely proportioned. The hair is parted and surrounded by a fillet which binds it into a knot in the back. The rendering of the hair is in the simple classical style. The result, however, is a lack of harmony between body and head.

The model which inspired the late Hellenistic artist has been rightly recognized in the Aphrodite of Capua, who was represented holding the shield of Ares, and with it holding the mantle in place around her hips.[8] Her head is almost identical with that of the Aphrodite of Melos (Fig. 673). In antiquity this real classical type was much more popular than the Hellenistic adaptation. The Romans made her a Victory by adding wings and often a chiton; an example is the Victory of Brescia.[9] On the column of Trajan, as well as on the column of Marcus Aurelius, the figure of such a Victory is used to separate from each other the two campaigns represented.[10] On both columns she is holding the shield of Ares, recording on it the victories attained by the emperor and his army. The type was used, too, for portrait statues of female members of the

[6] O. Walter in *Oest. Jahreshefte*, Vols. XIX–XX (1919), pp. 1 ff., Figs. 1–7, Pls. I–II. A. Hekler in *ibid.*, XXI–XXII (1920), pp. 120 ff. G. Becatti in *Riv. del Ist. Arch.*, Vol. VII (1940), pp. 25 ff., Figs. 6–7.
[7] A. Furtwängler, *Masterpieces of Greek Sculpture* (1895), pp. 367 ff. Brunn-Bruckmann, *Denkmäler*, Pl. 298. G. Rodenwaldt in *Die Kunst der Antike* (Berlin, Propyläen-Verlag, 1927; Propyläen-Kunstgeschichte, III), Pl. 458. *Encycl. phot.*, Vol. III, Pls. 200–203. S. Reinach in *Gazette des Beaux-Arts* (1890), pp. 376 ff. L. Laurenzi in *Riv. del Ist. Arch.*, Vol. VIII (1940), pp. 33 ff., Figs. 6–7. A. della Seta, *Il nudo nell' arte* (1930), p. 92, Fig. 249.

[8] Brunn-Bruckmann, *Denkmäler*, Pls. 297, 593.
[9] H. Bulle, *Der schöne Mensch im Altertum* (Munich, 1912), pp. 529 ff., Fig. 168, Pl. 252. F. Studniczka, *Die Siegesgöttin*, Pl. XII. K. Lehmann in *Röm. Mitt.*, Vols. XXXVIII–XXXIX (1923-24), pp. 185 ff., Beiblatt 7.
[10] W. Fröhner, *La Colonne Trajane* (1872–74), Pl. 107 in large edition, Pl. 120 in the small edition. C. Cichorius, *Die Reliefs der Trajanssäule* (1896–1900), Vol. I, Pl. LVIII. K. Lehmann, *Die Trajanssäule* (1926), p. 111, Pl. 37.

imperial court, sometimes together with another classical type of the end of the fifth century, the Borghese Ares in the Louvre, used to represent the emperor.[11]

The arms of the Aphrodite of Melos were certainly not holding a shield. It has been assumed that she held in her left hand an apple, the fruit for which Melos was named. Another possibility is suggested by a statuette in Rhodes, an Aphrodite which is very similar to the Melian. Here she lays her left arm around the shoulders of Eros, who shoots his arrow as he is seated on a rock pillar on the left side of his mother.[12] In any case, the statue of Melos has the open form, or centrifugal conception without a central axis, which Gerhard Krahmer has proved to be characteristic of the second half of the second century.[13]

The Aphrodite of Melos thus is one of the creations of this late Hellenistic period, which strove to impart new life into traditional types by combining retrospective traits with new realism and movement. It certainly is an eclectic work.

The same can be said of an Apollo which one might attribute to Timarchides I, an Athenian artist, the father of Timarchides II who, around 150 B.C., together with Timokles carved a statue of Asclepius for his temple in Elateia (Pausanias x. 34. 6). Timarchides I worked for Caecilius Metellus Macedonicus, who had defeated Macedonia in 146 B.C., whereupon Macedonia, including Attica, came under Roman rule. This is probably the time when Athenian artists began to follow the Roman conquerors to their homeland, where there had developed a great demand for original Greek works which even the plundering of Corinth and other places could not satisfy. Timarchides I may have been the first of many Attic artists to work for the

Romans (Chap. IX, p. 130). Thus in the porticus later known as the Porticus of Octavia there stood, together with Muses by Philiskos of Rhodes, a statue of Apollo holding the kithara (Pliny *Nat. hist.* XXXVI. 34–35). This statue is probably to be recognized in a type of which we have many variations [14] (Figs. 678–81). The most beautiful one has been found in Cyrene and is now in the British Museum (Figs. 678–79). It has soft features, developed from the Praxitelean Apollo Lykeios (see Figs. 17, 20–23). The hair is parted, with rich waves over the forehead, and adorned with fillet and wreath. Long locks fall forward on the shoulders. The right hand reposes on the crown of the head. It originally held the *plektron* for the lyre, as shown in the replicas—one of green basalt in Naples (Fig. 681), and one of white marble in the Museo Capitolino (Fig. 680). The left foot advances in a manner similar to that of the left foot of the Aphrodite of Melos. The mantle is wrapped around the thighs; one edge is held by the lyre instead of a tripod, as in the Capitolino replica, or a pillar, as in the one in Naples. The mantle looks as if it is about to slide down. The end hangs outside the left foot and seems to sweep the ground. A snake drinks from the basin on the tripod. There is something unbalanced and inharmonious in this figure, as there is in the Aphrodite of Melos, despite the attempt to recreate and enrich a classical statue like the Apollo Lykeios of Praxiteles.

A similar impression is received by the author from the Poseidon, also found on the island of Melos and now in Athens [15] (Fig. 684). In his raised hand Poseidon holds his trident. With the left hand he grasps the roll into which the upper edge of his mantle has been turned, so that the ends hang outside the left leg, as in the Apollo. A

---

[11] W. Fröhner, *Notice de la sculpture antique du Louvre* (4th ed., 1878), pp. 161 f., No. 131. *Encycl. Phot.*, Vol. III, p. 179. Furtwängler, *Masterpieces*, p. 384. M. Collignon, *Histoire de la sculpture grecque* (2 vols., Paris, 1892, 1897), Vol. II, p. 468. Two persons as Ares and Aphrodite: H. Stuart Jones, *A Catalogue of the Ancient Sculptures Preserved in the Municipal Collections of Rome. The Sculpture of the Museo Capitolino* (Oxford, 1912), pp. 297 f., Salone 34, Pl. 73. G. Richter, in *Proceedings of the American Philosophical Society*, Vol. XCV (1951), p. 187, Figs. 13–15.

[12] L. Laurenzi in *Clara Rhodos*, Vol. V, Part 2 (1932), pp. 148 ff., Fig. 36, and in *Riv. del Ist. Arch.*, Vol. VIII (1940), pp. 35 f., Fig. 8.

[13] G. Krahmer, "Stilphasen der hellenistischen Plastik," in *Röm. Mitt.*, Vols. XXXVIII–XXXIX (1923–24), pp. 140 f.

[14] A. H. Smith, *Brit. Mus. Cat.*, Vol. II, pp. 222 ff., No. 1380. G. E. Rizzo, *Prassitele* (Milan and Rome, Fratelli Treves, 1932), p. 83, Pl. 128. Brunn-Bruckmann, *Denkmäler*, Pl. 593. Jones, *Sculpt. Museo Capitolino*, pp. 279 f., Salone No. 7, Pl. 67. G. Becatti in *Bolletino Comunale*, LXIII (1935–36), 111 ff., and in *Riv. del Ist. Arch.*, Vol. VII (1940), pp. 29 ff., Figs. 9–12. M. Bieber in Thieme-Becker, *Künstlerlexikon*, Vol. XXIII (1929), p. 175 f. W. Klein, *Vom antiken Rokoko* (Vienna, Hölzel (1921), pp. 25 ff., Fig. 55. W. Klein, *Praxiteles* (Leipzig, 1898), pp. 163 ff. (replicas). O. Deubner, *Hellenistische Apollogestalten* (1934), pp. 30 ff., 64. Twelve replicas are known. See G. Lippold in Pauly-Wissowa, *Real-Enc.*, Second Series, Vol. VI, pp. 1233 f., s.v. Timarchides, No. 4.

[15] Brunn-Bruckmann, *Denkmäler*, Pl. 550. V. Staïs, *Marbres et bronzes du Musée national* (Athens, 1910), pp. 75 f., No. 235.

cushion-like roundel of folds lies on the shoulder, but again we have the impression of lability and the disagreeable feeling that the mantle will slip down at the back at any moment. The head looks to the left and somewhat upward. It is a dignified type with full hair and beard. It recalls the earlier type of the Asclepius, also from the island of Melos, in the British Museum; a replica of this, with the torso, has been found in the Piraeus harbor.[16] The hair standing up over the forehead in two strands like the lion's mane of Alexander, the locks falling down like a frame at the sides of the face, the deeply rolled single locks of the beard separated by strong shadowed areas, all are similar. This is the type which led to the Zeus of Otricoli and finally, probably, to the Jupiter on the Capitol which was made by Apollonios for Sulla.

A similar rhythm to that of the Poseidon of Melos, I believe, is to be seen in the much-discussed Hellenistic Ruler in the Museo Nazionale Romano in Rome [17] (Figs. 682–83 and 685). The left hand grasps the lance or scepter, the right is put behind the hip; the head has a lively turn to the right and the left foot is set so as to produce a forceful backward swing. It may be that the Alexander with the lance by Lysippos inspired this work, but the head (Figs. 682–83) shows all the realism and movement of small features which Hellenistic portraiture developed during the third and second centuries (see pp. 85 ff.). The hair, however, is rendered in a classical manner, with clear divisions but rather deeper undercutting than is seen even in Lysippos's heads.

The date of the statue has been set by Gerhard Krahmer at the beginning of the period of the open form, which is the middle of the second century

b.c.[18] This agrees with the interpretation of the statue as Demetrius I (Demetrius Soter) of Syria, who lived in Rome before he was king (162—150 b.c.). This name has been given to the statue on the basis of coins, which, unfortunately, are not absolutely identical.[19] They are, however, nearer to the bronze statue than are coins of Sulla and other early republican Roman coins, on the basis of which the statue has also been dated in the first century before Christ, with the name of Sulla or Lucullus attached to it.[20] To me there does not seem any possible doubt that the representation is that of a Greek of the second century, and as it has no diadem, Demetrius, before he became ruler, is still the best guess.

A dated portrait in relief takes us to the period 145—135 b.c. It is on a stele found in Clitor (Kleitor) in Arcadia, with an inscription, now lost, recording that it was set up for Polybius on account of his good deeds.[21] The original is now badly mutilated, but casts were exhibited in the Berlin Museum (Fig. 691) and at the Mostra Augustea in Rome. Pausanias (VIII. 9. 1; 30. 8; 37. 2; and 48. 8) mentions four other such steles and a statue (VIII. 44. 5) set up in Arcadia in honor of the great historian. Polybius was a cavalry officer in the Achaean League, and as such he was one of a thousand hostages sent to Rome after the defeat of Perseus of Macedon at Pydna in 168. He remained in Rome until 150 b.c. In this period he became a great admirer of the well-organized Roman state. Aemilius Paullus took him into his house and entrusted him with the education of his two sons; the younger son, Scipio Aemilianus, who later re-

[16] Staïs, *Marbres et bronzes*, pp. 89 f., No. 258. P. Wolters in *Athen. Mitt.*, Vol. XVII (1892), pp. 1 ff., Pls. II–IV. Collignon, *Sculpture grecque*, Vol. II, p. 249, Fig. 126. G. Becatti in *Bollettino Comunale*, LXIII (1935–36), pp. 44 f., Fig. 26. For a similar type see the Zeus or Asclepius in Rhodes: L. Laurenzi in *Clara Rhodos*, Vol. IX (1938), pp. 40 ff., Figs. 22–23, Pls. II–III. The head discovered in a shrine of Asclepius in Melos: A. H. Smith, *Brit. Mus. Cat.*, Vol. I, pp. 289 f., No. 550.

[17] P. Arndt, *Griechische und römische Porträts* (Munich, Bruckmann, 1891–1942), Pls. 358–60. Brunn-Bruckmann, *Denkmäler*, Pl. 246. *Ant. Denk.*, Vol. I, Pl. 5. R. Delbrück, *Antike Porträts* (1912), pp. XLIII ff., Pl. 30. A. Hekler, *Bildniskunst der Griechen und Römer* (1912), Pls. 82–84. L. Laurenzi, *Ritratti greci* (Florence, Sansoni, 1941), p. 129, No. 94, Pls. XXXVIII–XXXIX. O. Vessberg, *Studien zur Kunstgeschichte der römischen Republik* (Leipzig, 1941), pp. 171 f., Pl. XVII.

[18] G. Krahmer in *Röm. Mitt.*, Vol. XXXVIII–XXXIX (1923–24), pp. 138 ff., 151, and Vol. XLVI (1931), p. 236.

[19] For coins of Demetrius: Delbrück, *Porträts*, Pl. 61, Figs. 20–21; V. Müller in *Art Bulletin*, Vol. XX (1938), Pl. 26, Fig. 9.

[20] Rhys Carpenter in *Mem. Amer. Acad. at Rome*, Vol. XVIII (1941), pp. 81 ff., Pl. 25, and in *A.J.A.* (1945), pp. 353 ff. Phyllis Williams in *A.J.A.* (1945), pp. 330 ff.

[21] F. Studniczka in *Sitzungsberichte der Sächsischen Gesellschaft der Wissenschaften*, Phil.-Hist. Klasse, Vol. LXIII (1911), pp. 3 ff., Pls. 1–2. H. Möbius in *Jahrbuch d. Inst.*, Vol. XLIX (1934), pp. 52 f., Fig. 5 (the cast), Fig. 6 (the original). M. Rostovtzeff, *The Social and Economic History of the Hellenistic World* (Oxford, 1941), Vol. I, p. 54, Pl. VIII. G. Becatti in *Riv. del Ist. Arch.*, Vol. VII (1940), pp. 43 ff., Fig. 25. For the inscription see H. von Gaertringen, *Historische griechische Epigramme* (1926), No. 112; W. Dittenberger, *Sylloge Inscriptionum Graecarum* (3d ed., 1915–24), Vol. II, No. 686; *Insc. Graec.*, Vol. V, Part 2, No. 370.

ceived the name of Younger Africanus, became his friend. After the destruction of Corinth in 146 B.C. by Mummius, which he witnessed, Polybius was left in authority by the Romans to settle details of the administration of the Greek cities. He performed his task so wisely that the citizens of the Peloponnese regarded him as a public benefactor and set up many monuments to him.

The only preserved relief with the likeness of Polybius (Fig. 691) has the open form characteristic of this period. The lines do not converge on a center, but rather go away from it. Polybius appears as a broad-shouldered warrior, standing with legs rather wide apart, the right hand lifted in a gesture of adoration or salutation. He holds his spear in the left arm, while his shield and high-crested helmet are at his feet. He wears the long chlamys of the officer, and a chiton which leaves the right shoulder bare. The lower part of the right vertical edge of the mantle, which normally hangs at the back, is drawn forward by the left hand, so as to form a broad horizontal mass before the thighs. The other vertical edge is thrown back over the left arm. The end hangs with zigzag folds from the left hand down, covering part of the spear. The result is a complicated arrangement with many irregular and crossing lines. As the figure is over life size, it can serve as an example of a portrait statue of the second half of the second century.

The influence of Lysippos, which was so great in the early third century and had waned before the more brilliant Asiatic trend, can be seen returning in the Hellenistic Ruler, and seems to have been added during the late second century to the eclectic mixture of the classicized art. Adaptations of Lysippos's standing Heracles are found in Alexandria (see Chap. VI, p. 99, and Fig. 398). His seated Heracles Epitrapezios (see Chap. III, p. 36, Fig. 80) was transposed into a larger size in a newly found statue in Pompeii, now in Naples (Figs. 81 and 690), just as it was in the early Hellenistic period in a torso in the Metropolitan Museum of Art in New York.[22] The pose is made much more

effective by putting the club high up on a rock, so that the left arm is lifted, similarly to the right arm of the Poseidon of Melos (Fig. 684) and of Polybius (Fig. 691); there is also a marked similarity in the bulging muscles of this arm and of the torso. The head, too, is related in type to the Poseidon of Melos. I therefore would date the figure in the same period as the two related figures.

Another late Hellenistic adaptation, and exaggeration, of the style of Lysippos is the fighting warrior from the Borghese collection, now in the Louvre; it is signed on the tree trunk by Agasias, the son of Dositheos, the Ephesian[23] (Figs. 686, 688, 689). The possibilities of the third dimension, introduced by Lysippos, are here used to the full extent—indeed, almost misused. The body is stretched forward and there is one long line from the left foot through the leg, the slim body, and the head. The left arm, originally carrying the shield, is lifted upward and to the left. The right arm swings backward. The right leg strides widely forward. Thus each of the four members has a different direction. The violent action stretches the skin over the muscular body, under which there is visible a net of large and small muscles. This gives occasion for an unsurpassable display of anatomical knowledge, without giving the body the unity which classical sculptures always have. It is a factual result of anatomical research. Like the Doryphoros in the fourth century, the Borghese Warrior was used in the nineteenth century in Europe and America as a model from which young artists in art schools and drawing classes could get their knowledge of the forms of the human body. But, unlike the Doryphoros, this fighter gives more than what is essential for the build of the body.

The head of the Borghese Warrior (Fig. 686) shows less emotion than we would expect from the energetic action. It is close in conception to the seated Hermes from Herculaneum, belonging to the school of Lysippos (Figs. 106-8). The arrangement of the hair recalls the Hellenistic Ruler (Figs. 682-83). The date is probably around 100 B.C.

---

[22] Bronze statue found in Pompeii: R. Paribeni in *Notizie degli Scavi* (1902), p. 572. G. Richter in *Gazette des Beaux-Arts* (1950), pp. 53 f., Fig. 27. For the torso in the Metropolitan Museum, see G. A. Richter, *Handbook of the Classical Collection* (New York, Metropolitan Museum of Art, 1930), pp. 279 f., Fig. 198 and *Handbook of the Greek Collection* (1953), p. 142, Pl. 122b. Lawrence, *Later Greek Sculpture*, pp. 18, 109, Pls. 25b, 26.

[23] Brunn-Bruckmann, *Denkmäler*, Pl. 75. Bulle, *Der schöne Mensch*, pp. 174 ff., Pl. 88. G. Krahmer in *Jahrbuch d. Inst.*, XL (1925), pp. 190 f. *Encycl. phot.*, Vol. III, pp. 263-68.

This date, therefore, seems to be the high period for the centrifugal form, for the composition is as open as can be. A bronze statuette in Paris, with a similar movement, does not show the same exaggerations [24] (Fig. 687).

The influence of Lysippos also returned in portraiture. We can see this best in the portrait of Poseidonios (c. 130—50 B.C.). Poseidonios was the teacher of Cicero and Pompey, who visited him in his school on the island of Rhodes. Born in Syria, he studied in the Stoic school at Athens under Panaitios of Rhodes, whose books on Duty were used by Cicero in his *De officiis*. Poseidonios founded an eclectic school in Rhodes in 95 B.C., mixing Stoicism and Platonism, and here Cicero in 78 B.C. attended his lectures. Poseidonios was the most learned man of his age. His eclectic philosophy is the best parallel to the eclectic art of his time.

The portrait of this last great Hellenistic scholar is attested by a bust from the Farnese collection in Naples, inscribed ΠΟΣΙΔΩΝΙΟΣ on the chiton which covers the breast [25] (Figs. 696–97). The left shoulder, covered by a thick mantle, seems to indicate that the head was copied from a statue in strong movement, for it is considerably higher than the right one. The head has a lively turn to the right, so that the sinews of the skinny neck stand out strongly. It probably belonged to a seated statue in heavy drapery, like the one of a poet signed by the sculptor Zeuxis in the Metropolitan Museum of Art in New York [26] (Figs. 694–95). The chiton of the poet's statue has a protruding triangle over the breast similar to that of the bust of Poseidonios, although it is not identical, and also has similar thick folds of the mantle hanging from the left

shoulder. The torso has a lively movement with a marked turn to the left side, where a kithara was held in the left arm.

The features of Poseidonios (Figs. 696–97) and the simple rendering of the hair may have made a striking contrast to the body. Indeed, they remind one of the restrained psychological rendering of the Lysippean portraits (see Figs. 128–30). The thin strands of the hair are placed in flat layers and irregular rows. The broad forehead is deeply furrowed, and many small wrinkles encircle the eyes. The cheeks are thin, the mouth is broad, with deep corners. It looks as if the lecturer is just about to speak. The expression of the face is serious and energetic. He seems to be approximately fifty or sixty years old, hence the bust can be dated 85—75 B.C. The style in general recalls the early Hellenistic style of the Lysippean school, but the details, such as the emaciated neck, are in the late Hellenistic style. Thus it is an eclectic portrait, in agreement with the eclectic doctrine of Poseidonios. Like his teaching and writing, which profoundly affected Roman thought, this portrait, which must have been known to his immediate and later Roman followers, may have influenced the development of Roman portraiture. The Augustan style, with its soberness, is certainly a direct successor to the style of the head of Poseidonios.

The sober-looking man at Delphi, usually dated in the fourth century, is of a similar style [27] (Figs. 692–93). It certainly recalls the head of Menander (Figs. 151, 154–57) and other Lysippean heads. The extreme realism in the rendering of the lank hair and the thin beard, however, is so similar to that of the head of Poseidonios that it also must represent the eclectic trend of the first century B.C.

While in the last examples the head was classicized and the body realistically rendered in the Hellenistic manner, another combination is found in a bronze statuette in private possession in New York [28] (Figs. 700–701). An officer, perhaps a general, is standing in a Polycleitan pose, the left leg and the right arm relaxed, the right leg carrying

[24] Bibliothèque nationale, Paris, Bronzes, No. 3562, Cabinet des Médailles, No. 815. Formerly in the Blacas collection.

[25] J. J. Bernoulli, *Griechische Ikonographie* (2 vols., Munich, 1901), Vol. II, pp. 188 ff., Pl. XXV. Arndt, *Porträts*, Pls. 239–40. Hekler, *Bildniskunst*, Pl. 126. A. Hekler, *Bildnisse berühmter Griechen* (1940), Fig. 40. R. Paribeni, *Il ritratto nell' arte antica* (Milan, Fratelli Treves, 1934), Pl. LXVI. K. Schefold, *Die Bildnisse der antiken Dichter, Redner, und Denker* (Basel, Schwabe, 1943), pp. 150 ff.

[26] G. Richter in *A.J.A.*, XXIX (1925), 159; in Arndt, *Porträts*, Pls. 1121–22, Fig. 1, in text; in *Handbook* (1930), pp. 278 ff., Fig. 197, and *Handbook* (1953), p. 143, Pl. 124a; and in *Three Critical Periods in Greek Sculpture* (Oxford, The Clarendon Press, 1951), pp. 45, 49, Fig. 96. G. Lippold, *Griechische Porträtstatuen* (Munich, Bruckmann, 1912), pp. 83 f., Fig. 21. Schefold, *Bildnisse*, pp. 146 f., 213, Figs. 1, 3.

[27] C. Picard and P. de la Coste-Messelière, *Fouilles de Delphes*, Vol. IV (1927), p. 40, Pl. 73. Hekler, *Bildniskunst*, Pl. 80. F. Poulsen, *Delphi* (1920), pp. 318 ff., Figs. 158–59.

[28] The owner, Mr. E. Segredakis of New York City, kindly allowed the publication of Figs. 700–701. He told me that he had bought the statuette from a family in whose possession it had been for a hundred years.

the weight of the body, the left arm, which is vigorously bent, originally carrying a shield. The muscles in front also recall the Doryphoros, while at the back the muscles are rendered rather arbitrarily, in the manner of the Pergamene altar. The head, covered with a Corinthian helmet, has thick hair with deep shadows and the face has an emotional expression not possible in the classical period. I therefore believe that this is a late Hellenistic work of the classicizing period, perhaps not earlier than the first half of the first century. In this period Greek artists worked for their Roman conquerors, as they had done for the Hellenistic rulers in the earlier period. The technique is very fine. The eyeballs are of silver inlay, and the nipples were worked separately in lighter bronze. The crest of the helmet and the right hand seem modern to me in this New York statuette. It may be the statuette that was in the possession of a dealer in 1911,[29] but which had no crest and the right arm of which moved differently. Perhaps the crest was added and the right arm bent at the time that the right hand was restored. It looks as if it were copied from the ancient left hand.

Another mixture of Polycleitan style with not only Hellenistic, but also fourth century, features can be seen in the young athlete from Tralles in the Istanbul Museum[30] (Figs. 698–99). Except for the realistically swollen ears, the face recalls boys carved by Polykleitos. The crossed feet did not occur in the round before Skopas and Praxiteles used them (see Fig. 62), while the draping of the mantle, although on simple lines, shows the full realism of the Hellenistic period.

It is interesting to note that a classicized, retrograde style entered also into the architectural reliefs of Asia Minor during the second half of the second century B.C. The best examples are the friezes from the temple of Artemis Leukophryne in Magnesia on the Meander, and from the temple of Hecate at Lagina in Caria.

The temple of Artemis at Magnesia was built by Hermogenes. Already active around 175 B.C., he worked around 156 in Priene. It seems that after Priene he went to Magnesia, and that we can date his activity there about 150—130 B.C. He took the form of the Ionic capital from the archaic period and adapted it to Hellenistic taste, just as the classicizing sculptors adapted the earlier forms to the taste of their period. The rules for Ionic architecture, which Hermogenes codified, had a great influence on Roman architecture.[31] It seems as if the earliest sculptural work in Magnesia was the frieze of the altar, of which only fragments have been preserved.[32] The style recalls the Pergamon altar; the deep folds and creases of the drapery are in a similar style. The figures are like statues set before a smooth background.

The remains of the temple frieze are scattered between Paris, where about one third is preserved, Berlin (Figs. 702–3), and Istanbul.[33] There is only one subject on all four sides: the battle of the Greeks and the Amazons, so popular in the fifth century as a symbol of the victory of the Greeks over the Persians. Not only the subject matter, but the style also, is classicized. Whole groups of the frieze recall similar ones on the friezes of the temple of Apollo at Bassae (near Phigalia) and on the Nereid monument at Xanthos; examples are the Greek who pulls an Amazon backward from her wounded horse (Fig. 702), and the group of an Amazon protecting her wounded companion (Fig. 703). The single figures, however, are in much higher relief than the classical models. They are strongly undercut, standing out with much play of light and shade, meant to be looked at from a distance, just as are the contemporary one-sided groups of the same period (see Chap. X, pp. 146 ff., and Figs. 626–42). The movement—like that of the free-standing groups—often slants diagonally

[29] Bronze statuette in the sales catalogue *Vente Delessert*, June 13, 1911, Pl. 5. S. Reinach, *Répertoire de la statuaire grecque et romaine* (6 vols., 1906–30), Vol. V (1924), p. 267, Fig. 9.
[30] Istanbul Museum, No. 542. See *Mon. Piot*, Vol. X (1903), pp. 1 ff., Pl. IV; Lawrence, *Later Greek Sculpture*, p. 44, Pls. 74–75.

[31] W. B. Dinsmoor, *The Architecture of Ancient Greece* (1950), pp. 221 f., 272–75, Fig. 9 (plan), Pl. LXV (capital). R. Delbrück, *Hellenistische Bauten in Latium* (1912), Vol. II, pp. 161 f.
[32] A. von Gerkan, *Der Altar des Artemis-Tempels in Magnesia* (1929), pp. 27 ff. K. Humann, J. Kohte, and K. Watzinger, *Magnesia am Maeander* (Berlin, Reimer, 1904), pp. 91 ff., 175 ff., Pls. VI–VII. Dinsmoor, *Architecture of Ancient Greece*, p. 274 n., p. 288.
[33] Humann, Kohte, and Watzinger, *Magnesia*, pp. 184 f., Figs. 82–85, Pls. V, XII–XIV. E. Herkenrath, *Der Fries des Artemisions von Magnesia* (Berlin, 1902). G. Krahmer in *Jahrbuch d. Inst.*, Vol. XL (1925), pp. 185 ff., Figs. 4–6. *Encycl. phot.*, Vol. III, Pls. 250–51. G. Mendel, *Catalogue des sculptures grecques, romaines et byzantines, Musées Ottomanes* (3 vols., Constantinople, 1912–14), Vol. I, pp. 363 ff., Nos. 148–87.

toward the ground, so that there is a tension between figures and background unknown in the classical reliefs. There are indeed some groups of fighting Amazons which are so closely related to the frieze that they must belong to the same period.[34] They have been wrongly attributed to the groups of Attalus of Pergamon. They, like the frieze, are of rather coarse workmanship. Their muscles are conceived as a flat net over the surface of the bodies. Despite the strong movement the figures look like free standing ones pressed into a plane before a smooth background.

A similar style, but somewhat better work, is found in the friezes of the temple of Hecate at Lagina, near Stratonikeia in Caria [35] (Figs. 704–7). The temple was probably built in the last quarter of the second century, and perhaps finished in the early first century. Each side has a different subject: on the east the birth of Zeus in the presence of the Titanesses, the daughters of Cronus and of the nymphs, with Hecate helping Rhea to save the child from being swallowed by his father Cronus (Fig. 704); on the north, an alliance between the cities, mostly represented by Amazons, and Rome, represented by Roma in a similar guise, in the presence of heroes of tribes and other personifications (Fig. 705); on the west we have a battle of gods and giants, the giants with snakes for legs like those on the Pergamon altar (Fig. 706); on the south is an assembly of the gods who have to do with Caria, such as Zeus Karios and Hera, with children personifying the districts of Stratonikeia (Fig. 707). On each side it seems that Hecate was in the center.

In contrast to the dynamic movement on the Pergamon altar, this latest Greek monumental frieze shows the figures accumulated in repetitious sequence. They do not move in the deep space which surrounds them. Although some are seen from the back (see Artemis in Fig. 706) and some figures or parts of them disappear into the background, most figures are paratactic and static, appearing in frontal position (see examples in Figs. 706–7). They have depth, but are isolated against each other and the ground, like the contemporary one-sided groups. Here is found a crystallization of traditional types, with flattened and stiffened forms and linear rendering of details instead of the plastic roundness found in the high Hellenistic period of the second half of the third century and the first half of the second century. Greek art was on its way down when the Romans, with their enthusiasm and generosity, gave it new life and new tasks.

The decay of Greek art in the late Hellenistic period is best seen in a series of statuettes. These use motifs of older art, but transfer them into a more modern style without being able to rival the earlier statues or the great creations of the style which belongs mostly to the Asiatic school. There is, for example, an early Hellenistic statuette in Berlin (Fig. 709) of which there are several variations in later Hellenistic styles.[36] It is a youthful woman in a thin chiton, a mantle draped over the left shoulder, back, and right leg, which is slightly bent, so that the end rolled above the knee falls down in broad and deep folds between the legs. The left hand, with spread fingers, is laid on the left hip. The head with the melon coiffure and the graceful pose recall the school of Praxiteles. This type was used in the second century for a colossal statue in Pergamene style, found by T. Leslie Shear in Athens,[37] and also in statuettes, two in Rhodes and one in the British Museum, probably also from Rhodes,[38] enriched with greater movement, more details in the folds, and the addition of a belt directly below the breasts.

The characteristic spreading out of the fingers of the hand on the hip appears in a Hellenistic statu-

[34] B. Schweitzer in *Jahrbuch d. Inst.,* LI (1936), pp. 160 ff., Figs. 1–5; the right date is given by A. Schober in *Oest. Jahreshefte,* Vol. XXVII (1932), pp. 102 ff., Figs. 37–40. Aurigemma, *Le Terme di Diocleziano e il Museo Nazionale Romano* (2d ed., Rome, 1950), p. 71, No. 182, Pl. XXXVII. The others are in Naples and in Villa Patrizi. For the late Hellenistic reliefs, see also J. Sieveking in *Festschrift für Paul Arndt* (1925), pp. 14 ff.

[35] Mendel, *Catalogue Musées Ottomanes,* pp. 428 ff., Nos. 198–232. A. Schober in *Oest. Jahreshefte,* Vol. XXVII (1932), pp. 46 ff., Figs. 68–72, and *Der Fries des Hekateions von Lagina* (1933; Istanbuler Forschungen, No. 2). G. Krahmer in *Nachrichten Gött. Ges.* (1927), No. 1, pp. 61 ff., Pl. III, Figs. 7–8. Dinsmoor, *Architecture of Ancient Greece,* p. 282.

[36] Berlin, Altes Museum, No. 504. For replicas see R. Horn, *Stehende weibliche Gewandstatuen in der hellenistischen Plastik* (1931; Ergänzungsheft II to *Röm. Mitt.*), pp. 89–90, Note 9, No. II, 3.

[37] T. L. Shear in *Hesperia,* Vol. IV (1935), pp. 384 ff., Fig. 11.

[38] A. H. Smith, *Brit. Mus. Cat.,* Vol. III, p. 210, No. 2091, Pl. XXIII. L. Laurenzi in *Röm. Mitt.,* Vol. LIV (1939), pp. 57 ff., Pl. 16. Laurenzi dates the type in the second half of the second century and calls it Artemis.

ette of the second century in Athens. This statuette is also derived, judging from her head, from an early Hellenistic type, but has an added mantle in which the central fold stands out strongly from the figure [39] (Fig. 708).

We come to the first century B.C. with a statuette found in Athens [40] (Figs. 710–11). Its rhythm is somehow similar to that of the Nike of Samothrace, with the contrasting movement of the upper and the lower parts of the body. The mantle has a similar arrangement, but the left leg advances and the end of the mantle falls down outside this leg. Irregular grooves in the drapery are sunk in a rather coarse manner. The chiton clinging to the body has only a few thin-backed folds, while most of the folds are engraved, not modeled. Stiffness and schematism have transformed the originally lively movement of the drapery. The body is too long, considering its slimness; only the hips are strongly rounded.

[39] National Museum, Athens, No. 4748.
[40] National Museum, Athens, No. 2585. See G. Krahmer, "Stilphasen der hellenistischen Plastik," in *Röm. Mitt.,* Vols. XXXVIII–XXXIX (1923–24), p. 182, Fig. 6; Horn, *Gewandstatuen,* p. 89, Pl. 37, No. 3. Both authors correctly date this and related statuettes in the first century B.C.

The statuette in Athens probably represents Aphrodite, for there is a similar figure in Athens leaning on an archaistic idol of the goddess, and another one, now in Athens, found in Chaeronea in Boeotia, has a little Eros on her left arm and shoulder.[41] A variation found at Nikaia in Bithynia, now also in Athens [42] (Fig. 712), shows still more simplification in the mantle as well as in the engraved folds of the chiton.

The late Hellenistic works which have been discussed here practically represent the end of an entire era. When the Romans penetrated Greece and the Near East during the second century before Christ, the contemporary Hellenistic art at first attracted their attention, but gradually, specifically at Athens, they learned to know Greek art of the classical period which at once caught their admiration.

When, later, the Romans extended their influence to Asia Minor and Egypt, the great periods of art in those regions belonged to the past.

[41] Statuette leaning on idol, found in Athens, is in the National Museum, Athens, No. 1889. Statuette from Chaeronea is No. 680 in the National Museum, Athens.
[42] National Museum, Athens, No. 2230. The object under the left foot is an ox skull.

DETAIL OF THE BORGHESE KRATER BY ARKESILAOS[?]

XII

CONCLUSION

THE DETAILED STUDY of Hellenistic sculpture reveals that this period is one of the most important in the history of art. Nothing was lost of whatever previous periods have achieved: neither the charm and freshness of archaic art nor the grandeur and harmony of classical art was sacrificed by Hellenistic artists. On the contrary, infinitely more was added. After the artists of the fourth century had brought classical art to its highest refinement, the court sculptor of Alexander the Great conquered a new dimension for art. He and Attic artists developed portraiture to a point where not only the outer appearance of individuals, but also their spiritual and psychological inner life, was reflected. As most portraits can be fairly exactly dated, at least as a *terminus post quem* according to the age of the person represented, they form an important basis for the history of Hellenistic sculpture. Asiatic artists transferred this art of portraiture to the great personalities who ruled the new Hellenistic empires. They brought complicated grouping of several figures to perfection. Alexandrian artists added to the realm of figurative motifs taken from cosmopolitan and many-sided public life. The Rhodian and Pergamene artists lifted sculpture to a new grandeur; their works surpassed the fifth-century sculpture not only in scale but also in scope and depth of passion. Scholarship, philosophy, and natural sciences contributed to the development. Wild creatures of imagination were endowed with new meaning. The importance of the old Olympian gods declined and the gods became more and more human, while men became more important in all phases of their life: the innocence of childhood and the pathos of old age have never been grasped better than in this period. Man, in Hellenistic sculpture, is seen against his background and among his surroundings.

Then, when it seemed that sculpture had reached the boundaries of its possible achievement and, as a consequence, when it seemed that it must become stale, dry, and degenerate, a new people, the Romans, encouraged the return to older periods, which were by then considered classical. The Pergamene baroque did not appeal to them, and only in the Flavian and later Antonine periods did the baroque style again come to the fore. From the first the Romans preferred classical works, and it is due to their admiration that Polykleitos, Phidias, and Praxiteles have become classics—that is, model artists. The Romans preferred copies of these masterpieces to weak contemporary works such as those in our Figs. 708–12, just as today people with small means prefer to buy reproductions of well-known masterpieces rather than second-grade modern works of art. We owe to this taste of the Romans the survival of most Greek masterpieces, at least in copies made for the new masters. Thus the Romans not only gave commissions and bread to the Greek artists who could no longer get them from the Greek cities and decadent Hellenistic rulers, but they kept Greek tradition alive. They also gave new tasks to the artists: architecture, portraiture, and decoration were led into new fields.

Not everything made for the Romans was poor; nor was everything made for the Greek cities and sanctuaries good. When we compare the friezes of Magnesia and Lagina (Figs. 702–7) with a luxurious krater, the so-called Borghese Krater, in the Louvre [1] (p. 166), probably made for the Romans

[1] W. Fröhner, *Notice de la sculpture antique du Louvre* (4th ed., Paris, 1878), No. 235. F. Hauser, *Neuattische Reliefs* (1889), pp. 84 ff. Replica in the British Museum, *ibid.*, p. 86.

by a Greek artist, there can be no doubt that the decorative vase is of higher artistic quality than the architectural sculpture. The relief is much lower but has much more variety. Dionysos and one satyr are seen in front, one flute-playing satyr and a maenad with a tympanon are seen from the back. The others move parallel to the ground, but none is in full front or full profile. The drunken Silenus, held up with difficulty by a young satyr, the maenad beating the cymbals, and the flute-playing satyr are of great beauty and full of independent, inventive spirit. It has been assumed by Wilhelm Klein that this krater may be a product of Arkesilaos, who worked for Lucius Licinius Lucullus and for the Roman knight Octavius. For the latter he is known to have made the model of a bronze krater. I do not believe, however, that the Borghese Krater was created for bronze. In this period all artists probably worked in all materials with the same technical ease. A plaster, stucco, or wax model could have been executed in marble as well as in bronze. Apollonios of Athens, for example, worked in both materials, the famous torso of Belvedere in marble, and the boxer in bronze. It may be that the works of Arkesilaos, who worked in Rome, were not much different from works

---

W. Klein, *Vom antiken Rokoko* (Vienna, Hölzel, 1921), pp. 70 ff., Figs. 28–29. J. Charbonneaux, *La Sculpture grecque au Musée du Louvre* (Paris, 1936), Pl. XLIX. *Encycl. phot.,* Vol. III, Pls. 258–59. The fact that a replica was on the ship sunken near Mahdia (see *Arch. Anz.* [1909], pp. 213 f., Fig. 6) is against the assumption that the Borghese Krater was made in Rome.

made by Attic artists in Athens, or in Rome for the Romans. The borderline between late Hellenistic and Graeco-Roman art is very difficult to draw, because the eclectic tendencies of the Romans were shared by the Greeks of the last Hellenistic period. The poorer the present times were, the more the Greeks turned to their own great past, and thus they were ready to make the copies and adaptations of masterpieces which the Romans desired, and which now fill our museums. There can be no doubt that by demanding copies or adaptations of celebrated masterpieces the Romans saved Greek art for posterity. The Romans' eclectic taste often makes it difficult to distinguish between an exact copy and a new creation in a retrospective style. Thanks to the new tasks and ideas given to the late and exhausted Greek art, the stimulus and guidance of Roman patronage, Roman art emerged as an unbroken continuation of Greek art.[2]

This new art, which resulted from the addition of new blood and new vigor to the old forms, has lived on through all periods of European art. It was reborn not only in the Renaissance; each later period, and indeed the present one, has profited by taking stock of its relation to Greek or Roman art. Even in the United States the so-called "Greek revival" is based on Hellenistic-Roman art; and the most modern art returns from time to time to art forms which in the last analysis are Hellenistic.

---

[2] See G. Richter, "Who Made the Roman Portrait Statues—Greeks or Romans?" in *Proceedings of the American Philosophical Society,* XCV, No. 2 (1951), 184 ff.

Chronology

CHRONOLOGY

Historical Facts and Dated Works of Art

C.400—C.330 B.C.: TRANSITION FROM THE LATE
CLASSICAL TO THE EARLY HELLENISTIC PERIOD

395/4   Corinthian War. Tombstone of Dexileos, who fell in this war. War memorial for the dead.

395–375   Sculptures of the temple of Asclepius at Epidaurus, with Timotheos as the leading sculptor.

394   Temple of Athena Alea in Tegea destroyed.

375–372   The Eirene of Kephisodotos.

370–330   Activity of Praxiteles.

367–357   Portrait of Plato by Silanion.

364–361   Praxiteles becomes famous.

364–355   Temple of Tegea rebuilt and decorated by Skopas.

362/1   Relief above treaty of Athens with Arcadia.

356/5   Relief above treaty of Athens with Neapolis in Thrace.

356   Temple of Artemis of Ephesus is burnt. In the same night Alexander the Great is born.

353   Death of Mausolus.

351   Death of Artemisia.

350   Mausoleum completed with the help of Pytheos, Timotheos, Skopas, Bryaxis, and Leochares.

350–330   Temple of Artemis in Ephesus rebuilt and partly decorated by Skopas. An altar before the temple carved by Praxiteles.

350–300   Activity of Lysippos.

347/6   Relief stele in honor of princes of the Bosporus.

344–334   Statue of Agias by Lysippos dedicated by Daochos II, tetrarch of Thessaly.

340–330   Statue of Socrates by Lysippos in the Pompeion, Athens. Statues of the three great tragedians of the fifth century set up by Lycurgus in the theater of Dionysos. Statue of Aeschines.

338   Battle of Chaeronea. Philip conquers Greece. Lion of Chaeronea. Leochares makes statues of Philip and young Alexander for Delphi.

336–323   Alexander the Great rules Greece.

335/4   Choragic monument of Lysikrates, who won a victory with a chorus at the city Dionysia at Athens.

334   Battle on the river Granicus.

333   Battle of Issus. Alexander begins conquest of Persian Empire. Abdalonymos appointed King of Syria. Alexander sarcophagus carved for him.

332/1   Deinokrates builds Alexandria in Egypt.

330   Portrait of Corinna by Silanion.

C.330—C.250 B.C.: EARLY HELLENISTIC PERIOD

323/2   Relief of archon Kephisodoros.

319   Choragic monument of Thrasyllos in Athens.

317–307   Antiluxury decree of Demetrius of Phalerum puts an end to sculptured gravestones in Athens.

315–283   Demetrius Poliorcetes.

312–281   Seleucus I (Seleucus Nicator), king of Syria.

306/5   The successors of Alexander—Seleucus, Ptolemy, Antigonos, Demetrius Poliorcetes—take the title of king.

306–281   Ptolemy I, king of Egypt.

302–290   Chares of Lindos makes the Colossus of Rhodes.

300	Antioch on the river Orontes founded by Seleucus I.
296–293	Tyche of Antioch by Eutychides.
295–280	Themis of Rhamnus by Chairestratos. Group of Niobe and children.
283–247/6	Ptolemy II (Ptolemy Philadelphus).
282–263	Philetairos ruler of Pergamon.
281–261	Antiochus I (Antiochus Soter), king of Syria.
280/79	Statue of Demosthenes by Polyeuktos.
280	Portrait of Epicurus (342–270).
277	Portrait of Metrodorus.
272	The Romans conquer Tarentum.
271	Statue of Dionysos dedicated by Thrasikles.
270	Portraits of Hermarchus, successor of Epicurus, and of Zeno, the Stoic philosopher.
270–250	Doidalsas creates the Bathing Aphrodite for King Nikomedes of Bithynia (*c.* 278–250).

C.250—C.160 B.C.: MIDDLE HELLENISTIC PERIOD

246–222	Ptolemy III (Ptolemy Euergetes).
241–197	Attalus I of Pergamon.
241–228	Wars with the Gauls.
238	First victory.
228/7	Victory over the Gauls and Antiochus Hierax. Victory monument in bronze groups. First school of Pergamon. Leading artists: Phyromachos, Nikeratos, Stratonikos, Antigonos, and Isigonos (probably identical with Epigonos).
230–190	Euthydemos of Bactria.
223–187	Antiochus III (Antiochus the Great) of Syria.
222–205	Ptolemy IV (Ptolemy Philopator).
221–207	Altar at Magnesia.
212	Syracuse taken by the Romans.
210	Portraits of Antiochus III, Ptolemy IV and Arsinoë, and Chrysippos (280–206).
209	Sack of Tarentum by Fabius Maximus. Heracles of Lysippos taken to Rome.
*c.*200	Attalus I dedicates small groups on the Acropolis of Athens. Portrait of Euthydemos. The Barberini Satyr.
200–190	The Nike of Samothrace by Pythokritos of Rhodes.
197–159	Eumenes II of Pergamon.
197/6	Titus Quinctius Flamininus sets the Greeks free from Macedonian rule.
194	Titus Quinctius Flamininus brings works of Lysippos from Macedonia to Rome.

190–160	Eukratides, king of Bactria and India.
190–160	Boethos of Chalcedon. He made a portrait of Antiochus IV.
181–165	Great altar of Pergamon, with frieze of gigantomachy, erected.
181–145	Ptolemy VI (Ptolemy Philometor).
175–164	Antiochus IV (Antiochus Epiphanes) of Syria orders copies of the Zeus and Athena by Phidias.
*c.*175–*c.*150	Damophon of Messene's sculptures at Lycosura.
167	Aemilius Paullus defeats the Greeks at Pydna. Memorial at Delphi.
166	Delos established as a free port.
164–158	Telephos frieze carved on the great altar of Pergamon.

C.160—C.30 B.C.: LATE HELLENISTIC PERIOD

162–150	Demetrius I (Demetrius Soter) of Syria.
159–138	Attalos II of Pergamon.
150–130	Hermogenes works in Magnesia.
146	Caecilius Metellus Macedonicus defeats the Macedonians. Macedonia, including Attica, becomes the Roman province Achaia. Mummius sacks Corinth. Its art treasures are sent to Rome. Timarchides and his family, Philiskos of Rhodes, and other Greek artists begin to work for the Roman victors.
145–135	Stele of the historian Polybius.
138/7	Statues of Dioskurides and Cleopatra in Delos.
133	Rome inherits Pergamon from Attalus III (138–133).
130	Frieze of temple of Artemis at Magnesia.
127	The Parthians conquer the empire of the Seleucids. Hellenistic art extended to Bactria, Scythia, China.
125	Relief of Archelaos of Priene.
*c.*100	The centaurs of Apollonios and Tauriskos of Tralles. The Borghese warrior by Agasias of Ephesus. The *symplegma* by Heliodoros. The "pantoufle" group in Delos, and other one-view groups.

Late second to early first century. The Temple of Hecate at Lagina.

First century B.C.   Hellenistic reliefs.

88–84	First Mithridatic war. Mithridates VI (Mithridates Eupator) resides at Pergamon.
88	Pasiteles becomes a Roman citizen. His pupil Stephanos is a copyist.

86   Sulla conquers Athens.

85–75   Portrait of Poseidonios, founder of an eclectic philosophical school at Rhodes.

76   Syria becomes Roman.

70–60   Apollonios of Athens and other neo-Attic artists found eclectic Graeco-Roman art.

66   Mithridates defeated by Pompey.

51–30   Cleopatra VII of Egypt.

Middle of the first century. Laocoon by Hagesandros, Polydoros, and Athanadoros, of Rhodes.

31   Egypt, the last of the Hellenistic empires, is conquered and becomes Roman.

31B.C.–A.D.14 The Emperor Augustus: 13–9 B.C., Ara Pacis.

Selected Bibliography

SELECTED BIBLIOGRAPHY

ABBREVIATIONS FOR PERIODICALS AND SERIES PUBLICATIONS

Abh. Bayr. Akad.—*Abhandlungen der Bayrischen Akademie der Wissenschaften, Munich*

Abh. Preuss. Akad.—*Abhandlungen der Preussischen Akademie der Wissenschaften, Berlin*

Abh. Sächs. Akad.—*Abhandlungen der Sächsischen Akademie der Wissenschaften, Philologisch-Historische Klasse, Leipzig*

Abh. Sächs. Ges.—*Abhandlungen der Sächsischen Gesellschaft der Wissenschaften, Philologisch-Historische Klasse, Leipzig*

Africa Italiana—*Africa Italiana; Rivista di Storia e d'Arte a Cura del Ministero delle Colonie.* Rome, 1935–43

A.J.A.—*American Journal of Archaeology*

Amelung, Vatican Kat.—W. Amelung, *Die Skulpturen des Vaticanischen Museums.* 2 vols., Berlin, 1903–6

Ann. Arch. di Atene—*Annuario della Regia Scuola Archeologica di Atene e delle Missioni Italiani in Oriente*

Ann. Brit. Sch. at Athens—*Annual of the British School at Athens.* 1895——

Ant. Denk.—*Antike Denkmäler.* 4 vols., Berlin, Kaiserlich Deutsches Archaeologisches Institut, 1891–1931

Arch. Anz.—*Anzeiger des Deutschen Archaeologischen Instituts.* Part of *Jahrbuch des Deutschen Archaeologischen Instituts, Berlin*

Arch. Zeitung—*Archaeologische Zeitung.* Vols. I–XLIII, Berlin, 1843–85

Arndt-Amelung, Einzelaufnahmen—P. Arndt and W. Amelung, *Photographische Einzelaufnahmen antiker Skulpturen.* Munich, F. Bruckmann, 1893——

Arti—*Le Arti. Rassegna Trimestrale dell'Arte Antica e Moderna.* Vols. 1–5, 1938–43

Arti Figurative—*Arti Figurative, Rivista d'Arte, Antica e Moderna.* Vols. 1–3, 1945–47

Athen. Mitt.—*Mitteilungen des Deutschen Archaeologischen Instituts, Athenische Abteilung.* 1876——

Atti Pont. Accad. Rom.—*Atti della Pontifica Accademia Romana di Archeologia, Memorie*

Ausonia—*Ausonia, Rivista della Società Italiana di Archeologia e Storia dell'Arte.* Rome, Vols. I–X, 1906–21

B.C.H.—*Bulletin de Correspondance Hellénique.* École Française d'Athènes, 1877——

Bollettino Comunale—*Bollettino della Commissione Archeologia Comunale di Roma*

Bollettino d'Arte—*Bollettino d'Arte del Ministero della Publica Istruzione* (until 1929); *Bollettino d'Arte del Ministero della Educazione Nazionale* (1929–1931); *Notizie delle Gallerie, dei Musei, e dei Monumenti d'Italia,* 1907–38, 1948 to date; 1939–47 suspended

Brunn-Bruckmann, Denkmäler—H. Brunn and F. Bruckmann, *Denkmäler griechischer und römischer Skulptur.* Continued by P. Arndt and G. Lippold. Munich, 1888–1947

Bulletin de la Société royale d'Archéologie, Alexandrie—*Société royale d'Archéologie d'Alexandrie, Bulletin,* 1898–1934; N.S. (since 1934) X, Fascicules 32–33, 1938–39

C.A.H.—*Cambridge Ancient History*

C.I.G.—*Corpus Inscriptionum Graecarum.* 4 vols. in 8. Berlin, 1828–77

C.I.L.—*Corpus Inscriptionum Latinarum.* 38 vols. Berlin, 1862–1943

Clara Rhodos—*Clara Rhodos. Istituto Storico Archeologico di Rodi.* 9 Vols., 1927–38

Crit. d'Arte—*La Critica d'Arte. Rivista Bimestrale di Arti Figurative per il Mondo Antico.* 1935——

Die Antike—*Die Antike, Zeitschrift für Kunst und Kultur des Klassischen Altertums.* Vols. I–XX, Berlin, 1925–44

Encycl. phot.—*Encyclopédie photographique de l'art.* 5 vols., Paris, Edition "TEL," 1936–49. Vol. III, 1938: *Le Musée du Louvre, Grèce, Rome*

Ephemeris Arch.—*Ephemeris Archaeologike* or *Archaeologike Ephemeris.* 1837–1951

Hesperia—*Hesperia. Journal of the American School of Classical Studies at Athens.* 1932——

Insc. Graec.—*Inscriptiones Graecae, Akademie der Wissenschaften.* Berlin, 1873–1915. Editio minor, 1913–40

Jahrbuch d. Inst.—*Jahrbuch des Deutschen Archaeologischen Instituts.* Berlin, 1886——

J.H.S.—*Journal of Hellenic Studies.* 1880——

Jones, Sculpt. Museo Capitolino—H. Stuart Jones, *A Catalogue of the Ancient Sculptures Preserved in the Municipal Collections of Rome. The Sculptures of the Museo Capitolino.* Oxford, 1912

Jones, Sculpt. Palazzo Conservatori—H. Stuart Jones, *A Catalogue of the Ancient Sculptures Preserved in the Municipal Collections of Rome. The Sculptures of the Palazzo dei Conservatori.* Oxford, 1926

J.R.S.—*Journal of Roman Studies*

Kunstgesch. in Bildern—F. Winter, *Kunstgeschichte in Bildern.* 5 vols., Leipzig, 1898–1902. 2d ed., 1912

Lippold, Vatican Kat.—Lippold, G., *Die Skulpturen des Vaticanischen Museums.* Vol. III, Part 1, Berlin, 1936; Vol. III, Part 2, in press

Mem. Amer. Acad. Rome—*Memoirs of the American Academy in Rome*

Met. Mus. Studies—*Metropolitan Museum Studies*

M.F.A. Bulletin—Bulletin of the Museum of Fine Arts, Boston

Mitt. d. Inst.—Mitteilungen des Deutschen Archaeologischen Instituts. Berlin, 1948——

M.M.A. Bulletin—Bulletin of the Metropolitan Museum of Art, New York. 1906——

Mon. Accad. Lincei—Monumenti Antichi Publicati per Cura della Reale Accademia dei Lincei, Roma. 1890——

Mon. Piot—Monuments et Mémoirs publiées par l'Académie des Inscriptions et Belles-lettres. Fondation Eugène Piot, Paris, 1894——

Nachrichten Gött. Ges.—Nachrichten der Gesellschaft der Wissenschaften zu Göttingen, Philologisch-historische Klasse

Notiziario Archeologico—Notiziario Archeologico, Italia, Ministero delle Colonie. 4 vols., Rome, 1915–27

Notizie degli Scavi—Notizie degli Scavi di Antichità, Communicate alla Accademia dei Lincei, Roma. 1876——

Oest. Jahreshefte—Jahreshefte des Oesterreichischen Archaeologischen Instituts in Wien, 1898——

Pauly-Wissowa, Real-Enc.—A. Pauly, G. Wissowa, and W. Kroll, Real-Encyclopädie der klassischen Altertums-Wissenschaft, Stuttgart, 1894——

Poole, Brit. Mus. Cat. of Coins, The Ptolemies—R. S. Poole, British Museum Catalogue of Coins, The Ptolemies, London, 1883

Praktika—Praktika tes Akademias Athenon. Athens, 1926—— Also known as *Praktika Hellenike archaiologike hetairia, Athens*

Rend. Pont. Accad.—Rendiconti della Pontificia Accademia Romana di Archeologia. 1921——

Rev. Arch.—Revue Archéologique. Paris, 1844——

Riv. del Ist. Arch.—Rivista del Reale Istituto d'Archeologia e Storia dell'Arte. 1929——

Röm. Mitt.—Mitteilungen des Deutschen Archaeologischen Instituts, Römische Abteilung. 1886——

Sitzungsber. Bayr. Akad.—Sitzungsberichte der Bayrischen Akademie der Wissenschaften, Munich. Philosophisch-Historische Klasse

Sitzungsber. Preuss. Akad.—Sitzungsberichte der Preussischen Akademie der Wissenschaften, Berlin. Philosophisch-Historische Klasse

Sitzungsber. Sächs. Akad.—Sitzungsberichte der Sächsischen Akademie der Wissenschaften, Leipzig. Philosophisch-Historische Klasse

A. H. Smith, Brit. Mus. Cat.—A. H. Smith, *A Catalogue of Sculpture in the Department of Greek and Roman Antiquities of the British Museum.* Vol. I, 1892. Vol. II, 1900. Vol. III, 1904.

Thieme-Becker, Künstlerlexikon—U. Thieme and F. Becker, *Allgemeines Lexikon der bildenden Künstler, von der Antike bis zur Gegenwart.* 37 vols. Leipzig, Engelmann, 1907–50

Vid. Sels. Skrift.—Danske Videnskabernes selskab. Arkaeologisk-Kunsthistoriske (Meddelelser) Skrifter. Vol. I, Copenhagen, 1948

Winck.-Prog. Berlin—Winckelmanns-Programme der Archaeologischen Gesellschaft zu Berlin. 1840——

I. REFERENCE BOOKS

Anderson, W. J., R. Spiers, and W. B. Dinsmoor. The Architecture of Ancient Greece. London, 1927.

Arndt, P., and W. Amelung. Photographische Einzelaufnahmen antiker Skulpturen. Munich, F. Bruckmann, 1893——

Beazley, J. D., and B. Ashmole. Greek Sculpture and Painting to the End of the Hellenistic Period. Cambridge University Press, 1932.

Bieber, M. Entwicklungsgeschichte der griechischen Tracht. Berlin, 1934.

—— The History of the Greek and Roman Theater. Princeton University Press, 1939.

Brunn, H., and F. Bruckmann, Denkmäler griechischer und römischer Skulptur. Continued by P. Arndt and G. Lippold. Munich, 1888–1947.

Bulle, H. Der schöne Mensch im Altertum. Munich and Leipzig, 1912.

Buschor, E., Die Plastik der Griechen. Berlin, Rembrandt-Verlag, 1939.

Collignon, M. Histoire de la sculpture grecque. 2 vols. Paris, 1892 and 1897.

Cultrera, G. Saggi sull' arte ellenistica e greca-romana. Vol. 1: La corrente asiana, Rome, 1907.

Delbrück, R. Hellenistische Bauten in Latium. Strassburg, 1912.

Dickins, G. Hellenistic Sculpture. Oxford, The Clarendon Press, 1920.

Dinsmoor, W. B. The Architecture of Ancient Greece. London, 1950.

Dittenberger, W. Sylloge Inscriptionum Graecarum. 4 vols. 3d ed. Leipzig, 1915–1924.

Hicks, E. L. The Collection of Ancient Greek Inscriptions in the British Museum. 1874.

Hildebrand, A. Das Problem der Form in der bildenden Kunst. 1905.

Jones, H. Stuart. Select Passages from Ancient Writers, Illustrative of the History of Greek Sculpture, with a Translation. 1895.

Klein, W. Geschichte der griechischen Kunst. Vol. 3. Leipzig, Veit and Co., 1907.

Lawrence, A. W. Later Greek Sculpture and Its Influence on East and West. London, Cape, 1927.

Lippold, G. Die griechische Plastik. Munich, 1950. Vol. III, Part 1 of Handbuch der Archaeologie, ed. W. Otto and R. Herbig. 6 parts, Munich, 1937–53.

Loewy, E. Inschriften griechischer Bildhauer. 1885.

Murray, A. S. A history of Greek Sculpture. London, 1890.

Overbeck, J. Die antiken Schriftquellen zur Geschichte der bildenden Künste bei den Griechen. Leipzig, 1868.

Pauly, A., G. Wissowa, and W. Kroll. Real-Encyclopädie der klassischen Altertums-Wissenschaft. Stuttgart, 1894——

Picard, C. La Sculpture antique de Phidias à l'ère byzantine, pp. 165–310. Paris, Laurens, 1926. Manuels d'histoire de l'art.

—— Manuel d'archéologie grecque: La Sculpture antique. 3 vols., 1935–48. Vol. III, Période classique—IV. siècle. Paris, 1948.

Rayet, O. Monuments de l'art antique. Paris, 1884.

Reinach, S. Répertoire de la statuaire, grecque et romaine. Vols. I–VI, 1906–30.

Richter, G. The Sculpture and Sculptors of the Greeks. Rev. ed., New Haven, Yale University Press, 1950.

—— Three Critical Periods in Greek Sculpture. Oxford, The Clarendon Press, 1951. Chapters II–III, pp. 15–70.

Rodenwaldt, G. Die Kunst der Antike. Berlin, Propyläen-Verlag, 1927; Propyläen-Kuntgeschichte, III. Pp. 54 ff. and plates on pp. 425–73.

Roscher, W. H. Ausführliches Lexikon der griechischen und römischen Mythologie. 6 vols. Leipzig and Berlin, 1884–1937.

Rostovtzeff, M. I. The Social and Economic History of the Hellenistic World. 3 vols. Oxford University Press, 1941.

Rumpf, A. Griechische und römische Kunst. Vol. II, Part 3 of Alfred Gercke and Eduard Norden, Einleitung in die Altertumswissenschaft. 4th ed. Leipzig, Teubner, 1932.

Seltman, G. Approach to Greek Art. London and New York, 1948.

Winter, F. Kunstgeschichte in Bildern. . . . Leipzig, Seemann, 1900. Vol. I, pp. 289–384. New ed.: I. Das Altertum, Heft 10–12. Griechische Skulptur des vierten Jahrhunderts und hellenistische Skulptur, pp. 289–384. Leipzig, Kröner, 1912.

Zschietzschmann, W. Die hellenistische und römische Kunst. Potsdam, Akademische Verlagsgesellschaft Athenaion, c.1939. Vol. II, Part 2 of Handbuch der Kunstwissenschaft.

II. DATING

Binnebössel, R. Studien zu den attischen Urkundenreliefs. 1932.

Krahmer, G. "Die Artemis im Lateran und Verwandtes," Mitteilungen des Deutschen Archaeologischen Instituts, Athenische Abteilung, LV (1930), 237–72.

—— "Die einansichtige Gruppe und die späthellenistische Kunst," Nachrichten der Gesellschaft der Wissenschaften zu Göttingen, Philogisch-Historische Klasse, 1927, pp. 53–91.

—— "Eine Ehrung für Mithradates VI Eupator in Pergamon," Archäologisches Institut des Deutschen Reichs. Jahrbuch, XL (1925), 183–205.

—— "Eine Jünglingsfigur mittelhellenistischer Zeit," Mitteilungen des Deutschen Archaeologischen Instituts, Römische Abteilung, XLVI (1931), 139–49.

—— "Stilphasen der hellenistischen Plastik," Mitteilungen des Deutschen Archaeologischen Instituts, Römische Abteilung, XXXVIII–XXXIX (1923–24), 138–89.

Laurenzi, L. "Lineamenti di arte ellenistica," Arti Figurative, I (1945), 12–28, Plates I–IX.

Müller, V., "Chronology of Greek Sculpture 400—40 B.C.," Art Bulletin, XX (1938). 359–418.

Richter, G. "Chronologie hellénistique, le second et le premier siècle avant J.C." in Actes du Congrès de la Féderation internationale des associations d'études classiques. Paris, C. Klincksieck, 1951; pp. 185–92.

Süsserott, H. K. Griechische Plastik des vierten Jahrhunderts vor Christus: Untersuchungen zur Zeitbestimmung. Frankfurt, 1938.

III. SCULPTORS

Amelung, W. Die Basis des Praxiteles aus Mantinea; Archaeologische Studien. Munich, 1895.

Arias, P. E. Skopas. Roma, L'Erma di Bretschneider, 1952. (Quaderni e guide di archeologia, diretta da R. Bianchi Bendinelli e Luisa Banti. I.)

Collignon, M. Scopas et Praxitèle. 1907.

Dickins, G. "Damophon of Messene," Annual of the British School at Athens, XII (1905/6), 109–36.

Furtwängler, A. Masterpieces of Greek Sculpture. 1895.

Gardner, E. A. Six Greek Sculptors. London, Duckworth, 1910.

Johnson, F. P. Lysippos. Durham, N. C., Duke University Press, 1927.

Klein, W. Praxiteles. Leipzig, 1898.

Maviglia, A. L'Attività artistica di Lisippo. 1914.

Neugebauer, K. A. Studien über Skopas. Leipzig, 1913.

Rizzo, G. E. Prassitele. Milan and Rome, Fratelli Treves, 1932.

Thieme, U., and F. Becker. Allgemeines Lexikon der bildenden Künstler, von der Antike bis zur Gegenwart. 37 vols. Leipzig, Engelmann, 1907–50. (Contains articles on about 40 Hellenistic sculptors by Bruno Sauer, Walter Amelung, and Margarete Bieber.)

IV. PORTRAITS

Arndt, P. Griechische und römische Porträts. Continued by G. Lippold. F. Bruckmann, Munich, 1891–1942.

Bernoulli, J. J. Die erhaltenen Darstellungen Alexanders des Grossen. Munich, Bruckmann, 1905.

—— Griechische Ikonographie. 2 Vols., Munich, 1901.

Bieber, Margarete. "The Portraits of Alexander the Great," *Proceedings of the American Philosophical Society,* XCIII (1949), 373-427.

Boehringer, E., and R. Boehringer. Homer, Bildnisse und Nachweise. Breslau, 1939.

Boehringer, R. Platon, Bildnisse und Nachweise. Breslau, 1935.

Crome, J. F. Das Bildnis Vergils. Reale Accademia Virgiliana di Mantova, Atti e Memorie, Nuova Serie, Vol. XXIV (1935).

Delbrück, R. Antike Porträts. 1912.

Graindor, P. Bustes et statues-portraits d'Egypte romain. Cairo, 1939.

Hekler, A. Bildniskunst der Griechen und Römer. (Translated as Greek and Roman Portraits, London, Heinemann, 1912.)

—— Bildnisse berühmter Griechen. 1940.

Hinks, R. P. Greek and Roman Portrait Sculpture in the British Museum. London, 1935.

Imhoof-Blumer, F. Porträtköpfe auf antiken Münzen hellenischer und hellenisierter Völker. 1885.

Lange, K. Herrscherköpfe des Altertums im Münzbild ihrer Zeit. 1938.

Laurenzi, L. Rittratti greci. Florence, Sansoni, 1941.

Lippold, G. Griechische Porträtstatuen. Munich, Bruckmann, 1912.

L'Orange, H. P. Apotheosis in Ancient Portraiture. Cambridge, Harvard University Press, 1947.

Macurdy, G. H. Hellenistic Queens. Baltimore, The Johns Hopkins Press, 1932. The Johns Hopkins Studies in Archaeology, No. 14.

Michalowski, C. "Les Portraits hellénistiques et romains," *École française d'Athènes. Exploration archéologique de Delos,* XIII, 1932.

Paribeni, R. Il ritratto nell'arte antica. Milan, Fratelli Treves, 1934.

Pfuhl, E. Die Anfänge der griechischen Bildniskunst. Munich, Bruckmann, 1927.

—— "Ikonographische Beiträge zur Stilgeschichte der Hellenistischen Kunst," *Jahrbuch des Deutschen Archaeologischen Instituts,* Vol. XLV (1930), pp. 1 ff., Figs. 1-28, Pls. I-IV.

Poulsen, F. Greek and Roman Portraits in English Country Houses. Oxford, The Clarendon Press, 1923.

—— "Iconographic Studies in the Ny Carlsberg Glyptothek," in From the Collections of the Ny Carlsberg Glyptothek. Vol. I, 1931. Vol. II, 1938.

Schefold, K. Die Bildnisse der antiken Dichter, Redner, und Denker. Basel, B. Schwabe, 1943.

Studniczka, F. Das Bildnis des Aristoteles. Leipzig, 1908.

—— Das Bildnis Menanders. Reprinted from Illberg's Neue Jahrbücher für das klassische Altertum, Vol. 41 (1918).

Suhr, E. G. Sculptured Portraits of Greek Statesmen. Baltimore, The Johns Hopkins Press, 1931. The Johns Hopkins University Studies in Archaeology, No. 13.

Ujfalvy, C. de. Le Type physique d'Alexandre le Grand. Paris, A. Fontemoing, 1902.

Vessberg, O. Studien zur Kunstgeschichte der römischen Republik. 2 vols., Leipzig, 1941.

Visconti, E. Q. Iconographie grecque. 2d ed. 3 vols. Milan, 1824-26.

West, R. Römische Porträtplastik. Vol. I. Munich, 1933.

V. SCULPTURES FROM DEFINITE SITES

Adriani, A. Documenti e ricerche d'arte alessandrina. Vol. I: Scultura monumentale del Museo Greco-Romano di Alessandria, Rome, 1946. Vol. II: Testimonianze e monumenti di scultura alessandrina, Rome, 1948.

Altertümer von Pergamon. Vols. I-IX. Berlin, K. Museen, 1885-1912. Vol. III, Part 1: J. Schrammen, Der Grosse Altar, 1906. Vol. III, Part 2: H. Winnefeld, Die Friese des Grossen Altars, 1910. Vol. VII: F. Winter, Die Skulpturen, 1908. Vol. VIII: M. Fränkel. Die Inschriften von Pergamon, 2 parts, 1890-95.

Becatti, G. "Attikà—Saggio sulla scultura attica dell'ellenismo," in *Rivista del Reale Istituto d'Archeologia e Storia dell'Arte,* VII (1940), 7-116.

Benndorf, H. Neue Untersuchungen auf Samothrake. Vol. II, 1880.

Bevan, E. R. A History of Egypt under the Ptolemaic Dynasty. London, 1927.

Bieber, M. "Späthellenistische Frauenstatuen aus Kos," in Antike Plastik, Walter Amelung zum sechzigsten Geburtstag. Berlin and Leipzig, 1928, pp. 16 ff.

Blinkenberg, C., and K. F. Kinch. Lindos, Fouilles de l'Acropole, 1902-04, in Lindos, Fouilles et recherches, 1902-14. Berlin, 1931.

Breccia, E. Alexandrea ad Aegyptum. 1922.

Brückner, A. Der Friedhof am Eridanos. Berlin, 1909.

Bruns, G. Der grosse Altar von Pergamon. Berlin, 1949.

Calza, G. La necropoli del Porto di Roma. 1940.

Cavvadias, P. (Kabbadias). Fouilles d'Épidaure. Athens, 1891.

—— Fouilles de Lycosoura. Athens, 1893.

Clara Rhodos. Studi e materiali publicati a cura dell' Istituto Storico Archeologico di Rodi. 10 vols. 1928-39. Vol. I: A. Maiuri and G. Jacopich (Jacopi), Rapporto generale. Vol. II (1932): A. Maiuri, Monumenti di scultura del Museo Archeologico di Rodi, I. Vol. IV (1931): pp. 37 ff., G. Jacopi,

La stele di Crito e Timarista. Vol. V, Part 1 (1931): G. Jacopi, Monumenti di scultura del Museo Archeologico di Rodi, II. Vol. V, Part 2 (1932): pp. 9 ff., G. Jacopi, Monumenti di Scultura del Museo Archeologico di Rodi, II (continued); pp. 65 ff., L. Laurenzi, Monumenti di scultura del Museo Archeologico di Rodi, III, e dell' Antiquarium di Coo. Vol. IX (1938): pp. 9 ff., L. Laurenzi, Monumenti di scultura del Museo Archeologico di Rodi, IV, e dell' Antiquarium di Coo, II.

Comparetti, D., and G. de Petra. La Villa Ercolanese dei Pisoni. Turin, 1883.

Curtius, E., and F. Adler, eds. Olympia, die Ergebnisse der . . . Ausgrabung. 5 vols., Berlin, 1890–97. Vol. III: G. Treu, Die Bildwerke von Olympia in Stein und Thon, 1897. Vol. IV: A. Furtwängler, Die Bronzen und die übrigen kleineren Funde von Olympia, 1890.

Defrasse, A., and H. Léchat. Épidaure: Restauration et description des principaux monuments du sanctuaire d'Asclépios. Paris, 1895.

Deubner, O. Das Asklepieion von Pergamon. Berlin, 1938.

Dörpfeld, W. Troja und Ilion. Athens, 1902.

Dugas, C., J. Berchmans, and M. Clemmensen. Le sanctuaire d'Aléa Athéna à Tégée. Paris, 1924.

Dyggve, E., F. Poulsen, and K. Rhomaios. Das Heroon von Kalydon. Copenhagen, 1948.

École Français d'Athènes. Exploration archéologique de Delos, ed. Théophile Homolle and Maurice Holleaux. 19 vols. Paris, 1909–39.

—— Fouilles de Delphes, ed. Théophile Homolle. Vols. 2–5, Paris, 1902–43. Vol. II: F. Courby, Le Sanctuaire d'Apollon. La Terrasse du temple, 1927. Vol. IV: Ch. Picard, Sculpture, 1928–31. Vol. V: P. Perdrizet, Petits Bronzes, terres cuites, antiquités diverses, 1907–9.

Espérandieu, E. Recueil générale des bas-reliefs, statues, et bustes de la Gaule romaine. 13 vols., Paris, 1907–49.

Filow, B. D. L'Art antique en Bulgarie. Sofia, 1925.

Gerkan, A. von. Der Altar des Artemis-Tempels in Magnesia. 1929.

Goldman, H. Excavations at Tarsus. Vol. I: The Hellenistic and Roman Periods. Princeton, N.J., Princeton University Press, 1950.

Hamdy-bey, O., and T. Reinach. Une Nécropole royale à Sidon. Paris, E. Leroux, 1892.

Hansen, Esther. The Attalids of Pergamon. 1947.

Herkenrath, E. Der Fries des Artemisions von Magnesia. Berlin, 1902.

Humann, K. J. Kohte, J., and C. Watzinger. Magnesia am Maeander. Berlin, Reimer, 1904.

Kabbadias, P.: *see* Cavvadias, P.

Kähler, H. Der grosse Fries von Pergamon. Berlin, Gebrüder Mann, 1948.

—— Pergamon. Berlin, Gebrüder Mann, 1949. Bilderhefte antiker Kunst, Vol. IX.

Mau, A. Pompeii in Life and Art, 1904. (Translation of Pompeji in Leben und Kunst, 1900.)

Milet, Ergebnisse der Ausgrabungen und Untersuchungen seit dem Jahre 1899, ed. Th. Wiegand. Staatliche Museen zu Berlin, 1906–28. Vol. I, Part 3 (1914): G. Kawerau and A. Rehm, Das Delphinion in Milet. Vol. I, Part 9 (1928): A. von Gerkan, F. Krischen, and K. A. Neugebauer, Thermen und Palaestren.

Napp, A. E. Der Altar von Pergamon. Munich, 1936.

Piroli, T. Le antichità di Ercolano. 6 vols., 1789–1807. Vol. V: Bronzi II, 1794.

Pontremoli, E. and M. Collignon. Pergame: Restauration et description des monuments de L'Acropole. Paris, 1900.

Salis, A. von. Der Altar von Pergamon. Berlin, Reimer, 1912.

Schober, A. Der Fries des Hekateions von Lagina. Baden bei Wien, 1933. Istanbuler Forschungen, No. 2.

—— Die Kunst von Pergamon. Vienna, 1951.

—— "Zur Amazonengruppe des attalischen Weihgeschenkes," *Jahreshefte des Oesterreichischen Archaeologischen Instituts in Wien,* XXVIII, 102–11.

Schreiber, T. Der Gallierkopf des Museums in Gizeh bei Kairo. 1906.

Schuchhardt, C. Schliemanns Ausgrabungen im Lichte der heutigen Wissenschaft. Leipzig, 1890. Translated by E. Sellers as Schliemann's Excavations: An Archeological and Historical Study by Dr. C. Schuchhardt, London and New York, 1891.

Schuchhardt, W. H. Die Meister des grossen Frieses von Pergamon. Berlin, de Gruyter, 1925.

Sieglin, E. Expedition Ernst von Sieglin. Ausgrabungen in Alexandria unter Leitung von Theodor Schreiber und unter Mitwirkung von Friedrich Wilhelm Freiherrn von Bissing, Giuseppe Botti . . . hrsg. von Ernst Sieglin. 2 vols in 9. Leipzig, 1908–27. Vol. I: Theodor Schreiber, Die Nekropole von Kôm-Esch-Schukâfa, 1908. Vol. II: Die griechisch-ägyptische Sammlung Ernst von Sieglin; Part 1A, by Rudolf Pagenstecher, 1923; Part 1B, by Carl Watzinger, 1927; Part 2, Joseph Vogt, Terrakotten, 1924; Part 3, Die Gefässe in Stein und Ton. Knochenschnitzereien, 1913.

Squarciapino, M. La Scuola di Afrodisia. Rome, 1943.

Stier, H. E. Aus der Welt des Pergamonaltars. Berlin, 1932.

Stillwell, R., ed. Antioch-on-the Orontes. Vol. III (1941). The Excavations, 1937–39.

Wiegand, T., and H. Schrader, with Contributions by G. Kummer, W. Wilberg, H. Winnefeld, and R. Zahn. Priene: Ergebnisse der Ausgrabungen und Untersuchungen in den Jahren 1895–1896. Berlin, 1904.

Winter, F. Der Alexandersarkophag von Sidon. Strassburg, K. J. Trübner, 1912.

Winter, F., et al. Die Hellenistische Kunst in Pompeji. Vol. IV: E. Pernice. Gefässe und Geräte aus Bronze. Berlin, 1923.

VI. SPECIAL GROUPS OF SCULPTURE

Beardsley, G. H. The Negro in Greek and Roman Civilization. 1929. The Johns Hopkins Studies in Archaeology, No. 4.

Bernoulli, J. J. Aphrodite. Leipzig, 1873.

Biénkowski, P. R. von. Die Darstellung der Gallier in der hellenistischen Kunst. Vienna, A. Hölder, 1908.

—— Les Celtes dans les arts mineurs gréco-romains. Cracow, Imprimerie de l'Université des Jagellons, 1928.

Birt, T. Die Buchrolle in der Kunst. Leipzig, 1907.

Conze, A. Die attischen Grabreliefs. 4 vols. in 6. Berlin, 1893–1922.

Della Seta, A. Il Nudo nell'arte, 1930.

Deubner, O. Hellenistische Apollogestalten. Athens, 1934.

Diepolder, H. Die Attischen Grabreliefs des 5. und 4. Jahrhunderts v. Chr. Berlin, 1931.

Furtwängler, A. Antike Gemmen. Leipzig, 1900.

—— Beschreibung der geschnittenen Steine. Berlin, 1896.

Hauser, F. Die Neuattischen Reliefs. Stuttgart, 1889.

Horn, R. "Hellenistische Köpfe," Archäologisches Institut des Deutschen Reichs. Mitteilungen. Römische Abteilung, LII (1937), 140–63.

—— Stehende weibliche Gewandstatuen in der hellenistischen Plastik. (Ergänzungsheft II to the Römische Mitteilungen of the German Archeological Institute. 1931.)

Ippel, A. Der Bronzefund von Galjûb: Modelle eines hellenistischen Goldschmieds. Berlin, 1922. Pelizaeusmuseum, Hildesheim, Wissenschaftliche Veröffentlichung, Vol. II.

Klein, W. Vom antiken Rokoko. Vienna, Hölzel, 1921.

Lamb, W. Greek and Roman Bronzes. London, Methuen, 1929.

Lippold, G. Gemmen und Kameen. Stuttgart, 1922.

Noshy, I. The Arts in Ptolemaic Egypt: A Study of Greek and Egyptian Influences in Ptolemaic Architecture and Sculpture. London, 1937.

Richter, G. Ancient Furniture, Greek, Etruscan, and Roman. Oxford, 1926.

Rubensohn, O. Hellenistisches Silbergerät in antiken Gipsabgüssen. 1911. Pelizaeusmuseum, Hildesheim, Wissenschaftliche Veröffentlichung, Vol. I.

Schede, M. "Zu Philiskos, Archelaos und den Museen," Archäologisches Institut des Deutschen Reichs. Mitteilungen, Römische Abteilung, XXXV (1920) 70–82.

Schmidt, E. "Über einige Fälle der Übertragung gemalter Figuren in Rundplastik," Festschrift für Paul Arndt (Munich, Bruckmann, 1925), pp. 96–114.

Schreiber, T. Die Hellenistischen Reliefbilder. Leipzig, 1894.

—— Die Wiener Brunnenreliefs aus Palazzo Grimani: Eine Studie uber das hellenistische Reliefbild mit Untersuchungen über die bildende Kunst in Alexandrien. Leipzig, 1888.

Watzinger, C. Das Relief des Archelaos von Priene. 1903. Archäologische Gesellschaft zu Berlin, Winckelmanns-Programm No. 63.

Wickhoff, F. Einleitung zur Wiener Genesis. Wien, 1895. (Translated by Eugenie Strong-Sellers as Roman Art, London, 1900.)

Williams, C. R. Couches and Beds: Studies in Ancient Furniture. Chicago, 1905.

VII. TERRA COTTAS

Burr, D. Terra-cottas from Myrina in the Museum of Fine Arts, Boston. Vienna, printed by A. Holzhausens Nachfolger, 1934.

Charbonneaux, J. Les Terres cuites grecques. Paris, L. Reynaud, 1936.

Heuzey, L. Les Figurines de terre cuites du Musée du Louvre. Paris, 1883.

Kleiner, G. Tanagrafiguren. Berlin, W. de Gruyter, 1942. (Ergänzungsheft 15 to Jahrbuch des Deutschen Archaeologischen Instituts.)

Köster, A. Die griechischen Terrakotten. Berlin, Schoetz, 1926.

Leroux, G. Lagynos, recherches sur la céramique et l'art ornemental hellénistiques. Paris, 1913.

Perdrizet, P. Les Terres cuites d'Égypte de la Collection Fouquet. Nancy and Paris, 1921.

Pottier, E. Les Statuettes de terre cuite dans l'antiquité. Paris, 1890.

Pottier, E. and S. Reinach. La Nécropole de Myrina. Paris, E. Thorin, 1887.

Walters, H. B. Catalogue of the Terracottas in the Department of Greek and Roman Antiquities. London, The British Museum, 1899.

Weber, W. Die ägyptisch-griechischen Terrakotten. Berlin, Curtius, 1914. Vol. II of Mitteilungen aus der ägyptischen Sammlung der Museen Berlin.

VIII. SINGLE SCULPTURES

Bieber, M. Laocoon: The Influence of the Group since Its Rediscovery. New York, Columbia University Press, 1942.

Blinkenberg, C. Knidia. Beiträge zur Kenntnis der Praxitelischen Aphrodite. Copenhagen, 1933.

Carpenter, R. "Observations on Familiar Statuary in Rome," *Memoirs of the American Academy in Rome,* XVIII (1941), 73–104.

Schweitzer, B. "Das Original der sogenannten Pasquino-Gruppe," *Abhandlungen der Sächischen Akademie der Wissenschaften, Philologisch-historische Klasse,* XLIII, No. 4 (1936), Figs. 1–56.

Stark, K. B. Niobe und die Niobiden, Leipzig, 1863.

Studniczka, F. "Artemis und Iphigenie," *Abhandlungen der Sächsischen Akademie der Wissenschaften, Philologisch-historische Klasse,* XXXVII, No. 5 (1926).

—— "Der farnesische Stier," *Zeitschrift für bildende Kunst,* New Series, XIV (1903), pp. 171–82.

Thiersch, H. "Die Nike von Samothrake," *Nachrichten der Gesellschaft der Wissenschaften zu Göttingen, Philologisch-Historische Klasse* (1931), pp. 336–78.

—— "Pro Samothrake," *Sitzungsberichte der Akademie der Wissenschaften in Wien, Philosophisch-Historische Klasse,* 212 Band, 1 Abhandlung, 1930.

IX. CATALOGUES OF COLLECTIONS

Amelung, W. Führer durch die Antiken in Florenz. Munich, 1897.

—— Die Sculpturen des Vaticanischen Museums. Vols. I–II (2 vols. text, 2 vols. plates). Berlin, 1903–6.

Arndt, P. La Glyptothèque Ny Carlsberg. Munich, 1896–1912.

Ashmole, B. Catalogue of the Ancient Marbles at Ince Blundell Hall. Oxford, 1929.

Aurigemma, S. Le Terme di Diocleziano e il Museo Nazionale Romano. 2d ed., Rome, 1950.

Babelon, E., and J. A. Blanchet. Catalogue des bronzes antiques de la Bibliothèque nationale. Paris, 1895.

Babelon, J. Choix des bronzes de la collection Caylus. Paris and Brussels, 1928.

Bieber, M. Antike Skulpturen und Bronzen in Kassel. 1915.

Bloesch, H. Antike Kunst in der Schweiz. Zurich, Erlenbach, 1943.

Blümel, G. Staatliche Museen zu Berlin, Katalog der Sammlung antiker Skulpturen. Vol. III: Katalog der griechischen Skulpturen des fünften und vierten Jahrhunderts v. Chr., 1929. Vol. IV: Römische Kopien griechischer Skulpturen des fünften Jahrhunderts v. Chr., 1931. Vol. V: Römische Kopien des vierten Jahrhunderts, 1938.

Bothmer, D. von. Antiquities from the Collection of W. C. Baker. New York, 1950.

Calza, Raissa. Il Museo Ostiense. Rome, 1947.

Caskey, L. D. Catalogue of Greek and Roman Sculpture. Cambridge, Mass., published for the Museum of Fine Arts, Boston, by Harvard University Press, 1925.

Catalogue général des antiquités égyptiennes du Musée du Caire. 51 vols., Cairo, 1901–1939. Vol. IV: C. C. Edgar, Greek Sculpture, 1903. Vol. V: C. C. Edgar, Greek Bronzes, 1904. Vol. VI: C. C. Edgar, Greek Moulds, 1903.

Charbonneaux, J. La Sculpture grecque au Musée du Louvre. Paris, 1936.

Chase, G. H. Greek and Roman Sculpture in American Collections. Cambridge, Harvard University Press, 1924.

Coche de la Ferté, E. La Sculpture grecque et romaine au Musée du Louvre, 1951.

Dütschke, H. Antike Bildwerke in Oberitalien. Vol. III. 1882.

Edgar, C. C. Greek Bronzes. Cairo, 1904. Vol. V of Catalogue général des antiquités égyptiennes du Musée du Caire. 51 vols., 1901–39.

—— Greek Moulds. Cairo, 1903. Vol. VI of Catalogue général des antiquités égyptiennes du Musée du Caire.

—— Greek Sculpture. Cairo, 1903. Vol. IV of Catalogue général des antiquités égyptiennes du Musée du Caire.

Filow, B. D. Sofia, Führer durch das Nationalmuseum. Sofia, 1923.

Fröhner, W. Notice de la sculpture antique du Louvre. 4th ed., Paris, 1878.

Furtwängler, A. La Collection Sabouroff. 1883–87.

Furtwängler, A., and P. Wolters. Beschreibung der Glyptothek zu München. 2d ed., 1910.

Hekler, A. Die Sammlung antiker Skulpturen. Die Budapester Samlungen. Die Antiken in Budapest. 1. Abteilung: Die Skulpturen. Vienna, 1929.

Helbig, W. Führer durch die öffentlichen Sammlungen klassischer Altertümer in Rom. 3d ed. by W. Amelung. 2 vols. Leipzig, 1912–13.

Helbig, W., and G. Barracco. La Collection Barracco. Munich, 1893.

Herrmann, P. Verzeichnis der antiken Original-Bildwerke. Dresden, Skulpturen-Sammlung, 1915.

Hill, Dorothy K. Catalogue of Bronzes in the Walters Art Gallery. Baltimore, 1949.

Jacopi, G. Lo Spedale dei Cavalieri e il Museo archeologico di Rhodi. Rome, 1932.

Jones, H. Stuart. A Catalogue of the Ancient Sculptures Preserved in the Municipal Collections of Rome. The Sculptures of the Museo Capitolino. Oxford, 1912.

—— A Catalogue of the Ancient Sculptures Preserved in the Municipal Collections of Rome. The Sculptures of the Palazzo dei Conservatori. Oxford, 1926.

Kaschnitz-Weinberg, Guido von. Scultura del Magazzino del Museo Vaticano, 1936–37. Monumenti Vaticani di archeologia e d'arte IV, Città del Vaticano I. 1937.

Kekule von Stradonitz, R. Das Akademische Kunstmuseum, Bonn. 1872.

Levi, A. Sculture nel Palazzo Ducale di Mantova. Rome, 1931.

Lippold, G. Antike Skulpturen der Glyptothek Ny Carlsberg. 1924.

—— Die Sculpturen des Vaticanischen Museums. Vol. III, Part 1, Berlin, 1936. Vol. III, Part 2, in press.

Massow, W. von. Führer durch das Pergamon-Museum. 2d. ed., 1936.

Mendel, G. Catalogue das sculptures grecques, romaines et byzantines, Musées Ottomanes. 3 vols. Constantinople [Istanbul], 1912–14.

Merlin, A. Catalogue du Musée Aloui. 2d suppl., 1921.

Michaelis, A. Ancient Marbles in Great Britain. 1882.

Milani, L. A. Il Museo Archeologico di Firenze. 2 vols., 1912.

Morcelli, F., C. Fea, and E. Q. Visconti, La Villa Albani descritta. Rome, Salviucci, 1869.

Moretti, G. Guida illustrato del Museo di Ancona. 1915.

Mustilli, D. Il Museo Mussolini, Rome, Libreria dello Stato, 1939. (The name of this museum is now Museo Nuovo.)

Paribeni, Le Terme di Diocleziano e il Museo Nazionale Romano. 3d ed., Rome, 1920; 4th ed., 1922; 5th ed., 1932. English translation: The Roman National Museum in the Thermae of Diocletian, tr. by Rose Benetti. Milan, Fratelli Treves. 1925.

Poulsen, F. Catalogue of Ancient Sculpture in the Ny Carlsberg Glyptotek. Copenhagen, 1951. There were several Danish catalogues from 1906–1940. The English catalogue retains the old numerical arrangement, used also in the Glyptotek's Volumes of Plates: Billedtavler til Kataloget over antike Kunstvaerker, 1907, as well as in the supplementary Tillaeg til Billedtavler, 1915, and 2. Tillaeg til Billedtavler, 1941.

Reinecke, W. Einführung in die griechische Plastik an der Hand von Meisterwerken im Alten Museum. 1931.

Richter, G. M. A. Catalogue of Greek Sculptures in the Metropolitan Museum of Art. Cambridge, Harvard University Press, 1954.

—— Greek, Etruscan, and Roman Bronzes. New York, Metropolitan Museum of Art, 1915.

—— Handbook of the Classical Collection. New York, Metropolitan Museum of Art, 1930.

—— Handbook of the Greek Collection. Published for the Metropolitan Museum of Art, New York, by Harvard University Press, Cambridge, 1953.

Ridder, A. de. Les Bronzes antiques du Louvre. 2 vols. Paris, 1913–15.

Roeder, G., and A. Ippel. Die Denkmäler des Pelizaeusmuseums zu Hildesheim. 1921.

Ruesch, A. Guida del Museo Nazionale di Napoli. n.d.

Schede, M. Griechische und römische Skulpturen des Antikenmuseums. Meisterwerke der türkischen Museen zu Konstantinopel, Band 1. Berlin, de Gruyter, 1928.

Schneider, R. von. Album auserlesener Gegenstände der Antikensammlung des Kaiserhauses zu Wien. 1895.

Serra, L. Il Museo Nazionale in Ancona. 1934.

Sieveking, J. Bronzen, Terrakotten, und Vasen der Sammlung Loeb. Munich, 1930.

Smith, A. H. A Catalogue of Sculpture in the Department of Greek and Roman Antiquities of the British Museum. Vol. I, 1892. Vol. II, 1900. Vol. III, 1904.

Staïs, V. Marbres et bronzes du Musée national. Athens, 1910.

Strong, E. Catalogue of Antiques of Lord Melchior. 1928.

Svoronos, J. N. (I. N. Sboronos). Das Athener Nationalmuseum. 3 vols. Athens, Bede, 1908–37.

Villefosse, Héron de. Catalogue sommaire des marbres antiques. Musée du Louvre, 1896.

Visconti, C. L. Description de la Villa Albani. New ed., 1869.

Visconti, E. Q. I monumenti di sculture antichi, Museo Torlonia, reprodotti con la fototipia. Rome, 1884. (Atlas, 161 plates.)

—— Les monuments de la sculpture antique déscrits. Museo Torlonia. Rome, 1884.

Walter, O. Beschreibung der Reliefs im kleinen Akropolismuseum in Athen. Vienna, 1923.

Walters, H. B. Catalogue of the Bronzes, Greek, Roman and Etruscan, in the Department of Greek and Roman Antiquities. London, the British Museum, 1899.

—— Catalogue of the Silver Plate in the British Museum. London, 1921.

—— Select Bronzes, Greek, Roman and Etruscan. London, the British Museum, 1915.

Wyndham, M. Catalogue of the Leconfield Collection. London, 1915.

X. NUMISMATICS

Babelon, E. Traité des monnaies grecques et romains. Paris, 1901–32. Part II, Vol. 2 and Part III, Vol. 3 (plates), 1910.

Babelon, E., and T. Reinach. Recueil general des monnaies grecques d'Asie Mineure. 1925.

Gaebler, H. Die antiken Münzen Nord-Griechenlands. Berlin, Reimer. Vol. III, Part 1, 1906. Vol. III, Part 2, 1935: Die antiken Münzen von Makedonia und Paionia.

Gardner, Percy. The British Museum Catalogue of Indian Coins, Greek and Scythic Kings of Bactria and India, ed. by R. S. Poole. 1886.

—— The British Museum Catalogue of Coins of the Seleucid Kings of Syria, ed. by R. S. Poole. 1878.

Gnecchi, F. Medaglioni romani. Milan, 1912.

Grüber, H. Roman Medallions in the British Museum, ed. R. S. Poole. London, the British Museum, 1874.

Head, B. V. British Museum, A Guide to the Principal Gold and Silver Coins of the Ancients. 2d ed., 1881.

—— Catalogue of the Greek Coins of Caria, Cos, Rhodes. London, the British Museum, 1900.

—— Catalogue of the Greek Coins of Ionia, ed. by R. S. Poole, London, the British Museum, 1892.

—— A Guide to the Principal Coins of the Greeks in the British Museum. London, 1932.

—— Historia Numorum. 2d ed., Oxford, 1911.

Hill, G. F. Catalogue of the Greek Coins of Lycaonia, Isauria and Cilicia. London, the British Museum, 1900.

—— Historical Greek Coins. New York, 1906.

—— L'Art dans les monnaies grecques. Paris, 1927.

Imhoof-Blumer, F., and P. Gardner. Numismatic Commentary on Pausanias. Reprinted from the *Journal of Hellenic Studies*, Vol. VI–VIII (1885–87.)

Lehmann, P. Williams. Statues on Coins of Southern Italy and Sicily. New York, 1946.

Newell, E. T. Royal Greek Portrait Coins. New York, 1937.

Poole, R. S. British Museum Catalogue of Coins: Alexandria and the Nomes. London, 1892.

—— British Museum Catalogue of Coins: The Ptolemies. London, 1883.

Regling, K. L. Die Münzen von Priene. Berlin, 1927.

Seltman, C. Greek Coins. 1933.

Svoronos, J. N. (I. N. Sboronos). Die Münzen der Ptolemäer. 4 vols., 1904–8.

Wroth, W. Catalogue of the Greek Coins of Galatia, Cappadocia, and Syria. 1899.

—— Catalogue of the Greek Coins of Mysia, ed. by R. S. Poole. 1892.

XI. PAINTING

Dawson, C. M. Romano-Campanian Mythological Landscape Painting. New Haven, Yale University Press, 1944. Yale Classical Studies, No. IX.

Gabriel, M. Masters of Campanian Painting. New York, 1952.

Herrmann, P., and H. Bruckmann. Denkmäler der Malerei des Altertums. Munich, 1904–44.

Lehmann, P. Williams. Roman Wall Paintings from Boscoreale in the Metropolitan Museum of Art. Cambridge, 1953.

Maiuri, A. La Casa del Menandro. Rome, 1933.

Rizzo, G. E. La pittura ellenistico-romana. Milan, 1929.

—— Monumenti della pittura antica scoperti in Italia. Sezione terza. Rome, 1936.

Index

INDEX

In the names of Greek artists the *-os* ending instead of *-us* has been used in the majority of instances.

Textual references to illustrations have been indexed, but because there is a complete list of illustrations (pp. 205-32), the figures themselves have not been individually indexed.

Plates

LIST OF PLATES

THE CHRYSIPPOS OF EUBULIDES

FIG. 238. Side View of Statue, Louvre   *Photo Archives photographiques d'Art et d'Histoire, Paris*

FIG. 239. Front View of Fig. 238   *Photo Archives photographiques d'Art et d'Histoire, Paris*

FIG. 240. Reconstruction by Erika Schob of Statuette in Figs. 238–39
From G. Kleiner, Die Inspiration des Dichters, *Fig. 112*

FIG. 241. Statuette, Museo Nuovo, Rome   *From* American Journal of Archaeology, *XXIX (1925), p. 156*

FIG. 242. Reconstruction by Arthur Milchhöfer
From A. Milchhöfer, Archaelogische Studien Heinrich Brunn dargebracht, *p. 2, Fig. 1*

HEADS OF PERSIAN SATRAPS

FIG. 243. Coin of Tissaphernes   *From K. Lange*, Herrscherköpfe des Altertums im Münzbild ihrer Zeit, *p. 35*

FIG. 244. Coin of Pharnabazus   *From K. Lange*, Herrscherköpfe des Altertums im Münzbild ihrer Zeit, *p. 33*

FIG. 245. Mausolus: Head of Cast of Statue in Fig. 249, Metropolitan Museum of Art,
New York   *Photo Metropolitan Museum of Art 130856*

FIG. 246. Mausolus: Another View of Head in Fig. 249   *Photo Metropolitan Museum of Art 130857*

FIG. 247. Silver Coin of Orontas, from Colophon   *Photo Museum of Fine Arts, Boston*

FIG. 248. Gold Coin of Orontas, from Lampsacus   *Photo Museum of Fine Arts, Boston*

CULT STATUES FROM THE MAUSOLEUM AND FIGURES FROM SARCOPHAGI

FIG. 249. Mausolus and Artemisia, from the Mausoleum; British Museum
Photo Courtesy the Trustees of the British Museum

FIG. 250. Head of Persian, from Hunting Scene on the Alexander Sarcophagus
Photo Istanbul Museum

FIG. 251. Persian Adversary of Alexander, from Battle Scene on the Alexander Sarcophagus
Photo Istanbul Museum

FIG. 252. The Amazon Sarcophagus, Kunsthistorisches Museum, Vienna
Photo Paul Frankenstein, Vienna

THE NIOBID GROUP

FIG. 253. Niobid, Uffizi Gallery, Florence   *Photo Alinari 1277*

FIG. 254. Reconstructions of Figs. 253, 255, and 256–57
From Münchner Jahrbuch für bildende Kunst, Vol. VII (1912), p. 114, Fig. 1

FIG. 255. Niobid and Sister, Vatican Museum   *Photo Alinari 26994*

FIG. 256. Youngest Son of Niobe, Uffizi Gallery, Florence   *Photo Alinari 1285*

FIG. 257. Pedagogue, Uffizi Gallery, Florence   *Photo Alinari 1276*

THE NIOBID GROUP

FIG. 258. Niobe with Youngest Girl, Uffizi Gallery, Florence   *Photo Alinari 1270*

FIG. 259. Fleeing Son, Uffizi Gallery, Florence   *Photo Alinari 1279*

FIG. 260. Dead Son, Uffizi Gallery, Florence   *Photo Alinari 1273*

FIG. 261. Artemis and Niobe, Crete
From Jahrbuch des Deutschen Archaeologischen Instituts, *Vol. XLVII (1932), p. 58, Figs. 9, 10*

FIG. 262. Reconstruction of Niobid Group by Ernst Buschor
From Münchner Jahrbuch für bildende Kunst, *IX (1914–15), 200*

FIG. 263. Reconstruction of Niobid Group by Arthur Milchhöfer
From Münchner Jahrbuch für bildende Kunst, *Vol. VII (1912), p. 116, Fig. 2*

FIGURES AND GROUPS OF THE EARLY THIRD CENTURY

FIG. 264. Running Niobid, Uffizi Gallery, Florence   *Photo Alinari 1275*

FIG. 265. Running Girl, Vatican Museum   *Photo Vasari 1123*

FIG. 341. Bronze Medallion from Galjub, Egypt; Pelizaeusmuseum, Hildesheim
From A. Ippel, Der Bronzefund von Galjub, Pl. VII, No. 73

FIG. 342. Bust from Herculaneum, Museo Nazionale, Naples
Figs. 342–43 from P. Arndt, Griechische und römische Porträts, Plates 97, 98

FIG. 343. Front View of Bust in Fig. 342   *From P. Arndt, Griechische und römische Porträts*

PORTRAITS OF BERENICE II OF CYRENE

FIG. 344. Gold Decadrachm, Museum of Fine Arts, Boston   *Photo Museum of Fine Arts*

FIG. 345. Faience Vase, Bibliothèque nationale, Paris
From R. Horn, Stehende weibliche Gewandstatuen in der hellenistischen Plastik, Pl. X, Fig. 1

FIG. 346. Head from Cyrene, Museum of Benghazi   *Figs. 346–47 from Die Antike, Vol. V (1929), Plates II, III*

FIG. 347. Profile of Head in Fig. 346   *From Die Antike, Vol. V (1929)*

PORTRAITS OF PTOLEMAIC PRINCESSES IN GRAECO-EGYPTIAN STYLE

FIG. 348. Berenice II[?], Museo Nuovo, Rome   *Photo Alinari 28063*

FIG. 349. Profile of Head in Fig. 348   *Photo Alinari 28064*

FIG. 350. Black Granite Statue of a Princess as Isis[?], Glyptothek, Munich

Photo Ackermann, Munich

FIG. 351. Statuette, Metropolitan Museum of Art, New York   *Photo Metropolitan Museum of Art 48130*

FIG. 352. Statuette, Metropolitan Museum of Art, New York   *Photo Metropolitan Museum of Art 46726*

FIG. 353. Side View of Statuette in Fig. 352   *Photo Metropolitan Museum of Art 46727*

PORTRAITS OF ARSINOË III

FIG. 354. Bronze Head, Palazzo Ducale, Mantua
Figs. 354–55 from A. Levi, Sculpture nel Palazzo Ducale di Mantova, Plates XLIV, XLV

FIG. 355. Front View of Fig. 354   *From A. Levi, Sculpture nel Palazzo Ducale di Mantova*

FIG. 356. Gold Octadrachm   *From Bollettino d'Arte, Series II, Vol. VI (1926–27), p. 550, Fig. 1*

FIG. 357. Detail of Faience Vase in Fig. 358
From R. Horn, Stehende weibliche Gewandstatuen in der hellenistischen Plastik, Pl. X, Fig. 2

FIG. 358. Faience Vase from Alexandria, Stuttgart Museum
Figs 358–59 from E. Sieglin, Expedition Ernst von Sieglin, Vol. II, Part III, Plates XXXI, XXXII

FIG. 359. Drawing of Decorations on Vase in Fig. 358

From E. Sieglin, Expedition Ernst von Sieglin, Vol. II, Part III

PORTRAITS OF PTOLEMY VI (PTOLEMY PHILOMETOR), 181–145 B.C.

FIG. 360. Silver Tetradrachm Struck in Ake (Ptolemais), Cabinet de Médailles, Paris
Photo Bibliothèque nationale, Paris

FIG. 361. Head in Alexandria   *Figs. 361–63 from Bulletin de la Société royale d'Archéologie, Alexandrie, N. S.*

Vol. X, 1, No. 32 (1938), Plates X, XI, XII

FIG. 362. Profile of Head in Fig. 361   *From Bulletin de la Société royale d'Archéologie, Alexandrie*

FIG. 363. Front View of Fig. 361   *From Bulletin de la Société royale d'Archéologie, Alexandrie*

PORTRAITS OF CLEOPATRA VII, 51–30 B.C.

FIG. 364. Bronze Coin Struck in Alexandria, Museum of Fine Arts, Boston

Photo Museum of Fine Arts

FIG. 365. Silver Tetradrachm Struck in Ascalon
Photo from Cast in Museum of American Numismatic Society, New York

FIG. 366. Head, Vatican Museum   *From G. Lippold, Die Skulpturen des Vaticanischen Museums, Vol. III, Pl. LXII*

FIG. 367. Profile of Head in Fig. 366   *From G. Lippold, Die Skulpturen des Vaticanischen Museums, Vol. III, Pl. LXII*

APHRODITE IN ALEXANDRIAN ART

FIG. 393. Two Views of Marble Head, Stuttgart Museum
From E. Sieglin, Expedition Ernst von Sieglin, *Vol. II, Part 1B, Pl. XLI*

FIG. 394. Aphrodite Unfastening Her Sandal, Marble, Metropolitan Museum of Art, New York
Photo Metropolitan Museum of Art 45525

FIG. 395. Aphrodite Unfastening Her Sandal, Terra Cotta, Metropolitan Museum of Art, New York
Photo Metropolitan Museum of Art 56513

FIG. 396. Aphrodite from Cyrene, Museo Nazionale Romano, Rome
Photo Chauffourier 1715

FIG. 397. Back View of Statue in Fig. 396
Photo Chauffourier 1717

HERACLES AND ODYSSEUS IN ALEXANDRIAN ART

FIG. 398. Bronze Statuette of Heracles from Alexandria, Walters Art Gallery, Baltimore
Photo Walters Art Gallery

FIG. 399. Two Lamps and a Bowl from Alexandria
From E. Sieglin, Expedition Ernst von Sieglin, *Vol. I, Pl. LXX, Figs. 1, 2, 5*

FIG. 400. Polyphemus, Museo Capitolino, Rome
From H. Stuart Jones, A Catalogue of the Ancient Sculptures Preserved in the Municipal Collections of Rome. Sculptures of the Museo Capitolino, *Pl. V, No. 35*

FIG. 401. Ram Carrying Odysseus, Museo Torlonia, Rome
Photo German Archaeological Institute, Rome 35.81

FIG. 402. Ram Carrying Odysseus, Palazzo Doria, Rome
Photo Alinari 29773

ALEXANDRIAN SCHOLARSHIP

FIG. 403. Ptolemy IV on Silver Tetradrachm; Collection of Mrs. Edward T. Newell, New York
Photo American Numismatic Society

FIG. 404. Ptolemy IV and Arsinoë III on Relief by Archelaos of Priene
From Bollettino d'Arte, *Series II, Vol. VI (1926–27), p. 353, Fig. 3*

FIG. 405. Personification of the Nile, from Alexandria; Tübingen Museum
From E. Sieglin, Expedition Ernst von Sieglin, *Vol. II, Part 1B, Pl. XLIII*

FIG. 406. Three Views of a Muse with Kithara, from Alexandria; Tübingen Museum
From E. Sieglin, Expedition Ernst von Sieglin, *Vol. II, Part 1B, Pl. XLIII*

FIG. 407. Personification of the Nile, Vatican Museum
Photo Anderson 1426

ALEXANDRIAN PERSONIFICATIONS

FIG. 408. Personification of Cubits of the Nile Flood, from Fig. 407
Photo Anderson 5312

FIG. 409. Head of the Nile, from Fig. 407
Photo Anderson 5340

FIG. 410. Inside of the Tazza Farnese, Showing Symbolic Representation of the Fertility of Egypt; Museo Nazionale, Naples
Photo Alinari 19089

FIG. 411. Outside of Tazza Farnese (Fig. 410), Showing Head of Medusa
Photo Alinari 19090

PORTRAITS OF ALEXANDER THE GREAT

FIG. 412. Statuette from Priene
From E. Suhr, Sculptured Portraits of Greek Statesmen (Baltimore, The John Hopkins Press, 1931), *Fig. 12*

FIG. 413. Another View of Fig. 412
Figs. 413–14 from C. de Ujfalvy, Le Type physique d'Alexandre le Grand, *Plates XII, XIII*

FIG. 414. Profile of Fig. 412
From C. de Ujfalvy, Le Type physique d'Alexandre le Grande

FIG. 415. Coin of Lysimachos, Minted at Magnesia
Photo American Numismatic Society, New York

THE ATTALIDS OF PERGAMON

FIG. 416. Coin with Head of Philetairos, Museum of Fine Arts, Boston
Photo Museum of Fine Arts

GAY SATYRS

FIG. 573. Satyr, Red Marble, Vatican Museum   *Photo Anderson 1377*

FIG. 574. Head of Satyr, Louvre   *Photo Giraudon 2096*

FIG. 575. Satyr with Wineskin, Vatican Museum   *Photo Anderson 1326*

FIG. 576. Satyr Falling Asleep, Museo Nazionale, Naples   *Photo Alinari 11225*

DRUNKEN HERACLES

FIG. 577. Bronze Statuette, Metropolitan Museum of Art, New York   *Photo Metropolitan Museum of Art 29551*

FIG. 578. Side View of Fig. 577   *Photo Metropolitan Museum of Art 29552*

FIG. 579. Bronze Statuette, Walters Art Gallery, Baltimore   *Photo Walters Art Gallery No. 54.1035*

FIG. 580. Back View of Statuette in Figs. 577-78   *Photo Metropolitan Museum of Art 29553*

CENTAURS

FIG. 581. Heads of Old Centaur and Eros, Louvre   *From J. Charbonneaux, La Sculpture grecque au Musée du Louvre, Pl. XLVII*

FIG. 582. Head of Fauno colla Macchia, Glyptothek, Munich   *From Brunn-Bruckmann, Denkmäler griechischer und römischer Skulptur, Pl. 740*

FIG. 583. Old Centaur with Eros, Louvre   *Photo Alinari 22573*

FIG. 584. Young Centaur in Dark Grey Marble, Museo Capitolino, Rome   *Photo Edizione Inalterabile*

OLD DERELICTS

FIG. 585. Head of Old Nurse, Vollmer Collection, New York   *Photo Arndt-Amelung, Einzelaufnahmen No. 4738*

FIG. 586. Bronze Bottle in Form of Old Woman, Louvre   *Photo Archives photographiques d'Art et d'Histoire, Paris*

FIG. 587. Old Nurse with Baby, Metropolitan Museum of Art, New York   *Photo Metropolitan Museum of Art 113164*

FIG. 588. Old Pedagogue with Pupil, Metropolitan Museum of Art, New York   *Photo Metropolitan Museum of Art 56461*

FIG. 589. Two Old Men: Left, from Athens; Right, from Smyrna. Louvre   *Photo Louvre*

FIG. 590. Old Peasant Woman, Metropolitan Museum of Art, New York   *Photo Metropolitan Museum of Art 6028*

SHEPHERDS AND FISHERMEN

FIG. 591. Shepherdess Going to Market, Palazzo dei Conservatori, Rome   *Photo Anderson 1754*

FIG. 592. Fishermen, British Museum   *Photo Courtesy the Trustees of the British Museum*

FIG. 593. Torso of Fisherman, Metropolitan Museum of Art, New York   *Photo Metropolitan Museum of Art 46493*

FIG. 594. Old Shepherd: Relief Formerly in Pollak Collection, Rome   *Photo Courtesy of Dr. Ludwig Pollak*

FIG. 595. Fisherman, Black Marble, Louvre   *From Encyclopédie photographique de l'art, Vol. III, p. 266*

PORTRAITS OF OLD POETS

FIG. 596. Aristophanes[?], Bronze; Museo Nazionale, Naples   *Photo Alinari 11244*

FIG. 597. Aristophanes[?], Uffizi Gallery, Florence   *Photo Alinari 1315*

FIG. 598. Homer, Bronze, Museo Archeologico, Florence   *Photo Alinari 17053*

FIG. 599. Homer, Louvre   *Photo Giraudon 1257*

ELEGANT LADIES

FIG. 600. Draped Lady, Terra Cotta; Walters Art Gallery, Baltimore *Photo Walters Art Gallery*

FIG. 601. Terra Cotta, Metropolitan Museum of Art, New York
Photo Metropolitan Museum of Art 56464

FIG. 602. Terra Cotta, Metropolitan Museum of Art, New York
Photo Metropolitan Museum of Art 125106

FIG. 603. Kneeling Woman: Terra Cotta from Myrina, Louvre
From J. Charbonneaux, Les Terres cuites grecques, Pl. 68, Fig. 75

FIG. 604. Lady Arranging Her Hair, Palazzo Colonna, Rome
From Arndt-Amelung, Einzelaufnahmen No. 1144

FIG. 605. Lady Binding Her Hair with a Fillet, Walters Art Gallery, Baltimore
Photo Walters Art Gallery No. 23.83

APHRODITE

FIG. 606. Aphrodite Removing Her Sandal: Bronze, Museo Nazionale, Naples *Photo Sommer 7559*

FIG. 607. Aphrodite Removing Her Sandal: Bronze from Paramythia, British Museum
Photo Courtesy the Trustees of the British Museum

FIG. 608. Aphrodite Undressing: Statuette from Egypt, Louvre *Photo Giraudon 19235*

FIG. 609. Aphrodite, Louvre *From W. Klein, Vom antiken Rokoko, Pl. III*

FIG. 610. Aphrodite, Vatican Museum *Photo Alinari 6674*

FLYING EROS

FIG. 611. Two Flying Cupids, Terra Cotta; Metropolitan Museum of Art, New York
Photo Metropolitan Museum of Art 756

FIG. 612. Terra Cotta, Metropolitan Museum of Art, New York *Photo Metropolitan Museum of Art 143491*

FIG. 613. Eros with Kithara: Bronze from Mahdia, in Tunis
From Monuments et Mémoirs publiées par l'Académie des Inscriptions et Belles-lettres,
Fondation Eugène Piot, Vol. XVIII (1910), Pl. I

FIG. 614. Terra Cotta from Myrina, Louvre *Photo Alinari 23769*

FIG. 615. Eros in Chiton: Terra Cotta from Myrina, Louvre *Photo Alinari 23761*

INNOCENT SLEEP

FIG. 616. Head of the Eros in Fig. 617 *Photo Metropolitan Museum of Art 131041*

FIG. 617. Sleeping Eros, Bronze; Metropolitan Museum of Art, New York
Photo Metropolitan Museum of Art 131094

FIG. 618. Back View of Fig. 617 *Photo Metropolitan Museum of Art 131095*

FIG. 619. Sleeping Girl, Museo Nazionale Romano, Rome *Photo Moscioni 9206*

FIG. 620. Sleeping Eros, Palazzo dei Conservatori, Rome
From Journal of Hellenic Studies, Vol. XLII (1922), Pl. X, Fig. 3

RESTLESS SLEEP

FIG. 621. Endymion, Nationalmuseum, Stockholm
From Brunn-Bruckmann, Denkmäler griechischer und römischer Skulptur, Pl. 510

FIG. 622. Endymion, British Museum *Photo Mansell 1232, London*

FIG. 623. Hermaphrodite, Louvre *From J. Charbonneaux, La Sculpture grecque au Musée du Louvre, Pl. XLV*

FIG. 624. Ariadne, Museo Archeologico, Florence
From Brunn-Bruckmann, Denkmäler griechischer und römischer Skulptur, Pl. 168

FIG. 625. Hermaphrodite, Museo Nazionale Romano, Rome *Photo Anderson 2160*

FIG. 1. RECONSTRUCTION OF TOMB TERRACE

FIG. 2. MARBLE LEKYTHOS
Cleveland Museum of Art

FIG. 3. TOMB RELIEF OF HEGESO
Athens

FIG. 4. TOMBSTONE
Altes Museum, Berlin

ATTIC TOMB RELIEFS, EARLY FOURTH CENTURY B.C.

FIG. 5. TOMBSTONE OF TYNNIAS
National Museum, Athens

FIG. 6. TOMBSTONE
Cleveland Museum of Art

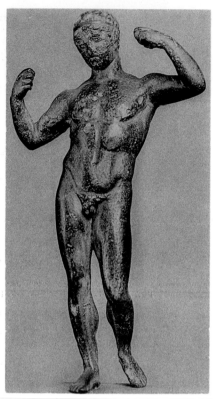

FIG. 7. BRONZE STATUETTE
Cabinet des Médailles, Paris

FIG. 9. BRONZE STATUETTE
Metropolitan Museum of Art, New York

FIG. 10. BACK VIEW OF FIG. 9,
WITHOUT FILLET

FIG. 8. TERRA-COTTA STATUETTE
Metropolitan Museum of Art, New York

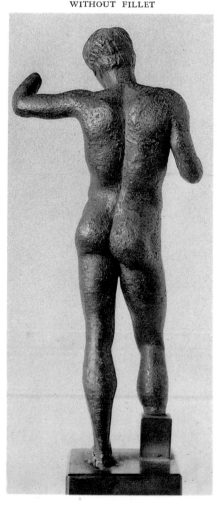

ATTIC TOMBSTONES AND STATUETTES BASED ON THE DIADUMENOS OF POLYKLEITOS

FIG. 11. HERMES BY PRAXITELES
Olympia Museum (Alinari Photo)

FIG. 12. HEAD OF FIG. 11
(Alinari Photo)

FIG. 14. HERMES OF ANDROS
National Museum, Athens (Alinari Photo)

FIG. 13. FOOT OF FIG. 11

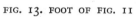

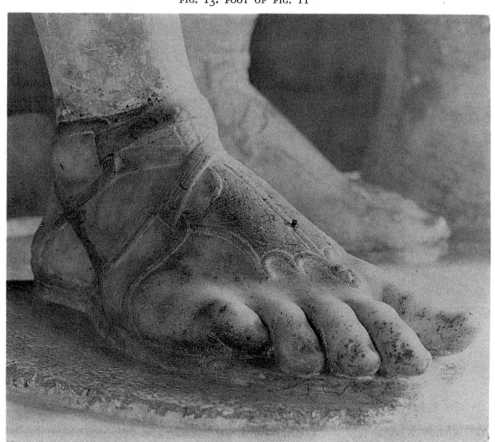

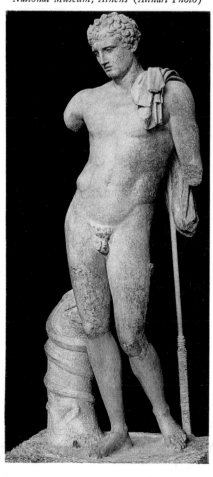

HERMES BY PRAXITELES

FIG. 15. POURING SATYR
Skulpturen-Sammlung, Dresden

FIG. 16. TORSO OF SATYR
Louvre (Alinari Photo)

FIG. 17. APOLLO LYKEIOS
Louvre (Alinari Photo)

FIG. 18. APOLLO SAUROCTONUS
Vatican Museum (Anderson Photo)

SATYRS AND APOLLO BY PRAXITELES

FIG. 21. HEAD OF FIG. 20

FIG. 19. YOUTH OF SUTRI
Museo Nazionale Romano, Rome
(Alinari Photo)

FIG. 20. IVORY STATUETTE
Agora Museum, Athens

FIG. 22. HEAD
Museo Barracco, Rome

FIG. 23. BRONZE HEAD
Museo Nazionale Romano, Rome (Alinari Photo)

COPIES AND ADAPTATIONS OF THE APOLLO LYKEIOS BY PRAXITELES

FIG. 24. HEAD OF CNIDIAN APHRODITE
Vatican Museum (Alinari Photo)

FIG. 25. CNIDIAN APHRODITE
Vatican Museum

FIG. 26. BRONZE STATUETTE
Metropolitan Museum of Art, New York

FIG. 27. SIDE VIEW OF FIG. 26

THE CNIDIAN APHRODITE AND HELLENISTIC ADAPTATION

FIG. 28. HEAD OF MEDICI APHRODITE
Uffizi Gallery, Florence (Anderson Photo)

FIG. 29. APHRODITE
Glyptothek, Munich

FIG. 30. MEDICI APHRODITE
Uffizi Gallery, Florence

FIG. 31. SIDE VIEW OF FIG. 30
(Alinari Photo)

EARLY HELLENISTIC APHRODITES DERIVED FROM PRAXITELES

FIG. 32. TORSO FROM KOS
Istanbul Museum

FIG. 33. HEAD FROM KOS
Stuttgart, Württembergisches Landesmuseum, Altes Schloss

FIG. 34. CAPITOLINE APHRODITE
Museo Capitolino, Rome (Alinari Photo)

FIG. 35. BACK VIEW OF FIG. 34

FIG. 34. CAPITOLINE APHRODITE
Museo Capitolino, Rome (Alinari Photo)

SONS AND LATER FOLLOWERS OF PRAXITELES

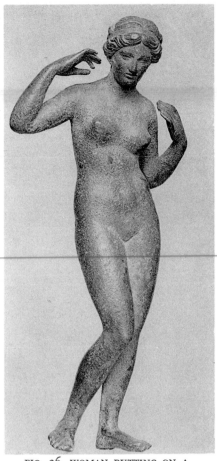

FIG. 36. WOMAN PUTTING ON A
NECKLACE
British Museum

FIG. 37. WOMAN ARRANGING HER HAIR

FIG. 38. WOMAN PUTTING ON A STEPHANE
Metropolitan Museum of Art, New York

FIG. 39. WOMAN HOLDING A STRAND OF HAIR
Skulpturen-Sammlung, Dresden

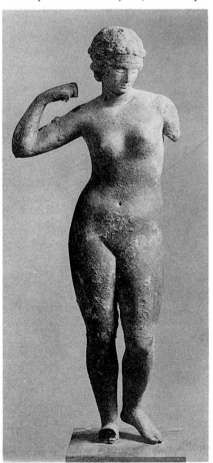

BRONZE STATUETTES OF WOMEN WITH PRAXITELEAN MOTIFS

FIG. 40. YOUTHFUL ARTEMIS
Skulpturen-Sammlung, Dresden

FIG. 41. ARTEMIS OF LARNACA
Kunsthistorisches Museum, Vienna

FIG. 42. TORSO OF ARTEMIS
Landgrafen-Museum, Kassel

FIG. 43. TORSO FROM KOS
Istanbul Museum

THE ARTEMIS OF PRAXITELES AND WORK OF FOLLOWERS

FIG. 44. THALIA
Vatican Museum (Alinari Photo)

FIG. 45. POLYHYMNIA
Vatican Museum (Anderson Photo)

FIG. 46. HEAD OF FIG. 45
(Anderson Photo)

FIG. 47. BRONZE STATUE OF ATHENA
Museo Archeologico, Florence

EARLY HELLENISTIC MUSES AND ATHENA

FIG. 48. BOY WITH KNUCKLEBONES
Metropolitan Museum of Art, New York

FIG. 49. GIRL WITH FAN
Louvre

FIG. 50. SEATED BOY
Metropolitan Museum of Art, New York

FIG. 52. GROUP OF TWO GIRLS
Louvre (Alinari Photo)

FIG. 51. SEATED GIRL
Louvre

FIG. 53. GIRL PLAYING KNUCKLEBONES
Metropolitan Museum of Art, New York

EARLY HELLENISTIC TERRA-COTTA STATUETTES FROM TANAGRA

FIG. 54. HEAD OF MELEAGER
Fogg Art Museum, Harvard University

FIG. 55. HEAD FROM TEGEA
National Museum, Athens (Alinari Photo)

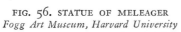

FIG. 56. STATUE OF MELEAGER
Fogg Art Museum, Harvard University

FIG. 57. BACK VIEW OF FIG. 56

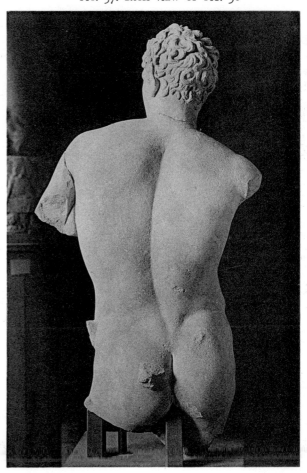

SKOPAS

FIG. 58. ATALANTA FROM TEGEA
National Museum, Athens

FIG. 59. MAENAD
Skulpturen-Sammlung, Dresden

FIG. 60. SIDE VIEW OF FIG. 59

FIG. 61. BATTLE OF GREEKS AND AMAZONS ON FRIEZE FROM MAUSOLEUM OF HALICARNASSUS
British Museum

SKOPAS

FIG. 62. STATUE OF POTHOS
Uffizi Gallery, Florence (Alinari Photo)

FIG. 63. TRITON
Vatican Museum (Anderson Photo)

FIG. 64. CHARIOTEER ON FRIEZE FROM MAUSOLEUM OF
HALICARNASSUS
British Museum

FIG. 65. AMAZON ON FRIEZE FROM MAUSOLEUM OF
HALICARNASSUS
British Museum

SKOPAS

FIG. 66. THANATOS, ALCESTIS, AND HERMES ON A COLUMN
DRUM FROM EPHESUS
British Museum

FIG. 67. HERMES, PERSEPHONE, AND HADES ON A COLUMN
DRUM FROM EPHESUS
British Museum

FIG. 68. COLUMN BASE FROM EPHESUS
British Museum

FIG. 69. TOMB RELIEF FROM THE ILISSOS
National Museum, Athens (Alinari Photo)

SCOPADIC ART IN EPHESUS AND ATHENS

FIG. 70. DEMETER OF CNIDUS
British Museum

FIG. 71. HEAD OF FIG. 70

FIG. 72. HELLENISTIC HEAD
British Museum

FIG. 73. HEAD FROM MAUSOLEUM OF HALICARNASSUS
British Museum

FIG. 72. HELLENISTIC HEAD
British Museum

WORKS IN THE SPIRIT OF SKOPAS

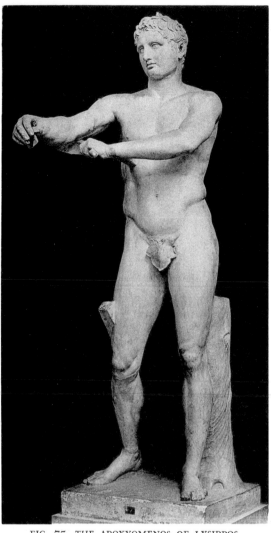

FIG. 76. STATUE OF AGIAS
Delphi Museum (Alinari Photo)

FIG. 74. THE APOXYOMENOS OF LYSIPPOS
Vatican Museum (Anderson Photo)

FIG. 75. THE APOXYOMENOS OF LYSIPPOS
Vatican Museum (Anderson Photo)

FIG. 77. RELIEF SHOWING ATHLETES SCRAPING THEMSELVES
Acropolis, Athens

LYSIPPOS'S APOXYOMENOS AND AGIAS

FIG. 78. HERACLES CAPTURING THE HIND, BRONZE
Museo Civico, Palermo (Alinari Photo)

FIG. 79. FARNESE HERACLES, BRONZE
Villa Albani, Rome (Alinari Photo)

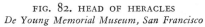

FIG. 80. HERACLES EPITRAPEZIOS
British Museum

FIG. 81. HERACLES EPITRAPEZIOS
Museo Nazionale, Naples (Alinari Photo)

FIG. 82. HEAD OF HERACLES
De Young Memorial Museum, San Francisco

FIG. 83. HEAD OF HERACLES
Taranto Museum (Alinari Photo)

HERACLES BY LYSIPPOS

FIG. 84. FARNESE HERACLES
Museo Nazionale, Naples (Alinari Photo)

FIG. 85. SILENUS WITH THE CHILD DIONYSOS
Vatican Museum (Anderson Photo)

FIG. 86. YOUNG SATYR PLAYING THE
FLUTE
Louvre

FIG. 87. EROS WITH BOW
British Museum

LYSIPPOS

FIG. 88. HEAD OF EROS
Walters Art Gallery, Baltimore

FIG. 89. HEAD OF EROS
British Museum

FIG. 91. DANCER
Museo Nazionale Romano, Rome
(Anderson Photo)

FIG. 90. DANCER
Museo Nazionale Romano, Rome

FIG. 92. DANCER
Bibliothèque nationale, Paris

FIG. 93. PRAYING BOY
IN BRONZE BY BOIDAS
Altes Museum, Berlin

FIG. 94. DANCING SATYR
Gallery of Villa Borghese, Rome (Anderson Photo)

FIG. 95. DANCING SATYR IN BRONZE
FROM CASA DEL FAUNO, POMPEII
Museo Nazionale, Naples (Alinari Photo)

FIG. 96. ANOTHER VIEW OF FIG. 95
(Alinari Photo)

SUCCESSORS OF LYSIPPOS

FIG. 97. HEAD OF STATUE FOUND IN ANZIO
Museo Nazionale Romano, Rome (Anderson Photo)

FIG. 98. ANOTHER VIEW OF FIG. 97
(Anderson Photo)

FIG. 99. STATUE
Museo Nazionale Romano, Rome (Anderson Photo)

FIG. 100. ANOTHER VIEW
OF FIG. 99
(Anderson Photo)

THE SACRIFICING WOMAN BY PHANIS, A PUPIL OF LYSIPPOS

FIG. 101. TEEN-AGE GIRL
Palazzo dei Conservatori, Rome (Anderson Photo)

FIG. 102. TYCHE OF ANTIOCH, BY EUTYCHIDES
Vatican Museum (Alinari Photo)

FIG. 103. THE LUDOVISI ARES
Museo Nazionale Romano, Rome (Anderson Photo)

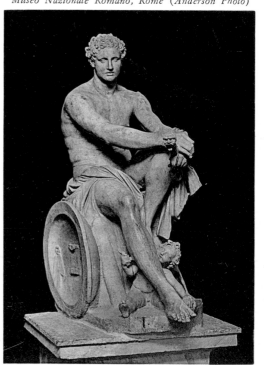

FIG. 104. TORSO OF ARES FROM PERGAMON

FIG. 105. TORSO OF ARES
Museo Nazionale, Naples

SEATED FIGURES OF THE SCHOOL OF LYSIPPOS

FIG. 106. HERMES
IN BRONZE FROM HERCULANEUM
Museo Nazionale, Naples (Alinari Photo)

FIG. 107. ANOTHER VIEW OF FIG. 106
(Alinari Photo)

FIG. 108. HEAD OF FIG. 106
(Alinari Photo)

FIG. 110. BRONZE STATUETTE
OF HERMES
Metropolitan Museum of Art, New York

FIG. 109. BRONZE STATUETTE
OF HERMES
Loeb Collection

FIG. 111. ANOTHER VIEW
OF FIG. 110

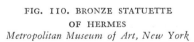

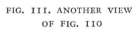

SEATED HERMES, SCHOOL OF LYSIPPOS

FIG. 112. HEAD OF PLATO
Vatican Museum

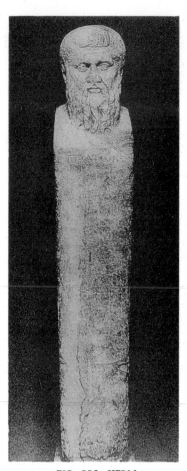

FIG. 113. HERM
Altes Museum, Berlin

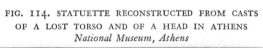

FIG. 114. STATUETTE RECONSTRUCTED FROM CASTS
OF A LOST TORSO AND OF A HEAD IN ATHENS
National Museum, Athens

FIG. 115. ANOTHER VIEW OF FIG. 114

THE PLATO OF SILANION

FIG. 116. HEAD OF PLATO

FIG. 117. FRONT VIEW OF FIG. 116

FIG. 118. RIGHT PROFILE OF FIG. 116

FIG. 119. LEFT PROFILE OF FIG. 116

THE PLATO OF SILANION: HEAD IN BOEHRINGER COLLECTION, GENEVA

FIG. 120. FRONT AND BACK VIEWS OF STATUETTE
Compiègne Museum

FIG. 121. HEAD OF FIG. 120

FIG. 122. PROFILE VIEW OF HEAD OF FIG. 120

FIG. 123. COIN FROM NORTHERN GREECE WITH ARTEMIS
RELATED TO SILANION'S CORINNA

THE CORINNA OF SILANION

FIG. 124. RELIEF
Museo Nazionale, Naples

FIG. 125. HERM
Vatican Museum

FIG. 126. BRONZE HEAD
Glyptothek, Munich

FIG. 127. FRONT VIEW OF FIG. 126

A CONTEMPORARY PORTRAIT OF SOCRATES

FIG. 128. PROFILE OF HERM
Louvre

FIG. 129. FRONT VIEW OF FIG. 128

FIG. 130. HEAD
Museo Nazionale Romano, Rome (Anderson Photo)

FIG. 131. MOSAIC IN COLOGNE

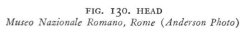

THE SOCRATES OF LYSIPPOS

FIG. 132. DRAWING MADE IN THE EIGHTEENTH CENTURY

FIG. 133. FORMER CONDITION OF STATUE IN FIG. 134

FIG. 134. RECONSTRUCTION OF STATUE
Ny Carlsberg Glyptotek, Copenhagen

FIG. 135. FRONT VIEW OF FIG. 134

STATUE OF SOCRATES BY LYSIPPOS

FIG. 137. ANOTHER VIEW OF FIG. 136
(*Alinari Photo*)

FIG. 136. HEAD
Villa Albani, Rome

FIG. 138. STATUETTE
British Museum

FIG. 139. ANOTHER VIEW OF FIG. 138

HELLENISTIC PORTRAITS OF SOCRATES

FIG. 140. TETRADRACHM STRUCK BY PHILETAIROS
Cabinet des Médailles, Paris

FIG. 141. BRONZE BUST FROM HERCULANEUM
Museo Nazionale, Naples

FIG. 142. PROFILE VIEW OF FIG. 141

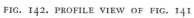

FIG. 143. FRONT VIEW OF FIG. 141

PORTRAITS OF SELEUCUS I (SELEUCUS NICATOR) OF SYRIA

FIG. 144. BRONZE HEAD FROM OLYMPIA
National Museum, Athens (Alinari Photo)

FIG. 145. PROFILE OF HERM FROM
HERCULANEUM
Museo Nazionale, Naples

FIG. 146. FRONT VIEW OF FIG. 145

FIG. 149. BRONZE STATUETTE FROM HERCULANEUM
Museo Nazionale, Naples (Alinari Photo)

FIG. 147. COIN OF DEMETRIUS
POLIORCETES

FIG. 148. REVERSE OF COIN IN
FIG. 147

LYSISTRATOS AND TEISIKRATES

FIG. 150. MEDALLION
Marbury Hall, England

FIG. 151. HEAD OF THE BUST OF MENANDER IN FIGS. 154–55

FIGS. 154–55

FIG. 153. ROMAN THEATER TICKET
FROM ALEXANDRIA, BOTH SIDES

FIG. 152. DRAWINGS OF LOST URSINUS MEDALLION, BY THEODORUS GALLAEUS

REPRESENTATIONS OF MENANDER

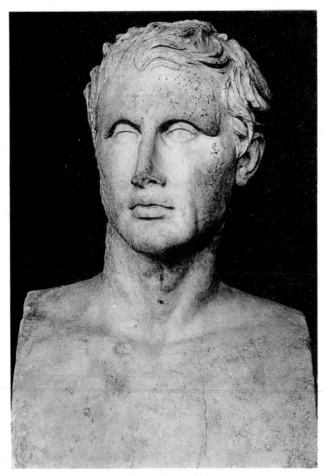

FIG. 154. BUST
Museum of Fine Arts, Boston

FIG. 155. PROFILE OF BUST IN FIG. 154

FIG. 156. BUST
Seminario Patriacale, Venice

FIG. 157. PROFILE OF FIG. 156

PORTRAITS OF MENANDER

FIG. 158. GEM

FIG. 159. BRONZE BUST FROM HERCULANEUM
Museo Nazionale, Naples

FIG. 160. HEAD FROM DOUBLE HERM
Museo Capitolino, Rome

FIG. 161. HEAD
Metropolitan Museum of Art, New York

FIG. 162. THREE-QUARTER VIEW OF FIG. 161

PORTRAITS OF EPICURUS

FIG. 163. STATUE
Ince Blundell Hall, England

FIG. 164. SIDE VIEW OF FIG. 163

FIG. 165. STATUE
Museo Archeologico, Florence

FIG. 166. STATUE
Formerly in Palazzo Margherita, Rome
Now in Ny Carlsberg Glyptotek, Copenhagen

STATUES OF EPICURUS

FIG. 167. BUST
Museo Capitolino, Rome

FIG. 168. PROFILE OF FIG. 167

FIG. 169. PROFILE OF BUST
National Museum, Athens

FIG. 170. FRONT VIEW OF BUST
National Museum, Athens

PORTRAITS OF METRODORUS

FIG. 171. BUST OF EPICURUS
Museo Capitolino, Rome

FIG. 172. HEAD OF METRODORUS FROM DOUBLE HERM
Museo Capitolino, Rome

FIG. 173. STATUE OF METRODORUS
Ny Carlsberg Glyptotek, Copenhagen

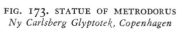

FIG. 174. FRONT VIEW OF FIG. 173

PORTRAITS OF METRODORUS AND EPICURUS

FIG. 175. BRONZE BUST FROM HERCULANEUM
Museo Nazionale, Naples

FIG. 176. STATUE
Museo Archeologico, Florence

FIG. 177. PROFILE OF BUST
Budapest Museum

FIG. 178. FRONT VIEW OF BUST
Budapest Museum

PORTRAITS OF HERMARCHUS

FIG. 179. BRONZE BUST OF AESCHYLUS
Museo Archeologico, Florence (Alinari Photo)

FIG. 180. BRONZE BUST OF SOPHOCLES
Museo Archeologico, Florence (Alinari Photo)

FIG. 181. INSCRIBED BUST OF SOPHOCLES
Vatican Museum (Anderson Photo)

FIG. 182. BRONZE BUST OF SOPHOCLES
British Museum

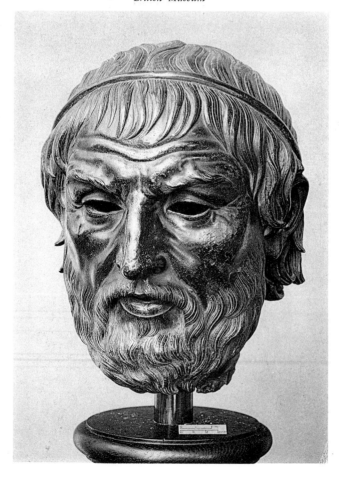

PORTRAITS OF AESCHYLUS AND SOPHOCLES

FIG. 183. HEAD OF SOPHOCLES IN THE LATERAN: CAST MADE BEFORE
RESTORATION
Cast in Villa Medici, Rome

FIG. 184. STATUETTE OF SOPHOCLES
Bibliothèque nationale, Paris

FIG. 187. DRAWING OF LOST
STATUETTE OF EURIPIDES

FIG. 185. EURIPIDES ON HERM FROM RIETI
Ny Carlsberg Glyptotek, Copenhagen

FIG. 188. DRAWING OF BUST
OF ARISTOTLE
Vatican Library

FIG. 189. DRAWING OF BUST
OF ARISTOTLE, BY RUBENS

FIG. 186. HEAD OF EURIPIDES
British Museum

PORTAITS OF SOPHOCLES, EURIPIDES, AND ARISTOTLE

FIG. 190. PROFILE OF HEAD
Kunsthistorisches Museum, Vienna

FIG. 191. FRONT VIEW OF HEAD IN FIG. 190

FIG. 192. BRONZE HEAD
Museo Nazionale, Naples

FIG. 193. PROFILE OF HEAD IN FIG. 192

PORTRAITS OF ARISTOTLE

FIG. 194. HERM
Vatican Museum (Alinari Photo)

FIG. 195. FRONT VIEW OF HERM IN FIG. 194

FIG. 196. HERM
British Museum

FIG. 197. STATUE
Museo Nazionale, Naples

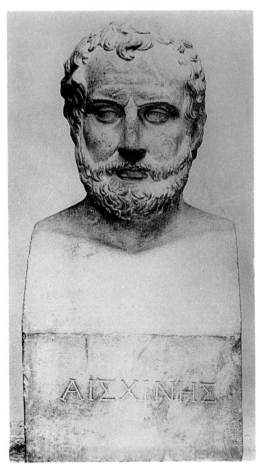

PORTRAITS OF AESCHINES

FIG. 198. GANYMEDE
Vatican Museum (Anderson Photo)

FIG. 199. THE APOLLO BELVEDERE
Vatican Museum

FIG. 200. THE APOLLO BELVEDERE
Vatican Museum (Anderson Photo)

FIG. 201. THE ARTEMIS OF VERSAILLES
Louvre

WORKS BY LEOCHARES

FIG. 202. HOUND OR LIONESS
Kerameikos, Athens (Alinari Photo)

FIG. 203. LOUTROPHOROS
National Museum, Athens (Alinari Photo)

FIG. 204. TOMB STATUE
OF MOURNING WOMAN FROM ACHARNAI
Altes Museum, Berlin

FIG. 205. ANOTHER VIEW OF TOMB STATUE
IN FIG. 204

ATTIC TOMB MONUMENTS

FIG. 206. FRAGMENT OF TOMB RELIEF
National Museum, Athens

FIG. 207. HEAD FROM TOMB RELIEF
National Museum, Athens

FIG. 209. WOMAN FROM TOMB
MONUMENT
Metropolitan Museum of Art, New York

FIG. 208. GIRL FROM TOMB MONUMENT
Metropolitan Museum of Art, New York

ATTIC TOMB MONUMENTS

FIG. 210. ATHENA
FROM CASTRA PRAETORIA, ROME
Museo Nuovo, Rome (Alinari Photo)

FIG. 211. BACK VIEW OF FIG. 210
(Alinari Photo)

FIG. 213. DIONYSOS FROM MONUMENT OF
THRASYLLOS
British Museum

FIG. 212. HEAD OF FIG. 210
(Alinari Photo)

ATTIC STATUES OF ATHENA AND DIONYSOS, EARLY HELLENISTIC PERIOD

FIG. 214. BRONZE BUST FROM HERCULANEUM
Museo Nazionale, Naples

FIG. 215. HEAD
Ashmolean Museum, Oxford University

FIG. 216. SILVER MEDALLION
Altes Museum, Berlin

FIG. 217. TWO VIEWS OF HEAD
Ny Carlsberg Glyptotek, Copenhagen

THE DEMOSTHENES OF POLYEUKTOS

FIG. 218. STATUE
Braccio Nuovo of the Vatican Museum

FIG. 219. HEAD OF STATUE
Ny Carlsberg Glyptotek, Copenhagen

FIG. 220. RIGHT PROFILE OF FIG. 219

FIG. 221. LEFT PROFILE OF FIG. 219

THE DEMOSTHENES OF POLYEUKTOS

FIG. 222. FRONT VIEW OF HEAD OF STATUE
Vatican Museum (Anderson Photo)

FIG. 223. PROFILE OF FIG. 222

FIG. 224. RECONSTRUCTION OF STATUE
Vatican Museum

FIG. 225. SIDE VIEW OF FIG. 224

THE DEMOSTHENES OF POLYEUKTOS

FIG. 226. BRONZE STATUETTE
Strauss-Hess Collection, New York

FIG. 227. FRONT VIEW OF FIG. 226

FIG. 228. BACK VIEW OF FIG. 226

FIG. 229. LEFT PROFILE OF FIG. 226

THE DEMOSTHENES OF POLYEUKTOS

FIG. 230. BRONZE STATUETTE
Metropolitan Museum of Art, New York

FIG. 231. FRONT VIEW OF FIG. 230
Metropolitan Museum of Art, New York

FIG. 232. SEATED PHILOSOPHER
Metropolitan Museum of Art, New York

FIG. 233. BRONZE STATUETTE
British Museum

STATUETTES OF PHILOSOPHERS, THIRD CENTURY B.C.

FIG. 234. HERM
Vatican Museum

FIG. 235. PROFILE OF FIG. 234

FIG. 236. HEAD
Metropolitan Museum of Art, New York

FIG. 237. FRONT VIEW OF FIG. 236

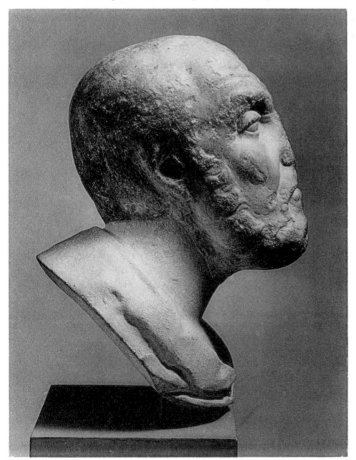

HEAD OF CHRYSIPPOS BY EUBULIDES

FIG. 238. SIDE VIEW OF STATUE
Louvre

FIG. 239. FRONT VIEW OF FIG. 238

FIG. 241. STATUETTE
Museo Nuovo, Rome

FIG. 240. RECONSTRUCTION BY ERIKA SCHOB
OF STATUETTE IN FIGS. 238–39

FIG. 242. RECONSTRUCTION
BY ARTHUR MILCHHÖFER

THE CHRYSIPPOS OF EUBULIDES

FIG. 243. COIN OF TISSAPHERNES

FIG. 244. COIN OF PHARNABAZUS

FIG. 245. MAUSOLUS: HEAD OF CAST
OF STATUE IN FIG. 249
Metropolitan Museum of Art, New York

FIG. 246. MAUSOLUS:
ANOTHER VIEW OF HEAD IN FIG. 249

FIG. 248. GOLD COIN OF ORONTAS, FROM LAMPSACUS

FIG. 247. SILVER COIN OF ORONTAS, FROM COLOPHON

HEADS OF PERSIAN SATRAPS

FIG. 249. MAUSOLUS AND ARTEMISIA, FROM THE MAUSOLEUM
British Museum

FIG. 250. HEAD OF PERSIAN
FROM HUNTING SCENE ON THE
ALEXANDER SARCOPHAGUS

FIG. 251. PERSIAN ADVERSARY
OF ALEXANDER, FROM BATTLE SCENE
ON THE ALEXANDER SARCOPHAGUS

FIG. 252. THE AMAZON SARCOPHAGUS
Kunsthistorisches Museum, Vienna

CULT STATUES FROM THE MAUSOLEUM AND FIGURES FROM SARCOPHAGI

FIG. 253. NIOBID
Uffizi Gallery, Florence (Alinari Photo)

FIG. 254. RECONSTRUCTIONS
OF FIGS. 253, 255, AND 256-57

FIG. 255. NIOBID AND SISTER
Vatican Museum (Alinari Photo)

FIG. 256. YOUNGEST SON OF NIOBE
Uffizi Gallery, Florence (Alinari Photo)

FIG. 257. PEDAGOGUE
Uffizi Gallery, Florence (Alinari Photo)

THE NIOBID GROUP

FIG. 258. NIOBE WITH YOUNGEST GIRL
Uffizi Gallery, Florence (Alinari Photo)

FIG. 259. FLEEING SON
Uffizi Gallery, Florence (Alinari Photo)

FIG. 260. DEAD SON
Uffizi Gallery, Florence (Alinari Photo)

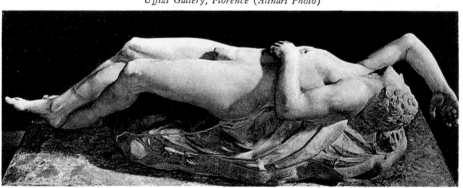

FIG. 261. ARTEMIS AND NIOBE
Crete

FIG. 263. RECONSTRUCTION OF NIOBID GROUP,
BY ARTHUR MILCHHÖFER

FIG. 262. RECONSTRUCTION OF NIOBID GROUP, BY ERNST BUSCHOR

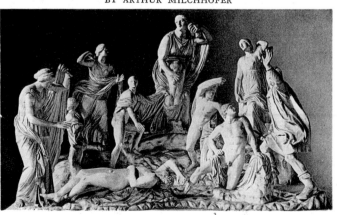

THE NIOBID GROUP

FIG. 264. RUNNING NIOBID
Uffizi Gallery, Florence (Alinari Photo)

FIG. 265. RUNNING GIRL
Vatican Museum

FIG. 266. YOUTH FROM SUBIACO
Museo Nazionale Romano, Rome (Anderson Photo)

FIG. 267. WRESTLERS
Uffizi Gallery, Florence

FIGURES AND GROUPS OF THE EARLY THIRD CENTURY

FIG. 268. ARTEMIS AND IPHIGENIA
Ny Carlsberg Glyptotek, Copenhagen

FIG. 269. ARTEMIS AND IPHIGENIA
RECONSTRUCTION BY FRANZ STUDNICZKA

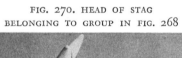

FIG. 270. HEAD OF STAG
BELONGING TO GROUP IN FIG. 268

FIG. 271. RECONSTRUCTION OF GROUP IN FIGS. 268–69
AFTER DRAWING BY INGEBORG CHRISTINE BIEBER

GROUP OF ARTEMIS AND IPHIGENIA

FIG. 272. GROUP
Loggia dei Lanzi, Florence

FIG. 273. THE PASQUINO GROUP
Before Palazzo Braschi, Rome

FIG. 274. RECONSTRUCTION OF GROUP
BY BERNHARD SCHWEITZER

FIG. 275. FRONT VIEW OF GROUP IN FIG. 274

MENELAOS WITH BODY OF PATROCLUS

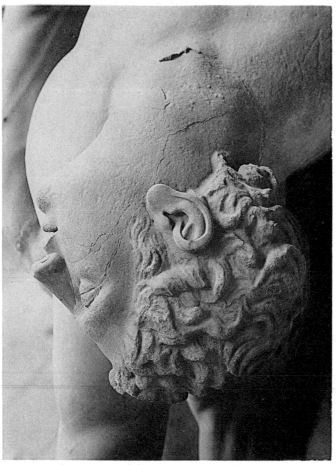

FIG. 276. HEAD OF PATROCLUS, FROM GROUP IN FIG. 272
(*Alinari Photo*)

FIG. 277. HEAD OF MENELAOS
Vatican Museum (*Alinari Photo*)

FIG. 278. PENTHESILEA, FROM SETTE BAGNI
Palazzo Borghese, Rome

FIG. 280. TORSO OF ACHILLES
Museo Nuovo, Rome (*Alinari Photo*)

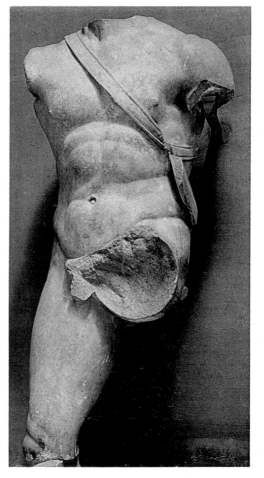

FIG. 279. TWO VIEWS OF GROUP OF ACHILLES WITH PENTHESILEA
RECONSTRUCTED BY GIUSEPPE LUGLI

HEROIC GROUPS, THIRD CENTURY B.C.

FIG. 281. GAULISH CHIEFTAIN
KILLING HIS WIFE AND HIMSELF
Museo Nazionale Romano, Rome (Anderson Photo)

FIG. 282. FRONT VIEW OF FIG. 281
(Anderson Photo)

FIG. 283. ANOTHER VIEW OF GROUP IN FIG. 281

FIG. 284. THE DRUNKEN WOMAN BY MYRON
Glyptothek, Munich

GROUPS OF THE SECOND HALF OF THE THIRD CENTURY B.C.

FIG. 285. BOY STRANGLING A GOOSE
Museo Capitolino, Rome (Anderson Photo)

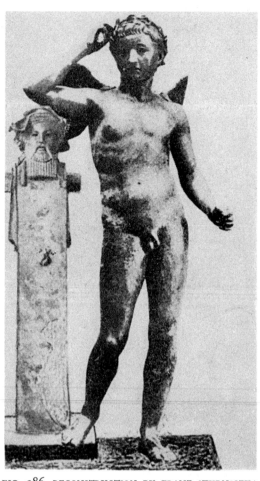

FIG. 286. RECONSTRUCTION BY FRANZ STUDNICZKA
OF THE AGON OF BOETHOS

FIG. 287. AGON
Musée du Bardo, Tunis

FIG. 288. HERM IN FIG. 286

FIG. 289. ANOTHER VIEW OF FIG. 287

WORKS OF BOETHOS

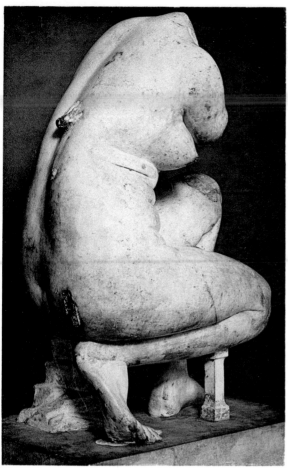

FIG. 290. APHRODITE FOUND IN VIENNE
Louvre

FIG. 291. ANOTHER VIEW OF FIG. 290
(*Alinari Photo*)

FIG. 292. BRONZE
Privately Owned, Paris

FIG. 293. APHRODITE
Formerly in Borghese Collection, Now in the Louvre

THE BATHING APHRODITE OF DOIDALSAS

FIG. 294. APHRODITE ARRANGING HER HAIR
Rhodes Museum

FIG. 295. BACK VIEW OF FIG. 294

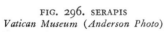

FIG. 296. SERAPIS
Vatican Museum (Anderson Photo)

FIG. 297. SERAPIS, BASALT
Villa Albani, Rome (Alinari Photo)

DOIDALSAS[?] AND BRYAXIS

FIG. 298. RIDER, PERHAPS DEMETRIOS OF BACTRIA
In Private Possession

FIG. 299. A RULER AS HERMES,
FROM POMPEII
Museo Nazionale, Naples

FIG. 300. PROFILE OF HEAD IN FIG. 299

FIG. 301. FACE OF RULER IN FIG. 299

BRONZE STATUETTES OF HELLENISTIC RULERS

FIG. 302. PROFILE OF HEAD
Ny Carlsberg Glyptotek, Copenhagen

FIG. 303. FACE OF HEAD IN FIG. 302

FIG. 304. SILVER COIN
Museum of Fine Arts, Boston

FIG. 305. PLASTER CAST
Pelizaeusmuseum, Hildesheim

REPRESENTATIONS OF PTOLEMY I

FIG. 306. GOLD COIN WITH BUSTS OF PTOLEMY I AND BERENICE I
Museum of Fine Arts, Boston

FIG. 307. STUCCO RELIEF OF PTOLEMY I AND BERENICE I
Alexandria Museum

FIG. 309. CAMEO WITH HEAD OF PTOLEMY I
Kunsthistorisches Museum, Vienna

FIG. 308. GOLD COIN WITH HEADS OF PTOLEMY II AND ARSINOË II
Museum of Fine Arts, Boston

THE FIRST AND SECOND PTOLEMIES AND THEIR WIVES

FIG. 310. COIN STRUCK IN BACTRIA
Museum of Fine Arts, Boston

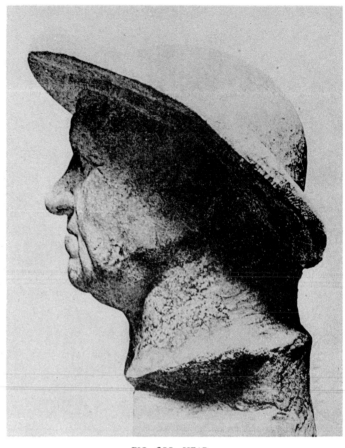

FIG. 311. HEAD
Villa Albani, Rome

FIG. 312. ANOTHER VIEW OF HEAD IN FIG. 311

FIG. 313. ANOTHER VIEW OF HEAD IN FIG. 311

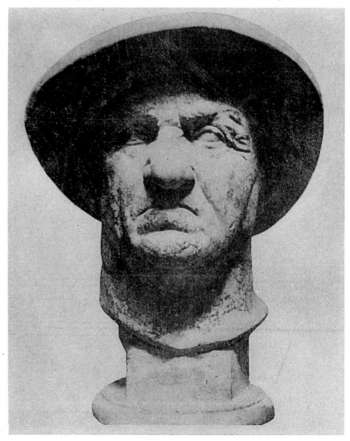

REPRESENTATIONS OF EUTHYDEMOS I OF BACTRIA

FIG. 314. COIN
WITH HEAD OF MITHRIDATES III

FIG. 315. COIN
WITH HEAD OF ARIARATHES III

FIG. 316. COIN
WITH HEAD OF ANTIMACHOS I OF BACTRIA
Museum of Fine Arts, Boston

FIG. 317. HEAD OF ANTIMACHOS I OF BACTRIA
Ny Carlsberg Glyptotek, Copenhagen

FIG. 318. PROFILE VIEW OF HEAD IN FIG. 317

RULERS OF THE MIDDLE HELLENISTIC PERIOD

FIG. 319. ANTIOCHUS III OF SYRIA
Louvre

FIG. 320. FRONT VIEW OF FIG. 319

FIG. 321. ANTIOCHUS III ON COIN
Metropolitan Museum of Art, New York

FIG. 322. NABIS OF SPARTA ON COIN

FIG. 323. TITUS QUINCTIUS FLAMININUS
ON COIN

RULERS OF THE MIDDLE HELLENISTIC PERIOD

FIG. 324. AGATHOKLES OF BACTRIA

FIG. 325. MITHRIDATES IV OF PONTUS

FIG. 326. OROPHERNES OF CAPPADOCIA

FIG. 327. ALEXANDER BALAS AND CLEOPATRA THEA

COINS OF MIDDLE HELLENISTIC RULERS

FIG. 328. HEAD WITH SHAWL
Alexandria

FIG. 329. ANOTHER VIEW OF FIG. 328

FIG. 330. HEAD
WITH ATTRIBUTES OF ISIS
Louvre

FIG. 331. HEAD WITH TWISTED LOCKS
Metropolitan Museum of Art, New York

FIG. 332. STATUE
Ince Blundell Hall, England

FIG. 333. STATUE
Uffizi Gallery, Florence

ALEXANDRIAN HEADS AND FIGURES WITH ISIS HEADDRESS

FIG. 334. ALEXANDER THE GREAT
Cleveland Museum of Art

FIG. 335. ANOTHER VIEW OF FIG. 334

FIG. 336. PTOLEMY IV
(PTOLEMY PHILOPATOR)
Museum of Fine Arts, Boston

FIG. 337. ANOTHER VIEW
OF HEAD IN FIG. 336

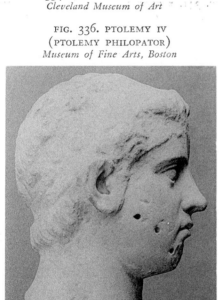

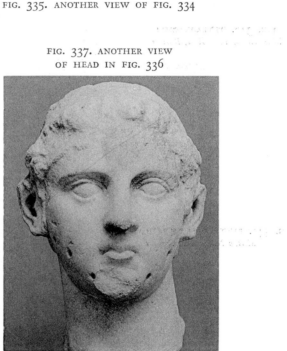

FIG. 338. ARSINOË III
Museum of Fine Arts, Boston

FIG. 339. ANOTHER VIEW OF HEAD IN
FIG. 338

ALEXANDRIAN PORTRAITS OF THE THIRD CENTURY B.C.

FIG. 340. TETRADRACHM
Museum of Fine Arts, Boston

FIG. 341. BRONZE MEDALLION FROM GALJUB, EGYPT
Pelizaeusmuseum, Hildesheim

FIG. 342. BUST FROM HERCULANEUM
Museo Nazionale, Naples

FIG. 343. FRONT VIEW OF BUST IN FIG. 342

PORTRAITS OF PTOLEMY III (PTOLEMY EUERGETES)

FIG. 344. GOLD DECADRACHM
Museum of Fine Arts, Boston

FIG. 345. FAIENCE VASE
Bibliothèque nationale, Paris

FIG. 346. HEAD FROM CYRENE
Museum of Benghazi

FIG. 347. PROFILE OF HEAD IN FIG. 346

PORTRAITS OF BERENICE II OF CYRENE

FIG. 348. BERENICE II[?]
Museo Nuovo, Rome (Alinari Photo)

FIG. 349. PROFILE OF HEAD IN FIG. 348
(Alinari Photo)

FIG. 350. BLACK GRANITE
STATUE OF A PRINCESS
AS ISIS[?]
Glyptothek, Munich

FIG. 351. STATUETTE
*Metropolitan Museum
of Art, New York*

FIG. 352. STATUETTE
*Metropolitan Museum
of Art, New York*

FIG. 353. SIDE VIEW
OF STATUETTE IN FIG. 352

PORTRAITS OF PTOLEMAIC PRINCESSES IN GRAECO-EGYPTIAN STYLE

FIG. 354. BRONZE HEAD
Palazzo Ducale, Mantua

FIG. 355. FRONT VIEW OF FIG. 354

FIG. 357. DETAIL OF FAIENCE VASE
IN FIG. 358

FIG. 358. FAIENCE VASE FROM ALEXANDRIA
Stuttgart Museum

FIG. 356. GOLD OCTADRACHM

FIG. 359. DRAWING OF DECORATIONS ON VASE
IN FIG. 358

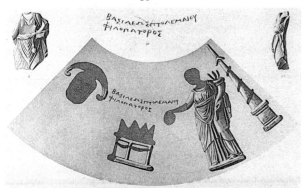

PORTRAITS OF ARSINOË III

FIG. 360. SILVER TETRADRACHM STRUCK IN AKE (PTOLEMAIS)
Cabinet des Médailles, Paris

FIG. 361. HEAD IN ALEXANDRIA

FIG. 362. PROFILE OF HEAD IN FIG. 361

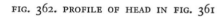

FIG. 363. FRONT VIEW OF FIG. 361

PORTRAITS OF PTOLEMY VI (PTOLEMY PHILOMETOR), 181–145 B.C.

FIG. 364. BRONZE COIN STRUCK IN ALEXANDRIA
Museum of Fine Arts, Boston

FIG. 365. SILVER TETRADRACHM STRUCK IN ASCALON
Cast in Museum of American Numismatic Society, New York

FIG. 366. HEAD
Vatican Museum

FIG. 367. PROFILE OF HEAD IN FIG. 366

PORTRAITS OF CLEOPATRA VII, 51–30 B.C.

FIG. 368. HEAD OF CLEOPATRA VII [?]
British Museum

FIG. 369. FRONT VIEW OF HEAD IN FIG. 368

FIG. 370. RELIEF FROM TEMPLE OF ISIS
AT PHILAE: PTOLEMY II BEFORE ANUKIT

FIG. 371. RELIEF FROM TEMPLE AT DENDERA:
CLEOPATRA VII

GRAECO-EGYPTIAN HEAD AND RELIEFS

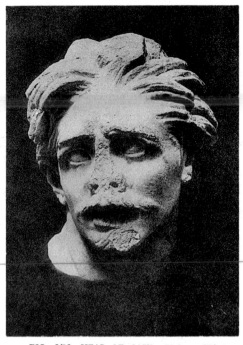

FIG. 372. HEAD OF GAUL
Cleveland Museum of Art

FIG. 373. HEAD OF GAUL, FROM GIZEH

FIG. 374. LITTLE GIRL
WITH GARLAND
Louvre

FIG. 375. "TANAGRA" FIGURINES
Alexandria Museum

FIG. 376. HUNCHBACK
IN MARBLE
*Metropolitan Museum of Art,
New York*

FIG. 377. HUNCHBACK
IN TERRA COTTA
*Metropolitan Museum of Art,
New York*

ALEXANDRIAN MARBLE AND TERRA-COTTA SCULPTURE

FIG. 378. DANCER
Baker Collection, New York

FIG. 379. ANOTHER VIEW OF DANCER IN FIG. 378

FIG. 380. RUNNING NEGRO
Metropolitan Museum of Art, New York

FIG. 381. STREET BOY
Bibliothèque nationale, Paris

ALEXANDRIAN LOW-CLASS TYPES IN BRONZE

FIG. 382. ACTOR OF THE NEW COMEDY
BRONZE
Art Museum, Princeton University

FIG. 383. BACK VIEW OF BRONZE
IN FIG. 382

FIG. 384. BOTTLE IN SHAPE OF NEGRO SLAVE
Fouquet Collection, Paris

FIG. 385. GROTESQUE HEADS
Sieglin Collection

FIG. 386. DEATH BRIDE
Sieglin Collection

FIG. 387. THE GODDESS BESA OR BESET
Sieglin Collection

ALEXANDRIAN GROTESQUES

FIG. 388. HEAD OF SERAPIS
Sieglin Collection

FIG. 389. ARES AND APHRODITE, TERRA COTTA
Sieglin Collection

FIG. 391. TWO FIGURES OF WOMEN ADORNING THEMSELVES: TERRA COTTAS
FROM CYRENE
Louvre

FIG. 390. APHRODITE
ARRANGING HER HAIR, FAIENCE
Brooklyn Museum, New York

FIG. 392. THREE TERRA-COTTA FIGURES OF HARPOKRATES
Sieglin Collection

SERAPIS, APHRODITE, AND HARPOKRATES

FIG. 393. TWO VIEWS OF MARBLE HEAD
Stuttgart Museum

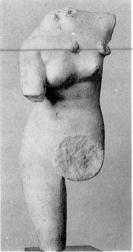

FIG. 394. APHRODITE UNFASTENING HER SANDAL, MARBLE
Metropolitan Museum of Art, New York

FIG. 395. APHRODITE
UNFASTENING HER SANDAL, TERRA COTTA
Metropolitan Museum of Art, New York

FIG. 396. APHRODITE FROM CYRENE
Museo Nazionale Romano, Rome

FIG. 397. BACK VIEW OF STATUE IN FIG. 396

APHRODITE IN ALEXANDRIAN ART

FIG. 398. BRONZE STATUETTE
OF HERACLES FROM ALEXANDRIA
Walters Art Gallery, Baltimore

FIG. 399. TWO LAMPS AND A BOWL
FROM ALEXANDRIA

FIG. 400. POLYPHEMUS
Museo Capitolino, Rome

FIG. 402. RAM CARRYING ODYSSEUS
Palazzo Doria, Rome (Alinari Photo)

FIG. 401. RAM CARRYING ODYSSEUS
Museo Torlonia, Rome

HERACLES AND ODYSSEUS IN ALEXANDRIAN ART

FIG. 403. PTOLEMY IV ON SILVER TETRADRACHM
Collection of Mrs. Edward T. Newell, New York

FIG. 404. PTOLEMY IV AND ARSINOË III
ON RELIEF BY ARCHELAOS OF PRIENE

FIG. 405. PERSONIFICATION OF THE NILE, FROM ALEXANDRIA
Tübingen Museum

FIG. 406. THREE VIEWS
OF A MUSE WITH KITHARA, FROM ALEXANDRIA
Tübingen Museum

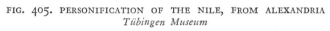

FIG. 407. PERSONIFICATION OF THE NILE
Vatican Museum (Anderson Photo)

ALEXANDRIAN SCHOLARSHIP

FIG. 408. PERSONIFICATIONS OF CUBITS
OF THE NILE FLOOD, FROM FIG. 407
(*Anderson Photo*)

FIG. 410. INSIDE OF THE TAZZA FARNESE
SHOWING SYMBOLIC REPRESENTATION OF THE FERTILITY OF EGYPT
Museo Nazionale, Naples (*Alinari Photo*)

FIG. 409. HEAD OF THE NILE, FROM FIG. 407
(*Anderson Photo*)

FIG. 411. OUTSIDE OF TAZZA FARNESE (FIG. 410)
SHOWING HEAD OF MEDUSA
(*Alinari Photo*)

ALEXANDRIAN PERSONIFICATIONS

FIG. 412. STATUETTE FROM PRIENE

FIG. 413. ANOTHER VIEW OF FIG. 412

FIG. 414. PROFILE OF FIG. 412

FIG. 415. COIN OF LYSIMACHOS, MINTED AT MAGNESIA

PORTRAITS OF ALEXANDER THE GREAT

FIG. 416. COIN WITH HEAD OF PHILETAIROS
Museum of Fine Arts, Boston

FIG. 417. COIN WITH HEAD OF EUMENES II

FIG. 418. BUST OF PHILETAIROS, FROM HERCULANEUM
Museo Nazionale, Naples

FIG. 419. FRONT VIEW OF BUST IN FIG. 418

THE ATTALIDS OF PERGAMON

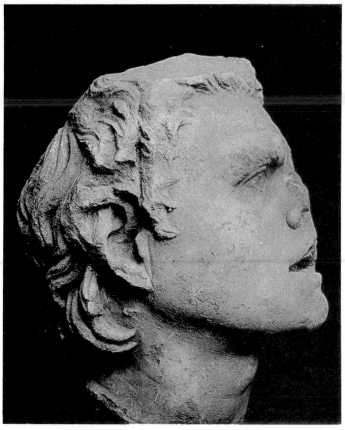

FIG. 420. PROFILE OF HEAD OF WARRIOR FOUND IN DELOS
Museum of Mykonos

FIG. 421. FRONT VIEW OF HEAD IN FIG. 420

FIG. 423. HEAD OF ASCLEPIUS
Museo Nazionale Romano, Rome (Anderson Photo)

FIG. 422. FALLEN WARRIOR FOUND IN DELOS
National Museum, Athens (Alinari Photo)

WORKS OF PHYROMACHOS AND NIKERATOS

FIG. 425. HEAD OF DYING PERSIAN
Museo Nazionale Romano, Rome

FIG. 424. HEAD OF GAULISH CHIEFTAIN
Museo Nazionale Romano, Rome

FIG. 426. HEAD OF DYING TRUMPETER SHOWN IN FIG. 427
Museo Capitolino, Rome (Alinari Photo)

FIG. 427. DYING TRUMPETER
Museo Capitolino, Rome
(Anderson Photo)

VICTORY MONUMENT OF ATTALUS I OF PERGAMON

FIG. 428. HEAD OF WARRIOR
Museo Comunale, Rome (Alinari Photo)

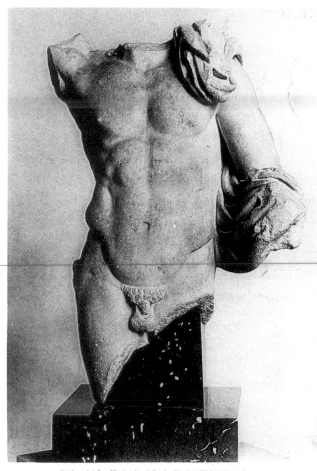

FIG. 429. TORSO OF A HELLENISTIC RULER
Altes Museum, Berlin

FIG. 431. WOUNDED GAUL
Louvre (Alinari Photo)

FIG. 430. GAUL FALLING BACKWARD
Museo Archeologico, Venice (Alinari Photo)

FIGURES FROM WAR MEMORIALS OF ATTALUS I

FIG. 432. HEAD OF THE
DEAD PERSIAN IN FIG. 435
Museo Nazionale, Naples

FIG. 433. HEAD OF
FIGHTING PERSIAN
Vatican Museum

FIG. 434. HEAD OF
DEAD GIANT IN FIG. 435

FIG. 435. CLOCKWISE FROM LOWER LEFT: DEAD PERSIAN, DYING GAUL, DEAD GIANT, AND DEAD AMAZON
Museo Nazionale, Naples

FIG. 437. FIGHTING PERSIAN
Museum of Aix, France

FIG. 436. DEAD GAUL
Museo Archeologico, Venice (Alinari Photo)

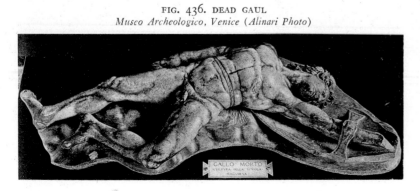

FIGURES DEDICATED BY ATTALUS I ON THE ACROPOLIS OF ATHENS

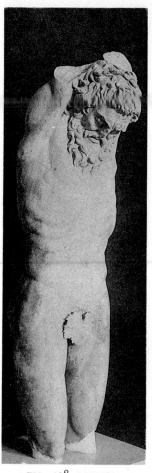

FIG. 438. MARSYAS
Istanbul Museum

FIG. 439. MARSYAS
Louvre

FIG. 440. MARSYAS
Uffizi Gallery, Florence
(Alinari Photo)

FIG. 442. ANOTHER VIEW OF SCYTHIAN IN FIG. 441

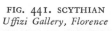

FIG. 441. SCYTHIAN
Uffizi Gallery, Florence

THE PUNISHMENT OF MARSYAS

FIG. 443. HEAD OF SCYTHIAN IN FIGS. 441–42

FIG. 444. HEAD OF SCYTHIAN IN FIGS. 441–43

FIG. 445. TWO VIEWS OF TORSO OF APOLLO FROM PERGAMON

FIG. 446. STATUETTE OF MARSYAS
British Museum

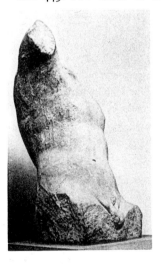

FIG. 447. SATYR WITH TORCH
STATUETTE
*Metropolitan Museum of Art,
New York*

FIG. 448. DANCING SATYR: STATUETTE
Metropolitan Museum of Art, New York

FIG. 449. GAY YOUNG SATYR
STATUETTE FROM PERGAMON

THE SCYTHIAN, APOLLO, AND BRONZE STATUETTES OF SATYRS IN PERGAMENE ART

FIG. 450. SLEEPING SATYR
Glyptothek, Munich

FIG. 451. ANOTHER VIEW OF SATYR IN FIG. 450

FIG. 452. SLEEPING MAENAD
Museo Nazionale Romano, Rome

FIG. 453. ANOTHER VIEW OF HEAD IN FIG. 452
(Alinari Photo)

PERGAMENE STYLE AROUND 200 B.C.

FIG. 454. ATTALUS I: HEAD IN ORIGINAL FORM
Pergamon Museum, Berlin

FIG. 455. HEAD OF ALEXANDER THE GREAT
Istanbul Museum

FIG. 456. HEAD IN FIG. 454, WITH ADDED WIG
Pergamon Museum, Berlin

FIG. 457. FRONT VIEW OF HEAD IN FIG. 456

PERGAMENE PORTRAITS OF ATTALUS I AND ALEXANDER THE GREAT

FIG. 458. RECONSTRUCTION OF ALTAR
Pergamon Museum, Berlin

FIG. 459. ZEUS AND THREE GIANTS
Pergamon Museum, Berlin

FIG. 460. GROUP OF ATHENA, ALCYONEUS, GE, AND NIKE
Pergamon Museum, Berlin

THE GREAT ALTAR OF ZEUS AT PERGAMON

FIG. 461. LETO
Pergamon Museum, Berlin

FIG. 462. ALCYONEUS FROM ATHENA GROUP
Pergamon Museum, Berlin

FIG. 464. DOG AND GIANT FROM ARTEMIS GROUP
Pergamon Museum, Berlin

FIG. 463. ARTEMIS AND OTOS
Pergamon Museum, Berlin

EAST FRIEZE OF THE GREAT ALTAR OF ZEUS AT PERGAMON

FIG. 465. HECATE AND KLYTIOS
Pergamon Museum, Berlin

FIG. 466. NYX, THE PERSONIFICATION OF NIGHT
Pergamon Museum, Berlin

FIG. 468. DIONYSOS AND SATYRS
Pergamon Museum, Berlin

FIG. 467. NEREUS AND DORIS
Pergamon Museum, Berlin

GODS AND GIANTS FROM GREAT ALTAR OF ZEUS AT PERGAMON

FIG. 469. TRITONS AS AKROTERIA
Pergamon Museum, Berlin

FIG. 470. NORTH WING OF ALTAR OF ZEUS
Reconstruction in Pergamon Museum, Berlin

THE GREAT ALTAR OF ZEUS AT PERGAMON

FIG. 472. STATUE OF ZEUS FROM TEMPLE IN FIG. 471

FIG. 471. TEMPLE OF HERA, PERGAMON

FIG. 473. TRAGOIDIA
Pergamon Museum, Berlin

FIG. 474. TWO VIEWS OF FIGURE OF CYBELE
Pergamon Museum, Berlin

PERGAMENE STATUES OF THE PERIOD OF ATTALUS II

FIG. 475. "THE BEAUTIFUL HEAD"
Pergamon Museum, Berlin

FIG. 476. HEAD OF HERACLES
Berlin Museum

FIG. 477. PART OF THE TELEPHOS FRIEZE,
SHOWING ALEOS, NEAIRA, AND HERACLES

FIG. 479. DANCER ON A RELIEF
Istanbul Museum

FIG. 478. PART OF THE TELEPHOS FRIEZE,
SHOWING BUILDING OF THE BOX FOR AUGE

HEADS AND RELIEFS FROM PERGAMON

FIG. 480. TETRADRACHM
Museum of Fine Arts, Boston

FIG. 481. TETRADRACHM
Museum of Fine Arts, Boston

FIG. 482. HEAD
Louvre

FIG. 483. PROFILE OF FIG. 482

PORTRAITS OF MITHRIDATES VI OF PONTUS

FIG. 484. COIN FROM ODESSUS
WITH MITHRIDATES AS HERACLES

FIG. 485. STATUETTE OF MITHRIDATES AS HERACLES
FROM PERGAMON
Pergamon Museum, Berlin

FIG. 486. FRONT VIEW OF HEAD OF FIG. 485

FIG. 487. PROFILE OF HEAD OF FIG. 485

PORTRAITS OF MITHRIDATES VI OF PONTUS

FIG. 488. HELIOS ON METOPE FROM TROY
Museum für Völkerkunde, Berlin

FIG. 489. VOTIVE RELIEF
Glyptothek, Munich

FIG. 490. TOMB RELIEF OF A TEACHER

RHODIAN RELIEFS

FIG. 491. GODDESS
Uffizi Gallery, Florence (Alinari Photo)

FIG. 492. STATUETTE OF HERMAPHRODITE
Tozzi Collection, New York

FIG. 493. NIKE OF SAMOTHRACE
Louvre (Alinari Photo)

FIG. 494. NIKE OF SAMOTHRACE
Louvre

RHODIAN STATUES

FIG. 495. NIKE OF SAMOTHRACE ON SHIP'S PROW
Louvre (Alinari Photo)

FIG. 496. ANOTHER VIEW OF NIKE OF SAMOTHRACE
Louvre

FIG. 497. RELIEF BY ARCHELAOS
DEPICTING APOTHEOSIS OF HOMER
British Museum

FIG. 498. TERPSICHORE, FROM MILETUS
Istanbul Museum

NIKE OF SAMOTHRACE AND THE MUSES

FIG. 499. KLIO
Istanbul Museum

FIG. 500. KLIO, FROM KOS

FIG. 501. MUSE FROM MILETUS
Istanbul Museum

FIG. 502. MELPOMENE
Berlin Museum

FIG. 503. LEANING WOMAN,
TERRA COTTA
Metropolitan Museum of Art, New York

FIG. 504. SEATED MUSE
Museo Nazionale Romano, Rome (Alinari Photo)

MUSES OF THE SECOND CENTURY B.C.

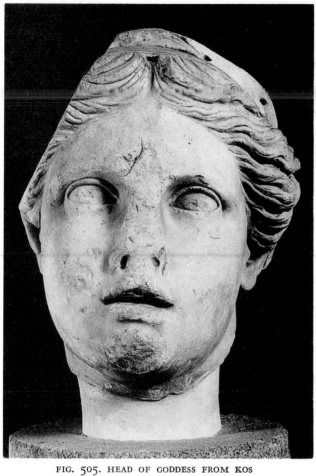

FIG. 505. HEAD OF GODDESS FROM KOS
Istanbul Museum

FIG. 506. HEAD OF MUSE FROM MILETUS
Istanbul Museum

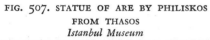

FIG. 507. STATUE OF ARE BY PHILISKOS
FROM THASOS
Istanbul Museum

FIG. 508. FRAGMENT OF WOMAN
FROM KOS
British Museum

FIG. 509. FRAGMENT OF WOMAN
FROM KOS
British Museum

HEADS AND DRAPERIES IN RHODIAN STYLE, AND A WORK OF PHILISKOS

FIG. 510. STATUE FROM KOS

FIG. 511. STATUE OF CLEOPATRA FROM DELOS
Delos

FIG. 512. STATUE FROM HERAION, SAMOS

FIG. 513. TERRA COTTA
OF WOMAN IN MANTLE
Metropolitan Museum of Art, New York

FIG. 514. STATUE OF WOMAN FROM
PERGAMON

FIG. 515. STATUE OF WOMAN FROM
PERGAMON

DRAPED WOMEN OF THE SECOND CENTURY B.C.

FIG. 516. STATUE OF THEMIS FROM
RHAMNUS
National Museum, Athens

FIG. 517. THE PRIESTESS NIKESO FROM
PRIENE
Pergamon Museum, Berlin

FIG. 518. WOMAN FROM THASOS
Istanbul Museum

FIG. 519. STATUE OF WOMAN
Louvre

FIG. 520. STATUE FROM MAGNESIA
Istanbul Museum

FIG. 521. STATUE BY APOLLODOROS OF
PHOCAEA
British Museum

DEVELOPMENT OF HELLENISTIC DRAPERY

FIG. 522. TWO VIEWS OF STATUE
Ashmolean Museum, Oxford University

FIG. 523. TOMBSTONE OF MENEPHILA
FROM EPHESUS
Louvre

FIG. 524. THE "PUDICITIA"
Vatican Museum (Anderson Photo)

FIG. 525. WOMAN
Louvre

STATUES OF THE PUDICITIA TYPE

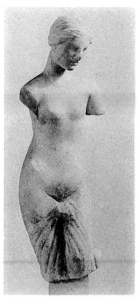

FIG. 526. APHRODITE
Metropolitan Museum of Art,
New York

FIG. 527. APHRODITE
FOUND IN HARBOR OF RHODES
Rhodes Museum

FIG. 528. TORSO OF APHRODITE[?]
FROM RHODES
Rhodes Museum

FIG. 529. AMPHION AND ZETHUS BIND DIRCE TO THE BULL
Museo Nazionale, Naples (Alinari Photo)

S BY APOLLONIOS AND TAURISKOS OF TRALLES, ADOPTED SONS OF MENEKRATES OF RHODES

FIG. 530. RECONSTRUCTION
Skulpturen-Sammlung, Dresden

FIG. 531. HEAD OF LAOCOON FROM GROUP IN VATICAN

FIG. 532. ENGRAVING BY MARCO DENTE
Metropolitan Museum of Art, New York

FIG. 533. COPY BY BACCIO BANDINELLI
Uffizi Gallery, Florence

THE LAOCOON GROUP BY HAGESANDROS, ATHENODOROS, AND POLYDOROS, OF RHODES

FIG. 534. BOY WITH FOX GOOSE
STATUE FROM EPHESUS
Kunsthistorisches Museum, Vienna

FIG. 535. TWINS, TERRA COTTA
National Museum, Athens

FIG. 536. THE INFANT HERACLES
STRANGLING SNAKES
Museo Capitolino, Rome (Anderson Photo)

FIG. 537. TERRA COTTA
OF BABY BOY ON MATTRESS
Museum antiker Kleinkunst, Munich

FIG. 538. TOMBSTONE OF METRODOROS
AND MATREAS, FROM SMYRNA
Louvre

FIG. 539. TOMBSTONE
OF AMYNTAS, FROM SMYRNA
Louvre

BABIES

FIG. 540. BOYS AT A COCK FIGHT, TERRA COTTA
Walters Art Gallery, Baltimore

FIG. 541. GIRL WITH PET
IN POUCH OF HER DRESS
Metropolitan Museum of Art,
New York

FIG. 542. THREE FIGURES OF GIRLS
DEDICATED TO EILITHYIA AT AGRAE
National Museum, Athens

FIG. 543. BOY WITH DEER AND GIRL WITH HARE, FROM MYRINA
Louvre

CHILDREN WITH PETS

FIG. 544. BRONZE STATUETTE OF GIRL
Palazzo Grazioli, Rome

FIG. 545. RUNNING BOY, BRONZE
Prado Museum, Madrid

FIG. 546. SMILING CHILD
British Museum

FIG. 547. TWO VIEWS OF HEAD OF SLEEPY CHILD
Glyptothek, Munich

FIG. 548. SLAVE BOY WITH LANTERN
Metropolitan Museum of Art, New York

FIG. 549. SLAVE BOY WITH LANTERN
Museo Nazionale Romano, Rome

FIG. 550. STREET BOY REMOVING A THORN
British Museum

CHILDREN OF RICH AND POOR FAMILIES

FIG. 551. PLAYING GIRLS, TERRA COTTA
Louvre

FIG. 552. GIRLS PLAYING
OSTRAKINDA, TERRA COTTA
*Metropolitan Museum of Art,
New York*

FIG. 553. DANCING GIRL
TERRA COTTA
Bibliothèque nationale, Paris

FIG. 554. DANCING GIRL
ON SNAIL, BRONZE
Walters Art Gallery, Baltimore

FIG. 555. DANCING GIRL
TERRA COTTA FROM TARENTUM
*Metropolitan Museum of Art,
New York*

FIG. 556. DANCING GIRL
TERRA COTTA FROM EGNATIA
Louvre

FIG. 557. DANCING GIRL
TERRA COTTA
Metropolitan Museum of Art, New York

FIG. 558. GIRL WITH STROPHION
TERRA COTTA
Metropolitan Museum of Art, New York

PLAYING AND DANCING TEEN-AGE GIRLS

FIG. 560. DANCING SATYR WITH THYRSUS
BRONZE STATUETTE FROM HERCULANEUM
Museo Nazionale, Naples

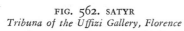

FIG. 559. BRONZE STATUETTE OF SATYR PLAYING FLUTE, FROM HERCULANEUM
Museo Nazionale, Naples

FIG. 561. DANCING SATYR, BRONZE
Bibliothèque nationale, Paris

FIG. 562. SATYR
Tribuna of the Uffizi Gallery, Florence

FIG. 563. NYMPH
Uffizi Gallery, Florence (Alinari Photo)

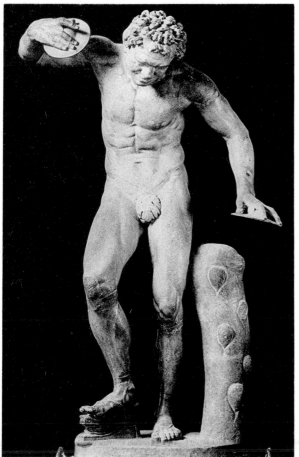

DANCING SATYRS AND NYMPH

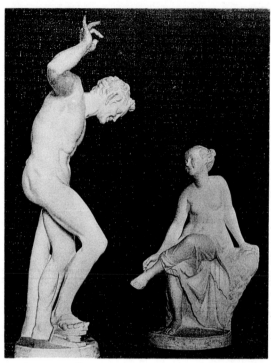

FIG. 565. COIN FROM CYZICUS
SHOWING SAME GROUP

FIG. 564. RECONSTRUCTION OF THE
"INVITATION TO DANCE" GROUP, FIGS. 562–63

FIG. 566. NYMPH FROM THE GROUP
Brussels Museum

FIG. 567. HEAD OF NYMPH
Museo Archeologico, Venice (Alinari Photo)

FIG. 568. SATYR WITH PANTHER
Villa Albani, Rome (Alinari Photo)

THE INVITATION TO DANCE

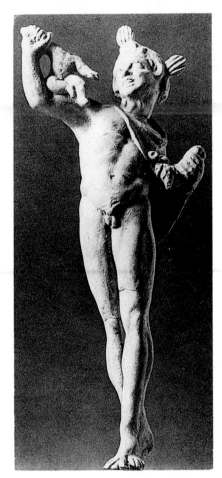

FIG. 569. SATYR
CARRYING THE CHILD DIONYSOS
Villa Albani, Rome (Alinari Photo)

FIG. 570. SATYR CARRYING THE
CHILD DIONYSOS: TERRA COTTA FROM MYRINA
Louvre

FIG. 571. SATYR CARRYING THE CHILD DIONYSOS
Walters Art Gallery, Baltimore

FIG. 572. DIONYSOS SUSTAINED BY SATYR: BRONZE
STATUETTE GROUP
Walters Art Gallery, Baltimore

THE SATYR AS A HELPFUL FELLOW

FIG. 573. SATYR, RED MARBLE
Vatican Museum (Anderson Photo)

FIG. 574. HEAD OF SATYR
Louvre

FIG. 576. SATYR FALLING ASLEEP
Museo Nazionale, Naples (Alinari Photo)

FIG. 575. SATYR WITH WINESKIN
Vatican Museum (Anderson Photo)

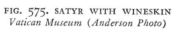

GAY SATYRS

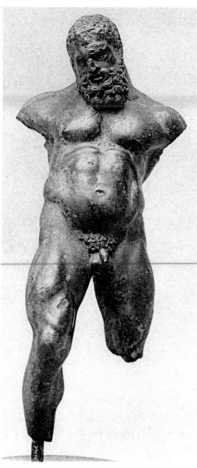

FIG. 577. BRONZE STATUETTE
Metropolitan Museum of Art, New York

FIG. 578. SIDE VIEW OF FIG. 577

FIG. 579. BRONZE STATUETTE
Walters Art Gallery, Baltimore

FIG. 580. BACK VIEW OF STATUETTE
IN FIGS. 577-78

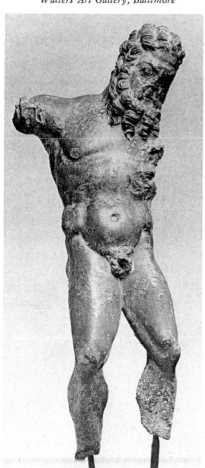

DRUNKEN HERACLES

FIG. 581. HEADS OF OLD CENTAUR AND EROS
Louvre

FIG. 582. HEAD OF FAUNO COLLA MACCHIA
Glyptothek, Munich

FIG. 583. OLD CENTAUR WITH EROS
Louvre (Alinari Photo)

FIG. 584. YOUNG CENTAUR IN DARK GREY MARBLE
Museo Capitolino, Rome

CENTAURS

FIG 585. HEAD OF OLD NURSE
Vollmer Collection, New York

FIG. 586. BRONZE BOTTLE
IN FORM OF OLD WOMAN
Louvre

FIG. 587. OLD NURSE
WITH BABY
*Metropolitan Museum of Art
New York*

FIG. 588. OLD PEDAGOGUE
WITH PUPIL
Metropolitan Museum of Art, New York

FIG. 589. TWO OLD MEN: LEFT, FROM ATHENS;
RIGHT, FROM SMYRNA
Louvre

FIG. 590. OLD PEASANT WOMAN
*Metropolitan Museum of Art
New York*

OLD DERELICTS

FIG. 591. SHEPHERDESS GOING TO MARKET
Palazzo dei Conservatori, Rome
(Anderson Photo)

FIG. 592. FISHERMAN
British Museum

FIG. 593. TORSO OF FISHERMAN
Metropolitan Museum of Art, New York

FIG. 595. FISHERMAN, BLACK MARBLE
Louvre

FIG. 594. OLD SHEPHERD
Relief Formerly in Pollak Collection, Rome

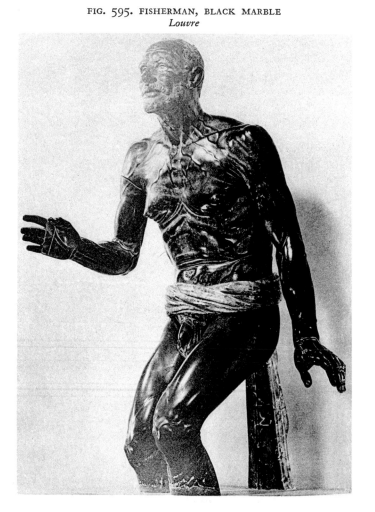

SHEPHERDS AND FISHERMEN

FIG. 596. ARISTOPHANES[?], BRONZE
Museo Nazionale, Naples (Alinari Photo)

FIG. 597. ARISTOPHANES[?]
Uffizi Gallery, Florence (Alinari Photo)

FIG. 598. HOMER, BRONZE
Museo Archeologico, Florence (Alinari Photo)

FIG. 599. HOMER
Louvre

PORTRAITS OF OLD POETS

FIG. 600. DRAPED LADY
TERRA COTTA
Walters Art Gallery, Baltimore

FIG. 601. TERRA COTTA
Metropolitan Museum of Art, New York

FIG. 602. TERRA COTTA
Metropolitan Museum of Art, New York

FIG. 603. KNEELING WOMAN
TERRA COTTA FROM MYRINA
Louvre

FIG. 605. LADY BINDING HER HAIR
WITH A FILLET
Walters Art Gallery, Baltimore

FIG. 604. LADY ARRANGING HER HAIR
Palazzo Colonna, Rome

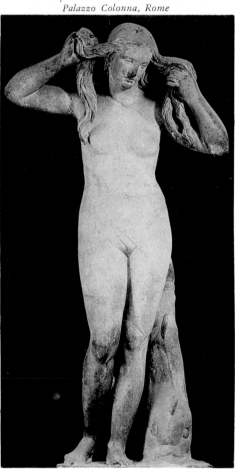

ELEGANT LADIES

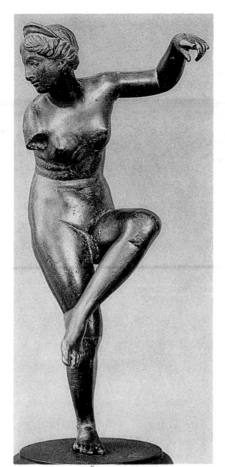

FIG. 606. APHRODITE
REMOVING HER SANDAL, BRONZE
Museo Nazionale, Naples

FIG. 607. APHRODITE
REMOVING HER SANDAL
BRONZE FROM PARAMYTHIA
British Museum

FIG. 608. APHRODITE UNDRESSING
STATUETTE FROM EGYPT
Louvre

FIG. 609. APHRODITE
Louvre

FIG. 610. APHRODITE
Vatican Museum (Alinari Photo)

FIG. 611. TWO FLYING CUPIDS, TERRA COTTA
Metropolitan Museum of Art, New York

FIG. 612. TERRA COTTA
Metropolitan Museum of Art, New York

FIG. 613. EROS WITH KITHARA
BRONZE FROM MAHDIA
Tunis

FIG. 615. EROS IN CHITON
TERRA COTTA FROM MYRINA
Louvre (Alinari Photo)

FIG. 614. TERRA COTTA FROM MYRINA
Louvre (Alinari Photo)

FLYING EROS

FIG. 616. HEAD OF THE EROS IN FIG. 617

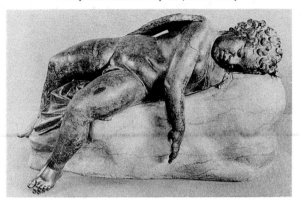

FIG. 617. SLEEPING EROS, BRONZE
Metropolitan Museum of Art, New York

FIG. 618. BACK VIEW OF FIG. 617

FIG. 619. SLEEPING GIRL
Museo Nazionale Romano, Rome

FIG. 620. SLEEPING EROS
Palazzo dei Conservatori, Rome

INNOCENT SLEEP

FIG. 621. ENDYMION
Nationalmuseum, Stockholm

FIG. 622. ENDYMION
British Museum

FIG. 623. HERMAPHRODITE
Louvre

FIG. 624. ARIADNE
Museo Archeologico, Florence

FIG. 625. HERMAPHRODITE
Museo Nazionale Romano, Rome (Anderson Photo)

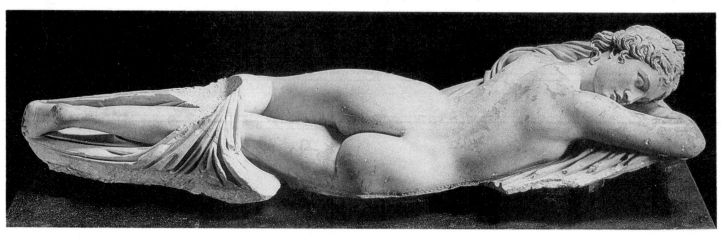

RESTLESS SLEEP

FIG. 626. HERMAPHRODITE AND SATYR
Skulpturen-Sammlung, Dresden

FIG. 627. SATYR AND NYMPH
Museo Nuovo, Rome (Alinari Photo)

FIG. 628. PAN AND DAPHNIS
Museo Nazionale Romano, Rome

CLOSELY KNIT GROUPS OF TWO PERSONS (*SYMPLEGMATA*)

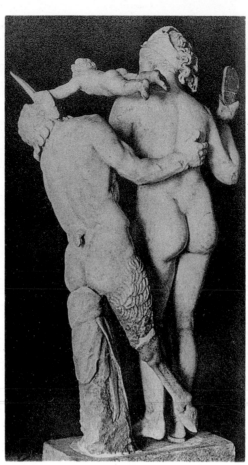

FIG. 629. PAN AND APHRODITE FROM DELOS
National Museum, Athens

FIG. 630. BACK VIEW OF FIG. 629

FIG. 631. PANISCA
Villa Albani, Rome

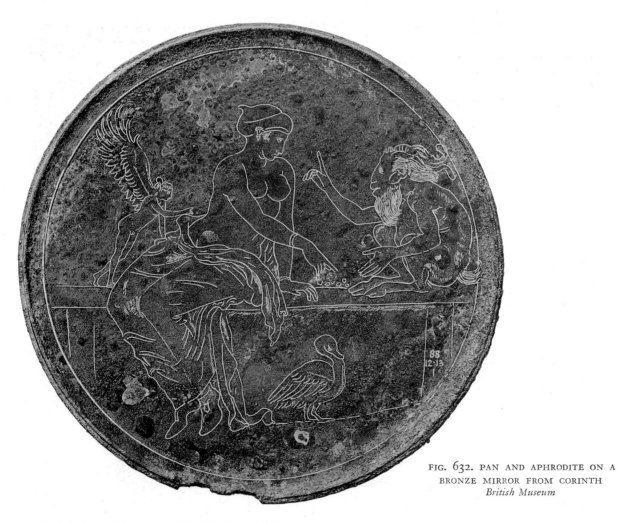

FIG. 632. PAN AND APHRODITE ON A
BRONZE MIRROR FROM CORINTH
British Museum

PAN, PANISCA, AND APHRODITE

FIG. 633. GROUP
Museum of Ostia

FIG. 634. GROUP
Louvre (Alinari Photo)

FIG. 635. GROUP
Vatican Museum (Alinari Photo)

PAN DRAWING THORN FROM FOOT OF SATYR

FIG. 636. PAINTED NYMPHS
IN HOUSE OF ROMULUS AND REMUS, POMPEII
(*Alinari Photo*)

FIG. 637. NYMPH WITH SHELL
BRONZE FROM POMPEII
Museo Nazionale, Naples

FIG. 638. EROS AND PSYCHE
Museo Capitolino, Rome
(*Anderson Photo*)

FIG. 639. HERACLES BATTLING WITH CENTAUR, BRONZE
Kunsthistorisches Museum, Vienna

NYMPH WITH SHELL, AND ONE-SIDED GROUPS

FIG. 640. TRITON CARRYING OFF A NEREID
Vatican Museum (Anderson Photo)

FIG. 641. TRITON CARRYING PAPPOSILENOS
Louvre

FIG. 642. NEWLY WED COUPLE, FROM MYRINA
Louvre (Alinari Photo)

ONE-SIDED LATE HELLENISTIC GROUPS

FIG. 643. BRONZE GROUP: WRESTLERS FROM
ALEXANDRIA
Walters Art Gallery, Baltimore

FIG. 644. ANOTHER BRONZE GROUP OF
WRESTLERS FROM ALEXANDRIA
Walters Art Gallery, Baltimore

FIG. 645. THREE KNEELING GIRLS, TERRA COTTA
Louvre

HELLENISTIC GROUPS OF DIFFERENT PERIODS

FIG. 646. TOMBSTONE FROM PERGAMON

FIG. 647. TOMBSTONE FROM SMYRNA
Altes Museum, Berlin

FIG. 648. COUPLE ON HORSEBACK, FROM CAPRI
Museo Nazionale, Naples (Alinari Photo)

EARLY HELLENISTIC RELIEFS OF THE THIRD AND SECOND CENTURIES B.C.

FIG. 649. POLYPHEMUS
Villa Albani, Rome

FIG. 650. ODYSSEUS AND DIOMEDES SPYING ON DOLON
Kunsthistorisches Museum, Vienna

FIG. 651. ARTEMIS AND SATYRS AT ALTAR: BRONZE FROM DELOS

FIG. 653. HELEN AND PARIS (ALEXANDROS)
Museo Nazionale, Naples (Alinari Photo)

FIG. 652. PEITHO
ON A FRAGMENT OF RELIEF
*Metropolitan Museum of Art,
New York*

HELLENISTIC RELIEFS

FIG. 654. YOUTH WITH COURTESANS
Museo Nazionale, Naples

FIG. 655. DIONYSOS VISITS A MORTAL
Louvre

HELLENISTIC RELIEFS OF THE SECOND CENTURY B.C.

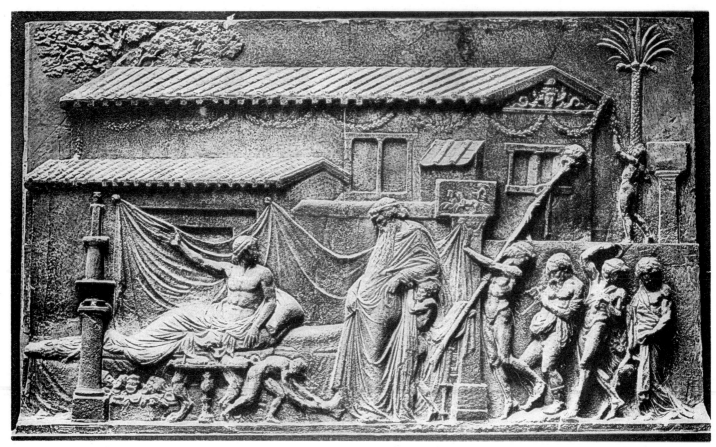

FIG. 656. RELIEF
British Museum

FIG. 657. RELIEF
Kephisia

DIONYSOS VISITING ICARIUS: LATE HELLENISTIC RELIEFS

FIG. 658. PEASANT WATERING A COW
Vatican Museum

FIG. 659. PEASANT DRIVING A COW
Glyptothek, Munich

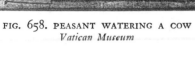

FIG. 660. BULLDOG
Vatican Museum (Anderson Photo)

FIG. 661. PLAYING HOUNDS
Vatican Museum (Alinari Photo)

FIG. 662. HEAD OF MULE
*Metropolitan Museum of Art
New York*

FIG. 664. PET DOG ON COUCH
Altes Museum, Berlin

FIG. 663. GREYHOUND
Metropolitan Museum of Art, New York

ANIMALS

FIG. 665. HEAD OF ANYTOS
National Museum, Athens

FIG. 666. FRONT VIEW OF FIG. 665

FIG. 667. BACK OF HEAD IN FIGS. 665–66

FIG. 668. COIN FROM LYCOSURA, SHOWING GROUP BY DAMOPHON

DAMOPHON OF MESSENE

FIG. 669. ATHENA BY EUBULIDES
National Museum, Athens (Alinari Photo)

FIG. 670. DESPOINA (KORE) BY DAMOPHON
National Museum, Athens (Alinari Photo)

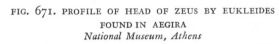

FIG. 671. PROFILE OF HEAD OF ZEUS BY EUKLEIDES
FOUND IN AEGIRA
National Museum, Athens

FIG. 672. FRONT VIEW OF FIG. 671

CLASSICIZED HEADS OF THE SECOND CENTURY B.C.

FIG. 673. UPPER PART OF FIGURE
Louvre (Alinari Photo)

FIG. 675. SIDE VIEW

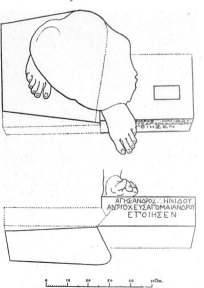

FIG. 676. GROUND PLAN
AND PROJECTION OF PLINTH

FIG. 674. THE FULL FIGURE
Louvre (Alinari Photo)

FIG. 677. SIDE VIEW OF PLINTH

APHRODITE OF MELOS (VENUS DE MILO)

FIG. 678. HEAD OF STATUE IN FIG. 679

FIG. 679. APOLLO OF CYRENE
British Museum

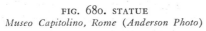

FIG. 680. STATUE
Museo Capitolino, Rome (Anderson Photo)

FIG. 681. STATUE
Museo Nazionale, Naples (Alinari Photo)

THE APOLLO CITHAROEDUS BY TIMARCHIDES[?]

FIG. 682. HEAD OF STATUE IN FIG. 685
(*Anderson Photo*)

FIG. 683. ANOTHER VIEW OF HEAD OF STATUE IN FIG. 685
(*Anderson Photo*)

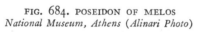

FIG. 684. POSEIDON OF MELOS
National Museum, Athens (Alinari Photo)

FIG. 685. "HELLENISTIC RULER," BRONZE
Museo Nazionale Romano, Rome

CLASSICIZED STATUES OF THE MIDDLE OF THE SECOND CENTURY B.C.

FIG. 686. HEAD OF FIGHTER IN FIGS. 688–89

FIG. 687. BRONZE STATUETTE OF WARRIOR FROM VIENNE
Bibliothèque nationale, Paris

FIG. 688. STATUE OF FIGHTER
Louvre (Alinari Photo)

FIG. 689. ANOTHER VIEW OF FIG. 688

AGASIAS OF EPHESUS

FIG. 690. SEATED HERACLES FROM POMPEII
Museo Nazionale, Naples

FIG. 691. STELE OF POLYBIUS FROM CLITOR
(KLEITOR), ARCADIA
Cast in Berlin

FIG. 692. PORTRAIT OF A MAN
Delphi Museum (Alinari Photo)

FIG. 693. SIDE VIEW OF FIG. 692
(Alinari Photo)

WORKS OF THE SECOND HALF OF THE SECOND CENTURY B.C.

FIG. 694. STATUE BY ZEUXIS
Metropolitan Museum of Art, New York

FIG. 695. FRONT VIEW OF FIG. 694

FIG. 696. POSEIDONIOS
Museo Nazionale, Naples

FIG. 697. FRONT VIEW OF FIG. 696

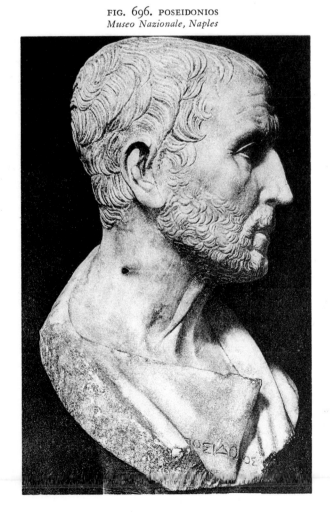

LATE HELLENISTIC PORTRAITS

FIG. 698. HEAD OF EPHEBUS IN FIG. 699
Istanbul Museum

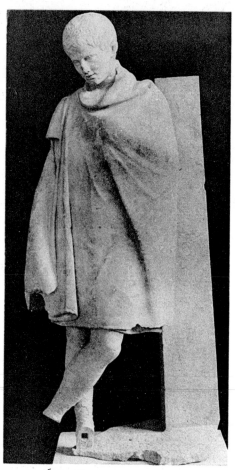

FIG. 699. AN EPHEBUS FROM TRALLES
Istanbul Museum

FIG. 700. BRONZE STATUETTE
OF WARRIOR
In Private Possession, New York

FIG. 701. SIDE VIEW
OF FIG. 700

CLASSICIZED STATUES

FIG. 702. FRIEZE FROM MAGNESIA
Pergamon Museum, Berlin

FIG. 703. ANOTHER PORTION OF FRIEZE FROM MAGNESIA
Pergamon Museum, Berlin

FIG. 704. EAST FRIEZE FROM TEMPLE OF HECATE
AT LAGINA IN CARIA: BIRTH OF ZEUS

FIG. 705. NORTH FRIEZE FROM LAGINA
ROMA AND OTHER PERSONIFICATIONS OF CITIES

FIG. 706. WEST FRIEZE FROM LAGINA
ARTEMIS, APOLLO, AND A GIANT

FIG. 707. SOUTH FRIEZE FROM LAGINA: CARIAN GODS

ARCHITECTURAL FRIEZES OF THE SECOND CENTURY B.C.

FIG. 708. STATUETTE
National Museum, Athens

FIG. 709. STATUETTE
Altes Museum, Berlin

FIG. 710. STATUETTE
National Museum, Athens

FIG. 711. FRONT VIEW OF FIG. 710

FIG. 712. STATUETTE FROM NIKAIA
National Museum, Athens

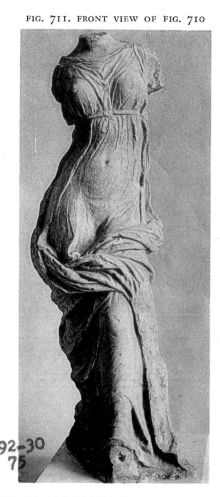

LATE HELLENISTIC STATUETTES FROM ATHENS